Fuel for Growth

FUEL FOR GROWTH

Water and Arizona's Urban Environment

DOUGLAS E. KUPEL

The University of Arizona Press
Tucson

The University of Arizona Press
© 2003 The Arizona Board of Regents
First printing
All rights reserved
☉ This book is printed on acid-free, archival-quality paper.
Manufactured in the United States of America
08   07   06   05   04   03   6   5   4   3   2   1

Library of Congress Cataloging-in-Publication Data
Kupel, Douglas E. (Douglas Edward), 1956–
Fuel for growth : water and Arizona's urban environment / Douglas E. Kupel.
p. cm.
Includes bibliographical references and index.
ISBN 0-8165-2169-7 (cloth : alk. paper)
1. Municipal water supply—Government policy—Arizona.   2. Water resources
development—Arizona.   3. Water-supply—Arizona—Phoenix.   4. Water-supply—
Arizona—Tucson.   5. Water-supply—Arizona—Flagstaff.   I. Title.
TD224.A7 .K87   2003
333.91'15'09791—dc21
2002010610

British Library Cataloguing-in-Publication Data
A catalogue record for this book is available from the British Library.

Publication of this book is made possible in part by grants from the Arizona
Humanities Council and the Friends of the Arizona Archives.

To my father

for his support, encouragement, and love

Contents

Maps

Illustrations

Preface

Despite water being a constant concern of Arizona's inhabitants, the state's water history has been largely ignored in comparison to other western states. But because Arizona is different from other areas in the arid West—most notably California—a study of its water history offers a different perspective from traditional treatments of water and the environment. This new perspective charts a divergent course from the West's water icons of Donald Worster's *Rivers of Empire* (1986) and Marc Reisner's *Cadillac Desert* (1986).[1]

An understanding of the Arizona experience follows a related intellectual genealogy, one first presented by Norris Hundley Jr. in *The Great Thirst* (1992). It also owes a considerable philosophical debt to urban historians specializing in the infrastructure of the modern city. Examining urban infrastructure, how services such as transportation, wastewater treatment, gas, electricity, and water are provided, is a necessary first step toward an understanding of urban growth.[2]

Traditional Western Water History

The growing field of environmental history has created an increasing interest in the relationship between humans and their natural environment. Because of the significant role water plays in the arid West, historians have devoted considerable attention to the impact of water on western culture. However, much of that literature is colored by a traditional view concerning the natural ecology of western water. A reexamination of water history reveals that western water development is a bit different from the traditional portrayal.

The conception that the arid West is a distinct region is one that has been promulgated since the early American explorers and scientists first visited the area. John Wesley Powell provided the best early distillation of the arid West thesis in 1878 with the publication of his *Report on the Arid Regions of the United States*. Powell argued that the arid West required new institutions and new technology in order to develop its resources in an efficient and orderly manner. Others built on this "West is different" theme in the intervening years, starting with Walter Prescott Webb in 1931 with the publication of his book *The Great Plains*. Webb documented the rise of a unique society in the West, based on new technology.[3]

Despite the obvious environmental differences between the arid West and humid East, a more accurate portrayal of water resources development in both areas shows many similarities. Water development infrastructure in both areas is capital intensive. In the East, water development focused on canals for transportation, harbor improvements, and flood control. Water development in the arid West took the form of irrigation projects, flood control, and hydroelectric power. The construction of water infrastructure in both regions facilitated economic development on a wider scale.

In the last fifteen years, writers in the new western history field such as Donald Worster have extended the "West is different" theme. Worster, writing in *Rivers of Empire* (1986), described the West as a hydraulic society based on control and ownership of water development infrastructure. According to Worster, the arid ecology of the West facilitated the creation of a new culture governed by water elites.[4]

The view that all western water decisions were dominated by an elite few flows from the experience of Owens Valley for Los Angeles and Hetch

Hetchy for San Francisco, both of which pitted urban water demand against what is often portrayed as a higher and better use. However, rather than being typical of events in the arid West, the California experience is atypical. In many cities, officials managed to meet the needs of urban residents without compromising the interests of other water users. Water projects frequently had the strong support of voters.

Instead of isolating water as a pivotal issue in western growth and development, a more conservative approach is to define the creation of a water infrastructure as one component in the expansion of urban areas. Only through an understanding of the complex components of urban infrastructure will historians provide more accurate descriptions of the interaction between humans and the environment. An examination of three traditional views of western water history charts a new path for the analysis of water ecology and culture in the arid West.

Tradition One: The West is Different

A common thesis advanced in western history is that a lack of water in the West sets the region apart from the rest of the country. This western water thesis had its roots in Frederick Jackson Turner's venerable frontier thesis. Turner stated that the presence of free land and the advancement of the settlement frontier westward affected the development of the United States by stimulating individualism, nationalism, and democracy. Similarly, the western water thesis states that the absence of water in the West fostered innovations in law, technology, and settlement patterns.[5]

The initial American perceptions of the West characterized it as a desert, first described by Zebulon Pike in 1810. In 1823, Major Stephen H. Long called it the Great American Desert. After the Civil War, Americans began to see possibilities for agricultural development in the West. The Great American Desert became the short grass plains and soon took its place in the national agrarian myth. The renunciation of the forbidding image of an American Sahara was led by the economic interests of eastern capital. Railroad promoters and land speculators shifted the perception of the Great American Desert to the great American garden.[6]

Some took issue with the conception of the West as an agricultural utopia made possible by the application of water. In 1878, John Wesley Powell presented his *Report on the Lands of the Arid Regions of the United*

States to Congress. Powell looked back toward the conception of the West as a desert, separated forever from the humid East by a boundary of sparse rainfall. Powell went on to construct a vision of how the arid regions could be developed, keeping in mind this drastic difference. He held an egalitarian view that resources should be put to use for the benefit of society as a whole, not just for the economically powerful. Reform of land laws in the West, in keeping with the arid ecology of the area, would preserve the resources.[7]

A second writer to question the application of agrarian ideas to the West was Walter Prescott Webb. A child of pioneer conditions in west Texas, Webb published *The Great Plains* in 1931. Like Powell, Webb questioned the optimistic overemphasis of reclamation possibilities in the West. He pointed to the promise of technology to enable settlers to carve farms from the desert plains and noted that natural limits placed boundaries on the success of these efforts.[8]

According to Powell and Webb, a clear line of demarcation separates the nation into East and West. The ninety-eighth meridian coincides with a natural climatic boundary separating two distinct environments. East of the line, rainfall averages twenty inches or more per year and agriculture is practiced with ease. West of the boundary, rainfall averages less than twenty inches per year, with isolated exceptions, and agriculture can only be practiced under certain conditions. Powell discussed these conditions and Webb documented some of them. Both stated that because of the dry climate, settlement patterns and agricultural production were different from the more humid East. New legal requirements, new technology, and new ways of living were required to conquer the arid West. The results of these adaptations made the West unique.

Like Turner's frontier thesis, the traditional view that the West is different may have outlived its usefulness. Western development is linked to larger factors that transcend the presence or absence of water. In fact, the West today mirrors conditions elsewhere in the nation. Western urban centers sit apart from their desert environment; they are in the desert but not of the desert. Rather than live with the desert environment, settlers have tried to recreate the same humid-region urban environment common in their areas of origin. Western growth focused on finding diverse solutions to water scarcity to achieve the realization of an urban vision.[9]

Tradition Two: The Hydraulic Society

A second traditional view in western water history is that water projects were the product of an elite group with a strong interest in construction. This idea has been most forcefully articulated by Donald Worster, who linked the arid environment of the West with the creation of a "hydraulic state" ruled by a small group of "water elites." In contrast to the freedom-loving, self-governing democracy envisioned by Powell and Webb, for Worster the "hydraulic mode" of production in the arid West has resulted in regimentation of water and human labor. Worster described a picture of the West in which agricultural users of water have joined forces with bureaucratic water elites to create a society where the many labor for the benefit of the few.[10]

Although Worster focused on the agricultural use of water, others have expanded the western water thesis to include the development of urban water systems. Here the case of Los Angeles sets the tone, with its infamous Owens Valley water project epitomizing urban growth at the expense of rural areas. In 1988, Robert Gottlieb extended the Los Angeles experience to the entire West: "By World War II, urban expansion in such places as Phoenix, Denver, Houston, and Dallas had become an industry in its own right. Many of the key interests for the policies of expansion came to dominate the politics and decision making of their communities. Those industries overlapped with an emergent water industry, which was busily devising projects bent on establishing continuing sources of supply and pricing mechanisms designed to encourage growth."[11]

In contrast, the history of water projects in Arizona tends to show that city leaders were responding to requests for service on the part of residents and neighboring subdivisions. As such, a better model for describing the growth and development of urban water services is the "urban infrastructure" school of writers such as Martin Melosi and Joel Tarr. These writers describe the construction of an urban infrastructure as a complex process linked to changing economic, political, and technological conditions.[12]

Perhaps one reason the approach of the new western historians falls short of presenting a clear picture of water development is that the scholars have emphasized agricultural water use and have overlooked the urban nature of the arid West. Writing in the *Journal of American History*, Worster advocated an "agroecological" approach to environmental history that stressed the study of farms and nature, not cities and human constructs. For the arid West, where much of the development in the twentieth century is concentrated in urban areas, the narrow focus of this approach tends to obscure the true process of environmental change.[13]

Writers in the urban infrastructure school are addressing the shortcomings of some environmental historians. Writing in the *Journal of Urban History*, Joel Tarr and Christine Rosen document the many impacts cities have had on the natural environment. In addition, Tarr and Rosen reflect on the impact nature has had on cities through geography and climate. The two authors advocate a synthesis of urban and environmental history, noting that "the natural and built environments evolved in dialectical interdependence and tension." By examining urban history in the context of its environment, historians and others can avoid single simplistic explanations for the growth of cities in the West.[14]

This more balanced approach may help others avoid the generalizations that too often serve as explanations for water history in the West. Instead of "busily devising projects" designed to expand the use of water, in the words of Robert Gottlieb, municipal leaders in Arizona struggled through the years to keep up with the demands placed on their water systems by an ever-increasing number of residents. These actions came about not because a few "key interests" could "dominate" decision making in the West, but because leaders were responsive to the demands of the residents and voters in the community.[15]

In his 1996 presidential address to the Western Historical Association, water historian Norris Hundley Jr. noted that several authors have contested the hydraulic society view. John Walton observed that the plans of Los Angeles to construct an aqueduct to Owens Valley were hotly contested by the resident farmers, in contrast to the view that Los Angeles officials had total control over the Owens Valley. Kazuto Oshio, in his doctoral dissertation on the Metropolitan Water District of Southern California, discovered that many smaller communities in coastal southern California battled the agency over control of water supplies. The shift toward a greater concern over the environmental consequences of large water projects in the last three decades is ample evidence that the general public has had a major role in the ultimate outcome of water planning.[16]

Tradition Three: As California Goes, So Goes the West

The third tradition of western water history is the idea that the California experience, exemplified by Los Angeles' taking of water from Owens Valley and San Francisco's damming of Hetch Hetchy, is typical of conflicts over water use in the West. After the turn of the century, boosters and leaders in California's two largest communities began to agitate for the construction of massive water projects to supply their growing populations and provide for future expansion and development. Of these two areas, the war waged by Los Angeles for control of water from Owens Valley and the Colorado River occupied greater attention. However, the struggle by San Francisco to construct the Hetch Hetchy reservoir and aqueduct had similar elements of tension.

Ray H. Taylor advanced San Francisco's municipal viewpoint in his 1926 publication *Hetch Hetchy: The Story of San Francisco's Struggle to Provide a Water Supply for Her Future Needs.* During the 1930s, at a time when conservation of natural resources came to the forefront of the national agenda, writers began to question the wisdom of the project. In recent years Richard Lowitt has revisited the Hetch Hetchy controversy, although he has not provided an alternate view of the debate.[17]

The campaign by Los Angeles to obtain water from the Owens Valley and the Colorado River attracted many more authors and publishers than San Francisco's story. Two writers are generally credited with painting Los Angeles as the West's biggest water hustler. William L. Kahrl and Abraham Hoffman portrayed Los Angeles as devious and scheming, a characterization that has colored our view of the Owens Valley conflict until the present.[18]

There is, however, an alternate view. Gordon R. Miller, in his 1977 doctoral dissertation at the Claremont Graduate School titled "Los Angeles and the Owens River Aqueduct," presented a skillful critique of the "conspiracy school." Miller questioned the portrayal of Los Angeles as a cunning and greedy entity that conspired to take water from Owens Valley farmers. He concluded that competition for water in California resulted from a natural shortage and that the bitter feelings associated with the Owens Valley project sprang from this competition.[19]

Rather than color the entire West, an alternate view of water history would portray the California experience as atypical. Many other large communities were able to construct large water projects with relatively little controversy—Seattle, Salt Lake City, and Portland are a few examples. The California experience has tarnished our view of western water development with a negative connotation. In the case of Portland and Seattle, the need for watershed protection to maintain water quality has resulted in the preservation of pristine forests, lakes, and rivers upstream from municipal diversions.[20]

The Arizona Experience

Examining the Arizona experience may not obliterate traditional views of water history in the West, but it will go a long way toward demonstrating that the historical pattern was more diverse. The development of Arizona water utilities passed through three stages of growth. The delivery of water began as a private enterprise in the fledgling cities of the nineteenth century. At the turn of the century, reformers within and without city government campaigned for municipal ownership of the private utilities. The successful battle to control water utilities led to a second stage, one of maturation, as municipal governments improved and perfected utility service. The final stage of development came after World War II when public officials confronted a new era of tremendous population growth. Municipal leaders transformed their utilities by reaching out to the Colorado with the Central Arizona Project as a means to provide water service to the new inhabitants. Today, Arizona has embraced new techniques of reuse, recharge, and restoration to meet the environmental concerns associated with a new century.

Acknowledgments

Like a traveler during an extended odyssey I have accumulated a debt of gratitude to a number of people that helped make this book a reality. First and foremost is George Britton, former deputy city manager for Phoenix. He had the foresight to determine that the City of Phoenix needed its own historian. He had strong support from Water Advisor Bill Chase who helped make the position a reality. In many ways this book is a tribute to the vision of these two men.

My colleagues at the Phoenix city attorney's office provided encouragement and understanding. These included former City Attorney Rod McDougall, City Attorney Peter Van Haren, Jesse W. Sears, M. James Callahan, Matt Palenica, Tom Buschatztke, Marilynn Turner, Cindy Fusselman, Charlene Zavala, and Paula Alberts. Water Services Department Director Mike Gritzuk fostered a climate of study and research. I owe a special debt of gratitude to Bing Brown. He served as author's muse and inspiration.

Outside the City of Phoenix colleagues at other government agencies provided assistance. These included Shelly Dudley, Catherine May, and Ileen Snoddy at the Salt River Project; Lynn D. Baker at the City of Tucson; and Barbara Tellman at the University of Arizona Water Resources

Research Center. I am particularly grateful to Shelly Dudley at SRP for helping to identify significant photos on short notice. Lynn Baker's exhaustive compilation of Tucson water history will guide researchers for the next hundred years.

The unsung heroes of any historical project are the archivists and librarians that preserve and organize the information that is the lifeblood of the historian's craft. The staff at a myriad of archives and libraries contributed to this work. Melanie Sturgeon and her staff at the Arizona State Archives did a monumental job under trying circumstances. Mike Wurtz at Sharlot Hall Museum in Prescott and Karen Underhill at NAU's Cline Library Special Collections dispensed needed assistance with good humor and charm.

Historian Pat Stein of Arizona Preservation Consultants in Flagstaff assisted with several research tasks for questions regarding northern Arizona. Her skill and expertise as a historian contributed to the final product.

I extend a special word of thanks to Bob Graham, AIA, of Metropolis Design Group in Phoenix for preparing the maps. His mastery of detail and art, reflected in the map drawings he contributed to the work, increased our understanding of the physical environment that provided a backdrop to Arizona water history. Staff at the University of Arizona Press are largely responsible for putting the book in its final form. Director Christine Szuter, acquiring editor Patti Hartmann, and editor Rose Byrne patiently guided the project to conclusion. The Friends of Arizona Archives and the Arizona Humanities Council graciously provided financial assistance toward publication costs.

While a great many individuals and institutions contributed to the success of this work, any errors of commission or omission are the responsibility of the author alone.

Abbreviations

af	acre-feet
cfs	cubic feet per second
gpm	gallons per minute
mgd	million gallons per day
AMA	Active Management Area
A&P	Atlantic and Pacific (railroad)
APS	Arizona Public Service
ANPP	Arizona Nuclear Power Project
ANRSG	Arizona Nuclear Resource Study Group
ASLB	Atomic Safety and Licensing Board
AT&SF	Atchison, Topeka and Santa Fe (railroad)
AWBA	Arizona Water Banking Authority
AWC	Arizona Water Commission
CAP	Central Arizona Project
CAWCD	Central Arizona Water Conservation District
CAWCS	Central Arizona Water Control Study
CAWS	Citizen Alliance for Water Security
CCAP	Citizens Concerned About the Project
CCC	Civilian Conservation Corps

DWR	Department of Water Resources
ECW	Emergency Conservation Work Program
EIS	Environmental Impact Statement
EPA	Environmental Protection Agency
FERA	Federal Emergency Recovery Act
FICO	Farmers Investment Company
GRUSP	Granite Reef Underground Storage Project
PIA	practicably irrigable acreage
PWA	Public Works Administration
RFC	Reconstruction Finance Corporation
SAWRSA	Southern Arizona Water Rights Settlement Act
SRP	Salt River Project
SRVWUA	Salt River Valley Water Users Association
TEP	Tucson Electric Power
USGS	U.S. Geological Survey
WPA	Works Progress Administration
WTP	water treatment plant
WWTP	wastewater treatment plant
YMCA	Young Men's Christian Association

Part I The Geographic and Cultural Background

A work of environmental history must have as its heart consideration for the environment within which historical events take place. A basic geographic and hydrographic background is a necessary starting point for a water history of Arizona's urban environment. Water use in Arizona took place within three main geographic areas: desert, mountains, and plateau. The state's major rivers also played a significant role in the ways Arizona's urban communities gained access to water supplies. The geographic pattern of Arizona provides a basic environmental context for consideration of the interaction between urban development and physical constraints.

Because environmental considerations play an important part in historical treatments of western water use, an understanding of Arizona's physical setting is necessary to understand how its urban areas have grown. However, the physical landscape is also a canvas upon which human activities take place. A second aspect to developing a basic understanding of water use requires an examination of early cultures that made the first human mark on Arizona's environment: prehistoric Native Americans, Spaniards, and Mexicans. These three cultural groups established the first patterns of water use that later American settlers would follow.

Chapter 1 Physical Patterns on the Land

Arizona's two largest urban areas, Tucson and Phoenix, could not be more different in their relationship with water. Tucson first relied on surface water for its domestic use, then for most of the twentieth century turned to pumping groundwater as its sole supply for municipal needs. Only in the last few years has Tucson once again tapped surface supplies through the mechanism of the Central Arizona Project. Phoenix, on the other hand, first relied on underground aquifers to supply its domestic water needs, then later turned to surface supplies. Today, pumped groundwater supplies only a small fraction of the total water supply delivered by Phoenix.[1]

While Phoenix and Tucson seem to share nothing more than their differences, Flagstaff is truly set apart from its counterparts. Known as the mountain community, Flagstaff sits atop Arizona's plateau country amidst evergreens and mountains. Although not a desert town, Flagstaff shares Arizona's lack of water. Its surface sources are few, so residents must depend on springs and wells for their needs.

The Physical Landscape

Desert

Desert is the word most closely associated with Arizona despite the presence of other types of physical landscapes. In Arizona, what people call the desert is categorized by geographers as the North American basin and range physiographic province. This is one of the most common landscape types in the arid Southwest, and home to nearly all of Arizona's urban population. Basin and range extends across the western United States and northern Mexico. Arizona's other two predominant landscapes are mountains and plateau.[2]

Basin and range consists of troughs and valleys between mountain ranges. The troughs are filled with alluvial deposits brought from the surrounding mountains and upstream areas through many years of erosion. Although cut by rivers, streams, creeks, and washes, the basin was not carved by water action but created by uplift of the surrounding mountains. This uplift created the troughs, which then filled with deposits. The deposits within the troughs are not uniform. At several places, geologic formations cut across the alluvial deposits, affecting the flow of surface and subsurface water. These formations create dikes that control the flow of water, concentrating surface flows and bringing groundwater to the surface.[3]

A good example of these cross-basin formations is near the San Xavier del Bac Mission south of Tucson, where a volcanic formation crosses the Santa Cruz Valley between Black Mountain and Martinez Hill. This formation creates a subsurface dike that raises the level of groundwater to the surface. The existence of water at San Xavier is preserved in the name "Bac" (Wa:K) which early historians and anthropologists recorded as meaning "place where the water emerges" in the language of the Tohono O'odham. Similar formations are found on other desert rivers. These formations helped create advantageous water conditions where settlement could exist.[4]

The alluvial deposits within the troughs themselves are filled with water. It took thousands of years for water to percolate from surface flows and fill the spaces between the rocks, gravels, and soil. Most of this filling took place during the Pleistocene epoch from 1.8 million to 8,000 years

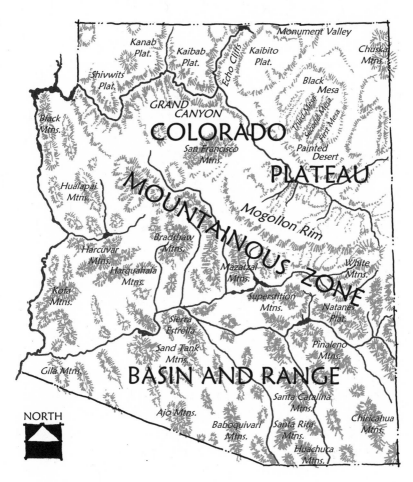

Arizona's physical geography

ago. This underground reservoir of ancient water provides most of the drinking supply for Tucson and many other smaller communities in Arizona. Agriculture is also heavily dependent on water stored in the underground aquifers of the basin and range physiographic province.

Arizona's desert mountain ranges form sky islands that rise abruptly above the desert floor. As the elevation increases, temperatures drop and vegetation changes. These mountain ranges serve as collectors of orthographic precipitation. Water vapor condenses as it rises to the tops of the highest mountains and collects as snow in winter and rain the rest of the year. This water finds its way to replenish the desert troughs below through mountain springs, seeps, and underground flows.

Despite the dry conditions that characterize Arizona's desert basins, the area supports a large variety of plant and animal life. Arizona is part of the Sonoran Desert region. In Arizona the Sonoran Desert is divided into two smaller regions, the Lower Colorado and the Arizona Upland. The Lower Colorado region is the drier of the two, with rainfall averaging less than five inches per year. A wide variety of cacti, shrubs, and small trees dominate the Arizona Upland region. Many species of cacti have adapted to the desert environment by quickly absorbing and storing water during infrequent rains. One of these cactus species, the barrel cactus, has been described as a good source of water in an emergency. However, the flesh and fluid of a barrel cactus—like other cacti—is very unpalatable. Drinking water from a barrel cactus would do a thirsty desert traveler more harm than good.[5]

Mountains

The mountains associated with the basin and range are generally small, seldom rising more than one or two thousand feet above the surrounding basins. Arizona does have a true mountainous region in the center of the state, with peaks rising to nearly eight thousand feet. This is a transitional zone between the basin and range that covers Arizona's southern and western quadrants and the plateau which dominates Arizona's northeast corner. The most conspicuous feature of this mountainous transitional zone is the Mogollon Rim.

This central mountainous region plays a key role in Arizona's water history because the mountains serve as a watershed for its urban population. Water collected in the winter months as snow provides the major portion of the flow for the Santa Cruz, Salt, Gila, and Little Colorado Rivers. The headwaters for these rivers are located in the mountainous central region of Arizona and western New Mexico.

While there is relatively little population in the mountainous transitional zone outside of mining communities, this area of Arizona sees tremendous use as a recreational area for residents of Phoenix and Tucson escaping the summer heat. While this recreational use has been compat-

Don't try this at home. A common misconception is that a barrel cactus is like a canteen, but drinking water from one could harm a thirsty traveler.

ible with watershed preservation, improved transportation and increasing population in Arizona has resulted in a growing number of permanent and part-time residents in this area. Communities such as Payson, Prescott, and Pinetop-Lakeside will face increasing demands on their water supply as more people take advantage of this particular climatic niche. Prescott is already facing restrictions on population growth until additional sources of water supply can be developed.

Plateau

Northeastern Arizona is characterized by a flat plateau. As with the basin and range province, this landscape feature extends beyond Arizona. The plateau province in Arizona is part of the larger Colorado Plateau that also includes portions of Utah, New Mexico, and Colorado. The plateau takes its name from the Colorado River which drains this vast area.

The Grand Canyon is the dominant feature of the plateau, formed only in part by the relentless action of erosion as the Colorado River cut into the earth. This downward erosive action was accompanied by an upward shift in the earth itself during the Cenozoic era and within the last ten million years. The combination of these two forces carved the Grand Canyon, one of the world's natural marvels. Today the Colorado River flows more than a mile below the level of the plateau at the rim of the canyon.

Beyond the depths of the Grand Canyon, high volcanic peaks punctuate the plateau. The highest peaks in Arizona rise from the plateau: Humphreys Peak in the San Francisco Mountains north of Flagstaff at 12,633 feet, and Mount Baldy in the White Mountains at 11,590 feet. Water deposited on the mountains as winter snow or summer thunderstorms provides a significant source for seeps, springs, and replenishment of underground aquifers.

The development of underground water sources in northern Arizona is hampered by the presence of the Grand Canyon. This deep declivity acts as a natural drain for the surrounding plateau, lowering the groundwater table to great depths. This situation has hampered the development of some communities in the area. Residents of Ash Fork, for example, had to have their water supply delivered by railroad tank car. The visitor facilities at the South Rim of the Grand Canyon and in the bustling park entrance community of Tusayan have water trucked in by tanker-trailers.

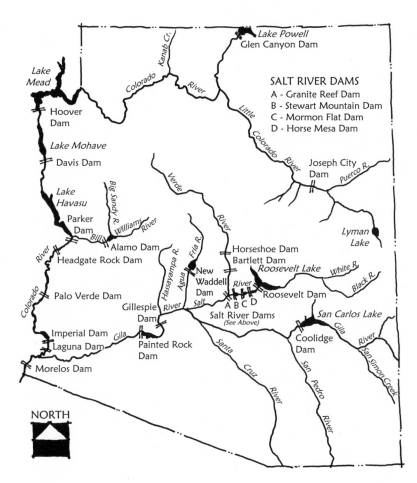

Major dams on Arizona's rivers and streams

Arizona's Rivers

Water flow in Arizona's rivers is directly related to precipitation. Arizona's climate is hot and dry in most parts of the state. The low desert along the Colorado River at the border with California has the lowest precipitation of all, ranging from 3.43 inches at Yuma to 4.72 at Parker. Precipitation in the Tucson area averages 11 inches a year, while Phoenix gets an average of 7.5 inches per year. Rainfall in Arizona's mountainous areas ranges up to 25 inches per year in the highest areas of the Mogollon Rim and White Mountains. On balance, more than half of Arizona receives less than 10 inches of precipitation per year, making it a very arid state. Arizona's rivers reflect this paucity of water.[6]

What little rain does fall in Arizona is concentrated into two periods: summer rains between July and September, and winter rains between December and March. Most of the precipitation occurs in the summer from thunderstorms of short duration and heavy intensity. As a result, there is little surface water and channels run only briefly after rains. Most of the precipitation percolates as recharge into groundwater or is lost through evapotranspiration. The average percentage of runoff from rainfall is estimated at only 3 percent.[7]

In addition to seasonal patterns of precipitation, Arizona's climate exhibits longer periods of drought and flood. A sharp and severe drought struck the Salt River Valley at the turn of the nineteenth century, extending over seventy-six months from September 1898 to December 1904. Many residents packed up and left. Those who remained redoubled their efforts to build a storage dam on the Salt River to conserve water in times of flood and release it gradually during periods of drought. Long, less severe droughts are also common. A mild drought began in 1920 in the Salt River Valley and did not break until 1941.[8]

While droughts slowly damage and destroy, floods take away in an instant what took years to create. All areas of Arizona have suffered from dramatic floods. In 1890 the poorly engineered Walnut Grove Dam, weakened by floodwaters, collapsed and took many lives. Floodwaters from Cave Creek once lapped at the state capitol in Phoenix. The Chase Creek floods in 1903 and 1983 not only wiped out large portions of Clifton, but also put an end to strikes when the water destroyed the miners' homes.[9]

Chapter 2 Prehistoric, Spanish, and Mexican Antecedents

Early pioneer Jack Swilling named the settlement that would eventually become Arizona's capitol Phoenix as a way of reminding inhabitants that others had come before. Arizona's unique character has its roots in prehistoric times and the earliest years of European settlement—the diversity of water control methods and sophisticated large-scale canal irrigation of the Hohokam, the water conservation practices of the Anasazi, and the introduction of Hispanic cultural influences that can be traced back to Islamic origins. This early cultural background set the stage for later adaptations to desert water management, including the reuse of Hohokam canals by American settlers in the Salt River Valley.

The cultures that adapted to the desert environment prior to the arrival of American settlers in Arizona left a legacy of water control techniques and perceptions. Much of what is different about patterns of water use in Arizona is a result of these groups and their contributions. These early strategies established points of comparison with later American water utilization patterns.

Prehistoric Water Use

Archaeologists generally categorize prehistoric water use into two types: irrigated and nonirrigated. Irrigation consists of diverting surface water flowing in streams into canals or ditches for delivery to crops. Agriculture was also practiced using nonirrigation techniques that captured and conserved rainfall, increasing the amount of soil moisture available for plants.[1]

The Hohokam occupied the area from the Salt River Valley south along the Gila and Santa Cruz Rivers to the Tucson basin. The Hohokam were superb irrigators and agriculturalists. They began canal construction in the Pioneer period (A.D. 300), then refined their skill at building canal systems over the next few centuries. Prior to A.D. 1100, Hohokam settlements consisted of villages of pit-houses. The larger villages had ball courts, where a type of ceremonial game was played. After A.D. 1100, the Hohokam began to construct aboveground adobe houses. Larger villages included mounds of earth and large structures. The Hohokam of this later period left a legacy of monumental architecture. The Casa Grande ruin along the Gila River and Pueblo Grande in the Salt River Valley is a testament to their high level of civilization.[2]

While the evidence of Hohokam accomplishments is strongest along the Salt and Gila Rivers, recent archaeological work in Tucson has revealed that the canals there are extremely old. There appears to be a long sequence of continuous habitation in the Santa Cruz Valley dating back at least three thousand years. Excavations near the San Agustín Mission uncovered a small canal constructed at least two thousand years ago. Other work has pushed back the development of agriculture in the Tucson area to 3100 B.P., with a continuous transition to irrigation use.[3]

By the time Spanish explorers found the ruins along the Gila River the Hohokam designers and builders were long gone. The word Hohokam means "those who have gone before" in the language of the Pima Indians (Akimel O'odham). Archaeologists estimate that the Hohokam constructed more than 350 miles of canals along the Salt River in the Phoenix area alone, with additional canals along other rivers in central and southern Arizona. This system of canals was the most extensive network of prehistoric irrigation in North America. The Hohokam irrigated about one hundred thousand acres of land in the Salt River Valley.[4]

Spanish explorers commented on the dimensions of the Hohokam canals. In 1699, Juan Mateo Manje described a canal in the Casa Grande area
that measured "10 varas [27.5 feet] wide and four varas [11 feet] deep."
Archaeologists have found fewer and smaller canals in the Tucson basin,
averaging 6 feet wide by 5 feet deep.[5]

While the Hohokam are renowned as the premier desert irrigation specialists in North America, they actually used many methods to control
and utilize water. In addition to canals, the Hohokam developed terracing,
check dams, rock piles, and linear and grid borders. As with other prehistoric cultures in Arizona, Hohokam water control features fall into two
categories: irrigation, such as canals and ditches; and nonirrigated or indirect methods, such as soil moisture conservation techniques.[6]

As distance increases from the Hohokam heartland of the Salt and Gila
Rivers, indirect methods of water control take on added significance. During an archaeological survey of Tumamoc Hill in Tucson, Bruce Masse
found considerable evidence of indirect water control features which included more than one thousand rock piles, thirty contour terraces, two
series of check dams, bordered gardens, and channeling borders. Archaeologists Paul and Suzanne Fish, during their survey of thousands of acres
in the northern Tucson basin, documented numerous indirect water control features, including some sites that measured hundreds of acres in
extent.[7]

Archaeologists have categorized indirect nonirrigation methods into
three types: floodwater, runoff, and dry farming. In floodwater farming,
native people followed floods to plant seeds in the moistened earth as
the water receded. This type of farming was practiced along the Colorado
River floodplain. Another type of floodwater farming is called *ak chin* farming, a technique that involves capturing and directing seasonal rainfall at
the outlet of washes to locations where crops could be grown.[8]

Runoff agriculture differed from ak chin agriculture in that it was most
often used on flat terraces and mesa tops rather than at the mouth of
washes. Farmers used similar techniques in these areas, such as check
dams and rock borders to direct and conserve water flow. Dry farming,
common in the mountain and plateau areas of the state, used stone terraces and rock piles to collect and preserve soil moisture from the little
rain that fell.[9]

Members of the Chaco culture, located in the Anasazi region of the plateau, became experts in nonirrigated agriculture. A variety of methods, from floodwater farming to stone terraces and gridlike fields, were used in Chaco Canyon. This allowed for the development of an advanced level of civilization for the Anasazi, including a network of roads for trading and monumental architecture.[10]

Archaeologists have long puzzled over what caused the rapid decline of cultures such as the Hohokam and Anasazi. By 1450, the Hohokam civilization abruptly vanished, leaving only traces of once prosperous villages. An environmental change may have rendered their technology obsolete. Social and cultural factors may also have played a part. A disruption in this society, one in which all members had to work in concert to survive, could have critically affected the community water supply.[11]

It may be simplistic to think that one reason can be cited for the decline of these great cultures. More likely, a number of factors contributed to their decline and demise. Most archaeologists believe the Hohokam faced problems with their water supply due to changes in the climate and environment that were exacerbated by dense populations. Their irrigated fields may have become waterlogged and covered with saline deposits, from which they saw no solution. Streams critical to water diversion may have become entrenched, leaving headgates for canals and ditches above the water level. Evidence exists that a change in summer-dominant rainfall occurred after A.D. 1200, and that headcuts caused channel erosion. At first, headcutting was discontinuous and the Hohokam could move their water control features to more auspicious locations. Over time the effect may have become more widespread, leading to a disruption of direct control methods and an increasing reliance on indirect water control.[12]

For the Anasazi, less dependent on irrigated agriculture, it appears that population may have outstripped the supply of available resources. Locating finite resources such as timber, water, and agricultural land required greater effort as residents exhausted nearby supplies. Climate change in northern Arizona may also have played an important role. A long drought in the middle of the twelfth century appears to have made shortages of raw materials even worse, thus contributing to famine and population decline.[13]

In the end, the decline of prehistoric cultures might be traced to changes in the environment for which they could not adapt new tech-

The demise of the Hohokam, often attributed to problems with their water supply, provides a cautionary tale. This Reg Manning editorial cartoon appeared in the *Arizona Republic* newspaper on February 23, 1947.

nology. While optimistic Anglo settlers named their new community Phoenix in honor of an earlier civilization, others may have taken a different lesson from the past. The experience of the Hohokam is a cautionary tale for modern residents of the desert. The water supply must be protected and conserved, because it is the basic resource of society.

Spain Sets a Pattern

A near complete break in human habitation marked the period between the fall of the Hohokam and the arrival of the Spanish. When the Spanish first sent settlers to what is now Arizona in the late 1680s and early 1690s there were no permanent Indian settlements on the Salt River, and only a few small villages on the Gila. The Spaniards concentrated their settlement efforts in the area they called the Pimeria Alta, the northern portion of the region inhabited by the Pima-speaking Indians that is now southern Arizona and northern Mexico. This was one of the few places the missionaries found enough native inhabitants to make the effort of settlement worth pursuing.

The Spaniards established the first missions in what became Arizona from their base in Santa Fe. In 1629 the Franciscans opened missions at the Hopi villages of Awatovi, Shgópovi, and Oraibi. However, Spanish officials were unable to extend much influence so far from Santa Fe, even less so after the Pueblo Revolt of 1680 against the Franciscan priests and Spanish settlers.

Father Eusebio Francisco Kino visited what is now Arizona as early as 1691, when he held services at the Indian village of Tumacácori on the Santa Cruz River. He ventured further north the following year, visiting the Indian village called Bac. Kino named the location for his patron saint, Francisco Xavier. Combining native and European names, Kino christened the location San Xavier del Bac. In 1694, he pushed on to the Gila River and recorded the location of the Casa Grande ruin. He also revisited Bac and a second village, further north along the Santa Cruz, which he named San Cosme del Tucson. Kino eventually established three missions in Arizona: Guevavi, Tumacácori, and San Xavier.

We owe much of what we know about early Spanish activities in the Tucson basin to Captain Juan Mateo Manje. Manje and a company of soldiers accompanied Kino in 1697 when the Jesuit brought domesticated animals and sheep north to share with the native inhabitants. Captain Manje noted that San Xavier possessed rich land, all of which was under irrigation. Two years later, on a return visit in March, he recorded that the natives had "sufficient cultivated lands watered by means of good ditches" to support two thousand people. At that time, approximately eight hundred people lived at the San Xavier site. Manje described Father Kino's personal observation about the agricultural potential of San Xavier on his visit to the village on October 27, 1699: "The fields and lands for sowing were so extensive and supplied with so many irrigation ditches running along the ground that the father visitor said they were sufficient for another city like Mexico."[14]

The Spaniards traced the agricultural zone along the Santa Cruz downstream to the north, encountering two other villages with sizeable populations. Three leagues (eight miles) north of Bac, on the west bank, they visited San Cosme and two leagues farther on the village of San Agustín, on the east bank. In 1697 at San Agustín, Manje noted "numerous irrigation ditches watered the abundant crops of corn, beans, cotton, squash, cantaloupes, and watermelons." The next year Kino described the area between Bac and San Agustín as "the most populous and most fertile spot in the whole valley. The natives had extensive fields under irrigation, raised large crops of maize, frijoles, cotton, calabashes, watermelons and cantaloupes, wove the cotton and wore it for clothing." Further north, in the "Valle de Correa," near the Rillito narrows, the Spanish explorers and missionaries found another village. Here a deep well and crops dependent on seasonal rainfall supported a population of one hundred people. These conditions impressed Kino so much that in 1706 he recommended San Agustín as the site for a mission.[15]

Mission building at San Agustín would have to wait while the Spaniards concentrated their efforts at the more populous village of Bac. Here an adequate water supply and a diversion system were the primary reasons for locating a mission. The Spaniards brought stone from the nearby mountains and drew water for the mortar from irrigation ditches. Their first mission, begun April 26, 1700 (south of the present structure), became a base for Spanish activity in the area. They introduced domestic animals and new crops. Kino opened agricultural fields and brought herds of animals from the Altar Valley to the mission during the period from 1691 to 1702. In 1700 alone, he drove in seven hundred head of cattle.[16]

Spanish Urban Water Traditions

The Spaniards were adept at water control technology. Spain was also an arid environment, and had been exposed to new ideas of engineering during the long Moorish occupation from 711 to 1492. When the Spaniards established settlements in the New World, they chose locations where water could be easily put to use for irrigation. They brought skilled hydraulic engineers and a well-established system of laws. Because of their experience living in a dry climate, Spaniards did little to change native methods of water use that resembled their own traditional patterns.[17]

Both Spanish and Indian cultures depended on irrigation. However, the presumed similarity of Spanish and Indian water use actually masked the great level of control the Spaniards exerted over the Native American inhabitants of the Southwest. More often than not, they exercised this power through control of water resources.

The Spaniards tempered their control over water because of their missionary activities. If they appropriated too much water or land, the Indians were not very receptive to proselytizing. Water systems were necessary for the successful operation of the mission program, but too much control could prove disastrous. Father Kino, writing of his 1691 visit to the Santa Cruz Valley, noted that the native inhabitants expressed concern that the ranching activities of the missionaries had dried up local springs.[18]

The Spaniards had a tremendous impact on native agriculture. They introduced new crops, including wheat, kidney beans, lentils, vetch, and chickpeas. They brought in livestock and domestic animals. As a result, the use of land, dams, and ditches increased. The language of water use in Arizona dates to Spanish times. The Spanish word for canal, *acequia*, is still used today. Water users in Arizona still refer to a ditch tender as a *zanjero*.

The most far-reaching Spanish impact on water resources was in the area of law. The Europeans brought a complex of legal institutions which they modified for the New World. Their interest in water regulation is reflected in land grant documents mentioning both land and water, in contrast to English grants which usually mention only land. The most significant Spanish impact on water is reflected in the Latin phrase "qui prior est in tempore, potior est in jure" (first in time, first in right). This doctrine of prior appropriation became the keystone of western water law.[19]

Although Spanish law recognized that the first person to put the water to use had the first right to it, in actual practice Spanish settlers in the New World adopted a more pragmatic approach. Spanish and later Mexican settlers negotiated a communal approach to water that recognized the value of the resource in arid regions. This belief can be traced to

Islamic influence in Spain that emphasized cleanliness. Legal historian Peter Reich observed that "priority was just one of many criteria used to resolve water disputes" in Hispanic Arizona.[20]

In 1770, the Spaniards established a mission at the village of San Agustín on the east bank of the Santa Cruz. Prior to this time, Tucson existed as an outlying village to the mission of Bac. By February of 1771, the mission residence was completed and the next year church construction began. In 1775, Hugo O'Conor, an Irish soldier employed by the Spanish crown, selected a location on the east bank of the Santa Cruz across from the mission as the location of a *presidio* (fort). In 1776, Spanish authorities moved the presidio of Tubac to Tucson to afford protection to local Pima and Sobaipuri villages and for land travel to California. By 1782 soldiers had enclosed the presidio at Tucson with a fortified wall of adobe.[21]

At the Tucson presidio, Spanish farmers built acequias to supply their fields in the Santa Cruz River floodplain, the largest known as the acequia madre. Inside the presidio, a large well provided water to the soldiers. Outside the walls, a water-filled ditch left after excavating soil for making adobes on the presidio's north side was used for bathing and laundering. The soldiers also hauled water from the Santa Cruz and, in times of drought, dug shallow wells and procured water with a bucket and rope. The increase in Spanish population caused clashes with local Indians. Encroachment by Spanish settlers aggravated the scarcity of water and led to an agreement in 1776 that guaranteed the Indians three-fourths of the water from the Santa Cruz, while one-fourth would go to the presidio.[22]

Stock raising and agriculture provided the mainstay of Tucson's economy during the Spanish period. In 1804, the total community agricultural production averaged less than four thousand bushels a year, two-thirds in the form of wheat. This limited production may have been due to continuing tensions between Spanish settlers and Indians over water availability. The local Spanish population remained small; in 1819 Tucson had between eighty and ninety soldiers and three hundred settlers.[23]

The walled settlement of Tucson was one of the final outposts of the Spanish empire in the New World. Spain's grip on its empire began to slip in 1810 when Father Hidalgo called for a war of independence from Spain. Mexico achieved this goal in 1821, and Tucson became part of a new nation. Despite the political change, residents on Mexico's northern frontier continued their traditional patterns of water use. Communal ditches watered small agricultural plots. Residents obtained domestic water from wells.

Mexican Antecedents

Mexican independence from Spain in 1821 had little immediate impact on Arizona in terms of water utilization. While the change in political control would later have far-reaching consequences for American settlement in Arizona, the immediate environmental impact of Mexican independence remained small. Recent research by historian Michael F. Logan places the population of the Tucson area at two thousand souls near the end of Spanish political control in 1800. Logan compares this figure to a population of between five thousand and ten thousand at the height of the Hohokam occupation of the Santa Cruz river valley. The impact of European diseases had contributed to the decline in population.[24]

The withdrawal of Spanish religious and military authority after Mexico achieved its independence had a negative effect on urban and agricultural development in Arizona. This change began when the Mexican government secularized the missions by federal decree late in 1827. Local residents plundered mission lands and agricultural fields went untilled. Mission herds, no longer controlled, roamed wild. Civil authorities took advantage of the situation to increase their proportion of water rights by reducing the Indian allocation of the Santa Cruz River from three-fourths to one-half in 1828.[25]

Perhaps the most far-reaching effect of the removal of Spanish military forces was the disruption in relations between the Apache and local residents. The Spaniards and the Apache had reached an agreement that allowed for payments of food and goods by the Spanish in exchange for peace. This agreement lapsed with the departure of the Spanish, and in 1831 the Apache rose in revolt and resumed traditional cycles of raiding. These raids made the practice of agriculture difficult in the Santa Cruz and San Pedro river valleys. Relative newcomers themselves, the Apache competed with Mexican settlers for control of land and resources.[26]

As a means to combat Apache raiding and to encourage settlement, the Mexican government made a number of land grants in its northern provinces. Most of the grants were filed between 1821 and 1833, although one was filed as late as 1841. While some grants were eventually confirmed in Arizona, an even larger number of grants were found to be fraudulent. Those that were legitimate had often passed out of the hands of the original Mexican settlers and into the ownership of American speculators by the time the grants were confirmed. These claims are significant for defining some of the earliest water rights in Arizona.

Summary

Each of the earliest cultures in Arizona depended on a series of adaptations to subsist in the region. Prehistoric Indian groups used a variety of water control methods. The Spaniards, although skilled in the technology of water use, tempered their control to achieve their religious aims. The Mexicans, abandoning Spanish ecclesiastical concerns, began to develop water resources on a larger scale. Mexican residents were more concerned with economic pursuits and with permanent settlement in the area. For all of these groups, their water control methods and perceptions reflected their goals and attitudes toward the environment.

By the end of the Mexican era Hispanic settlers had adapted to the dry desert valleys of southern Arizona. Farmers maintained acequias and planted crops. Skillful in the management of water, Hispanic residents of Arizona relied on traditional engineering systems for their agricultural practices. They excavated new wells and continued to use burros to haul water from the Santa Cruz for sale in Tucson.[27]

Although Spanish legal authorities developed the doctrine of prior appropriation, in order to pursue their religious goals officials involved in day-to-day relations with native groups used a communal approach to water development. Available resources were shared in order to produce the harvests of grain that assisted with the conversion process. The Spaniards learned that native peoples would not stand for too much disruption in their traditional ways of water use.

Part II The Fledgling Cities, 1825-1912

The period from 1825 to 1880 highlights the early reactions of American explorers and settlers to Hispanic patterns of water use. After an initial period of interaction that culminated in the War with Mexico, American settlers began to establish communities in Arizona. These frontier towns would eventually grow into the dense urban centers of today's Arizona.

Business enterprises dominated the provision of urban services in the fledgling cities. Private entrepreneurs constructed the earliest municipal water supply systems in Arizona in the 1880s. Around 1900, municipal leaders in the territory's larger communities began to take control of these private water systems and convert them to public entities. By the first decade of the twentieth century several of the larger city governments had achieved municipal ownership of the water utilities in their community. In the second decade of the twentieth century, during which Arizona attained statehood in 1912, mature municipal governments began to develop their own plans to improve and expand public water systems.

The era from 1880 to 1900 can be characterized as a period of private solutions to the water question. This emphasis had its roots in institutional factors, particularly the limit on municipal indebtedness in territories that prevented city leaders from operating utilities. Technology and access to capital also limited the options of government and led private individuals to find their own solutions to water supply problems. When these individuals determined that utilities could be profit-making entities, business leaders expanded their operations into several arenas. The developers of water systems also established electrical utilities, gas works, and street railways.

As city leaders became more sophisticated in their relations with entrepreneurs and speculators, they began to demand increased levels of service. In doing so public officials established standards for water service and for the provision of municipal services as a whole. By 1912 most larger Arizona towns and cities had assumed ownership of the water infrastructure in their communities.

Chapter 3 First Impressions

Early American Settlement in Arizona

Sylvester Pattie and his son James Ohio Pattie were the first American explorers to enter what is now Arizona when they trapped along the Gila River in 1825. The period from 1825 to 1880 was one of dramatic transition, beginning with the arrival of the first American trappers and concluding with the arrival of the railroad at Tucson. Significant events in the transition to American political control include the War with Mexico from 1846 to 1848, the creation of the Territory of New Mexico in 1850 (which included today's Arizona north of the Gila River), the Gadsden Purchase of Arizona south of the Gila River from Mexico in 1854, and the creation of a separate Arizona territory in 1863.

Trappers and Transportation in Arizona

Trappers such as the Patties and Ewing Young followed the Gila River in search of beaver, and in doing so they identified an early transportation route across Arizona. Although topography in its upper reaches proved difficult, the Gila River formed an easy travel corridor across Arizona. After their trapping days were over many mountain men served as guides for later explorers, U.S. Army expeditions, and prospectors.

In 1846 war broke out between the United States and Mexico over the annexation of Texas. The war resulted in the first arrival of American military forces in Arizona. After capturing Santa Fe without a shot, on October 21, 1846, Colonel Stephen Watts Kearney and his "Army of the West" began a journey to California by following the Gila River. Kearney reached the Colorado River and California on November 22, 1846. This pioneering route became known as the Gila Trail and in a few years would carry thousands of gold-seekers across Arizona to California in search of wealth.

After Kearney had occupied Santa Fe, and before he began his march to California, he legitimized his control of the Southwest by preparing a code of basic laws to govern the area. Although he delegated this task to some of the lawyers in his party of Missouri volunteers, this first legal document became known as the Kearney Code. The basic thrust of the Kearney Code was to protect existing land and water rights. This was done to preserve the investments of the residents of New Mexico and Arizona. The result was to continue Hispanic traditions of water use.[1]

A second military expedition crossed Arizona during the War with Mexico. Led by Captain (later Lt. Colonel) Phillip St. George Cooke, the "Mormon Battalion" consisted of volunteer Latter-day Saints organized in Council Bluffs, Iowa, in July of 1846. Cooke and his party reached California in January of 1847, proving that wagons could traverse the territory and further linking the conquered territory with the United States. In contrast to Kearney, who bypassed Tucson, the Mormon Battalion passed through the Mexican village on the Santa Cruz.

The Treaty of Guadalupe Hidalgo, ratified in 1848, brought an end to the war. The treaty also brought a tremendous amount of new land into the United States. As a result of the war, the present states of Texas, New Mexico, Nevada, California, Utah, and portions of Colorado and Arizona were taken from Mexico. These new lands were the culmination of the concept of Manifest Destiny, the idea that the United States was destined to reach from the Atlantic Ocean to the Pacific. In Arizona, lands north of the Gila River became part of the United States for the first time. This area did not include Tucson, which remained a part of Mexico.

Like the Kearney Code that preceded it, the Treaty of Guadalupe Hidalgo protected the existing land and water rights of the inhabitants. While the drafters of the treaty gave residents of the conquered area the option of leaving the United States, few did so. Those who remained were to receive equal treatment with respect to their property rights as U.S. citizens. Although the objective of the treaty was not always achieved in practice, the clear intent was to limit any disruption in land tenure caused by the change in government.[2]

Initial Encounters: Tucson, 1846–1854

The unsettled conditions caused by the War with Mexico led to increased raiding activity by the Apache, resulting in a population loss and the abandonment of many ranches in southern Arizona. In December of 1846, when the Mormon Battalion passed through Tucson, its members noted that most of the city's inhabitants had left because of the war. The Mormons described seeing green patches of winter wheat and fruit trees along the Santa Cruz. The soil looked dark and rich but irrigation was needed for crops. In 1848, Tucson had 760 inhabitants, while 249 lived in Tubac. In December of that year Apaches killed 9 people in Tubac, inciting the residents of both Tubac and Tumacácori to move to Tucson in 1849.[3]

The California gold rush brought John Durviage through Tucson and San Xavier on May 28, 1849. Durviage noted that the lands "are rich and fertile in the extreme." The occupants of San Xavier managed to raise just enough corn for their own consumption but the old mission garden in Tucson was "well stocked with fruit." After obtaining a small quantity of flour and corn, Durviage continued on his journey to California.[4]

In October of 1849 Joseph Aldrich described the Tucson basin, noting that he had "passed a number of deserted ranches" and attributed this to Apache "hostilities and incursions." During his 1849 visit, Robert Eccelston estimated there were approximately eight hundred inhabitants in Tucson and several burro-powered flour mills. Eccelston had no trouble obtaining wheat, flour, and corn, as the harvest season had just ended. The only fruits available were quinces and the only vegetables pumpkins and peppers. Benjamin Hayes observed that the village of San Xavier produced "fine corn, wheat, and beans," along with garden vegetables. Most of the forty-niners seemed impressed with the agricultural potential of the Santa Cruz Valley.[5]

What we now know as Arizona first came into the United States as part of the Territory of New Mexico. Congress brought New Mexico into the United States as part of the Compromise of 1850, the result of a bitter debate over whether the lands obtained during the War with Mexico would be slave or free. Congress adopted New Mexico's Organic Act on September 9, 1850. This act created the Territory of New Mexico, which included Arizona. Like earlier legislative enactments, New Mexico's Organic Act had little immediate effect on traditional patterns of land and water use in the Southwest.[6]

As a means to open the new territory for development, Americans began to consider construction of a transcontinental railroad. Surveyors identified several possible routes. One proposal focused on the thirty-fifth parallel, and another followed the thirty-second parallel. Because the thiry-second parallel route ran through Mexico, its supporters—Southerners who would benefit from a railroad though the South—convinced Congress to purchase additional land to accommodate the southern route.

On December 30, 1853, James Gadsden executed an agreement with Mexico to purchase territory south of the Gila River. The U.S. Congress ratified the $10 million deal and President Franklin Pierce signed the legislation on June 30, 1854. The Gadsden Purchase brought what is now southern Arizona into the United States. This action opened the area for development and the eventual Southern Pacific railroad route through Arizona. From 1854 until the Civil War, a stream of American surveyors, freighters, cattle drovers, and immigrants crossed the new territory.

Early Private Water Efforts in Tucson, 1854–1865

Economic growth in the Tucson area during the period from 1854 to 1865 was unsteady. Conflict with the Apache, poor transportation, difficulty in commerce, and primitive ventures in both mining and agriculture characterized this era. Yet Tucson emerged as a center of urban development as an increasing number of Americans struggled to make permanent homes in the desert.[7]

Tucson in 1854 served mainly as a way station to protect settlers on the northern road to California. Mexican troops remained for two years after the Gadsden Purchase although Tucson was now part of the American Territory of New Mexico. Finally, in March of 1856, the United States sent troops to take over the region. In the bottomlands south and west of Tucson, farmers raised crops for the soldiers and settlers but produced no surplus.

Surveyor W. H. Emory, who visited Tucson in 1855, estimated that seventy families engaged in agriculture. "Some fine fields of wheat and corn were ready for the sickle," Emory reported. "Many varieties of fruit and all kinds of vegetables were also to be had, upon which we indulged our long-famished appetites." Agricultural pursuits still took great courage because of the constant threat from the Apache. So many settlers concentrated on defense and neglected agriculture that Tucson suffered from a food shortage in 1858.[8]

That same year, 1858, traveler Phocion Way estimated the population of Tucson at two hundred people, only a dozen of whom were Americans. Way described local water utilization and the contrasting attitudes of the two cultures in Tucson. Members of the Hispanic community obtained their water from the Santa Cruz River or irrigation ditches, while newly arrived Americans dug wells for domestic water use. A Mexican observer the 1850s described conditions a bit differently: "The women washed what clothes they had out in a ditch that ran along near the west wall [of the presidio]. Whenever they went out to do their washing the guards always went with them. For washboards they used big rocks. Inside the wall was a well and folks had plenty of water to use."[9]

The Civil War

The Civil War interrupted economic growth in Arizona and hindered the development of water technology. Military forces left Arizona for the war in the East. The Apache, already emboldened by the defeat of Mexican troops by the Americans, seized the opportunity to increase raiding activities. Until the arrival of California volunteer troops in May of 1862, Arizona was essentially without a U.S. military presence. This atmosphere of uncertainty adversely affected agricultural and industrial water use. So little forage or flour was produced in the Tucson area the military garrison imported food from Sonora.[10]

While wartime disruptions curtailed water development, the Civil War generated changes that would later have a profound effect on water use. Mineral discoveries, principally gold, led the administration of Abraham Lincoln and Congress to carve a separate Territory of Arizona from New Mexico Territory in 1863. Arizona's gold would provide desperately needed revenue for the Union forces during the Civil War. To protect these re-

Women washed clothes in the Santa Cruz River in Tucson near the ruins of the
San Agustín Mission.

sources, Union leaders designated loyal Republicans as governor and territorial officials.

One of the first actions of the territorial legislature was to enact a comprehensive legal code. Known as the Howell Code for its author, Judge William T. Howell, the document contained several provisions to govern water resources. The code retained Spanish and Mexican customs regarding the regulation of acequias and stated that water should be held appurtenant to the land, following Mexican law.[11]

Legal precedent going back to Spanish law had established the principle of "first in time, first in use." With respect to water, this became known as the prior appropriation doctrine, meaning the first person to put the water to use had the first right to it. Mining law in the West also followed this theory, giving rights to the first person to discover the minerals. This doctrine would become increasingly significant in later years when competition and droughts created a scarcity of water resources. As a result of the doctrine of prior appropriation, long-time water users had priority over those who had only recently begun to put water to use.

The Aftermath of the Civil War in Tucson

After the Civil War, Tucson's fortunes brightened as Americans once again looked west for economic potential. Beginning in 1866, the area's population grew considerably as advances in mining, commerce, and territorial government activities drew American settlers to the banks of the Santa Cruz. New firms located in southern Arizona. The county seat since 1864, Tucson also served as the territorial capital from 1867 until 1877.[12]

Tucson residents continued to obtain water from the Santa Cruz River and from springs and wells. "Water, when not bought from the old Mexican who hauled it in barrels in a dilapidated cart from the cool spring on the Bishop's farm, was obtained from wells, which were good and sweet in the first months of their career," wrote James Bourke during his 1869 visit. These wells averaged fifteen to twenty feet in depth, and water was drawn up with a rope and bucket. Bourke added that the wells soon became impregnated with alkali and because of this, the city possessed "innumerable abandoned wells which were to be met with in every block."[13]

Industrial use of water increased in Tucson with the demands of the local population and economic growth. In 1870, the Eagle Flour Mill was operating at capacity, working night and day to process grain from Santa Cruz Valley farms. The steam-powered mill consisted of six buildings and could grind seven thousand pounds of flour in twelve hours. Governor Anson P. K. Safford estimated in 1874 that the mill ground six hundred thousand pounds of flour per year. Owners James Lee and William F. Scott "delighted to blow the steam whistle, its loud shriek sent dogs howling." Even the steam-powered mill could not keep up with demand, and older methods continued. James Bell, during an 1874 visit, mentioned several flour mills powered by burros.[14]

Enterprising Americans soon took advantage of the situation. Solomon Warner planned a water-powered mill and negotiated an agreement with Bishop John B. Salpointe for water rights. The agreement, signed on October 17, 1874, granted Warner the right to construct a water ditch on the west side of the mission garden, gave him right-of-way for the ditch, and allowed use of the acequia madre in the Santa Cruz floodplain west of the mission for his tailrace. In exchange, Warner would grind wheat for the church.[15]

Warner constructed a dam at the base of Sentinel Peak and by 1875 had machinery in place to complete his mill. Warner's Lake, extending south from the Sentinel Peak dam, covered thirty-seven acres with a water depth of fifteen feet. Always the entrepreneur, Warner stocked the lake with fish, which he sold to Tucson residents. In 1879 he added an ore-reduction stamp mill to complement his flour mill.[16]

Water was also used for recreation. In 1879 Leopoldo Carrillo purchased thirteen acres of land south of the road to San Agustín (the old Convento, built after 1800) and Warner's Mill. Carrillo converted several acres, "then covered with the usual growth of bushes," into what became known as Carrillo Gardens. Carrillo apparently patterned his gardens after the Woodward Gardens of San Francisco. He excavated a main ditch and several side ditches into the mesa and diverted the water into a fifty-foot square stone tank with a pump. Carrillo used this water to irrigate the former wasteland. Traveler Richard J. Hinton described the site as "a beautiful flower, fruit, and vegetable garden with sand and gravel paths." In later years it became known as Elysian Gardens. Carrillo School now stands on the site.[17]

The windmill, introduced by Americans in the 1870s, revolutionized water procurement and many windmills dotted the city. Even so, conditions still seemed crude to some travelers. James Bell described his visit in 1874: "We will move to-day—such is the last order, and I am very glad of it, if only to get good drinking water, for we have been using the water that the cattle are running through and drinking it."[18]

This situation inspired the entrepreneurial spirit in Tucson business-men. Adam Saunders and Joseph Phy took over the water trade from Mexican peddlers and established a monopoly. They sold buckets of water for five cents each, delivered by wagon from house to house. For the convenience of residents, they also offered coupon books of twenty-five-cent tickets for one dollar.[19]

In the late 1870s a "waterworks fever" hit Arizona. Generated by abuses such as water monopolies and the danger of fire in the bustling communities, cities and towns struggled to create municipal water utilities. Tucson awarded its first municipal water contract in 1875 to develop a supply from artesian wells. When the venture proved unsuccessful, Tucson tried again in 1879, this time awarding a contract to Thomas J. Jeffords. On April 11, Mayor James H. Toole gave Jeffords a twenty-five-year franchise. For the first well drilled, the city would give one block of land, and for each additional well one lot. Jeffords could sink as many wells as necessary to supply the city with water. In May, Jeffords began to erect machinery on a site south of the city, consisting of a well drilling rig with a thirty-horsepower steam engine to drill an eight-inch-diameter well. Most of the equipment for the project came from California, and by the end of June thirty-five thousand pounds of machinery had arrived. Jeffords hoped to have the well in operation by the Fourth of July. After an expenditure of twenty-five thousand dollars Jeffords failed to hit an artesian flow, but the well did provide some water to the city. This pioneering effort would see fruit in later years.[20]

Early Settlement in Phoenix and the Salt River Valley

The establishment of Phoenix in 1865 coincided with a growing interest in irrigation development across the West. At this time a network of pre-historic Hohokam canals was still evident in the Phoenix area. Entrepreneurs and farmers quickly realized the time and money to be saved by following the course laid out by the master irrigators who had gone before.[21]

On November 11, 1867, Jack Swilling and a group of Salt River Valley farmers claimed six thousand miner's inches of water from the Salt River for irrigating purposes and recorded the filing with the Yavapai County Recorder in Prescott. Five days later, at a meeting in Wickenburg, the group organized the Swilling Irrigating and Canal Company. In December, Swilling and a group of twenty other men began construction of an irrigation canal on the north side of the Salt River near Tempe Buttes. When they were stopped by a hard formation of caliche, they moved downstream and began work on a canal three or four miles west of their initial attempt. It soon became evident that the canal could not be completed in time for the planting season. The group then constructed a temporary ditch and planted several hundred acres of corn and beans. Work continued on the Swilling Ditch during the interim, later known as the Salt River Valley Canal or Town Ditch.[22]

Swilling's efforts proved successful and opened the Salt River Valley to agricultural enterprise. In 1868, Swilling and Thomas Barnum took out a new ditch three-fourths of a mile upstream from the Swilling Ditch head. Organized as the Phoenix Ditch Company, this "north extension" ditch later became known as the Maricopa Canal. To the south of the Swilling Ditch, Jacob and Andrew Starer completed the Dutch Ditch. Columbus H. Gray, James Murphy, and John B. Montgomery also settled along the Dutch Ditch. By 1870 a thriving farming community of 240 souls had fifteen hundred acres under cultivation.[23]

During the 1870s, Phoenix residents relied on the Salt River, irrigation ditches, or wells for their domestic water supplies. In August of 1870 a correspondent to the Prescott *Arizona Miner* reported about Phoenix: "Digging wells has commenced. One of sixteen feet has a large supply of delicious water. At present the ditches supply nearly every demand of man, beast and crop." In a letter dated August 31, 1872, a Phoenix resident reported "Recent rains have damaged the ditches—so town has no water for a week, except that which has been hauled from river or drawn from wells."[24]

The town commissioners arranged to supply irrigation ditches with water from the Salt River Valley Canal which ran along Van Buren Street at the north edge of town. Although wealthier inhabitants managed to dig wells for personal household needs, most residents used water from the irrigation ditches for both irrigation and domestic purposes. For community use, the town commissioners contracted for a dug well in the town plaza. In 1879 Judge John T. Alsap erected the first windmill in Phoenix for pumping water.[25]

Saloons and hotels, charged with meeting the demands of residents and travelers alike, led the way in the installation of plumbing fixtures and distribution systems. In 1878, Phoenix Hotel owner John J. Gardiner made news when he introduced shower baths. Toilets added the following year completed the indoor plumbing system and made the hotel a "resort" for the "dusty traveler." Gardiner later added a swimming pool.[26]

In the 1870s, the owners of the Capitol Saloon at Twenty-seven East Adams Street built a small water distribution system. Using a good well located in back of the saloon, the barkeepers pumped water to an elevated tank and from there distributed it to five or six other businesses, including a Chinese laundry, a bathhouse, and one or two other saloons. Early resident John Rau recalled that he first saw the system in operation in 1879 and said "it was old then." The fountain from the well at the Capitol Saloon provided most of the residents of Phoenix with drinking water. In 1879, the general public found only three other wells convenient for obtaining water: one in Doctor Thibido's backyard, a second in Monihon's Corral, and the third in the stage corral.[27]

By 1880, census takers recorded a population of 1,708 residents in Phoenix. That fall, a group of citizens raised money by subscription to place a pump in the plaza well. By the end of October, the public-spirited boosters completed the project, placing a secure cover over the old dug well to prevent debris and garbage from contaminating it and installing a hand pump for the benefit of the citizenry.[28]

Summary

The Territory of Arizona was an arid land, but one that had seen successful development by prehistoric Hohokam and Anasazi, contemporary Native American groups, Spaniards, and Mexicans. In Tucson, occupation by different cultural groups had been continuous since the Hohokam era. The process of water development continued after Americans took over the area. For much of the period between 1825 and the coming of the railroad in 1880, American water development followed the pattern of earlier cultures. While growth was slow and uneven, the seeds for later growth were planted.

Pioneering efforts in the early years of American political control in Arizona proved that the area had tremendous potential for economic development. Every success eroded the general belief of many Americans that Arizona was an inhospitable desert. The Carrillo Gardens in Tucson provides the best example of how settlers might transform a "wasteland" into a productive and attractive area. The success of Jack Swilling's transformation of old Hohokam irrigation canals in Phoenix to new agricultural uses demonstrated that a great urban civilization might someday rise again in Arizona.

Chapter 4 Water Entrepreneurs

The Private Era

Private business interests dominated water service in Arizona from 1880 to 1900. Entrepreneurs ranged from the corporate owners of the Atlantic and Pacific Railroad in Flagstaff to Hispanics in Tucson who carried water from house to house on the backs of burros. More typical were the pioneering businessmen such as John J. Gardiner in Phoenix or Thomas J. Jeffords in Tucson who attempted to build the first municipal water systems.

Corporate owners followed the early individual entrepreneurs. Water systems required an amount of capital beyond the reach of smaller business owners. In addition to hard money, owners of water systems often had to manipulate political capital as well. Larger corporate entities often proved more adept at manipulating the political system to their advantage, a key asset for the success of corporate water utilities.

Arizona Was Urban

The private era of water development took place in an increasingly urban environment. Despite the popular image of the West as wide-open spaces, vast landscapes, and a sparse population, even in the nineteenth century the vast majority of Westerners were urban dwellers. Mining towns serve

Arizona's urban centers and political boundaries

as the best example. These boomtowns went up quickly, gained a large population in close proximity to the mine or smelter, and often vanished just as quickly. Even agricultural communities were centralized close to the location of the economic enterprise. In many instances this was for protection of the settlers from Native Americans who were hostile to the new arrivals. For both mining and agricultural towns, the location of particular resources—metal-bearing ore or water—played a key role in the founding of American settlements. Western communities are often described as "oases in the desert" and in the sense that they were isolated locales of habitation this is an accurate picture.

Towns in the territory (Arizona did not become a state until 1912) were truly fledgling communities. Compared to other cities in the West, Arizona's largest towns were small indeed. In 1900, the year many Arizona communities were asserting municipal control over their water resources, Phoenix had a population of 5,600 people; for comparison, San Francisco had 342,800, Denver 133,900, and Los Angeles 102,500. Even El Paso, a community that Phoenix boosters would eventually perceive as their chief rival for control of the Southwest economy, had 16,000. Tucson in 1900 had a population of just over 7,500. New arrivals encountering the sprawling Phoenix metropolitan area may think Phoenix was always the dominant community in Arizona, with Tucson a close second. The 2000 U.S. Census indicated that Phoenix rose to the sixth largest city in the United States, but it only became the largest city in Arizona in 1920.[1]

Tucson's Private Water Systems, 1880–1900

Following the 1880 arrival of the Southern Pacific Railroad in Tucson, land speculation became the new driving force in Tucson's economy. In 1881, a company called Real Estate Associates purchased four hundred acres of land northwest of the city and made plans to sell lots to settlers. The developers promised that each plot of land would have a hydrant, from which the residents could "water the lawns, shrubbery, and flower gardens." Water was the key to land development and its distribution became increasingly sophisticated.[2]

When the army first established Fort Lowell on the Rillito River, soldiers used mule teams to haul water from the stream. When this became inadequate, the men constructed an acequia for bathing and washing, irrigation, and for watering the livestock and the post garden. They obtained drinking water from wells powered by windmills.[3]

By January of 1884, the military had opened four wells with an average depth of thirty-seven feet to supply domestic water to the fort. Pumped water was stored in a three-thousand-gallon tank. By the next year this was inadequate, and the military planned to divert water from Sabino Canyon. On May 15, 1886, an executive order extended the military reservation up the canyon where a dam site had been selected. However, settler

Calvin A. Elliot had claimed water rights to the canyon in 1883. Faced with this prior claim, the military decided to install a steam pump and new tanks instead. For an expenditure of $2,585, in August of 1887 the army purchased two ten-thousand-gallon tanks and a fifteen-horsepower pump. These changes solved the water supply problem, and the soldiers gained the luxury of a steam-powered ice machine as part of the project.[4]

Agricultural development along the Rillito brought additional settlers to Tucson. John Davidson organized the Santa Catalina Ditch and Irrigating Company to build a canal from the Rillito. He planned to irrigate nearly thirty-five hundred acres. In June of 1887, sixty workers labored on the project and finished two hundred feet of concrete flume. The plans called for a concrete infiltration gallery four feet wide and five feet high, which would be buried eleven feet beneath the surface. Holes in the gallery would allow water to collect and empty into a canal that ran along the south side of the Rillito to the location of present Dodge Avenue. There, an inverted siphon underneath the Rillito would carry water to a canal for irrigating lands on the north side. A late summer flood in 1887 washed out the canal and ended the project.[5]

Industrial water use in the 1880s centered on the two mill sites in the Santa Cruz Valley: Solomon Warner's Mill and Silver Lake. In 1881, J. F. Rickey and J. O. Bailey leased land from James Lee at Silver Lake to construct a hotel, bathhouses, pavilion, and picnic grove. In 1884, following the death of Lee, Fred Maish and Thomas Driscoll acquired the property and renovated the facilities. In late 1886 heavy floods hit the valley and damaged Silver Lake dam. Subsequent floods in 1887, 1889, and 1890 further damaged the property and in 1890 the hotel burned down.[6]

Solomon Warner also made improvements to his facilities during this period. In 1883, he constructed an earthen dam south of Sentinel Peak and built a rock-lined ditch to divert the collected waters to his mill. The dam impounded approximately twenty acres of water. These water diversions altered the amount of water available to agriculture in the central Tucson basin and would later lead to a legal dispute between downstream users and upstream diverters.[7]

By 1881, most of the water available from the Santa Cruz River was being diverted into acequias. Irrigation water sold in 1886 for $1.25 an acre. The *Arizona Mining Index* commented on the level of development: "Eight streams of water run through the Santa Cruz Valley opposite Tucson. Five of these ditches are 7 ft. wide that now contain a foot and a half of running water. The other three are narrower and contain less."[8]

In the Santa Cruz district irrigators employed a zanjero, or water overseer, to regulate the flow of water in the acequias. A water judge settled disputes and levied assessments of fifty cents an acre for improvements to ditches and water facilities. An informal water users association elected the overseer and the judge and paid them small salaries. During the spring, the irrigators pooled labor to repair and weed the ditches.[9]

Environmental change accompanied the increasing use of land and water in Tucson. Exceptionally heavy floods that began in 1887 were the immediate cause of erosion and channel entrenchment in the Santa Cruz River, but overgrazing, wagon roads, railroad construction, and poor farming practices aggravated these conditions. Gullies formed along linear paths created by cattle trails, roads, and ditches, leading to entrenchment. Water following these paths eroded soil. Although natural climatic changes played a part in the situation, the conversion of much of southern Arizona's once extensive grasslands to mesquite scrubland may have been caused by overuse of land and water in the 1880s.[10]

In the face of this situation, Tucson continued its efforts to obtain a reliable supply of drinking water. After an expenditure of twenty-five thousand dollars, Thomas J. Jeffords failed to secure a flow of artesian water in his well south of the city. Jeffords shifted his plan to utilizing the flow of water that could be pumped from the well. On March 24, 1881, the Tucson City Council granted Jeffords another water franchise, this time for developing a reservoir and system of mains to bring water into the city. Jeffords continued working on the project, and on August 11, 1881, assured the council that water would soon be flowing in the system.[11]

More months passed, but still no water. Tucson officials decided to cut their losses with Jeffords and put their support behind a new competitor. On December 15, the council passed Ordinance 35, awarding Tucson's water franchise to R. N. Leatherwood. The council hoped the former mayor would have better luck.[12]

The Parker and Watts Franchise

Leatherwood devised a scheme to tap the underground flow of the Santa Cruz River south of town and divert it to the city through a series of gravity mains. He enlisted the help of Sylvester Watts and James W. Parker, who had successfully developed water systems in El Paso, Texas, and in Atchison, Kansas. On April 11, 1882, the city transferred the franchise first awarded to Leatherwood under Ordinance 35 to Sylvester Watts. On April 23, Watts brought Parker into the business and the two men incorporated the Tucson Water Company. Using capital from the Midwest, Parker and Watts attempted to implement Leatherwood's plan.[13]

As their first move, Parker and Watts purchased one thousand acres of land surrounding the water supply, some six miles south of the city. In May, they started constructing pipe for the project, using heavy sheet metal formed into ten-inch diameter pipe and riveted together. By August, they stockpiled enough pipe to begin construction at the diversion point. Workers excavated a trench four feet wide into a water-bearing stratum. This infiltration trench contained a triangular redwood collector which led to a forebay constructed of heavy timbers, twenty feet deep. Here the stored water discharged into a twenty-inch main leading to the ten-inch pipe, continuing to the corner of Main and McCormick Streets, where it connected with six-inch and eight-inch mains for distribution to the city.[14]

Parker and Watts were successful. On September 16, 1882, the first water flowed through the gravity system to the city. The advent of a reliable water source quickly changed the appearance of Tucson as the city began watering streets to keep down dust and residents set about landscaping. A writer for the Tucson *Star* believed the benefits went beyond mere surface beauty, stating that the landscaping "will result in greatly reducing the temperature of the summer months, as vegetation absorbs the heat, and more growing trees absorb many kinds of poisonous gasses and thus they are not liable to be inhaled by people." A large number of trees were planted on Tucson's streets, and the transformation of the dusty city into a garden began.[15]

Still, the transformation took time and many Tucson homes were not yet connected to the city water system. Lloyd Vernon Briggs, in his 1882 visit, noted that on the way from San Xavier to Tucson "we met a great many barefooted Indian women, walking to town with a loaded *olla* on their backs. The *olla* is a jar which keeps water cool for a long time." On April 2, 1885, the Tucson *Star* reported that John Hart hauled clear mountain water to sell in Tucson, which he claimed superior to the local product.[16]

The City of Tucson purchased the private Tucson Water Company in 1900 along with this building and the steam engine booster pumps.

To meet increasing needs, the Tucson Water Company constructed their first steam-driven pumping plant in December of 1889. Located in city block 137, at Eighteenth Street and Osborne Avenue, Plant 1 consisted of a large dug well thirty feet in diameter and forty feet deep. Four drilled wells, located within the dug well and drilled to a depth of two hundred feet with a diameter of five inches, provided additional water. A Barr steam-powered pump with a capacity of 1,250 gallons per minute (gpm) diverted the water into the city mains.[17]

Tucson suffered a slowdown in water development during the early 1890s, caused more by environmental conditions than the economy. A series of floods followed the drought of the mid-1880s, culminating in a major flood in the summer of 1890. Water raged over the Santa Cruz floodplain destroying dams and irrigation works. Floodwaters followed a ditch constructed by Sam Hughes to divert water from the river, rushing with such force it eroded the soft soil in the bed of the river. The Santa Cruz became entrenched below its banks, leaving points for surface diversions far above the water level in the channel.[18]

The entrenchment of the Santa Cruz and the destruction of the older water control system was a substantial change in the local environment, but undaunted residents searched for new institutional and technological approaches to water utilization. Although not fully articulated until much later, there were those who thought that agriculture was not critical in the area. For them, entrenchment opened the way for urban development in the floodplain.[19]

Despite the progress made in supplying water to the city, the 1890s were difficult years for Tucsonans. Now that a municipal water system existed, under franchise to Parker and Watts, citizens demanded adequate service. This required close attention to operations and to the need for improvements in the system.

City beautification and dust treatment increased the demand for water. In August of 1892, a combination of heat and drought led Mayor Fred Maish to shut off the mains in the city parks to conserve water. In 1893, the city applied five thousand gallons a day to streets to keep dust down in the winter, and up to ten thousand gallons in the summer. To resolve shortages, the city considered regulating water for irrigating gardens, lawns, and trees. In February of 1893, the city council discussed a plan to limit all such irrigation to between six o'clock in the evening and four o'clock in the morning.[20]

Tucson attempted to remedy its water problems by both increasing supply and reducing demand, but the standard response was to apply technology to increase supply. In its water history Tucson actually made few moves to reduce demand. As a writer for the Tucson *Star* noted, "a change in the waterworks of the city will soon be made, which will do away with all the old trouble of scarcity of water in time of need." However, taking more of a scarce resource for one area meant leaving less for another.[21]

To increase the city's supply, the Tucson Water Company drilled a well on the San Xavier Reservation upstream from the gravity system and diverted water into the city mains. The company installed a special water system known as a Cook Well, consisting of a vertical perforated tube connected to horizontal tubes radiating out from the central collector for a distance of fifty feet. The system was propelled by a sixty-horsepower steam engine. The new well began operating on March 31, 1893, but by the summer the water supply became inadequate and customers complained.

Even after improvements in water service, laundry remained a laborious task as these Winslow girls demonstrate circa 1925.

Residents discovered that the underground water supply had limits when J. R. Watts reported a significant drop in the water table near San Xavier in June of 1895. The lower water table interfered with the gravity supply, and the city had to rely increasingly on pumped water. During the twenty-seven months the Cook Well operated (up to June of 1895), the steam engine that powered it consumed 1,782 cords of mesquite wood at a cost of forty-five hundred dollars.[22]

To combat these problems, in May of 1898 Parker and Watts upgraded the system by installing a high-pressure pump and twenty-six miles of new main. The pumping plant, located at Eighteenth Street and Eleventh Avenue, had a capacity of 3 million gallons per day. They also constructed a 450,000-gallon standpipe at Eighteenth Street and Fourth Avenue to provide additional pressure and backup supplies in the event of an emergency. The standpipe stood eight feet high, with a diameter of thirty feet.[23]

These improvements solved the problem of water distribution for a time. However, not all Tucson citizens shared in the new system. Mexican inhabitants continued to rely on older methods. A Mexican resident of Tucson's barrio recalled the situation in the 1890s: "At that time water was very precious in Tucson. The only water we had, we fetched from wells, and lucky indeed, was the family that could afford a windmill."[24]

Private Water Entrepreneurs in Phoenix after 1880

Phoenix incorporated as a city in 1881, and officials soon encountered the familiar bane of public servants: complaints about the provision of services. In the middle of June 1881, just over a month after the first city election, a newspaper reporter for the *Gazette* berated the recently elected officials over the condition of the water supply ditches. The reporter noted that "fully one-half of the population" received its domestic supply from the irrigation ditches that ran along both sides of major streets in the city. Asserting that the ditches were "filthy," the *Gazette* reporter expressed the opinion that residents had received better service before incorporation.[25]

The conflict between the level of municipal water service and its cost to the taxpayer eluded resolution in the summer of 1881, and controversy over the provision of water service continued. Concerns over water quality as well as the amount of water available remained constant. The sanitary condition of the Phoenix water supply was of particular concern to the less affluent members of the community.

Wealthier citizens had their own wells with tanks to reserve water for periods of drought or contamination. Families too poor to dig their own wells used community irrigation ditches and risked contamination from upstream pollution. In December of 1881 a *Gazette* subscriber complained of a flock of ducks living at the head of the town ditch and polluting the water supply. On March 10, 1882, *Herald* readers who frequented downtown saloons received a warning from the editor: "We have noticed for some time in front of several saloons spittoons put into the ditches stay there to soak. This is a very bad habit and, according to the law, a nuisance. Many citizens use this water for drinking and culinary purposes. Desist, gentlemen, from this foul practice."[26]

During the early 1880s, residents and business owners with the necessary means and resources continued to develop water supply and distribution systems for their own use. Citizens dug private wells to provide for their household needs, sometimes incorporating systems of pumps and tanks to improve performance. As Phoenix grew and entrepreneurs invested in property improvements, fire protection became a leading incentive for water development. Business owners installed pumps to draw water from wells or the irrigation ditches to safeguard buildings and merchandise. Other entrepreneurs developed water supplies for the comfort and cleanliness of residents. Shumaker's Barber Shop provided "hot, cold, clear shower and plunge baths for both sexes." Those unwilling to pay for the privilege of bathing took advantage of the town ditch at Central north of Van Buren where nearly fifty people swam nightly during the summer of 1884.[27]

Construction of the Arizona Canal, begun in May 1883 and completed in June 1885, stimulated interest in the creation of a domestic water supply system for Phoenix. The Arizona Canal proposal took advantage of the roughly two-hundred-foot drop in elevation between the canal and Phoenix, which would have provided gravity pressure for the water distribution system.[28]

In April of 1886, Phoenix leaders considered issuing bonds for waterworks construction. Before any bonds were issued, President Grover Cleveland signed the Harrison Act on July 30, 1886. The new law effected a major institutional change in the relationship between the federal government and its territorial wards. The legislation, sponsored by Senator (later President) Benjamin Harrison, restricted the amount of indebtedness allowed territorial governments to 1 percent of the total assessed valuation of real property in the territory. The act also limited the indebtedness of territorial municipalities to 4 percent of the assessed valuation of real property in the city. The bonding limitation placed by the Harrison Act circumscribed the ability of Phoenix to issue bonds to build its own water plant, forcing the city to issue a franchise for private construction.[29]

During the summer of 1886, two cases of typhoid fever in the city scared residents and caused city officials to fear a major epidemic. Doctors linked the contamination to the close proximity of wells to privies and cesspools in the business district. With the increased density of residents and businesses in the city in the 1880s, the amount of wastewater multiplied. As sewage and wastewater drained into the water table that residents tapped with wells for their water supply, the contagion spread.

When citizens drew more and more water from wells, the sewage followed to the pumps. Concerns about the sanitary condition of underground water resources spurred agitation for an organized water distribution system.[30]

The Gardiner Franchise

It fell to pioneer businessman and long-time resident John J. Gardiner to construct the first waterworks system for Phoenix. Gardiner operated his own water supply and delivery system for the Phoenix Hotel and his wood-working and wagon shop. These enterprises depended on water to meet customers' needs, produce power through steam engines, and provide fire protection. Gardiner's familiarity with the mechanics of water production facilitated the expansion of his personal system to serve additional customers in the business district. In December of 1886, Gardiner began laying a two-and-one-half-inch diameter cast iron water main to serve the stores and saloons in the heart of the city.[31]

Building from his base of satisfied customers, Gardiner intended to extend his system along Washington Street through the entire business district. He planned to raise his tanks to sixty feet and install a six-inch main down Washington Street from Pinal (Fourth Street) to Yuma (Fourth Avenue). Gardiner's promises of improved service failed to sway the city council. At its meeting of April 16, 1887, its members voted to award a waterworks franchise to Colonel C. S. Masten. The council denied Gardiner's franchise request. Masten promised to have a complete system in place before the end of the year.[32]

Even while the plans of Masten's group progressed, John J. Gardiner continued to improve and expand his system. In July of 1887, Gardiner had three thousand feet of mains and seventy connections in place and charged a rate of two to three dollars each month. Gardiner hoped to expand his capacity to serve five hundred customers by the first of August. The need for a dependable supply of water to combat fires continued. During July, the residence of Beverly Cox burned to the ground as a lack of water hampered the efforts of firefighters.[33]

Gardiner continued to lobby the common council to grant him a franchise for his waterworks system. On August 16, 1887, he again approached the council with a franchise proposition only to have his request placed on file. Moses H. Sherman's Arizona Improvement Company also wanted a franchise, and on September 10, the company presented a draft ordinance for a system of waterworks. The council referred it to the ordinance committee.[34]

On November 7, 1887, Gardiner brought another franchise request to the common council, and finally met with success. On December 1, 1887, Gardiner's workmen began excavating a trench for the pipes in front of his Phoenix Hotel at Third Street and Washington. Working west, within a few days the ditch diggers reached Center Street (now Central Avenue) where they extended a lateral main south. Gardiner installed six-inch-diameter pipes, a large increase in size from his original two-and-one-half-inch mains.[35]

The Phoenix Water Works Company, with Gardiner as president, purchased Lots 1 and 10 of Block 2 in the Dennis Addition for four thousand dollars on April 2, 1889. The directors selected this location, near today's Ninth and Polk Streets, because of a small hill where the slight elevation above the city would increase the pressure of the system.[36]

April 3, 1889, marked the beginning of a large construction program. The Phoenix Water Works Company employed over one hundred men to excavate trenches and lay pipe. The company planned a twenty-foot-diameter dug well to the water table. Two pumps and boilers provided a capacity of two million gallons per day, but one set would be held in reserve for emergencies. The standpipe would extend 110 feet high, with a fourteen-foot diameter. The company expected the system to be finished by May 1, 1889, but because of many delays, on April 9 the common council extended the completion date until May 15.[37]

By April 19, 1889, construction had progressed far enough that the Phoenix Water Works Company began to solicit customers. John J. Gardiner's son, John M. Gardiner, advertised in the *Herald*: "All persons desiring to make contracts for water for domestic purposes within city limits from the new water supply are requested to call and make arrangements at the office at Adams and Maricopa Street."[38]

On April 24, 1889, the *Herald* reported that the company had completed the installation of all eight miles of pipe for the new system. The company still needed to connect the new system to old lines in the core of the business section, a two-day process requiring the water supply to be shut off; customers were requested to "make other arrangements."[39]

The improvements were completed by midsummer and on June 26, Boston engineer M. M. Tidd and St. Louis stockholder Edward Worcester arrived to inspect the new system. Tidd put the system to a severe test. He started the pumps at noon and ran them until sundown, drawing an enormous amount of water from the well. Tidd estimated the flow at 1.25 million gallons. Company officials predicted customers in Phoenix would demand 280,000 gallons per day, leaving a comfortable margin of safety.[40]

Phoenix Mayor George F. Coats and council members E. M. Mills and B. Heyman visited the waterworks during the test. The elected officials sent a message of congratulation to President John J. Gardiner of the Phoenix Water Works Company, which read in part: "We found your well to contain an apparently inexhaustible supply of perfectly clear, pure, delicious water. Its sparkling flow can best be appreciated by a personal visit. We believe that you will now be able to furnish all the water that can be possibly needed by our city for domestic, fire, and irrigating purposes, and we do hereby congratulate you upon the successful solution of the water question achieved by you."[41]

A reporter for the *Gazette* described the waterworks as "the most complete water system in Arizona." During the remainder of 1889, the Phoenix Water Works Company continued to expand the distribution system. By the end of the year the system included twelve miles of mains, extending through Collins Addition to the end of the streetcar line, along Van Buren, and up Center Street.[42]

Despite the expansion, the distribution system was still concentrated in the business section of town and many citizens in outlying residential areas found connecting with the pipes beyond their means. Some used wells from fifteen to fifty feet deep, of varying quality from sweet to salt, while others continued to take their chances with the water in the irrigation ditches that lined almost every street. Travelers to Phoenix also faced a lack of easily available drinking water. Phoenix possessed only one public fountain, located in the county courthouse plaza. Those unwilling to walk that far for a drink could request one at a business establishment or saloon. According to resident H. A. Bigelow, one saloon keeper stated he dispensed over four hundred drinks of water daily. Editors of the *Herald* advocated placing hydrants at convenient locations where cups could be chained for the use of the public at large that did not care to patronize saloons.[43]

After bringing the complicated waterworks project to fruition, John J.

Gardiner decided to reap the profits of his labor. On December 10, 1889, Gardiner completed negotiations with engineer and banker Thomas W. Hine and Hine's brother-in-law, attorney Jerry Millay, for the sale of Gardiner's seventy-five shares of stock in the Phoenix Water Works Company. Gardiner received fifty-five thousand dollars for his 75 percent interest from Hine and Millay. Hine took over as president, E. H. Hiller remained treasurer, and son John M. Gardiner continued as secretary.[44]

The Phoenix Water Company

On May 8, 1890, Hine and Millay completed incorporation papers for the Phoenix Water Company, and on May 21 the new corporation took title to the property, franchise, and equipment owned by the Phoenix Water Works Company. The corporate ownership transfer facilitated the next financial maneuver, raising money for expanding the water company. On May 29, 1890, the Phoenix Water Company executed a trust deed with the People's Home Savings Bank of San Francisco for a mortgage in the amount of $250,000. The San Francisco bank, where M. H. Sherman served as director after January 1891, issued bonds for the Phoenix firm.[45]

Over the next few years the Phoenix Water Company struggled to keep up with growing consumer demand. Hine served as president of the company, M. H. Sherman became vice president, and Sherman's brother-in-law B. N. Pratt held the office of secretary, dividing his time between the water company and Sherman's electric street railway. By the summer of 1892, Phoenix residents consumed seven hundred thousand gallons of water daily, an average of one hundred gallons each for its population of seven thousand. The increasing use led officials of the Phoenix Water Company to ask customers to conserve, threatening to disconnect flagrant water wasters. The company limited lawn and garden sprinkling to the hours between five and seven o'clock in the evening and prohibited sprinkling using hoses without nozzles. Three years later, in the summer of 1895, water use increased to over one million gallons per day.[46]

As he prepared for the annual meeting of the Phoenix Water Company Board of Directors in 1896, President Hine faced an uncertain future. The national depression beginning in 1893 and the collapse of the People's Home Savings Bank in San Francisco left the company in financial trouble and Hine in a precarious position. In contrast, M. H. Sherman emerged from the crisis intact and managed to profit from the bank collapse by purchasing the outstanding debts of the San Francisco bank at fifty cents on the dollar. At the June 23, 1896 board meeting, Sherman managed to engineer Hine's resignation. Sherman placed his brother-in-law, B. N. Pratt, in charge of the water company as manager. This action consolidated Sherman's interest in the street railway and water franchises, two important Phoenix utilities. Since 1893, these two utilities operated from the same property at Ninth Street and Polk where Sherman constructed the powerhouse for the electric railway.[47]

At the end of the year Sherman sealed his control over the Phoenix Water Company. On December 1, 1896, he executed a trust deed with the Broadway Bank and Trust Company of Los Angeles in the amount of $350,000. This placed the total bonded indebtedness of the company at $660,000, including the $60,000 note held by the Boston Safe Deposit and Trust Company and the $250,000 note acquired by Sherman's Pacific Bank after the People's Home collapse. Sherman obtained the bonds on the basis of the franchise value of the company in terms of its future profits, instead of using the value of its equipment and physical plant.[48]

By 1898 growing discontent with the private Phoenix water system and its methods of operation led to agitation for municipal ownership. A change in legislation at the national level that liberalized bonding limits for municipalities would also lead to demands for a municipally owned water utility in Phoenix.

Railroad Construction and Water Development in Flagstaff

In contrast to railroad construction in southern Arizona, where engineers were able to take advantage of existing towns such as Yuma, Tucson, and El Paso, the construction of a railroad across northern Arizona took place in a true wilderness. The Colorado Plateau of northern Arizona, a relatively flat and treeless plain, had long been an east-west travel corridor along the thirty-fifth parallel. The natural barrier of the Grand Canyon funneled trails south onto the plateau.

The settlement of Flagstaff began before the arrival of the railroad. Two groups of pioneers from Boston came to the area in 1876 and celebrated the U.S. centennial on the Fourth of July by flying a flag from a tall pine; the tree became a landmark known as the flagstaff. The pioneers organized a townsite near Leroux Spring, about seven miles north of the present location of Flagstaff. The spring took its name from Antoine Leroux, a mountain man who led several expeditions across northern Arizona. Leroux Spring had its source in the snow of the San Francisco Peaks. By the time railroad surveyors arrived in the summer of 1880, this early settlement at Leroux Spring had been all but abandoned.[49]

The construction of the Atlantic and Pacific Railroad (A&P) across northern Arizona, beginning in 1880, offered an outlet for the mineral resources discovered in the central part of the territory at Prescott and Jerome. The A&P also provided a means to supply the material requirements of the growing mining industry.[50]

Railroad crews established their camp at Antelope Spring, at the base of Mars Hill, in 1881. By August of 1882 a small community developed around the spring and camp. However, steep grades along the railroad route at Antelope Spring made it a poor location for trains to stop. The railroad then established a temporary depot at a more level location about one mile to the east of the spring by placing an old railroad boxcar beside the tracks. A second settlement, known as New Town to distinguish it from the original camp at Antelope Spring, grew up around the boxcar depot. This location quickly became the railroad's center of operations.[51]

After the shift in location, Antelope Spring was more commonly known as Old Town Spring and provided the only source of water for early Flagstaff. As the village grew, Flagstaff residents needed new sources of water and turned again to Leroux Spring. Entrepreneurs Charles Veit and Frank Cavanaugh transported spring water to town in barrels, stopping wherever residents requested delivery by displaying a white flag on a stick. By the fall of 1881, the partnership of Jack Smith and Frank Hart located City Springs in the crater of the San Francisco Peaks and began to offer Veit and Cavanaugh competition.[52]

Officials of the Atlantic and Pacific Railroad provided water for their enterprise from springs as well. Railroad workers pumped spring water into tank cars which were then delivered to a water tank in Flagstaff for transfer to the boilers of steam locomotives. This was costly and time consuming. In May of 1886 the A&P simplified its operations at Flagstaff by constructing a pipeline from the Old Town (Antelope) Spring to its water tank at the depot. In July of 1886, the railroad constructed a pipeline to the tank from Rogers Lake as a backup supply. From this point forward the water supply of Flagstaff was closely linked to the railroad.[53]

The presence of the railroad did not stop private entrepreneurs from trying their hand at the water business. The example of the railroad showed that water could be easily delivered by pipes to the business district of Flagstaff. In November of 1887, the *Champion* newspaper promoted the idea of developing a reservoir at Smith Springs and piping water to the town. In the summer of 1888 J. M. Simpson began a pipeline from a railroad spring eight miles south of the town, thus continuing the town's reliance on the railroad. Flagstaff received a patent for its townsite in January of 1889, and officials recorded the town plat on January 24, 1890.[54]

Summary

The decade of the 1880s brought increasing water use and development to Arizona as a result of improved transportation and technology. The arrival of the railroad provided business owners access to new methods of water production. These developments benefited agriculture, attracting many new settlers to Arizona. The population of Arizona's urban areas increased to serve the needs of increased agricultural production. As the era progressed, the provision of water service shifted from the purview of small entrepreneurs to the control of large corporate interests. The gains made by corporate developers of city water supplies facilitated the transformation of Arizona's communities into settled towns by 1900. These advances were not without cost, however, as the conflict over water rights, stream entrenchment, and falling water tables illustrated. These occasional setbacks soon began to give rise to demands for municipal ownership.

A shift from private development to incorporated groups of individuals characterized the era as small entrepreneurs were pushed out by poor economic conditions. Corporate development of water resources increased during the latter half of the 1890s. In 1893, the territorial legislature recognized this trend by passing a law setting rules for water appropriation. The law required that a notice of intent be posted at the place of diversion stating the nature of the works planned, and represented an early attempt by the territory to regulate the increasing number of corporate developments utilizing water resources.[55]

By the end of the 1890s Arizona's urban residents and public officials began to express dissatisfaction with corporate stewardship of water resources. Complaints about poor service usually led the list, but customers also complained of gouging and high prices. Others believed the high profits generated by water systems could be better put to public use. These factors led to a campaign for municipal ownership in Arizona.

Chapter 5 The Drive for Municipal Ownership

Arizona community leaders waged contentious political campaigns to bring private water utilities under public ownership. A change in legislation at the national level facilitated the drive for municipal ownership in territories such as Arizona. On March 4, 1898, President William McKinley signed an amendment to the 1886 Harrison Act that removed limitations for municipalities with respect to specific public works projects, including sanitary and health measures, the construction of sewers and waterworks, and street improvements.[1]

The drive for municipal ownership of Arizona waterworks at the turn of the century coincided with the Progressive Era, an overall reform movement to make government at all levels more responsive to the electorate and eliminate corruption. Nationwide in scope, the progressive reforms concentrated at the municipal level.[2]

Achieving Municipal Ownership in Tucson

Tucson at the turn of the century enjoyed a vibrant economic climate. The increased prosperity led to an expansion of the town to the north and west, following a natural pattern away from the floodplain of the Santa

Cruz River on the west and toward the University of Arizona northeast of downtown. The city of Tucson expanded from a railroad center to a tourist center as the university, the automobile, and boosterism attracted health-seekers to the Santa Cruz Valley.[3]

As did residents of other cities in Arizona, Tucsonans found themselves disappointed with the service they received from the owners of the private Tucson Water Company. At a city council meeting on November 4, 1895, political leaders authorized a special committee to investigate a public water system for Tucson. The group found their options limited by the cost of the proposed system. Since Tucson was located within a territory, the improvements would exceed the city's debt limit under the terms of the 1886 Harrison Act. The city needed congressional approval to sell water-works bonds beyond the parameters of the 1886 law. Consequently, the mayor and council charged the committee with the task of preparing a report for Congress requesting an exception that would permit Tucson to issue the bonds.[4]

By June 1, 1896, Tucson Water Company owner Sylvester Watts assisted the committee in preparing the report. On July 6, 1896, the U.S. House of Representatives adopted Resolution no. 14638, which authorized the City of Tucson to sell water bonds. Sponsors of the bill noted that only 15 percent of the city had fire protection and insurance rates were excessively high beyond areas containing fire hydrants. At the time, Tucson had only fourteen miles of water mains and needed thirty-six miles to adequately protect the city from fire.[5]

Despite congressional approval, it took some time for the mayor and council to set a date for voter approval of bonds to allow for the purchase of the Tucson Water Company. Because action in Congress regarding a change in the Harrison Act looked eminent, Tucson officials decided to wait. After Congress passed the amendment to liberalize the amount of debt municipalities in territories could undertake, Tucson officials set the date for the bond election. On March 25, 1898, the mayor and council of Tucson set May 5, 1898, as the day Tucson voters would decide whether to issue $100,000 in water and sewer bonds. Also on March 25, the mayor and council created a water and sewer commission to oversee the new system.[6]

Tucson voters responded favorably, and on July 21, 1898, the city council passed an ordinance for sale of the waterworks bonds to N. W. Harris and Company of Chicago. In 1899 James W. Parker transferred his interest in the Tucson Water Company to H. A. Lawton. This paved the way for the transfer of the company to the city. On July 24, 1900, the city purchased the Tucson Water Company for $110,000. The City of Tucson was officially in the public water business.[7]

The deed signed by Sylvester Watts and H. A. Lawton on July 24, 1900, included all of the land, equipment, pipes, and rights the company had received under the terms of Ordinance 35. Not only did the deed cover Plant 1 at Eighteenth Street and Osborne, it also included a 720-acre parcel of land called the city water farm. Plant 1 contained Tucson's only well field and pumping plant, while the water farm contained the diversion point for the gravity system. The system served 625 customer connections out of a service area population of 4,225.[8]

The city council subsequently enacted regulations to govern the new utility. Resolution 33 on August 3, 1900, created a water and sewerage department. Ordinance 140 on October 1, 1900, prohibited the use of water without permission and levied penalties for such acts. The final organizing measure was Ordinance 143, passed in March of 1901, establishing the duties and responsibilities of the water department.[9]

The city's purchase of the Tucson Water Company did not mean that private ownership of utilities in the Tucson area ended, only that the city now owned the company serving the central portion of the city. As developers platted additional subdivisions adjacent to the city, they also established new private water companies to serve the additions. In later years, these private water companies were purchased by the city for the same reasons: improved service, greater accountability, and access to additional capital for improvements. With the change to municipal ownership, city engineers considered new technology to obtain water. Public officials continued to pursue water projects after the turn of the century, but now these initiatives were a product of municipal leadership.

The Battle for Municipal Ownership in Phoenix

In contrast to the relatively calm transition to public ownership in Tucson, it took a dedicated group of municipal reformers to gain control of the water utility in Phoenix. Reformers faced a worthy adversary in Moses H. Sherman, the Los Angeles real estate developer who owned the Phoenix waterworks. The battle for municipal control brought the small city of Phoenix squarely into the twentieth century.

A severe drought starting in the late 1890s in the Salt River Valley added to the problems of the Phoenix Water Company and contributed to the clamor for municipal ownership. Climatologists documented a six-month dry period from March to August of 1896. This six-month drought set the stage for a seventy-six-month drought that began in September of 1898 and lasted until December 1904. It reached its peak in 1902, recorded as the most severe drought year between 1895 and 1983. The dry conditions lowered the water table from which the water company supplied Phoenix. At the same time, consumers increased demands as the dry conditions magnified water needs for irrigation and domestic use. As the private company strove to maintain its system in the face of severe drought, Phoenix residents and city officials continued to complain when it failed to meet its obligations.[10]

In December of 1898, the common council met in special session to debate the merits of the waterworks bond issue. City attorney Walter Bennett presented a resolution calling for a single $265,000 bond issue for improvements to both the waterworks and sewerage system. The council passed the measure unanimously, setting the election date for January 24, 1899.[11]

Phoenix voters defeated the $265,000 proposal by a margin of 140 to 199. In order to meet the requirements of the 1898 amendment to the Harrison Act, the proposal needed to pass by a two-thirds majority. Mayor J. C. Adams considered the election a stunning defeat. On January 25, he resigned his official position, citing the need to devote additional time to his business ventures. However, most observers believed he resigned as a result of the bond issue defeat.[12]

Nearly a year later, on December 29, 1899, supporters of municipal ownership presented a report to the common council asking for another bond election. The council approved the report, which called for a $305,000 waterworks and sewerage bond election. The council adopted February 23, 1900, as the date for the election.[13]

With the bond election set for just over a month away, Phoenix voters braced themselves for an onslaught of invective from supporters of municipal ownership and backers of the water company. The editors of the *Republican* newspaper sustained the drive for municipal ownership and published numerous articles in favor of the bond issue. The *Gazette*'s Democratic editors backed the water company and tended to publish articles critical of municipal ownership. Unsatisfied with the portrayal of the issues in local papers, water company owner Moses H. Sherman established his own tabloid. He titled his sheet *The Taxpayer* and used the phrase "the greatest good for the greatest number" as his masthead slogan. Municipal ownership supporters listed familiar arguments: the present poor service would be improved, increased fire protection would reduce fire insurance rates, future growth would be facilitated as water service could be extended, property values would increase due to improved sanitation, and the protection of a healthy atmosphere in Phoenix would continue the influx of settlers. Water company backers alleged that Phoenix would be saddled with a tremendous debt burden and taxes would increase if the bond issue passed. Sherman also claimed that many small property owners in the suburban additions to the city, such as the Churchill, Dennis, Simms, University, East Capitol, Linville, and Montgomery Additions, already had their own wells and would not benefit from the extension of the municipal system.[14]

On February 23, voters defeated the water bond proposal by a wide margin. The final tally was 64 votes in favor and 273 votes opposed. The defeat of the bond proposals quieted the supporters of municipal reform for the next eighteen months. The citizens committee in charge of the waterworks campaign disbanded. Its members pledged to organize a citizens' league to work on the annexation of outlying areas, but this idea failed to garner much enthusiasm.[15]

The water company worked to capitalize on the political situation. In June of 1902 Sherman circulated a proposal to provide four hundred additional fire hydrants at a cost of $12.50 each per year. In exchange for this offer, Sherman requested a fifty-year extension of his waterworks franchise. On August 6, 1902, Sherman felt comfortable enough to publish a draft copy of the ordinance extending his franchise for fifty years in exchange for providing additional fire hydrants.[16]

Sherman committed a grave miscalculation with his franchise extension request. The citizens of Phoenix greeted the attempt to extend the franchise for fifty years with derision. During the evening of August 6, 1902, the forces of reform held a meeting in the county district court room.

Those present dedicated themselves to bringing another proposal for municipal ownership before the voters.[17]

The franchise proposal rekindled interest in reform and the municipal ownership movement. The common council supported the decision adopted at the mass meeting and on October 6, 1902, voted to postpone action on a proposal of its own until a committee appointed by the citizens could issue a report.[18]

The citizens committee spent the remainder of the year compiling information and contacting other municipalities that had established public utilities. It prepared plans and specifications for the Phoenix system. On January 3, 1903, the committee presented the common council with a precise estimate for the cost of the municipal waterworks: $299,576.12. Rather than set an election date at its regular meeting, the council decided to meet with the citizens committee on January 8, 1903, to evaluate the details of the committee's proposal. Opposition soon developed to the proposed course of events. Municipal ownership supporters felt that since the committee originated at a mass meeting, the final report of the committee should be delivered at another mass meeting. For this reason the committee delayed the presentation of its report until a mass meeting could be organized.[19]

On March 2, 1903, representatives of the citizens committee appeared before the common council. J.L.B. Alexander, the chairman of the committee on laws appointed by the citizens committee, and George Bullard, Phoenix city attorney, presented the election resolution to the council. The council promptly ordered the election for April 15, 1903.[20]

On April 14, 1903, municipal control supporters capped their campaign with a mass meeting at the Dorris Opera House. The meeting featured Tucson City Attorney John B. Wright as the main speaker. Wright described Tucson's experience with municipal ownership in favorable terms. The reformers conceded that they could not muster enough votes at the election to pass the bond issue, but expressed the opinion that the tide of support had shifted in their direction. On election day, April 15, backers of the bond issue failed to muster the two-thirds majority needed to pass the measure. It received 487 votes in favor and 288 votes opposed, thirty votes short of the necessary number for adoption. Both sides claimed victory. The Phoenix Water Company cited the vote as evidence that the demand for municipal ownership had been blunted. Supporters stated the election results proved voters approved of the concept of municipal ownership.[21]

Municipal ownership forces kept the pressure on the council. Citizens created a new committee to work for municipal ownership, calling themselves the Municipal Water Works League. On June 15, 1903, the league persuaded council member John T. Dennis to introduce a motion calling for a waterworks bond election on November 12. The council adopted the motion, putting the water company on notice that municipal ownership supporters planned to continue their fight, despite Sherman's plans to improve his system.[22]

The delay over the bond election continued through the summer and into the fall. On October 6, 1903, J. C. Adams appeared before the council with a request to hold a waterworks bond election on December 12. The council then adopted two resolutions, one setting the election date for December 12 and one calling for voter registration.[23]

The water company took a different approach toward the fifth election held to consider municipal ownership. Instead of mounting a publicity campaign as it had in the past, water company officials concentrated on the task of making improvements in the system as a way to placate opponents. On October 27, 1903, Superintendent Harry Heap had twenty-five men excavating trenches on Van Buren Street while other laborers unloaded pipe in preparation for installation. By November 4, the company employed sixty men and installed two new 150-horsepower boilers, oil pumps, and condensers at its Ninth and Polk waterworks plant.[24]

Faced with growing indignation from the voters and little response to their proposals to delay the vote, Phoenix Water Company officials decided to take more direct action to influence the outcome of the election. On November 25, the editors of the *Enterprise* newspaper accused water company superintendent Harry Heap and his project manager Pedro de Lama of registering straw votes for the upcoming election. The large construction project underway gave the water company an inducement in the form of jobs to offer prospective laborers if they could pass the property qualification and register. On November 27, registrars expelled de Lama from the area where voters signed the election roll for alleged interference with the process.[25]

In the few days remaining before the election both sides mobilized to get their message to the voters. Each held meetings and lobbied prominent citizens. On December 12, 1903, Phoenix voters passed the bond proposal with a two-thirds majority, 735 in favor and 336 opposed. Eugene Brady O'Neil, chairman of the citizens committee, indulged in a bit of gloating when he summed up the results: "The integrity and intelligence of Phoenix voters has triumphed over bribe givers and bribe-takers."[26]

The Development of a Municipal System in Flagstaff

Officials in Flagstaff managed to chart a course between the divisive battle waged in Phoenix and the relative ease of the Tucson acquisition. Faced with railroad control of critical springs in the Flagstaff area, town officials found themselves forced to negotiate with the railroad over access to water supplies. The result was a cooperative enterprise with the railroad to create a new water system for Flagstaff. A consequence of this approach was that Flagstaff failed to establish total control over its public water system.

As an incentive to railroad construction in the West, Congress had provided both generous land grants and cash subsidies to the railroad companies. As part of its original grant, on July 27, 1866, Congress awarded the Atlantic and Pacific Railroad (A&P) forty odd-numbered sections of land for every mile of track constructed in Arizona and New Mexico (a section equals one square mile or 640 acres).[27]

While this generous grant made the A&P land-rich, the railroad was cash-poor. The company had trouble scraping a profit from the small amount of freight it hauled long distances across northern Arizona. The line was costly to operate. On July 1, 1897, the Atchison, Topeka and Santa Fe Railway acquired the holdings of the A&P. From this time forward the railroad would be known as the AT&SF or Santa Fe.

By 1897 Flagstaff residents began to express dissatisfaction with their water system. A disastrous fire in the downtown business district in April of 1896 led to demands for improved water service for fire fighting and domestic use. The town council appointed David Babbitt to head a committee to assemble data for the new system. Babbitt and the committee reported a good source of water at Jack Smith Springs in the inner basin of the San Francisco Peaks. Jack Smith and Jim Lamport had located and claimed water rights from Jack Smith Springs in 1893.[28]

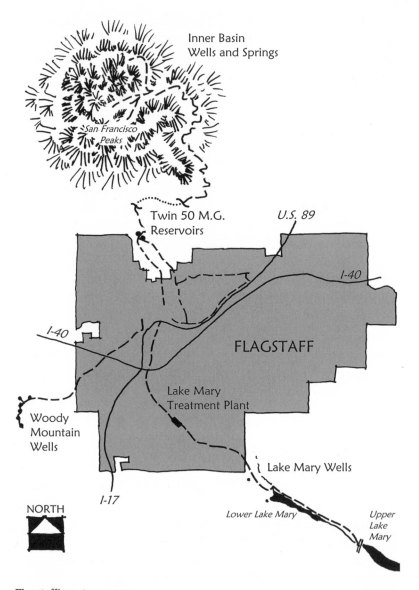

Inner Basin
Wells and Springs

San Francisco
Peaks

Twin 50 M.G.
Reservoirs

U.S. 89

I-40

I-40

FLAGSTAFF

Woody
Mountain
Wells

Lake Mary
Treatment Plant

Lake Mary Wells

NORTH

I-17

Lower Lake Mary

Upper
Lake
Mary

Flagstaff's water sources

The only problem with the plan was that the springs were located within the railroad's land grant. At the time Flagstaff leaders did not consider this an insurmountable obstacle, since town officials already had a working relationship with the railroad regarding use of the company's springs at Old Town, its pipeline from Rogers Lake, and the water tank near the depot. A continuation of business as usual with the railroad seemed a natural course of events.[29]

Flagstaff voters made several trips to the polls before construction began on the municipal system, not due to any real opposition to the project but rather to legal complications. Because of its status as a city in a territory, Flagstaff needed permission from Congress to take on debt through a bond issue. The town accomplished this early in 1897, allowing officials to present a bond issue of $65,000. Voters endorsed the measure by a margin of 168 to 5.[30]

It turned out that the $65,000 figure was too optimistic. Town officials could not find a contractor willing to do the job for that amount of money. In March of 1898 Congress relaxed the provisions of the Harrison Act, allowing municipal governments in territories to increase the amount of bond indebtedness for public health projects.[31]

Flagstaff leaders revised the bond issue by increasing the amount to $85,000. Voters responded favorably again, approving the new measure in the spring of 1898 by a margin of 119 to 9. Questions were raised about the way the election notice was published, so to be prudent town officials scheduled another election. Voters approved the bonds unanimously, 86 in favor and none opposed. Many thought this would settle the matter once and for all, but questions over legal procedure were raised once again. On the third and final vote for the $85,000 bond issue, Flagstaff voters approved the measure 124 to 1. Lawyers finally gave the green light to construction.[32]

Flagstaff Mayor Julius Aubineau spearheaded the design and construction of the new system. The town purchased a reservoir site from the A-I Bar ranch. The town also agreed to pay Joseph R. Treat and Henry C. Lockett $750 each to acquire any water rights the two men might have for Jack Smith Springs as prior users.[33]

These accomplishments were but mere sparring matches compared to negotiations with the railroad. In the end, the railroad agreed to a thirty-year contract that allowed the town to use the springs at a cost of $100

Teamsters made use of available technology to deliver supplies for Flagstaff's 1898 pipeline.

per year. In addition, the town agreed to deliver seventy-five thousand gallons per day to the railroad for use in AT&SF facilities. This amounted to 27 million gallons per year, for which the railroad would pay nine cents for each one thousand gallons delivered. This proved to be a very advantageous deal for the railroad, but town officials believed there were ample supplies for both railroad and town use.[34]

Construction began in the summer of 1898. Crews of mule skinners hauled pipes up the mountain, and ditchdiggers plowed through the streets of Flagstaff. As with many projects, the water system went over budget and town officials had to go back to the voters for an additional $10,000 in December of 1898. The first water flowed through the taps of Flagstaff in time for Christmas.[35]

In addition to reaching an agreement with the railroad, Flagstaff officials entered into contracts with other entities to deliver water in bulk from the new system. The Coconino County Board of Supervisors signed up for water delivery to the courthouse grounds. Timothy A. Riordan, president of the Arizona Lumber and Timber Company, signed up to purchase a minimum of fifteen thousand gallons per day for his sawmill.[36]

While the decision to sell water in bulk made good economic sense to town officials concerned with repaying a large bond issue, the contracts placed too great a demand on the water system. Almost as soon as the water began to flow in December of 1898, the railroad took it all to fill their tank cars and left the reservoir dry. Flagstaff leaders addressed the situation in the summer of 1899 by improving the intake at the springs at an expense of $4,000. Despite the additional expenditure, town officials limited water use for lawns and gardens.[37]

The first municipal system in Flagstaff served about three hundred customers. Despite the introduction of municipal water service, residents who could not afford residential fees of two dollars per month still depended on home delivery of water from barrels. Others continued to use the Old Town Spring for their water supply.[38]

Summary

Municipal leaders across Arizona and the United States pushed for control of public utilities during the Progressive Era. In addition to water utilities, campaigns for municipal ownership of transportation, gas, and electric systems occurred in communities from East to West. In many instances corporate utility owners unwittingly encouraged these campaigns by allowing franchise abuse on the local level. Charges of corruption and bribe-taking were common. To combat the heavy hand of corporate influence that operated in detriment to the public, reformers at all levels of government during the Progressive Era established the provision of basic urban services as public duty.

Municipal leaders in Arizona faced some unique challenges. Arizona's territorial status resulted in a limitation in the form of the 1886 Harrison Act. The liberalization of the act in 1898 facilitated the movement toward municipal ownership in Arizona.

In 1900 the residents of Tucson achieved complete control of their municipal water supply through purchases from private owners. Phoenix voters finally authorized the purchase of the water utility in 1903, but the corporate owners were not content to let the voters have the final say. It took four more years for Phoenix officials to achieve full compliance with the will of the voters. Flagstaff established a public water utility in 1898, but the Santa Fe railroad still controlled key springs. Flagstaff's failure to break completely free from corporate ownership would later have negative consequences.

Chapter 6 Strengthening Municipal Ownership

Inhabitants in three very different parts of Arizona, faced with unique environments and cultures, managed to create three very similar municipal utilities by 1903. The campaigns for municipal ownership—carried out at the insistence of the voters in each community—shows that water development in the West was undertaken with strong public support. That these three communities reflect the broad patterns of the Progressive Era suggests that water development in Arizona cities was influenced more by overall national trends than the local environment.

Improved economic conditions led to growth and increased water utilization in Arizona at the precise time that the conversion to public ownership took place. Both local and national factors influenced this growth. The state as a whole witnessed tremendous economic development as Roosevelt Dam rose at the confluence of the Salt River and Tonto Creek starting in 1905. The start of construction corresponded with the end of a long drought. Farming was once again profitable. By the time the dam was completed in 1911, the agricultural economy of Arizona had rebounded. The mining economy also prospered as new techniques and increased demand put more money in the hands of shareholders. With massive federal expenditures associated with the Salt River Reclamation Project (SRP) and a booming economy, Arizona residents persuaded Congress and President William Howard Taft to grant Arizona statehood. Arizona finally emerged from territorial status on February 14, 1912.

Strengthening Municipal Ownership in Tucson

After purchasing the city's private water system in 1900, Tucson officials worked diligently to improve and enhance the system. Drought continued to tax the city supply. In the summer of 1903, the council curtailed water use for plants and landscaping in the city. Irrigation was allowed only between the hours of five and eight o'clock in the morning and between five and eight o'clock in the evening. Officials believed that the entrenchment of the Santa Cruz River beyond the old Silver Lake location and continuing to the San Xavier Reservation aggravated the water shortage. The deep cut in the river drew off underflow in the channel previously available for pumping and gravity diversion. In the summer of 1906, the city council established a maximum fine of fifty dollars for anyone violating the irrigation restrictions.[1]

Eventually, however, the city turned to technological improvements rather than conservation to see it through the crisis. On October 7, 1905, the council authorized the sale of bonds to finance improvements to the water system. It took some time for voters to approve the measure and for the council to fight back several legal challenges. Finally, on January 7, 1908, the American Light and Water Company received a $245,940 contract to build additional water mains and provide service to the area between downtown and the University of Arizona. Two days later the city awarded a contract to E. J. Merkle in the amount of $23,000 for the purchase of a pump and two steam boilers to power a new well drilled at the site of the original gravity infiltration gallery south of town.[2]

This major expenditure by the Tucson Water Department created Plant 2 at Irvington Road and the Santa Cruz River in 1908. This location was within the original 720-acre parcel that contained the forebay for the gravity supply constructed in 1882 under the Watts and Parker franchise. The theory behind Plant 2 was to build the pumping plant at a location closer to the source of the water. To connect Plant 2 with the existing distribution system, the city constructed a sixteen-inch concrete main down Irvington Road. The length of the main offset any savings from reduced pumping costs, but Plant 2 developed into a productive well field for the City of Tucson as urban growth expanded to surround the plant.[3]

Tucson's population grew from 7,250 in 1900 to 9,500 in 1905, and by 1910 there were 13,193 people living in the city. In contrast to previous eras, many of these migrants brought wealth with them from the East. The value of land escalated, with improved land selling for upwards of one hundred dollars an acre. Less wealthy migrants filed homestead and desert land claims expanding the town into the surrounding desert.[4]

Achieving Municipal Ownership in Phoenix

Supporters of municipal ownership in Phoenix achieved success in 1903 when voters authorized a public water system, but this accomplishment constituted only half the battle for municipal control. Actually creating a new system proved exceedingly difficult. The 1903 election approved $300,000 in bonds to raise funds to construct a city water system that would compete with Moses H. Sherman's private plant. Municipal ownership supporters soon began to question the wisdom of establishing a competing plant. Citizen leaders such as W. C. Foster and businessman Vernon L. Clark proposed using the bonds to purchase the Sherman system, but a citizens' committee carried forward its program for an independent municipal system.[5]

On February 1, 1904, the Phoenix common council authorized the issuance of the water bonds. In spite of the progress on the bond issue, municipal reformers harbored fears regarding Sherman's reaction. Few expected Sherman to remain passive as the city pushed its bond program forward. Harry Heap, superintendent of the waterworks plant for Sherman, confirmed the fears after he returned from a trip to New York at the end of February. Heap revealed that Sherman had retained the New York law firm of Dillon and Hubbard to assist local attorney C. F. Ainsworth in filing a lawsuit challenging the city bond issue.[6]

On April 2, 1904, C. F. Ainsworth of the Phoenix law firm Chalmers and Wilkinson filed suit in district court against the common council. In his complaint, Ainsworth asked for a temporary injunction against the city to prevent it from issuing the bonds. He also asked the court to declare the bond election null and void. In addition, Ainsworth requested that the court restrain Phoenix from building its own waterworks plant. The complaint, prepared with the assistance of counsel Dillon and Hubbard of New York, listed four principal reasons for requesting the injunction. Sherman's lawyers stated that the common council had no authority to call the bond election, the city was bound to a "no competition" clause in the waterworks franchise, the public system would not serve the community interest, and that voting irregularities marred the election.[7]

The filing of the lawsuit began a second great battle for those in favor of municipal ownership. After working for five years to gain voter approval of the bond issue, the reformers now faced a lengthy lawsuit. On April 4, 1904, members of the common council discussed the lawsuit and planned a course of attack.[8]

Phoenix Mayor Walter Bennett and city attorney T. J. Prescott worked at a frantic pace to respond to the lawsuit. On June 20, 1904, the two filed an amended answer with the court. The amended answer outlined the basic premise of the city's case: the water company's opposition to the bond issue was "irrelevant, immaterial, and superfluous." After hearing arguments in October and early November, Judge Edward Kent prepared his decision and on November 5 issued an opinion sustaining the city's position. On November 11 Kent issued a judgment dismissing the case.[9]

Although the water company appealed the decision, city leaders eventually prevailed on the merits of the case. On November 5, 1905, the council accepted the latest bond offer and awarded the sale to Todd & Company of Cincinnati. After authorizing the bond sale contract, the council instructed city recorder Frank Thomas to notify water company owner Moses H. Sherman that the city now stood ready to entertain any proposal for the sale of the waterworks plant.[10]

With the bond sale awarded, the council then considered alternatives to purchasing Sherman's plant. Council members hired an outside engineer to examine the situation. On June 12, 1906, engineer Alexander Potter arrived in Phoenix from New York. Expressing disappointment at the $300,000 limit of the bond issue, Potter advocated as an improved alternative spending $600,000 to build a gravity system from the Verde River to Phoenix. The gravity system would utilize the difference in elevation between the diversion point on the Verde River and Phoenix to develop pressure for delivery. Potter recommended taking the water from the Verde near Fort McDowell. As a second option, Potter explored taking water from the Agua Fria River west of Glendale.[11]

In the fall of 1906, negotiations between Sherman attorney L. H. Chalmers and city attorney Roy S. Goodrich came to fruition. On October 15, a reporter for the *Republican* newspaper revealed that the two men were closing in on an agreement for the purchase of the Sherman plant and delivery system. Both Goodrich and Chalmers realized that any sale had to be made contingent on Congress granting Phoenix authority to acquire a system, and on approval from Phoenix voters to spend the bond funds for the purchase of the existing plant instead of the construction of a separate system.[12]

The negotiators put the finishing touches on the agreement on January 10, 1907. The contract called for the city to pay Sherman $150,000 for the waterworks plant and distribution system, consisting of $90,000 in cash and $60,000 in outstanding bonds to be assumed by the city. In addition, the contract specified that the city would apply to Congress before March 4, 1907, for permission to acquire the plant under the terms of the Harrison Act amendment. On January 15, 1907, the council authorized the mayor and city recorder to sign the contract on behalf of the city.[13]

The council then moved to arrange for the needed congressional approval to purchase the water plant. Since the 1898 Harrison Act amendment allowed municipalities in territories only to "construct" waterworks, Phoenix had to receive permission from Congress to "acquire" the Sherman plant. On January 21, 1907, the council mailed copies of the contract and proposed legislation to Marcus A. Smith, Arizona's delegate to Congress. By January 23, Smith introduced the bill in the House of Representatives. On March 3, 1907, Smith notified the council that the Senate Committee on Territories had amended the bill to provide for ratification of the contract by the voters. Despite the amendment, the full Senate had yet to take action on the measure. Smith summed up the situation in a telegram: "Time very short. Am doing my best." On March 4, 1907, Smith managed to pull the bill from committee and receive congressional approval from both houses. The legislation (34 Stat. 1414) confirmed the contract between the city and the Phoenix Water Company, authorized the use of bonds for the purchase of the plant and for improvements, and called for approval of the sale by a majority of voters at the next general election.[14]

In contrast to the high level of interest generated by the waterworks bond elections, the campaign for ratification proved uneventful. Phoenix voters understood the immediate need to acquire the present system

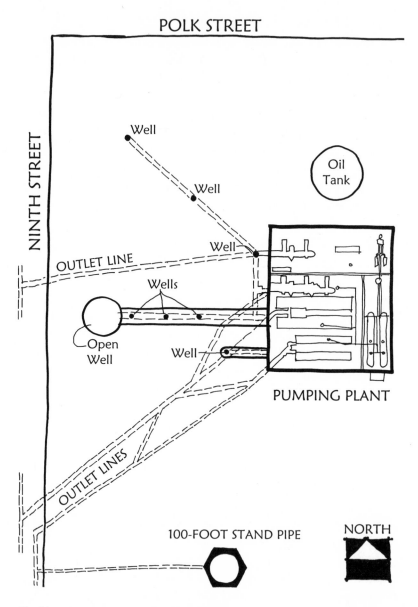

POLK STREET

NINTH STREET

Well

Well

Oil
Tank

Well

OUTLET LINE

Wells

Open
Well

Well

PUMPING PLANT

OUTLET LINES

100-FOOT STAND PIPE

NORTH

The Phoenix waterworks at Ninth and Polk

and begin upgrading with the remainder of the $300,000 bond issue. Observers noted little opposition to the purchase contract. On election day, May 7, 1907, the editor of the *Republican* newspaper outlined the two choices for voters: a yes vote would ratify the contract for a new system, while a no vote would mean "a dusty village with high fire insurance rates." The city recorder tallied 1,033 yes votes and 140 no votes.[15]

The council spent the next two months planning the transfer of the private water plant. On June 12, 1907, members selected Walter Bennett to serve as special counsel to assist with the details of the change of ownership. The council surveyed other cities to determine the best methods for operating and organizing the plant. Officials settled on a superintendent plan similar to the current operation of the waterworks. The superintendent would have an office in city hall where all transactions would take place. With the assistance of a chief clerk, the superintendent would be responsible for all water rentals and business correspondence. The council planned to retain most of the Sherman employees at the waterworks plant, and selected Sherman employee Robert W. Craig for the position of superintendent.[16]

On June 28, 1907, S. H. Mitchell, superintendent of Sherman's street railroad, returned from Los Angeles with the signed deed turning over control and ownership of Sherman's waterworks property. The next day, L. H. Chalmers presented the papers to the council. The council responded by adopting Resolution 309, resolving that upon delivery of the deed the city would deliver $90,000 to the Phoenix Water Company. On July 1, 1907, Chalmers met city recorder Frank Thomas to exchange the deed for the check, thus establishing municipal ownership of the water utility in Phoenix.[17]

Flagstaff Adjusts Its System

Flagstaff faced a formidable adversary in the Atchison, Topeka and Santa Fe Railroad (AT&SF) in its quest to strengthen its municipal water system. In 1898, Flagstaff constructed a new system supplied by springs in the inner basin of the San Francisco Peaks at Jack Smith Springs. The system was based on sound engineering principles, but to get access to the water the town had to make a deal with the railroad. The agreement resulted in constant friction between the town and the railroad over the supply of water.

Rather than depend on the municipal supply, many large water users in Flagstaff developed alternate sources. In 1903 lumber mill owner Timothy A. Riordan engineered a dam to create Lake Mary, naming the lake after his daughter. Water impounded behind the dam in the reservoir provided a needed resource for many uses on Riordan's sawmill property.[18]

Action by the federal government spurred Flagstaff to take on the Santa Fe. As part of his conservation program associated with the Progressive Era, President Theodore Roosevelt set aside millions of acres in the West as forest reserves, precursors to today's national forests. In Arizona, the forest reserves covered vast areas of the northern and central portion of the territory. Many of the reserves encompassed lands within the original land grant to the Atlantic & Pacific Railroad, the predecessor to the AT&SF. The railroad had been slow to survey and develop the land because of its isolated and mountainous location. The creation of the forest reserves gave railroad officials an incentive to give up ownership of the land in the reserves in exchange for more attractive lands controlled by the federal government elsewhere in the territory.[19]

In 1908 newly elected mayor Charles A. Keller seized upon the idea of persuading the railroad to trade the section of land containing Jack Smith Springs and the town water supply. Judge E. M. Doe argued that since the land was within the forest reserve the railroad could be enticed to part with the land along with other parcels under consideration. Fred S. Breen, the federal government's supervisor of the forest reserve, supported the idea and encouraged the town to present a proposal to the railroad. At this stage Flagstaff officials were a bit more idealistic about their relationship with the railroad and expressed surprise when they were turned down flat.[20]

Flagstaff leaders believed they needed a new reservoir at the springs to store an ample supply of water to protect the town from drought. The city sued the railroad to gain access to the springs, seeking to condemn the property for municipal use. While municipal officials in Arizona have been very reluctant to use powers of condemnation to acquire water supplies for fear of adverse public reaction, in this case Flagstaff leaders knew the railroad would engender little sympathy.

In addition to pressing forward on the legal front, Flagstaff officials dedicated a portion of the proceeds from water sales to fund construction of a new, larger reservoir at the springs. By 1910, convinced that town leaders meant business, Santa Fe stepped forward with a proposal of its own. If the town would drop its lawsuit, the railroad would transfer title of the springs and pipeline to the town and build a fifty- to sixty-million-gallon reservoir. Santa Fe engineers estimated the project would cost $92,000, but railroad management was willing to advance the funds to the town at only 5 percent interest.[21]

While some Flagstaff residents believed the railroad's offer was made in good faith, many others saw it as a delaying tactic. Delay worked in the railroad's favor by allowing it to continue to obtain cheap water while the lawsuit worked its way through the courts. The skeptics felt vindicated when the railroad announced that, upon further review, the price for the reservoir had risen to $125,000. Caught between a rock and a hard place, town officials capitulated and informed the Santa Fe that they would accept the offer.[22]

Time passed without any response from the railroad. Flagstaff leaders who took the railroad at its word complained that they were left twisting in the wind. Time itself eventually turned from ally to enemy of the railroad. The spring of 1912 brought statehood for Arizona, freeing municipalities in the baby state from the restrictions of the Harrison Act. Flagstaff town government could now borrow up to 15 percent of the assessed valuation of the town, up from the paltry 4 percent of territorial days. Now the town had the ability to construct the reservoir on its own without the railroad's assistance with financing.[23]

Mayor Joseph R. Treat declared in 1912 that not only would the town vigorously pursue litigation to condemn the springs, it would also begin plans to finance and construct the reservoir itself. Railroad officials now began to negotiate in earnest. The Santa Fe offered to give its section of land containing the springs to the town and construct a new fifty-million-gallon reservoir at a cost of $162,000, paid for by the railroad. In exchange, the Santa Fe would receive two hundred thousand gallons per day for a nominal fee. At the end of twenty-five years, the town would have the option of purchasing the reservoir and the water rights to the spring by reimbursing the railroad what it had spent on the system.[24]

Statehood gave the town council real power and railroad officials knew it. This time their offer was genuine, and Flagstaff residents believed the agreement benefited both parties. It would allow Flagstaff to acquire water rights to the spring, construct a new pipeline and large reservoir, and end the condemnation proceedings that had been a financial drain on the town. The railroad would benefit from the improved water supply and continue to pay a nominal fee for water. The drawback for Flagstaff residents was that the rocky relationship with the railroad would continue. The system would be improved but the link to the Santa Fe remained.[25]

Work began in 1914 when the town purchased the forty-acre reservoir site from Katherine McMillan for $4,500. The project was completed in November of that year at a total cost at $235,000, a substantial increase from the railroad's original $162,000 estimate.[26]

Flagstaff residents expressed pleasure at the increased water supply as the reservoir filled with water during the winter of 1915. They were less pleased when the railroad filled its big tanks and the tremendous draw on the system dropped water pressure all over town. Like many engineering projects the new system needed some adjustments. To solve the problem engineers designed a second pipeline from the reservoir directly to the Santa Fe's facilities to eliminate the draw on the town system and allow the railroad to access the reservoir directly.[27]

While this solution looked good on paper, putting it into practice proved difficult. The railroad simply refused to contribute to the $17,000 cost of the project. After some tense discussions, the railroad finally agreed to assist the project by charging only half its regular freight rate for delivery of the pipes.[28]

The new line was completed in 1916, and heavy rains filled the reservoir. In 1917 town officials noticed a swift drop in the level of the reservoir when it should have been filling. Some quick calculations determined that the railroad had been using its direct line to consume nearly all the water flowing into the reservoir. Flagstaff officials established a strict metering program at the reservoir to monitor the railroad's water use and provide a basis to ask the railroad to conserve when the company consumed more than its share. By 1920, municipal leaders in Flagstaff had made engineering adjustments to improve water delivery but could not address the basic problem: the AT&SF still owned the springs.[29]

The Salt River Project and Urban Water Use

Urban residents were not the only ones complaining about water infrastructure in Phoenix at the turn of the nineteenth century. Farmers complained that a lack of reservoir storage limited agriculture in the Salt River Valley. Water flowed down the Salt River unused during the wet season, but the river remained dry when farmers needed water most. To solve the problem, farmers and business leaders began to call for the construction of a dam on the Salt River to accumulate water during rainy periods and release it later for irrigation. In 1902 Congress passed the National Reclamation Act to fund projects such as dams that were beyond the financial ability of local government. On February 4, 1903, local businessmen and farmers formed the Salt River Valley Water Users Association to lobby the federal government for funds. Construction of Roosevelt Dam began in 1905.[30]

In preparation for distributing water from the storage reservoir into valley canals, U.S. Reclamation Service officials wanted to settle conflicting water rights in the valley. To do this, the government and settlers decided on a "friendly" lawsuit, meaning there was no antagonism between the parties. On January 16, 1905, P. T. Hurley brought the suit before district court judge Joseph Kibbey. On July 22, 1905, the common council appointed city attorney Roy S. Goodrich to represent Phoenix in the suit. The council directed the attorney to file answers for property owners within the corporate limits of the city. The answers arrived slowly, so to speed the process the court set a deadline of June 15, 1906, to file answers.[31]

City officials urged property owners to deed their rights to the mayor of Phoenix so the answers could be filed to meet the deadline. In 1906 the city held water rights for the original townsite, the Bennett Addition, the west half of the Churchill Addition, the Murphy Addition, the Irvine Addition, the Montgomery Addition, and the Dennis Addition. Other property owners in the city received water by private arrangement with the canal companies. In order to assure complete filings, city attorney Goodrich offered to file answers on behalf of property owners. He charged fifteen cents per answer for owners of property with rights deeded to the city and thirty-five cents for owners with property not under city trust. It took several years to compile testimony in the case and to arrive at a decision. On March 1, 1910, Judge Edward Kent delivered the decision in the case. Known as the Kent Decree, *Hurley v. Abbott* determined the relative priorities of water rights in the Salt River Valley.[32]

Roosevelt Dam was nearly complete by the time of the Kent Decree, although it would not be dedicated until 1911. The government took steps to regulate water distribution from the dam. On April 28, 1910, the Reclamation Service approved water distribution regulations. On October 1, 1910, Phoenix officials executed a contract with the Reclamation Service for the delivery of irrigation water.[33]

The 1902 Reclamation Act was designed to develop water for agricultural irrigation and had to be modified for the provision of urban irrigation water as part of the Salt River Project. The original act prevented the federal government from contracting with corporations for the delivery of irrigation water, including municipal corporations. In 1906 Congress changed the law, passing the Townsite Act. This law included provisions for contracting with municipalities within or near reclamation projects.[34]

Judge Kent recognized the urban nature of portions of the Salt River Valley in the Kent Decree. The map which accompanied his decision in the *Hurley v. Abbott* case designated the urban areas in Phoenix. Later, when the Reclamation Service conducted a formal analysis of the lands in the Salt River Project area by an independent group called the Board of Survey, project officials designated urban acres as "townsite lands" based on the provisions of the 1906 Townsite Act. By 1914, when the Reclamation Service's Board of Survey completed its report, the number of acres designated as urban had increased. As the basis for designating urban lands, the Board of Survey followed the plat maps of subdivisions filed at the office of the Maricopa County Recorder.[35]

The renewal of contracts with the Department of Interior's Reclamation Service for water delivery to townsite lands became an annual event for the Phoenix council. This relationship lasted until 1917 when the Salt River Valley Water Users Association (SRVWUA or Water Users) took control of the Salt River Project. On March 20, 1919, the city executed its first water contract with the water users association. After that date, the council made all arrangements for irrigation water with the SRVWUA.[36]

Wastewater as a Water Resource

The development of municipal sewer systems paralleled the growth of municipal water utilities. Increased use of water in cities hastened the need for sewage treatment. Most residents considered the issue a basic health measure, as excess sewage menaced the municipal environment. Even before 1912, Arizona residents put sewage effluent to productive use for irrigation. This practice anticipated the last few decades of the twentieth century, when Arizona would come full circle and rediscover effluent as another source of supply.[37]

As in other cities, municipal boosters in Phoenix and Tucson believed an adequate sewer system was part of the healthy business atmosphere needed to lure entrepreneurs and investors to their community. For Arizona, which owed a portion of its growth to a climate that attracted health-seekers, leaders considered an adequate sewer system an absolute necessity. The development of municipal sewer systems paralleled water utility development in several ways.[38]

Both water and sewer utilities went through an initial stage of private ownership. As with water utilities, municipal leaders initially lacked the financial resources to tackle public construction of sewer systems. Sewer utilities also shifted to municipal ownership as residents demanded improvements in services that private owners were reluctant to provide. However, in contrast to the prolonged battles of municipal reformers to obtain ownership of city water systems, most considered the provision of sewer service a natural public responsibility.[39]

The desert environment of the Santa Cruz Valley made surface water a precious commodity. The City of Tucson capitalized on the value of surface water by selling sewage for irrigation purposes. In February of 1918, the city passed Ordinance 473 providing for the sale of sewer outfall for two dollars per acre-foot per year (an acre-foot of water is enough to cover one acre of land one foot deep, or about 325,851 gallons). Later, in April, Ordinance 474 changed the rate to not less than fifty cents per acre-foot per year. The sale of sewage for irrigation originated in Europe, but by 1894 the city of Los Angeles pioneered this method in the West. In 1919, area farmers irrigated 483 acres of land using Tucson city sewage. This practice continued until 1930 when the city constructed a sewage treatment plant.[40]

The city of Phoenix granted a franchise to sewer company officials to construct a system in 1892. One important question to be resolved concerned the outfall of the sewer. Preliminary plans called for the sewer line to follow Center Street (today's Central) straight south to the Salt River where the effluent would be discharged. Some residents objected to this plan for fear the sewer outfall would contaminate the good swimming hole at the foot of Center Street. To keep costs down, sewer company officials wanted to reduce the amount of large pipe used by discharging the sewage short of the river. To solve the problem, company officials acquired a portion of the farm of Hosea G. and Elizabeth A. Greenhaw (today the quarter-section between Seventh and Fifteenth Avenues south of the I-17 freeway) where the sewage effluent could be used for irrigation.[41]

On December 5, 1892, the city council accepted the completed sewer system. After the system was operational, on January 6, 1893, the council ordered all "cesspools, cess-pits, dug-outs and open drains" in the sewer district closed. The council allowed residential privy vaults to remain as long they were constructed and maintained according to specifications promulgated by the city health officer.[42]

The sewer system operated without incident after its construction. Despite the general satisfaction with the system, as early as 1896 the city health officer recommended that the city consider the eventual purchase of the private sewer system. Phoenix purchased the system in 1911 and embarked on an ambitious expansion program. By 1915, Phoenix had upgraded the system and adopted a septic tank and filter bed method of treatment. This method worked well until 1932, when Phoenix constructed a new treatment plant at Twenty-third Avenue and the Salt River.[43]

Summary

Establishing municipal water supply systems in Arizona from 1903 to 1912 proved much more difficult than supporters first imagined. Backers of public ownership represented a wide range of professions and included members from both political parties, although Republicans dominated. Business owners and merchants formed the largest percentage of reformers. Real estate speculators, lawyers, construction contractors, and doctors rounded out the group.

This diverse group supported municipal ownership for different reasons. The business community desired the continued growth improved water facilities would bring, as well as better fire protection for their investments. Real estate speculators wanted a system with added capacity so that as they developed outlying areas water would be available for residential service. Given the complex legal nature of the many challenges to municipal ownership, attorneys found ample opportunity to practice their trade. Contractors gave technical advice on construction costs and supported the movement for the boost it would give their industry. Doctors wanted improved sanitary conditions to protect the health of the community.

Public waterworks contributed to the maturation of Arizona cities in two significant ways. In a physical sense, municipal ownership placed control of an important resource in the hands of elected officials accountable to the public rather than under the jurisdiction of a private monopoly. This meant that calls for additional fire protection, expanded service, and improved quality by citizens now had a forum at the common council. The development of a secure water infrastructure enabled Arizona towns and cities to grow and mature as urban communities at a rapid pace through the first two decades of the twentieth century.

The fight to establish municipal ownership advanced the political maturation of Arizona's urban centers as well. The campaign forged a coalition of reformers from a wide variety of professions into an organized group of advocates. In Phoenix, these forward-looking citizens ensured the domestic water supply future for Phoenix by battling a powerful business interest. In Flagstaff, municipal leaders honed their political skills against a formidable corporate opponent in the Santa Fe Railroad.

After establishing municipal waterworks, public officials relied on the knowledge and skills of professional engineers to run the systems. This practice fit well with the city manager form of government, which delegated decision making to a specialist to remove the daily business operations of the city from political influence. The battle for control of water systems and the experience of operating them ushered in a new era of growth for Arizona after 1912.

Statehood for Arizona brought to a close the first era of American settlement. In less than a century from the arrival of the first trappers in 1825 to the completion of Roosevelt Dam in 1911, Americans left a profound imprint on established patterns of Hispanic water use. Water use in Arizona increased dramatically with the arrival of the Americans and the demands of agriculture, mining, and urban development. The introduction of railroad transportation increased water use exponentially. The last three decades from 1880 to 1912 resulted in a rapid transformation of Arizona's environment.

Part III Maturation, 1912–1950

The achievement of statehood in 1912 marked the start of a new era in the urban development of Arizona. Although the state itself was new, by this time its urban communities showed signs of greater maturity. Local officials achieved control of municipal utilities and started to manage them as true public ventures. City leaders began to consider how the development of municipal utilities could enhance the business climate of Arizona's urban centers. By 1950, after two world wars and the Great Depression, Arizona's urban centers were fully mature. In the years following 1950 Arizona cities would emerge as leaders in the growth of the Sunbelt.

During the period from 1912 to 1950 Arizona municipal leaders actively encouraged growth and took steps to make utilities attractive assets to additional business and investment. Urban leaders used improvements in municipal utilities to gain a competitive advantage over their counterparts in neighboring towns and states. Both officials and citizens made a conscious effort to make their town more attractive for business.

Although municipal leaders promoted growth, Arizonans often found themselves reacting to economic changes on the national level. World War I created a great demand for Arizona's mineral and agricultural products and the economy soared. After a brief postwar slump, Arizona's economy remained strong through the twenties as tourism became an important source of income. Like the rest of the nation, Arizona suffered during the Great Depression and received its share of federal government public works projects to help lift its economy. World War II brought the nation, and Arizona, out of the Depression. In many ways throughout this period, public officials were reacting to growth rather than encouraging it.

Between 1912 and 1950 the relationship between Arizona cities and the federal government blossomed and matured. While a grizzled pioneer who lived through Arizona's long territorial tutelage by appointed officials might disagree, the decade of the 1930s resulted in the first sustained interaction between the federal government and Arizona municipalities. Unlike territorial times, there was now a direct working relationship between municipal officials and federal officials. The interaction between these two levels of government expanded and deepened during World War II.

By 1950, Arizona was at the brink of a great transformation. A tremendous amount of deferred and delayed growth, spurred by the baby boom, demanded attention from urban planners. The population increase after the war taxed municipal infrastructure to its limit. While officials addressed the immediate needs as best they could, it would soon become apparent that more permanent solutions were necessary. In the aftermath of the transformation that forever changed Arizona in the second half of the twentieth century, residents would look back on the first half as a quaint era in the desert state.

Chapter 7 Municipal Achievements, 1912–1929

City officials embarked on engineering initiatives soon after gaining public ownership of water systems. Although improvements occurred in all three cities, the change was most dramatic in Phoenix where city leaders constructed a redwood pipeline to the Verde River. This novel solution soon generated a host of problems as the wooden pipe shrank in the hot Arizona sun and cowboys took potshots at it to quench their thirst. Tucson, faced with a falling water table in the Santa Cruz River, gave up on surface supplies and converted completely to groundwater. Flagstaff continued battling the railroad.

The second decade of the twentieth century saw continued growth in Arizona as a whole. The completion of Roosevelt Dam in 1911 sparked tremendous agricultural development near Phoenix and helped push Arizona to statehood in 1912. World War I created a great demand for Arizona copper to manufacture armaments. The mining industry introduced the flotation process for refining copper ore, and mine owners' profits soared. The war curtailed the supply of Egyptian cotton, so the Goodyear Corporation pushed the development of long-staple pima cotton in Arizona. The robust mining and agricultural economies led to population growth in the urban centers that supplied workers and goods to the outlying areas. The increase in mining, agriculture, and urban populations during these years all created heavy demands on water resources.[1]

Increased use of land and water required increased regulation. In 1909, the Arizona territorial legislature passed the Irrigation District Act, patterned after California's Wright Act of 1887, and by 1921 water associations had formed nine separate districts in the state. Due to the demands on underground aquifers, the state passed its first water code covering groundwater in 1919. Largely written by University of Arizona professor George E. P. Smith, the act required associations to file a permit with the state land department. The department would evaluate the application and, if no objections could be found, authorize construction. Companies and individuals had to prove the project would entail beneficial use of the water. If the requirements were satisfied, the land department would issue a certificate of water rights.

A third important development on the state level was Arizona's quest to capture its share of Colorado River water. This pitted Arizona against formidable opponents in California as the new state competed with its established neighbor to the west for water. During the early years Arizona envisioned using Colorado River water for additional agricultural development, but by the time the water arrived from the Colorado in the last two decades of the twentieth century urban dwellers and Native Americans became the prime beneficiaries of the Central Arizona Project.

Technology kept up with the increased water demands. As hydrology became a scientific discipline, managers looked to hydrologists for advice on water mechanics. Engineers installed electric motors to power pumps on a larger scale. New advances in refining techniques, generated by the war effort, led to increased use of gasoline as engine fuel for groundwater pumps after wartime restrictions ended.[2]

World War I

Agricultural production in Arizona increased between 1910 and 1920, with cotton becoming a major commercial crop. First introduced to Arizona as an experimental crop in 1901, Egyptian cotton did not see commercial production until 1912, when Maricopa County farmers planted four hundred acres. University of Arizona agronomists perfected strains of Egyptian and pima cotton.

After World War I broke out in Europe in 1914, high cotton prices encouraged additional agricultural development across Arizona, particularly in the Salt River Valley of central Arizona. The war disrupted cotton production in traditional areas of supply, such as Egypt and the Sudan, because Britain imposed restrictions to ensure its own supply during the war. Manufacturers in the United States faced a severe shortage of the fiber, which was used for clothing and in the fabrication of tires. The development of a long-staple variety of pima cotton in Arizona, combined with the long growing season and ample water supplies of the Salt River Valley, transformed Arizona into one of the world's largest producers of cotton. Farmers prospered with high cotton prices, which meant that urban merchants and residents also benefited as more money circulated in the state.

Pima County farmers cultivated only 150 acres of cotton in 1918, but this increased to 1,100 by 1919 and to 4,000 in 1920. Other crops came into production as developers brought new areas "under ditch." A writer for the Tucson *Star* observed: "So remarkable is the recent agricultural development of the vicinity of Tucson that the mere statement of facts of the development, without verbal decorations, excites the suspicion of exaggeration and, in some quarters, envy."[3]

World War I had a positive impact on mining as well. Wartime demand for copper caused prices to rise and companies took advantage of the situation to make heavy profits. Here again, residents of Arizona's urban areas benefited from a vigorous mining economy as companies purchased supplies from town merchants and miners spent bigger paychecks in town businesses.

Tucson Water Development in the Teens

The fledgling city water department entered its second decade facing the perennial problem of mounting water demands. In 1911, the city supplied 1.2 billion gallons a year to Tucson residents at a cost of $21.70 per million gallons. To save costs, only a few of the services were metered. If a customer complained about a bill, the water superintendent would install a meter to measure the flow.[4]

The city attempted to curtail water use and waste. Low water pressure between the hours of four and eight o'clock in the evening particularly concerned the department, as it left streams from fire hoses incapable of reaching tall buildings. On May 17, 1913, City Engineer Moss Ruthrauff issued a warning against wasting water. The water department directed citizens to stop irrigating lawns and gardens when the fire whistle blew.[5]

The city took the matter to the voters on September 2, 1913, asking them to authorize a bond election to provide funds for improvements. The voters approved the measure and the city made plans to spend $85,000 for new pumps at both water plants, a gravity main between the plants, and another reservoir.[6]

On March 16, 1914, the city awarded a contract to the Griffith Construction Company for the construction of a 1.5-million-gallon reservoir at Plant 1 and a thirty-inch concrete gravity main from one-half mile north of Valencia Road to the new reservoir. The reservoir consisted of reinforced concrete construction with a corrugated metal roof supported by timber trusses atop precast concrete columns. The inside diameter measured 150 feet, with a uniform water depth of twelve feet, six inches. The floor slab was eight inches thick. The reservoir cost the city $13,660, while the concrete pipeline cost $70,972.[7]

With the new system in place the city took steps to protect its investment. This included installing meters on all services and eliminating free service to several charitable organizations, such as the YMCA. Ordinance 447, adopted by the mayor and council on July 3, 1916, specified that all services would receive a five-eighths-inch meter for a charge of fifteen dollars. If a customer wanted a larger meter, other sizes were available.[8]

The meter policy drew some complaints but most customers understood the need for water conservation. After the United States entered World War I in April of 1917, conservation and rationing of scarce resources became a patriotic duty. City officials adopted a pragmatic attitude toward the meters. In May, the mayor and council restored free water service to the YMCA in recognition of the many benefits the organization provided the community.[9]

In addition to protecting its investment financially, Tucson officials had to physically protect their facilities. Starting in 1915, Arizona had been under the influence of a wet climactic cycle with frequent storms and flooding. Heavy flow in the Santa Cruz River shifted the channel closer to the location of Plant 2 and the gravity main. On September 10, 1917, the mayor and council authorized the city engineer to take any steps necessary to protect the water system. Work crews completed the job by early November. Although this action preserved city facilities in the near term, the situation would repeat as channel changes in the Santa Cruz continued.[10]

The increasing investment of the city at Plant 2 underscored the need for protection. Tucson drilled six new wells at Plant 2 between 1915 and 1919. The exposed nature of this investment led Tucson officials to consider decentralizing their well operations. As Tucson expanded in size, it made more sense to drill additional wells closer to the location of the residents.[11]

Tucson Water Development in the Twenties

The Roaring Twenties were so named because of the tremendous economic expansion during the decade. However, in the mining and agricultural sectors of Arizona's economy, the 1920s were anything but roaring. The end of World War I brought a reduction in demand for the mineral and agricultural products of Arizona. The years following the war were particularly difficult for farmers who had invested heavily in cotton production. A drastic drop in cotton prices starting in 1921 left many bankrupt. Cotton, when it paid to ship it to market, brought only a fraction of its wartime price.

The slump in agricultural prices had a ripple effect in Arizona's urban economy. Merchants who catered to the farm trade saw sales and profits fall. Bankers who had loaned money to farmers had to write off loans as uncollectible. It took several years for farmers to diversify into truck crops, melons, and grapes, and begin to pull themselves out of the slump.

Although the agricultural and mining economy suffered, the decade was prosperous in other areas. One part of the economy that was particularly healthy was automobile production, which in turn spurred the mobility of many Americans. Automobiles allowed Americans to travel with ease and many of them discovered Tucson. After they discovered it, many wanted to stay. Historian C. L. Sonnichsen called the 1920s Tucson's "gold-plated decade" for the development of tourist amenities and suburban residential growth.[12]

The development of the tourist industry had a great impact on Tucson. Long popular with tubercular invalids who came to improve their health in its salubrious climate, in the twenties Tucson became a destination for fun seekers. In 1922, Tucson boosters organized the Sunshine Climate Club for visitors seeking relaxation in the city's warm winters. Health-seekers continued to arrive as well, lured by a new Southern Pacific Hospital and a United States Veterans Hospital, both opened in Tucson in the 1920s. Landmarks such as the Temple of Music and Art, the San Xavier Mission, and the University of Arizona drew their share of visitors.[13]

As Tucson's reputation for tourism grew, a shortage of hotel rooms frustrated visitors and businessmen alike. Conventions chose towns with better accommodations. To resolve this situation, investors opened the El Conquistador Resort Hotel on Tucson's east side on November 22, 1928. The construction of the hotel was a calculated gamble on the part of local business owners to boost visitation to Tucson. Although the hotel never lived up to the hopes of its financial backers, its construction spurred additional residential subdivisions on the city's east side.[14]

Water control technology continued to develop in the Tucson basin during the 1920s. The increased use of surface and groundwater before 1920 caused a drop in the water table so severe that the centrifugal pump used throughout the West could no longer cope with the increased draft. The device became impractical because of excessive costs and inconvenience of operation when placed on deep wells.[15]

To combat these problems, engineers perfected the deep turbine pump. This pump used a small turbine which, when lowered through a cylinder to the bottom of the well, could operate at the water level rather than relying on suction from above to draw water. The turbine derived its motive power from motors or engines at the top of the well transferred to the turbine by a shaft. While the turbine pump could be powered by petroleum distillate or electricity, its ease of operation and low maintenance made it particularly useful when used with electric motors.[16]

After a slow initial acceptance, the turbine pump became increasingly popular after 1920 because of its efficient operation in deep wells. Compared to the 50 to 55 percent efficiency of centrifugal pumps, deep-well turbines achieved from 65 to 75 percent. The turbine pump found wide acceptance in the late 1930s and helped generate a new era in groundwater pumping. But, as is often the case, this technological solution eventually caused problems itself by greatly accelerating groundwater depletion.[17]

Tucson grew as the active campaign by the chamber of commerce attracted more tourists and health-seekers, and the city water department struggled to keep up with increasing demand and dwindling supplies. The city's population multiplied from 20,292 in 1920 to 32,506 by 1930. Water tap installations increased from 4,543 metered services in 1923 to 6,882 in 1929.[18]

The real estate boom in Tucson prompted residential building in the area on the east and north sides of town. Developers filled in the land between the city and the university and spilled over into desert lands beyond the campus. Between 1920 and 1930 developers platted eighty-five subdivisions in Tucson.

On April 5, 1920, the mayor and council adopted Ordinance 497 authorizing the city to extend and improve the water system. In May, the city floated bonds to finance the water improvements. The $140,000 raised by the bond sale provided enough funds for a new reservoir, booster plant, and additional wells.[19]

On November 5, the city awarded a contract to the Littlejohn and Singleton Construction Company in the amount of $36,400 to construct a 1.5-million-gallon reservoir at Campbell and Second Streets. This became known as Plant 3. The city awarded J. W. Belt the contract to drill the first of several north side wells on February 7, 1921. To carry the water from the north side wells to the new reservoir, on August 25, 1921, Tucson awarded S. B. Shumway the contract for construction of a concrete gravity main to the new reservoir.[20]

The new reservoir at Plant 3 consisted of a circular reinforced concrete structure with an inside diameter of 150 feet, a conical bottom and vertical sidewalls, and a capacity of 1.5 million gallons. It carried a galvanized corrugated metal roof supported by timber framing atop precast concrete columns. The two ten-inch booster pumps each possessed a capacity of 1,500 gpm. Plant 3 and the north side well field served the rapidly developing area surrounding the University of Arizona. The north side well field associated with Plant 3 eventually grew to be a significant portion of the entire Tucson supply. The later purchase of private water companies expanded the number of wells linked to Plant 3.[21]

After expending the money on the north side well system and reservoir, the city took steps to ensure that residents did not waste water. In May of 1922, the water department hired an employee to distribute educational information on water use to citizens. This two-pronged approach reflected the reality faced by city officials in Tucson and elsewhere in the state. Residents demanded additional water supplies and officials worked hard to provide it, but water remained a scarce commodity in Arizona. This approach was very different from the situation in Los Angeles, where William Mullholland's speech at the dedication of the Owens Valley aqueduct consisted of the words "There it is. Take it." [22]

In addition to efforts to reduce demand, Tucson continued to seek new technology to meet shortages in the water supply. On May 9, 1927, voters approved another bond issue, this one in the amount of two hundred thousand dollars, for the construction of a belt-line system of water mains to serve the east side of town. The project increased the size of the water main down Campbell Avenue from First Street to Eighth Street to twelve inches and provided for increasing other mains to eight inches. The bond issue also enabled the city to purchase a third booster pump at Plant 3, a gasoline stand-by unit, and to convert the pumps at Plant 1 from steam power to electricity. Finally, the bond issue authorized construction of a thirty-thousand-gallon water storage tank in Randolph Park. [23]

The shortage of water led many to capitalize on the precious resource. Speculators found that water sold to the city could be as lucrative as water developed for agriculture, and approached the city with propositions to convert agricultural water to municipal use. On October 28, 1927, the city council discussed a proposal to hire Los Angeles hydrologist Reed G. Brady to investigate possible water sources developed by private groups and offered to the city. [24]

On May 27, 1928, Brady presented his report. Brady noted that while Tucson suffered from an insufficient water supply and storage capacity, several sources could be tapped to alleviate the situation. One group quickly capitalized on Brady's recommendations. The Rillito River Development Company presented a proposal to the city for the development of water in Pantano and Rillito creeks by means of an infiltration gallery and reservoir. The plan also called for the utilization of turbine pumps to augment the gravity flow. [25]

Downstream users opposed the Rillito diversion for fear it would jeopardize their supply by removing water from the Rillito watershed. In a stormy city council session on June 19, 1928, a large group of citizens voiced their protests. In response, Tucson terminated its negotiations with the Rillito River Development Company. Opposition from the agricultural sector pushed Tucson city officials to consider purchasing ground-water supplies from private domestic water companies.[26]

Adjustments and Big Dreams: Phoenix and the Verde Project

After acquiring the private water company in 1907 and embarking on an expansion program, Phoenix city leaders looked for a better source than the salty groundwater wells used at the waterworks pumping plant at Ninth and Polk. The search for pure water led to the Verde River and the Fort McDowell Indian Reservation. The history of the Verde River water project and the interaction between Phoenix officials, Yavapai Indians at Fort McDowell, and representatives of the United States government charged with the regulation of Indian affairs offers a revealing look at the changing nature of resource development in the twentieth-century West.

The possibility of using water from the Verde River at Fort McDowell for the city of Phoenix had long intrigued engineers and entrepreneurs. As early as 1886, Los Angeles water entrepreneur J. W. Potts advocated bringing Verde water to the city because groundwater would always cause some "dissatisfaction" for household use "as the water is a little salty." The fresh Verde water, only twenty-eight miles from Phoenix, would make an excellent alternative.[27]

During the battle to win control of the Phoenix waterworks from Moses H. Sherman, Phoenix officials commissioned several engineering studies to evaluate possible water supply sources. In 1906, Alexander Potter reported that a gravity supply system from the Verde River offered an improved alternative over the city's wells, which contained a high percentage of dissolved minerals. After the city purchased the pumping plant, waterworks superintendent V. A. Thompson once again raised the possibility of the Verde gravity supply project. On July 29, 1913, the common council authorized Thompson to hire an independent contractor to study the water system. Thompson chose noted hydraulic engineer Hiram Phillips of St. Louis, who in turn enlisted the services of local engineer Howard S. Reed. On November 10, 1913, Phillips and Reed presented their findings to the council. The engineers concluded that Verde River water was of superior quality and could be easily obtained by situating an intake four and one-half miles above its confluence with the Salt River.[28]

In the spring of 1915 Phoenix Mayor George V. Young requested the city commission examine methods to obtain a supply of soft water. On June 4, 1915, Mayor Young called on City Manager Robert W. Craig to investigate the situation and take action. On July 29, Craig and City Engineer James Girand left for the Verde to conduct a survey for the gravity supply line. After examining possible sources of supply, on August 5, 1915, the two men posted a notice of location for a municipal water supply water right. City Clerk Frank Thomas filed the notice with the county recorder the next day.[29]

The water rights filing began a seven-year effort by Phoenix to authorize, design, and build the Verde River gravity water supply project. Receiving authorization from the U.S. government to build the pipeline on the Fort McDowell Reservation was the first challenge. Phoenix operated under the provisions of a February 15, 1901, congressional act (31 Stat. 790) governing permits for right-of-way on federal reservations. In accordance with the act, Phoenix prepared a map and verbal description of the proposed right-of-way for the project. On January 16, 1916, Phoenix forwarded its application to the commissioner of the General Land Office.[30]

As city officials waited for a response to the application, they planned other aspects of the project. The city commission hired another engineer with a national reputation, William L. Church of New York, to conduct additional investigations of the proposal. On February 16, 1916, Church's report to the commissioners echoed the findings of the other engineers, concluding that the project was feasible and that the Verde water was superior in quality.[31]

The Verde project was delayed by World War I, but on March 12, 1919, the city commission directed the city engineer to prepare a cost estimate for the pipeline. L. B. Hitchcock presented the results of his cost estimates on May 14. The commissioners then requested advice from the city attorney regarding the right-of-way situation. Howard Sloan reported favorably and on May 28, 1919, the commissioners directed him to prepare an ordinance calling for a bond election to fund the project. The commission adopted the ordinance for $1.3 million in bonds on June 11. Originally set for July 19, a second ordinance passed on June 18 delayed the election until July 26. If passed, the Verde supply system would be the largest project ever constructed by the City of Phoenix. Little opposition to the bond issue emerged, and on July 26, 1919, Phoenix voters approved the bonds by a 25 to 1 ratio, 810 votes in favor and 33 votes against.[32]

City officials then began the daunting task of constructing the supply system. As the initial phase, financing for the project needed to be secured. On August 11, the funding bonds were offered for sale and the city engineer was authorized to negotiate with Hiram Phillips to oversee the project. On September 20, 1919, Phillips accepted the job and the bonds were sold. These actions set the project on its way.[33]

Postwar inflation and a shortage of materials rendered the original budget insufficient. As bids for the project came in during January of 1920, commission members sought alternatives to reduce the project's cost. The commission eliminated a 25-million-gallon concrete reservoir and considered a proposal using redwood pipe. The redwood pipe, constructed of staves bound with steel straps like a barrel and placed end-to-end, would be less expensive than concrete or metal pipe. On January 30, 1920, the commission accepted the bids of the Pacific Tank Company and the Redwood Manufacturing Company for construction of the line. Each contractor would build a portion of the project. The choice of redwood pipe was opposed by residents who believed concrete or steel would make a better investment in the long run, but after much discussion and second thoughts the commission approved the contract for the redwood pipeline.[34]

Construction on the Verde project began during the summer of 1920 and proved to be a massive undertaking. Workers constructed an infiltration gallery at the head of the system on the Fort McDowell Reservation. Consisting of twelve thousand feet of open-jointed concrete pipe, engineers designed the gallery to lie in a trench parallel to the Verde River so that the subsurface flow which filtered through the sand and rocks would pass into the pipe. From here the water flowed by gravity through the redwood pipeline to Phoenix, a distance of over twenty-eight miles. Much of the pipeline remained above ground, but workers buried some of it below the surface. The construction of the gallery and pipeline provided jobs for a number of Yavapai and Pima Indian workers from the Fort McDowell and Salt River Reservations. The jobs generated by the pipeline project provided an important source of income to Native American workers, exposing tribal members to the cash economy and enabling them to acquire new skills.[35]

Phoenix engineers designed a concrete infiltration gallery at the upper end of the redwood pipeline.

Water began to flow into the city on December 15, 1921, but did not reach consumers immediately. Due to problems with bacterial contamination, Phoenix needed to arrange for a chlorination plant. After it was installed, Verde water first reached the taps of Phoenix residents on February 13, 1922.[36]

On October 1, 1924, the city commission adopted an ordinance which provided for free use of water on the reservation for domestic purposes through seven three-quarter-inch taps, and for the use of the Salt River Indian Agency and School through a two-and-one-half-inch pipeline. The ordinance formed the basis for an August 5, 1925, contract between the city and Charles S. Young, superintendent of the Salt River Agency, whereby Superintendent Young waived any damage claims resulting from the pipeline construction in exchange for the water taps. This agreement facilitated the final approval of the project by the federal government. On December 23, 1925, Phoenix filed its final "proof of construction," accepted by the Department of the Interior on January 13, 1926.[37]

The 1925 contract represented the beginning of a change in the relationship between the Yavapai and the city. The Yavapai discovered that the

The redwood pipeline carried Verde River water twenty-eight miles across the desert to Phoenix.

permit process gave them leverage against the city for obtaining benefits from the project. These included benefits over and above employment for tribal members which had formed the only compensation heretofore received. Although tribal leadership remained poorly developed during the 1920s, the discovery that the permit process could be used to the Yavapai's advantage set the pattern for later interaction. This situation notwithstanding, the Yavapai still needed to rely on the intervention of Indian office representatives on their behalf.

Completion of the Verde pipeline did not mean an end to work for the city. Plagued with constant maintenance needs and increasing demands, city officials faced continual challenges in the operation of the Verde system. Design problems complicated matters. The redwood used for the pipeline shrank in the hot Arizona sun and caused leaks. The infiltration gallery could not keep the line full so as the top half of the pipe baked the bottom half rotted. The redwood also proved an attractive target for water rustlers who shot holes in the pipe to capture a cool drink.

In 1927, city engineers made the first of many changes to the Verde system. On February 16, the commission received bids on four wells to be constructed at the infiltration gallery. In March, commissioners approved the bid of C. L. Maddox and established a right-of-way for an electrical transmission line to serve the wells from Granite Reef Dam. Engineers placed three of the wells in operation by June 13, with the fourth to follow. On June 25, Phoenix filed an amendment to its right-of-way application to cover the transmission line and the wells. Acting Commissioner Thomas Howell of the General Land Office approved the change on January 16, 1928.[38]

Even as the Department of the Interior considered the application for the well project, the city faced rapid deterioration in the redwood pipeline. During the August heat of 1927, leaks in a five-mile section of the pipe limited the city's water supply. On November 9, 1927, officials opened bids for reconstruction of the deteriorated segments. The city awarded the bid to Western Concrete Pipe Company on November 16. The company used precast reinforced concrete pipe for the job. By the end of March in 1928, Western Concrete finished the patchwork with the new pipe.[39]

Phoenix officials determined from this experience that the redwood pipeline needed a massive overhaul. Rather than work on the project in a piecemeal fashion, the commissioners wanted a thorough solution. On July 18, 1928, the commission contracted with the Black and Veatch engineering firm to complete a study of the Verde system and the anticipated water needs for a growing population. On January 16, 1929, City Manager C. E. Griggs presented the Black and Veatch report to the commission. The engineers advocated a second line from the Verde, additional wells near its confluence with the Salt River, and a 20-million-gallon reservoir. A citizen's group called the Greater Phoenix Committee examined the recommendations carefully, and on March 14, 1929, presented its own report. The committee called for the construction of a forty-two-inch-diameter concrete line from the Verde. Commissioners acted on one of the recommendations of the Black and Veatch report swiftly. During the summer of 1929, they directed contractor Scott Coburn to drill test wells for the delineation of possible locations for a well field along the Verde pipeline.[40]

Flagstaff from 1917 to 1926

After getting only grudging support from the railroad for a second line to the new reservoir in 1917, Flagstaff town officials found it necessary to closely monitor water use by the Santa Fe. Completion of the new 50-million-gallon reservoir in 1914 greatly increased the town's storage capacity from the 2.5 million gallons contained in the 1898 reservoir. Engineers had estimated this would take care of the town's needs for many years to come, but the same economic forces that increased the pace of development elsewhere in Arizona had an influence on Flagstaff as well.

World War I increased the demand for wood products and three sawmills worked on extended shifts. These required large amounts of water for processing and for fire protection. The development of the tourist industry had a tremendous impact on the railroad. In 1904, the Grand Canyon Railway forged a direct rail link from Williams to the Grand Canyon. In 1919 Grand Canyon officially became a national park, bringing with it increased rail traffic. More trains meant more water, and the Santa Fe continued to draw heavily on the reservoir. A cold dry spell in the winter of 1919 curtailed runoff and made the situation worse. Town officials began making plans for additional storage.[41]

Flagstaff residents had differing opinions on how to best remedy the water shortage. Mayor Earl Slipher supported constructing a new and larger reservoir. George Babbitt advanced a proposal in September of 1919 to construct a dam in Switzer Canyon. Babbitt argued that in addition to providing water storage, the dam would have the added advantage of providing recreational opportunities. Another dry winter in 1921 underscored the need for additional storage, as runoff fell far below average. As the situation worsened, others stepped forward with new proposals. Arthur H. "Al" Beasley offered a dam site on his ranch in Fort Valley, and Charles H. Spencer advocated diverting runoff from the inner basin springs into Crater Lake as a natural reservoir.[42]

As ideas proliferated, Flagstaff leaders decided to hire an outside professional engineer to evaluate the situation and recommend a course of action. Late in the fall of 1922, Mayor Thomas E. Pulliam and the town council chose the Burns and McDonnell engineering firm to complete a study. The firm rejected all three dam proposals as too costly and impractical. The engineers stated that Flagstaff's best course of action was to continue to develop the inner basin springs and construct a new reservoir to capture the flow.[43]

While augmenting the inner basin springs made sense from an engineering standpoint, the project required continuing participation from the

Santa Fe Railroad. George C. Davenport, the railroad's hydraulic engineer, agreed that constructing a second large reservoir was the most practical solution, but a final decision needed to come from Santa Fe management. Railroad officials seemed in no hurry to make a decision. They were under pressure from Flagstaff leaders on another issue, the construction of a new passenger depot. In December of 1923 the railroad responded favorably to the depot proposal, stating that construction would begin soon.[44]

A hot and dry summer in 1924 brought conditions to a crisis. The council ordered major industrial users, such as the sawmills and the railroad, to cut back on water use. This convinced railroad management that Flagstaff's water problem was its problem as well. In October of 1924, the railroad proposed to turn over the deed to the springs and $235,000 worth of improvements made in 1914 if the town would pay the railroad $125,000 in cash at $15,000 per year. The railroad would take the remaining debt of $110,000 plus interest in water deliveries. This would allow the town to put forward a $485,000 bond issue for the second large reservoir, second pipeline, and distribution improvements. The Santa Fe reserved the right to construct a third reservoir for its own use at the site.[45]

The town council thought this was a fair arrangement and set a bond election for December 30, 1924. Voters approved the measure by an overwhelming margin, five hundred in favor and sixteen opposed. The council awarded the construction contracts in April of 1925.[46]

Mayor Ignacio B. "Tony" Koch led the Flagstaff community in a dedication of the new water facility on June 18, 1926. Approximately one thousand residents attended the ceremony. This was truly a cause for celebration because the town had doubled its storage capacity to just over 100 million gallons. Flagstaff had matured as a town and the improvements to its water system provided ample evidence of its new standing. On September 6, 1926, Flagstaff left town status behind and incorporated as a city. It had come of age.[47]

Summary

The period from statehood in 1912 to the end of the 1920s brought large-scale economic development to Arizona. Economic growth caused by World War I raised the value of crops and land which further fueled growth. After a brief postwar slump, the rise of the tourism industry brought new areas for economic growth. Increased economic activity led to residential growth and an increased demand for water in Arizona's urban areas. The increasing application of new pump technology and sources of energy facilitated the expansion of water service by providing the means to achieve it. Despite the gains, municipal water managers found themselves just able to keep up with growth—not able to get ahead of it.

Arizona municipalities tried different ways to better serve the needs of their residents from 1912 to 1929. Tucson explored new sources of supply by looking to surrounding agricultural lands. This had its limits, so officials turned to improving the basic infrastructure of wells, pumping plants, and reservoirs within the city. Phoenix struck out dramatically for the Verde River, developing a surface supply to replace the old pumping plant downtown. Flagstaff officials also considered surface supplies of water, but found the proposals expensive and complex. In the end, Flagstaff managed to rid itself of railroad influence over its water supply, and continued to develop its traditional source at the inner basin springs.

Chapter 8 Big Brother Arrives

The Depression Decade

Arizona city governments developed a strong relationship with the federal government during the Great Depression. Changed economic conditions left urban leaders reacting rather than initiating municipal projects, and federal policies governed the solutions available from 1930 to 1939. Many communities took advantage of federal public works programs to improve and expand their water infrastructure.

In 1933, Arizona's water situation was aggravated by the widespread drought that created the dust bowl. This affected Arizona by further depressing agricultural prices and irrigation decreased. The federal government moved to rectify the situation for Arizona and the nation as a whole by enacting the Taylor Grazing Act in 1934, installing the Soil Conservation Service in 1935, and passing the Flood Control Act in 1936.[1]

Other federal programs addressed different sectors of the economy. In Arizona, significant relief programs included the Civilian Conservation Corps (CCC), the Federal Emergency Relief Act (FERA), and the Public Works Administration (PWA), all created in 1933. President Franklin Roosevelt and Congress added the Works Progress Administration (WPA) in 1934, among others.[2]

The Great Depression in Tucson

In the late 1920s, faced with a dwindling water supply and continued groundwater depletion, Tucson officials contemplated purchasing private water systems in agricultural areas surrounding the city. The water systems could easily be connected to the municipal infrastructure to better meet the needs of an expanding urban population. The first purchase occurred on June 30, 1929, when the city acquired Jack Ryland's Queen City Farms. The Ryland tract included two wells and one hundred acres of land, easily attached to the city water system on the south side of town. The total cost of the acquisition was about thirty thousand dollars.[3]

Rather than purchasing private water sources in a piecemeal fashion, on January 1, 1930, Tucson commissioned the Kansas City firm of Black and Veatch to study the costs to expand its water supplies. The consultants evaluated sources at Flowing Wells, Sahuarita, and along the Rillito. In a report presented to the city council on April 6, 1930, Black and Veatch favored the purchase of private water supplies, particularly those at Sahuarita. The owners of these properties, suffering low prices for agricultural products, promptly offered the city their water systems. The first to approach the city was the Flowing Wells Irrigation District. On August 19, 1930, the district proposed constructing a thirty-nine-inch main to deliver twenty-five million gallons per day into the city's Osborne Reservoir at Plant 1. On September 13, Midvale Farms proposed transferring water developed on its agricultural land south of the city to domestic use.[4]

After reviewing the matter, the city decided to purchase a tract of land at Sahuarita. On September 21, a group appeared before the city, asking for a monetary settlement. Continued pumping from south side wells had lowered the water level in their own wells. The city council denied the petition of Mary J. Lynn, I. F. Nichols, the L. H. Manning Company, and H. A. and H. C. Kinnison, whereupon the petitioners threatened a court suit if the matter could not be successfully arbitrated.[5]

On November 14, the city signed a contract with M. B. and Verdie Ora Watson to purchase 350 acres of water-bearing land at Sahuarita containing twelve pumps powered by eight belt-driven 2,200-volt motors for a total cost of $141,000. However, a court suit brought by Ben C. Hill and Thomas J. Elliot opposed the transaction because the funds for the purchase did not constitute an appropriated portion of the city budget and thus violated state budget law. Superior Court Judge Fred W. Fickett ruled for the plaintiffs, and on December 7, declared the Sahuarita purchase illegal.[6]

The court case did not stop Tucson from seeking new sources of water. In 1931, the city explored the water situation on the San Xavier Indian Reservation. The proposed water projects on the reservation caught the attention of Congress, and the Senate held hearings in Tucson. Indian Irrigation Service engineers strongly opposed the plan, citing the continued water problems on the reservation itself. In 1932, H. C. Kinnison joined those landholders asking the city to purchase their water supplies. Based on his previous difficulty with the city over lowering water levels, he decided the best solution lay in city purchase of his land. He offered to sell 804 acres of land containing nine wells producing 4.32 million gallons for $329,000. The city declined the offer.[7]

Some residents still focused on developing surface diversions. In the 1930s, Tucsonans tried once again to erect a dam in Sabino Canyon. This time the chamber of commerce presented the effort as both a recreational project and a water diversion scheme. The drive started in 1931 when the chamber appointed Roy Long to chair a committee studying the situation. Long commissioned Charles McCash to conduct a survey for a proposed dam seventy-five feet high.[8]

On December 4, 1933, the committee applied to the forest service for water rights and a permit to dam Sabino Creek, this time envisioning a 250-foot-high structure. The depression meant the county had little money for such an undertaking, so on October 1, 1934, the Tucson Chamber of Commerce applied and received Federal Emergency Relief Administration (FERA) funds to launch the project. A year later, FERA started building a road up Sabino Canyon to the dam site. FERA planners estimated the dam would create a two-mile-long lake to an average depth of seventy-six feet and contain nine thousand acre-feet of water storage.[9]

FERA crews were only able to construct the road before the federal government cancelled the permit for lack of progress. Undaunted, the chamber of commerce submitted a $750,000 request for Works Progress Administration (WPA) funds to continue the project and persuaded Army Corps of Engineers Major Theodore Wyman to make a visit and endorse the project in the summer of 1935. After two years the chamber finally persuaded the board of supervisors to make a formal request for WPA funds, which they did on June 16, 1937. By this time, the cost for the Sabino Canyon dam had jumped to $1,063,506. In order to approve the request, the WPA stipulated that Tucson must put up at least $600,000 of the cost. The local residents, through their representatives in city hall and on the board of supervisors, decided that the cost in relation to the benefits seemed too high and abandoned the project.[10]

After the frustrated attempts to purchase private water systems in the late 1920s and early 1930s, the city moved to develop additional supplies and storage capacity on its own. In 1930, the city drew on fifteen wells, eleven located in the south side well field. The other four wells served the north side; three were at Campbell and Second Street and one at Campbell and Eighth Street.[11]

On November 15, 1932, the city approved a plan to construct a 5-million-gallon reservoir at the south side pumping plant for an estimated cost of $27,000. The city asked the Reconstruction Finance Corporation to put up $10,000 of the total cost. Construction started in 1933. The following year, when the government approved a $250,000 loan to the city, plans were made to increase the reservoir size to 7.5 million gallons. Because of continued funding problems, the new reservoir was not completed until 1939.[12]

In 1935, the city began to explore the possibility of using PWA funds to improve the water system. At the time, 65 to 75 percent of city power use went to pump water because the city lacked elevated tanks. The city planned to use the PWA funds to construct two elevated tanks to solve the problem. On August 1, 1938, city voters approved a $226,636 bond issue for the improvements. The PWA put in $277,000 toward the total cost of $503,636.[13]

To improve water pressure in the city through the use of the elevated tanks, engineers divided the city into two zones based on altitude. A 1-million-gallon elevated storage reservoir would be located in each zone to reduce pumping costs. Workers constructed the high zone tank in Randolph Park and the low zone tank at Third and Elm.[14]

In 1938, the city again considered purchasing private water systems. This time the rationale differed. Rather than acquire agricultural water systems, city officials looked to private water companies serving residential areas. As the city expanded through annexation it encompassed many

The Elm Street reservoir was constructed in 1938 to provide greater water pressure for Tucson residents.

real estate developments served by private water facilities. As with the purchase of the original water company in 1900, the primary reason for the acquisition of the private companies was to upgrade consumer service, not to obtain more water. Homeowners in the real estate developments petitioned the city to acquire the systems to lower rates and improve water quality.[15]

Tucson purchased the first of many private residential water utilities, the San Clemente Water Company serving the subdivision of the same name, in 1938. The city purchased only one more water company before the war, Jefferson Park, in August of 1939. However, the strategy established before the war provided a blueprint for the later expansion of Tucson's water infrastructure.[16]

The Verde Project in the Thirties

At the end of the 1920s, Phoenix officials were faced with the failure of the old redwood pipeline. Workers had already replaced a section, but the entire line needed replacement. Given the cost and the changed economic conditions, city officials were reluctant. The Greater Phoenix Committee led the discussion, presenting various options to the commission on September 20, 1929. The commissioners directed City Engineer William Jamieson to examine the propositions. After discussing the matter at two meetings on October 16 and 18, the commissioners asked the city attorney to prepare an ordinance for a $2.7 million bond issue for a new concrete pipeline. Based on their experience with the redwood pipeline city voters were skeptical of the new proposal and on December 3, 1929, they rejected the bonds by a margin of 1,515 votes in favor to 1,840 votes against.[17]

The defeat forced city officials to reconsider the proposal. One faction advocated holding a special election as soon as possible while another called for delay until after the general election on April 1 so the new commission could consider the bond issue. The forces of action carried the day and persuaded the commission to schedule the election for February 11, 1930. They regretted their haste. Voters again rejected the issue, this time by a margin of 1,335 in favor and 1,777 opposed. The political difficulties forging a consensus did not delay the continuing problems with the redwood pipeline. On February 14, 1930, a section four miles east of

Scottsdale blew out and sent a geyser of water one hundred feet in the air, wasting millions of gallons of water and creating a vast sea of mud. Several days later sections eight miles below the gallery broke, discovered when workmen observed water bubbling out of the ground and forming a large lake.[18]

The water bond issue was one of the first items of business for the new commission taking office May 1. City Manager George Todd addressed the commissioners on May 7, recommending the early submission of a new bond proposal. After much consideration and deliberation, the commission approved a $2.3 million water bond election for June 25. Voters responded with enthusiasm to the new administration and expressed their confidence by approving the bonds with 2,219 in favor and 954 against.[19]

City Manager Todd pushed the bond program forward. On July 31, 1930, he wrote to John B. Brown, the new superintendent of the Fort McDowell agency, requesting permission to drill additional test wells to locate more water for the line. On August 25, 1930, the first assistant secretary of the interior approved the well drilling program and granted permission to the city to apply for a new pipeline right-of-way.[20]

With the permit approval granted, the commission contracted with consulting engineer C. C. Kennedy on October 16, 1930, to supervise construction of the new pipeline. On November 5 the commissioners authorized construction of the project. Engineer Kennedy recommended awarding the construction contract to joint bidders American Concrete Pipe Company and Schmidt-Hitchcock Contractors. The commissioners accepted the bid on December 4, and the contractors announced they would begin construction in three weeks.[21]

With the pipeline program underway, City Manager Todd turned his attention to the well field. The results of three test wells drilled near the Verde indicated that a good supply of water could be obtained by pumping. City engineers identified a parcel for the well field containing a groundwater aquifer. Todd enlisted the help of Senator Carl Hayden on February 9 to secure title to the 120.68-acre parcel, informing Hayden that "the immediate water needs of Phoenix make it imperative that title to this acreage be secured at the earliest possible date."[22]

On December 10, 1931, Senator Hayden introduced Senate Bill 1438 in the 1st Session of the 72nd Congress to authorize the sale of reservation land. The bill passed the Senate side on February 5, 1932, and went to the

House of Representatives. It took over a year before the bill passed out of committee to the full House. On March 1, 1933, the House failed to pass the bill. The adoption of the Indian Reorganization Act in 1934 put an end to the well field purchase, as it prohibited the sale of reservation land.[23]

As the city pursued its ill-fated attempt to acquire title to the well field, construction on the concrete pipeline was completed. On August 20, 1932, acting City Manager Joseph C. Furst applied to the commissioner of Indian Affairs to amend its right-of-way application to cover the "as built" location of the line. The commissioner directed Dr. Carl H. Skinner, superintendent of the Phoenix Indian School, to examine the situation. On June 25, 1933, Skinner held a special meeting at the Fort McDowell Catholic Church to consider compensation. The Yavapai stipulated that the present free water taps continue, two more faucets be added, and no additional charges besides the annual well field rental be made. On July 7, 1933, Skinner recommended approving the application according to the stipulations.[24]

The Commissioner of Indian Affairs did not immediately respond to Skinner's recommendation since water was already flowing through the concrete pipeline and it did not seem urgent. In 1936, the Yavapai organized their tribal council under authority of their community constitution. Supervision of the Fort McDowell Reservation passed to the Pima Agency at Sacaton the same year.[25]

The change in administrative location set the approval process back. In 1938 City Engineer Girand opened talks with Superintendent A. E. Robinson of the Pima Agency. Both sides expressed a desire to reach an agreement on a long-term lease for the property used by the city at Fort McDowell and Salt River. By the end of December in 1938, Girand prepared a draft contract for submission to Robinson. Robinson's negative response on April 29, 1939 put a damper on future negotiations. The superintendent noted "there seems to be quite a difference of opinion on many of the features of this agreement." This sent both sides back to the drawing board. The stalemate continued until World War II.[26]

Phoenix Fights the Depression

The 1930s created opportunities for the development and expansion of the Phoenix water system beyond the Verde project. With the completion of

the concrete pipeline to the Verde River in 1931 city officials found themselves with a good supply of water available for city growth. The only
drawback was that the economic slowdown curtailed the steady progress
made during the 1920s. Phoenix was fortunate that the Salt River Valley
had a diversified economic base of agriculture, manufacturing, and transportation to soften the impact of the depression. Even so, business expansion came to a stop and residential home construction slowed until late
in the decade.[27]

Faced with an ample water supply and a stagnant economy, Phoenix
officials looked for ways to market the resource to keep revenues flowing
into the general fund and pay off the debt incurred by the construction of
the pipeline. The federal government came to the rescue, providing funds
for public works construction programs that enabled the city to expand
its water distribution network.

The improved water supply generated a constant stream of requests
for water service from areas outside Phoenix city limits. Before a policy
was developed to handle these requests they were discussed individually
and often raised controversy. The pipeline also created the possibility for
profits from selling water to those outside the city limits. Consumers in
these areas, dependent on shallow wells often contaminated by cesspools
and septic tanks, clamored for the pure Verde water.

The short-term water surplus and the need for additional revenue
linked the city's water utility to its annexation program. Suburban residents wanted city services but the infrastructure to provide them had
been paid for by Phoenix residents through taxes and bond issues. For
city leaders to be fair to the taxpayers who elected them, they needed to
charge outside residents more for services or encourage the outside areas
to annex to the city. City officials preferred annexation because it brought
additional taxable property into the city and expanded its bonding capability. Throughout the 1930s Phoenix officials struggled to provide water
service both within and without the city limits in an equitable manner. The
economic conditions exacerbated the situation.[28]

Prior to the concrete pipeline project, city policy did not allow additional taps on the water system outside city limits. This policy made sense
in the late twenties when Phoenix faced water shortages caused by problems with the redwood pipeline. With construction on the concrete pipeline underway in 1930 it became more difficult for commission members to

deny water service to those living adjacent to city limits or near the Verde gravity supply pipeline. The case of T. A. Christian illustrates the tough choices faced by commissioners. On April 9, 1930, Christian approached the commission and asked for a permit to tap into the city water system for his lot near Eighteenth and Adams Streets. Christian wanted to sell the lot to obtain money for a medical operation and water service would improve the property's marketability and value. In this instance the commission authorized the tap.[29]

City officials looked for federal help with the water system even before Franklin Delano Roosevelt took office and created a massive public works program. In December of 1932, the city applied for a $150,000 loan from the Reconstruction Finance Corporation (RFC) to extend city water facilities into portions of nineteen residential subdivisions adjacent to the city. Little came of this application, as the change of administrations in Washington soon presented a whole new slate of federal agencies to which the city could apply for aid.[30]

During the summer of 1933, Phoenix received assistance from the RFC to add 281 new customers to the water system. The RFC furnished the labor to extend water lines to areas outside the city that relied on wells for their only supply of water. For its part, the city provided free water to needy families of RFC workers. As a result of this project alone, city officials anticipated an increase of $17,000 in revenues for the water department during 1933.[31]

The success of the small RFC contribution served as a prototype for other water improvement projects during the decade. On August 22, 1933, the City of Phoenix filed preliminary applications for five projects with the Arizona Public Works Advisory Board, including a $150,000 waterworks extension program and $350,000 for sanitary sewer construction outside city limits in areas served only by cesspools and septic tanks. Officials stressed that the water extension would increase revenue and improve the health of residents.[32]

Over the next few months the city refined its application. On October 18, 1933, the city commission adopted resolutions endorsing final applications for $1,899,500. Water service extensions comprised $250,000 and the sewer system extension made up $420,000 of the total. The remainder included improvements for parks and storm sewers.[33]

On November 11, 1933, the commissioners met in special session to set

December 9 as the date of the bond election. The commissioners also reduced the amount of the sanitary sewer project to $340,000 while leaving
the water extension at $250,000. On November 15, the commission re-
scinded its 1932 application for $150,000 in funds from the Reconstruc-
tion Finance Corporation because this earlier request would conflict with
the public works application made under the terms of the National Recovery Act.[34]

With the legal preliminaries out of the way the city concentrated on
selling the proposals to the voters. On December 8, 1933, the night before the election, supporters organized several hundred marchers carrying
torches through downtown Phoenix to show support for the bond issues.
A phalanx of automobiles followed the marchers and the entire parade
stretched for five blocks. Supporters needed every bit of strength they
could muster. The bond issues passed by narrow margins, the water system extension by only 116 votes and the sewer extension by 164 votes.[35]

On January 3, 1934, City Manager S. McNeil Johnston received good
news. Phoenix attorney Harold A. Elliot wired from Washington that President Roosevelt approved the $250,000 water extension project and that
approvals were expected shortly for the other public works projects.
Roosevelt approved the sanitary sewer extension two days later. The city
commission limited employment on the projects to residents of Phoenix
and began compiling a list of unemployed local citizens who qualified. In
addition to alleviating economic hardship by providing jobs to Phoenix
residents, officials anticipated that the water and sewer extensions would
fatten the coffers of the city treasury.[36]

On July 27, 1934, the city delivered the form for the bond issue and sale
to state PWA engineer Howard S. Reed, along with plans and specifications for the water project. The commission retained attorney Orme Lewis
of the law firm of Elliot and Lewis to facilitate the legal aspects of the
bond sale, scheduled for September 4.[37]

PWA state engineer Howard S. Reed, city special legal counsel Orme
Lewis, and City Manager W. C. LeFebvre negotiated an agreement on the
bond sale. On August 29, the city sweetened the pot by agreeing to furnish a water credit of not more than five hundred dollars per month to
the Federal Emergency Relief Administration (FERA), which would then
channel the money to people unable to meet their water bills. For its part,
FERA agreed to furnish labor for city projects. On August 31, the com-

mission adopted the final plans and specifications for the water extension project and issued a call for construction bids.[38]

Commissioners approved the contract with O. F. Fisher on October 23, and two days later $1.52 million worth of bonds arrived in Phoenix from the federal government. Fisher spent the next month assembling equipment and men. Carloads of pipe arrived the week of December 10. On December 17, sixty men began excavating trenches for pipes to link the suburban residential areas with the city water system.[39]

As workers rushed to finish the project, city officials announced that the engineering department was working on plans for a second unit of the water system extension. On February 15, the city announced plans to ask for federal Public Works Administration (PWA) assistance with the construction of lateral mains and service connections. This secondary infrastructure network would link the large mains of the first unit with individual dwellings. Fisher completed the first unit in mid-March.[40]

Early in April of 1935, City Attorney Hess Seaman traveled to Washington, D.C. to confer with PWA officials on the second unit of the water extension project. On April 4, he reported that he had received assurances that the city would be awarded one hundred thousand dollars for the second unit. This second unit would consist of over thirteen miles of connecting pipe and laterals.[41]

Despite the grand plans for the initial water extension project, it soon became apparent that without a means of connecting the mains to the customers the investment in the first unit could not be realized. When the new mayor and commission took office in May of 1935 they faced a budget crisis. As envisioned in the original plan, the city would simply connect to the suburban private water systems and sell the water for distribution. However, the economic downturn had left these small companies in financial difficulty and many had let their plant and equipment run down. Without the money or means to rehabilitate the private systems, Phoenix was unable to sell the water and increase city revenues. It took the mayor and commission the better part of a year to find a way out of the situation.

On March 11, 1936, the commission adopted an amended application to the PWA for the second unit of the water system extension. The plans called for the purchase and rehabilitation of seven private water utilities, the installation of connections to fourteen private water utilities, and permission to provide connections and water to thirty-seven other subdivisions should the city and the private utilities reach agreement on terms for water sale. In addition, the city asked for funds to extend the infiltration gallery at the Verde River, to add a pump and booster station at the lower end of the infiltration gallery, and to purchase a new pump for Well 1 at the Verde River.[42]

Before PWA officials in Washington could act on the amended request, another periodic political storm swept a new mayor and commission into office on May 1. They appointed a new city engineer, James Girand, who decided to reevaluate and revise the application. On May 27, Girand submitted a second amended application to the city commission. His plan abandoned the idea of rehabilitating the private suburban water systems because the cost this entailed would limit the number of utilities that could be improved and thus reduce the number of potential customers for the city. Instead, Girand proposed that the city forego the rehabilitation aspect in favor of purchasing as many private water utilities as could be obtained with the money remaining. Girand also changed the Verde River improvements slightly, eliminating the infiltration gallery extension and instead drilling a new well to provide additional water. The plan for well no. 1 remained the same. On May 28, the commission approved the second amended application.[43]

State PWA engineer Howard S. Reed spent the next month examining the proposal and on July 13, 1936, forwarded the application to Washington. Reed noted that he had "devoted considerable study" to the second amended application and he believed that it was "the best thing possible for the City of Phoenix." Horatio R. Hackett, PWA assistant administrator in Washington, approved the second amended application on August 24. City Manager Evan S. Stallcup announced that the project would begin soon. After receiving approval from Washington, the city commission on September 1, 1936, adopted the plans and specifications for the second unit of the water system extension.[44]

The commission accepted construction bids on October 15, 1936. City Manager Stallcup signed contracts the next day with Arizona Concrete Company, Lewis Brothers Contractors, and Hanson Pump and Machine works. The work itself proceeded just as smoothly.[45]

On July 20, 1937, the city commission authorized the final payment on the water construction projects. The PWA program resulted in an increase in total water supply available to the city from 21 million gallons per day to 24 million gallons per day (mgd). Peak daily usage at that time was 20 mgd, so the project provided a safety margin of nearly 20 percent. The project also proved its worth as a revenue producer for the city. Annual water department revenues increased from $480,000 in FY 1935–36 to $543,000 in FY 1936–37. Officials anticipated water department revenues to increase to $593,000 in FY 1937–38.[46]

Flagstaff during the Thirties

Flagstaff leaders thought the 1926 project to double the city's storage capacity to just over one hundred million gallons would solve their water problems for a long time. They were wrong. Continued rapid growth during the late 1920s increased demand by industrial and municipal users. In 1931 a cold dry winter descended on northern Arizona and what little snow fell soon evaporated. The water level in Flagstaff's reservoirs dropped and dropped.[47]

The water shortage forced Flagstaff city officials to purchase water from the Santa Fe's Del Rio Springs in the lower Chino Valley and have it shipped in. This additional expense, combined with the absence of revenue from municipal water sales, quickly put the city budget in the red. Federal hydrologist A. H. Womack advised lowering the intake at the city's inner basin springs to below the frost line to allow an uninterrupted flow during the cold winter months. Womack also suggested that the city locate another source of water.[48]

During the summer of 1932 the city tapped into two additional springs in the inner basin and lowered the intake lines. For an alternate supply, the city drilled twenty-six shallow wells at Clark Ranch. This sufficed for the summer and fall, but in the winter of 1932–33 the city had to resume water shipments from Del Rio. The next winter was warmer, but 1934 was the coldest and driest on record. City officials scrambled to find more water.[49]

Flagstaff city officials tried several temporary measures to augment the water supply, including tapping into O'Neill Springs, running a pipeline to Lindberg Springs, and placing an infiltration gallery in a well field at Clark Ranch. While these plans were being considered, forest supervisor E. G. Miller took matters into his own hands. He coordinated a Civilian Conservation Corps crew that built a five-mile line to tap springs on the north slope of the San Francisco Peaks and divert the flow to the inner basin intake.[50]

Supervisor Miller named the springs area on the north slope Aubineau Springs in honor of early Flagstaff Mayor Julius Aubineau. Mayor Aubineau had played an instrumental role in developing Flagstaff's first reservoir in 1898. In addition to CCC labor, the U.S. Resettlement Administration contributed just under eighteen thousand dollars to the project.[51]

Flagstaff leaders realized these were just stopgap measures and that the community needed a comprehensive solution. The city council contracted with Phoenix engineer John Carollo to conduct a study. Carollo discredited the idea of a dam in Fort Valley and stressed development of underground supplies as the most feasible solution. Carollo recommended that the city drill at O'Neill Springs or in Oak Creek near Riordan.[52]

Despite Carollo's negative evaluation of surface water proposals, some Flagstaff leaders, including scientist V. M. Slipher from Lowell Observatory, combat veteran J. D. "Jim" Walkup, and newspaper editor Columbus P. Giragi, continued to pursue dam construction. In 1934–35, a wet winter encouraged surface water proponents as floodwaters rushed through the bed of the Rio de Flag. Proponents called for construction of a dam in Switzer Canyon.

Despite an active campaign in support of the dam led by newspaper editor Giragi, other Flagstaff leaders urged caution and additional study. The city council contracted with another hydraulic engineer, J. J. Jakowsky of Los Angeles. Jakowsky issued a report on the Riordan and Fort Valley areas in 1937, and prepared a second report based on an expanded survey area the following year. His findings echoed those of his colleagues. Jakowsky recommended additional development of groundwater supplies, either in Oak Creek or Fort Valley.[53]

Flagstaff leaders decided to pursue the well option in Fort Valley. City officials prepared an application to the Public Works Administration (PWA) for funding for both the well and dam in Switzer Canyon. Engineers estimated the total project cost at $126,000, of which $50,000 was a grant from the PWA. The remaining $76,000 would be a PWA loan the city would have to repay from the proceeds of a bond sale. In October of 1937 Flagstaff voters approved the bond sale by a margin of 173 to 48.[54]

The project turned out to be a disappointment for several reasons. In November of 1937 state PWA administrators reported that all PWA funds for Arizona had been expended and that there would be no money available for the Flagstaff project. City leaders went ahead with the well anyway, but drillers found only a meager supply of water. It became clear to everyone involved that Flagstaff needed to look elsewhere for more water.[55]

Summary

The federal government played the dominant role in Arizona's water history during the 1930s. Depression-era public works programs helped Arizona's urban leaders improve their water production and distribution infrastructure. What was different about the federal presence in Arizona during the thirties was the urban emphasis of government involvement.

Arizona residents had long been accustomed to federal agents on Indian reservations, as forest supervisors, and as park rangers. The federal government controlled—and still controls—vast tracts of Arizona real estate. Arizona residents chafed under a long line of appointed territorial officials that were more concerned with personal wealth than with advancing the territory. During the thirties, the federal government first began to have an extensive involvement with the needs of urban areas.

In Phoenix, federal funds allowed the city to expand water service into suburban areas. While touted as a public works project to provide jobs and boost the local economy, the water infrastructure improvement projects also allowed Phoenix to expand and improve its water system at a very small cost while providing income for the city. The thirties established the provision of water service as an important part of municipal income.

As relatively smaller communities, Tucson and Flagstaff reaped fewer rewards from the federal government. However, public works projects in these smaller cities had a correspondingly greater effect. Programs such as the WPA, PWA, and CCC allowed both Tucson and Flagstaff to make needed improvements to their water infrastructure that would have been very difficult without federal funds.

Federal actions during the thirties helped tribal leaders gain new levels of sophistication and equality in their relationships with other government entities. The long and complex history of the Verde project on the Fort McDowell Indian Reservation reveals the evolving relationship between American Indians, the federal government, and resource users.

Over the years, the Yavapai exerted greater control over decisions affecting their resources. Through this process, the Yavapai developed skills to function in the urbanizing region surrounding Phoenix.

The dissatisfaction with officials of the Indian office expressed by the Yavapai and similar complaints by other Native American groups resulted in the Indian Reorganization Act of 1934. At this same time, Phoenix officials moved to replace the redwood pipeline that was partly on reservation land. The establishment of a community constitution and tribal council under the terms of the 1934 act facilitated a more active role for the Yavapai with the project during the 1930s and beyond.

Chapter 9 World War II

World War II had a dramatic impact on the state as increased defense spending brought military and civilian workers to Arizona. Although the war increased water use by agriculture and industry, completing water projects to keep up with demand was difficult because of restrictions on construction supplies. This led to an increase in spending after the war when urban leaders addressed deferred needs.

Prior to 1940, water consumption in Tucson averaged less than the annual recharge, but when the war began consumption outpaced recharge for the first time. Recharge is the amount of water that returns to the earth from rainfall or river floods. When more groundwater is removed than recharged, the condition is known as *overdraft* and usually results in falling groundwater levels. Water users in Tucson pumped 60 percent more groundwater in 1945 than 1941, causing a critical depletion of groundwater. A dramatic lowering of water tables occurred across the state. Low average rainfall between 1920 and 1940 and little winter rainfall or major floods to contribute to groundwater recharge aggravated the situation.[1]

Although much of the nation had been gearing for war since Germany invaded Poland in 1939, the United States joined the allied countries as a full partner in the war effort after the Japanese attack at Pearl Harbor in 1941. City officials in Arizona turned their attention to facilitating the training of fighting personnel and the construction of defense industries. Water supplies for these new activities formed a crucial part of their planning.

World War II in Tucson

World War II generated increases in mining and agriculture, traditional areas of Tucson's economy, and for the first time there was industrial growth as military spending brought aircraft firms to the basin. The population grew as workers moved to Tucson to take jobs at the mines, farms, and aircraft plants. All of these factors spurred the increased use of groundwater between 1943 and 1947.[2]

Environmental conditions aggravated the problem of low water tables. A twenty-year dry period culminated with a deep drought in 1940 which left virtually all surface reservoirs in the state with very little water. Although 1941 was a wet year, another ten-year drought began in 1942. This hit Tucson particularly hard because the area was almost entirely dependent on groundwater by 1945.[3]

The federal government militarized Davis-Monthan Field in 1940 to prepare for the war effort. Named for two Tucson aviators who lost their lives in the line of duty, Davis-Monthan was the largest municipally owned airport in the United States. Noted aviator Charles A. Lindbergh dedicated the facility on its opening day, September 23, 1927. In the years that followed the Army Air Corps maintained a constant presence at the municipal field, taking advantage of the clear air and wide open spaces to practice.[4]

On August 6, 1940, the federal government announced plans to take over and expand Davis-Monthan into a center for military aviation. Plans called for increasing the size of the field from three hundred to sixteen hundred acres. The expansion would allow the largest bombers to use the facility, and employ more than three thousand military and civilian workers.[5]

Plans progressed quickly. By December of 1940 the federal government terminated the use of all city facilities at Davis-Monthan and Tucson leaders were forced to relocate the municipal airport. Tucson businessman Mike Mansfield proved instrumental in finding a new location not far away, giving Tucson a civilian airport facility as well as a military field. The municipal airport became the center of civilian defense industries during and after the war.[6]

Tucson agriculture in the 1940s relied almost exclusively on water pumped from wells. Agriculture expanded rapidly with wartime needs, resulting in further groundwater depletion. As in World War I, cotton was the major crop. The University of Arizona College of Agriculture developed new strains of high-producing cotton. The Farmers Investment Company (FICO) started a major cotton farming operation during the 1940s, similar to the corporate investment in agriculture that occurred during World War I in the Salt River Valley.[7]

The Tucson Water Department grappled with the problems of increased use and lower water tables. The expansion of its system in the late 1930s, fueled by the influx of federal funds, enabled the city to enter the war economy with a good base of municipal water facilities to meet the growing demands.[8]

In the immediate aftermath of the attack on Pearl Harbor, Mayor Henry Jaasted believed the city's water facilities might be vulnerable to sabotage and ordered the erection of chain-link fences topped with barbed wire around Tucson's water reservoirs. As an additional precaution, in December of 1941 City Manager Phil J. Martin provided key business owners with maps showing the location of critical valves in case sabotage made it necessary to stop the flow of water from the reservoirs.[9]

While Davis-Monthan Air Field was the largest federal facility in Tucson, the government located two other facilities close by to provide additional space for pilot training. Ryan Field west of Tucson and Marana Field north of the city played key roles in the defense effort. Marana developed into one of the most active locations for pilot training in Arizona. By the end of the war more than ten thousand pilots had trained there.[10]

The protected inland location of Tucson combined with its normally cloud-free days and surrounding open space made it a prime location for military activities. In addition to official military installations, conditions in Tucson also attracted defense industries. Civilian contractors set up shop at Tucson's new municipal airport. The largest of these was Consolidated Aircraft. Consolidated workers put the finishing touches on B-24 airplanes flown in from factories in other locations.[11]

Military training facilities and civilian defense contractors put a strain on the urban infrastructure of Tucson. The influx of workers, both military and civilian, made housing scarce. The federal government provided assistance by creating housing tracts for the new residents. In 1941 the City of Tucson executed an agreement with the government to provide water service to a 135-unit federal housing project. More residents meant more water connections as the war effort continued.[12]

Despite the increased activity, Tucson constructed no new major water facilities during the war. Municipal officials continued to acquire private water companies to bring those wells and distribution systems into the city distribution grid. During the war four private companies were added to the city system: Mundo Vista (1942), Catalina Vista (May 1942), Samos (June 1943), and Colonia Solana (March 1944).[13]

Overview: World War II in Phoenix

Phoenix officials also struggled to provide water service to a rapidly expanding number of residential and industrial customers while wartime restrictions on materials limited their flexibility. To meet the demand for water, Phoenix increased its well capacity to supplement its surface water supply from the Verde River.

The clear skies and even climate of the Salt River Valley brought service personnel and war workers to Phoenix by the thousands and stressed urban services. As early as 1939 Sky Harbor Airport in Phoenix became home to an aviation training facility as part of the federal government's war preparedness program. In 1940 contractors opened a second facility near Glendale (Thunderbird Field) followed by Falcon Field in Mesa in September of 1941. These small sites paved the way for two large aviation facilities, Luke Field in the west valley and Williams Field in the east valley. By the end of the war in 1945, thousands of American and foreign cadets had trained at these posts.[14]

Defense industries formed the second aspect of the economic expansion. The inland location of Phoenix offered protection to vital war industries which might be vulnerable to attack. The federal government encouraged the dispersal of defense industries, offering an opportunity for transportation and commercial centers such as Phoenix to develop an industrial base. In July of 1941 the Goodyear Aircraft Corporation announced plans for an airplane manufacturing facility near Litchfield Park in the west valley. The City of Phoenix assisted this effort by purchasing land for an airport at the Goodyear site. In March of 1942 the Federal Defense Plant Corporation and the Aluminum Company of America (Alcoa) started construction of an aluminum plant at Thirty-fifth Avenue and Van Buren. In November of 1942 AiResearch Corporation, a manufacturer of airplane parts, opened a facility south of Sky Harbor Airport. These industries further increased the demand for water resources.[15]

This greater water use came on top of a technological innovation in home cooling which further taxed the municipal water supply. In the late 1930s garage mechanics perfected the design of the evaporative cooler. Installed on a home's roof or outside wall, this device used a fan to force hot dry outside air through pads made of wood shavings and kept wet with a small but steady stream of water. Air cooled through evaporation then flowed into the home. By 1940 the use of evaporative coolers had spread across Phoenix as manufacturers refined commercial production, resulting in a large increase in water consumption during the hot summer months.[16]

Phoenix, 1940–1941: The Calm before the Storm?

In the summer of 1940 increased water use caught up with limited production. While Phoenix had expanded its service area in the 1930s, it had not increased water production. On Thursday, June 13, 1940, the hot dry weather caused Phoenix residents to use water faster than the system could supply it, and reserves in the Phoenix reservoir system sunk to two million gallons out of a total capacity of thirty-five million gallons. To combat the situation City Manager Roy R. Hislop declared an immediate ban on all lawn sprinkling in the city until Monday, June 17. Water Department Superintendent Ira W. Bellinger installed an in-stream pump to divert raw Verde River water into the city system in an effort to boost production. In the meantime, Hislop dispatched City Engineer James Girand to the Verde River to make a personal examination of the situation. Hislop also directed the water department to prepare auxiliary wells in the city for pumping.[17]

With a complicated set of factors contributing to the water shortage, City Engineer Girand recommended a series of steps to get the city through the crisis. He advised placing a second in-stream pump at the Verde River, installing a pump at an available well in the city's lower Verde well field, moving two drilling rigs to the Verde to drill new wells, hiring new personnel, keeping the level of Bartlett Reservoir high to prevent silting of intakes, and cleaning the river of silt to improve flow to the infiltration gallery and wells. Within the city, Girand recommended continued conservation efforts and directed that the city well at Coronado Park, normally used to supply Coronado Pool, be diverted directly into the city mains.[18]

These changes managed to bolster the city water supply, and reservoir storage rose to nearly thirty million gallons on Saturday, June 15. City Manager Hislop responded by lifting the complete ban on lawn sprinkling, effective Sunday. In its place Hislop established an even/odd rationing of irrigation water; residents with odd-numbered addresses could water their lawns and gardens on Monday, Wednesday, and Friday, those with even numbers could do so on the alternating days of Tuesday, Thursday and Saturday. Hislop exempted Sundays from the water restrictions. The easing of restrictions, combined with the increased production of two million gallons per day (mgd) from the Coronado Park well, slowed the drain on the city reservoir system. Despite their efforts, demand continued to outpace water production and the water levels in the reservoirs continued to drop.[19]

By June 21, City Engineer Girand's improvements at the Verde had raised the city's water production capacity enough to meet the current demand without depleting reservoir storage. Girand accomplished this by drilling and equipping a twenty-inch well at the Verde well field. City Park Superintendent George H. Hollis stopped diverting water from the Coronado Park well into the city system and reopened Coronado Pool on June 22. On June 24, 1940, City Manager Hislop lifted the restrictions on water use and abandoned the alternating address rationing plan. As a final step in crisis management, on June 29 the city commission adopted an ordinance requiring the installation of water meters at all locations that used evaporative coolers and directed the city manager to explore the abandonment of "flat rate" water service.[20]

Despite the improvements, during the last week of August in 1940 Phoenix experienced another water shortage. Storms in the Verde River watershed released silt-laden water downstream, reducing the effectiveness of the city's wells and infiltration galleries. The backup well at Ninth and Polk went into operation again on August 22. On August 30, Thomas M. Sullivan, taking over as acting city manager for Roy R. Hislop, issued an "earnest appeal" to Phoenix citizens for water conservation. Sullivan asked the public to stop wasting water and to desist from watering lawns or yards.[21]

By September cooler weather and continued conservation moderated the water shortage. The city began to look for long-term solutions. University of Arizona consulting hydrologist H. C. Schwalen recommended that the city drill more wells. Schwalen located sites for wells east of Scottsdale and recommended drilling a deep well in Encanto Park. Water that proved to be of high quality could be turned into the city system. Schwalen also suggested obtaining permission to use wells owned by the Salt River Valley Water Users Association that were located near the city's water main from the Verde River and could be put to municipal use.[22]

On January 7, 1941, the commission purchased two parcels of land east of Scottsdale for the well sites, and authorized contracts with the firm of Lyon Brothers to drill two wells at the Scottsdale location and a single well in Encanto Park. The Scottsdale wells would add 8 mgd to the city's total water production.[23]

In March, the commission augmented the improvement program by purchasing an additional well site east of Scottsdale, and again contracted with Lyon Brothers to drill the well. After some delays, the job was completed in May. The three wells east of Scottsdale added a total of 14 mgd to the water production capability of the city.[24]

In an ironic turn of events, the delay on the well project was partly attributed to wet weather causing difficult construction conditions along the Verde River. Heavy runoff during the last three months of 1940 filled the reservoirs of the Salt River Project on the Salt and Verde Rivers. This was the largest runoff in seven years and followed a record drought year. The wet cycle continued in 1941, with March setting a record for rainfall in Phoenix. Precipitation on the Salt and Verde watersheds filled the reservoirs to capacity, resulting in flooding downstream in March and April.[25]

The end of the drought prompted Arizona Governor Sidney Osborn to declare Saturday, April 26, 1941, "Day of Thanksgiving for Water." The

Governor Sidney Osborn declared April 26, 1941, "Day of Thanksgiving for Water" to celebrate the end of a long drought.

Water Users, Arizona Federation of Farm Bureaus, and the Phoenix Chamber of Commerce organized a celebration with an all-day program of events that included a chuck-wagon lunch served in downtown Phoenix on Central Avenue, which was closed for the occasion. The Water Users erected a display of Roosevelt Dam in front of the Heard building. Governor Osborn addressed the crowd, as did Phoenix Mayor Dr. Reed Shupe and City Commissioner M. F. Wharton. On Saturday, "confidence and cheer radiated" in Phoenix as residents danced in the streets to celebrate the end of the drought.[26]

Phoenix Water Adjusts for the Duration of the War

In November of 1941 the city manager executed a contract with D. K. Murphy to remove the steel bands on the old redwood pipeline as a war salvage effort. Described by a contemporary as "an ambitious individual," Murphy used a power shovel to excavate the buried pipeline. The city agreed to backfill the ditch to eliminate open holes and cave-in hazards. After Pearl Harbor, in March of 1942, resident George O. Ford raised the question of protecting the city's water supply in case of attack. City Manager Scott and City Engineer R. Gail Baker assured Ford that the city was doing everything possible to protect the system.[27]

The emergency situation created by the war led to a final agreement between the City of Phoenix and the tribal government at Fort McDowell over the right-of-way for the Verde pipeline. On January 6, 1942, both parties agreed to a contract. The articles of agreement signed by Superintendent A. E. Robinson on behalf of the Fort McDowell Mohave-Apache Indian community called for a lump-sum payment to clear all past due rentals up to 1940. Thereafter, the Yavapai would receive an annual rental fee. The contract contained no expiration date, but the parties agreed it would be subject to redetermination after June 30, 1960. In addition, Phoenix agreed to "continue its past policy of giving preference to Indians for all unskilled labor performed in connection with the operation and maintenance" of the Verde project.[28]

As summer approached in 1943, the city commission asked City Engineer Richard Bennett to outline the water situation. Bennett reported that the city water system produced 30 to 31 mgd from its Verde infiltration gallery and wells. Demand in 1942 peaked at 30.6 mgd, so the city system operated at the edge of its capacity. To prepare for an emergency, the water department placed an additional well in operation on the Verde during April and had men clearing the river channel to remove silt and improve flow. Bennett had already checked and readied the auxiliary wells in the city. He reported that the city was as prepared as it could be, but the water situation depended on river conditions and weather. If the river remained silt-free and the weather cool, the city would have ample supplies for the summer.[29]

By July, the demand on the system from the new war plants and defense workers became evident. Consumption averaged 4 to 6 mgd over use a year earlier in July of 1942. Drought conditions again curtailed the production from the Verde River, forcing the city to rely on its high-capacity wells drilled east of Scottsdale in 1941. On July 8, 1943, City Manager Roy J. Heyne asked residents to conserve water by preventing waste.[30]

Although Phoenix survived the summer heat without a repeat of the drastic water crisis that paralyzed the city in 1940, city officials knew they must find a solution to the summer water shortage problem. Because the problem could be traced to silt accumulation caused by the construction of Bartlett Dam by the Salt River Valley Water Users Association, many in the city looked to the Water Users for help. In August of 1943 City Manager Heyne approached the management of the Water Users with a proposal to tap four of the association's existing wells located near the city's Verde River pipeline for municipal use.[31]

By October Water Department Superintendent Joe S. Thurman reached a tentative agreement with the Water Users for the use of four wells east of Scottsdale, and the city commission made plans to incorporate the new wells into the city system. On January 4, 1944, the city adopted plans and specifications for a pipeline extending from the wells to the city's Verde pipeline. The next day the commission authorized a contract with Jules L. Vermeersch to purchase pumps for the four wells.[32]

On January 18, 1944, after months of negotiations between the city and the Water Users, the commission authorized the tentative auxiliary water supply contract reached on October 20, 1943. The lease agreement cost the city $185,000 and would boost production by 24.8 mgd. The contract noted that the agreement was temporary in nature due to the war emergency. Since the city could not develop an additional supply under wartime restrictions, the Water Users agreed to the use of their wells for a period not to exceed ten years or until such time as the city developed additional supplies.[33]

On January 27, 1944, the commission opened the bids for the construction of the pipeline. Two bids, one by N. P. Van Valkenburg of Southgate, California, and one by Tiffany Construction Company of Phoenix, came in very close. Van Valkenburg had a lower bid, but because Tiffany was located in Phoenix it was eligible for a 5 percent local preference. However, Van Valkenburg challenged Tiffany's bid by claiming the local company failed to pay its taxes. Rather than make an award that might be disputed in court, the commission members rejected all bids and called for a new round of bidding.[34]

The commission then decided to revise the project to eliminate one of the wells. The city had applied to the War Production Board to cover the cost of the wells as a war emergency measure, and after studying the situation board officials agreed to fund only three wells. When the bids came back on the three wells, pipeline, and connections, Van Valkenburg remained the low bidder. This time the commission accepted the

bid and awarded the contract to the California firm. Van Valkenburg bid
$136,196.15 for the total project.[35]

Van Valkenburg spent the spring of 1944 connecting the wells to the
city system and completed the project the first week of June. The water
supplied by the additional wells boosted the city's production capacity in
time for the summer demand peak.[36]

Although the wells expanded production enough to get the city through
the summer of 1944, city officials realized the program was an emergency war measure. As early as February of 1944 Mayor Newell Stewart
stressed the need for postwar planning. In a speech to the Phoenix Junior
Chamber of Commerce, Stewart noted that the lease of the Water Users
wells was a temporary measure, but the changes caused by the war and
the widespread use of evaporative coolers were permanent. Stewart
stated that Phoenix must find ways to expand its production and delivery
of surface water.[37]

Flagstaff Water Projects during the War

Flagstaff leaders investigated several possible locations for surface water
diversions during the 1930s. Despite this interest in surface supplies,
each engineer the city consulted recommended additional development of
groundwater. The results of these studies failed to dissuade Flagstaff's
dam proponents in the years prior to World War II.

In 1935 a new contender for a reservoir location came into play. Lumber
mill owner Joseph C. Dolan transferred the real estate title of Lake Mary
to the Forest Service. The lake had been created in 1903 by Timothy A.
Riordan to supply the lumber company with water for its operation. Dolan
emphasized the recreational attributes of the lake, but also suggested the
reservoir as a source of municipal water.[38]

In 1939 Flagstaff hired consulting engineer Walter Johannessen to evaluate ways to augment the city's water supply. Johannessen found fault
with the Lake Mary project and instead supported a proposal to construct
a dam in Switzer Canyon. City leaders wanted another opinion and engaged the services of Santa Fe railroad hydraulic engineer George C. Davenport and University of Arizona professor of geology A. A. Stoyanow.[39]

The two men worked independently to evaluate potential reservoir

Completed in 1941, the Lake Mary Water Treatment Plant gave Flagstaff residents access to a large supply of surface water.

sites in Lake Mary and Switzer Canyon. When they completed their reports in February of 1940, both came to the conclusion that Lake Mary was a better location for a surface water diversion. Davenport pointed out the size difference in the two watersheds—a 60-square-mile drainage area behind Lake Mary compared with only 2.6 square miles in Switzer Canyon. Stoyanow suggested constructing the dam at the upper end of Lake Mary.[40]

Flagstaff officials considered the reports the definitive word on the development of a surface water supply. The city council proposed a

$200,000 bond issue, and on December 5, 1940, Flagstaff voters approved the measure by a margin of 178 to 12.[41]

The city council found additional funds to cover the total project cost of just under $280,000 including the dam, pipelines, pumping plant, and treatment plant. Fisher Contracting Company had actually started construction on the earthen dam before the vote, on November 5, 1940. The council opened bids for other portions of the project on January 3, 1941, and contractor James W. Huntley constructed the water treatment plant. Flagstaff residents attended the grand opening of the new facility in August of 1941.[42]

On January 30, 1942, Flagstaff city leaders learned that the federal government had selected Coconino County as the location for a massive ammunition depot. The $17 million project had a tremendous impact on the area. Located at the small community of Bellmont west of Flagstaff, the Navajo Ordnance Depot was one of several constructed by military planners. As with other military facilities in Arizona, the inland location would protect the depot from possible enemy attack.[43]

The depot project employed more than six thousand laborers. With relatives and dependents included, local officials estimated that fifteen thousand workers and family members relocated to Flagstaff. The construction project and influx of workers strained available water supplies. Until Volunteer Springs could be developed at the site for a local source of water, workers hauled in thirty tank cars of water each day from the Flagstaff water system. When completed, the Navajo Ordnance Depot employed just over eight hundred civilian workers.[44]

Summary

Historian Gerald D. Nash called World War II a "watershed event" in the development of the West. According to Nash, prior to the war the West was a "colony" of the east. Westerners sent their raw materials and resources east to line the pockets of eastern investors and capitalists. World War II thrust the West into the national picture as a leading producer of manufactured goods for the war effort. After the war, the West developed its own industry and economy. Profits from these activities stayed in the West to further the tremendous economic expansion of the postwar years.[45]

The relationship between military spending and urban growth was not confined to the West, nor was it a phenomenon limited to World War II. Historian Roger W. Lotchin has defined this relationship as the "martial metropolis" and notes that it has a long history in urban areas. For cities in Arizona, however, which had a limited military involvement prior to the Second World War, the impact of increased federal spending was striking. Lotchin considers the hallmark of a martial metropolis a federal-urban partnership. In Arizona, that partnership extended to the urban water infrastructure as well.[46]

Chapter 10 The Postwar Boom to 1950

Adjustment and transition followed World War II as Arizona's urban leaders came to the realization that things had changed forever. The increasing demand for water led to a major conflict between the City of Phoenix and the Salt River Valley Water Users Association that operated the Salt River Project (SRP). Officials at SRP threatened to cut off the city's supply unless municipal leaders provided funds for improvements to Horseshoe Dam. Events in Tucson and Flagstaff were not as dramatic, but also underscored the profound implications the war had for Arizona.

Tucson after the War

Like their counterparts elsewhere in the state, Tucson municipal officials struggled to keep up with a growing population in the postwar period. From 10,684 service connections in 1945, the Tucson distribution system grew to 15,074 connections in 1950. While some of these new connections represented customers of existing water systems that had been purchased by the city and brought into the distribution grid, many more were the result of new residents.[1]

Following World War II, the conditions that first drew the military to

Tucson Water Department consulting engineer George Barr (left) and chief engineer John Rausher inspect a new well site in 1954.

Tucson and Arizona proved to be strong lures for many new residents. The wonderful climate, plenty of open space, and a friendly western hospitality pulled thousands to the Old Pueblo. Residential home construction multiplied at a strong pace. Many who came to Tucson during the war to work in the defense industry or while serving in the military decided to make the desert community their permanent home.

The Tucson water system expanded through the purchase of private water utilities from 1945 to 1950. With no available source of surface water, city officials turned to wells to tap underground aquifers, and acquired most of these wells by incorporating private companies into the city service area. At the end of the war Tucson had nineteen wells in active service, including the wells at its two pumping plants and the north side well field. In 1950, the number of wells in active service had increased to thirty-three.[2]

In a very real sense the city was not anticipating growth but reacting to it. Developers of subdivisions put in wells and distribution grids to serve residents of that subdivision. As city limits expanded to include developed areas, the city negotiated the purchase of the wells and distribution systems from the private companies. Private water company purchases between 1945 and 1950 included El Encanto (January 1947), Monterey (May 1947), North Campbell Estates (June 1949), South Gate (July 1949), Beard (October 1949), Parkview (1950), and Kilburn (1950).[3]

The Postwar Boom to 1950 in Phoenix

In 1946 Phoenix faced a critical water shortage. Increased population and economic activity generated by World War II combined with drought conditions to push municipal water services to the limit. The difficulty of providing water to the new industries and residents in the sprawling community threatened to slow growth and expansion. To supply water for municipal needs, Phoenix embarked on a plan to construct a water treatment plant on the Verde River near its confluence with the Salt River. This proposal came under opposition from the Salt River Valley Water Users Association, which managed the Salt River Project (SRP).

Salt River Project officials advocated a plan to construct control gates on the spillway of Horseshoe Dam in the Verde River Valley, fifty-five miles northeast of Phoenix. During winter storms the control gates would impound and store additional floodwater by effectively raising the height of the dam; this water would then be available during the water-short summer months. The careful negotiations and compromise necessary to win approval for the gates project from voters, government administrators, and other water users in central Arizona occupied Phoenix officials from 1946 to 1950, but proved essential to obtaining new water for Phoenix.

Between 1943 and 1945, Phelps-Dodge Corporation had constructed Horseshoe Dam on the Verde River with the assistance and support of the U.S. government's Defense Plant Corporation and the Salt River Valley Water Users Association. By 1945 the dam could impound up to 60,000 acre-feet (af) of water. Under an agreement with the Salt River Project, the federal government facilitated a water diversion by Phelps Dodge from the Black River upstream from SRP dams on the Salt River. Because this removed water that might otherwise flow into SRP dams, the federal government and Phelps Dodge assisted SRP to construct Horseshoe Dam to impound additional water to make up for what might be lost. Phelps-Dodge used the water at the Morenci mine and smelter, and the Water Users managed the dam for the benefit of valley agriculture.[4]

Leeds, Hill, Barnard and Jewett, a Los Angeles engineering firm, designed the dam. The foundation of Horseshoe Dam was built to support a potential expansion that could impound up to 240,000 af. The dam could be enlarged if it became part of the massive Central Arizona Project (CAP) then under consideration by the Interior Department's Bureau of Reclamation.[5]

The end of World War II reduced the demand for copper but the need for water in the Salt River Valley was greater than ever. After two decades of dry years, a drought in the late 1940s signaled the beginning of a new dry cycle at a time of increased development. These two conditions caused a marked decline in groundwater levels by 1945. State officials passed a weak groundwater regulation measure that year.[6]

Government officials at three levels soon considered ways to provide additional water for the valley. The federal Bureau of Reclamation concentrated on developing a system to bring Colorado River water to central Arizona. State legislators studied methods for stricter groundwater controls. Phoenix, faced with increasing demands and dwindling supplies, took action as well.[7]

Phoenix city commissioners held a special meeting on July 31, 1946. The mayor's emergency water committee, the water development committee, and the finance committee each presented separate reports with recommendations to solve the crisis. The committees reviewed the city's needs and proposed a bond issue to build a new water intake and filtration plant on the Verde River for domestic supply. The commissioners adopted the recommendations of the joint committees and backed the proposal to issue $4.8 million in bonds for the Verde water treatment plant.[8]

Phoenix engineers spent the month of August setting the details and presented the bond package at a special meeting of the commission on September 10, but the commissioners adjourned without approving the bond issue. Action by the valley's major agricultural water supplier caused the delay. At a meeting the previous day, the Salt River Valley Water Users Association board of governors proposed that Phoenix add $800,000 to the bond issue for construction of spillway gates at Horseshoe Dam.

Greig Scott, attorney for the Water Users, stated that the plan to build a new intake and filtration plant on the Verde depended on new supplies of water, and that the present stream flow was inadequate during the summer period of peak use. The Water Users believed the gates were needed immediately and seized on the water bond issue as a way to guarantee construction. This intervention by the Water Users delayed approval of the bond election, and the water development committee took the proposal under advisement.[9]

A week later, on September 17, the water development committee presented a second report. The committee determined that improvements to the distribution system and mains, the Verde intake, filtration plant, and new reservoir would cost $5 million. In addition, members recommended that Phoenix spend $200,000 to repair roofs on two existing municipal reservoirs and $800,000 to build the gates on Horseshoe Dam. The Water Users emphasized that the gates would assure Phoenix of 20,000 af of water annually, in addition to the 30,000 af it was using. Phoenix needed the additional water to increase line pressure during the summer months and reduce concerns about fire safety. An *Arizona Republic* newspaper correspondent observed that in the event of a major fire during the summer, the water system was incapable of generating enough pressure to stop the spread of flames.[10]

On October 8, the city commission set November 19 as the date for the bond election. Representatives from three Phoenix engineering firms completed the plans, and City Engineer R. Gail Baker and the emergency water committee approved the specifications. City Attorney Jack Choisser resolved the legal issues.[11]

Contract negotiations to provide an operating agreement between Phoenix and the Water Users for the gates and water supply culminated three days before the bond election. On November 16, the Water Users board approved the contract after meeting with Phoenix representatives. City Engineer Baker expressed dissatisfaction with several parts of the document and the *Republic* reported that the Water Users drove a hard financial bargain in the face of the city's need for water. Baker objected to a provision that called for Phoenix to pay an annual maintenance fee to the Water Users and a second provision that reduced the city's storage space in proportion to silt accumulation in both Horseshoe and Bartlett Dams. Baker believed the city's portion of storage space could eventually be lost to silt accumulation. Despite these concerns, and the claim that the Water

Users obtained the best part of the deal, the commissioners gave tentative approval to the contract.[12]

On November 19 the voters endorsed the bonds by a wide margin. The official canvass revealed 2,396 votes in favor and 801 cast in opposition. Armed with this support, the city commission approved the contract. Water Users President Lin B. Orme and City Manager Odd S. Halseth signed the contract on November 22.[13]

The operating contract provided for the construction of spillway gates on Horseshoe Dam to create an additional 75,000 af of storage space for Phoenix. In return for financing the gate construction Phoenix received the right to divert up to 25,000 af of the stored water annually. The contract stated that Phoenix could accumulate up to 150,000 af of water, starting when the combined storage capacity of both Bartlett and Horseshoe Dams exceeded 246,283 af. The contract also stipulated that one or both (or neither) party might participate in any enlargement of Horseshoe Dam, that the city had no rights of ownership in the dam or power it produced, and that the contract be approved by the secretary of the interior.[14]

As spring turned to summer in 1947, Phoenix officials prepared applications to the state land commissioner to build the gates and divert water. The 1919 state water code, as amended, specified that the state land commissioner also served as state water commissioner with the power to review applications and grant permits to divert water. As Phoenix prepared its case, vocal opposition to the gates project arose.

On May 26, 1947, E. W. Michael, president of the Verde River Irrigation and Power District, wrote to Secretary of Interior Julius A. Krug about the contract between Phoenix and the Water Users submitted to the land commissioner for approval. Michael's board of directors believed a long-range plan for Horseshoe Dam should be considered first, prior to the addition of spillway gates. They believed gate construction would sidetrack the need to later enlarge the dam to the full capacity of its foundation as part of the CAP.[15]

The next day, Michael's letter to Krug prompted State Land Commissioner Orlando C. Williams to write E. A. Moritz, the regional director of the Bureau of Reclamation in Boulder City. Williams enclosed a copy of Michael's letter and told Moritz to expect a formal protest. Williams suggested that no decision on the application would be appropriate until the claims of opponents were heard and until the Bureau of Reclamation could complete its evaluation of the contract.[16]

On June 13, director Moritz responded to Williams' letter. He agreed that Horseshoe Dam was a valuable water reservoir and acknowledged that it was being considered for inclusion in the Central Arizona Project, but reiterated that Phoenix and the Water Users believed the need for the project was urgent. He asked whether Williams planned to hold a public hearing on the application and, if so, when it would occur. Williams replied that he was awaiting the outcome of meetings between the Verde District and elected officials in Washington, D.C., before scheduling a public hearing.[17]

On December 6, 1946, Phoenix submitted the contract to the Interior Department for approval. The Interior Department's Bureau of Reclamation had reservations about the impact of the gates project on construction of the Central Arizona Project. Under one proposal, Horseshoe Dam would serve as a storage reservoir for water diverted from the Colorado at either Marble Canyon or Glen Canyon and transferred by a lengthy tunnel to the Verde River. Some engineers believed the gates might affect CAP plans by reducing the dam's capacity.[18]

On July 22, 1947, Williams issued a public notice informing the public that Phoenix had filed an application to draw 25,000 af of Verde floodwaters annually from increased storage behind Horseshoe Dam. The water division of the State Land Department sent the notice under Williams' signature to several downstream users that might be affected by the project. Anyone who wanted to protest the permit had thirty days to do so.[19]

A steady stream of protesters arrived to dispute the city's claim that it intended to store only "unappropriated" waters from the Verde River. Downstream users asserted that all waters of the Verde had been appropriated. The Verde River Irrigation and Drainage District opposed the permit because "it would mutilate the ultimate development for the storage of the flood and surface waters of the Verde," meaning the gates would prevent expansion of Horseshoe Dam.[20]

On August 21, C.H.W. Smith, an engineer in the state water division, sent city engineer Baker copies of the protests. Smith gave the city thirty days to reply. The number of protests indicated tremendous concern.[21]

On September 12, City Attorney Choisser filed a reply. He stated that the city sought only to appropriate floodwaters stored behind the gates. This water was available only in time of floods, and was not subject to vested rights. Choisser also stressed the immediacy of the problem, because the summer demand for water was already beyond the capacity of the city system to furnish. Land Commissioner Williams then set September 22 as a tentative hearing date.[22]

On September 18 Williams changed plans and decided to schedule an informal hearing on October 1. His special assistant, Kenneth C. Chatwin, notified the interested parties. Williams would hear testimony at the hearing, but hoped that some of the issues raised in the protests could be resolved informally.[23]

On October 1, Williams began the meeting in the hearing room of the Arizona industrial commission. He wanted to expedite the applications and avoid delay on the floodgates. By conducting an informal meeting he hoped objections could be reconciled and withdrawn, canceling the need for a formal hearing.[24]

Water Users attorney Greig Scott made the first presentation. He stressed the serious nature of the situation, saying that in outlying areas of Phoenix water faucets failed to run on summer afternoons because of low water pressure. Coolers quit working because the water lacked enough pressure to reach the roof units. To meet summer needs in wartime, Phoenix had leased several pumps from the Water Users. The city now planned to install a new intake and filtration plant on the Verde. Scott contended that during the summer the Verde flow was too low to support the new diversion, and Phoenix must obtain its summer supply from stored water captured during winter months behind floodgates at Horseshoe Dam. No user had appropriated the floodwater, so Phoenix could not be accused of taking another user's water.[25]

City Attorney Choisser then explained the peculiar nature of the problem. Because demand peaked in summer at the precise time that flow in the Verde diminished, this combination of factors increased the water shortage. Phoenix needed storage water and a system to regulate the flow of the Verde so that impounded water could be available during peak demand.[26]

The protesters spoke next. The downstream water users, located on the lower Gila River, claimed they were entitled to some of the floodwater of the Verde. Floodwaters had a low mineral content that flushed accumulated salts from agricultural fields. The Verde Irrigation and Drainage District raised a different objection. William C. Fields, attorney for the Verde District, expressed concern that construction of the spillway gates would preclude later expansion of Horseshoe Dam.[27]

Phoenix and the Water Users failed to mollify the protesters at the informal October 1 hearing. Land Commissioner Williams responded by announcing he would convene a formal hearing on November 4. This led to serious reconsideration of the project. City Engineer Baker questioned the relative value of the project to the city compared to the Water Users. Baker, who had earlier criticized the annual maintenance fee and silt provisions, now said Phoenix would be paying for water it would not use for several years. In the meantime, Phoenix would pay $800,000 while the Water Users received the benefit.[28]

City Water Superintendent James Girand attempted to refocus the debate, emphasizing the real and acute water shortage Phoenix faced in the summer months. While Girand remained neutral as to whether the Water Users contract took unfair advantage of the city, he championed the city stand on the issue of water rights. Girand believed the city was in a good position because under state law appropriations for domestic purposes took precedence over other uses.[29]

On October 28 city plans received a tremendous blow. The city commission received a letter from Land Commissioner Williams that the city must have a signed agreement with the owner of the dam, the United States, to meet state statutory requirements before the project could proceed. As yet, the Interior Department had neglected to sign the agreement. The city commission asked for a continuance of the November 4 hearing to consider its options.[30]

Upon reflection, the commission decided to press the United States for approval of the gates project. Engineer Hill appeared before the commission with a draft letter requesting approval and proposed that it be sent with the signature of the mayor and the president of the Water Users Association to Secretary of Interior Julius Krug. The commission hoped that Krug would approve the contract before the scheduled November hearing.[31]

In the meantime, Williams announced that he would not open the November 4 hearing to further testimony. He felt there was little to discuss because the joint letter from the Water Users and the city had failed to motivate Krug to sign the contract. Interior Department officials remained concerned over the effect of the gates on the dam's role in the Central Arizona Project.[32]

At the hearing, Williams considered arguments from engineer Girand and attorney Choisser. Girand documented the severity of the city's water shortage and emphasized that the situation was desperate. Customers had complained about bad-tasting water and lack of water. Moreover, the city was unable to maintain adequate pressure for fire protection or domestic service. Choisser focused on the legal issues. He contended that because the city had asked for a primary permit on a new reservoir, and not a secondary permit on an existing reservoir, the state statute requiring federal government approval did not apply.[33]

The hearing ended in a stalemate. Williams refused to approve the permit without the secretary of the interior's signature and the secretary would not sign until the state's concerns over the CAP were resolved. Girand labeled the situation a "squeeze play" to force Phoenix to support the CAP. This seemed unreasonable because the city had always supported the CAP. At the end of the hearing Williams issued an order that gave the city sixty days to complete the applications.[34]

Phoenix scrambled to obtain Interior Department approval. The city, the Water Users, and the Reclamation Bureau exchanged proposals. After considerable disagreement over which parties would participate, the bureau agreed to attend a conference with the city and the Water Users in Phoenix.

The conference began on March 18. The Bureau of Reclamation charged that the installation of the Horseshoe gates gave Phoenix the cheapest water available in the CAP scheme and might jeopardize the entire project. Phoenix officials reiterated that they had always been a supporter of the CAP and that construction of the gates would have a very minor impact on the project. The bureau proposed that the city then accept a 10 percent interest in an expanded Horseshoe reservoir. City officials opposed this formula because it would have guaranteed just 23,000 af of storage and only 4,000 af of annual use. Mayor-elect Nicholas Udall felt strongly that because the bond issue voters approved called for up to 150,000 af of storage and 25,000 af of annual use, the city must have that amount.[35]

In the evening on March 18, a small group of city officials met in Phoenix City Manager J. T. Deppe's office with Water Users consulting engineer Hill. After they discussed several proposals, they settled on a solution. Phoenix would accept 23,000 af of storage, provided that the bureau completed expansion of Horseshoe Dam as part of the Central Arizona Project within twenty-five years. The twenty-five-year figure incorporated an estimate of ten years to complete CAP, plus another ten to fifteen years to develop demand for the water. Phoenix accepted the lower annual water amount because it desperately needed stored water during the summer months.[36]

The next morning, bureau and city officials reconvened at the Hotel Adams. After reiterating their support for the CAP and discounting its possible impact on the gates project, Phoenix presented its twenty-five-year plan. The plan recognized the November 22, 1946, agreement as valid and stipulated that it would remain in effect for twenty-five years and beyond until the United States had expanded the capacity of Horseshoe Dam by 100,000 af and completed the Central Arizona Project.[37]

Bureau officials accepted this provision, but a lengthy discussion over silt accumulation followed. Phoenix finally agreed to participate in periodic surveys of silt conditions and to prorate any accumulations recorded. The conference concluded with officials negotiating minor revisions to the 1946 agreement.[38]

After the conference, consulting engineer Hill prepared a tentative draft of the proposal and circulated it to the three parties. They agreed to meet on April 7, 1948, to discuss the language of the contract and debate the silt issue. After long and difficult discussions, the negotiators reached a compromise on April 9. The Water Users board of governors tentatively approved the contract. Formal approval awaited the results of the Interior Department's review.[39]

Department of Interior approval of the contract came during the hot dry summer of 1948. After careful examination, Assistant Secretary of the Interior William Warne approved the form of the contract on August 5. The final step of federal government approval took two more months. Secretary Krug finally authorized Warne to sign the contract and he did so on October 7.[40]

Phoenix now sought approval from State Land Commissioner Williams. Williams had to decide the merits of the project from the perspective of state government. The application had languished since the expiration of the sixty-day extension on January 4, 1948.

On January 18, 1949, the land commissioner opened a second formal hearing on the application. Over a year had passed since the first hearing, but downstream opposition remained unchanged. On the eve of the hearing one user vowed to oppose the gates proposal "into the next century." Neil Clark, attorney for dam-builder Bernard Gillespie, threatened a lawsuit. Downstream users believed losing the use of the water the dam gates would impound would cause them hardship.[41]

In the face of the wide disparity between Phoenix and the Verde water users, Williams recessed the hearing until January 20. Perhaps the parties could resolve their differences if they had more time to discuss the issue of unappropriated floodwaters. The downstream users on the Gila River claimed they needed the floodwaters to flush salts from their land and thus considered such waters appropriated. Phoenix contended that a great deal of water flowed down the Verde to the Gila in times of flood, far in excess of downstream need. The parties solved the impasse by agreeing to define surplus water in the Gila River system as that which flowed over the crest of Gillespie Dam.

On January 20 the contending parties appeared before Williams. Phoenix agreed to limit its use to surplus water as defined. This quieted the opposition. Williams ended the hearing and announced he would soon rule on the permit application. On January 25, 1949, he issued an order that gave the city permission to begin construction of the Horseshoe gates project.[42]

On June 14, 1950, Mayor Nicholas Udall and Salt River Valley Water Users Association President Richard D. Searles traveled the long, hot, dusty road to Horseshoe Dam to inspect the completion of the spillway gates after eighteen months of construction. The two leaders found little cause for celebration at the site. Only a pitiful 1,300 af of water filled the 144,030 af capacity reservoir that day.[43]

When the city placed the gate construction on the 1946 bond issue ballot, few realized the negotiation and compromise required to bring the project to completion. Federal and state officials, intent on the pursuit of the CAP and groundwater legislation, made certain that their own water projects remained on schedule. As the severity of the water shortage increased, engineers, attorneys, and managers fashioned a solution to the

The gates across the Horseshoe Dam spillway were completed in 1950.

postwar water crisis. Although each level of government approached the problem differently, the period following World War II marks the beginning of a concerted effort to find permanent solutions in Phoenix to the ever increasing demand for water.[44]

The gates functioned smoothly, capturing peak flood flows and storing the water for use during the summer months. By 1952, the gates impounded 77,982 af of water. The building of the gates stood as a monument to those who had the foresight to recognize the value of additional water storage to the continued growth of Phoenix at midcentury. Although few appreciated the significance of the project at the time, the gates provided an entry to the success of modern Phoenix.

The Verde Water Treatment Plant

Almost lost in the struggle over approval of the gates was construction of the Verde Water Treatment Plant (WTP). The controversy over the spill-

The Verde River Water Treatment Plant was designed to take water from either the Salt or Verde Rivers.

way control gates on Horseshoe Dam had been set off by the city's plans to construct a water treatment plant at the confluence of the Salt and Verde Rivers. Engineers located the plant just downstream from the confluence so that it could take water from either the Salt or Verde river, depending on stream flow conditions. The primary purpose of the plant was to take the city's allocation of Verde River water.

On May 13, 1947, N. P. Van Valkenburg received the contract for constructing the river pumps and pipelines for the plant. Phoenix plans called for the water to be collected in small ponds and pumped to the plant. This portion of the project cost just under $187,000.[45]

On June 17, 1947, the city commission awarded the larger portion of the construction contracts for the Verde WTP. A co-venture between Arizona Sand and Rock and the Del E. Webb Construction Company submitted the low bid of $1.16 million to construct the treatment plant itself. Construction began shortly thereafter.[46]

With the construction contracts let, the city then needed to finalize details of the right-of-way across the Salt River Indian Reservation. Construction of the new plant required additional right-of-way above and beyond that needed for the pipelines from the Fort McDowell Indian Reservation. On June 15, 1948, the commission approved the new right-of-way for the Verde WTP. Construction was completed within a year, and the Verde WTP began delivering water to Phoenix residents in 1949.[47]

The Immediate Postwar Era in Flagstaff

Operation of the Lake Mary treatment plant during the war revealed several areas that could be improved with minor modifications. In 1943, Flagstaff added a second pump at the Lake Mary pumping plant as a wartime protection measure. This nearly doubled the capacity of the plant and provided an important measure of safety. If one of the pumps failed, there would be a second pump ready to continue operation.[48]

When the war was over Flagstaff leaders were in a position to address their deferred water needs. In 1946 the city council hired the Los Angeles engineering firm of Taylor and Taylor to examine the city system and make recommendations for improvement. The California consultants spent the months of July, August, and September in the mountain city conducting field surveys and investigations. They issued their report in January of 1947.[49]

The engineers recommended that Flagstaff construct additional coagulation and sedimentation basins at the treatment facility, build sludge settling basins, and add a chemical building for chlorination and storage for clean water. Workers finished these modifications to the Lake Mary treatment plant by the end of 1947.[50]

Taylor and Taylor also recommended construction of a separate pipeline from Upper Lake Mary directly to the Lake Mary WTP. Common practice since the plant was first constructed had been to divert water from Upper Lake Mary to Lower Lake Mary and then to the plant. The more direct pipeline would avoid contamination problems with the lower lake and reduce water transport losses.[51]

A drought in the summer of 1947 underscored the importance of the bypass pipeline. Water levels dropped in Lake Mary. Although Flagstaff still had a comfortable supply, recreational uses on the lower lake increased the risk of contamination. Municipal leaders asked Flagstaff residents to approve one hundred thousand dollars in bonds to construct the bypass line. Voters responded enthusiastically, and contractors completed the project in 1948.[52]

Summary

In the immediate postwar era from 1945 to 1950, local attempts to improve water infrastructure dominated the agenda of municipal officials as they faced increasing growth. In a very real sense municipal government reached maturity during this period, as measured in the acquisition of knowledge and personnel able to run the complex water systems. The decisions made by officials during this era established the parameters for later development: Tucson would remain dependent on groundwater while Phoenix and Flagstaff pursued new surface sources.

The larger period from 1912 to 1950 is a period of maturity as well. Arizona's municipal leaders emerged from territorial status with the means and motivation to pursue improvements to their water infrastructure that would make the state a location for business investment. While national trends dominated the economy of Arizona, local boosters and outside investors capitalized on the unique attractions of the state for business opportunities.

The links to the national economy are very apparent during the period from 1912 to 1929. World War I created a heavy demand for the mining and agricultural products of Arizona. Profits in these industries attracted investment and residents to Arizona. Following the war, a tourism boom in the 1920s brought more residents and visitors to Arizona, increasing demand for water. Municipal governments responded, constructing projects such as the redwood pipeline in Phoenix, the north side well field in Tucson, and additional reservoir capacity in Flagstaff.

During the thirties Arizonans were reminded that their relationship with national economic cycles includes both good times and bad. Urban historian Jon C. Teaford observed that the Great Depression changed the relationship between municipalities and the federal government. Although the depression decade saw few physical changes in cities, for Teaford "it was a revolutionary era" in terms of the federal/city relationship. In the 1930s municipal governments began to look toward Washington, D.C., for financial aid. Much of this aid came in the form of public works assistance, which had the result of improving the water and sewer infrastructure of municipalities as well as providing unemployment assistance.[53]

For the West this revolutionary era represented a marked economic shift. For years, the West had supplied the East with raw materials and saw the profit from its natural resources go east as well. In the 1930s the economic pipeline began to run in reverse, with the West receiving a return in the form of government assistance programs. A modest change at first, the reversal reached full force during World War II.[54]

By 1950, the entire economic tilt of the country had begun a trend to the south and west, bringing new residents and industry to Arizona. Arizona had been a state for only thirty-eight years at midcentury, but had achieved a sense of mature status for its contributions to the nation in times of war and depression. At midcentury, Arizona was poised to transform itself into one of the fastest-growing states in the nation.

Part IV Transformation since 1950

Arizona's municipal leaders confronted increased water demand caused by a tremendous influx of urban residents in the last half of the twentieth century. While this influx transformed the physical environment of urban Arizona, reactions to the population boom also transformed how Arizonans thought about the environment. Leaders of the environmental movement, supported by strong and vocal followers, influenced the design of several major components of the Central Arizona Project and other water projects.

By 1950, the water systems of Arizona's urban centers had reached maturity. City staff and elected officials had mastered the design and construction of water facilities. To move beyond this basic level required a great transformation in the approach used by Arizona municipalities. In the Phoenix area, city leaders reached an understanding with the Salt River Project (SRP) that governed the transformation of agricultural lands to urban uses. Tucson officials tapped underground aquifers in Avra Valley to help supply city residents.

While the transfer of water from agricultural to urban uses proved to be the key to the successful development of municipal water resources, it was dependent on an adequate supply of agricultural water. In Phoenix, the city expanded its water service area to include land outside the original boundaries of the Salt River Project, but the only source of water they could use for this "off-project" land was that generated by the gates at Horseshoe Dam. Phoenix leaders needed to develop other water sources. Tucson leaders also had to look elsewhere as they encountered increasing challenges to the continued use of groundwater.

In the Salt River Valley, there are several major municipalities that manage water within city and town boundaries, often with competing goals and agendas. Outside these agencies are agricultural water providers, private water companies serving subdivisions in unincorporated county areas, and smaller incorporated communities without a municipal utility served by private companies. While Tucson and Flagstaff do not have the same level of interaction between municipal governments, a multitude of water agencies complicates the decision-making process with regard to urban water use.

Arizona's municipal leaders became ever stronger supporters of the Central Arizona Project because it provided the best means of supplementing scarce local supplies of water. First viewed as an agricultural "rescue" project for central Arizona, by the end of the twentieth century the CAP emerged as urban Arizona's lifeline and a boon to Native American tribes. Not all Arizonans accepted CAP salvation with equanimity. While its arrival went relatively unheralded in the Phoenix area, in Tucson city residents rejected CAP water after it left a bad taste in their mouths. Ever since, Tucson has been grappling with ways to use its allocation of CAP water and in so doing has provided innovative solutions to the water challenges facing urban Arizona.

Because the quest for the Central Arizona Project played such a significant role in the water history of urban Arizona during the last half of the twentieth century, the milestones of water history are closely associated with the CAP. Significant dates that represent turning points included Arizona's 1963 victory in the U.S. Supreme Court, and the Arizona Groundwater Management Act adopted in 1980 to assure continued federal support for the project. Although federal involvement in Arizona's water affairs remained heavy, these events represent a transformation of another type: rather than reacting to broad national political and economic trends, Arizona took responsibility for managing its own water future during this time period.

Chapter 11 Confronting the Urban Influx, 1950–1963

Officials across Arizona struggled to keep up with a rapid increase in population during the fifties and sixties. Tucson again looked to agricultural lands as a source of urban water during this period, this time moving beyond its immediate surroundings. In Phoenix, this era is marked by a ground-breaking agreement between the city and the Salt River Project that secured a stable water supply for Arizona's capital city. In northern Arizona, growth was less spectacular but steady nonetheless.

The rapid population growth that began in the immediate postwar period continued unabated in the 1950s and early 1960s. It became clear that population growth for the nation as a whole was tilting to the south and west, giving rise to the term *Sunbelt* to describe the tier of states stretching across the southern United States from Florida to California. Although the term has fallen into disuse, the growing economic power of the region has remained. A shift to conservative politics accompanied the population shift and economic growth in service and defense industries, typified by the rise of Barry Goldwater to Phoenix city council member, to senator, to Republican presidential candidate in 1964.[1]

Confronting the Urban Influx in 1950s Tucson

In the 1950s, demand for water increased in Tucson. The economic conditions of the 1940s that led to increased water use persisted: high farm prices, population increase, military spending, and mining activity. Industrial development topped the list of new water users. In 1951, Hughes Aircraft Company purchased twenty thousand acres south of town and constructed the first air-to-air missile plant for the U.S. Air Force. Between 1952 and 1958, Hughes became one of the largest employers in the state with 5,858 workers. Other large companies included the Arizona Portland Cement Company, the Chapman-Dyer Steel Manufacturing Company, and the Krieger Air Conditioning Company. The number of industrial firms in the city grew by 115 percent from 1951 to 1958.[2]

Population growth, mining, and agriculture also increased groundwater pumping. Between 1952 and 1962, Tucson annexed 61.4 square miles of land consisting of numerous subdivisions developed in the years after the war. Between 1956 and 1960, urban and mining uses in the Tucson basin consumed 49,500 acre-feet of water and agriculture 45,600 af. Natural recharge, the amount of water flowing back into aquifers from rain and stream flow, was 50,400 acre-feet during the period. This left an overdraft of 48,500 acre-feet, depressing Pima County water levels to a record low.[3]

Agriculture expanded in the early 1950s in the Tucson area, spurred by the demand for cotton for the Korean War and continued cold war spending. The potential for profits from cotton and other agricultural goods led to a 400,000-acre increase of irrigated land in the state between 1948 and 1953. Agriculture made up a substantial part of the water used in the Tucson basin. In 1957 alone, farms used 5,000 acre-feet.[4]

Tucson embarked on another round of water supply and storage projects in the 1950s, hoping to meet pent-up demands from the late 1940s. In 1951, the city floated $1.25 million in revenue bonds. Portions of this money went to acquire rights-of-way and well sites in the Avra Valley. The city purchased its first Avra Valley well in 1952.[5]

In 1953, Tucson sold an additional $5.5 million in water revenue bonds. The construction of a 20-million-gallon reservoir near Craycroft Road and Twenty-second Street comprised the major project. Finished in 1954, the reservoir, built by the San Xavier Rock and Sand Company, drew water from eight new city wells and brought the storage capacity of the city to 32.3 million gallons.[6]

The purchase of private water companies continued. By 1959, a total of forty-three companies had been incorporated into the city system. While most of these companies were established to provide water service to the many new subdivisions that developed in Tucson in the fifties, some served the speculative needs of investors rather than providing adequate service to consumers. The speculative nature of these enterprises is illustrated by the case of the Polar Water Company. The valuation of the company listed for tax purposes ($30,750) differed considerably from its value for rate-making assessments ($410,000). In a move reminiscent or the drive for public ownership at the turn of the nineteenth century, Tucson citizens favored the acquisition of private water companies to reduce the speculative profit gained at the expense of ratepayers.[7]

The expansion of Tucson water use brought the city into conflict with agricultural water providers. In 1957, the Midvale Farms Company challenged Tucson's plan to drill additional wells in the floodplain of the Santa Cruz River. In filings before the state land commissioner, attorneys for Midvale Farms contended that additional pumping would have a negative effect on their own water supply. On December 16, 1957, the two sides executed an agreement that recognized a prior right of Midvale Farms to six thousand acre-feet per year from the Santa Cruz River. City officials acknowledged that this right predated Tucson's planned pumping project.[8]

Transforming Water Use in Phoenix

As Phoenix grew, agricultural lands were transformed to urban use. Although they were no longer being used for agriculture these lands were still part of the Salt River Project and land owners were required to pay association dues to SRP. As lands passed from agricultural to urban use the new owners of the property often let their dues to SRP lapse, causing a financial crisis for the project. These parcels still used water, of course, except that it was now delivered through the Phoenix municipal system.

The hot dry summer of 1951 baked urban and rural residents alike across Arizona. In urban areas, larger populations increased demand and supplies ran low. The 1946 contract with the Salt River Project for construction of the gates at Horseshoe Dam recognized the city's historical

This view from 1956 shows former citrus orchards outside Phoenix growing a new crop of tract homes.

diversion of 20,193 af of of water per year plus any additional water provided by the gates. During several dry years, no water had accumulated behind the gates.[9]

By 1951 several years of drought limited the amount of water available. On July 2, 1951, Salt River Valley Water Users' Association (SRVWUA or Water Users) President W. W. Pickrell informed Phoenix officials that in 1951 the city had consumed more than half of the annual amount allotted under the 1946 contract. Pickrell implied that the Water Users would curtail water deliveries when Phoenix reached its limit and suggested that Salt River Project (SRP) officials and city leaders meet to discuss the situation. When the Water Users made the announcement, the city had used 16,000 af of the 20,193 af described by the 1946 contract. This left the city with a ten-day supply of water.[10]

At the meeting on July 6, 1951, Pickrell suggested that the city take over assessment payments on lots that were no longer receiving agricultural water so that this water could be transferred to municipal use. Project officials contended that they did not begrudge Phoenix the water, but objected to the city taking it without remuneration. The city had been taking Verde water since 1922 without making any payments to the Water Users that operated the Salt River Project. Transferring former agricultural lands to domestic water delivery would alleviate the financial crisis facing the project and relieve pressure on the city to find additional supplies of water. Pickrell suggested that the city and the project approach the problem in two stages, a temporary fix for the summer shortage and a permanent long-term solution.[11]

City officials had few options. As they had in 1941, they considered bringing emergency wells into production, including the old pumping plant wells at Ninth and Polk and wells recently purchased from the Arizona Water Company. Officials were reluctant to take this step because groundwater pumped from these wells contained high salt and mineral content.[12]

Events went from bad to worse. In early July water consumption in Phoenix reached an all-time high of 77 million gallons per day (mgd). City officials called for stringent conservation measures, and residents cut consumption to 62 mgd. On July 16, 1951, a summer monsoon thunderstorm knocked out electricity to the Verde River pumps. The water level in the city's reservoirs began to drop quickly. Phoenix officials dispatched police patrols throughout the city to look for people washing cars or sprinkling lawns and ask them to stop using water.[13]

In the midst of this dire situation, city and SRP officials continued negotiations. Project officials requested that the city pay $87,000 for delinquent assessment accounts for lands within the city and $119,165 for lands outside city boundaries but within the city's water service area. When city officials balked at this demand, project officials suggested that it might be appropriate to charge the city for the 20,193 af of water use recognized in the 1946 Horseshoe gates contract. As a means to bolster their negotiating position, the project intimated that the city might be in debt for all the water it ever diverted from the Verde—more than 450,000 af used since 1922.[14]

On July 31, W. W. Pickrell issued an ultimatum to the city. He served notice on Mayor Nicolas Udall that the project would not permit any further withdrawal of water after August 7 unless arrangements were made for the delivery of water throughout the remainder of 1951. Pickrell wrote the mayor that "our purpose in so advising you, at this time, is to give you ample opportunity to take whatever action may be proper to provide an uninterrupted water supply of the city." Meeting on August 1, city and project negotiators hammered out an agreement. The city agreed to pay the project $75,000 for about 15,000 af of additional water used in 1951 beyond the baseline 20,193 af mentioned in the 1946 agreement. This amount would be enough to get the city through the summer emergency. The city council ratified the agreement on August 10, 1951. To cover water used by the city during the crisis, the agreement was retroactive to July 24, 1951, the day on which the city had used 19,135 af. The contract allowed the city to divert an additional 15,865 af up to December 31, 1951. Thus, the contract allowed the city to divert up to 35,000 af for calendar year 1951.[15]

City officials clearly felt backed into a corner and forced to capitulate. On August 11, 1951, the city council discussed the agreement "and so that there will be no misunderstanding in the future we are setting forth our position and our objections" in a letter addressed to project officials. Noting that the agreement was "purely temporary," city officials objected to having to pay for diversion and delivery of water to townsite lands within city boundaries. Townsite lands were a special class of land that was already urbanized when lands eligible for project water were chosen. These lands were not eligible for inclusion in the project and owners did not pay project assessments, but they were eligible to receive water.[16]

Reaching a permanent agreement took negotiators just over a year. In 1952, city officials had the luxury of negotiating without the threat of a water crisis. Winter and spring rains increased the flow in the Verde River and backed up water behind the gates at Horseshoe Dam. By April of 1952, the city had a large amount of floodwater stored behind the gates.[17]

Negotiators circulated several draft agreements during the fall of 1951, and by January of 1952 the basic points of the agreement had been worked out. Some additional disagreements delayed the final contract. Although negotiators completed the agreement in September of 1952, like the 1951 contract, its provisions were retroactive.[18]

Key elements of the agreement were that the city would pay project assessments on lands it owned within the project, pay back and current assessments for lands that had already passed from agriculture to urban use, and pay the assessments for agricultural lands that became urbanized in the future. The 1952 contract was called the domestic water service agreement and required the city to assume responsibility for assessments on parcels no longer used for agriculture. The Salt River Project agreed to use its facilities to deliver water to the city for urban use on the parcels.[19]

The domestic water service agreement proved to be the key to providing water for continued urban growth in the Phoenix area. Instead of the Salt River Project delivering agricultural water directly through its canals and ditches, the 1952 contract called for the city to take the water from those canals and ditches and deliver water through its municipal system as the lands became urbanized. In one sense the 1952 contract recognized a situation that already existed, since many acres of former agricultural land in the project had already been urbanized. In another sense the contract was a prescient document because it anticipated continued growth in the Salt River Valley and provided a mechanism to deliver water as lands urbanized.

Phoenix Water in the Late 1950s

A key provision of the 1952 domestic water service agreement allowed Phoenix to construct a water treatment plant on the Arizona Canal in the vicinity of Twenty-fourth Street. Soon known as the Squaw Peak Water Treatment Plant after the mountain of the same name in close proximity, this facility permitted the city to take water directly from the valley's system of agricultural canals, treat it for municipal use, and deliver the water to customers. Because the contract provision allowing the city to construct a plant on the Arizona Canal had been settled before other outstanding issues, the city was able to begin construction before final contract approval. Construction of the Squaw Peak WTP provided a model for other water treatment plants in the years ahead.

The city began purchasing land for the Squaw Peak plant in June of 1952, and added more in September and October. The T.G.K. Construction Company received the construction contract for the Squaw Peak WTP in November. Construction went quickly, and the plant began to deliver water to Phoenix municipal customers in 1953. The Squaw Peak WTP had an initial capacity to treat and deliver 30 mgd.[20]

Completion of the Squaw Peak WTP enabled city officials to entirely

The Squaw Peak Water Treatment Plant was constructed in Phoenix in 1952.

shut down production from downtown wells during the winter months. Water from the Squaw Peak WTP, the Verde WTP, and the infiltration gallery and wells on the Fort McDowell Indian Reservation provided all the water the city needed. Up to 1956, the city could shut down the filter plants during the winter and rely solely on water developed on the Fort McDowell Reservation.[21]

In the late 1950s the city embarked on another buying spree of private water companies. Although this event was a repeat of the practice used heavily during the thirties, in the fifties the city had a different rationale for the purchases. In the thirties, the city acquired private water companies on its boundaries in order to bring new customers into the system as part of a program of public works to improve the economy during the depression. In the early fifties the city caught annexation fever. Phoenix annexed huge amounts of suburban land north and south of the traditional urban core. Once annexed, city officials brought new residents into the municipal water system by purchasing private water companies.

City officials called the newly annexed subdivisions "fringe areas." In May of 1957 Phoenix voters approved a $35 million bond issue for a water expansion program to purchase privately owned water companies in the northern, western, and southern fringe areas. Many of the voters that approved the bond issue were residents that had only recently been taken into the boundaries of the city. Improved water service had been one of the arguments in favor of annexation.[22]

By the end of 1957, the city purchased five private water companies: Suburban, Valley, Mariposa, North Central, and that portion of the Consolidated Water Company east of Forty-third Avenue. The combined purchase price reached just over $10 million. Purchasing the companies added 35,100 new customers to the city system. Former customers of North Central and Consolidated joined the city on December 1, 1957, and the remainder began to receive city water service on January 1, 1958.[23]

City officials included expansion of the Squaw Peak WTP in the bond issue. Phoenix allocated nearly $6 million for a 60 mgd expansion of the plant, bringing its total capacity to 90 mgd. The bond issue also covered a 20-million-gallon reservoir at Sixty-fourth Street and Thomas Road. John Carollo Engineers designed the treatment plant addition and Stephens & Associates designed the reservoir. F. H. Antrim began work on the reservoir in August of 1958, and Fisher Contracting started work on the addition in December of that year.[24]

In September of 1959, Phoenix officials began planning for the future by entering into an agreement with the City of Mesa for construction of a joint venture treatment plant. Phoenix and Mesa agreed to purchase land for the water treatment plant from the Val Vista Investment Company on September 29, 1959. This turned out to be a project far ahead of its time. Before the plant could be built, Mesa officials needed to execute a domestic water service agreement of their own with the Salt River Project. This took some time, and development in Phoenix shifted toward the west. Mesa and Phoenix officials later completed the Val Vista WTP in 1975 when growth in the area increased the demand for water.[25]

Growth in Phoenix during the fifties surged west, not east. This was the work of master developer John F. Long. He took advantage of the demand for housing in the Phoenix area to develop the community of Maryvale, which he named after his wife. He eventually constructed thousands of low-cost homes on the west side of the Salt River Valley that suited the needs of former military personnel who settled in the valley and helped produce the postwar baby boom.

The growing population on the west side increased the demand for water. To meet the need, Phoenix officials purchased land at Thirty-first Avenue and the Arizona Canal in 1961 for a surface water treatment plant. On the day after Christmas, the city council named the new facility the Deer Valley Water Treatment Plant. Engineer John Carollo designed the plant to treat 80 mgd of surface water diverted from the Arizona Canal. The city council issued construction contracts in March of 1963 and the plant began operation in September of 1964.[26]

The Deer Valley WTP comprised just a portion of the city's water program funded in 1961. Other portions included a 20-million-gallon reservoir at the Deer Valley WTP, a 20-million-gallon reservoir at the Squaw Peak WTP, a 20 mgd addition to the Squaw Peak WTP, and a 10-million-gallon reservoir at Shaw Butte. The city continued to purchase private water companies. In 1960, for example, the city added five new companies and acquired 6,256 service connections.[27]

Flagstaff Water Development in the 1950s

Flagstaff continued to find and develop sources of water from 1950 to 1963. At the same time, city leaders continued to build upon their existing infrastructure of water production and distribution facilities. While Flagstaff leaders cóped with continued growth in the postwar period, the pace of residential growth in northern Arizona was not as great as in the central part of the state. Industrial growth continued at a steady clip, as demand for the timber products of northern Arizona increased in proportion to the postwar boom of new home construction throughout the West.

One of the greatest changes in postwar Flagstaff concerned the relationship between the community and the railroad. In many ways World War II marked the high point of railroad activity in the twentieth century. More and more freight traveled by truck after World War II, and more and more people traveled by personal car. Although airplane travel had yet to make a substantial impact on the percentage of business still held by railroads, air transportation would gradually take an increasing number

The City of Phoenix added the Deer Valley Water Treatment Plant at Thirty-first Avenue in 1964.

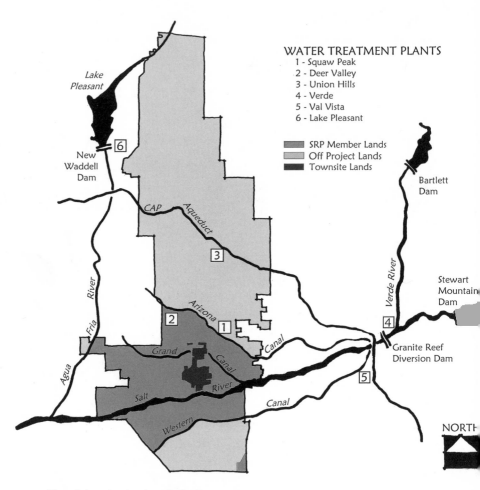

Phoenix's water treatment plants

of customers away from trains as time went on. The development of the interstate highway system, started in the 1950s, gradually took more and more business from the railroads.

While the Santa Fe remained a constant presence in Flagstaff, the introduction of the first main line diesel locomotives in 1947 eliminated the decades-old conflict with the railroad over water supplies. The old steam engines that required copious amounts of water to fill their ever thirsty boilers were a thing of the past. Of the two major railroads in Arizona, the Santa Fe through northern Arizona and the Southern Pacific through central and southern Arizona, the Santa Fe was more aggressive in rolling out the new diesel engines. The last regularly scheduled run with a steam engine by the Santa Fe took place in 1953. As a consequence the old water tank that had been a significant landmark in downtown Flagstaff came down, a victim of progress and marking the end of an era.[28]

Although the reduction in demand for water on the part of the Santa Fe had great symbolic significance, the actual impact on the water system was small. Flagstaff officials had begun to consider modifications to the city's production system in 1952. Improvements proceeded in two directions: modifications to the surface water collection system at Lake Mary and the development of a groundwater production unit.

Based on recommendations in the 1947 report by Taylor and Taylor consulting engineers, in 1953 Flagstaff officials decided to raise the dam at Lower Lake Mary. Because of the relatively flat topography of the area, a small increase in the height of the dam—Taylor and Taylor recommended between five and eight feet—would increase the size of the reservoir by 50 percent. In the years since the publication of the Taylor and Taylor report, Flagstaff officials had determined that the dam could be raised by twelve feet and contracted for this amount.[29]

Workers took on the project during the late summer of 1953 when water levels in the lake were low. During the course of construction workers took dirt for the dam modification from an area too close to the lake, causing a sinkhole that broke through into the fractured limestone bedrock below the lake. Workers managed to fill the sinkhole, but the accident revealed a problem with water storage in Lower and Upper Lake Mary: the geology of the area contributed to water loss through the bottom of the lakes.[30]

This experience convinced Flagstaff leaders that development of groundwater resources was a better alternative for future water production. The 1937 report by consulting engineer J. J. Jakowsky identified the Woody Mountain area seven miles southwest of the city as a prime location for the establishment of a well field. In 1954 the Flagstaff city council engaged the services of U.S. Geological Survey (USGS) district geologist John Harshberger, who confirmed Jakowsky's opinion. Harshberger recommended a joint investigation by the USGS and the city to confirm the presence of groundwater at Woody Mountain. In May of 1954 the council contracted with the Perry Brothers firm from Winslow to drill the test well.[31]

The well drillers at Woody Mountain encountered extremely difficult conditions caused by thick layers of volcanic basalt. Workers pushed a sixteen-inch-diameter hole into the ground. At a depth of 1,250 feet they encountered a good flow of water, estimated at five hundred thousand gallons per day. This convinced the Flagstaff council of the value of the well field and members quickly voted to drill a second well. The council then voted to put the cost of drilling two additional wells before the voters, who responded by approving the funds by a large margin.[32]

Flagstaff drilled a total of four wells at the Woody Mountain well field in the years from 1954 to 1956. Development of the well field came at an opportune time for Flagstaff residents. A dry winter in 1955–56 continued into a dry spring and summer. Water in Lake Mary was at a record low and the inner basin springs were producing well below capacity. Workers completed a pipeline to the Woody Mountain wells on July 9, 1956, which allowed the water to flow into the city distribution grid. Adjustments and modifications were needed to get the pumps running properly and they were shut down entirely for one week. City officials pleaded for conservation until the pumps could be restored to service. After an initial period of adjustment, the Woody Mountain well field developed into a significant source of water production for Flagstaff.[33]

The success of the Woody Mountain project encouraged city officials to pursue additional groundwater sources as time went on. Flagstaff again had the benefit of expert advice from USGS officials. In 1959 district geologist P. Eldon Dennis of Tucson recommended construction of a fifth well at Woody Mountain. Dennis also suggested that groundwater resources could be successfully developed by drilling wells in the vicinity of Lake Mary and in the inner basin well field.[34]

Summary

The years from 1950 to 1963 resulted in profound changes that transformed Arizona's urban water infrastructure. The 1952 domestic water service agreement ushered in the modern era of water development in Phoenix. The agreement allowed the construction of a series of water treatment plants in the valley that took raw water from Salt River Project canals and treated it for urban use. Phoenix constructed the first of these plants, the Squaw Peak treatment plant, in 1953 along the Arizona Canal just west of Twenty-fourth Street.

The 1952 contract is referred to as the Rosetta stone of Phoenix water history because it allows us to understand and interpret the development of the Salt River Valley. Looked at in another way, the 1952 contract is a blueprint for the future. Its provisions guided Phoenix water development for the next quarter century, and continues to govern the relationship between the project and the city.

Officials in Tucson searched for new supplies of water to meet growing demands, but achieved no similar breakthrough. Tucson continued the past practice of locating and acquiring private agricultural and urban water systems that could be incorporated into the municipal infrastructure. This resulted in an increasing number of groundwater wells connected to the city system. In Flagstaff, officials also pursued the development of additional groundwater. The completion of the Woody Mountain well field and the reduction of railroad demand combined to leave Flagstaff in a good water supply position by the mid-1960s.

Chapter 12 Mastering the Present, Facing the Future

By 1963, municipal leaders in Tucson, Phoenix, and Flagstaff had mastered the major challenges of providing water for the booming postwar economy of Arizona. Flagstaff had identified four main sources of water that continue to serve the city today. Phoenix officials came to an understanding with the Salt River Project for water delivery to former agricultural lands now transformed to urban use. Tucson residents, lacking any other source of water, relied on groundwater and the purchase of private water companies.

While Arizona's municipal officials believed they had mastered the postwar boom, a water infrastructure plateau was illusory. The influx of new residents continued unabated and water engineers found themselves pushed to the limit to accommodate them. In Phoenix, growth beyond the limits of the Salt River Project led engineers to embark on a new program of groundwater development. In Tucson, conflict over high water rates attributed to increased pumping costs left the city in turmoil. City officials in all areas called on creativity and innovation to meet the challenges of water demand.

A significant milestone in the struggle to make progress on the CAP was reached in 1963 when the U.S. Supreme Court ruled in Arizona's favor after a lengthy dispute with California over Colorado River water. The battle shifted to Washington, D.C., and culminated in 1968 with congressional authorization for the project. Construction began in 1973, but disputes over the cost and extent of the project continued until negotiators reached a breakthrough agreement in 1980. The promise of a new source of water spawned litigation between Native American tribes, agricultural interests, and urban centers over its allocation and distribution.

The Central Arizona Project

On June 3, 1963, the U.S. Supreme Court rendered its decision in *Arizona v. California*. The decision upheld the major provisions spelled out by Special Master Simon Rifkind in his 1960 report. On March 9, 1964, the Supreme Court issued a final decree confirming Arizona's entitlement to 2.8 million acre-feet of annual diversions and proportionate surpluses from the Colorado River. The decision paved the way for the eventual authorization of the Central Arizona Project. The Colorado River Basin Project Act (Public Law 90-537, 82 Stat. 885), passed by Congress on September 30, 1968, gave the Bureau of Reclamation permission to start the CAP.[1]

The groundbreaking ceremony for the Central Arizona Project took place on May 6, 1973, on the shores of Lake Havasu. The initial construction contract consisted of the creation of a half-mile breakwater to form an impoundment channel for the intake plant at Lake Havasu, and initial site clearance for the Lake Havasu pumping structure. Although small in relation to the entire project, this activity signaled a new phase in the long history of the CAP: construction.[2]

Even as the bureau's construction crews organized, opponents to the project began to mobilize. In 1973 a group of environmentalists formed Citizens Concerned About the Project (CCAP). Dave Campbell founded the group and Frank Welsh took the post of executive director. Gil Venable served as its attorney. Venable also served as the attorney for the Maricopa Audubon Society which joined forces with CCAP to oppose the project.[3]

These opponents directed their first efforts at Orme Dam. The 1968 act authorizing the project included Orme Dam "or a suitable alternative" to provide regulatory storage for the CAP. The storage capacity was needed to even out seasonal fluctuations in CAP use. Since most water use in

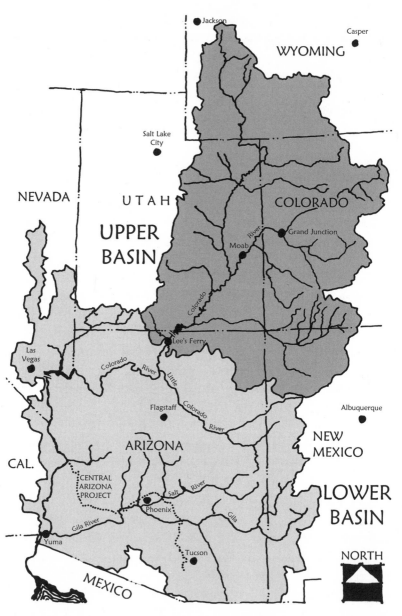

The Central Arizona Project and the Colorado River basins

Arizona occurs in the summer months, demand at that time would be more than the capacity of the canal. In the winter when demand was low, the canal would be capable of carrying more water than was immediately needed. Orme Dam, located at the confluence of the Salt and Verde Rivers, was planned to store excess water during the winter months so the water could be used during the summer when demand was high. This regulatory storage was considered an integral part of the CAP, because if water could not be stored it would be lost for use. Regulatory storage also allowed for the generation and sale of hydroelectric power in the summer, and the use of profits from that power sale to fund CAP pumping in the winter.[4]

Critics opposed the dam for a variety of reasons. The Maricopa Audubon Society charged that construction of the dam would flood important habitat for rare and endangered species, including the bald eagle. CCAP opposed the dam on more general grounds, charging that it was too expensive, would inundate significant recreational areas on the Salt River, and would be unsafe. In June of 1975 CCAP and the Maricopa Audubon Society filed suit against the bureau to stop construction of a portion of an aqueduct they believed would eliminate possible alternatives to Orme Dam. The lawsuit failed to stop construction.[5]

The CCAP organized recreational users of the Salt River, specifically those who liked to float down the river on inner tubes, to join in the battle against Orme Dam. The "tubers" proved to be vocal opponents. The Audubon Society mobilized its members and took their case to the public. In this atmosphere of opposition, in July of 1976 the bureau held public hearings on the draft of the Orme Dam environmental impact statement. Opposition was fierce.[6]

The 1976 hearing on Orme Dam failed to placate the critics. The publicity it generated seemed to further inflame passions against the dam. In the aftermath of the hearing, Native Americans on the Fort McDowell Reservation began to organize formal opposition to the Orme component of the CAP. Orme Dam would inundate the reservation if constructed. In 1976 John Williams, a resident of the reservation, and Carolina Butler, a Hispanic homemaker who lived near the reservation, organized the Committee to Save Fort McDowell to stop Orme Dam on the basis of damage it would cause on the Fort McDowell Reservation.[7]

Residents of Fort McDowell had taken an informal poll in 1975 and found 140 opposed to the dam, 1 in favor, and 8 with no opinion. Early in 1976 the bureau held a series of informational meetings on the reservation to discuss plans for the dam and plans to relocate the residents of the reservation. In September of 1976 the tribal council held a referendum on the subject of Orme Dam, asking if tribal members would be willing to sell their land and relocate to allow the dam construction. The results of this vote showed 144 opposed and 57 in favor.[8]

In the midst of the environmental debate, on October 15, 1976, the secretary of the interior issued water allocations for Indian tribes in central Arizona. These totaled 257,000 af until the year 2005, with a 10 percent priority for CAP water after that time. Indian tribes challenged the allocations in court, a process which took the remainder of the decade to resolve. Also in 1976, the Arizona Water Commission (AWC) issued its recommendations on state water allocations. The recommendations were released by the AWC on November 26, 1976. The AWC then organized public hearings in Phoenix, Tucson, and Yuma to obtain additional comments on the recommended allocations. On June 22, 1977, the AWC transmitted its final recommendations on CAP water allocations to the secretary of the interior.[9]

Although environmental concerns seemed to dominate discussion regarding the CAP, critics found many reasons to question the project. Two University of Arizona economists, W. E. Martin and Robert A. Young, attacked the project on an economic basis. Using a "typical" farm as an example, the economists estimated that it would be cheaper for farmers to continue to pump groundwater than to take CAP water. While this situation would result in the negative impact of continued groundwater depletion, from a purely economic perspective Martin and Young were correct that pumping groundwater was expected to be less expensive than CAP water. This finding anticipated the later problem of CAP underutilization because many farmers could not afford the imported CAP water.[10]

The mining industry expressed concerns that the quality of CAP water might have a negative effect on their operations. Colorado River water delivered through the CAP aqueduct would have a higher level of dissolved solids than either surface water or pumped groundwater. Because much of the dissolved solids consisted of salts, the water might interfere with chemical reactions. The salinity issue was of concern to farmers as well, fearful of introducing additional salts into the topsoil. Mine operators also objected to the expected price they would have to pay for CAP water.[11]

The continuing debates over the future of the project and the gradual refinement of its design represented controversial but expected conflict. But in 1977, difficulties arose from an entirely unexpected quarter. In February President Jimmy Carter decided to attack the ever-growing federal deficit by striking out at what he perceived as ill-conceived pork barrel water projects. Carter identified a list of nineteen such projects, including the CAP in Arizona. In March, President Carter initiated a review of the water projects, and his list gradually grew to more than eighty projects. This review came under heavy criticism by Congress, the public, and the press, but Carter persevered.[12]

The crisis over Carter's "hit list" reached its zenith on April 18, 1977, when the president recommended the withdrawal of funding for Orme Dam, Hooker Dam, and Charleston Dam as part of the CAP. The secretary of the interior was then charged with finding "suitable alternatives." In Arizona, Governor Raul Castro then appointed a group of citizens to study the alternatives.[13]

Over the next few years the Carter administration retreated from its strong stance in opposition to the water projects. Congress restored funding to most of the projects identified by Carter. For the CAP, however, the blow to the three dams would change the project permanently. After the Carter debacle, the combination of environmental opposition to dams and criticism on financial grounds would be very difficult for CAP planners to overcome. On September 30, 1977, the director of the Lower Colorado region of the bureau issued a memorandum to the Arizona Projects Office to halt all studies of Orme Dam and concentrate on finding alternatives instead.[14]

While the bureau had managed to keep the project going through political troubles in Washington and environmental opposition in Arizona, in March of 1978 severe floods hit the Salt River Valley and presented new challenges to CAP planners. A second flood occurred in December of 1978. Two years later, in February of 1980, a third major flood hit the Valley. These floods caused tremendous destruction in the Phoenix area and disrupted traffic patterns when bridges were damaged.[15]

The floods renewed calls for the construction of Orme Dam on the Salt

River and for other construction projects upstream on the Verde and Salt Rivers to reduce the danger from floods. This planning effort was combined with the search for Orme Dam alternatives started in the wake of President Carter's hit list. The bureau called the new investigation, initiated in July of 1978, the Central Arizona Water Control Study (CAWCS).[16]

The bureau challenged CAWCS staffers to find alternatives to Orme Dam and ways to increase flood protection for the Salt River Valley. The bureau enlisted the help of the Army Corps of Engineers for flood control planning and analysis. The task of the CAWCS planners was to link the need for flood control as demonstrated by the recent flooding with the need for regulatory storage as part of the CAP, and to design both in a manner acceptable to the environmentalists that opposed Orme Dam. In 1978 Congress spurred these planning actions when it passed the Safety of Dams Act. This federal legislation provided funding to repair and improve existing dams, but did not include funding for the construction of new dams.[17]

While state leaders grappled with the flooding problem and integrating regulatory storage into the project, they also worked on finalizing CAP water allocations submitted to the secretary of the interior in 1978. However, the allocation process became enmeshed with the Carter administration's campaign against water projects. Secretary of the Interior Cecil Andrus announced on October 5, 1979, that Arizona must demonstrate a greater commitment to controlling groundwater use in the state before he could issue final recommendations on the proposed allocations. Since the CAP had been billed as a rescue project to save Arizona from overdrafting its groundwater supply, Andrus wanted the state to show that it was willing to curtail groundwater use in exchange for CAP water. While this demand had obvious conservation and environmental benefits, it was also designed to ensure the financial solvency of the project. By limiting groundwater pumping, the federal government forced Arizona water users to purchase water from the CAP.[18]

Arizona officials responded by adopting the Groundwater Management Act of 1980. This legislation changed Arizona water law in many significant ways. It created the Arizona Department of Water Resources (DWR) to take the place of the Arizona Water Commission. This placed all water management decisions in the hands of a state agency, rather than a governor-appointed commission as had been the case previously. The Arizona Water Commission remained as an advisory body to the director of DWR.[19]

More significant from a policy standpoint, the 1980 act created Active Management Areas and Irrigation Non-Expansion Areas. Water planners hoped the designation of these groundwater basins where pumping could be limited and strictly controlled would lessen the state's dependence on groundwater. The act established a timetable for the gradual reduction and eventual elimination of groundwater overdraft in designated areas. For municipalities, the act created the concept of an "assured water supply," an amount of water presumed to be adequate to satisfy the needs of proposed developments for at least one hundred years.[20]

As an immediate effect of the act, the federal government put CAP activities back on track. This included addressing Indian water claims and finalizing CAP allocations. An agreement on land classification for the Gila River Indian Reservation early in 1980 allowed work on both fronts to move forward.[21]

Facing the Future: Tucson Encounters Limits to Growth

By 1965, the Tucson Water Department served 250,000 customers through 61,000 connections, up from 23,000 connections in 1956. The city possessed a total storage capacity of 52 million gallons and had 1,260 miles of distribution lines. Private water systems served another 70,000 customers. By 1965, the city had added two hundred private water companies to its system since it started the practice in 1938.[22]

Tucson also continued to purchase agricultural lands for water development. In 1960, the city purchased 2,200 acres of farmland in the San Pedro Valley for pumping groundwater to Tucson. Although this project never reached fruition, a 1962 amendment to the Arizona Water Code authorized the transfer of water rights between hydrologic basins and gave the city legal authority to expand its acquisition of agricultural water systems. In 1965, the city acquired eleven thousand acres of farmland in Avra Valley for $19 million to serve increasing urban needs. Most of the farmland purchased had been affected by the continued depletion of groundwater in the Tucson basin and its use for agriculture was limited by the increased costs of pumping water. Between 1947 and 1965, groundwater levels dropped twenty to forty feet.[23]

As part of the development of the Avra Valley well field, the city of Tucson constructed its second 20-million-gallon reservoir in 1963–64. City leaders named the structure the Martin Reservoir after Phil Martin, who had served as director of the Tucson Water Department for thirty years and as Tucson city manager for ten years. Engineers located the Martin Reservoir at the southeast corner of Old Nogales Highway and Valencia Road.[24]

Tucson residents faced a water crisis in the mid-1970s. Arizona and the nation experienced an economic downturn associated with increased energy prices. In the aftermath of the Yom Kippur War of 1973 during which the United States supported Israel, oil-producing states in the Middle East placed an embargo on oil exports. Increased fuel costs led to inflation, causing a decline in the American economy. To make matters worse, Arizona suffered from a decline in copper and agricultural profits as the Vietnam War came to an end. This hit Tucson particularly hard because the city was heavily dependent on payrolls from nearby mines and agricultural production facilities. Because Tucson pumped all of its water supply from deep wells, increased energy costs and inflation made the city's water utility more expensive to operate.[25]

Long years of deferred capital improvements in the city's water infrastructure further complicated the situation. Water officials had been reacting to growth by purchasing private water companies in the wake of development and adding those companies to the city system. This approach worked fairly well while the number of new connections remained small, but as the number grew Tucson water officials found it difficult to meet the demand. The infrastructure built by private water companies often failed to meet quality standards expected of municipal systems, burdening the city with considerable expense to retrofit substandard equipment.[26]

A study by engineer John Carollo in 1975 detailed severe problems with undercapitalization at the Tucson water utility. Carollo called for a 42 percent increase in Tucson water rates, including a conservation component that increased the cost of water as the amount used increased. Carollo also recommended a "lift charge" for users in higher elevations where additional pumping resulted in higher costs. Carollo issued his report in January of 1976, which coincided with a political change on the Tucson city council. A group called the "new Democrats" took office that same month. Constituting a majority of the Tucson City Council, the new political faction linked the water and growth issues.[27]

The council followed the recommendations of the Carollo report and instituted the new rate structure in June of 1976. While the increase in rates was more closely associated with national energy prices and local problems of deferred capital improvements, the public linked the conservation rate structure and lift charge with the ideology of the new political faction. That ideology was perceived as being more supportive of the environment and less supportive of growth. In July, when customers began receiving bills based on the new rates that sometimes doubled prior bills, reaction was swift. Opponents of the rate hike took out recall petitions against members of the council that voted for the increase.[28]

Council members backtracked and rescinded the lift charge, but the damage was done and the recall movement spread. In a recall election held in January of 1977, members who supported the new rates and represented the "new Democrats" were defeated. Opposition members took their place. The new council members who had run on the basis of opposition to the rate hike now found themselves in a peculiar situation. After their election, and some time to more thoroughly investigate the situation, they found pressing and legitimate needs for higher water rates.[29]

Tucson water officials attacked the problem in two ways: they increased water rates so that charges more accurately reflected the cost of its production and delivery, and they embarked on a program of conservation. The first action addressed the issues of deferred maintenance and undercapitalization. The conservation approach focused on peak demands in the summer months. During hot dry Tucson summers demand increased as residents watered lawns, filled swimming pools, and ran evaporative coolers. The period of peak demand lasted only a short time but required an extensive water infrastructure to meet it. By reducing peak demand, Tucson water planners could use a smaller system more attuned to average levels of demand.[30]

While the Tucson water crisis in 1975–76 may have been painful to those who lost their council seats, it gave birth to a successful water conservation program still in use today. Called "Beat the Peak," the program asked residents to reduce summertime peak demand usage. Through a combination of advertising and public relations announcements, Tucson residents got the message that reducing peak water use during the summer could keep costs down. While Beat the Peak remains a useful program, it appears that cost was the greatest factor in reducing consumption.[31]

Reducing peak demand meant that the system could be engineered to a smaller capacity, reducing capital expenditures. Although the final result was positive, Tucson elected officials and city staff learned a hard lesson about anticipating change and future growth: officials needed to plan for the future, not react to it.

Mastering What Works: Phoenix Water Development, 1963–1980

In the 1960s and 1970s the City of Phoenix concentrated on perfecting what worked. With the completion of the Deer Valley water treatment plant in 1964, the city had accumulated a total production capacity of 360 mgd. When the city acquired land on the southeastern side of the valley, Phoenix and the City of Mesa built the Val Vista treatment plant to meet the needs of both cities. This plant had an initial capacity of 80 mgd. The City of Phoenix continued the proven approach of purchasing private water systems as municipal boundaries extended ever outward.

Toward the end of the period Phoenix leaders faced a new challenge: finding a supply of water for areas outside the boundaries of the Salt River Project. The 1952 domestic water service agreement allowed the city to deliver water to former agricultural lands transformed to urban uses. When new subdivisions extended beyond SRP boundaries, however, the city could not divert SRP water to these off-project lands.

Development in the 1960s moved south toward the border with Tempe. In 1972 Preseley Development Company started planning a massive area of residential homes that became the Phoenix suburb of Ahwatukee. Other valley cities experienced similar growth.[32]

Federal environmental legislation enacted during the Nixon administration assisted Phoenix and Mesa with the construction of the Val Vista water treatment plant. In 1971 the two cities applied to the Environmental Protection Agency (EPA) for a grant under the terms of the Clean Water Act for construction assistance. John Carollo provided engineering services on the project. Construction began in February of 1973 when workers for M. M. Sundt Company broke ground. Completed at a total cost of $13.5 million with federal assistance, the Val Vista WTP had an initial capacity of 80 mgd. Carollo situated the plant on the site to allow for a future expanded capacity of 280 mgd.[33]

Continued development at greater distances from the city core resulted in a greater reliance on groundwater supplies. Most of the surface water available to the city was part of the Salt River Project's supply and could only be used within SRP boundaries (on-project). The only source of surface water that could be used off-project was that generated by the gates at Horseshoe Dam. The city addressed growth in off-project areas through increased development of groundwater, but also developed effluent for sale to agricultural users.

A dispute over effluent between the city and SRP arose in the late sixties. The project wanted effluent that came from water diverted for project purposes to remain on-project. The valley cities that operated the Ninety-first Avenue Wastewater Treatment Plant (WWTP) as a joint venture wanted to sell effluent to downstream farmers to raise money and conserve water. The cities of Phoenix, Mesa, Glendale, Scottsdale, and Tempe reached an agreement with SRP in 1969 with regard to the disposition of effluent. As part of the agreement, Phoenix and SRP extended the 1952 domestic water service agreement for twenty-five years.[34]

In 1972, as a result of continued growth in areas of Phoenix not originally designated as project lands, the city and SRP executed a contract designed to provide water to these areas. The 1972 agreement provided for the exchange and transfer of water between project and nonmember lands provided that the transfer of water did not result in a net loss of water to project lands. Nonmember lands were within project boundaries but without rights to project water because these lands could not be irrigated at the time the project was developed (land that was too low or too high to be irrigated, for example).[35]

Flagstaff Water Projects in the 1960s

By the 1960s the Flagstaff city council moved firmly behind continued groundwater development. Council members returned to the voters for permission to expand the groundwater program, this time asking for funds to drill a fifth well at Woody Mountain and a test well at Lake Mary. Voters were more cautious with taxpayer dollars this time around, and the bonds for the water project passed in June of 1961 by only thirty-seven votes. Contemporary observers attributed voter reluctance to increases in water rates to fund previous projects, too many bond issues in too few years, and an influx of newcomers unfamiliar with Flagstaff's water situation.[36]

Any remaining doubts about the wisdom of pursuing groundwater development vanished in the summer of 1963 when the fifth well at Woody Mountain came on-line. This raised the total capacity of the Woody Mountain system to 2.5 mgd, surpassing the 2 mgd output of the Lake Mary system. Even so, this amount just covered the daily demand of Flagstaff water users. The test well at Lake Mary authorized by the 1961 bond issue proved to be a good producer and justified the expenditure of more funds to develop a well field at Lake Mary.[37]

The biggest problem facing Flagstaff water planners was increasing the size of the transmission main from Lake Mary to the distribution grid. In September of 1963 voters approved a $3.5 million bond issue to upgrade the transmission main and drill a sixth well at Woody Mountain. This permitted the development of an additional well at Lake Mary.[38]

In 1966 Flagstaff officials renewed consideration of a suggestion first made by USGS geologist P. Eldon Dennis. Working in conjunction with engineers from the Bureau of Reclamation, the city sponsored a series of test wells in the inner basin. Confirming Dennis' expectation, well drillers encountered a good flow at depths from 150 to 200 feet. While the amount of water that could be developed from underground aquifers turned out to be limited, the inner basin wells were very valuable additions to the Flagstaff water supply. The relatively short distance to groundwater (the wells at Woody Mountain were ten times deeper) resulted in low pumping costs. Ease of pumping and the ability to divert the flow into the existing gravity distribution system serving the inner basin combined to produce water at a very small cost for Flagstaff consumers.[39]

The construction of wells in the inner basin completed the basic parameters of water sources for Flagstaff. There have been some additional modifications and improvements over the years, but the four main sources of supply have remained constant: the inner basin springs and wells, Lake Mary surface water, the Lake Mary well field, and the Woody Mountain well field.[40]

Summary

In many ways Arizona had mastered its water future in the 1960s and 1970s. Winning congressional authorization for the Central Arizona Project and starting construction was a tremendous victory against what appeared to be insurmountable opposition from California water users. The City of Phoenix mastered a productive working relationship with the Salt River Project, compared to the tempestuous relationship between the two entities in the 1950s. This allowed Phoenix, and other valley cities, to meet the demands of urban water users on former agricultural lands through a series of surface water treatment plants. Flagstaff established the basic parameters of its water production systems that continue to serve the city today. Tucson leaders, shocked by a situation for which they were ill prepared, developed a conservation strategy that suited the area's reliance on pumped groundwater.

Although Arizona's urban leaders had mastered the present, they faced an uncertain future. Continued heavy demand for water outside the boundaries of the Salt River Project required Phoenix to rely on wells or find an alternate supply. Tucson had a program of conservation in place, but the demand reduction campaign did not and could not satisfy the needs of the many new residents that moved to the Tucson area.

Construction and authorization of the Central Arizona Project spawned a series of lawsuits over the new supply of water. Many saw the opportunity to settle old wrongs with new water. As Arizona municipal leaders faced the future, decisions about water supply would be more often made by lawyers in courtrooms than by engineers behind drafting tables.

Chapter 13 Environmental Reactions since 1980

Environmental concerns regarding water resource development and a continuing debate over the Central Arizona Project dominated Arizona's water history over the last two decades of the twentieth century. During this period environmental opposition to large water development projects became increasingly sophisticated and widespread. Events in Arizona demonstrated that strong public input could change many basic assumptions about water development.

As water planners and environmentalists battled over details of the Central Arizona Project, municipal leaders and water officials readied themselves for water delivery. This process required municipal officials to plan, design, and construct water production facilities to take water from the CAP aqueduct, treat it, and deliver it to customers. Officials accomplished this task with varying degrees of success, as the examples of Phoenix and Tucson illustrate.

Lawyers came to dominate water activities during this period. Disputes over water rights had been settled in the courtroom over the years, but the arrival of Central Arizona Project water brought new conflicts. Attorneys hammered out several significant Indian water rights settlements to address the needs of Arizona's first inhabitants. At the same time, Arizona embarked on a general adjudication of water rights as a means to determine the relative priority of water use for Indians and non-Indians alike.

CAP: Modifications and Maneuvering, 1980–1993

In 1980, Governor Bruce Babbitt signed the Arizona Groundwater Management Act creating four Active Management Areas (AMAs) where groundwater pumping could be regulated to achieve specific water management goals. Passed under threat of federal withdrawal of funding for the CAP, the Arizona legislative action underscored the determination of the state's political leaders. The passage of the act opened the way to finalize some of the water allocation decisions for the CAP.[1]

On July 31, 1980, Secretary of the Interior Cecil Andrus announced preliminary allocations for Arizona Indian tribes. The State of Arizona then brought suit in U.S. District Court objecting to the proposed Indian allocations. Secretary Andrus issued final Indian allocations on December 1, 1980, but the district court granted a preliminary injunction to prevent the secretary from implementing them.[2]

Following the election of President Ronald Reagan in November of 1980, new Secretary of the Interior James Watt announced three tentative decisions with regard to the CAP. These took the form of "proposed actions" to expedite environmental clearance for the project and included the allocation of 309,828 af for Indian users, the selection of "Plan 6" of the CAWCS as a means of regulatory and flood control for the project, and the termination of the CAP aqueduct south of Tucson at the San Xavier Indian Reservation. In late 1981, the U.S. District Court allowed the allocations selected by Watt to stand when it dismissed the suit brought by Arizona. The final allocations took effect on March 24, 1983, when they were published in the Federal Register. Municipal and industrial users were awarded 640,000 af per year. Indian water users received 309,828 af, with the remaining water to be allocated to non-Indian agriculture.[3]

The designation of Plan 6 as the preferred alternative for consideration did not end the Central Arizona Water Control Study (CAWCS). Work continued to refine the features of the proposed action. Plan 6 takes its name from the CAWCS list where it was sixth in a series of alternative plans to Orme Dam. Plan 6 included the construction of New Waddell Dam, the construction of Cliff Dam to replace existing Horseshoe Dam upstream from Bartlett Dam on the Verde River, the reconstruction of spillways at Stewart Mountain Dam to improve safety, and the modification of Roosevelt Dam to increase storage capacity, improve flood control, and improve safety by increasing its ability to withstand floods.[4]

By the end of 1982, Secretary Watt finalized the extension of the CAP aqueduct to the San Xavier Indian Reservation. This was part of the Southern Arizona Water Rights Settlement Act designed to settle a lawsuit brought by the Tohono O'odham tribe against water users in Tucson. In December of 1982, the bureau eliminated Hooker Dam in New Mexico from the project, the result of a study begun in 1981 known as the Upper Gila Water Supply Study.[5]

On April 29, 1983, the bureau issued its draft environmental impact statement on Plan 6. However, the bureau undertook further study of Cliff Dam because of continued opposition from CCAP and the Maricopa Audubon Society. The continuing environmental opposition to portions of the project resulted in construction delays.[6]

In the late summer of 1984, U.S. Representative for Arizona John J. Rhodes met with leaders of the Arizona legislature and Governor Babbitt to find state funding for portions of the CAP to keep it on schedule. In January of 1985, Governor Babbitt appointed an eighteen-member task force to study CAP financing. The group, known as the Executive Committee on CAP Financing, completed its study in September of 1985, and Governor Babbitt presented it to the state's congressional delegation with a request that it be forwarded to the Reagan administration for consideration. The proposal called for the contribution of funds by the CAWCD, the Flood Control District of Maricopa County, several Arizona municipalities, and the Salt River Project.[7]

Construction on other parts of the CAP continued as the Plan 6 portion of the project was being discussed. By the end of 1983, the project was 41 percent complete. This rose to 55 percent by the end of 1985. On March 8, 1985, Unit 6 at the Havasu pumping plant was turned on and water flowed from the Colorado River into the first reach of the CAP canal. On May 22, 1985, the first water for agricultural use was delivered into a CAP sublateral of the Harquahala Valley Irrigation District. The water was used to irrigate a cotton field about eighty-six miles west of Phoenix.

This first delivery of water from the CAP was cause for a small celebration. Bill Plummer, the regional director for the Bureau of Reclamation, turned the wheel to lift a gate and divert water into the lateral.[8]

It took five more months for CAP water to reach the Phoenix area. On October 8, 1985, the first water for municipal use was turned out from the Granite Reef Aqueduct into an impoundment at the Union Hills water treatment plant in the city of Phoenix. On November 15, 1985, a group of dignitaries gathered at the Union Hills water treatment plant to celebrate the completion of the project to Phoenix.[9]

These water deliveries were facilitated by the execution of subcontracts for CAP water delivery between the CAWCD and the water users. The secretary of the interior had approved the draft form of these subcontracts on April 26, 1984, allowing them to go through. The subcontract for Phoenix was executed on October 10, 1984. By the end of 1986, fifty municipal and industrial use water service contracts had been executed, accounting for 464,175 af or 72.6 percent of the available municipal and industrial (M&I) supply. Ten agricultural contracts had been executed by the end of that year, accounting for 70.7 percent of the non-Indian agricultural allocation.[10]

While the CAP was finally delivering water to central Arizona, the Plan 6 portion of the project calling for Cliff Dam continued to be mired in controversy. On August 16, 1985, the U.S. Fish and Wildlife Service issued an opinion that Cliff Dam could be built without jeopardizing the bald eagle habitat in the vicinity of the proposed dam. However, on September 19, 1985, the Maricopa Audubon Society and other environmental groups filed suit to prevent the construction of Cliff Dam. These groups coalesced into an umbrella organization called the National Coalition to Stop Cliff Dam.[11]

Despite the continuing environmental opposition to Cliff Dam, a negotiating committee made up of representatives of state entities and the federal government met to formulate a contractual arrangement for state funding of portions of Plan 6. On December 12, 1985, the CAWCD board of directors approved a Plan 6 funding agreement that followed the formula outlined in the report published by Governor Babbitt's Executive Committee on CAP Financing. On April 15, 1986, the federal government and Arizona entities agreed on the Plan 6 funding agreement.[12]

Although the multiparty agreement provided funding for Plan 6 and

Cliff Dam, it did not address the opposition of environmental groups continuing to press their case in court and the public arena. On June 18, 1987, the Arizona congressional delegation reached an agreement with the National Coalition to Stop Cliff Dam that called for the elimination of Cliff Dam from Plan 6. In exchange, the congressional delegation pledged that it would find other sources of water and flood control for the Arizona entities—including Salt River Valley municipalities—that Cliff Dam would have provided.[13]

On June 22, 1987, the Phoenix City Council authorized the city to join other Plan 6 participants to negotiate a supplemental agreement to continue state funding for the project. The final agreement pledged the participants to continue funding Plan 6 and for the federal government to find replacement water. The supplemental Plan 6 funding agreement was completed in October of 1987. Under the terms of the agreement, the contract carried an execution date of July 1, 1987.[14]

The elimination of Cliff Dam smoothed the way for the CAP to move forward, and the years to completion were filled with activity: in 1986, ground was broken on Reach 4 of the Phase B aqueduct to Tucson; construction of New Waddell Dam began on September 16, 1987; in 1988, construction contracts were awarded on the last two of fourteen CAP pumping plants; in 1990 repairs began on siphons suffering from corrosion damage; on October 4, 1991, Colorado River water for delivery to municipal customers reached Tucson; on October 29, 1992, a "topping out" ceremony was held at New Waddell Dam; modifications to Roosevelt Dam got underway.[15]

In October of 1992, the secretary of the interior indicated that he planned to issue a notice that the CAP was complete, a step that would begin the repayment obligations of the CAWCD and water users. Although water deliveries to Tucson had begun, the CAWCD board believed that in light of continuing siphon repair problems and the financial hardships among Arizona water districts, the federal government should not issue its notice. The CAWCD board asked the federal government to delay the start of CAP repayment for one year.[16]

Governor Fife Symington appointed a sixteen-member task force in 1993 to address the financing and repayment problems and discuss underutilization issues. The task force verified that forecasts of agricultural

The Bureau of Reclamation raised the height of Roosevelt Dam and covered it with a layer of concrete as part of the Plan 6 program.

water use had been overly optimistic. The CAWCD board responded by reducing the price of agricultural water in an attempt to improve cash flow. Although this action was not considered a long-term solution, it did result in increased use of CAP water.[17]

In 1993 the Bureau of Reclamation granted the CAWCD a one-year extension of the repayment period for reimbursable project costs. This extension allowed the local entities additional time to establish an acceptable repayment schedule.[18] In October of 1993, the secretary of the interior issued his notice of completion for the CAP, and in January of 1994 the CAWCD made its first payment under the provisions of the 1972 master repayment contract.[19]

Constructing CAP Facilities in Phoenix

The City of Phoenix continued its established pattern of constructing surface water treatment plants during the last two decades of the twentieth century. What made the new plants different was the source of water. Engineers located these new plants on the Granite Reef Aqueduct of the Central Arizona Project to treat Colorado River Water.

Completion of the Central Arizona Project to the Phoenix area required several treatment and delivery facilities to get the water to area residents. Phoenix officials planned for the delivery of CAP water well in advance. The city acquired the first parcel for the Union Hills WTP for treating CAP water in May of 1974, and engineer John Carollo completed a preliminary plan for the plant by that fall. The city purchased additional parcels in February and October of 1977 and in January of 1978.[20]

Carollo returned to the drafting table in 1981 to prepare plans and specifications for the Union Hills WTP. Dillingham Construction Company received the construction contract on January 10, 1984. The plant would take water from the Central Arizona Project canal diverted from the Granite Reef Aqueduct for treatment and delivery to north Phoenix. The Union Hills WTP began operating in October of 1985 with an initial capacity of 80 mgd, and was expanded to 160 mgd in 1992. Engineers designed the plant for eventual expansion to 240 mgd.[21]

After completion of the Union Hills WTP, water officials in Phoenix and other valley cities began planning for another facility to divert water from the CAP aqueduct. In December of 1985, city water advisor Bill Chase presented a report on an interconnection facility between SRP and CAP. Although Phoenix had planned to take most of its CAP allocation at the Union Hills WTP, the CAP interconnect would allow CAP water to be diverted into SRP canals and from there into any of the city's water treatment plants. The interconnect would also facilitate diversion of CAP water into the Salt River in the vicinity of Granite Reef Dam for use in future groundwater recharge projects.[22]

The interconnect facility built on a tradition of cooperation between valley cities regarding water and wastewater infrastructure. The interconnect between the CAP and SRP system permitted other valley cities to take their CAP allocations and participate in the groundwater recharge project. Under the auspices of the Arizona Municipal Water Users Association, city representatives developed a cost-sharing agreement that spread the cost of the project among Phoenix, Glendale, Scottsdale, Tempe, Mesa, and Chandler.[23]

Locating the interconnect at Granite Reef Dam was intended to allow

The interconnect of the Central Arizona and Salt River Projects allowed Colorado River water to be diverted into SRP canals, and then to municipal water treatment plants.

for the diversion of water stored behind the future Cliff Dam. With the elimination of Cliff Dam (itself a replacement for Orme Dam), CAP water planners concentrated their efforts at Lake Pleasant. The Bureau of Reclamation constructed a new, larger dam to replace the original Waddell Dam. This expanded Lake Pleasant, which became a storage reservoir for CAP water.

The elimination of Cliff Dam led Phoenix water planners to look toward Lake Pleasant for the site of a new water treatment plant. Locating the plant as far north as possible would allow for gravity delivery of water and reduce costs. Increased growth in the north Phoenix area along the corridor of Interstate 17 north of the CAP canal was also a factor. In 1991 consulting engineers recommended Lake Pleasant as the location for the new water treatment plant.[24]

The City of Phoenix purchased the plant site from the State of Arizona

in 1998. Initial plans developed in 2001 specified construction of a plant
with a capacity of 80 mgd, with planned expansion to a final capacity of
320 mgd over the next few decades. The planned completion date for the
project is 2007.[25]

Tucson Readies Itself for the Future

After the many years it took to plan, prepare, and construct the Central
Arizona Project, one would expect that the 1992 arrival of CAP water in
Tucson would be an uneventful affair. As it turned out, Tucson residents
reacted with shock and dismay as the unaccustomed fluid wreaked havoc
with pipes in the Old Pueblo. The acidic chemical composition of the CAP
water scoured rust and corrosion from pipes and deposited the resulting
mixture in sinks, bathtubs, and evaporative coolers.

As had Phoenix, Tucson began preparations for the arrival of CAP
water far in advance of the actual event. Although the extra distance from
the Colorado meant that the CAP arrived later in Tucson, uncertainty over
funding and routing left Tucson Water officials with comparatively little
time to evaluate treatment alternatives. In October of 1989, Tucson began
construction of the Hayden/Udall Water Treatment Plant. The name of the
plant honored Senator Carl Hayden and Congressman Morris Udall, long-
time advocates of the CAP. The Clearwell Reservoir, with a capacity of 60
million gallons, stored finished water. Workers completed the Clearwell
Reservoir in 1990.[26]

Tucson officials selected ozone as the primary means of treatment
at the Hayden/Udall WTP. Although no other city in Arizona used this
method, ozone treatment, while not common, had been used in Europe and
in some parts of the United States. Ozone gas passed through the water
and killed any viruses and bacteria, then dissipated in a short amount
of time. Tucson officials selected chloramine as a residual disinfectant
for protection after the water left the plant. Officials selected chloramine
rather than the more common chlorine because they believed many people
found the taste and odor of chlorine objectionable.[27]

While Tucson officials had ample scientific research to back up their
decisions, many residents felt less than comfortable with the treatment
choices. Informational material distributed by the water utility warned
that chloramine had a dangerous effect on kidney dialysis patients whose

blood came in direct contact with the chemical. The chemical also had a harmful effect on fish because water came in contact with their blood stream when it passed through their gills. Tucson Water officials warned people with fish tanks and aquariums that the water needed a special filter or specific chemicals to neutralize chloramine.[28]

Colorado River water arrived at the Hayden/Udall treatment plant on October 4, 1991. A reporter for the *Arizona Daily Star* described the fluid as "brown-tinged" on its first day in the treatment plant. While Governor Fife Symington, former Governor Jack Williams, and former Arizona senator Paul Fannin presented remarks that underscored the importance of reducing groundwater use, nearly a dozen protestors marched outside the facility with signs in opposition to the project. Reporter Enric Volante reminded readers about the public relations campaign directed at kidney dialysis patients and fish owners: "The city's use of chloramine to disinfect the water means it could be toxic to human blood cells through dialysis, and to pet fish that swim in it."[29]

Although Tucson Water officials expected to begin delivery of CAP water during the summer of 1992, it took until October before it arrived at customer's taps. This period allowed technicians to fine-tune the filtration and treatment process. After a flurry of inquiries, the number of complaints about taste and odor fell to about normal within two weeks and most residents seemed to accept the introduction of CAP water in stride. More than 225,000 Tucsonans received CAP water during the first month of service, representing 84,000 service connections and about 58 percent of Tucson's water service area.[30]

Over time serious problems developed with CAP water in Tucson. It had a relatively high level of acidity compared to Tucson groundwater and a corrosive effect that released rust, dirt, salts, and other deposits accumulated in pipes over the years. Complaints reached a crescendo in August of 1993. Tucson Water received an estimated one thousand complaints about discoloration and odor out of the 84,000 service connections that received CAP water. Beyond discoloration and taste, some residents reported damage to water heaters, evaporative coolers, and washing machines. As water officials scrambled to find a solution to the problem, members of the Tucson City Council and the Pima County Board of Supervisors called for the termination of CAP water delivery.[31]

After defeating a motion to shut down the CAP supply, Tucson City

Council members gave the project a show of support on August 24 when they voted to continue delivery of CAP water and take steps to solve the problem. But complaints continued, and on October 5, 1993, the council voted to cut off CAP water to Tucson residents. This action generated a storm of controversy from critics who thought the decision was rash. Tucson Water Director Mike Tubbs resigned in the aftermath of the vote. The council reversed itself one week later, voting on October 12 to keep using CAP water in the system. However, the council voted to exclude it from the east side of Tucson's water delivery area which contained the older galvanized pipes most seriously affected by CAP water.[32]

While Tucson Water struggled over the next few months to find a solution to the corrosion problem, residents opposed to CAP water took their complaints to the voters. Activists organized an initiative petition to stop delivery of CAP water. The Arizona Department of Environmental Quality provided the activists with additional ammunition in June of 1994 when it slapped Tucson with fines up to $400,000 for violations of drinking water regulations. In November of 1994 Tucson Water pulled the plug on the CAP, not because of demands by residents or activists, but because routine maintenance tasks required officials to drain the canal. Once the maintenance was finished, the council voted not to resume CAP deliveries.[33]

As the temporary maintenance shutdown evolved into a firm rejection of CAP water by the council, activists took matters into their own hands. Richard Wiersma and city council member Molly McKasson helped form a group that lobbied for the Citizens' Water Protection Initiative. These opponents of the CAP gathered enough signatures to place an initiative on the ballot in November 1995 asking Tucson voters to approve proposition 200, the Water Consumer Protection Act. Voters approved the measure, which barred Tucson Water from using chemical treatment and outlawed direct delivery of CAP water for five years unless it matched the quality of pumped groundwater. In the aftermath of the election, Tucson Water began to explore options for CAP water such as groundwater recharge and recovery.[34]

If the Water Consumer Protection Act of 1995 can be considered Tucson's water revolution, in 1997 Tucson experienced a counterrevolution. Business leaders and developers took a page from the book of CAP opponents and placed an initiative on the ballot that would have repealed most of the provisions of the 1995 Water Consumer Protection Act. Voters rejected this measure, and many perceived the defeat as a reaffirmation of recharge and reuse of CAP water. This left Tucson Water officials in the position of finding an alternative to direct delivery of CAP water.[35]

Opponents of the CAP struck again in 1999. Led by automobile dealer Bob Beaudry, the Citizens Alliance for Water Security (CAWS) pressed an initiative that would have strengthened the protection provisions of 1995's proposition 200 and extended the moratorium on the domestic use of CAP water. Voters rejected this measure as well, with many stating that it was too stringent and needlessly limited the options available to the municipal water agency. This vote opened the way for Tucson Water to complete a compromise program to return a blend of recharged CAP water and groundwater to Tucson taps. This compromise blend managed to address the water quality issue with regard to CAP water in Tucson, but still left Tucson short of using its full allocation.[36]

The delivery of CAP water brought with it a realization that groundwater levels were continually depleted as Tucson used more water each year than could be replaced naturally from rainfall and river flow. Tucson had outpaced its natural recharge since 1940, resulting in falling water tables. While this situation was of primary concern to scientists and environmentalists, others in the Tucson area had a more direct experience with falling water tables.

The Impact of Falling Water Tables: A Retrospective

The experience of Tohono O'odham farmers at the San Xavier Indian Reservation south of Tucson reflected the difficulties that had plagued farmers along the Santa Cruz River since the 1920s. The construction of pumping plants and wells, combined with flood protection works, had increased the water supply and the number of cultivated acres by 1920. This success proved to be short lived. Within three years the falling water table rendered the supply inadequate. Late in 1923, A. L. Wathan, who later became director of the Indian Irrigation Service, proposed the construction of an infiltration gallery on the reservation to collect the subsurface flow of the Santa Cruz River.[37]

Construction of infiltration gallery 1 began in November of 1923. The Irrigation Service built the gallery in the bed of the west branch of the

Santa Cruz River. The gallery consisted of 6,500 feet of open ditch cut twenty-two feet deep into the subsurface flow of the river at its southern end, and 3,488 feet of thirty-inch creosoted fir pipe with drilled perforations to allow the water to enter buried between ten and eighteen feet deep on the northern end. At the north end of the infiltration gallery, engineers diverted the flow into irrigation ditches. Gallery 1 was nearly two miles long.[38]

To excavate the trench for the perforated pipe collector, the Irrigation Service hired crews of Native American workers who used picks and shovels to move the hard dirt. Teams of horses pulled fresnos (scrapers) to remove earth from the center of the ditch. The cost of the labor alone for the job neared $37,000. The Irrigation Service completed the project in July of 1925.[39]

At first, infiltration gallery 1 seemed successful. It produced 8.79 cfs (cubic feet per second) in December of 1925. However, by June of 1926, the flow shrunk to 7.5 cfs. In 1927, engineers added 2,613 feet of concrete pipe to increase the flow, but this effort achieved little because the groundwater was depleted and the water table continued to fall. In 1929, infiltration gallery no. 1 produced a flow of only 2 cfs. Despite "considerable assistance" provided by the government, the attempts to obtain more water at San Xavier proved futile.[40]

The San Xavier Reservation also experienced water difficulties during the 1930s. President Franklin D. Roosevelt appointed an able administrator, John Collier, to be commissioner of Indian affairs. Collier organized a special division of the Civilian Conservation Corps (CCC) made up entirely of Indian labor. Other New Deal programs used for water development at San Xavier included Public Works Administration (PWA) funds, the Emergency Conservation Work Program (ECW), and the Soil Conservation Service. Despite these programs, the water table at San Xavier dropped almost thirty feet from 1930 to 1940.[41]

The Indian Irrigation Service drilled four wells in 1935, using PWA funds. The pumps had a capacity to irrigate fifteen hundred acres, but because of sagging farm prices and a low water table only one thousand acres were planted. The wells ranged from 92 to 232 feet in depth and produced from 690 to 1,465 gpm (gallons per minute). Electric-powered turbine pumps ran the wells, which were gravel packed and had eighteen-inch-diameter casings.[42]

In 1935 the Irrigation Service constructed a concrete dam in the Santa Cruz to help with reservation irrigation and flood control. The engineers designed the structure to furnish water to the existing distribution system. They also hoped that the new dam would control erosion by preventing channel entrenchment further upstream. Started on April 6, work on the dam neared completion by June 8. Unfortunately, a flood on September 2 wrecked the structure and prevented its use.[43]

The government then began construction of infiltration gallery 2 in February of 1938, and by August had completed 12,500 feet of trench and laid 7,000 feet of pipe. In November and December, the Irrigation Service excavated an additional 1,240 feet of trench and laid 6,640 feet of pipe. The total length of infiltration gallery 2 measured 13,725 feet. Gallery 2 started in Sahuarita Wash at the eastern boundary of the reservation and ran west in the wash to the Santa Cruz. There, the Irrigation Service built a small earthen dam to constrict the river flow. The gallery then proceeded in a northwesterly direction, paralleling the west bank of the Santa Cruz. At the northern end of the infiltration gallery, the water flowed into the distribution system.[44]

The Irrigation Service used a dragline with a one and one-half cubic foot bucket to excavate the trench for gallery no. 2. Hurrying to complete the project before the summer flood season, the Tohono O'odham worked in shifts. One group started at four o'clock in the morning and worked until noon; the second shift worked until eight o'clock at night. The project cost an estimated $110,000, and produced between 4 and 5 cfs when completed.[45]

By 1945, gallery 1 produced little water and by 1947 gallery 2 produced less than 0.5 cfs. After this time, the reservation converted entirely to pump irrigation as the water table continued to drop below the level of surface diversions and the infiltration galleries. The era of diversions from the Santa Cruz had ended. The arrival of the CAP brought with it the potential of a new source of supply for Native American agriculture at San Xavier and elsewhere in Arizona. In the 1980s, Native Americans began to use the legal system as a means to obtain additional sources of water for agriculture and environmental restoration.[46]

Federal Reserved Water Rights

Attorneys for Arizona achieved a tremendous victory in 1963 when the U.S. Supreme Court ruled that water diverted from the Colorado River must follow the allocations set forth in the "law of the river" that originated with the Colorado River Compact of 1922. But while the decision resolved one conflict, it opened many new ones. The court ruled that Native American tribes on the Colorado River were also entitled to water, whether they had been using it or not. The ruling had its roots in a U.S. Supreme Court ruling made in 1908 that created the concept of a reserved water right for Indian reservations.[47]

The 1908 Court decision concerned the Fort Belknap Indian Reservation bordering the Milk River in Montana. The government planned to use waters from the Milk River for an irrigation project to benefit the residents of the reservation. However, irrigation planners found that much of the water had been put to use by non-Indian settlers in the area. These settlers claimed the water under the terms of state law based on the prior appropriation doctrine (first in time, first in right).[48]

In the case titled *Winters v. United States* (1908), the Supreme Court ruled that when the federal government created reservations such as Fort Belknap it reserved not just the land but also the water. While the reservation of land was specific, the reservation of water need not be. The Supreme Court ruled that the mere fact that the government had created the reservation implied that it had also reserved enough water to fulfill the purposes for which the reservation had been created. The water rights created by the Supreme Court are often called "Winters" rights after the name of the decision. They are also referred to as "federal Indian reserved rights" to distinguish them from rights established under state law (state rights).[49]

In contrast to state law, which dates water rights from the first beneficial use, federal reserved rights have no beneficial use requirement. The water is reserved until such time as it is needed by the reservation. Rather than a date of first use, federal Indian reserved rights date from the time the reservation was created.[50]

Since many of the federal Indian reservations in the West were created well before non-Indian settlement, after the Winters case these later arrivals found that their state water rights had later priorities as well. Considerable development took place in the West based on state law water rights, despite the fact that, according to Winters, Native Americans had senior water rights. Then, in 1963, the U.S. Supreme Court addressed the reserved rights issue when it provided a method of quantification for Winters rights.

In its *Arizona v. California* decision the U.S. Supreme Court established the concept of "practicably irrigable acreage" (PIA) as a means to determine the amount of water Native American tribes might be entitled to use on their reservations. The court based its decision on data gathered for the case on five tribes with reservations on the main stream of the Colorado River: Chemehuevi, Cocopah, Yuma, Colorado River, and Fort Mohave. The PIA standard set forth that the measure of a reservation's water right should be the amount of water needed to irrigate all of the acreage within the reservation that could be practicably irrigated—in other words, all of the land that it was feasible to use for agriculture with irrigation.[51]

The decision in *Arizona v. California* delineated large amounts of water that could be reserved for tribal use. Because the PIA concept was based on irrigated agriculture, most reservations in the West had large potential water rights claims based on vast amounts of land that could be put to use for agriculture if water was physically and economically available. These two elements proved to be the key parts of the PIA issue, since by the time of the 1963 decision most water in the West had been appropriated.

The Central Arizona Project provided a new source of water. Arizona's water planners had envisioned the project as a means to protect and preserve agriculture in the state. However, the very U.S. Supreme Court decision that made the project possible ultimately resulted in a basic change in the goal of the CAP. The 1963 decision meant that a considerable portion of the water delivered by the project would later be allocated to meet the federal reserved rights of Arizona's Native American tribes.

Arizona's General Stream Adjudications

Two factors contributed to the creation of a process to examine and determine the relative priority of water rights in Arizona during the 1970s. The first was the start of construction for the CAP. The second was continuing depletion of groundwater with its associated problems of land subsidence and increased pumping expense caused by greater depths to underground water.

The CAP triggered a need for water planning in Arizona. In order to get information for the CAP water allocation process, hydrologists evaluated the sources of supply, quantities available, and uses. The construction of the Salt River Project early in the century brought with it a need to determine the relative priority of water rights in the Salt River Valley, a process that resulted in the Kent Decree of 1910. As construction began on the CAP, attorneys contemplated the need to repeat this historical pattern.

Arizona officials had convinced Congress and federal budget planners of the need for the CAP based on declining water tables. The federal government asked Arizona to adopt the Groundwater Management Act of 1980 in recognition of the seriousness of the problem and to make sure that the water delivered by the CAP addressed the problem of groundwater decline. At the same time, there was an increased level of activism on the nation's Indian reservations. The civil rights movements of the 1960s and 1970s prepared Native American leaders to use all methods available to protect their water supply.

These separate trends in the early 1970s convinced water officials there was a need for an overall judicial review of Arizona's water rights, called a general adjudication, in anticipation of CAP completion and to address lawsuits filed by Native American tribes to determine their federal reserved rights. Salt River Project officials took the first step on April 30, 1974, when they filed a petition with the State Land Department for an adjudication of the water rights of the Salt River above Granite Reef Dam.[52]

Water officials at SRP were also concerned with state right holders, and the impact new upstream uses of the Salt and Verde rivers would have on the amount of water available for direct delivery and for storage behind SRP dams. On February 26, 1976, SRP filed a petition with the State Land Department for a general adjudication of the Verde River. Other large water interests followed SRP's lead. On February 17, 1978, Phelps-Dodge Corporation filed a petition for an adjudication of the Little Colorado and Upper Gila Rivers, and on April 3, 1978, the American Smelting and Refining Company (ASARCO) filed a petition for the San Pedro River.[53]

Many other western states also embarked on general adjudications of water rights during this period, usually over federal reserved water rights. Because those rights were federal in origin, the normal course of action would require the issue to be litigated in federal court. However, in 1952 Congress adopted the McCarran Amendment, which allowed state courts to assume jurisdiction for general stream adjudications under certain circumstances. Under the terms of the McCarran Amendment, state courts could assume jurisdiction as long as the adjudication was "comprehensive," meaning that all water users and all water sources came under scrutiny.[54]

Partly as a means to make sure the general stream adjudication in Arizona met the terms of the McCarran Amendment, in 1979 the Arizona state legislature amended the adjudication statute. As a result of the legislation, responsibility for the water rights investigation moved from the State Land Department to the Arizona Superior Court. Prior to the change the adjudication was an administrative proceeding before a state agency and not a judicial proceeding. Subsequent to the legislation, in 1979 large water users refiled their petitions to adjudicate in superior court.[55]

One reason for conducting the adjudication in superior court rather than a state administrative proceeding was to protect the interests of Native Americans who expressed concern that they could not get a fair hearing before an agency so closely aligned with state government. Despite the move to superior court, many Native Americans contended that only federal court would offer them a neutral arena. In June of 1981, the San Carlos Apache filed a motion to dismiss the adjudication in superior court. This case eventually reached the U.S. Supreme Court, which upheld the constitutionality of the superior court adjudication in 1983 and allowed the adjudication to move forward at an accelerated pace.[56]

Native American Water Rights Settlements

The court consolidated Arizona's general stream adjudications into two main cases: the Little Colorado Adjudication and the Gila River Adjudication. The adjudications included streams tributary to each river. To facilitate the legal process, in 1991 the Arizona Supreme Court appointed a special master to serve as a court commissioner. The master could take testimony, hear legal arguments, and prepare reports. The adjudications provided a mechanism for determining federal reserved rights, but the pace of the lawsuits was exceedingly slow. Instead of relying on a court to determine water rights, the parties involved turned to negotiation in an attempt to settle the dispute.[57]

Negotiators crafted the Ak-Chin water settlement in 1978, Arizona's first Native American water rights settlement. The settlement addressed the severe decline in groundwater levels on the Ak-Chin Reservation caused by intense pumping for non-Indian agriculture. The Ak-Chin settlement did not necessarily provide a model for future settlements, but it did suggest that solutions to water problems might be better resolved by negotiation than by litigation.[58]

In 1975, attorneys for the Tohono O'odham tribe filed a complaint in U.S. District Court that contended increasing water use in the Tucson area by the city, mines, and agriculture violated their water rights. The tribe based its suit on the Winters Doctrine. Continued depletion of groundwater in the Tucson area led the Tohono O'odham to seek legal redress as practicing agriculture on the reservation became more and more difficult. In 1975, the average underground water depth in the basin stood at 174 feet, down from 142 feet in 1947.[59]

Tribal leaders encountered intense pressure from water users in the Tucson area to settle the lawsuit. On February 18, 1980, the Tohono O'odham tribal council approved a tentative out-of-court settlement to the water rights suit. Representative Morris Udall then introduced the Southern Arizona Water Rights Settlement Act (SAWRSA) in Congress to guarantee the Tohono O'odham a firm entitlement to water from the Central Arizona Project and other sources. Although both houses of Congress passed the measure, President Ronald Reagan vetoed it on June 1, 1982. The president expressed concern over the total cost of the measure.[60]

After a reduction in funding, Reagan signed the Southern Arizona Water Rights Settlement Act on October 12, 1982. The settlement guaranteed the Tohono O'odham firm delivery of 66,000 annual acre-feet of water for the San Xavier and Schuk Toak districts of the reservation, to be obtained from pumping, reclaimed wastewater, and the CAP, and paid for by a cooperative fund of private and government money.[61]

The successful resolution of water rights litigation in southern Arizona encouraged tribal and municipal leaders in the Phoenix area to begin the

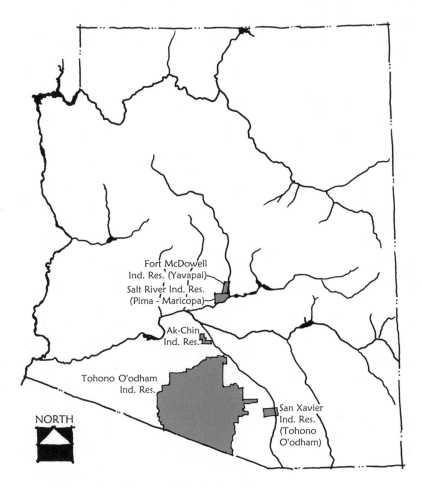

Indian reservations with water rights settlements

settlement process for the Salt and Verde Rivers. Officials pursued settlements in separate negotiations for the Salt River Pima-Maricopa Indian
Community and the Fort McDowell Indian Community. Negotiations regarding these settlements proved to be more complicated because Native
American claims included both federal reserved rights and rights to water
under state law. Both tribes had received rights to surface flows under the
terms of the Kent Decree in 1910.[62]

In addition to federal reserved rights, lands of the Salt River Indian

Community had water rights from both the 1910 Kent Decree and a 1935 agreement to construct Bartlett Dam on the Verde River, as well as from CAP allocations. Disputes over the amount of water delivered from the 1910 decree, the 1935 agreement, and Winters rights formed the basis of the tribe's complaints in several lawsuits filed in the mid-1980s. By 1987, negotiators managed to draft a preliminary agreement that contained a series of complex water exchanges, transfers, and leases.[63]

Congress approved the terms of the agreement in 1988. The tribe received a total of 122,400 af of water per year for the irrigation of 27,200 acres on the reservation. Congressional authorization paved the way for the parties to put their final signatures on the agreement in 1989. As part of the settlement, the special master assigned to Arizona's general stream adjudication reviewed its terms. The special master filed his report on October 16, 1991, approving the terms of the settlement. The superior court gave its approval on November 7, 1991, which allowed the parties to sign a stipulation dismissing the pending water rights lawsuits in favor of the negotiated settlement.[64]

Settlement of water rights claims for the Fort McDowell Indian Community passed through a series of stages very similar to that of the Salt River Pima-Maricopa. The two reservations are adjacent to each other near the confluence of the Salt and Verde Rivers, and the issues involved were similar. Fort McDowell residents claimed both federal reserved rights and state rights. The reservation received an allocation of water by the terms of the 1910 Kent Decree. Congress approved the Fort McDowell settlement in 1990.[65]

According to the terms of the 1990 settlement, residents at Fort McDowell received an entitlement to 36,350 af of water per year. The water could be used on the reservation for agriculture and a portion of the water could be leased to the City of Phoenix. The agreement ensured a minimum in-stream flow of 100 cfs (cubic feet per second) in the Verde River. The parties executed the final agreement in December of 1992. The superior court approved the Fort McDowell Indian Community Water Rights Settlement on November 3, 1993.[66]

Summary

Arizona's leaders created several new mechanisms to push the CAP to completion, including the Arizona Department of Water Resources and the Central Arizona Water Conservation District. The CAWCD gradually took on more and more responsibility for the project. With the official completion of the project in 1993, the CAWCD took on its greatest responsibility of all: paying for the project. The CAP entered the repayment phase when it made the first payment in 1994.

Once the CAP water arrived, municipal water officials faced the task of treating it and delivering it to customers. The results were a dramatic tale of two cities as Phoenix used traditional technology and approaches to treat the water while Tucson embarked on an innovative and ultimately unsuccessful method previously untried in Arizona. Hindsight is always nearly perfect, and it is clear that Tucson officials made several mistakes, including errors in public relations by alarming its residents about possible hazards from CAP water, and errors in management by not responding to the actual problems that existed.

The environmental movement was in many ways a product of the sixties, as was the struggle for civil rights by minority groups. In the eighties and nineties, Arizona's Native American tribes expressed themselves by exerting sovereignty over their land and water rights through litigation and negotiation. This process generated legal activity on many fronts at a level unmatched by any period of Arizona water history, even including the ten-year battle with California over the rights to the Colorado River. Decisions regarding Arizona's water future are now more likely to be made by judges and attorneys than by hydrologists and engineers.

Chapter 14 Planning for the Future

Reuse, Recharge, Restoration

Municipal leaders embarked on new directions for water use and development in the late twentieth century that serve as models for the future. These new directions are usually limited by the assumption that the days of large water projects are over. While new large-scale construction projects cannot be ruled out, Arizona's water future is more likely to include reuse of water that has already passed through the system, recharge of water back into the ground to replace depleted aquifers, and restoration or re-creation of water environments.

The use of effluent originating in the Phoenix area to cool reactors at the Palo Verde Nuclear Generating Station provided an early example of water reuse for others to follow. Both Phoenix and Tucson have developed recharge projects, designed at first to stop land subsidence and later as a means to store water for future use. The creation of "engineered wetlands" in both Phoenix and Tucson represented a new means of effluent treatment that originated in the last two decades.

These are just a few examples of how the development of technology and water projects has evolved through the years to address the needs and desires of a changing urban population. In the Phoenix area, the city of Tempe used CAP water to create Tempe Town Lake in the normally dry Salt River bed. This urban oasis has become an attraction for recreational users from all parts of the metropolitan region. In Tucson, the Sonoran Desert Conservation Plan under consideration by Pima County includes several riparian restoration projects. While both of these are a far cry from the once ubiquitous urban lakes associated with suburban real estate developments in the Salt River Valley, these new uses for water provide strong evidence that public perceptions and goals have a decided influence on water policy decisions. There is a growing realization today that water has multiple values.[1]

A New Fuel for Growth: Effluent

The use and sale of effluent (wastewater) is nothing new. One of the earliest methods of sewage treatment in both Phoenix and Tucson was to divert sewage flow to farmlands and use effluent for irrigation. Today, effluent has become a valuable commodity for agricultural and industrial use.

In the early 1980s developer John F. Long led a series of unsuccessful legal challenges to the ability of Phoenix to sell effluent. The Arizona Supreme Court upheld the right of municipalities to control the method of wastewater disposal in 1989. The decision confirmed the contract executed by Phoenix to sell effluent for use at the Palo Verde Nuclear Generating Station. The decision paved the way for increased use of effluent in Arizona by affirming the right of municipal governments to dispose of effluent in new and innovative ways that benefit the public good.

The effluent contract with the Arizona Nuclear Power Project (ANPP), known as Palo Verde, resulted from two seemingly unrelated events: the construction of the Ninety-first Avenue wastewater treatment plant (WWTP) and the desire for Arizona utilities to increase power production. Although effluent and electricity may appear to have nothing in common, the increased volume of effluent generated from the Ninety-first Avenue plant and the increased demand for electricity are both results of the dramatic population explosion that began in the 1960s when Phoenix emerged as a major population center. The population influx taxed sewage treatment facilities and prompted the construction and expansion of the Ninety-first Avenue WWTP. Population growth also increased the demand for electrical energy and led Arizona utilities to explore alternate power sources.

In the late 1960s, SRP, APS, and Tucson Electric Power (TEP) joined forces to construct several fossil fuel power plants. This cooperative effort formed the basis for a joint study of new sources of power. In 1970 the three energy companies funded a private research arm, the Arizona Nuclear Resource Study Group (ANRSG), and directed it to investigate the feasibility of nuclear-fueled power plants for the Southwest. In 1971, ANRSG released the results of its study recommending that the utilities pursue construction of a nuclear power plant. In 1972, El Paso Electric and the Public Service Company of New Mexico joined the project. The utilities then began a site selection study.[2]

Locations in Arizona proved difficult to find because an assured supply of water for cooling the nuclear reactors constituted the primary basis for site selection. Since groundwater sources could not supply enough water over the projected life of the facility, and since surface water streams had been appropriated for other uses, ANPP planners turned to sewage effluent as the source of supply. After examining many sites in Arizona and elsewhere, the group settled on a location called Palo Verde about fifty miles west of Phoenix where effluent might be diverted from the Ninety-first Avenue WWTP.[3]

Preliminary discussions between representatives of the city, APS, and SRP regarding the availability of effluent began in the spring of 1972. It took just over a year to complete the negotiation process. All parties executed the contract on April 23, 1973. The signed contract constituted proof of an assured water supply for federal regulatory authorities.[4]

Although the effluent question occupied the time and effort of Phoenix water officials, it represented only one small part of the many considerations necessary for construction of the Palo Verde nuclear plant. In 1973, ANPP purchased the Palo Verde site and began to conduct environmental impact studies on the property. It issued a draft report in 1974 and a final EIS in 1975. With the approval of the environmental documents, construction began in 1976. The original plans called for five reactors, making Palo Verde the largest nuclear plant in the country.[5]

The Three Mile Island nuclear plant accident in 1979 increased concerns about the safety of nuclear power. In the aftermath of the near meltdown, ANPP planners eliminated two of the reactor units at Palo Verde. Despite the reduction in size, the construction project remained a massive undertaking. Employment reached its peak in 1980 and 1981 when more

The Palo Verde nuclear plant uses effluent from the Ninety-first Avenue Wastewater Treatment Plant.

than eight thousand workers labored at the site. Workers topped out the three containment buildings in 1980, 1981, and 1983.[6]

The Atomic Safety and Licensing Board (ASLB) granted Palo Verde a license to load fuel rods in 1982. It still took several years for the three reactor units at Palo Verde to come on line: unit 1 in January of 1986, unit 2 in September of 1986, and unit 3 in January of 1988. The ANPP contract demonstrated that effluent had value. Its disposition could be managed to preserve higher quality surface and groundwater for other uses.[7]

Any nuclear project generated plenty of controversy, and Palo Verde had its share of opponents. Environmental activists and others opposed to the project had tried to derail the effluent sale during the ASLB licensing process. Although this strategy failed, opponents did not abandon their objections. The dispute then moved into the judicial arena.[8]

On November 3, 1982, Ronald Rayner and William T. Gladden, two Buckeye area farmers, filed suit against the cities and APS. They complained that they had a right to utilize the effluent discharge and that this right was prior to the ANPP contract. On December 12, 1983, valley homebuilder John F. Long filed suit in federal district court. Long challenged the contract on federal antitrust grounds. The Buckeye farmers then filed a second suit on January 23, 1984, duplicating many of the same complaints that Long had made in federal court. To complete the picture, on November 22, 1985, the City of Phoenix filed suit against Long when it asked the Maricopa County Superior Court to declare the effluent contract valid.[9]

These court cases took some time to wind through the judicial process. *City of Phoenix v. Long* reached the Arizona Supreme Court first. The court ruled on February 11, 1988, and upheld the contract provisions. Attorneys for both sides had agreed to dismiss the case in federal court on November 22, 1985, pending resolution of the effluent dispute in Maricopa County Superior Court. The court consolidated the two cases contesting the sale of effluent.[10]

The consolidated superior court cases eventually reached the Arizona Supreme Court. On April 17, 1989, the supreme court made a significant ruling that opened the way for increased use of effluent in Arizona. The state supreme court defined effluent as neither groundwater nor surface water. Based on this definition, the court held that effluent could be sold for use on lands regardless of the water's original appropriation. Not only did the court find that this was the law in Arizona, but that it was good public policy: "the cities can put its sewage effluent to any reasonable use that it sees fit. This will allow municipalities to maximize their use of appropriated water and dispose of sewage effluent in an economically feasible manner." The court went on to rule that municipalities had no obligation to continue to discharge effluent for the benefit of downstream users.[11]

The decision in *APS v. Long* permitted the delivery of effluent to Palo Verde under the terms of the ANPP contract. By giving Arizona municipalities the ability to control effluent the supreme court guaranteed greater use of the scarce resource. The court clearly understood that to limit the use of effluent would be a setback for Arizona because it "would deprive the cities of their ability to dispose of effluent in the most economically and environmentally sound manner." The court noted that this "would be contrary to the spirit and purpose of Arizona water law, which is to promote the beneficial use of water and to eliminate waste of this precious resource."[12]

Recharge Projects in Phoenix and Tucson

The continued depletion of groundwater in both Phoenix and Tucson caused land subsidence in some areas. As water is withdrawn from underground aquifers, soils can compact. If enough water is withdrawn and soil conditions are suitable, land in the area where the water was withdrawn may sink. This phenomenon is called land subsidence and it can be an expensive problem if it occurs in areas with aboveground structures such as homes and streets.

In Phoenix, the city council first began to examine the issue of land subsidence in 1978. The city contracted with Arizona State University professor Troy Pewe to conduct a study of land subsidence in east Phoenix. The cities of Scottsdale and Tempe signed separate agreements to study their communities.[13]

The identification of groundwater withdrawal as a source of environmental problems led the Phoenix City Council to explore groundwater recharge. A second interest in recharge was the possibility that Central Arizona Project water could be stored underground during times of low demand or excess supply and withdrawn at a later time. In 1983 the council executed an agreement with Cella-Barr Associates to explore the possibility of constructing recharge facilities in the Cave Creek Wash area for storage of CAP water. In 1985, Phoenix installed a monitoring well to measure the recharge phenomena.[14]

Based on the success of projects like the one in Phoenix, in 1986 the Arizona legislature adopted regulations that allowed entities to store water underground for later use. The law specified that the stored water would retain its original legal character when withdrawn and could be used in the same manner. For example, if entities recharged CAP water, it would still be considered CAP water when it was withdrawn. This was a significant distinction because the recharged water withdrawn would not constitute groundwater under the terms of the Groundwater Management Act of 1980.[15]

The Arizona legislature again stepped into the picture in 1990 when it authorized state demonstration projects for groundwater recharge. The legislation provided funding through the creation of the Arizona Water Storage Fund. The fund received revenues from a four-cent tax in Maricopa and Pima counties from 1991 to 1996.[16]

The City of Phoenix and the Cities of Chandler, Mesa, Scottsdale, and Tempe, along with the town of Gilbert, pooled their resources to plan an underground storage project. The valley municipalities leased a 350-acre parcel from the Salt River Pima-Maricopa Indian Community in the Salt River channel. The project used the SRP-CAP interconnect to divert water into the South Canal and then into a series of spreading basins that would allow the water to percolate into the ground. The municipalities executed an intergovernmental agreement authorizing the Granite Reef Underground Storage Project (GRUSP) on February 26, 1993. The initial phase of the project limited the size of the spreading basins to 130 acres.[17]

Workers completed the project in May of 1994 and placed it in operation. In addition to storing CAP allocations from municipal government, the Central Arizona Water Conservation District also stored excess CAP water in the GRUSP facility. By 1998, the project had recharged more than 300,000 acre-feet of CAP water. The valley municipalities participating in GRUSP expanded the project in 1998 to allow for additional space in the recharge basins.[18]

Recharge projects received a boost in 1996 when Governor Fife Symington and the Arizona legislature created the Arizona Water Banking Authority (AWBA). The state created this agency to store unused portions of Arizona's CAP allocations and proportionate shares of any Colorado River surplus flows. The water bank paid for the acquisition and storage cost of CAP water, which could then be redeemed when Arizona communities needed to withdraw the water. AWBA became a large user of the GRUSP facility. In 1997, it entered into an agreement to use GRUSP for five years to store a minimum of 50,000 acre-feet of water per year.[19]

The City of Tucson also undertook groundwater recharge projects associated with the CAP. With funds from the state demonstration project program authorized by the legislature in 1990, Tucson developed two recharge projects. Engineers located the first project near Marana in 1996. Called the Avra Valley Recharge Project, the demonstration project utilized eleven acres of spreading basins north of the Avra Valley Airport that could recharge up to 8,300 af per year during an initial phase. Tucson also participated in a second demonstration project. Located near the southern boundary of the Tohono O'odham San Xavier district near Pima Mine Road and Interstate 19, engineers designed the second recharge project in 1996 to address groundwater depletion in the area along the Santa Cruz River.[20]

The Pima Mine Road project south of Tucson also received AWBA support. Officials at AWBA planned to recharge 2,500 af of CAP water during the winter months at a fourteen-acre area of recharge basins at the Pima Mine Road site. AWBA also contracted to recharge water at the existing demonstration project in Marana near the Avra Valley Airport. Officials at AWBA planned two other recharge areas in the Tucson area, one in Marana near the Santa Cruz River and a second site in central Avra Valley. This fourth site in central Avra Valley would later develop into Tucson's major CAP treatment facility.[21]

The concept of using Tucson's allocation of CAP water for recharge instead of direct delivery predated the 1993 fiasco when Tucson officials terminated CAP delivery to customers. During the early 1980s hydrologists at the University of Arizona called for using Tucson's entire CAP allocation for recharge. Hydrologist C. Brent Cluff helped organize Citizens for CAP Recharge in 1986. The group pressed plans for a large-scale recharge project in the Rillito River and Cañada del Oro Wash.[22]

After Tucson voters approved the Water Consumer Protection Act in 1995, water officials found themselves precluded from direct delivery of CAP water unless it matched the quality of local groundwater. In December of 1995, in the aftermath of the vote, officials began plans for a large-scale recharge facility in central Avra Valley. Initial estimates placed the cost of the project at $61.5 million.[23]

Based on the success of the demonstration projects, Tucson Water officials moved forward with plans for the recharge project. By 1998, the cost of the project had increased to $70 million. In addition to the central Avra Valley recharge and treatment facility, Tucson spent more than $25 million since 1993 improving 225 miles of water transportation and distribution mains.[24]

After the failure of the 1999 voter initiative that would have further restricted the delivery and use of CAP water in the area, Tucson officials moved quickly to put the finishing touches on the central Avra Valley facility. During 1999 and 2000 Tucson Water delivered a blend of recharged CAP water and groundwater to four volunteer Tucson neighborhoods to evaluate any potential problems to pipes and fixtures. Residents

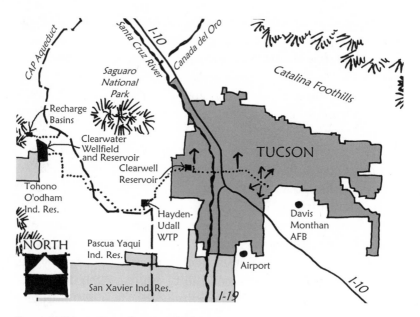

Tucson's Clearwater recharge project

reported no adverse reactions and many expressed a favorable impression of the blended water.[25]

To further restore public confidence in the project officials called it the Clearwater Renewable Resource Facility. It consisted of a series of three recharge basins with the capacity to recharge up to 5 billion gallons of CAP water each year. Engineers placed nine wells surrounding the recharge basins to recover the water, which after recharge consisted of a blend of groundwater and CAP water. Eleven miles of pipelines connected the wells to the Clearwater Reservoir, which had a capacity of 8.5 million gallons. From the reservoir, booster pumps could deliver water to Hayden-Udall WTP where it received additional treatment for ph balance. Following treatment, the blend traveled to the existing 20-million-gallon Clearwell Reservoir for connection into the city's system of distribution mains.[26]

On May 3, 2001, Tucson Mayor Bob Walkup reintroduced CAP water to Tucson customers. Although the day marked a key event in Tucson water history, officials planned for a gradual introduction of the blend into Tucson homes. The first phase called for the Clearwater project to meet approximately 15 percent of the average daily demand for water in Tucson. Officials expected the blend to make up 50 percent of daily demand by 2003.[27]

Restoration and Reconstruction

The final piece of the water puzzle for Arizona is restoration or reconstruction of natural environments. This trend is related to the reuse of treated effluent from wastewater treatment plants. In Phoenix, projects such as the Palo Verde nuclear plant already used a large amount of wastewater, as did farmers in the Buckeye Irrigation District and the Roosevelt Irrigation District downstream of the sewage treatment plant. In Tucson, reclaimed water use began in 1984 and expanded to include several customers with large areas to irrigate, such as golf courses. However, treated effluent continued to be discharged into Arizona's rivers despite increasing use.

Changes to water quality standards in 1990 threatened to completely eliminate continued discharge of treated effluent into Arizona's rivers. To meet increasingly strict proposed standards would have cost municipalities many millions of dollars in upgrades to sewage treatment plants. In the Phoenix area alone, engineers estimated that improvements to the Ninety-first Avenue WWTP to meet the proposed stringent standards would cost nearly $635 million.[28]

Given the tremendous cost associated with the proposed standards, Phoenix-area municipalities that used the Ninety-first Avenue plant began exploring alternatives to improve the condition of the effluent without having to treat it to near drinking-water quality. The valley cities received some assistance from the U.S. Army Corps of Engineers in 1992 when it proposed using constructed wetlands to provide additional treatment of effluent while incorporating added benefits of wildlife habitat and downstream flood protection. After exploring several alternatives, the Army Corps recommended construction of a wetlands project downstream of the Ninety-first Avenue WWTP near the confluence of the Salt, Gila, and Agua Fria Rivers.[29]

Based on the positive recommendations contained in the Army Corps study, the City of Phoenix worked in conjunction with other federal, state, and municipal governments to design a pilot program. The goals of the pilot program included testing the capacity of constructed wetlands to improve effluent water quality, and to assess the environmental benefits of the wetlands to plant and animal life. Completed in 1993, the study resulted in a full planning program.[30]

On May 11, 1994, the Bureau of Reclamation reached an agreement with the valley cities using the Ninety-first Avenue WWTP to jointly build the Tres Rios Constructed Wetlands Demonstration Project. The project took its name from the Spanish words for three rivers and was a reference to the rivers that came together in the vicinity of the plant (Gila, Salt, and Agua Fria). Work began on a series of constructed wetlands in 1995. The initial plan called for the construction of two separate wetlands areas. The Hayfield site, constructed in an old agricultural field, consisted of two 3-acre ponds. A second site, called the Cobble site, consisted of a single 4.3-acre pond in the bed of the Salt River. These two areas allowed the evaluation of different soil types. A second phase of the project, consisting of smaller research cells to evaluate a variety of conditions, began in 1996.[31]

The Tres Rios project proved to be a tremendous success. The constructed wetlands became home to a wide variety of plant and animal life. The water emerging from the wetlands had been "polished" or finished to a very high quality as it passed through natural systems of biological filtration. Tres Rios represented the investment of just over $8 million, with about half coming from the Bureau of Reclamation and half coming from the consortium of valley cities participating in the Ninety-first Avenue WWTP. Plans are currently under consideration to expand Tres Rios to approximately eight hundred acres of wetlands.[32]

The City of Tucson faced the same tightening of discharge standards encountered by municipalities in the Salt River Valley. In 1993, Tucson contracted with an engineering firm for a constructed wetlands to treat a portion of the water from Tucson's reclaimed wastewater facility. In September of 1994, Tucson contracted with a consortium of engineering firms to construct a larger, multi-use facility. This project included constructed wetlands, recharge, and biotic habitat.[33]

Tucson officials called the project the Sweetwater Wetlands and Recharge Facility. Planning began in the fall of 1994 and it took more than a year before the consultants delivered a final design to Tucson Water officials. The consultants devoted considerable attention to an extensive public involvement component headed by the Sweetwater Wetlands Recharge Citizens Advisory Committee. The Sweetwater project reached completion in August of 1997.[34]

As completed, the Sweetwater project consisted of two acres of settling basins, seventeen acres of wetlands ponds, and fourteen acres of recharge basins. City officials dedicated the plant on March 19, 1998. It had a design capacity to process up to 1.5 mgd of backwash water and to recharge 3,250 af of reclaimed water per year.[35]

Summary

The last few years offer a tantalizing glimpse of an exciting and innovative water future for Arizona. While it is too soon to make broad generalizations, it seems clear that Arizona residents have begun to explore new ways of using what little water they have. While no one can rule out the possibility of new water projects such as dams or aqueducts to develop additional supplies of water, it seems more likely that Arizona will reuse, reclaim, and conserve its existing water supplies. In many ways this is the second phase of the environmental movement that started in the 1960s. From the sixties to the eighties, the movement focused on protection of the environment and the prevention of additional damage. Starting in the nineties and continuing into the twenty-first century, the environmental movement is increasingly directed toward the restoration of watersheds and ecosystems. This substantial paradigm shift is likely to govern water decisions in the next century.[36]

Projects such as Tres Rios and Sweetwater will pave the way for new and innovative approaches to water utilization. Recharge of CAP water represented by the GRUSP and Clearwater projects has the potential of extending the useful life of Arizona's groundwater resources for many more years. More traditional uses of treated effluent, exemplified by the use of reclaimed wastewater for industrial or agricultural use, will continue.

Part V Conclusion

Chapter 15 A New Water Vision for Urban Arizona

The development of Arizona water utilities passed through three stages of growth. The delivery of water began as a private enterprise in the fledgling cities of the nineteenth century. At the turn of the century, reformers within and without city government campaigned for municipal ownership of the private utilities. The successful battle to control water utilities led to maturation as municipal governments improved and perfected utility service. The final stage of development came after World War II as public officials confronted tremendous population growth. Municipal leaders transformed their utilities by reaching out to tap the Colorado River through the Central Arizona Project and provide water service to the new inhabitants. Today, Arizona has embraced new techniques to meet environmental concerns associated with rapid growth.

By the end of the twentieth century, having spent many millions of dollars constructing an elaborate system of water facilities, city officials still faced their perennial problem: more people meant greater demand for more water. In this sense the Arizona experience demonstrates what political scientists Mohamed T. El-Ashry and Diana C. Gibbons have called the conservative approach of urban water agencies. Urban water managers believed that their mandate was to meet present and anticipated demand.[1]

The urban water history of Arizona suggests that several traditional viewpoints regarding water in the West are misleading. The belief that the simple aridity of the West requires new means and methods of water production is undermined by the example of humid cities like New York and Boston that also rely on distant sources of water. The traditional view that water projects are conceived, engineered, and run by a small elite isolated from the public is at odds with the experience of Tucson residents who altered Central Arizona Project delivery plans through grassroots efforts. Part of the problem is that much of what passes for gospel in water history has been generated in California, which, as Cary McWilliams has observed, is the great exception. When each of these three situations are examined from the other side of the river—the Arizona side—the western water picture is a bit different.[2]

Geography, the Environment, and Urbanism

Although Arizona's urban water systems developed in the arid West, the solutions pursued by its officials are similar to those used throughout the country. The hot dry environment of Arizona may have resulted in increased per capita water consumption, but the general approach to supplying water was the same for Tucson, Phoenix, and Flagstaff as for any other urban area in the nation. Faced with continual demands to improve the system, Arizona officials explored many possibilities to bring fresh water to municipal residents. Because the successful development of water resources was a key element that helped create an attractive lifestyle in Arizona, water is truly Arizona's fuel for growth.

But water as fuel for growth also has the capacity to limit and contain the impact of urbanization on the environment. Attorney and urban observer Grady Gammage Jr. calls water in the West "liquid glue" because it has had the effect of containing development in the small geographic area where urban planners have been able to provide water service. Although people may bemoan the high population and concentration of development in the Salt River Valley, it is contained by the availability of water. Without the liquid glue of water, people and buildings might be spread across the environment without any means of control. The national forests established in Arizona and elsewhere in the West protect valuable watersheds as a source of water for irrigation and urban use. Without the ability to concentrate use and development in a relatively small area, growth might spread into the pristine areas set aside to protect the watersheds.[3]

In the past, water provided the means to achieve an attractive and healthful environment. The relationship between the development of Arizona's water resources and its urban areas is likely to become more controversial in the future as urban residents face increasing competition over a scarce resource. Judged by the rapid growth and population influx characteristic of Arizona's urban areas, public officials and municipal leaders have been successful in creating an environment that attracts new residents to the state.

But rather than being the single most important determinant of municipal growth, the arid nature of the West had comparatively little impact on the development of modern municipal water infrastructure in Arizona. The provision of water to municipal residents is now understood as just one component of a wide array of amenities demanded by increasing numbers of inhabitants. Cities in Arizona, like their eastern counterparts, have gone about the acquisition of water supplies in response to urban demand. While cities in the West may have gone farther and deeper to secure an adequate supply, the availability of water is only one of many elements required for development in the West.

A more balanced approach places water within the context of other development forces, including railroads, mineral resources, national economic trends, and federal government policies. Water is not the single catalyst for western development. If water is just one part of a complex interplay of forces contributing to western culture, the role of aridity in determining the unique ecology of the West is also due for new thinking. The examination of aridity as the single most important characteristic of the West blurs our focus on other factors, such as the contributions of various ethnic groups. For Native Americans and Hispanics, access to technology governed their response to aridity. American settlers, with a different set of technologies, responded to the same ecological situation by reproducing farming and town communities similar to those in the humid East. In the end, it was not aridity that controlled our response to the ecology of the West, but our culture.

The Public and the Water Elite

Development elsewhere in the West is often characterized as the product of a small group of water leaders, a water elite. Yet, development of each of Arizona's urban centers reflects the broad hopes and aspirations of its inhabitants rather than the desires of a select few, revealing a new vision of water history based on the Arizona experience.

There are several examples of Arizona residents exerting pressure on political and community leaders to create water systems more to their liking. At the turn of the century, residents in Arizona's three signature communities of Tucson, Phoenix, and Flagstaff challenged entrenched private interests to wrest control of their municipal water systems. This trend was part of a broader pattern in American history, that of Progressive Era reform. While there were many reasons for the change, the goals of improving service, ending abuses, and reducing costs created the groundswell of support for municipal ownership.

Controlling its own water destiny took Flagstaff residents longer than most. While residents of the northern Arizona town established municipal service, they still had to negotiate with the private owners of the springs for access and use. Flagstaff residents persevered, gaining control of their water supply and achieving status as an incorporated city in 1926.

The most noteworthy case of local control and responsiveness occurred in Tucson, where citizens seized the initiative on more than one occasion to exert their will over a municipal utility many residents believed was unresponsive. In 1975 and 1976, Tucson residents took matters into their own hands to recall city council members that many felt were responsible for raising water rates too high, too fast. In the 1990s, Tucson residents successfully placed three citizen initiatives on the ballot to modify and control how the Tucson Water Department handled CAP water.

The entire history of the CAP is one of Arizonans reaching for and achieving their goals. Viewed from an Arizona perspective, the completion of the CAP is a triumph over California water interests that tried to block the project at every turn and continue to use more than their share of Colorado River water. Within Arizona, the shape and form of the project changed over time to meet a growing consensus that environmental issues should have greater importance. The elimination of Orme Dam and Cliff Dam from CAP plans is not evidence of a powerful water elite, but rather documentation of the power of individuals to modify water projects to meet their own goals.

The advantage of viewing water history as a product of the hopes and aspirations of many individuals is that it gives control of water projects to the people. In the past, residents of Arizona and elsewhere in the West were most interested in having adequate supplies of pure water at reasonable cost. These residents persuaded their elected leaders and public officials to construct water projects to meet those goals. Now, residents in the West recognize that water has many values. People today may be more willing to compromise on issues of cost and convenience to achieve environmental restoration and enhancement. In a sense this is a liberating view, because it allows residents of the West to control their own destiny.

The Arizona Experience

Much of our understanding of water in the West is based on the California experience. The early environmental battle over Hetch Hetchy and the schemes of Los Angeles to import water from Owens Valley and the Colorado have provided fertile ground for an entire literature of water analysis, but this focus on one state has blurred our impressions of other parts of the West. Writing from California on Arizona is colored by the decades-long battle between the two states over the Colorado River.

Like Los Angeles, Arizona's largest urban center sought and found a source of surface water to meet the water demands of its residents. Unlike the California experience, municipal officials in Phoenix worked closely with the residents of the Fort McDowell Reservation and with federal officers charged with protecting the rights of Native Americans. The result has been more cooperation than conflict.

The long and complex history of the Verde project on the Fort McDowell Indian Reservation reveals the changing relationships between American Indians, the federal government, and resource users in Phoenix. The permit and permission process pursued by Phoenix to gain approval for water use from the Verde River went through several different stages depending on the period within which the parties operated. Over the years, the Yavapai exerted greater control over decisions that affected their resources. Through this process, the Yavapai developed skills to function in the urbanizing region surrounding Phoenix. These skills were very much in evidence during the debate over the future of Orme Dam, when the Yavapai joined with others opposed to the dam and were successful in having it removed from plans for the CAP.

When the city of Phoenix first filed its notice of appropriation for a municipal water supply from the Verde River in 1915, the Yavapai at Fort McDowell were in the midst of a battle for control of their reservation. At that time, the Indian Office and the Reclamation Service advocated moving the Yavapai to allotments on the Salt River Reservation. This off-reservation administration of affairs continued to cause problems through the early decades of the twentieth century.

The dissatisfaction with officials of the Indian Office expressed by the Yavapai during the 1931 congressional hearings and similar complaints by other Native American groups resulted in the Indian Reorganization Act of 1934. At this same time, Phoenix officials moved to replace the redwood pipeline that crossed reservation land with a concrete alternative. The establishment of a community constitution under the terms of the 1934 act and the more active role of the tribal council facilitated an agreement with Phoenix regarding water resources. The 1942 agreement established a mechanism for future negotiations between Phoenix and the Yavapai for the use of water facilities on the reservation and has provided the basis for a contractual relationship for more than sixty years.

Arizona's Water Future

What makes a historical perspective on water issues valuable is that the study of where we have been gives us insight into where we are going. As we move forward into the twenty-first century Arizona needs to develop a balanced approach on future water issues. These fall into three broad categories of protecting our environment, protecting water quality, and protecting our water supply.

Protecting the Environment

One of the most exciting developments in the past twenty years is the growth of environmental restoration and water recharge programs. During the next few years, programs such as Rio Salado, Tres Rios, and restoration of riparian habitats on the Santa Cruz and San Pedro will become even more significant. Organizations such as the Nature Conservancy are increasingly active in purchasing and retiring farmland to reduce impacts on water supplies. Native American tribes have expressed interest in using portions of their CAP allotments to restore riparian habitats along the Gila and Santa Cruz rivers.[4]

The goal of protecting endangered species within the environment will have a substantial impact on water production and distribution in the future. Significant lawsuits have been filed regarding the protection of endangered species at Roosevelt Dam and the Colorado River delta. Other lawsuits concern the impact of Arizona water laws and diversions on many of the state's watersheds, including those of the Verde, Salt, and Gila Rivers. These lawsuits have the potential to stop diversions from rivers that might affect endangered species, and could have tremendous consequences for Arizona water users by classifying dams, canals, and water control features as impediments to the survival of native species. It will require careful compromise and negotiation to protect Arizona's investment in its water infrastructure while achieving environmental goals.[5]

Protecting Water Quality

The issue of water quality has not received much attention, but the quality issue will take on added significance in the next few years. In particular, revised water quality standards for arsenic may significantly raise treatment costs. Poor groundwater quality could limit production at municipal wells in the near future.

The presence of arsenic in Arizona groundwater is of particular concern in Tucson, where an estimated sixty-two wells may have arsenic contamination. The Environmental Protection Agency (EPA) is considering changing the allowable levels of arsenic in drinking water. Arsenic, a naturally occurring mineral in many parts of the West, has been permitted in drinking water since the 1970s at fifty parts per billion. Proposed EPA regulations anticipate reducing this to five parts per billion. Treating water to reduce arsenic to this level would cost Tucson an estimated $75 million.[6]

In the Salt River Valley, meeting the proposed EPA standard does not present a substantial challenge because there is less of the mineral present in groundwater. However, even if the standard were raised to ten parts per billion it would still cost the city of Phoenix from $1 to 2 million for the needed filters. Outside the major metropolitan area, many small private water companies may have considerable difficulty achieving the standard while continuing to provide water at a reasonable cost.[7]

Protecting Water Supplies

While Arizona is in the enviable position of having an adequate supply of water for the short-term future thanks to the CAP, municipal officials need to remain vigilant to protect water supplies. Specific issues to be addressed during the next few years include competition over surface water supplies between municipal users, and finalizing methods to ensure the use of Arizona's full CAP allocation.

The most pressing issue facing Phoenix during the next two decades is finding additional supplies of water for off-project areas, expected to be needed by 2017. Phoenix will need to finish work on additional CAP water allocations and reallocations, implement a lease of CAP water based on a proposed settlement with the Gila River Indian Community, and continue to make water conservation a priority.[8]

Competition between municipal providers has been almost nonexistent in Arizona. Most competition over water supplies has been between different sectors of the economy, such as agriculture and urban use. In the future, as Arizona's rural areas attract more permanent residents, water use in those areas could place significant demands on existing supplies. Plans by Prescott, Prescott Valley, and Chino Valley to develop additional water supplies from the Big Chino Valley through increased pumping of groundwater has the potential to deplete aquifers supporting the Verde River. Since many Salt River Valley municipalities depend on water from the Verde, as supplied from the Salt River Project, additional upstream development could result in competition between urban communities over a finite supply.[9]

Competition between municipalities is a potential problem as the gap between urban "haves" and "have nots" threatens to grow larger. Communities such as Flagstaff that have invested the time and money to develop an adequate water infrastructure may feel pressure from smaller urban and rural communities that did not have the ability or foresight to meet their own needs. In the dry summer of 2000, the city of Williams approached Flagstaff with a request for water-sharing on a temporary basis. Other smaller communities may approach the legislature for a type of municipal "cost sharing" to develop water resources in portions of the state where small private and municipal water systems are challenged by increased growth.[10]

Paradoxically, the problem for Tucson is achieving better utilization of its CAP allocation. Part of the challenge for Tucson will be recognizing the environmental cost associated with continued groundwater depletion and achieving a balance with the economic cost of delivering CAP water. While CAP water may cost more, increasing its use has the potential to reduce reliance on a precious resource. Reducing groundwater pumping will help alleviate problems with subsidence and poor groundwater quality, and preserve a backup supply of underground water for future generations.[11]

Achieving more efficient use of CAP water will include working with mines to ensure that industry makes better use of Colorado River surface water rather than depleting groundwater. ASARCO has taken steps to experiment on a trial basis with CAP water for its mine south of Tucson. Communities in the Tucson area that did not receive CAP allocations, such as Marana and Oro Valley, could be allowed to use the resource through agreements with Tucson. Because Marana and Oro Valley were not water providers at the time of the original CAP allocations in 1982, those communities were not included in the allocations. Providing CAP water to these communities now may reduce their reliance on pumped groundwater.[12]

Flagstaff constructed its own water system in 1898, Tucson celebrated its centennial of municipal service in 2000, and in 2007 Phoenix will mark a century of municipal water delivery. The history of urban water service in Arizona is the story of achievement, dedication, and attentiveness to the desires of Arizona's residents. Municipal officials have met and surpassed many significant challenges and obstacles in the past century. In the next, Arizona must address changes and improvements in water service that will continue to make the state an attractive place to live.

Notes

Preface

1. Donald Worster, *Rivers of Empire: Water, Aridity, and the Growth of the American West* (New York: Pantheon Books, 1986); and Marc Reisner, *Cadillac Desert: The American West and its Disappearing Water* (New York: Viking, 1986).

2. Norris Hundley Jr., *The Great Thirst: Californians and Water, 1770s–1990s* (Berkeley: University of California Press, 1992).

3. John Wesley Powell, *Report on the Lands of the Arid Regions of the United States* (Washington: U.S. Government Printing Office, 1878); and Walter Prescott Webb, *The Great Plains* (Boston: Ginn and Company, 1931).

4. Worster, *Rivers of Empire*, pp. 261–266.

5. For a contemporary view of Turner's frontier thesis, see William F. Deverell, "Fighting Words: The Significance of the American West in the History of the United States," in *A New Significance: Re-Envisioning the History of the American West*, edited by Clyde A. Milner II (New York: Oxford University Press, 1996), p. 30.

6. Elliot Coues, ed., *The Explorations of Zebulon Montgomery Pike* (New York, 1895), vol. II, p. 525; B. C. Buffum, *Arid Agriculture* (n.p.: privately printed, 1909), p. 12; and Henry Nash Smith, *Virgin Land: The American West as Symbol and Myth* (Cambridge: Harvard University Press, 1975), p. 179.

7. Powell, *Report*, pp. 77–80. For a recent analysis of the report, see Donald Worster, *A River Running West: The Life of John Wesley Powell* (New York: Oxford University Press, 2001), pp. 354–360.

8. Webb, *The Great Plains*, pp. 385–387 and 510–512. See also W. Eugene Hollon, "Walter Prescott Webb's Arid West: Four Decades Later," in *Essays on Walter Prescott Webb*, Kenneth R. Philp and Elliot West, ed., (Austin: University of Texas Press, 1976), pp. 54–55.

9. Norman Smith, *Man and Water: A History of Hydro-Technology* (London: Peter Davies, 1976), p. 73.

10. Worster, *Rivers of Empire*, pp. 40–45.

11. Robert Gottlieb, *A Life of its Own: The Politics of Water and Power* (San Diego: Harcourt, Brace, Jovanavich, 1988), p. 123.

12. For a description of writers in the urban infrastructure school, see Douglas E. Kupel, "Investigating Urban Infrastructure," *Journal of Urban History* 27:4 (May, 2001): 520–525. See also Joel A. Tarr, *The Search for the Ultimate Sink: Urban Pollution in Historical Perspective* (Akron, Ohio: University of Akron Press, 1996) and Martin V. Melosi, *The Sanitary City: Urban Infrastructure in America from Colonial Times to the Present* (Baltimore: Johns Hopkins, 2000).

13. Donald Worster, "Transformations of the Earth: Toward an Agroecological Perspective in History," *Journal of American History* 76 (March, 1990): 1,087–1,106.

14. Christine Meisner Rosen and Joel Arthur Tarr, "The Importance of an Urban Perspective in Environmental History," *Journal of Urban History* 20:3 (May, 1994): 299–310.

15. Gottlieb, *A Life of its Own*, p. 123.

16. Norris Hundley Jr., "Water and the West in Historical Imagination," *Western Historical Quarterly* 27 (Spring, 1996): 22; John Walton, *Western Times and Water Wars: State, Culture, and Rebellion in California* (Berkeley: University of California Press, 1992), p. 297; Kazuto Oshio, "Urban Water Diplomacy: A Policy History of the Metropolitan Water Supply in Twentieth Century Southern California" (Ph.D. diss., University of California, Santa Barbara, 1992), p. 5.

17. Ray H. Taylor, *Hetch Hetchy: The Story of San Francisco's Struggle to Provide a Water Supply for Her Future Needs* (San Francisco: R. J. Orozco, 1926); M. M. O'Shaughnessy, *Hetch Hetchy: Its Origin and History* (San Francisco: Recorder Printing and Publishing, 1934); Robert Sterling Yard, "The Unforgotten Story of Hetch Hetchy," *American Forests* 40 (December, 1934): 566–69; Suzette Dornberger, "The Struggle for Hetch Hetchy, 1900–1913," (master's thesis, University of California Berkeley, 1935); Richard Lowitt, "The Hetch Hetchy Controversy, Phase II: The 1913 Senate Debate," *California History* 74 (Summer, 1995): 190–203.

18. William L. Kahrl, *Water and Power: The Conflict Over Los Angeles' Water Supply in the Owens Valley* (Berkeley: University of California Press, 1982); Abraham Hoffman, *Vision or Villainy: Origins of the Owens Valley–Los Angeles Water Controversy* (College Station: Texas A&M Press, 1981).

19. Gordon R. Miller, "Los Angeles and the Owens River Aqueduct," (Ph.D. diss., Claremont Graduate School, 1977), pp. 227–260.

20. Fisher Sanford Harris, *100 Years of Water Development* (Salt Lake City: Metropolitan Water District of Salt Lake City, 1942); Mary McWilliams and Roy Morse,

Seattle Water Department History, 1854-1954 (Seattle: City of Seattle, 1955); Roy P. Wilson, "Cooperation and Conflict in a Federal-Municipal Watershed: A Case Study of Portland, Oregon" (Ph.D. diss., Oregon State University, 1989); Douglas E. Kupel, "Urban Water in the Arid West: Municipal Water and Sewer Utilities in Phoenix, Arizona" (Ph.D. diss., Arizona State University, 1995).

Chapter 1. Physical Patterns on the Land

1. In the year 2000, groundwater supplied less than 4 percent of the water supplied to Phoenix customers. City of Phoenix, *2000 Water Quality Annual Report* (Phoenix: City of Phoenix, 2001), p. 1.

2. The best map reference on Arizona history is Henry P. Walker and Don Bufkin, *Historical Atlas of Arizona* (Norman: University of Oklahoma Press, 1979). See also Melvin Hecht and Richard Reeve, *The Arizona Atlas* (Tucson: University of Arizona Office of Arid Lands Studies, 1981).

3. A good summary of the basin and range province, as well as Arizona's other physiographic provinces, is found in Tom Miller, *Arizona: The Land and the People* (Tucson: University of Arizona Press, 1986).

4. George E. P. Smith, "The Physiography of Arizona Valleys and the Occurrence of Ground Water," *University of Arizona Agricultural Experiment Station Technical Bulletin* no. 77 (Tucson: University of Arizona, 1938), p. 51.

5. For a description of the Sonoran Desert region, see Roger Dunbier, *The Sonoran Desert: Its Geography, Economy, and People* (Tucson: University of Arizona Press, 1968).

6. William D. Sellers and Richard H. Hill, ed., *Arizona Climate: 1931-1972* (Tucson: University of Arizona Press, 1974), pp. 112-115. The best summary of Arizona's rivers is found in Barbara Tellman, Richard Yarde, and Mary G. Wallace, *Arizona's Changing Rivers: How People have Affected the Rivers* (Tucson: University of Arizona Water Resources Research Center, 1997). To place Arizona's rivers in a broader perspective, see Tim Palmer, *America by Rivers* (Washington, D.C.: Island Press, 1996).

7. H. M. Babcock and E. M. Cushing, "Recharge to Groundwater From Floods in a Typical Desert Wash, Pinal County, Arizona," *Transactions of the American Geophysical Union* XXII, part 1 (1942), p. 56.

8. Sellers and Hill, *Arizona Climate*, p. 82.

9. I. H. Parkman, "Hassayampa Dam Disaster," *Desert* 18:11 (November, 1955): 11-12, and David B. Dill Jr., "Terror on the Hassayampa: The Walnut Grove Dam Disaster of 1890," *Journal of Arizona History* 28:3 (Autumn, 1987): 283-306.

Chapter 2. Prehistoric, Spanish, and Mexican Antecedents

1. The Arizona State Historic Preservation Office (SHPO) has sponsored two historic context studies of prehistoric agriculture. See Alan Dart, *Prehistoric Irrigation in Arizona: A Context for Canals and Related Cultural Resources* (Tucson: Center for Desert Archaeology, 1989) and David E. Doyel, *Prehistoric Non-Irrigated Agriculture in Arizona:*

A Historic Context for Planning (Phoenix: Estrella Cultural Research, 1993). The context for irrigated agriculture is in the process of being updated.

2. Dart, *Prehistoric Irrigation*, p. 3.

3. For a brief summary of the work at San Agustín, see Jonathan B. Mabry, "Three Thousand Years of Irrigation in a Riverine Oasis," *Archaeology Southwest* 15: 2 (Spring, 2001): 14–15; for the archaic to agricultural transition, see Barbara Roth and Kevin Wellman, "New Insights into the Early Agricultural Period in the Tucson Basin: Excavations at the Valley Farms Site (AZ AA:12:736)," *Kiva* 67: 1 (Fall, 2001): 75.

4. Emil Haury, *The Hohokam, Desert Farmers and Craftsmen: Excavations at Snaketown, 1964–1965* (Tucson: University of Arizona Press, 1976), p. 5, and Linda M. Nicholas, "Irrigation and Sociopolitical Development in the Salt River Valley, Arizona: An Examination of Three Prehistoric Canal Systems" (master's thesis, Arizona State University, 1981).

5. Harry J. Karns, *Luz de Tierra Incognita: Unknown Arizona and Sonora 1693–1721* (Tucson: Arizona Silhouettes, 1954) p. 287; Frank Midvale, "Prehistoric Irrigation in the Salt River Valley," *Kiva*, 34:1 (October, 1968): 28; O. A. Turney, "Prehistoric Irrigation," *Arizona Historical Review*, 2:1 (April, 1929): 40; Gay M. Kinkade and Gordon Fritz, "The Tucson Sewage Project: Studies at Two Archaeological Sites in the Tucson Basin," *Arizona State Museum Archaeological Series* 64 (1975); and Suzanne K. Fish, Paul R. Fish, and John H. Madsen, "A Preliminary Analysis of Hohokam Settlement and Agriculture in the Northern Tucson Basin," in *Proceedings of the 1983 Hohokam Symposium, Part 1*, ed. Alfred E. Dittart Jr. and Donald E. Dove (Phoenix: Arizona Archaeological Society, 1985).

6. Anne Woosley, "Agricultural Diversity in the Prehistoric Southwest," *Kiva*, 45:4 (Summer, 1980): 322; Emil Haury, "Snaketown: 1964–1965," *Kiva*, 31:1 (October, 1965): 8; and Michael F. Logan, "Head-Cuts and Check-Dams: Changing Patterns of Environmental Manipulation by the Hohokam and Spanish in the Santa Cruz River Valley, 200–1820," *Environmental History* 4 (July, 1999): 405–430.

7. David E. Doyle, "Rillito and Rincon Period Settlements in the Middle Santa Cruz River Valley: Alternative Models," *Kiva* 43 (Winter, 1977): 103; W. Bruce Masse, "An Intensive Survey of Prehistoric Dry Farming Systems near Tumamoc Hill in Tucson," *Kiva* 45:1–2 (Fall-Winter, 1979): 142; and Fish, Fish, and Madsen, "Preliminary Analysis," p. 79.

8. Doyle, *Prehistoric Non-Irrigated Agriculture*, p. 9. For a description of ak chin agriculture, see Edward F. Castetter and Willis H. Bell, *Pima and Papago Indian Agriculture* (Albuquerque: University of New Mexico Press, 1942), pp. 168–170. For a more impressionistic view, see Gary Paul Nabhan, *The Desert Smells Like Rain: A Naturalist in Papago Indian Country* (San Francisco; North Point Press, 1982).

9. Doyle, *Prehistoric Non-Irrigated Agriculture*, p. 10.

10. R. Gwinn Vivian, "Chacoan Water Management," in *Anasazi Regional Organization and the Chaco System*, ed. by David E. Doyle (Albuquerque: Maxwell Museum, 1992), pp. 45–57.

11. T. Lindsay Baker and Steven R. Rae, *Water for the Southwest: Historical Survey and Guide to Historic Sites* (New York: American Society of Civil Engineers Historical Publications, 1973), p. 7.

12. David R. Wilcox, "Warfare Implications of Dry-Laid Masonry Walls on Tumamoc Hill," *Kiva* 45:1–2 (Fall-Winter, 1979): 33; Paul Grebinger and David P. Adam, "Hard Times? Classic Period Hohokam Cultural Development in the Tucson Basin," *World Archaeology* 6 (1974): 226–241.

13. For a discussion of the possible relationship between the decline of both the Anasazi and Hohokam cultures, see Patricia L. Crown and W. James Judge, "Synthesis and Conclusions," in *Chaco and Hohokam Prehistoric Regional Systems in the American Southwest*, ed. Patricia L. Crown and W. James Judge (Santa Fe: School of American Research Press, 1991), pp. 303–305. For a discussion of possible reasons for the decline in the most recent prehistoric period in the Four Corners area, see Timothy A. Kohler, "The Final 400 Years of Prehispanic Agricultural Society in the Mesa Verde Region," *Kiva* 66:1 (Fall, 2000): 191–204.

14. Ernest J. Burrus, *Kino and Manje, Explorers of Sonora and Arizona: Their Vision of the Future* (St. Louis: Jesuit Historical Institute, 1971), p. 246; and Herbert Eugene Bolton, *Kino's Historical Memoir of Pimeria Alta* (Cleveland: Arthur H. Clark, 1919), p. 205.

15. Herbert Eugene Bolton, *Rim of Christendom* (New York: MacMillan and Company, 1936), p. 376, 503.

16. Annetta L. Cheek, "The Evidence for Acculturation in Artifacts: Indians and Non-Indians at San Xavier del Bac, Arizona," (Ph.D. diss., University of Arizona, 1977), p. 42; Michael C. Meyer, *Water in the Hispanic Southwest, A Social and Legal History, 1550–1850* (Tucson: University of Arizona Press, 1984), p. 55; and Guyneth H. Xavier, *The Cattle Industry of the Southern Papago Districts* (New York: Garland Publications, 1974), p. 1.

17. Betty Eakle Dobkins, *The Spanish Element in Texas Water Law* (Austin: University of Texas Press, 1959), p. 83.

18. Tellman et al., *Arizona's Changing Rivers*, p. 18.

19. William E. Colby, "The Freedom of the Miner and Its Influence on Water Law," in *Legal Essays in Tribute to Orrin Kip McMurray*, ed. Max Radin (Berkeley: University of California Press, 1935), p. 80.

20. Peter L. Reich, "The 'Hispanic' Roots of Prior Appropriation in Arizona," *Arizona State Law Journal* 27:2 (Summer, 1995): 650.

21. H. H. Bancroft, *History of Arizona and New Mexico, 1530–1888* (San Francisco: The History Company, 1889), p. 594.

22. Bernice Cosulich, *Tucson* (Tucson: Arizona Silhouettes, 1953), p. 95; and Meyer, *Water in the Hispanic Southwest*, p. 57.

23. Wallace W. Elliot, *History of Arizona Territory* (1884; reprint ed., Flagstaff: Northland Press, 1964), p. 255.

24. Logan, "Head-Cuts and Check-Dams," pp. 421–422.

25. Richard J. Morrisey, "The Early Range Cattle Industry in Arizona," *Agricultural History* 24:3 (July, 1950): 151.

26. For examples of the conflicts between the Apache and Mexican settlers, see Angie Debo, *Geronimo* (Norman: University of Oklahoma Press, 1976), pp. 35–36.

27. R. H. Forbes, "History of Irrigation Development in Arizona," *Reclamation Era* 26 (October, 1936): 226.

Chapter 3. First Impressions

1. The best source for the early history of water in the Territory of New Mexico, which included Arizona until 1863, is Ira G. Clark, *Water in New Mexico: A History of its Management and Use* (Albuquerque: University of New Mexico Press, 1987). For the Kearney Code see p. 24.

2. Clark, *Water in New Mexico*, pp. 24–25.

3. Henry W. Bigler, "Extracts from the Journal of Henry W. Bigler," *Utah Historical Quarterly* 5 (April, 1932): 49; and Philip St. George Cooke, *The Conquest of New Mexico and California, An Historical and Personal Narrative* (Albuquerque: Horn and Wallace, 1964), p. 158.

4. John E. Durviage, "Through Mexico to California: Letters and Journal of John E. Durviage," in *Southwestern Historical Series*, ed. Ralph P. Bieber, vol. V, *Southern Trails to California* (Glendale, California: Arthur H. Clark, 1937), pp. 210–211.

5. Durviage, "Through Mexico to California," p. 211; L. D. Aldrich, *A Journal of the Overland Route to California and the Gold Mines* (Los Angeles: Dawson's Book Shop, 1950), pp. 49–50; Robert Eccleston, *Overland to California on the Southwestern Trail: 1849* (Berkeley: University of California Press, 1950), p. 202; and Benjamin Hayes, "Diary of Judge Benjamin Hayes," (Arizona Historical Society, 1850), p. 39.

6. A good summary of territorial era water use in New Mexico is John O. Baxter, *Dividing New Mexico's Waters, 1700–1912* (Albuquerque: University of New Mexico Press, 1997). For the Organic Act, see p. 65.

7. William H. Lyon, "The Corporate Frontier in Arizona," *Journal of Arizona History* 9:1 (Spring, 1968): 12; and Forbes, "History of Irrigation," p. 226.

8. W. H. Emory, *Notes of a Military Reconnaissance from Fort Leavenworth, in Missouri, to San Diego, in California, Including Part of the Arkansas, Del Norte, and Gila Rivers* (Washington: Wendell and Van Benthuysen, Printers, 1848), p. 95; and W. Clement Eaton, "Frontier Life in Southern Arizona, 1858–1861," *Southwestern Historical Quarterly* 36 (January, 1933): 179.

9. Phocion R. Way, "Overland Via Jackass Mail in 1858: The Diary of Phocion R. Way," ed. and annotated by William A. Duffen, *Arizona and the West* 2 (Summer, 1960): 159–160; and Hilario Gallego, "Reminiscences of an Arizona Pioneer," *Arizona Historical Review* 6:1 (January, 1935): 78.

10. U.S. Department of War, "Letter of Secretary of War Communicating Copy of Report of Major D. Ferguson on the Country, Its Resources and the Route between Tucson

and Lobos Bay," 37th Congress Special Session, *Senate Ex. Doc. no. 1*, (Washington: U.S. Government Printing Office, 1863), p. 14; and Richard J. Hinton, *The Handbook of Arizona: Its Resources, History, Towns, Mines, Ruins, and Scenery* (San Francisco: Payot, Upham and Company, 1878; reprint ed., Tucson: Arizona Silhouettes, 1954), p. 286.

11. Territory of Arizona, *Acts, Resolutions, and Memorials* (Prescott: First Legislative Assembly, 1864), pp. 25–28.

12. John Gregory Bourke, *On the Border With Crook* (New York: Charles Scribner's Sons, 1891), p. 63; and Michael James Box, *Capt. James Box's Adventures and Explorations in New and Old Mexico* (New York: J. Miller, 1869), pp. 325–326.

13. Bourke, *On The Border*, pp. 63, 75–76.

14. Bell, "Log," p. 47; Anson P. K. Safford, *The Territory of Arizona, A Brief History and Summary* (Tucson: Arizona Citizen, 1874), p. 15; and Thomas H. Peterson, "A Tour of Tucson—1874," *Journal of Arizona History* 11:3 (Autumn, 1970): 13.

15. Solomon Warner, "Personal Notes and Papers," (Arizona Historical Society); and C. C. Wheeler, "History and Facts Concerning Warner and Silver Lake and the Santa Cruz River," (Arizona Historical Society).

16. Safford, *Territory of Arizona*, p. 15.

17. *Tucson Citizen* (Tucson newspaper, hereafter *Citizen*), May 2, 1879; and Hinton, *Handbook of Arizona*, p. 267.

18. Bourke, *On the Border*, p. 63; and Bell, "Log," p. 48.

19. *Citizen*, July 21, 1952; and Cosulich, *Tucson*, p. 96.

20. *Arizona Weekly Star* (Tucson newspaper; later known as the *Arizona Daily Star*; hereafter *Star*), May 1, 1879; May 8, 1979; May 17, 1879; May 18, 1879; June 28, 1879; June 29, 1879; March 24, 1881; City of Tucson Mayor and Council *Minutes* (hereafter Tucson *Minutes*), March 31, 1879, and April 11, 1879.

21. John T. Ganoe, "The Beginnings of Irrigation in the United States," *Mississippi Valley Historical Review* 25:1 (June, 1938): 69; and Salt River Project, *The Taming of the Salt* (Phoenix: Salt River Project, 1979), pp. 11–15.

22. *Phoenix Herald*, (Phoenix newspaper, hereafter *Herald*) May 4, 1878. For a description of early irrigation efforts in Phoenix, see Earl Zarbin, *The Swilling Legacy* (Phoenix: Salt River Project, 1978), pp. 11–12. Swilling recorded his filing in Prescott because it was the county seat for that portion of the Salt River Valley. Maricopa County was created in 1871 from portions of Yavapai County. A miner's inch is a measurement of flowing water, and in Arizona equals 0.025 cubic feet per second (cfs). This earlier unit of measurement was not a fixed and definite quantity, and varied from place to place. The flow was measured by passing water under six inches of head through a one-inch square opening.

23. *Arizona Miner* (Prescott newspaper), September 3, 1870; March 2, 1872; April 27, 1872; November 23, 1872.

24. *Arizona Miner*, August 27, 1870, and August 31, 1872.

25. *Herald*, January 26, 1878; September 28, 1878; October 17, 1879; and October 27, 1879.

26. *Republic*, October 2, 1937, and July 29, 1940; *Republican*, September 1, 1890. The *Republican* newspaper changed its name to the *Arizona Republic* on November 11, 1930; references to this newspaper after that date are cited as *Republic*.

27. *Herald*, June 29, 1878, and June 28, 1879.

28. *Herald*, September 25, 1880, and October 12, 1880; *Territorial Expositor*, (Phoenix newspaper, hereafter *Expositor*) October 22, 1880.

Chapter 4. Water Entrepreneurs

1. Charles Sargent, *Metro Arizona* (Scottsdale: Buffington Books, 1988), 6 and 46. For the Phoenix/El Paso rivalry, see Bradford Luckingham, *The Urban Southwest: A Profile History of Albuquerque, El Paso, Phoenix, and Tucson* (El Paso: Texas Western Press, 1982).

2. C.M.K. Paulison, *Arizona the Wonderful Country* (Tucson, Arizona Star, 1881), p. 29; and *Star*, June 5, 1884.

3. Teresa Turner, *The People of Fort Lowell* (Tucson: Fort Lowell Historic District Board, 1982), p. 10.

4. John M. Weaver, "The History of Fort Lowell," (master's thesis, University of Arizona, Tucson, 1947), pp. 94–95, 101.

5. Linda M. Gregonis and Lisa W. Huckell, "The Tucson Urban Study," *Cultural Resource Management Section Archaeological Series* no. 138 (Tucson: Arizona State Museum, 1980): 60.

6. *Citizen*, December 27, 1884; and *Arizona Mining Index* (Tucson newspaper), August 7, 1886.

7. Warner, "Personal Notes," and *Citizen*, November 17, 1883.

8. Paulison, *Arizona The Wonderful*, p. 15; Patrick Hamilton, *Arizona, For Homes, For Health, For Investments*, (Phoenix, n.p., 1886), p. 36; and *Arizona Mining Index*, February 13, 1886.

9. Charles Rivers Drake, "Transcript of Court Proceedings in the Trial of *Dalton et al. v. Carrillo et al.*," manuscript, Arizona Historical Society, Tucson, 1885, pp. 3, 7–9.

10. S. C. Martin and R. M. Turner, "Vegetation Change in the Sonoran Desert Region, Arizona and Sonora," *Journal of the Arizona Academy of Science* 12:2 (June, 1977): 68; and Luna B. Leopold, "Vegetation of Southwestern Watersheds in the Nineteenth Century," *Geographical Review* 41:2 (1951): 296.

11. *Star*, March 3, 1881; March 24, 1881, and August 11, 1881.

12. Tucson *Minutes*, December 15, 1881.

13. Ibid., April 11, 1882, and April 13, 1882.

14. *Star*, September 24, 1882; and Harold W. Yost and Leigh O. Gardiner, "City of Tucson, Arizona; Report on Water Systems Investigations," (Tucson Water Department, 1948), pp. 2–3.

15. *Star*, October 26, 1882; February 5, 1885; January 15, 1888.

16. Lloyd Vernon Briggs, *Arizona and New Mexico, 1882, California 1886, Mexico 1891* (Boston, n.p., 1932), p. 21; and *Star*, April 2, 1885.

17. Yost and Gardiner, "City of Tucson," p. 2.

18. Tellman, et al., *Arizona's Changing Rivers*, p. 21.

19. *Star*, August 26, 1891.

20. *Star*, August 8, 1892; January 9, 1893; February 15, 1893.

21. *Ibid.*, February 17, 1893.

22. *Ibid.*, February 17, 1893; March 21, 1893; March 31, 1893; June 11, 1893; June 13, 1895.

23. *Star*, May 5, 1898; Lynn D. Baker, "Standpipe, 4th Avenue and 18th Street," in *Tucson Water History: A Reference Book*, ed. Lynn D. Baker (Tucson: Tucson Water Department, 2000), vol. I, 13-8 to 13-9. The mayor and council of Tucson ordered the removal of the standpipe on October 28, 1927; see Tucson *Minutes*, October 28, 1927.

24. Manuella S. Yeatts, "A River is Born," *Arizona Quarterly* 5:3 (Autumn, 1949): 256.

25. *Arizona Gazette* (Phoenix newspaper, hereafter *Gazette*), June 16, 1881.

26. *Gazette*, December 15, 1881; *Herald*, March 10, 1882.

27. *Herald*, May 20, 1880; August 17, 1881; June 19, 1884; May 28, 1885.

28. *Gazette*, April 22, 1884; *Herald*, September 22, 1884; June 22, 1885. For a discussion of W. J. Murphy and the construction of the Arizona Canal, see Merwin Murphy, *W. J. and the Valley* (Alhambra, California: Merwin Murphy, 1975).

29. *Herald*, April 28, 1886; Thomas G. Alexander, *A Clash of Interests: Interior Department and Mountain West, 1863–96* (Provo: Brigham Young University Press, 1977), pp. 75–76, 24 Stat. 470.

30. *Gazette*, July 28, 1886; *Herald*, September 2, 1886.

31. *Herald*, March 8, 1884; December 17, 1886; January 5, 1887; *Gazette*, December 14, 1886; Chapman Publishing Co. *Portrait and Biographical Record of Arizona* (Chicago: Chapman Publishing Co., 1901), pp. 353–354.

32. *Herald*, April 15, 1887; April 18, 1887; *Gazette*, April 17, 1887; April 20, 1887; Ordinance 58, April 16, 1887, on file with the Phoenix City Clerk Department.

33. *Gazette*, July 3, 1887; *Herald*, August 19, 1887.

34. *Herald*, August 16, 1887; September 12, 1887; September 29, 1887.

35. *Minutes*, Book 1, p. 423 (November 7, 1887) and p. 425 (November 9, 1887); *Gazette*, November 8, 1887; November 10, 1887; November 15, 1887; November 23, 1887; December 1, 1887; *Herald*, November 8, 1887; November 10, 1887; December 5, 1887.

36. Maricopa County Book 21 of Deeds, pp. 238–239; Maricopa County Book 6 of Mortgages, p. 27.

37. *Minutes*, Book 2, p. 72 (April 9, 1889); *Herald*, April 3, 1889.

38. *Herald*, April 19, 1889.

39. *Herald*, April 24, 1889.

40. *Herald*, June 26, 1889; June 28, 1889; June 27, 1889; *Gazette*, June 27, 1889.

41. *Herald*, June 27, 1889.

42. *Minutes*, Book 2, p. 100 (July 1, 1889); *Gazette*, June 29, 1889; *Herald*, July 2, 1889; July 12, 1889; August 5, 1889.

43. *Herald*, March 23, 1888; February 9, 1889; *Gazette*, November 13, 1887.

44. *Herald*, December 10, 1889.

45. Maricopa County Book 17 of Deeds, pp. 601–603; Maricopa County Book 6 of Mortgages, pp. 515–530; *Gazette*, June 1, 1890; *Herald*, June 20, 1890.

46. *Herald*, May 8, 1891; May 24, 1892; July 18, 1892; August 26, 1895.

47. *Herald*, June 24, 1896; Lawrence J. Fleming, *Ride a Mile and Smile the While: A History of the Phoenix Street Railway, 1887–1948* (Phoenix: Arizona Historical Society, 1978), p. 11.

48. Maricopa County Book 28 of Mortgages, pp. 91–110; San Francisco *Call*, November 11, 1898.

49. Platt Cline, *They Came to the Mountain: The Story of Flagstaff's Beginnings* (Flagstaff: Northland Press, 1976), pp. 66–68.

50. For a discussion of railroad land acquisition, see Thomas E. Sheridan, *Arizona: A History* (Tucson: University of Arizona Press, 1995), pp. 134–136.

51. Ryden Architects, *An Historic Building Analysis of the Santa Fe Freight Depot, Flagstaff, Arizona* (Phoenix: Ryden Architects, 1995), pp. 11–12.

52. Cline, *They Came to the Mountain*, p. 127.

53. Ibid., p. 237.

54. Ibid., p. 243.

55. F. H. Newell, "Irrigation Developments in the United States," *Engineering Record* 64:25 (December 16, 1911): 712; and Arizona Water Commission, *Inventory of Resources and Uses, Phase 1, Arizona State Water Plan* (Phoenix: Arizona Water Commission, 1975), p. 63.

Chapter 5. The Drive for Municipal Ownership

1. *Minutes*, Book 3, p. 436 (March 7, 1898): 30 Stat. 252; *Herald*, March 5, 1898.

2. Charles Waldo Haskins and Joseph French Johnson, "The Recent History of Municipal Ownership in the United States," *Municipal Affairs* 4 (1902): 524–528; William R. Hill, "City Ownership of Water Supply," *Municipal Affairs* 4 (1902): 730–737. For an examination of the relationship between the progressive movement and municipal reform see Jon C. Teaford, *The Municipal Revolution in America* (Chicago: University of Chicago Press, 1975). On the Progressive Era in Arizona, see David R. Berman, *Reformers, Corporations, and the Electorate: An Analysis of Arizona's Age of Reform* (Niwot: University Press of Colorado, 1992).

3. Samuel F. Turner, *Groundwater Resources of the Santa Cruz Basin, Arizona* (Tucson: U.S. Department of Interior, Geological Survey, 1943), p. 12; and Harry F. Blaney and Martin R. Huberty, "Irrigation in the Far West," *Agricultural Engineering* 38:6 (June, 1957): 415.

4. Tucson *Minutes* November 4, 1895.

5. Tucson *Minutes*, June 1, 1896; Yost and Gardiner, "City of Tucson," p. 3.

6. Tucson *Minutes*, May 5, 1898.

7. Ibid., July 21, 1898.

8. Lynn D. Baker, "Tucson Water—The First 25 Years" in Baker, *Tucson Water History*, vol. I, 1-1 to 1-5.

9. Tucson *Minutes*, August 3, 1900; October 1, 1900, and March 15, 1901.

10. Anthony J. Brazel, "Statewide Temperature and Moisture Trends, 1895–1983," in Sellers and Hill, *Arizona Climate*, pp. 79–84.

11. *Minutes*, Book 4, p. 54 (December 19, 1898); Book 4, p. 55 (December 21, 1898); *Republican*, December 20, 1898 and December 22, 1898.

12. *Minutes*, Book 4, p. 66 (January 25, 1899); Book 4, pp. 68–70 (January 26, 1899); *Herald*, January 25, 1899; *Republican*, January 26, 1899.

13. *Minutes*, Book 4, p. 220 (December 29, 1899); *Gazette*, December 30, 1899; *Republican*, December 30, 1899.

14. *Gazette*, January 9, 1900; *Republican*, January 26, 1900; February 2, 1900; February 9, 1900; February 12, 1900; February 13, 1900. The only surviving copy of *The Taxpayer* (vol. 1, no. 21, April 13, 1903) is located in the J.L.B. Alexander papers in the Arizona Collection at Arizona State University.

15. *Minutes*, Book 4, pp. 247–248 (February 26, 1900); *Gazette*, February 21, 1900; February 24, 1900; *Republican*, February 23, 1900; February 24, 1900.

16. *Arizona Enterprise* (Prescott newspaper, hereafter *Enterprise*), June 6, 1902; June 7, 1902; August 7, 1902; *Republican*, June 2, 1902; July 27, 1902.

17. *Republican*, August 7, 1902; *Gazette*, August 7, 1902.

18. *Minutes*, Book 5, pp. 89–90 (October 6, 1902); *Republican*, August 8, 1902; September 24, 1902; *Gazette*, August 8, 1902.

19. *Minutes*, Book 5, pp. 104–106 (January 5, 1903); *Republican*, January 9, 1903.

20. *Minutes*, Book 5, pp. 113–114 (March 2, 1903); *Republican*, March 3, 1903.

21. *Minutes*, Book 5, p. 133 (April 17, 1903); *Republican*, April 15, 1903; April 16, 1903; *Enterprise*, April 15, 1903; April 16, 1903; *Gazette*, April 15, 1903; April 16, 1903.

22. *Minutes*, Book 5, pp. 160–161 (June 15, 1903); *Enterprise*, June 16, 1903.

23. *Minutes*, Book 5, p. 173 (August 3, 1903) and p. 193 (October 6, 1903); *Enterprise*, September 4, 1903; October 7, 1903; *Republican*, September 12, 1903.

24. *Republican*, October 28, 1903; November 11, 1903.

25. *Enterprise*, November 25, 1903; November 27, 1903; December 1, 1903.

26. *Minutes*, Book 5, pp. 215–216 (December 14, 1903); *Republican*, December 13, 1903; *Enterprise*, December 14, 1903.

27. Sheridan, *Arizona*, pp. 134–135.

28. Platt Cline, *Mountain Town: Flagstaff's First Century* (Flagstaff: Northland Publishing, 1994), pp. 50–51.

29. Ibid., p. 52.

30. Ibid.

31. Ibid.

32. Ibid.

33. City of Flagstaff, "Souvenir of the Completion of Flagstaff's New Four Billion Gallon Water Storage Project," 1941, pamphlet, Flagstaff Public Library Vertical File, p. 2.

34. Cline, *Mountain Town*, p. 53.

35. A. Barman and J. Aubineau, *Reports on the Water Works of the Town of Flagstaff, Arizona* (Flagstaff: Funston Press, 1901), pp. 6–7.

36. Cline, *Mountain Town*, p. 54.

37. Ibid., p. 56.

38. Ibid.

Chapter 6. Strengthening Municipal Ownership

1. *Star*, June 19, 1903; June 24, 1905; June 24, 1906.

2. Tucson *Minutes*, October 7, 1905; January 6, 1908; August 26, 1908; Yost and Gardiner, "City of Tucson," p. 3.

3. J. B. Lippincott, "Report on the Available Water Supply from the Midvale Farms for the City of Tucson," unpublished report, Tucson Water Department, 1930, p. 5; Lynn D. Baker, "Water Pumping Plant no. 2" in Baker, *Tucson Water History*, vol. II, pp. 26–57.

4. Ray Stannard Baker, "The Great Southwest, Part III, Irrigation," *Century Magazine* 64: 3 (July, 1902): 366–367; F. H. Newell, "The Human Side of Irrigation," *Engineering News-Record* 70:9 (August 29, 1914): 236; and *Star*, May 25, 1932.

5. *Minutes*, Book 5, p. 222 (January 4, 1904); *Enterprise*, January 1, 1904; *Republican*, December 16, 1903; December 17, 1903; December 19, 1903; January 3, 1904.

6. *Minutes*, Book 5, p. 231 (February 1, 1904); *Gazette*, February 2, 1904; *Enterprise*, February 5, 1904; *Republican*, February 26, 1904.

7. *Phoenix Water Company v. Common Council of City of Phoenix*, Maricopa County Superior Court case no. 4283, "Complaint," filed April 2, 1904, pp. 26–27; *Gazette*, April 3, 1904; *Republican*, April 3, 1903; *Enterprise*, April 4, 1904.

8. *Minutes*, Book 5, p. 253 and p. 256 (April 6, 1904); *Gazette*, April 5, 1904.

9. *Phoenix Water Company v. Common Council of Phoenix*, "Answer," filed April 16, 1904; "Amended Answer," filed June 20, 1904; "Opinion," filed November 5, 1904; "Judgment," filed November 11, 1904.

10. *Minutes*, Book 5, p. 427 (July 22, 1905); Book 5, p. 429 (July 22, 1905); Book 5, p. 476 (October 30, 1905); Book 5, pp. 478–479 (November 2, 1905); *Republican*, July 23, 1905; October 31, 1905; November 3, 1905.

11. *Republican*, June 13, 1906; July 27, 1906.

12. *Republican*, October 15, 1906.

13. *Minutes*, Book 6, p. 100 (January 15, 1907); *Republican*, January 10, 1907; January 16, 1907.

14. *Minutes*, Book 6, p. 101 (January 21, 1907); Book 6, p. 113 (March 4, 1907); *Republican*, January 29, 1907; March 5, 1907.

15. *Republican*, May 3, 1907; May 7, 1907; May 8, 1907.

16. *Minutes*, Book 6, p. 132 (May 16, 1907); Book 6, p. 137 (June 3, 1907); Book 6, p. 139 (June 7, 1907); Book 6, p. 140 (June 12, 1907); Book 6, p. 142 (June 17, 1907); *Gazette*, May 29, 1907; June 13, 1907.

17. Maricopa County Book 75 of Deeds, pp. 614–620 (July 1, 1907); *Minutes*, Book 6, pp. 144–146 (June 29, 1907); *Gazette*, June 25, 1907; June 28, 1907.

18. Cline, *They Came to the Mountain*, pp. 162–163.

19. For a good summary of public land disposition in the territories, see Jon A. Souder and Sally K. Fairfax, *State Trust Lands: History, Management, and Sustainable Use* (Lawrence: University Press of Kansas, 1996).

20. Cline, *Mountain Town*, p. 96.

21. Ibid., p. 96.

22. Ibid., p. 97.

23. Ibid.

24. Ibid.

25. Ibid., p. 98.

26. Ibid.

27. Ibid., p. 99.

28. Ibid.

29. Ibid., p. 100.

30. On the early history of the Salt River Project and Roosevelt Dam see Karen L. Smith, *The Magnificent Experiment: Building the Salt River Reclamation Project, 1890–1917* (Tucson: University of Arizona Press, 1986).

31. *Minutes*, Book 5, pp. 425–426 (July 22, 1905); *Republican*, January 17, 1905; July 23, 1905; June 3, 1906.

32. *Republican*, June 3, 1906; "Decision and Decree," *Patrick J. Hurley v. Charles F. Abbott*, Maricopa County Superior Court case no. 4564.

33. Contract no. 74, October 1, 1910, on file with Phoenix City Clerk Department; *Republican*, June 24, 1910.

34. 34 Stat. 116.

35. District Counsel E.W.R. Ewing to District Counsel in Charge E. E. Roddis, November 23, 1916, Records of the Bureau of Reclamation, Record Group 115, Office of Chief Engineer, General Correspondence, National Archives, Rocky Mountain Region, Denver; U.S. Reclamation Service, *Salt River Project, Arizona: Limiting Irrigable Area of Land* (Washington, D.C.: U.S. Reclamation Service, 1914). For additional information on the Board of Survey see Smith, *The Magnificent Experiment*, pp. 130–135.

36. There are many references to the contracts with the Reclamation Service in the *Minutes* between 1911 and 1917. For the contract with the Water Users, see *Minutes*, vol. 2, p. 368 (March 19, 1919). The Phoenix City Clerk changed the numbering system of the *Minutes* after the 1914 charter revision and started a new set of minute books. To distinguish the later set from the earlier one, *Minutes* after 1914 are designated by "vol." (rather than "book") number.

37. For a discussion of early sewage treatment methods in Phoenix, see Kupel, "Urban Water in the Arid West," pp. 205–235.

38. For the relationship between water and sewer systems, see Eugene P. Moehring, "Public Works and Urban History: Recent Trends and New Directions," *Essays in Public Works History* 13 (1982): 13. On sewers as part of the improvements boosters

lobbied for, see Charles C. Euchner, "The Politics of Urban Expansion: Baltimore and the Sewerage Question, 1859–1905," *Maryland Historical Magazine* 86 (Fall, 1991): 272.

39. For the private ownership era, see Stanley K. Schultz and Clay McShane, "To Engineer the Metropolis: Sewers, Sanitation, and City Planning in Late Nineteenth Century America," *Journal of American History* 65 (September, 1978): 389.

40. *Star*, October 10, 1907; November 15, 1930; and S. H. Orme, "Sewage Irrigation," *Engineering News* 32: 1 (July 5, 1894): 17.

41. Maricopa County Recorder Book 29 of Deeds, 532–534, May 31, 1892; *Minutes*, Book 2, p. 267 (May 23, 1892); Book 2, p. 269 (June 10, 1892); *Herald*, May 24, 1892.

42. *Minutes*, Book 2, pp. 301–305 (December 5, 1892).

43. *Gazette*, August 1, 1893; December 22, 1953; *Herald*, May 5, 1896; Kupel, "Urban Water in the Arid West," pp. 230–235.

Chapter 7. Municipal Achievements, 1912–1929

1. A. J. Harshberger, "Mining in Pima County," *Tucson* 2: 6 (June, 1929): 3–4; C. B. Brown, "Agriculture in Pima County, 1920–1928," *Tucson* 2:3 (March, 1929): 3; and George E.P. Smith, "Pump Irrigation in the Santa Cruz Valley," *Arizona* 11:7 (December, 1920): 9.

2. M. B. Levick, *Tucson, Arizona* (San Francisco: Sunset Magazine Homeseekers Bureau, 1911), p. 29; Newell, "Human Side," p. 236; Smith, "In the Santa Cruz Valley," p. 9; W. H. Holcomb, "The Development of the Deep-Well Turbine Pump," *Mechanical Engineering* 51:11 (November, 1929): 833; and Oscar Edward Meizner, "The History and Development of Ground-Water Hydrology," *Journal of the Washington Academy of Science*, 24:1 (January 15, 1934): 19.

3. *Star*, February 1, 1913; R. Brooks Taylor, "Cotton," in *Arizona the Grand Canyon State: A History of Arizona*, ed. Florence Wachholtz (Westminster, Colorado: Western States Historical Publishers, 1975), p. 49; and Richard N. Davis, *History of Dairying in Arizona*, (Tucson: University of Arizona Agricultural Experiment Station, 1959), pp. 6, 8–9.

4. Levick, *Tucson, Arizona*, p. 7; *Star*, June 10, 1910; and Tucson *Minutes*, April 11, 1910.

5. *Star*, June 7, 1912; March 16, 1913; May 17, 1913.

6. *Star*, July 20, 1913; July 27, 1913.

7. *Star*, March 9, 1914; March 16, 1914; Tucson *Minutes*, January 5, 1914; January 13, 1914; March 5, 1914; March 11, 1914.

8. Tucson *Minutes*, July 3, 1916.

9. Ibid., May 7, 1917; June 4, 1917.

10. Sellers and Hill, *Arizona Climate*, pp. 81–83; Tucson *Minutes*, September 10, 1917; November 5, 1917.

11. Yost and Gardiner, "City of Tucson," appendix III-3, p. 1; Tucson *Minutes*, October 8, 1919; November 10, 1919; December 24, 1919; December 29, 1919.

12. C. L. Sonnichsen, *Tucson: The Life and Times of an American City* (Norman: University of Oklahoma Press, 1982; 2d ed., 1987), p. 202.

13. The best discussion of tourism in Tucson is Alex Jay Kimmelman, "Luring the Tourist to Tucson: Civic Promotion in the Twenties," *Journal of Arizona History* 28:2 (Summer, 1987): pp. 135–154.

14. Ibid., 148–151.

15. Holcomb, "Deep-Well Pump," p. 833.

16. Edward A. Ackerman and George O. G. Lof, *Technology in American Water Development* (Baltimore: Johns Hopkins Press, 1959), p. 281.

17. Roy Bainer, "Science and Technology in Western Agriculture," *Agricultural History* 49: 1 (January, 1975): 71; Holcomb, "Deep-Well Pump," pp. 833–834; and Ackerman and Lof, *Technology*, p. 281.

18. Sonnichsen, *Tucson*, pp. 202–203.

19. Tucson *Minutes*, April 5, 1920; July 19, 1920; September 2, 1920.

20. Tucson *Minutes*, November 5, 1920; February 7, 1921; August 25, 1921.

21. Yost and Gardiner, "City of Tucson," p. 4; Lynn D. Baker, "Water Pumping Plant no. 3," in Baker, *Tucson Water History*, vol. II, pp. 26–79.

22. For the Tucson water awareness campaign, see Tucson *Minutes*, May 1, 1922. For the Mulholland quote, see Reisner, *Cadillac Desert*, p. 86.

23. *Star*, August 13, 1927; Tucson *Minutes*, January 24, 1928; and Yost and Gardiner, "City of Tucson," p. 4.

24. Tucson *Minutes*, October 28, 1927.

25. *Star*, May 31, 1928; Tucson *Minutes*, June 4, 1928.

26. *Star*, June 20, 1928.

27. *Herald*, February 6, 1886.

28. *Minutes*, Book 7, p. 412 (July 29, 1913); *Republican*, June 13, 1906; July 30, 1913; November 11, 1913.

29. Phoenix switched from a mayor and council form of government to a mayor, commission, and city manager in 1914; thus the reference in the text to the city commission rather than the common council. *Minutes*, Book 7, p. 180 (April 12, 1915); Book 7, p. 265 (June 4, 1915); vol. 1, p. 210 (June 15, 1915); *Republican*, July 29, 1915; August 6, 1915; "Municipal Water Supply Water Right," Maricopa County Recorder's Office Book of Canals no. 2, p. 401.

30. *Minutes*, vol. 1, p. 319 (September 30, 1915), *Republican*, October 1, 1915; Letter from Register Phoenix Office to General Land Office Commissioner, January 16, 1916, City of Phoenix Archives (unless specifically noted, all correspondence cited in this chapter is found in this archive).

31. *Minutes*, vol. 1, p. 396 (February 16, 1916), *Republican*, February 17, 1916.

32. *Minutes*, vol. 2, p. 365 (March 12, 1919); vol. 2, p. 410 (May 14, 1919); vol. 2, p. 425 (May 26, 1919); vol. 2, p. 436 (June 11, 1919); vol. 2, p. 440 (June 18, 1919); *Republican*, May 15, 1919; May 29, 1919; June 11, 1919; July 26, 1919; July 27, 1919; and *Gazette*, June 18, 1919.

33. *Minutes*, vol. 2, p. 475 (August 11, 1919); vol. 2, p. 506 (September 20, 1919), *Republican*, August 12, 1919; September 21, 1919.

34. *Minutes*, vol. 2, p. 575 (January 21, 1920); vol. 2, p. 584 (January 30, 1920); vol. 3, p. 12 (February 25, 1920); vol. 3, p. 42 (March 19, 1920), *Republican*, January 31, 1920; March 20, 1920.

35. "Verde River Water Project of the City of Phoenix, Arizona." Unpublished report, ca. 1925, pp. 20–27.

36. "Permit," filed by Phoenix Mayor Willis H. Plunkett with Department of Interior, December 13, 1921; *Gazette*, December 15, 1921; February 13, 1922.

37. William Spry to Commissioner of Indian Affairs, March 14, 1923; "Indenture" between City of Phoenix and U.S. Indian Service, August 5, 1925; William Spry to Phoenix Land Office Register, December 12, 1925; "Affidavit as to Construction" signed by City Engineer Henry Rieger, December 23, 1925; William Spry to Phoenix Land Office Register, January 13, 1926; *Minutes*, vol. 5, pp. 356–357 (August 20, 1924); vol. 5, p. 375 (October 1, 1924).

38. "Proof of Construction" signed by City Engineer William Jamieson, June 25, 1927; Acting Land Commissioner Thomas Howell to Secretary of the Interior, January 16, 1928; *Minutes*, vol. 6, p. 371 (February 16, 1927); vol. 6, p. 403 (March 20, 1927), *Republican*, June 13, 1927.

39. *Minutes*, vol. 6, p. 567 (August 31, 1927); vol. 7, p. 25 (November 9, 1927), *Republican*, November 16, 1927.

40. Contract no. 346, July 18, 1928, on file Phoenix City Clerk Department; *Minutes*, vol. 8, p. 168 (July 10, 1929); *Republican*, January 27, 1929; March 15, 1929.

41. Cline, *Mountain Town*, p. 275.

42. Ibid., 276–279.

43. Ibid., p. 279.

44. Ibid.

45. Ibid., p. 282.

46. Ibid., p. 283.

47. Ibid., pp. 284–285.

Chapter 8. Big Brother Arrives

1. C. B. Brown, "Agricultural Adjustments," *Tucson* 4:6 (June, 1931): 3; W. Eugene Hollon, *The Southwest: Old and New* (New York: Prentice Hall, 1961), 318, 320; and Forbes, "History of Irrigation," p. 227.

2. The definitive work on federal programs in Arizona is William S. Collins, *The New Deal in Arizona* (Phoenix: Arizona State Parks Board, 1999).

3. J. B. Lippincott, "Report on the Available Water Supply from the Midvale Farms for the City of Tucson," unpublished report, Tucson Water Department, 1930, p. 5.

4. *Star*, April 6, 1930; August 19, 1930; September 13, 1930.

5. *Ibid.*, September 21, 1930.

6. *Star*, November 14, 1930; December 5, 1930; December 7, 1930; and Raymond A. Hill, "Additional Water Supply for City of Tucson, Arizona," report on file, City of Tucson Water Department, 1930, p. 112.

7. *Star*, May 8, 1932; and Hill, "Additional Water Supply," p. 128.

8. A. H. Condron, "What Sabino Canyon Means to Tucson," *Tucson* 9:4 (April, 1936): 5.

9. Condron, "Sabino Canyon," p. 5; and William Holzhauser, "Lake in Catalinas Assured," *Tucson* 7:11 (November, 1934): 5.

10. *Star*, August 4, 1937; and Condron, "Sabino Canyon," pp. 5, 12.

11. *Star*, February 1, 1930.

12. *Star*, November 15, 1932; January 10, 1934; and Lynn D. Baker, "Reservoirs—Storage Tanks," in Baker, *Tucson Water History*, vol. I, pp. 13-5.

13. *Star*, July 24, 1935; August 1, 1938; and Burns and McDonnell Engineering Company, "Report on Municipal Power Plant, Tucson, Arizona," (Tucson Water Department, 1933), p. 5.

14. Yost and Gardiner, "City of Tucson," Appendix III-5, p. 1; and Lynn D. Baker, "Reservoirs—Storage Tanks," in Baker, *Tucson Water History*, vol. I, 13-5.

15. *Ibid.*, p. 5.

16. Lynn D. Baker, "Known Private Water Company Purchases," in Baker, *Tucson Water History*, vol. II, 21-1.

17. *Minutes*, vol. 8, pp. 253–256 (September 9, 1929); vol. 8, pp. 284–286 (October 16, 1929); vol. 8, pp. 289–291 (October 21, 1929); vol. 8, pp. 362–367 (December 11, 1929); *Republican*, September 20, 1929; September 21, 1929.

18. *Minutes*, vol. 8, pp. 433–434 (January 29, 1930); vol. 8, pp. 444–445 (February 18, 1930); *Republican*, February 23, 1930.

19. *Minutes*, vol. 8, pp. 535–536 (May 7, 1930); vol. 8, pp. 567–568 (May 21, 1930); *Republican*, May 22, 1930.

20. Phoenix City Manager George Todd to Superintendent of Fort McDowell Indian Agency John B. Brown, July 31, 1930; Brown to Commissioner of Indian Affairs, July 31, 1930; Brown to Todd, October 27, 1930, City of Phoenix Archives (unless specifically noted, all correspondence cited in this chapter is found in this archive).

21. Contract no. 491, October 16, 1930, on file Phoenix City Clerk Department; *Minutes*, vol. 9, pp. 164–165 (November 5, 1930); vol. 9, pp. 194–195 (December 4, 1930); *Republican*, December 7, 1930.

22. Todd to Brown, January 15, 1931; Brown to Commissioner of Indian Affairs, February 3, 1931; Todd to Carl Hayden, February 9, 1931; Hayden to Todd, February 27, 1931.

23. Isabella Greenway to City Manager McNeil Johnson, February 20, 1934.

24. Superintendent of Phoenix Indian School Carl H. Skinner to City Manager William F. Clark, February 3, 1933.

25. Report of City Engineer James Girand, June 15, 1936; Assistant Commissioner of Indian Affairs William Zimmerman to Phoenix City Clerk, July 13, 1936.

26. City Engineer James Girand to Superintendent A. E. Robinson of Fort McDowell and Salt River Indian Reservations, December 29, 1938; Robinson to Girand, April 21, 1939.

27. For an examination of the depression in Phoenix, see Jay Edward Niebur, "The Social and Economic Effects of the Great Depression on Phoenix, Arizona, 1929–1934," (master's thesis, Arizona State University, 1967). Niebur concludes (pp. 83–84) that the Great Depression had only a slight impact on Phoenix, with the exception of increased demands for welfare caused by transients and unemployed miners.

28. The best discussion of the annexation question is John D. Wenum, "Spatial Growth and the Central City: Problems, Potential, and the Case of Phoenix, Arizona," (Ph.D. diss., Northwestern University, 1968).

29. *Minutes*, vol. 8, p. 507 (April 9, 1930).

30. *Republic*, December 10, 1932.

31. *Republic*, August 19, 1933.

32. *Republic*, August 16, 1933; August 22, 1933.

33. *Minutes*, vol. 11, p. 264 (October 18, 1933); *Republic*, October 18, 1933; October 19, 1933.

34. *Minutes*, vol. 11, p. 277 (November 2, 1933); Resolution no. 6106, on file with Phoenix City Clerk Department, November 15, 1933; *Republic*, November 3, 1933; November 16, 1933; *Gazette*, November 15, 1933.

35. *Gazette*, December 2, 1933; December 4, 1933; December 11, 1933; *Republic*, December 8, 1933; December 9, 1933; December 10, 1933.

36. *Republic*, January 4, 1934; January 5, 1934; January 6, 1934.

37. *Republic*, July 28, 1934; August 12, 1934.

38. *Minutes*, vol. 12, p. 264 (August 31, 1934); *Republic*, August 28, 1934; August 29, 1934; August 30, 1934.

39. Contract no. 661, October 23, 1934, on file with Phoenix City Clerk Department; *Republic*, October 19, 1934; October 25, 1934; December 4, 1934; December 9, 1934; December 13, 1934.

40. *Gazette*, Jan. 14, 1935; *Republic*, Feb. 12, 1935; Feb. 16, 1935; March 17, 1935.

41. *Republic*, April 4, 1935; May 12, 1935.

42. *Minutes*, vol. 14, p. 181 (March 11, 1936); National Archives and Records Center, Washington, D.C., RG 135, Records of the Public Works Administration, PWA Docket 2636; *Republic*, March 12, 1936.

43. *Minutes*, vol. 14, pp. 376–377 (May 28, 1936); PWA Docket 2636 Records of the Public Works Administration, RG 135, National Archives, Washington, D.C.; *Republic*, May 21, 1936 (I, 5: 2–3); *Gazette*, May 28, 1936.

44. National Archives; PWA Docket 2636; Ordinance 2400, September 1, 1936, on file with the Phoenix City Clerk Department; *Gazette*, August 31, 1936; *Republic*, September 1, 1936.

45. Resolution no. 6384, October 15, 1936; Contract no. 944, October 17, 1936; Contract no. 945, October 16, 1936; Contract no. 950, October 16, 1936; all on file with the Phoenix City Clerk Department.

46. *Minutes*, vol. 15, pp. 429–430 (July 20, 1937); *Gazette*, July 20, 1937.

47. Cline, *Mountain Town*, pp. 320–321.

48. Ibid., p. 321. For Del Rio Springs, see C. E. Yount, "Notes on the History of Prescott's Water Supply," manuscript, Sharlot Hall Museum, Prescott, 1939, p. 13.

49. Yount, "Notes," p. 13.

50. Cline, *Mountain Town*, p. 322.

51. City of Flagstaff, "Souvenir," p. 2.

52. Ibid.

53. Cline, *Mountain Town*, p. 323; International Geophysics, Inc., *Geophysical Survey Report, Riordan and Fort Valley Areas* (Flagstaff, City of Flagstaff, 1937), pp. 21–24; International Geophysics, Inc., *Geophysical Survey Report, Clark Valley–Riordan Area, Switzer Mesa Area, and Fort Valley Area* (Flagstaff, City of Flagstaff, 1938).

54. Cline, *Mountain Town*, p. 323.

55. Ibid., p. 324.

Chapter 9. World War II

1. Samuel F. Turner, "Water Resources Available to the City of Tucson, Pima County, Arizona," (Tucson Water Department, 1959), p. 3; and A. H. Griffin, "An Economic and Institutional Assessment of the Water Problem Facing the Tucson Basin" (Ph.D. diss., University of Arizona, Tucson, 1980), p. 2.

2. Samuel F. Turner, *Further Investigations of the Groundwater Resources of the Santa Cruz Basin, Arizona* (Tucson: U.S. Geological Survey, 1947), p. 2; Don Bufkin, "From Mud Village to Modern Metropolis: The Urbanization of Tucson," *Journal of Arizona History* 22:1 (Spring, 1981): 82; and R. G. Fowler, "Where Tucson's Water Level Stands," *Tucson Business* 2:1 (April, 1976): 40.

3. W. S. Gookin, "Central Arizona Project," *Reclamation Era* 35 (January, 1949): 6; and W.G.V. Balchin and Norman Pye, "The Drought in the Southwestern United States," *Weather* 8:8 (1953): 233.

4. Sonnichsen, *Tucson*, pp. 220–221.

5. Ibid., p. 263.

6. Ibid., pp. 268–269.

7. Turner, *Groundwater Resources*, p. 51; R. Brooks Taylor, "Cotton," p. 51; Gregonis and Huckell, "Tucson Urban Study," p. 23; and Siegfried Birle, *Irrigation Agriculture in the Southwest United States*, (Marburg, West Germany: University of Marburg Press, 1976), pp. 148–149.

8. *Star*, December 1, 1946; and Yost and Gardiner, "City of Tucson," p. 5.

9. Sonnichsen, *Tucson*, p. 270.

10. Ibid., p. 272.

11. Ibid.

12. Ibid.; Lynn D. Baker, "Tucson Water Department Contract/Bid Documents," in Baker, *Tucson Water History*, vol. I, 7-2.

13. Lynn D. Baker, "Known Private Water Company Purchases," in Baker, *Tucson*

Water History, vol. II, 21-1. By acquiring the Colonia Solana system, the city purchased what later became a local landmark, the El Con water tower. Built by Martin Schwerin for Colonia Solana Estates, the 1927 tower is now listed on the National Register of Historic Places.

14. Bradford Luckingham, *Phoenix, The History of a Southwestern Metropolis*, (Tucson: University of Arizona Press, 1989), pp. 136–138. The best discussion of Phoenix during World War II is found in Dennis Preisler, "Phoenix, Arizona, During the 1940s: A Decade of Change," (master's thesis, Arizona State University, 1992).

15. Luckingham, *Phoenix*, pp. 139–141.

16. For a discussion of the evaporative cooler, see Bob Cunningham, "The Box that Broke the Barrier: The Swamp Cooler Comes to Arizona," *Journal of Arizona History* 26:2 (Summer, 1985): 163–174.

17. *Republic*, June 14, 1940; *Gazette*, June 14, 1940.

18. *Republic*, June 15, 1940.

19. *Republic*, June 16, 1940; *Gazette*, June 17, 1940; June 18, 1940; June 19, 1940; June 21, 1940.

20. *Minutes*, vol. 18, 314 and 316 (June 29, 1940); *Republic*, June 22, 1940; June 30, 1940; *Gazette*, June 24, 1940; August 2, 1940.

21. *Republic*, August 23, 1940; August 30, 1940.

22. *Republic*, November 28, 1940; H. C. Schwalen, "Outline of Verbal Report," October 2, 1940, H. C. Schwalen papers, collection AZ-563, University of Arizona Special Collections Library, Tucson.

23. *Minutes*, vol. 18, pp. 490–492 (January 7, 1941); *Republic*, January 8, 1941; *Gazette*, January 8, 1941.

24. *Minutes*, vol. 19, p. 8 (March 4, 1941); vol. 19, pp. 20–21 (March 14, 1941); vol. 19, pp. 79–80 (May 6, 1941); *Republic*, March 5, 1941; May 7, 1941; *Gazette*, March 5, 1941; May 7, 1941.

25. *Gazette*, January 20, 1941; March 5, 1941; March 13, 1941; March 15, 1941; April 14, 1941; *Republic*, March 4, 1941; March 5, 1941; March 6, 1941; March 14, 1941; March 16, 1941.

26. *Gazette*, April 22, 1941; April 26, 1941; *Republic*, April 22, 1941; April 23, 1941; April 26, 1941; April 27, 1941.

27. Contract no. 1302, November 13, 1941, on file with Phoenix City Clerk Department; *Minutes*, vol. 19, p. 414 (March 5, 1941); *Republic*, November 29, 1941.

28. Contract no. 1335, January 6, 1942, on file Phoenix City Clerk Department.

29. *Minutes*, vol. 20, p. 297 (May 1, 1943); *Republic*, May 2, 1943; May 8, 1943; *Gazette*, April 15, 1943; May 7, 1943.

30. *Gazette*, July 9, 1943.

31. *Republic*, August 17, 1943.

32. *Minutes*, vol. 20, p. 532 (January 4, 1944); vol. 20, p. 534 (January 5, 1944); *Gazette*, January 4, 1944; *Republic*, January 4, 1944.

33. *Minutes*, vol. 20, p. 539 (January 18, 1944); Contract no. 1417, October 20, 1943, on file with Phoenix City Clerk Department; *Gazette*, January 18, 1944.

34. *Minutes*, vol. 20, pp. 547–549 (January 27, 1944); *Gazette*, January 27, 1944; *Republic*, January 28, 1944.

35. *Minutes*, vol. 20, pp. 558–559 (February 3, 1944); *Gazette*, February 3, 1944; *Republic*, February 4, 1944.

36. *Minutes*, vol. 21, p. 42 (May 1, 1944); *Gazette*, May 2, 1944.

37. *Republic*, February 3, 1944; *Gazette*, February 3, 1944.

38. Cline, *Mountain Town*, p. 324.

39. Ibid.

40. Ibid, pp. 324–325.

41. Ibid., p. 325; City of Flagstaff, "Souvenir," pp. 3–4.

42. Cline, *Mountain Town*, p. 325; City of Flagstaff, "Souvenir," pp. 5–6.

43. John S. Westerlund, "U.S. Project Men Here: Building Navajo Ordnance Depot at Flagstaff," *The Journal of Arizona History* 42:2 (Summer, 2001): 206–207.

44. Westerlund, "Project Men Here," pp. 217–219.

45. Gerald D. Nash first articulated his "World War II as watershed" thesis in *The American West in the Twentieth Century: A Short History of an Urban Oasis* (Albuquerque: University of New Mexico Press, 1977). He expanded his treatment in *The American West Transformed: The Impact of the Second World War* (Bloomington, Indiana: Indiana University Press, 1985), which examined cultural and social impacts, and his *World War II and the West: Reshaping the Economy* (Lincoln: University of Nebraska Press, 1990), which focused on the economic impact of the war effort.

46. For the definition of the martial metropolis, see Roger W. Lotchin, "Conclusion," in Roger W. Lotchin, ed., *The Martial Metropolis: U.S. Cities in War and Peace* (New York: Praeger, 1984), pp. 223–232.

Chapter 10. The Postwar Boom to 1950

1. Phil J. Martin, "Annual Statistical Report of the City Water Department," in Baker, *Tucson Water History*, vol. I, 2-60.

2. City of Tucson, "Tucson Water General Statistical Information," in Baker, *Tucson Water History*, vol. II, 18-10.

3. Lynn D. Baker, "Known Private Water Company Purchases," in Baker, *Tucson Water History*, vol. II, 21-1.

4. "Agreement Between Salt River Valley Water Users Association, Phelps Dodge Corporation, and Defense Plant Corporation," March 1, 1944, Records of the Bureau of Reclamation, Record Group 115, National Archives, Rocky Mountain Region, Denver.

5. "Dam Contract Award is Scheduled Today," *Gazette*, 28 April 1944, p. 3. The actual capacity of the dam as built approximated 67,900 af.

6. Balchin and Pye, "Drought," p. 33; Charles C. Colley, "Water Under the Earth: Robert H. Forbes and the Fight for Control," *Journal of Arizona History* 16:3 (Autumn, 1975): 255.

7. U.S. Bureau of Reclamation, *Report on Central Arizona Project* (Boulder City, Nevada: U.S. Bureau of Reclamation, 1947): B-85, B-86; Paul Kelso, "The Arizona Ground

Water Act," *Western Political Quarterly* 1:2 (June, 1948): 180–181; Rich Johnson, *The Central Arizona Project* (Tucson: University of Arizona Press, 1977), p. 116.

8. *Minutes*, vol. 22, July 31, 1946, p. 340; Charles A. Esser, "Bond Election is Set," *Republic*, August 1, 1946, p. 1.

9. *Minutes*, vol. 22, September 10, 1946, p. 391; Esser, "City Bond Election Delayed," *Republic*, September 11, 1946, p. 1.

10. *Minutes*, vol. 22, September 17, 1946, p. 412; Esser, "$5,000,000 Water Bond Urged," *Republic*, September 18, 1946, p. 1.

11. *Minutes*, vol. 22, October 8, 1946, 434–435; Esser, "Bond Vote Set Nov. 19—Three Big Projects Proposed," *Republic*, October 9, 1946, p. 1.

12. *Minutes*, vol. 22, November 16, 1946, p. 482; "Verde Water Supply Assured City," *Republic*, November 16, 1946, p. 1.

13. *Minutes*, vol. 22, November 19, 1946, p. 483 and November 26, 1946, 503–509; "$9,600,000 Bond Issues Pass," *Republic*, November 20, 1946, p. 1; Contract No. 1604, November 22, 1946, on file with Phoenix City Clerk Department, p. 13.

14. *Republic*, November 16, 1946; Contract no. 1604, pp. 4–6.

15. E. W. Michael, President Verde River Irrigation and Power District, to Julius A. Krug, Secretary of the Interior, Phoenix, May 26, 1947, Arizona Department of Water Resources Archives (unless specifically noted, all correspondence cited in this chapter is found in this archive).

16. O. C. Williams, State Land Commissioner to E. A. Moritz, Bureau of Reclamation Regional Director, Phoenix, May 27, 1947.

17. Moritz to Williams, Boulder City, June 13, 1947; Williams to Moritz, Phoenix, June 23, 1947.

18. James G. Girand, "Notes of Meeting on Horseshoe Gates," March 18, 1948, City of Phoenix Archives.

19. "Notice of Application to Appropriate Water," July 22, 1947.

20. Michael to Williams, Phoenix, August 15, 1947.

21. C.H.W. Smith, State Land Department Water Division Engineer, to R. Gail Baker, Phoenix City Engineer, Phoenix, August 21, 1947.

22. Phoenix City Attorney Jack Choisser to Williams, Phoenix, September 12, 1947.

23. Lin B. Orme, President Salt River Valley Water Users Association to Williams, Phoenix, September 19, 1947.

24. "Notes of Meeting Held in Hearing Room, Arizona Industrial Commission, October 1, 1947, Re: Application nos. A-2853 and R-943 of the City of Phoenix for Permit to Store and Appropriate Surplus Waters of the Verde River," October 1947, p. 1.

25. Ibid., pp. 2–6.

26. Ibid., pp. 7–8.

27. Ibid., pp. 20–23.

28. "Notice of Hearing Before State Land Commissioner of the State of Arizona," October 2, 1947; Herb Nelson, "City Will Buy Water That Association Uses," *Gazette*, October 6, 1947, p. 1.

29. Girand to Phoenix City Manager J. T. Deppe, Phoenix, October 9, 1947, City of Phoenix Archives.

30. Williams to Phoenix City Commission, Phoenix, October 28, 1947; *Minutes*, vol. 24, October 28, 1947, p. 241; Esser, "Approval Delay Hits Flood Gate Project," *Republic*, October 29, 1947, p. 4.

31. *Minutes*, vol. 24, October 30, 1947, pp. 242–246.

32. Claiborne Nuckolls, "Floodgate Talks Are Doubtful" *Republic*, November 4, 1947, p. 3.

33. James Girand and Jack Choisser, "Transcripts of Statements Before O. C. Williams," November 4, 1947, pp. 1–2.

34. O. C. Williams, "Order in the Matter of Application A-2853," November 4, 1947, p. 1; David F. Brinegar, "Water Users; City Given 60 More Days," *Arizona Times* (Phoenix newspaper), November 4, 1947, p. 1; "City Water Seizure Hinted," *Gazette*, November 5, 1947, p. 6; "Squeeze on Water Charged by City," *Arizona Times*, November 5, 1947, p. 4; "Verde Gates Delay Cited as Project Squeeze Play," *Republic*, November 6, 1947, p. 3.

35. City of Phoenix, "Report of Conferences with United States Bureau of Reclamation Officials in Regard to Spillway Gates on Horseshoe Dam," March 18, 1948.

36. Ibid.

37. Ibid.

38. Ibid.

39. "Technicalities Snag Floodgate Parlay," *Gazette*, April 9, 1948, p. 3; "Head Gates Agreement Is Reached," *Republic*, April 10, 1948, Raymond A. Hill, Consulting Engineer, to Girand, Los Angeles, April 10, 1948, City of Phoenix Archives; Hill to R. J. Coffey, Bureau of Reclamation Regional Counsel, Los Angeles, April 10, 1948, City of Phoenix Archives.

40. William W. Warne, Assistant Secretary of the Interior, telegram to O. L. Norman, Water Users General Manager, Washington, D.C., August 5, 1948, City of Phoenix Archives; "U.S. Okays Verde River Floodgates — Interior Department Approval Is Next to Final Step," *Republic* October 15, 1948, p. 1; "Horseshoe Dam Floodgates Approved by U.S. Officials," *Gazette*, October 15, 1948.

41. Nuckolls, "Bitter Fight Assured on Dam Project," *Republic*, January 19, 1949, p. 2; "Flood Gates Delay Granted," *Gazette*, January 18, 1949, p. 3.

42. Formal Okay Given Horseshoe Project," *Republic*, January 26, 1949, p. 1.

43. "Only 1,300 Acre Feet Behind Enlarged Dam," *Gazette*, June 16, 1950, p. 1; Ben Avery, "Horseshoe Dam Capacity Now More Than Doubled," *Republic*, June 16, 1950, p. 1.

44. Robert G. Dunbar, "The Arizona Groundwater Controversy at Mid-Century," *Arizona and the West 19* (Spring, 1977): 22–24; Dean E. Mann, "*The Politics of Water in Arizona*" (Tucson: University of Arizona Press, 1963), pp. 49, 51.

45. *Minutes*, vol. 23, p. 381 (May 13, 1947); *Republic*, May 14, 1947.

46. *Minutes*, vol. 23, pp. 482–483 (June 17, 1947).

47. Ibid., vol. 25, p. 461 (June 15, 1948).

48. Taylor and Taylor Consulting Engineers, *Engineering Report, Municipal Water System, City of Flagstaff, Arizona* (Los Angeles: Taylor and Taylor, 1947), p. 53.

49. Ibid., p. 1.

50. Ibid., p. 53; John A. Carollo, *Water Works Report, City of Flagstaff, Arizona* (Phoenix: John Carollo Engineers, 1971), pp. 5–12.

51. Taylor and Taylor, *Engineering Report*, p. 51.

52. Cline, *Mountain Town*, p. 370.

53. Jon C. Teaford, *The Twentieth Century American City: Problem, Promise, and Reality* (Baltimore: Johns Hopkins University Press, 1986), pp. 74–75.

54. For the impact of federal programs on the West during the depression, see Richard Lowitt, *The New Deal and the West* (Bloomington: Indiana University Press, 1984). Although Lowitt fails to devote much attention to urban areas, he does include an entire chapter on the impact of federal reclamation water policy on the West at pp. 81–99.

Chapter 11. Confronting the Urban Influx, 1950–1963

1. For a discussion of the accuracy of the Sunbelt term, see Sargent, *Metro Arizona*, pp. 78–79. Some of the more noteworthy works on the Sunbelt phenomenon include Steven C. Ballard and Thomas E. James, ed., *The Future of the Sunbelt: Managing Growth and Change* (New York, Praeger, 1983); Richard M. Bernard and Bradley R. Rice, ed., *Sunbelt Cities: Politics and Growth Since World War II* (Austin: University of Texas Press, 1983); Carl Abbott, *The New Urban America: Growth and Politics in Sunbelt Cities* (Chapel Hill: University of North Carolina Press, 1987); and Raymond A. Mohl, ed., *Essays on Sunbelt Cities and Recent Urban America* (College Station: Texas A&M Press, 1990).

2. Robert V. Boyle, "Southwest Gets Thirstier as Water Problem Grows," *Soil Conservation* 17:9 (April, 1952): 195; John A. Carollo, "Water Works Survey Report, Tucson, Arizona" (Tucson: Tucson Water Department, 1959), p. 2; and John Riddick, "Tucson Transformed," *Tucson Business* 1:1 (April, 1975): 12.

3. L. C. Halpenny and R. L. Cushman, "Pumpage and Groundwater Levels in Arizona in 1951," (University of Arizona Special Collections, 1951); and Andrew W. Wilson, "Tucson: A Problem in Uses of Water," in *Aridity and Man; The Challenge of the Arid Lands in the United States*, ed. Carle Hodge and Peter C. Duisberg (Washington: American Association for the Advancement of Science, 1963), p. 483.

4. H. C. Schwalen and R. J. Shaw, "Ground Water Supplies of Santa Cruz Valley of Southern Arizona Between Rillito Station and the International Boundary," *University of Arizona Agricultural Experiment Station Bulletin* 288, (Tucson: University of Arizona, 1957).

5. Carollo, "Water Works Survey," p. 6.

6. Ibid., p. 6; and Lynn D. Baker, "Reservoirs—Storage Tanks," in Baker, *Tucson Water History*, vol. I, pp. 3-5.

7. Carollo, "Water Works Survey," p. 6; and *Star*, May 6, 1953.

8. Resolution no. 3724, December 16, 1957, on file with Tucson City Clerk Department.

9. *Gazette*, July 4, 1951.

10. Ray W. Wilson, "Report on Verde River Water Problem," July 20, 1951, p. 4, City of Phoenix Archives.

11. *Gazette*, July 6, 1951.

12. Ibid., July 9, 1951.

13. Ibid., July 16, 1951.

14. Ibid., July 17, 1951.

15. Ibid., August 2, 1951; August 3, 1951; *Minutes*, vol. 30, pp. 128–129 (August 10, 1951); Contract no. 2345, July 24, 1951, on file with Phoenix City Clerk Department.

16. *Minutes*, vol. 30, pp. 128–129 (August 10, 1951). For a discussion of townsite lands, see chapter 4.

17. *Republic*, April 16, 1952.

18. *Republic*, August 6, 1952; August 8, 1952; September 10, 1952.

19. Contract no. 2538, January 1, 1952, on file with Phoenix City Clerk Department.

20. *Minutes*, vol. 31, 66 to 67 (June 5, 1952); vol. 31, p. 266 (September 2, 1952); vol. 31, p. 331 (October 14, 1952); vol. 31, pp. 371–372 (November 25, 1952); vol. 31, p. 498 (February 10, 1953).

21. City of Phoenix, *Monthly Review: City Manager's Summary of Activities* (July, 1954), p. 7; and (November, 1956), p. 4.

22. Ibid., (November, 1957), p. 4.

23. Ibid., (March, 1958), p. 6.

24. Ibid, (March, 1958), p. 6 and (April, 1959), p. 3.

25. *Minutes*, vol. 40, p. 349 (September 29, 1959); vol. 41, p. 121 (January 26, 1960).

26. City of Phoenix, *Monthly Review*, (December, 1961), p. 3; (March, 1964), p. 4; *Minutes*, vol. 44, p. 503 (November 21, 1961).

27. City of Phoenix, *Monthly Review*, (January, 1961), p. 7; (December, 1961), p. 3.

28. Cline, *Mountain Town*, p. 402.

29. Taylor and Taylor, *Engineering Report*, p. 45; City of Flagstaff, *City of Flagstaff Water Program* (Flagstaff: City of Flagstaff, 1962), p. 6.

30. City of Flagstaff, *Water Program*, p. 6.

31. Cline, *Mountain Town*, p. 403.

32. Ibid., p. 404.

33. Ibid., pp. 404–405.

34. Ibid., p. 428.

Chapter 12. Mastering the Present, Facing the Future

1. The classic work on Arizona and the Central Arizona Project is Johnson, *The Central Arizona Project*. A recent treatment is Jack L. August Jr., *Vision in the Desert: Carl Hayden and Hydropolitics in the American Southwest* (Fort Worth: Texas Christian University Press, 1999). For a discussion of the 1964 decree from a distinctly California

viewpoint, see Norris Hundley Jr., "Clio Nods: Arizona v. California and the Boulder Canyon Act: A Reassessment," *Western Historical Quarterly* 3 (January, 1972): 50–51.

2. Linda Micale, *A Review of Key CAP-Related Decisions From 1965 to Present* (Tucson: Dames & Moore, 1995), 1–3 and 1–4.

3. Frank Welsh, *How to Create a Water Crisis* (Boulder, Colorado: Johnson Books, 1985), p. 142. See also Tony Davis, "Frank Welsh Hopes He Can Retire CAP," *Citizen*, January 2, 1985.

4. For a good summary of the controversy over Orme Dam, see Ron K. Schilling, "Indians and Eagles: The Struggle Over Orme Dam," *Journal of Arizona History* 41:1 (Spring, 2000): 57–82.

5. Schilling, "Indians and Eagles," pp. 68–69.

6. Welsh, *How to Create*, p. 144.

7. Schilling, "Indians and Eagles," p. 71–72.

8. Ibid., p. 72.

9. Micale, *Review*, pp. 1–5.

10. Robert A. Young and William Martin, "The Economics of Arizona's Water Problem," *Arizona Review* 16:3 (March, 1967): 13–17.

11. For a good brief summary of the CAP, see Joe Gelt et al., *Water in the Tucson Area: Seeking Sustainability* (Tucson: University of Arizona Water Resources Research Center, 1999), pp. 11–12.

12. Welsh, *How to Create*, p. 151.

13. Central Arizona Water Conservation District, "Chronological History of the Central Arizona Project and the Central Arizona Water Conservation District," manuscript, Central Arizona Water Conservation District, Phoenix, 1992, p. 6.

14. Ibid.

15. For a description of the floods, see U.S. Army Corps of Engineers, *Flood Damage Survey, Phoenix, Arizona, February 1980* (Los Angeles: U.S. Army Corps of Engineers, 1981).

16. For a discussion of the genesis of the planning process, see U.S. Bureau of Reclamation, *Factbook, Public Forums, November-December 1980: Central Arizona Water Control Study* (Phoenix: Arizona Projects Office, 1981) and U.S. Bureau of Reclamation, *Central Arizona Water Control Study Factbook* (Phoenix: Arizona Projects Office, 1981).

17. Bureau of Reclamation, *Central Arizona Water Control Study*, pp. 3–4.

18. Central Arizona Water Conservation District, "Chronological History," pp. 7–8.

19. James W. Johnson, *Summary of the 1980 Arizona Groundwater Management Act* (Phoenix: State Bar of Arizona, 1980), pp. 2–4.

20. Desmond D. Connall, "A History of the Arizona Groundwater Management Act," *Arizona State Law Journal* 2 (1982): 313.

21. Dale E. Pontius, "Groundwater Management in Arizona: A New Set of Rules," *Arizona Bar Journal* (October, 1980): 28–29.

22. Paul Beerman, "Tucson has its Water Supply under Constant Study," *Western City Magazine* 41 (June, 1965): 28.

23. *Star*, May 7, 1960; W. G. Matlock, H. C. Schwalen, and R. J. Shaw, "Progress

Report on Study of Water in the Santa Cruz Valley, Arizona," *University of Arizona Agricultural Experiment Station Report* 233 (Tucson: University of Arizona, 1965), p. 14; Arizona Water Commission, *Inventory of Resources*, p. 64; and Sonnichsen, *Tucson*, pp. 314–315.

24. Baker, "Reservoirs—Storage Tanks," in Baker, *Tucson Water History*, vol. I, 13-5.

25. Sonnichsen, *Tucson*, p. 315.

26. The problems in the Tucson water system are detailed in John A. Carollo, *Report Submitted to Metropolitan Utilities Management Agency* (Tucson: City of Tucson, 1976).

27. William E. Martin et al., *Saving Water in a Desert City* (Washington, D.C.: Resources for the Future, 1984), pp. 14–15.

28. Ibid., pp. 20–21.

29. Ibid., p. 22.

30. Ibid., p. 24.

31. Ibid., p. 25. For a good summary of the 1975–1976 controversy, see Gelt et al., *Water in the Tucson Area*, pp. 9–10.

32. *Minutes*, vol. 85, p. 439 (June 27, 1972).

33. *Minutes*, vol. 83, p. 11 (October 5, 1971); vol. 88, p. 22 (January 2, 1973); vol. 88, p. 213 (February 6, 1973); City of Phoenix, *Monthly Review* (November, 1974), p. 4.

34. Contract no. 11535, December 30, 1969, on file with Phoenix City Clerk Department.

35. Contract no. 12921, February 9, 1972, on file with Phoenix City Clerk Department.

36. Martin et al., *Saving Water*, pp. 428–429.

37. Ibid., p. 429.

38. Ibid.

39. Ibid.

40. Jack Rathjen, "Water Quality Data and Distribution," March 24, 2000, Flagstaff Public Library Vertical File.

Chapter 13. Environmental Reactions since 1980

1. Mary A. M. Gindhart, "The Babbitt Legacy: Water Management," in *Arizona Waterline*, ed. Athia L. Hardt (Phoenix: Salt River Project, 1988), p. 165.

2. John DeWitt and Steve Meissner, "State Suit Greets Final CAP Allocations," *Star*, December 2, 1980.

3. John Ellement, "Clark Picks Plan 6 For CAP Work," *Citizen*, April 4, 1984.

4. Mary A. M. Gindhart, "The Debate Over Funding Plan 6," in Hardt, *Arizona Waterline*, p. 149.

5. Micale, *Review*, p. x.

6. Thomas Clark, "Cliff Dam and the CAP," in Hardt, *Arizona Waterline*, p. 163.

7. John D. Leshy, "Implications of Federal Water Project Cost-Sharing," in Hardt, *Arizona Waterline*, p. 153.

8. Tony Davis, "First CAP Water Flows Wednesday," *Citizen*, May 20, 1985; "CAP Water Flows Out of Ditch 38 Years and 45 Minutes Late," *Citizen*, May 22, 1985.

9. Micale, *Review*, p. xi.

10. Contract no. 36282, October 25, 1984, on file with Phoenix City Clerk Department.

11. Micale, *Review*, p. xii.

12. Contract no. 41742, April 15, 1986, on file with Phoenix City Clerk Department.

13. Micale, *Review*, p. xiii.

14. Supplement to Contract no. 41742, July 1, 1987, on file with Phoenix City Clerk Department.

15. Enric Volante, "Long-Planned CAP Water Finally Welcomed to Tucson," *Star*, October 5, 1991.

16. Robert Jerome Glennon, "Coattails of the Past: Using and Financing the Central Arizona Project," *Arizona State Law Journal* 27:2 (Summer, 1995): 680–681.

17. Ibid., pp. 689–690.

18. Ibid., p. 690.

19. Ibid.

20. *Minutes*, vol. 83, p. 191 (April 4, 1974); vol. 104, p. 156 (February 1, 1977); vol. 107, p. 157 (October 25, 1977); vol. 108, p. 168 (January 31, 1978).

21. *Minutes*, vol. 123, p. 763 (December 15, 1981); vol. 132, p. 58 (January 10, 1984).

22. *Minutes*, vol. 139a, pp. 613–614 (December 4, 1985).

23. William L. Chase Jr., to City Manager Marvin Andrews, "City Council Report, CAP/SRP Interconnect Facilities," December 3, 1985, City of Phoenix Archives.

24. City of Phoenix, *Request for Proposals, Lake Pleasant Water Treatment Plant* (Phoenix: City of Phoenix, 2001), pp. 1–2.

25. Ibid., p. 2–1.

26. Ries Lindley, "The Central Arizona Project," in Baker, *Tucson Water*, vol. I, 3-1.

27. City of Tucson, "CAP Water—What it Will Mean to You," in Baker, *Tucson Water*, vol. I, pp. 3-4.

28. Ibid., pp. 3-7.

29. Enric Volante, "Long-Planned CAP Water Finally Welcomed to Tucson," *Star*, October 5, 1991.

30. Enric Volante, "CAP Water Flow to Tucson Taps Starts Tuesday," *Star*, October 30, 1992; Ibid., "Not Bad, Say Some of the First Sippers of CAP Water," *Star*, November 6, 1992; Tom Shields, "Tucsonans Accepting CAP Water," *Citizen*, November 27, 1992. A good summary of the events associated with the delivery of CAP water to the Tucson area is found in Gelt et al., *Water in the Tucson Area*, pp. 12–13.

31. Douglas Kreutz, "Wheeler Calls for Total Halt of CAP Deliveries," *Star*, August 17, 1993; Ann-Eve Pedersen, "Council, Water Officials Ready to Shut Off CAP Tap," *Citizen*, August 19, 1992; Mike Graham, "CAP Water Users Voice Their Anger," *Citizen*, August 19, 1993; Mark Thomas Swenson, "CAP Officials: Zinc Will Clear Up Rust," *Citizen*, September 11, 1993.

32. Joe Burchell, "City Council Votes to Keep Up CAP Deliveries," *Star*, August 25,

1993; "Council Orders Shut-off of CAP Water Delivery," *Star*, October 5, 1993; "Council Votes to Keep Using CAP System" *Star*, October 12, 1993; and Gelt et al., *Water in the Tucson Area*, p. 13.

33. Gelt et al., *Water in the Tucson Area*, p. 13.

34. Christina Valdez Diaz, "CAP Plan will Cost $61.5 Million," *Citizen*, December 6, 1995; and Gelt et al., *Water in the Tucson Area*, p. 13.

35. Gelt et al., *Water in the Tucson Area*, p. 13.

36. Mitch Tobin, "Answers to Common Questions On CAP Water," *Star*, May 3, 2001.

37. A. L. Wathan, "Report on Water Development San Xavier Indian Reservation, Arizona," manuscript on file, Bureau of Indian Affairs, Phoenix, June 23, 1923, p. 4; and F. Ellis Nielson and L. W. Holloway, "Irrigation Development for San Xavier," *Aw-o-tahn* 4:8 (1938): 1.

38. Nielson and Holloway, "Irrigation Development," p. 1.

39. Herbert V. Clotts, "Letter to A. L. Wathan, Director of Indian Irrigation Service," manuscript on file, Bureau of Indian Affairs, Phoenix, July 25, 1939, p. 3; and T. B. Hall, "Superintendent's Annual Report, Sells Agency," University of Arizona Special Collections, 1936, p. 70.

40. S. D. Clark, "Lessons from Southwestern Indian Agriculture," *University of Arizona Agricultural Experiment Station Bulletin* 125 (Tucson: University of Arizona, 1928), p. 246.

41. Turner, *Groundwater Resources*, p. 12; and Henry F. Dobyns, "The Papago People," manuscript on file, University of Arizona Special Collections, 1972, p. 58.

42. G. B. Keesee, "Report on the Status of the San Xavier Indian Irrigation Project at the Close of Fiscal Year 1940," manuscript on file, Bureau of Indian Affairs, Phoenix, 1940, p. 2.

43. Keesee, "Report," p. 2; and Clotts, "Letter," p. 3.

44. Keesee, "Report," pp. 3–5.

45. Nielson and Holloway, "Irrigation Development," p. 2; H. C. Schwalen, "San Xavier Collecting Pipeline Notes," H. C. Schwalen papers, collection AZ-563, University of Arizona Special Collections, 1940; and Keesee, "Report," p. 13.

46. Keesee, "Report," pp. 9–10; and Clotts, "Letter," p. 7.

47. A good early summary is Michael C. Nelson and Bradley L. Booke, "The Winters Doctrine: Seventy Years of Application of 'Reserved' Water Rights to Indian Reservations," *Arid Lands Resource Information Paper* 9 (Tucson: University of Arizona, 1977), p. 26. The definitive work on the Winters Doctrine from a historical perspective is John Shurts, *Indian Reserved Water Rights: The Winters Doctrine in its Social and Legal Context, 1880s–1930s* (Norman: University of Oklahoma Press, 2000).

48. Shurts, *Indian Reserved Water Rights*, pp. 43–55.

49. Ibid., pp. 150–157. The Fort Belknap case is cited as *Winters v. United States*, 207 U.S. 564 (1908). For a good summary of Indian water rights from an Arizona perspective, see Elizabeth Checchio and Bonnie G. Colby, *Indian Water Rights: Negotiating the Future* (Tucson: University of Arizona Water Resources Research Center, 1993).

50. Checchio and Colby, *Indian Water Rights*, pp. 9–10.

51. *Arizona v. California*, 373 U.S. 546 (1963).

52. A good summary of the early years of the adjudication is found in Mikel L. Moore and John B. Weldon Jr., "General Water Rights Adjudication in Arizona: Yesterday, Today, and Tomorrow," *Arizona Law Review* 27:3 (1985): 709.

53. Ibid.

54. The full text of the McCarran Amendment can be found at 43 U.S.C. section 666(a) (1952). The McCarran Amendment took its name from Nevada Senator Patrick McCarran, who devised it at the behest of the Department of Justice to assist a determination of rights concerning the Santa Margarita River in California; see Clark, *Water in New Mexico*, pp. 570–572.

55. A good summary of the later years of the adjudication is John E. Thorson, "State Watershed Adjudications: Approaches and Alternatives," *Rocky Mountain Mineral Law Institute Proceedings* 42 (1996): 22–36 to 22–37.

56. The decision that validated Arizona's approach to the adjudication of water rights is *Arizona v. San Carlos Tribe*, 463 U.S. 545 (1983).

57. Thorson, "State Watershed Adjudications," pp. 22–38. The relative merits of litigation and negotiation as methods to resolve Native American water rights claims is addressed by Peter Sly, *Reserved Water Rights Settlement Manual* (Washington, D.C.: Island Press, 1991), pp. 192–193. Sly includes an excellent summary of the lawsuits that underlie Arizona's general stream adjudications at pp. 194–198.

58. Checchio and Colby, *Indian Water Rights*, p. 49.

59. The lawsuit is cited as *United States v. City of Tucson*, U.S. District Court case no. Civ. 75-39 TUC-JAW. The Tohono O'odham were formerly known as the Papago. An excellent analysis of the issues involved with the Tohono O'odham is found in Lloyd Burton, *American Indian Water Rights and the Limits of Law* (Lawrence: University Press of Kansas, 1991), pp. 87–123.

60. John C. Hare, *Indian Water Rights: An Analysis of Current and Pending Indian Water Rights Settlements* (Washington, D.C.: Bureau of Indian Affairs, 1996), p. 44.

61. Ben MacNitt, "Papago OK Effort to Settle Water Suit," *Citizen*, February 18, 1980; Anne Q. Hoy, "Papago Bill Too Costly," *Citizen*, June 2, 1982; James R. Wyckoff, "Papago Water-Rights Act is Signed," *Citizen*, October 13, 1982; and John A. Folk-Williams, *What Indian Water Means to the West: A Sourcebook* (Santa Fe, New Mexico: Western Network 1982), p. 40.

62. For the Salt River Reservation, see John E. Thorson, "Report of the Special Master on the Proposed Salt River Pima-Maricopa Indian Community Water Rights Settlement; Motion for Approval of Report and Entry of Final Judgment; and Notice of Deadline for Filing Exceptions to the Report and Hearing on Those Objections," *In Re: General Adjudication of the Gila River System and Source*, Maricopa County Superior Court case no. W-1, W-2, W-3, W-4; Consolidated Contested case no. W1-200, filed October 16, 1991. For the Fort McDowell Reservation, see John E. Thorson, "Report of the Special Master on the Proposed Fort McDowell Indian Community Water Rights Settle-

ment; Motion for Approval of Report and Entry of Final Judgment; and Notice of Deadline for Filing Exceptions to the Report and Hearing on Those Objections," *In Re: General Adjudication of the Gila River System and Source*, Maricopa County Superior Court case no. W-1, W-2, W-3, W-4; Consolidated Contested case no. W1-201, filed October 13, 1993.

63. Hare, *Indian Water Rights*, p. 30.

64. Ibid., pp. 32–33.

65. Ibid., p. 20.

66. Thorson, "Fort McDowell Indian Community Water Rights Settlement," p. 3.

Chapter 14. Planning for the Future

1. For Tempe Town Lake, see CH2M Hill, Inc., *Rio Salado Town Lake Feasibility Study* (Tempe: CH2M Hill, 1992) and BRW, Inc., *Town Lake Capacity and Needs Study, Rio Salado Project, City of Tempe* (Phoenix: BRW, 1997). For the SDCP, see Barbara Tellman, *Water Resources in Pima County: A Report for the Sonoran Desert Conservation Plan* (Tucson: University of Arizona Water Resources Research Center, 2001), pp. 49–51.

2. *Republic*, March 26, 1987.

3. Management Research, Inc., *Economic Benefits of Alternative Uses for Effluent from the 23rd Avenue and 91st Avenue Sewage Treatment Plants* (Phoenix: Management Research, 1978).

4. Contract no. 13904, April 23, 1973, on file with Phoenix City Clerk Department.

5. U.S. Nuclear Regulatory Commission, *Final Environmental Impact Statement Related to Construction of Palo Verde Nuclear Generating Station, Units 1, 2 and 3* (Washington, D.C.: U.S. Nuclear Regulatory Commission, 1975).

6. *Republic*, March 26, 1987.

7. *Republic*, July 5, 1982.

8. *Republic*, April 28, 1982.

9. *Ronald Rayner and W. T. Gladden v. City of Phoenix, et al.*, Maricopa County Superior Court case no. C-473318 (1982); *John F. Long v. Salt River Project et al.*, U.S. District Court case no. CIV-83-2397 PHX CAM (1983); *Ronald Rayner and W. T. Gladden v. City of Phoenix, et al.*, Maricopa County Superior Court case no. C-505023 (1984); *City of Phoenix v. John F. Long*, Maricopa County Superior Court case no. C-562763 (1985).

10. *City of Phoenix v. Long*, 158 Ariz. 59 (1988).

11. *APS v. Long*, 160 Ariz. 429 (1989).

12. Ibid., p. 438.

13. *Minutes*, November 7, 1978.

14. *Minutes*, December 13, 1983; October 2, 1985.

15. William Chase, "Granite Reef Underground Storage Project Agreement City Council Report," September 30, 1992, City of Phoenix Archives.

16. Margaret Bushman LaBianca, "The Arizona Water Bank and the Law of the River," *Arizona Law Review* 40:2 (Summer, 1998): 659–660.

17. Chase, "Granite Reef Underground," p. 1.

18. William Chase, "City Participation in Granite Reef Underground Storage Project Expansion City Council Report," October 26, 1998, City of Phoenix Archives.

19. Chase, "City Participation," p. 2.

20. Christina Valdez Diaz, "S. Arizona CAP Recharge Begins," *Citizen*, July 31, 1996.

21. Keith Bagwell, "Water Banking Authority to Begin CAP Recharge in Pima," *Star*, January 9, 1997.

22. Ric Volante, "Plant to Treat Water From CAP Under Fire," *Star*, April 6, 1986.

23. Christine Valdez Diaz, "CAP Plan Will Cost 61.5 Million," *Citizen*, December 6, 1995.

24. Michael R. Graham, "$6M Pipe Fix to Help Solve CAP Woes," *Citizen*, July 18, 1998; Rhonda Bodfield, "Half of City's Water to be CAP Pumped From the Ground," *Star*, September 6, 1998.

25. City of Tucson, *A Comprehensive Guide To Clearwater, Tucson's New Blended Water Resource* (Tucson City of Tucson, 2001), p. 5.

26. Ibid., pp. 2–3.

27. Mitch Tobin, "Walkup Turns on Tucson's CAP Water Tap," *Star*, May 4, 2001.

28. U.S. Environmental Protection Agency, *Guiding Principles for Constructed Treatment Wetlands: Providing for Water Quality and Wildlife Habitat* (Washington, D.C.: U.S. Environmental Protection Agency, 2000), pp. 16–17.

29. Ibid., pp. 1–2.

30. City of Phoenix, *Phoenix Water Reclamation and Re-Use Study, Tres Rios Demonstration Wetlands* (Phoenix: City of Phoenix, 1993).

31. Michael Gritzuk, "Intergovernmental Agreement with the U.S. Bureau of Reclamation to Jointly Conduct the Tres Rios Demonstration Wetlands Construction and Research Project City Council Report," April 11, 1994, City of Phoenix Archives.

32. Michael Gritzuk, "Tres Rios Constructed Wetlands Project Summary City Council Report," January 28, 1999, City of Phoenix Archives.

33. Arizona Water and Pollution Control Association, "Tucson's Sweetwater Wetlands and Recharge Facility: A Practical and Innovative Alternative to Recycle Treated Wastewater," in Baker, *Tucson Water*, vol. II, pp. 26-101.

34. Ibid.

35. Ibid., pp. 26–100.

36. On the paradigm shift, see Robert Jerome Glennon and John E. Thorson, "Federal Environmental Restoration Initiatives: An Analysis of Agency Performance and the Capacity for Change," *Arizona Law Review* 42: 2 (Summer, 2000): 488–489.

Chapter 15. A New Water Vision for Urban Arizona

1. Mohamed T. El-Ashry and Diana C. Gibbons, *Troubled Waters: New Policies for Managing Water in the American West* (Washington, D.C.: World Resources Institute, 1986), pp. 39–40.

2. For New York, see Gerard T. Koeppel, *Water for Gotham: A History* (Princeton:

Princeton University Press, 2000). For an interesting comparison of Boston and Oakland, California, that points out many similarities between East and West, see Sarah S. Elkind, *Bay Cities and Water Politics: The Battle for Resources in Boston and Oakland* (Lawrence, Kansas: University Press of Kansas, 1998). For California, see Carey Mc-Williams, *California: The Great Exception* (New York: Current Books, 1949).

3. Grady Gammage Jr., *Phoenix in Perspective: Reflections on Developing the Desert* (Tempe, Arizona: Herberger Center for Design Excellence, College of Architecture and Environmental Design, Arizona State University, 1999), pp. 30–31.

4. For the Nature Conservancy, see Mitch Tobin, "Trying to Revive the San Pedro," *Star*, April 19, 2001.

5. For a sampling of recent lawsuits filed concerning endangered species and water infrastructure, see Mark Shaffer, "Verde Waters at Issue in Filing," *Republic*, May 26, 2001; Shaun McKinnon, "Taxpayers May Get $12 Million Fish Bill," *Republic*, October 10, 2000; Judd Slivka, "Environmental Group Files Suit Over Gila Watershed Diversion," *Republic*, July 10, 2001; and Mitch Tobin, "Suit Seeks To Safeguard Waterways," *Star*, January 8, 2002.

6. Joe Burchell, "Arsenic in Water Topic for Council," *Star*, September 11, 2001; and Maureen O'Connell, "New Rules on Arsenic May Hit 62 City Wells," *Star*, December 28, 2001.

7. Mitchell Vantrease, "New Water Standard No Problem in Valley," *Republic*, January 4, 2001.

8. City of Phoenix, *Water Resources Plan Update 2000* (Phoenix: City of Phoenix, 2000), IV-1 to IV-3.

9. N. Carl Tenney, "Pumping Water to Supply North Central Arizona Won't Hurt Valley," *Republic*, January 24, 2001; and Mark Shaffer, "Verde Valley Fears Prescott Will Dry River," *Republic*, February 5, 2001.

10. "Thirsty Williams Renews Request for Flagstaff Water," *Star*, August 14, 2000.

11. Shaun McKinnon, "State Facing Water Crisis With Growth," *Republic*, May 7, 2000.

12. Joe Burchell, "ASARCO to Try Using CAP Water in Mining," *Star*, October 17, 2000; and Ibid., "Marana, Oro Valley Might Get CAP Share," *Star*, November 28, 2001.

Bibliography

Archives and Manuscript Collections

Denver, Colorado. National Archives, Rocky Mountain Region
    Record Group 115, Records of the Bureau of Reclamation
Flagstaff, Arizona. City of Flagstaff
    Flagstaff Public Library Vertical File
Phoenix, Arizona. Bureau of Indian Affairs
    Archives
Phoenix, Arizona. Central Arizona Water Conservation District
    Archives
Phoenix, Arizona. City of Phoenix
    City Clerk Department
        Minutes of the Common Council and City Commission
        Contracts
        Ordinances
        Resolutions
        Archives
    City Manager's Office
        Monthly Review: City Manager's Summary of Activities
Phoenix, Arizona. Department of Water Resources
    Archives
Phoenix, Arizona. Maricopa County Recorder's Office

Book of Canals
Book of Deeds
Book of Mortgages
Prescott, Arizona. Sharlot Hall Museum
    Archives
Tempe, Arizona. Arizona State University. Hayden Library. Arizona
Collection
    J.L.B. Alexander papers
Tucson, Arizona. Arizona Historical Society
    Manuscript Collections
Tucson, Arizona. City of Tucson
    City Clerk Department
        Mayor and Council Minutes
        Resolutions
    Tucson Water Department
    Archives
Tucson, Arizona. University of Arizona. Special Collections
    H. C. Schwalen papers
Washington, D.C. National Archives
    Record Group 135, Records of the Public Works Administration

Unpublished Materials

Burns and McDonnell Engineering Company. "Report on Municipal Power Plant, Tucson, Arizona." 1933. Tucson, Arizona: Tucson Water Department.

Carollo, John A. "Water Works Survey Report, Tucson Arizona." 1959. Tucson, Arizona: Tucson Water Department.

Central Arizona Water Conservation District. "Chronological History of the Central Arizona Project and the Central Arizona Water Conservation District." 1992. Phoenix, Arizona: Central Arizona Water Conservation District.

City of Flagstaff. "Souvenir of the Completion of Flagstaff's New Four Billion Gallon Water Storage Project." Pamphlet, Flagstaff Public Library Vertical File, 1941.

Clotts, Herbert V. "Letter to A. L. Wathan, Director of Indian Irrigation Service." July 25, 1939. Phoenix, Arizona: Bureau of Indian Affairs.

Dobyns, Henry F. "The Papago People." 1972. Tucson, Arizona: University of Arizona, Special Collections.

Drake, Charles Rivers. "Transcript of Court Proceedings in the Trial of *Dalton et al. vs. Carrillo et al.*" 1885. Tucson, Arizona: Arizona Historical Society.

Hall, T. B. "Superintendent's Annual Report, Sells Agency." 1935. Tucson, Arizona: University of Arizona, Special Collections.

———. "Superintendent's Annual Report, Sells Agency." 1936. Tucson, Arizona: University of Arizona, Special Collections.

Halpenny, L. C., and R. L. Cushman. "Pumpage and Groundwater Levels in Arizona in 1951." 1951. Tucson, Arizona: University of Arizona, Special Collections.

Hayes, Benjamin. "Diary of Judge Benjamin Hayes." 1850. Tucson, Arizona: Arizona Historical Society.

Hill, Raymond A. "Additional Water Supply for City of Tucson, Arizona." 1930. Tucson, Arizona: Tucson Water Department.

Keesee, G. B. "Report on the Status of the San Xavier Indian Irrigation Project at the Close of Fiscal Year 1940." 1940. Phoenix, Arizona: Bureau of Indian Affairs.

Lippincott, J. B. "Report on the Available Water Supply from the Midvale Farms for the City of Tucson." 1930. Tucson, Arizona: Tucson Water Department.

Rathjen, Jack. "Water Quality Data and Distribution." March 24, 2000. Flagstaff Public Library Vertical File.

Turner, Samuel F. "Water Resources Available to the City of Tucson, Pima County, Arizona." 1959. Tucson, Arizona: Tucson Water Department.

Warner, Solomon. "Personal Notes and Papers." Tucson, Arizona: Arizona Historical Society.

Wathan, A. L. "Report on Water Development San Xavier Indian Reservation, Arizona." June 23, 1923. Phoenix, Arizona: Bureau of Indian Affairs.

Wheeler, C. C. "History and Facts Concerning Warner and Silver Lake and the Santa Cruz River." Tucson, Arizona: Arizona Historical Society.

Yost, Harold W. and Leigh O. Gardiner. "City of Tucson, Arizona: Report on Water Systems Investigations." 1948. Tucson, Arizona: Tucson Water Department.

Yount, C. E. "Notes on the History of Prescott's Water Supply." 1939. Prescott, Arizona: Sharlot Hall Museum.

Court Cases

Arizona Supreme Court

APS v. Long, 160 Ariz. 429 (1989).
City of Phoenix v. Long, 158 Ariz. 59 (1988).
Phoenix Water Co. v. Common Council of Phoenix, 9 Ariz. 430 (1906).

Maricopa County Superior Court

City of Phoenix v. John F. Long, case no. C-562763.
Hurley, Patrick J. v. Charles F. Abbott et al., case no. 4564.
In Re: General Adjudication of the Gila River System and Source, case no. W-1, W-2, W-3, W-4; Consolidated Contested case no. W1-200.
In Re: General Adjudication of the Gila River System and Source, case no. W-1, W-2, W-3, W-4; Consolidated Contested case no. W1-201.
Phoenix Water Co. v. Common Council of Phoenix, case no. 4283.
Rayner, Ronald and W. T. Gladden v. City of Phoenix et. al., case no. C-473318.
Rayner, Ronald and W. T. Gladden v. City of Phoenix et. al., case no. C-505023.

United States Supreme Court

Arizona v. California, 373 U.S. 546 (1963).
Arizona v. San Carlos Tribe, 463 U.S. 545 (1983).
Winters v. United States, 207 U.S. 564 (1908).

United States District Court

John F. Long v. Salt River Project et al., case no. CIV-83-2397 PHX CAM.
United States v. City of Tucson, case no. Civ. 75-39 TUC-JAW.

Newspapers

Arizona Daily Star (Tucson, Arizona)
Arizona Enterprise (Prescott, Arizona)
Arizona Gazette (Phoenix, Arizona)
Arizona Miner (Prescott, Arizona)
Arizona Mining Index (Tucson, Arizona)
Arizona Republic (Phoenix, Arizona)
Arizona Republican (Phoenix, Arizona)
Arizona Times (Phoenix, Arizona)
Arizona Weekly Star (Tucson, Arizona)
Phoenix Herald (Phoenix, Arizona)
San Francisco Call (San Francisco, California)
Territorial Expositor (Phoenix, Arizona)
The Taxpayer (Phoenix, Arizona)
Tucson Citizen (Tucson, Arizona)

Published Materials

Abbott, Carl. *The New Urban America: Growth and Politics in Sunbelt Cities*. Chapel Hill: University of North Carolina Press, 1987.
Ackerman, Edward A., and George O. G. Lof. *Technology in American Water Development*. Baltimore: Johns Hopkins Press, 1959.
Aldrich, L. D. *A Journal of the Overland Route to California and the Gold Mines*. Los Angeles: Dawson's Book Shop, 1950.
Alexander, Thomas G. *A Clash of Interests: Interior Department and Mountain West, 1863–96*. Provo, Utah: Brigham Young University Press, 1977.
Arizona Water and Pollution Control Association. "Tucson's Sweetwater Wetlands and Recharge Facility: A Practical and Innovative Alternative to Recycle Treated Wastewater." In *Tucson Water History: A Reference Book*, ed. Lynn D. Baker, vol. II, 26–100 to 26–101. Tucson: Tucson Water Department, 2000.

Arizona Water Commission. *Inventory of Resources and Uses, Phase 1, Arizona State Water Plan*. Phoenix, 1975.

August, Jack L. Jr. *Vision in the Desert: Carl Hayden and Hydropolitics in the American Southwest*. Fort Worth, Texas: Texas Christian University Press, 1999.

Babcock, H. M. and E. M. Cushing. "Recharge to Groundwater from Floods in a Typical Desert Wash, Pinal County, Arizona." *Transactions of the American Geophysical Union* 23: 1 (1942): 49–56.

Bainer, Roy. "Science and Technology in Western Agriculture." *Agricultural History* 49: 1 (January, 1975): 56–72.

Baker, Lynn D. "Tucson Water—The First 25 Years." In *Tucson Water History: A Reference Book*, ed. Lynn D. Baker, vol. I, 1-1 to 1-5. Tucson: Tucson Water Department, 2000.

——. "Tucson Water Department Contract / Bid Documents." In *Tucson Water History: A Reference Book*, ed. Lynn D. Baker, vol. I, 7-1 to 7-2. Tucson: Tucson Water Department, 2000.

——. "Reservoirs—Storage Tanks." In *Tucson Water History: A Reference Book*, ed. Lynn D. Baker, vol. I, 13-4 to 13-5. Tucson: Tucson Water Department, 2000.

——. "Standpipe, 4th Avenue and 18th Street." In *Tucson Water History: A Reference Book*, ed. Lynn D. Baker, vol. I, 13-8 to 13-9. Tucson: Tucson Water Department, 2000.

——. "Known Private Water Company Purchases." In *Tucson Water History: A Reference Book*, ed. Lynn D. Baker, vol. II, 21-1 to 21-3. Tucson: Tucson Water Department, 2000.

——. "Water Pumping Plant no. 2." In *Tucson Water History: A Reference Book*, ed. Lynn D. Baker, vol. II, 26-57. Tucson: Tucson Water Department, 2000.

——. "Water Pumping Plant no. 3." In *Tucson Water History: A Reference Book*, ed. Lynn D. Baker, vol. II, 26-79 to 26-99. Tucson: Tucson Water Department, 2000.

Baker, Lynn D., ed. *Tucson Water History: A Reference Book*. Tucson: Tucson Water Department, 2000.

Baker, Ray Stannard. "The Great Southwest. III. Irrigation." *Century Magazine* 64: 3 (July, 1902): 361–373.

Baker, T. Lindsay, and Steven R. Rae. *Water for the Southwest: Historical Survey and Guide to Historic Sites*. New York: American Society of Civil Engineers Historical Publications, 1973.

Balchin, W.G.V., and Norman Pye. "The Drought in the Southwestern United States." *Weather* 8: 8 (1953): 232–236.

Ballard, Steven C. and Thomas E. James, ed. *The Future of the Sunbelt: Managing Growth and Change*. New York: Praeger, 1983.

Bancroft, Hubert H. *History of Arizona and New Mexico: 1530–1888*. San Francisco: The History Company, 1889.

Barman, A. and J. Aubineau. *Reports on the Water Works of the Town of Flagstaff*. Flagstaff: Funston Press, 1901.

Baxter, John O. *Dividing New Mexico's Waters, 1700–1912*. Albuquerque: University of New Mexico Press, 1997.

Beerman, Paul. "Tucson has its Water Supply Under Constant Study." *Western City Magazine* 41 (June, 1965): 28.

Bell, J. G. "A Log of the Texas-California Cattle Trail, 1854." *Southwestern Historical Quarterly* 35 (April, 1932): 290–316; 36 (July, 1932): 47–66.

Berman, David R. *Reformers, Corporations, and the Electorate: An Analysis of Arizona's Age of Reform*. Niwot: University Press of Colorado, 1992.

Bernard, Richard M. and Bradley R. Rice, ed. *Sunbelt Cities: Politics and Growth Since World War II*. Austin: University of Texas Press, 1983.

Bigler, Henry W. "Extracts From the Journal of Henry W. Bigler." *Utah Historical Quarterly* 5 (April, 1932): 35–64; (July, 1932): 87–112; and (October, 1932): 134–160.

Birle, Siegfried. *Irrigation Agriculture in the Southwest United States*. Marburg, West Germany: University of Marburg Press, 1976.

Blaney, Harry F. and Martin R. Huberty. "Irrigation in the Far West." *Agricultural Engineering* 38: 6 (June, 1957): 414–417.

Bolton, Herbert Eugene. *Kino's Historical Memoir of Pimeria Alta*. Cleveland: Arthur H. Clark, 1919.

———. *Rim of Christendom*. New York: MacMillan and Company, 1936.

Bourke, John Gregory. *On the Border With Crook*. New York: Charles Scribner's Sons, 1891.

Box, Michael James. *Capt. James Box's Adventures and Explorations in New and Old Mexico*. New York: J. Miller, 1869.

Boyle, Robert V. "Southwest Gets Thirstier as Water Problem Grows." *Soil Conservation* 17: 9 (April, 1952): 195–198.

Brazel, Anthony J. "Statewide Temperature and Moisture Trends, 1895–1983." In *Arizona Climate*, ed. William D. Sellers and Richard H. Hill, 79–84. Tucson: University of Arizona Press, 1985.

Briggs, Lloyd Vernon. *Arizona and New Mexico 1882, California 1886, Mexico 1891*. Boston: n.p., 1932.

Brown, C. B. "Agriculture in Pima County, 1920–1928." *Tucson* 2: 3 (March, 1929): 3–6.

———. "Agricultural Adjustments." *Tucson* 4: 6 (June, 1931): 3–4.

BRW Inc. *Town Lake Capacity and Needs Study, Rio Salado Project, City of Tempe*. Phoenix: BRW, 1997.

Buffum, B. C. *Arid Agriculture*. N.p., 1909.

Bufkin, Don. "From Mud Village to Modern Metropolis: The Urbanization of Tucson." *Journal of Arizona History* 22:1 (Spring, 1981): 63–98.

Burrus, Ernest J. *Kino and Manje, Explorers of Sonora and Arizona: Their Vision of the Future*. St. Louis: Jesuit Historical Institute, 1971.

Burton, Lloyd. *American Indian Water Rights and the Limits of Law*. Lawrence: University Press of Kansas, 1991.

Carollo, John A. *Report Submitted to Metropolitan Utilities Management Agency*. Tucson: City of Tucson, 1976.

———. *Water Works Report, City of Flagstaff, Arizona*. Phoenix: John Carollo Engineers, 1971.

Castetter, Edward F. and Willis H. Bell. *Pima and Papago Indian Agriculture*. Albuquerque: University of New Mexico Press, 1942.

CH2M Hill. *Rio Salado Town Lake Feasibility Study*. Tempe: CH2M Hill, 1992.

Chapman Publishing Co. *Portrait and Biographical Record of Arizona*. Chicago: Chapman Publishing Co., 1901.

Checcio, Elizabeth and Bonnie G. Colby. *Indian Water Rights: Negotiating the Future*. Tucson: University of Arizona Water Resources Research Center, 1993.

Cheek, Annetta L. "The Evidence for Acculturation in Artifacts: Indians and Non-Indians at San Xavier del Bac, Arizona." Ph.D. diss., University of Arizona, 1977.

City of Flagstaff. *City of Flagstaff Water Program*. Flagstaff: City of Flagstaff, 1962.

City of Phoenix. *Phoenix Water Reclamation and Re-Use Study, Tres Rios Demonstration Wetlands*. Phoenix: City of Phoenix, 1993.

———. *2000 Water Quality Report*. Phoenix: City of Phoenix, 2000.

———. *Water Resources Plan Update, 2000*. Phoenix, City of Phoenix, 2000.

———. *Request for Proposals: Lake Pleasant Water Treatment Plant*. Phoenix: City of Phoenix, 2001.

City of Tucson. "Cap Water—What it Will Mean to You." In *Tucson Water History: A Reference Book*, ed. Lynn D. Baker, vol. I, 3-3 to 3-11. Tucson: Tucson Water Department, 2000.

———. *A Comprehensive Guide to Clearwater, Tucson's New Blended Water Resource*. Tucson: City of Tucson, 2001.

———. "Tucson Water General Statistical Information." In *Tucson Water History: A Reference Book*, ed. Lynn D. Baker, vol. II, 18-1 to 18-19. Tucson: Tucson Water Department, 2000.

Clark, Ira G. *Water in New Mexico: A History of its Management and Use*. Albuquerque: University of New Mexico Press, 1987.

Clark, S. D. "Lessons From Southwestern Indian Agriculture." *University of Arizona Agricultural Experiment Station Bulletin* 125. Tucson, University of Arizona, 1928.

Clark, Thomas. "Cliff Dam and The CAP." In *Arizona Waterline*, ed. Athia L. Hardt, 161–164. Phoenix: Salt River Project, 1988.

Cline, Platt. *They Came to the Mountain: The Story of Flagstaff's Beginnings*. Flagstaff: Northland Press, 1976.

———. *Mountain Town: Flagstaff's First Century*. Flagstaff: Northland Publishing, 1994.

Colby, William E. "The Freedom of the Miner and its Influence on Water Law." In *Legal Essays in Tribute to Orrin Kip McMurray*, ed. Max Radin, 67–84. Berkeley, University of California Press, 1935.

Colley, Charles C. "Water Under the Earth: Robert H. Forbes and the Fight for Control." *Journal of Arizona History* 16:3 (Autumn, 1975): 253–266.

Collins, William S. *The New Deal in Arizona*. Phoenix: Arizona State Parks Board, 1999.

Condron, A. H. "What Sabino Canyon Means to Tucson." *Tucson* 9:4 (April, 1936): 5, 12.

Connall, Desmond D. "A History of the Arizona Groundwater Management Act." *Arizona State Law Journal* 2 (1982): 313–344.

Cooke, Philip St. George. *The Conquest of New Mexico and California, An Historical and Personal Narrative.* Albuquerque: Horn and Wallace, 1964.

Cosulich, Bernice. *Tucson.* Tucson: Arizona Silhouettes, 1953.

Coues, Elliott, ed. *The Explorations of Zebulon Montgomery Pike.* New York: Harpers, 1895.

Crown, Patricia L. and W. James Judge, eds. *Chaco and Hohokam Prehistoric Regional Systems in the American Southwest.* Santa Fe: School of American Research Press, 1991.

Crown, Patricia L. and W. James Judge. "Synthesis and Conclusions." In *Chaco and Hohokam: Prehistoric Regional Systems in the American Southwest,* ed. Patricia L. Crown and W. James Judge, pp. 293–308. Santa Fe: School of American Research Press, 1991.

Cunningham, Bob. "The Box That Broke the Barrier: The Swamp Cooler Comes to Arizona." *Journal of Arizona History* 26 (Summer, 1985): 163–174.

Dart, Alan. *Prehistoric Irrigation in Arizona: A Context for Canals and Related Cultural Resources.* Tucson: Center for Desert Archaeology, 1989.

Davis, Richard N. *History of Dairying in Arizona.* Tucson: University of Arizona Agricultural Experiment Station, 1959.

Debo, Angie. *Geronimo.* Norman: University of Oklahoma Press, 1976.

Deverell, William F. "Fighting Words: The Significance of the American West in the History of the United States." In *A New Significance: Re-Envisioning the History of the American West,* ed. Clyde A. Milner II, pp. 29–55. New York: Oxford, 1996.

Dill, David B., Jr. "Terror on the Hassayampa: The Walnut Grove Dam Disaster of 1890." *Journal of Arizona History* 28:3 (Autumn, 1987): 283–306.

Dobkins, Betty Eakle. *The Spanish Element in Texas Water Law.* Austin: University of Texas Press, 1959.

Dornberger, Suzette. "The Struggle for Hetch Hetchy, 1900–1913." Master's thesis, University of California, Berkeley, 1935.

Doyle, David E. *Prehistoric Non-Irrigated Agriculture in Arizona: A Historic Context for Planning.* Phoenix: Estrella Cultural Research, 1993.

——. "Rillito and Rincon Period Settlements in the Middle Santa Cruz River Valley: Alternative Models." *Kiva* 43 (Winter, 1977): 93–110.

Dunbar, Robert G. "The Arizona Groundwater Controversy at Mid-Century." *Arizona and the West* 19:1 (Spring, 1977): 5–24.

Dunbier, Roger. *The Sonoran Desert: Its Geography, Economy, People.* Tucson: University of Arizona Press, 1968.

Durviage, John E. "Through Mexico to California: Letters and Journal of John E. Durviage." In Southwestern Historical Series, vol. V: *Southern Trails to California,* ed. Ralph P. Bieber. Glendale, California: Arthur H. Clark, 1937.

Eaton, W. Clement. "Frontier Life in Southern Arizona, 1858–1861." *Southwestern Historical Quarterly* 36 (January, 1933): 173–192.

Eccleston, Robert. *Overland to California on the Southwestern Trail: 1849*. Berkeley: University of California Press, 1950.

El-Ashry, Mohamed T. and Diana C. Gibbons. *Troubled Waters: New Policies for Managing Water in the American West*. Washington, D.C.: World Resources Institute, 1986.

Elkind, Sarah S. *Bay Cities and Water Politics: The Battle for Resources in Boston and Oakland*. Lawrence: University Press of Kansas, 1998.

Elliot, Wallace W. *History of Arizona Territory*. 1884; reprint ed., Flagstaff: Northland Press, 1964.

Emory, W. H. *Notes of a Military Reconnaissance from Fort Leavenworth, in Missouri, to San Diego, in California, Including part of the Arkansas, Del Norte, and Gila Rivers*. Washington: Wendell and Van Benthuysen, Printers, 1848.

Euchner, Charles C. "The Politics of Urban Expansion: Baltimore and the Sewerage Question, 1859–1905." *Maryland Historical Magazine* 86 (Fall, 1991): 270–91.

Fish, Suzanne K., Paul R. Fish, and John H. Madsen. "A Preliminary Analysis of Hohokam Settlement and Agriculture in the Northern Tucson Basin." In *Proceedings of the 1983 Hohokam Symposium, Part 1*, ed. Alfred E. Dittart Jr. and Donald E. Dove, pp. 53–85. Phoenix: Arizona Archaeological Society, 1985.

Fleming, Lawrence J. *Ride a Mile and Smile the While: A History of the Phoenix Street Railway, 1887–1948*. Phoenix: Arizona Historical Society, 1978.

Folk-Williams, John A. *What Indian Water Means to the West: A Sourcebook*. Santa Fe: Western Network, 1982.

Folk-Williams, John A., Susan Fry and Lucy Hilgendorf. *Western Water Flows to the Cities*. Santa Fe: Western Network, 1985.

Forbes, Robert H. "History of Irrigation Development in Arizona." *Reclamation Era* 26 (October, 1936): 226–227.

Fowler, R. G. "Where Tucson's Water Level Stands." *Tucson Business* 2:1 (April, 1976): 40–41.

Gallego, Hilario. "Reminiscences of an Arizona Pioneer." *Arizona Historical Review* 6:1 (January, 1935): 75–81.

Gammage, Grady, Jr. *Phoenix in Perspective: Reflections on Developing the Desert*. Tempe, Arizona: Herberger Center for Design Excellence, College of Architecture and Environmental Design, Arizona State University, 1999.

Ganoe, John T. "The Beginnings of Irrigation in the United States." *Mississippi Valley Historical Review* 25:1 (June, 1938): 59–78.

Gelt, Joe, Jim Henderson, Kenneth Seasholes, Barbara Tellman, and Gary Woodard. *Water in the Tucson Area: Seeking Sustainability*. Tucson: Water Resources Research Center, 1999.

Gindhart, Mary A. M. "The Debate Over Funding Plan 6." In *Arizona Waterline*, ed. Athia L. Hardt, pp. 149–151. Phoenix: Salt River Project, 1988.

——. "The Babbitt Legacy: Water Management." In *Arizona Waterline*, ed. Athia L. Hardt, pp. 165–167. Phoenix: Salt River Project, 1988.

Glennon, Robert Jerome. "Coattails of the Past: Using and Financing the Central Arizona Project." *Arizona State Law Journal* 27:2 (Summer 1995): 677–756.

Glennon, Robert Jerome and John E. Thorson. "Federal Environmental Restoration Initiatives: An Analysis of Agency Performance and the Capacity for Change." *Arizona Law Review* 42: 2 (Summer, 2000): 483–524.

Gookin, W. S. "Central Arizona Project." *Reclamation Era* 35 (January, 1949): 28.

Gottlieb, Robert. *A Life of its Own: The Politics of Power and Water*. San Diego: Harcourt, Brace, Jovanavich, 1988.

Grebinger, Paul and David P. Adam. "Hard Times? Classic Period Hohokam Cultural Development in the Tucson Basin." *World Archaeology* 6 (1974): 226–241.

Gregonis, Linda M. and Lisa W. Huckell. "The Tucson Urban Study." *Cultural Resource Management Section Archaeological Series* 138. Tucson: Arizona State Museum, 1980.

Griffin, Adrian H. "An Economic and Institutional Assessment of the Water Problem Facing the Tucson Basin." Ph.D. diss., University of Arizona, 1980.

Hamilton, Patrick. *Arizona, For Homes, For Health, For Investments*. Phoenix: n.p., 1886.

Hare, John C. *Indian Water Rights: An Analysis of Current and Pending Indian Water Rights Settlements*. Washington, D.C. Bureau of Indian Affairs, 1996.

Harris, Fisher Sanford. *100 Years of Water Development*. Salt Lake City: Metropolitan Water District of Salt Lake City, 1942.

Harshberger, A. J. "Mining in Pima County." *Tucson* 2:6 (June, 1929): 3–5.

Haskins, Charles Waldo and Joseph French Johnson. "The Recent History of Municipal Ownership in the United States." *Municipal Affairs* 4 (1902): 524–28.

Haury, Emil W. *The Hohokam, Desert Farmers and Craftsmen: Excavations at Snaketown, 1964–1965*. Tucson: University of Arizona Press, 1976.

——. "Snaketown: 1964–1965." *Kiva* 31:1 (October, 1965): 1–13.

Hecht, Melvin and Richard Reeve. *The Arizona Atlas*. Tucson: University of Arizona Office of Arid Lands Studies, 1981.

Hill, William R. "City Ownership of Water Supply." *Municipal Affairs* 4 (1902): 730–737.

Hinton, Richard J. *The Handbook of Arizona: Its Resources, History, Towns, Mines, Ruins, and Scenery*. San Francisco: Payot, Upham and Company, 1878; reprint ed., Tucson: Arizona Silhouettes, 1954.

Hoffman, Abraham. *Vision or Villainy: Origins of the Owens Valley–Los Angeles Water Controversy*. College Station, Texas: Texas A&M Press, 1981.

Holcomb, W. H. "The Development of the Deep-Well Turbine Pump." *Mechanical Engineering* 51:11 (November, 1929): 833–836.

Hollon, W. Eugene. *The Southwest: Old and New*. New York, Prentice-Hall, 1961.

——. "Walter Prescott Webb's Arid West: Four Decades Later." In *Essays on Walter Prescott Webb*, ed. by Kenneth R. Philp and Elliot West, pp. 53–72. Austin, University of Texas Press, 1976.

Holzhauser, William. "Lake in Catalinas Assured." *Tucson* 7:11 (Nov. 1934): 5, 17.

Hundley, Norris, Jr. "Clio Nods: *Arizona v. California* and the Boulder Canyon Act: A Reassessment." *Western Historical Quarterly* 3 (January, 1972): 17–51.

——. *Water and the West: The Colorado River Compact and the Politics of Water in the American West*. Berkeley: University of California Press, 1975.

———. *The Great Thirst: Californians and Water, 1770s–1990s.* Berkeley: University of California Press, 1992.

———. "Water and the West in Historical Imagination." *Western Historical Quarterly* 27: (Spring, 1996): 5–31.

International Geophysics, Inc. *Geophysical Survey Report, Riordan and Fort Valley Areas.* Flagstaff: City of Flagstaff, 1937.

———. *Geophysical Survey Report, Clark Valley–Riordan Area, Switzer Mesa Area, and Fort Valley Area.* Flagstaff: City of Flagstaff, 1938.

Johnson, James W. *Summary of the 1980 Arizona Groundwater Management Act.* Phoenix: State Bar of Arizona, 1980.

Johnson, Rich. *The Central Arizona Project.* Tucson: University of Arizona Press, 1977.

Kahrl, William L. *Water and Power: The Conflict Over Los Angeles' Water Supply in the Owens Valley.* Berkeley: University of California Press, 1982.

Karns, Harry J. *Luz de Tierra Incognita: Unknown Arizona and Sonora, 1693–1721.* Tucson: Arizona Silhouettes, 1954.

Kelso, Paul. "The Arizona Ground Water Act." *Western Political Quarterly* 1: 2 (June, 1948): 178–182.

Kimmelman, Alex Jay. "Luring the Tourist to Tucson: Civic Promotion in the Twenties." *Journal of Arizona History* 28:2 (Summer, 1987): 135–154.

Kinkade, Gay M. and Gordon Fritz. "The Tucson Sewage Project: Studies at Two Archaeological Sites in the Tucson Basin." *Arizona State Museum Archaeological Series* 64. Tucson: University of Arizona, 1975.

Koeppel, Gerard T. *Water for Gotham: A History.* Princeton, New Jersey: Princeton University Press, 2000.

Kohler, Timothy A. "The Final 400 Years of Prehispanic Agricultural Society in the Mesa Verde Region." *Kiva* 66:1 (Fall, 2000): 191–204.

Kupel, Douglas E. "Investigating Urban Infrastructure." *Journal of Urban History* 27:4 (May, 2001): 520–525.

———. "Urban Water in the Arid West: Municipal Water and Sewer Utilities in Phoenix, Arizona." Ph.D. diss., Arizona State University, 1995.

LaBianca, Margaret Bushman. "The Arizona Water Bank and the Law of the River." *Arizona Law Review* 40:2 (Summer, 1998): 659–680.

Leopold, Luna B. "Vegetation of Southwestern Watersheds in the Nineteenth Century." *Geographical Review* 41:2 (1951): 295–316.

Leshy, John D. "Implications of Federal Water Project Cost-Sharing." In *Arizona Waterline*, ed. Athia L. Hardt, pp. 152–156. Phoenix: Salt River Project, 1988.

Levick, M. B. *Tucson, Arizona.* San Francisco: Sunset Magazine Homeseekers Bureau, 1911.

Logan, Michael F. "Head-Cuts and Check Dams: Changing Patterns of Environmental Manipulation by the Hohokam and Spanish in the Santa Cruz River Valley, 200–1820." *Environmental History* 4 (July, 1999): 405–430.

Lotchin, Roger W. "Conclusion." In *The Martial Metropolis: U.S. Cities in War and Peace*, ed. Roger W. Lotchin, 223–232. New York: Praeger, 1984.

Lowitt, Richard. "The Hetch Hetchy Controversy, Phase II: The 1913 Senate Debate." *California History* 74 (Summer, 1995): 190–203.

——. *The New Deal and the West*. Bloomington: Indiana University Press, 1984.

Luckingham, Bradford. *Phoenix: The History of a Southwestern Metropolis*. Tucson: University of Arizona Press, 1989.

——. *The Urban Southwest: A Profile History of Albuquerque, El Paso, Phoenix, and Tucson*. El Paso: Texas Western Press, 1982.

Lyon, William H. "The Corporate Frontier in Arizona." *Journal of Arizona History* 9:1 (Spring, 1968): 1–17.

Mabry, Jonathan B. "Three Thousand Years of Irrigation in a Riverine Oasis." *Archaeology Southwest* 15:2 (Spring, 2001): 14–15.

Martin, Phil J. "Annual Statistical Report of the City Water Department." In *Tucson Water History: A Reference Book*, ed. Lynn D. Baker, Volume I, 2-60. Tucson: Tucson Water Department, 2000.

Martin, S. C. and R. M. Turner. "Vegetation Change in the Sonoran Desert Region, Arizona and Sonora." *Journal of Arizona Academy of Science* 12: 2 (June 1977): 54–69.

Masse, W. Bruce. "An Intensive Survey of Prehistoric Dry Farming Systems near Tumamoc Hill in Tucson." *Kiva* 45:1–2 (Fall-Winter, 1979): 141–186.

McWilliams, Carey. *California, The Great Exception*. New York: Current Books, 1949.

McWilliams, Mary and Roy Morse. *Seattle Water Department History, 1854–1954*. Seattle: City of Seattle, 1955.

Management Research, Inc. *Economic Benefits of Alternative Uses for Effluent From the 23rd Avenue and 91st Avenue Sewage Treatment Plants*. Phoenix: Management Research, 1978.

Mann, Dean E. *The Politics of Water in Arizona*. Tucson: University of Arizona Press, 1963.

Martin, William E., Helen M. Ingram, Nancy K. Laney, and Adrian H. Griffin. *Saving Water in a Desert City*. Washington, D.C.: Resources for the Future, 1984.

Matlock, W. G., H. C. Schwalen, and R. J. Shaw. "Progress Report on Study of Water in the Santa Cruz Valley, Arizona." *University of Arizona Agricultural Experiment Station Report* 233. Tucson: University of Arizona, 1965.

Meizner, Oscar Edward. "The History and Development of Ground-Water Hydrology." *Journal of the Washington Academy of Science* 24:1 (January 15, 1934): 6–32.

Melosi, Martin V. *The Sanitary City: Urban Infrastructure in America From Colonial Times to the Present*. Baltimore: Johns Hopkins, 2000.

Meyer, Michael C. *Water in the Hispanic Southwest: A Social and Legal History, 1550–1850*. Tucson: University of Arizona Press, 1984.

Micale, Linda. *A Review of Key CAP-Related Decisions from 1965 to Present*. Tucson: Dames & Moore, 1995.

Midvale, Frank. "Prehistoric Irrigation in the Salt River Valley." *Kiva* 34:1 (October, 1968): 28–32.

Miller, Gordon R. "Los Angeles and the Owens River Aqueduct." Ph.D. diss., Claremont Graduate School, 1977.

Miller, Tom. *Arizona: The Land and the People*. Tucson: Univ. of Arizona Press, 1986.

Moehring, Eugene P. "Public Works and Urban History: Recent Trends and New Directions." *Essays in Public Works History* 13 (1982): 1–60.

Mohl, Raymond H., ed. *Essays on Sunbelt Cities and Recent Urban America*. College Station: Texas A&M Press, 1990.

Moore, Mikel L. and John B. Weldon, Jr. "General Water Rights Adjudication in Arizona: Yesterday, Today, and Tomorrow." *Arizona Law Review* 27:3 (1985): 709–729.

Morrisey, Richard J. "The Early Range Cattle Industry in Arizona." *Agricultural History* 24:3 (July, 1950): 41–58.

Murphy, Merwin. *W.J. and the Valley*. Alhambra, California: Merwin Murphy, 1975.

Nabhan, Gary Paul. *The Desert Smells Like Rain: A Naturalist in Papago Indian Country*. San Francisco: North Point Press, 1982.

Nash, Gerald D. *The American West in the Twentieth Century: A Short History of an Urban Oasis*. Albuquerque: University of New Mexico Press, 1977.

———. *The American West Transformed: The Impact of the Second World War*. Bloomington: Indiana University Press, 1985.

———. *World War II and the West: Reshaping the Economy*. Lincoln: University of Nebraska Press, 1990.

Nelson, Michael C. and Bradley L. Booke. "The Winters Doctrine: Seventy Years of Application of 'Reserved' Water Rights to Indian Reservations." *Arid Lands Resource Information Paper* 9. Tucson: University of Arizona, 1977.

Newell, F. H. "Irrigation Developments in the United States." *Engineering Record* 64: 25 (December 16, 1911): 711–715; and 64: 26 (December 23, 1911): 745–747.

———. "The Human Side of Irrigation." *Engineering News-Record* 70: 9 (August 29, 1914): 236–237.

Nichols, Linda M. "Irrigation and Sociopolitical Development in the Salt River Valley, Arizona: An Examination of Three Prehistoric Canal Systems." Master's thesis, Arizona State University, 1981.

Niebur, Jay Edward. "The Social and Economic Effects of the Great Depression on Phoenix, Arizona, 1929–1934." Master's thesis, Arizona State University, 1967.

Nielson, F. Ellis and L. W. Holloway. "Irrigation Development for San Xavier." *Aw-o-tahn* 4:8 (1938): 1–3.

Officer, James E., Mardith Schuetz-Miller, and Bernard L. Fontana. *The Pimería Alta: Missions and More*. Tucson: Southwestern Mission Research Center, 1996.

Orme, S. H. "Sewage Irrigation." *Engineering News* 32:1 (July 5, 1894): 17–18.

O'Shaughnessy, M.M. *Hetch Hetchy: Its Origin and History*. San Francisco: Recorder Printing and Publishing, 1934.

Oshio, Kazuto. "Urban Water Diplomacy: A Policy History of the Metropolitan Water Supply in Twentieth Century Southern California." Ph.D. diss., University of California, Santa Barbara, 1992.

Palmer, Tim. *America By Rivers*. Washington, D.C. Island Press, 1996.

Parkman, I. H. "Hassayampa Dam Disaster." *Desert* 18:11 (November, 1955): 11–12.

Paulison, C.M.K. *Arizona, The Wonderful Country*. Tucson: Arizona Star, 1881.

Peterson, Thomas H. "A Tour of Tucson—1874." *Journal of Arizona History* 11:3 (Autumn, 1970): 180–201.

Pontius, Dale E. "Groundwater Management in Arizona: A New Set of Rules." *Arizona Bar Journal* (October, 1980): 28–29.

Powell, John Wesley. *Report on the Lands of the Arid Region of the United States*. Washington: U.S. Government Printing Office, 1878.

Preisler, Dennis. "Phoenix, Arizona During the 1940's: A Decade of Change." Master's thesis, Arizona State University, 1992.

Reich, Peter L. "The 'Hispanic' Roots of Prior Appropriation in Arizona." *Arizona State Law Journal* 27:2 (Summer, 1995): 649–662.

Reisner, Marc. *Cadillac Desert: The American West and its Disappearing Water*. New York: Viking, 1986.

Riddick, John. "Tucson Transformed." *Tucson Business* 1:1 (April, 1975): 11–14.

Ries, Lindley. "The Central Arizona Project." In *Tucson Water History: A Reference Book*, ed. Lynn D. Baker, vol. I, 3-1 to 3-2. Tucson: Tucson Water Department, 2000.

Rosen, Christine Meisner and Joel Arthur Tarr. "The Importance of an Urban Perspective in Environmental History." *Journal of Urban History* 20 (May, 1994): 299–310.

Roth, Barbara and Kevin Wellman. "New Insights Into the Early Agricultural Period in the Tucson Basin: Excavations at the Valley Farms Site." *Kiva* 67:1 (Fall, 2001): 59–79.

Ryden Architects. *An Historic Building Analysis of the Santa Fe Freight Depot, Flagstaff, Arizona*. Phoenix: Ryden Architects, 1995.

Safford, Anson P. K. *The Territory of Arizona, A Brief History and Summary*. Tucson: Arizona Citizen, 1874.

Salt River Project. *The Taming of the Salt*. Phoenix: Salt River Project, 1979.

Sargent, Charles. *Metro Arizona*. Scottsdale, Arizona: Buffington Books, 1988.

Schilling, Ron K. "Indians and Eagles: The Struggle Over Orme Dam." *Journal of Arizona History* 41:1 (Spring, 2000): 57–82.

Schultz, Stanley K. and Clay McShane. "To Engineer the Metropolis: Sewers, Sanitation, and City Planning in Late Nineteenth Century America." *Journal of American History* 65 (September, 1978): 389–411.

Schwalen, H. C. and R. J. Shaw. "Ground Water Supplies of Santa Cruz Valley of Southern Arizona Between Rillito Station and the International Boundary." *University of Arizona Agricultural Experiment Station Bulletin* 288. Tucson: University of Arizona, 1957.

Sellers, William D. and Richard H. Hill, ed. *Arizona Climate: 1931–1972*. Tucson: University of Arizona Press, 1974.

Sheridan, Thomas E. *Arizona: A History*. Tucson: University of Arizona Press, 1995.

Shurts, John. *Indian Reserved Water Rights: The Winters Doctrine in its Social and Legal Context, 1880s–1930s*. Norman: University of Oklahoma Press, 2000.

Sly, Peter W. *Reserved Water Rights Settlement Manual*. Washington, D.C. Island Press, 1991.

Smith, George E. P. "The Physiography of Arizona Valleys and the Occurrence of Ground Water." *University of Arizona Agricultural Experiment Station Technical Bulletin 77*. Tucson: University of Arizona, 1938.

———. "Pump Irrigation in the Santa Cruz Valley." *Arizona* 11:7 (December, 1920): 9, 11.

Smith, Henry Nash. *Virgin Land: The American West as Symbol and Myth*. Cambridge, Massachusetts: Harvard University Press, 1975.

Smith, Karen L. *The Magnificent Experiment: Building the Salt River Reclamation Project, 1890–1917*. Tucson: University of Arizona Press, 1986.

Smith, Norman. *Man and Water: A History of Hydro-Technology*. London: Peter Davies, 1976.

Sonnichsen, C. L. *Tucson: The Life and Times of an American City*. Norman, Oklahoma: University of Oklahoma Press, 1982. Second edition, 1987.

Souder, Jon A. and Sally K. Fairfax. *State Trust Lands: History, Management, and Sustainable Use*. Lawrence: University Press of Kansas, 1996.

Tarr, Joel A. *The Search for the Ultimate Sink: Urban Pollution in Historical Perspective*. Akron, Ohio: University of Akron Press, 1996.

Taylor and Taylor Consulting Engineers. *Engineering Report, Municipal Water System, City of Flagstaff, Arizona*. Los Angeles: Taylor and Taylor, 1947.

Taylor, Ray H. *Hetch Hetchy: The Story of San Francisco's Struggle to Provide a Water Supply for Her Future Needs*. San Francisco: R. J. Orozco, 1926.

Taylor, R. Brooks. "Cotton." In *Arizona the Grand Canyon State: A History of Arizona*, ed. Florence Wachholtz, pp. 49–59. Westminster, Colorado: Western States Historical Publishers, 1975.

Teaford, Jon C. *The Municipal Revolution in America*. Chicago: University of Chicago Press, 1975.

———. *The Twentieth Century American City: Problem, Promise, and Reality*. Baltimore: Johns Hopkins University Press, 1986.

Teiwes, Helga and Bernard L. Fontana. *Mission San Xavier Del Bac: A Photographic Essay on the Desert People and Their Church*. Tucson: University of Arizona Press, 1996.

Tellman, Barbara. *Water Resources in Pima County: A Report for the Sonoran Desert Conservation Plan*. Tucson: University of Arizona Water Resources Research Center, 2001.

Tellman, Barbara, Richard Yarde, and Mary G. Wallace. *Arizona's Changing Rivers: How People Have Affected the Rivers*. Tucson: University of Arizona Water Resources Research Center, 1997.

Territory of Arizona. *Acts, Resolutions, and Memorials*. Prescott: First Legislative Assembly, 1864.

Thorson, John E. "State Watershed Adjudications: Approaches and Alternatives." *Rocky Mountain Mineral Law Institute Proceedings* 42 (1996): 22-1 to 22-58.

Turner, Samuel F. *Groundwater Resources of the Santa Cruz Basin, Arizona.* Tucson: U.S. Geological Survey, 1943.

——. *Further Investigation of the Groundwater Resources of the Santa Cruz Basin, Arizona.* Tucson: U.S. Geological Survey, 1947.

Turner, Teresa. *The People of Fort Lowell.* Tucson: Fort Lowell Historic District Board, 1982.

Turney, O. A. "Prehistoric Irrigation." *Arizona Historical Review* 2:1 (April, 1929): 12–52.

U.S. Army Corps of Engineers. *Flood Damage Survey, Phoenix, Arizona, February, 1980.* Los Angeles: U.S. Army Corps of Engineers, 1981.

U.S. Bureau of Reclamation. *Report on Central Arizona Project.* Boulder City, Nevada: U.S. Bureau of Reclamation, 1947.

——. *Factbook, Public Forums, November–December 1980: Central Arizona Water Control Study.* Phoenix: Arizona Projects Office, 1980.

——. *Central Arizona Water Control Study Factbook.* Phoenix: Arizona Projects Office, 1981.

U.S. Department of War. "Letter of Secretary of War Communicating Copy of Report of Major D. Ferguson on the Country, Its Resources and the Route between Tucson and Lobos Bay." 37th Congress, Special Session, *Senate Ex. Doc.* no. 1. Washington: U.S. Government Printing Office, 1863.

U.S. Environmental Protection Agency. *Guiding Principles for Constructed Treatment Wetlands: Providing for Water Quality and Wildlife Habitat.* Washington, D.C.: U.S. Environmental Protection Agency, 2000.

U.S. Nuclear Regulatory Commission. *Final Environmental Impact Statement Related to Construction of Palo Verde Nuclear Generating Station, Units 1, 2, and 3.* Washington, D.C.: U.S. Nuclear Regulatory Commission, 1975.

U.S. Reclamation Service. *Salt River Project, Arizona: Limiting Irrigable Area of Land.* Washington: U.S. Reclamation Service, 1914.

U.S. Statutes at Large.

Vivian, R. Gwinn, "Chacoan Water Management." In *Anasasi Regional Organization and the Chaco System*, ed. David E. Doyle, pp. 45–57. Albuquerque: Maxwell Museum, 1992.

Walker, Henry P. and Don Bufkin. *Historical Atlas of Arizona.* Norman: University of Oklahoma Press, 1979.

Walton, John. *Western Times and Water Wars: State, Culture and Rebellion in California.* Berkeley: University of California Press, 1992.

Way, Phocion R. "Overland Via Jackass Mail in 1858: The Diary of Phocion R. Way," ed. William A. Duffen. *Arizona and the West* 2 (Spring, 1960): 35–53; (Summer, 1960): 147–164; (Autumn, 1960): 279–292; and (Winter, 1960): 353–370.

Weaver, John M. "The History of Fort Lowell." Master's thesis, University of Arizona, 1947. Webb, Walter Prescott. *The Great Plains.* Boston: Ginn & Co., 1931.

Welsh, Frank. *How to Create a Water Crisis.* Boulder, Colorado: Johnson Books, 1985.

Wenum, John D. "Spatial Growth and the Central City: Problems, Potential, and the Case of Phoenix, Arizona." Ph.D. diss., Northwestern University, 1968.

Westerlund, John S. "U.S. Project Men Here: Building Navajo Ordinance Depot at Flagstaff." *Journal of Arizona History* 42:2 (Summer, 2001): 201–226.

Wilcox, David R. "Warfare Implications of Dry-Laid Masonry Walls on Tumamoc Hill." *Kiva* 45:1–2 (Fall-Winter, 1979): 15–38.

Wilson, Andrew W. "Tucson: A Problem in Uses of Water." In *Aridity and Man: The Challenge of the Arid Lands in the United States*, ed. Carle Hodge and Peter C. Duisberg, pp. 483–505. Washington: American Association for the Advancement of Science, 1963.

Wilson, Roy P. "Cooperation and Conflict in a Federal-Municipal Watershed: A Case Study of Portland, Oregon." Ph.D. diss., Oregon State University, 1989.

Woosley, Anne. "Agricultural Diversity in the Prehistoric Southwest." *Kiva* 45:4 (Summer, 1980): 317–335.

Worster, Donald E. *Rivers of Empire: Water, Aridity, and the Growth of the American West.* New York: Pantheon Books, 1986.

——. *A River Running West: The Life of John Wesley Powell.* New York: Oxford University Press, 2001.

——. "Transformations of the Earth: Toward an Agroecological Perspective in History." *Journal of American History* 76 (March, 1990): 1087–1106.

Xavier, Guyneth H. *The Cattle Industry of the Southern Papago Districts.* New York: Garland Publications, 1974.

Yard, Robert Sterling. "The Unforgotten Story of Hetch Hetchy." *American Forests* 40 (December, 1934): 566–69.

Yeatts, Manuella S. "A River is Born." *Arizona Quarterly* 5:3 (Autumn, 1949): 254–257.

Young, Robert A. and William Martin. "The Economics of Arizona's Water Problem." *Arizona Review* 16:3 (March, 1967): 9–18.

Zarbin, Earl. *The Swilling Legacy.* Phoenix: Salt River Project, 1978.

Illustration Credits

Drinking from a barrel cactus. (Courtesy of the Arizona Historical Society, Tucson, Muriel Upham Collection, no. 92948)

Reg Manning editorial cartoon on the demise of the Hohokam. (Used with permission of Colonel David C. Manning)

A woman washing clothes in the Santa Cruz River in Tucson. (Courtesy of the Arizona Historical Society, Tucson, no. 21969)

Tucson Water Company building. (Courtesy Lynn Baker, City of Tucson)

Winslow girls doing laundry circa 1925. (Courtesy Arizona State Library, Archives and Public Records, Archives Division, Phoenix, no. 98-0676)

Delivering supplies for Flagstaff's 1898 pipeline. (Courtesy Arizona Historical Society, Northern Arizona Division, Flagstaff, no. AHS.0338.00005)

Concrete infiltration gallery on the redwood pipeline. (Courtesy City of Phoenix)

The redwood pipeline for Verde River water. (Courtesy City of Phoenix)

The Elm Street reservoir in Tucson. (Courtesy Lynn Baker, City of Tucson)

A "Day of Thanksgiving for Water" April 26, 1941. (Courtesy of SRP Research Archives)

The Lake Mary Water Treatment Plant in Flagstaff. (Courtesy Cline Library, Northern Arizona University, Flagstaff, Fronske Collection, NAU.PH.85.3.0.223)

Inspecting a new well site in Tucson, 1954. (Courtesy Lynn Baker, City of Tucson)

The gates across the Horseshoe Dam spillway. (Courtesy SRP Research Archives)

The Verde River Water Treatment Plant in Phoenix. (Courtesy Arizona Historical Foundation, Arizona State University, Tempe, R. Gail Baker Collection, AHF no. BA-93)

New tract homes in former citrus orchards outside Phoenix. (Courtesy Arizona State Library, Archives and Public Records, Archives Division, Phoenix, no. 97-0970)

The Squaw Peak Water Treatment Plant in Phoenix. (Courtesy SRP Research Archives)

The Deer Valley Water Treatment Plant in Phoenix. (Courtesy SRP Research Archives)

Roosevelt Dam. (Courtesy Salt River Project)

The interconnect of the Central Arizona and Salt River Projects. (Courtesy SRP Research Archives)

The Palo Verde nuclear plant. (Courtesy Arizona Public Service Company, Phoenix)

Index

33; groundwater, 4–6, 121, 177, 229; growth, 156–157, 177–180; municipal water systems, 70–71, 89–95, 123, 136–137, 177–180; Parker and Watts franchise, 41–46; private water systems, 33, 39–46, 57–58, 177; recharge, 212–215, *214*; sale of effluent, 81, 215; water crisis of 1970s, 177–180; wetlands, 216–217; and World War I, 89–91; and World War II, 121–124, 135–137
Tucson Electric Power (TEP), 208
Tucson Water Co., 42–44
Tucson Water Department, 58; and CAP, 192–195; infrastructure and growth, 70–71, 89–91, 123, *136*, 137, 177–180; recharge, 213
Tumacácori, 27
Typhoid fever, 47

Udall, Morris, 192, 202
Udall, Nicolas, 144, 146, 159
Underground water storage. *See* Recharge
Union Hills Water Treatment Plant, 187, 190
U.S. Army Corps of Engineers, 215–216
U.S. Bureau of Reclamation, 171, 189, 216
U.S. Fish and Wildlife Service, 187
U.S. Reclamation Service, 79–80
U.S. Resettlement Administration, 118
Upper Gila Water Supply Study, 186

Val Vista Investment Co., 163
Val Vista Water Treatment Plant, 163, 180–181
Van Valkenburg, N. P., 130–131, 148
Veit, Charles, 53
Venable, Gil, 171
Verde River: infiltration gallery, 116; irrigation and drainage district, 141; irrigation and power district, 140; and Phoenix water crisis, 125–127;

pipeline project, 87, 95–100, 109–112, 225–226; water rights adjudication, 200; water treatment plant, 147–149, *148*, 162. *See also* Salt River Project
Volante, Enric, 193
Volunteer Springs, 133

Walkup, Bob, 214
Walkup, J. D. "Jim," 118
Warne, William, 145
Warner, Solomon, 32, 40
War Production Board, 130
Wastewater treatment plants (WWTPs): and constructed wetlands, 215–217; Ninety-first Avenue Wastewater Treatment Plant, 181, 207–210, 215–216; *See also* Effluent; Water treatment plants
"Water elite," 222, 224–225
Water legislation, city level: Phoenix/SRP domestic water agreement (1952), 157–161, 168–169; Water Consumer Protection Act and Tucson citizen initiative (1995), 194–195, 213
Water legislation, federal: *Arizona v. California* (1963), 154, 170–171, 199; Colorado River Compact (1922), 198; federal Indian reserved rights, 198–199; Fort McDowell Indian Community Water Rights Settlement (1993), 203–204; general stream adjudications (1970s), 199–201; Groundwater Management Act (1980), 176–177, 211; Horseshoe Dam floodwater appropriations, 140–145; *Hurley v. Abbott* (1910), 79–80; Kent Decree (1910), 79–80, 200, 203, 204; McCarron Amendment (1952), 201; National Reclamation Act (1902), 79–80; SAWRSA (1982), 186, 202; Townsite Act (1906), 80; *Winters v. United States* (1908), 198–199
Water legislation, state: *APS v. Long*

About the Author

Doug Kupel has worked for the City of Phoenix Law Department since 1988, where he conducts historical research for environmental litigation. He received his doctoral degree from Arizona State University and his master's degree from the University of Arizona. Prior to joining the City of Phoenix, he worked as a historian for the Arizona State Historic Preservation Office. Before moving to Arizona in 1984, he worked as a historian and archaeologist for government agencies in California, Nevada, and Illinois. He maintains an active membership in several professional organizations in the fields of archaeology and history, including registration as a professional archaeologist by the Register of Professional Archaeologists. His articles and book reviews have been published in the *Mining History Journal*, the *Journal of Urban History*, the *Journal of Arizona History*, the *Public Historian*, the *Journal of Urban Affairs*, and *Western Legal History*. He has taught history courses at Phoenix College, Gateway Community College, and Arizona State University.

Carol,

Thank you

Scott King

**Cancer Only Sucks On Days
That End In "Y"**

4/C+/

Cancer Only Sucks On Days That End In "Y"

Scott D. Finestone

To order additional copies of this book, contact:
Xlibris Corporation
1-888-795-4274
www.Xlibris.com
Orders@Xlibris.com
50620

Contents

Introduction

I am beyond clueless as to what actually constitutes an "introduction." But, I am very aware that any person stumbling across this book, and reading through the table of contents, will be either shocked or insulted by the descriptions that are given. To that end, I felt it necessary to forewarn you that I am a sarcastic animal by nature. This book is a combination of our history fighting this disease and advice for families that are joining the battle. I have a long history of hiding my pain behind my words, so inside the following pages you will learn about our journey through this wonderful disease known as cancer. If after reading my book you are at all interested in boring yourself to tears, you can go online to *www.caringbridge.org/fl/zacharyfinestone* and select the 'Read Journal History' tab where you will find all of my journal entries dating back to May of 2002 when I started to post them online.

Inside the following pages, you will not only find the topics that are mentioned in the Table of Contests, but intertwined amongst those you will also find "Classic Journal" entries. These are actual journal entries that were written and posted on the date shown. I have gone to great lengths to select relevant entries that will hopefully give you a unique insight into what was going on in our lives at the time of each entry. Please keep in mind that some of the context contained in these dated entries will have references to subjects that are not included in the story, so it may at times be a little bit confusing. Having said that, I have carefully (somewhat) chosen specific entries that have some relevance to the chapter that they are included in, so read them through completely before passing judgment. There is a nickname that we starting using for Zachary when he was first diagnosed, and I am certain that it is not explained anywhere in the journal entries that I have included in this book. So, when you see the name "Zman," you will know that I am speaking of the man, the myth, the legend . . . . Zachary.

As of the writing of this book (5/1/08) there had been over 600,000 hits to that web page. That's over 100,000 hits/year. Many of the visitors who have posted comments in our guestbook over the years have suggested that I should write a book. It is because of those pesky, prodding, lurkers that this book even exists. So blame them!

Acknowledgements:

There are so many organizations, family, friends, and acquaintances to thank, that I am CERTAIN if I try to list them all, I will fail miserably. Mine and Rebecca's families have been amazing and unwavering in their support, both emotionally and financially over the past 8 years. Through personal illnesses, and geographical, financial and logistical challenges, they have always found a way to be there for us. Through sickness and in health, my parents have gone above and beyond the call of duty by making themselves available to us even when they were facing life changing illnesses of their own. My two brothers and their families live far away, but they have repeatedly shown how much they value the bond of our family by making themselves and their resources available to us when we have needed them. My cousins in Atlanta have also been there for us, providing moral support and advice when we have needed it. Rebecca's father and grandparents have always made Zachary and our family a priority in their lives, even when they too were facing uncertainty and medical turmoil. I would like to make a special mention of Ian, Rebecca's brother, who through extreme adversity has always found time for Zachary and for our family.

The only way that I could ever do justice to the numerous charities that have helped us is by listing their contact information the way that I did. I truly hope that my stories and your curiosity will drive you to read up on or research one or more of the many charities that I have mentioned. All of them are wonderful organizations that help families like ours each and every day. They rely on the support of people like you, so please never underestimate how powerful your time, resources or donations can mean to them. My business partner for 11 years and friend of over 30 years and his family have been an amazing source of help and comfort since diagnosis. From day 1, the Weekman family was standing alongside us in the hospital, making sure that we had them as a crutch to lean on. For that, we will always be grateful. I would also like to thank the Palmer's our "second" family here in Florida. They have always included us in their family gatherings and made us a part of their lives. Their support and advice on issues from life to school to pharmacy questions has proven to be invaluable over the years. Zachary's two public schools, their administrators and entire staff have been an integral part in not only keeping Zachary on pace with his classmates, but by improving Zachary's quality of life by going above and beyond to help us out. I would like to make a special mention of the two Beth's, one from elementary school and the other from middle school. They both have figured enormously in our success with school. The fundraisers that were done early in Zachary's diagnosis saved us from certain bankruptcy and financial ruin, and for that, we will be eternally grateful to Jensen Beach Elementary School.

To the many friends and local companies that have helped us over the years, we thank you from the bottom of our hearts. The dinners, money, chores, gift cards, prayers, etc. that you embraced us with helped us to survive during times where the survival of our family was very much in question. I applaud you for stepping up and helping a family like ours when many of you had no personal connection to us. You have shown that the true spirit of giving and helping a neighbor is alive and well in Jensen Beach, Florida.

The many doctors and hospitals that I have repeatedly ridiculed and lambasted in my journal entries deserve to be recognized for something other than errors and problems. Rebecca and I know how fortunate we are to have been blessed with a parade of qualified and caring medical personnel over the past 8 years. To date, we have been in 10 hospitals in four states, and received medicine from an eleventh in yet another state. The many specialists, support staff and administrators who have contributed to Zachary's longevity will always hold a special place in our hearts.

In that last paragraph I purposely did not mention the nurses who have treated Zachary over the years. To mention them as part of a larger group would not do justice to what the many nurses who have treated Zachary have meant to us. From Zachary's first day of diagnosis, we were introduced to a level of care that we had never known existed. Zachary's many treating nurses have contributed so much to our quality of life and to Zachary's well-being that I feel guilty for not having dedicated an entire chapter to them. I recall many occasions when the nurses acted on our behalf to prevent the administration of the hospital from mistreating the cancer families, and I remember at least two times when a visiting specialist (doctor) was suggesting treatments that the nurses warned us about. Without them, this journey would have been even more of a nightmare than it has been.

An acknowledgement page in this book would be incomplete without mentioning the legions of faithful "lurkers" and "posters" who have "plagued" the pages of our guest book since May of 2002. In the past 8 years you have visited our page to check on Zachary over 600,000 times. Many of you have passed along Zachary's web page address to friends and family, thus resulting in the accumulation of an amazing network around the world of caring people who have added us to their prayer lists and made us a part of their lives. As I mentioned in the introduction, it is because of the many urgings of guest book signers that I finally got off of my butt and wrote this book.

Last but certainly not least, there are the numerous cancer families who have either directly or indirectly touched our lives. The original Cancer Sucks Club included the following families: Us, the Charlton's, the Mathis's, the Schmidt's, the Jorgensen's, the Pacheco's, and the Baileys. There were many other families who were a part of our club locally and remotely, however, the above-mentioned families were together at the hospital on many occasions and made it a point to make time for each other away from the cancer floor. I credit all of the cancer families for helping to inspire me with their stories and for lighting a fiery rage against this disease in me that stoked the flames of creativity and kept me sane (or insane depending on your perspective) for all of these years.

I would also like to give a special thanks to Michael Price for allowing me to use the amazing photograph that appears on the cover of this book. Please check out his other great photos at: *www.michaelpricephotography.com*.

P.S. In keeping with my most common ending for journal entries, there has got to be a post script. Zachary and Rebecca have been with me since early in 1995. Rebecca was only 18 at the time, and Zachary was about 9 months old. I am the only father that Zachary has ever known. Many of you were already aware of the fact that after Rebecca and got married in 1998, I adopted Zachary to make it official. I was with him for his first words, his first steps, and of course when we started this journey together with his battle with cancer. I have never viewed him as my adopted son, but rather as just . . . . . my son! I am truly blessed to have a loving, caring and understanding wife who tolerates my sarcastic take on the world and allows me to vent via the web page and now this book. I am continually inspired and humbled by the strength, courage and veracity with which Zachary has fought this disease and I am quite certain that had I ever faced a fraction of the adversity that he has faced, I would surely have succumbed to its powers and lost miserably. Zman rocks!

Chapter 1

Life before Cancer

"It is hard to remember our life before diagnosis, but I read about those years on the internet, so they must have existed."

It is difficult to remember a life before cancer because we have been fighting it for over eight years. I however am a firm believer that ALL stories should begin and end on a good note. Nothing is more depressing than seeing a movie where the good guy loses in the end!

Our story began in October of 1994. I was working as an assistant manager for a large pharmacy chain, and Rebecca was working next door in a flower shop. I had been in there a few times to buy flowers for my girlfriend, so I had met her on a couple of occasions. My girlfriend and I ended our relationship, and about a month later, Rebecca lost her job with the florist and she came into my store looking for a job as a cashier. She was an 18 year old single mom who carried herself with the maturity of someone in their twenties. I was 33 at the time, (no spring chicken), but until I read her application, I had no idea that she was only 18 years old. Her son Zachary was only 7 months old at the time, and I distinctly remember thinking that he looked like an angel. Whenever Rebecca would bring him into the store, people would gravitate towards him. His personality and disposition were both electrifying and calming to me at the same time. Shortly after Rebecca was hired, we began to date. And shortly after that, I had to inform my boss that I was dating an employee and that I needed to be transferred. (Companies frown upon that kind of stuff these days.)

Zachary played an integral part in our relationship from when Rebecca and I first started dating. He had never known his biological father, so his only male

13

influence was Rebecca's younger brother who was living with her. Ian was 13 years old at the time. Ian's father had passed away a couple of years before I met them and Rebecca's father lived up north in New Hampshire. Rebecca's mother was supposed to be living with her, taking care of Ian, but she was dealing with her own demons, and was gone more than she was around. So Rebecca, at age 18, was taking care of her younger brother, and her baby. (As I wrote earlier, she was very mature for her age.) Within six months of beginning our relationship, we had moved in together. We were an instant family, (just add water and stir.) I was there with her when Zachary uttered his first words, and when he took his first steps, I was there to hold his hand. I am the only father Zachary has ever known.

Rebecca, Zachary and I very quickly formed a bond which has helped to carry us through our current battles with cancer. When Rebecca and I got married in March of 1998, Zachary was only four years old, but he participated by handing Rebecca a bouquet of flowers during the ceremony. I adopted him about two months after our wedding. To this day, when folks meet us, they comment that he looks and acts more like me than her. There have been a few times when he has tried to use the fact that I am not his biological father against me, but in the end, when the dust settles, I think that all of us would agree that we were destined to be a part of each other's lives.

In addition to personality quirks, Zachary has always taken after me when it comes to sports. He excelled at soccer at a very young age, and when I used to play roller-blade hockey, he would be there with his skates, wanting to pass the puck or practice shooting with me between periods or after my games. My competitiveness also rubbed off on him, he hates to lose! I imagine in some ways this has helped him to battle his cancer for so long, Zachary has never been a quitter! Rebecca has also shown that she is a survivor. Through extreme adversity, she raised her son, raised her brother, finished high school, and even completed some college courses and earned her elementary teacher's aide certificate while we were first dating. All of that may seem trivial to some folks who have faced adversity themselves, but there is more to this story than meets the eye. When Rebecca was 18 years old, she was diagnosed with lupus and rheumatoid arthritis. By the time she was diagnosed, she had lost a fair amount of bone density, especially in her hands. Having the odds stacked against her has never stopped her from forging ahead and finding a way to keep us bonded tightly as a family. She just recently started an online course to become a medical transcriptionist. Rebecca is currently working for a local bowling alley while studying for her degree; she expects to complete that program within the next few months.

As for me, I was raised in a tight-knit family with two brothers, one older and one younger. My older brother is a Senior Vice-President with a major automotive retail company, and my younger brother has a degree in physical therapy which he uses in his position as the sales manager for a large medical supply company. My father is a retired anesthesiologist and my mother is a retired nurse/counselor. I am the oddball of the family. I completed my associate's degree and jumped from one job to another before landing with the pharmacy chain that I mentioned earlier. I was there about five years before I purchased a fishing lure business with my friend of 30 years. We turned that little business into a respected tackle distribution company that we ran successfully for 11 years before selling it. I now work in sales when I am not helping with Zachary's numerous doctors' visits.

So there you have it, a little taste of our history. Now that you know who the players are, we can get to the "game."

Chapter 2

Diagnosis

"Also known as 'D-Day,' or 'The End of Days,' or 'Holy Shit What Am I Going To Do Now, Day.'"

On March 16, 2000, our world drastically changed. Actually, it changed long before that date, but we just hadn't figured it out yet. In February of 2000, our son Zachary who was 5 at the time, started to experience frequent fevers and then mild to moderate back pain that eventually became severe. He had just joined a t-ball league, and after each practice, his back would be hurting for a day or so. There were other more subtle changes in him that we as parents had missed. (This is the part where, as a parent, you get to beat yourself up and then blame each other. But, more on the "Blame Game" later.) Zachary's frequent fevers had us running back and forth to the pediatrician's office, where our son was placed on the conveyor belt of children waiting to see one of the many doctors who worked at that practice. The "conveyor belt" would move, your child would get placed in an examination room, and then a doctor would come in and proceed to NOT examine your child. Sure, they would LOOK at your child, but God-forbid they would actually TOUCH them. After the cursory 8.4 second exam, a diagnosis of a pulled muscle from t-ball and a flu bug would be made, a prescription for antibiotics would be written, and then you would be on your way.

Now, at this point in my diagnosis story, you are probably getting the impression that we blame the pediatrician for not catching the disease earlier. Yeah, he screwed up, a little bit, for not being more hands-on with Zachary, but in all reality, the odds were stacked against him of ever making a diagnosis.

(More on that later.) After several weeks of the fever/pain thing not going away, it was suggested to me by my father (a retired physician) that six-year olds do NOT usually have the strength to pull muscles. His suggestion was that we have Zachary seen by an orthopedic surgeon. I called the pediatrician's office and asked for a referral for an orthopedic surgeon. The receptionist there very bluntly informed me that they do NOT give referrals. I returned the favor by very bluntly informing her that we had a PPO, and that I didn't NEED her permission to see another doctor. I further informed her that if she was unwilling to give me the name of an orthopedic surgeon that I would play 'Eenie, meenie, minie, moe" with the doctor list to choose one myself. She responded by saying, "Well, if you are going to be that way about it, then here is the name of the doctor who we sometimes use." (Problem solved.)

We called the new doctor's office and asked for an appointment. We were informed that the earliest one that was available would be about three weeks away. At that point, I relayed to the receptionist that I had a 5-year old son who was in pain, crying at night and unable to sleep. She promptly squeezed us in for an appointment two days out. (As a parent, YOU are responsible for being your child's #1 advocate. There will be doors slammed in your face; however it is your job to find a way to open them. Sometimes, the doors remain shut. In those cases, you either find another way into the building, or you choose an entirely different building (doctor) to gain access to. There are organizations that will help you, but in the end, you need to step up to the plate and start swinging the bat.) [I hate sports references, but they just seem to fit sometimes.]

We made it to the new doctor's office and got our exam. He didn't like the way Zachary looked, so after reviewing some x-rays, he ordered an immediate MRI for that afternoon. (In retrospect, we probably should have picked up on his anxiousness to find answers, but we were so caught up in finally having someone listen to us that we were still oblivious to what was coming.) At the MRI facility, we were very fortunate that Zachary was able to lie still for over three hours as they scanned and rescanned him from a billion different angles. Once again, having a medical degree would have been REAL handy at this point. (In fact, for all of you parents of healthy kids who are reading this, you may want to use your spare time on weekends to go ahead and get your degree in medicine . . . . you just never know when you're going to need it.) OK, back to the MRI place. Once again, we probably should have picked up on the concerned looks of the technicians and radiologist, but we were focusing on keeping young Zachary from moving around during the procedure. After finishing up, we were told that our doctor would call us the next morning with results.

Thursday morning March 16, 2000 will be a day that we will never forget. I was on the road selling fishing tackle in Ft. Lauderdale, about an hour and a half away from home, and Rebecca was with Zachary at the house, waiting to hear from our doctor. My mother, who is a retired nurse and counselor, had somewhat of a premonition that the news might be serious, if not confusing to Rebecca, so she had my father drive down to be with her when the call came. He made it to within 10 minutes of our house when the fateful call arrived. The news was not good. (Duh . . . . this book isn't about falling off a bike and skinning your knee, it's CANCER! What did you expect?) The doctor informed Rebecca that they had found multiple tumors in Zachary's spine and that he had a large tumor in his belly. The doctor further informed Rebecca that she was to pack a bag and immediately take Zachary to St. Mary's Hospital in West Palm Beach (about 45 minutes away) where there was a team waiting for her. Rebecca immediately tried to call me, but at the time we were using a cell phone provider (that will remain nameless), and we were constantly battling to find coverage. Shortly after that, my business partner was able to get me on the phone, and I immediately knew that something was amiss, because he told me that I needed to call Rebecca right away. I did, and my world was turned upside down. She told me of the tumors, and in my "shock", I was unable to process that this meant cancer. I left Ft. Lauderdale and told her that I would meet her at the hospital. While driving up the highway, I called my mother and through sobs of agony, I asked her what this all meant. She tried to reassure me that we would get through it, and that we would get answers together. All of it was a blur of emotions, fear and confusion.

I ended up arriving at the hospital before Rebecca and Zachary. I found the oncologist's office and walked in. Almost immediately, one of the doctors was walking by the sign-in window and saw me. He must have seen the distraught look on my face, because after confirming who I was, he ushered me back to his office where he proceeded to give me the "good" news.

"We believe that Zachary has stage IV neuroblastoma. He has a large tumor in his left adrenal gland. He has multiple tumors in his spine and hips. We believe that his bone marrow is compromised. After an initial evaluation today, he will need immediate surgery tomorrow to implant a port, to give us easy access to his blood stream. Two days after that, he will begin an intense chemotherapy regimen that will last almost 3 months. If he survives that, he will then have surgery to remove the tumor in his adrenal gland. After that he will need a stem cell bone marrow transplant and radiation. If we are correct in our diagnosis of the disease being stage IV, then he has about a 40% survival rate. Approximately 80% of the kids like this will make it through chemotherapy to the transplant, and of those, about 50% will survive and live to be cancer-free. The rest either die during the process, or relapse where they have a 0% chance of long-term survival."

GREAT! . . . . Sounds perfect! . . . . Where can I sign up?

The only "good" news that we received that day was when Rebecca and Zachary arrived. When the doctor saw Zachary walk in, he turned to me and commented that he had fully expected Zachary to be brought in using a wheelchair. He went on to say that with Zachary's level of disease, he was impressed at how he was "carrying himself." Other than that, it was pretty much a suck-fest of a day. The other interesting (or not) data that we were given was the fact that about 550 kids each year are diagnosed with this particular disease. Using those numbers, and doing rough math, that meant that each state would have about 11 kids each year who would get this type of cancer. You spread those 11 kids over a state the size of Florida, and you start to realize why local pediatricians are not too adept at picking up these diagnoses. Now, having said that, there are many other childhood cancers that ARE detectable through simple blood work.

During that first day of hell, you get to give your history and personal information about five or six times to a variety of doctors and nurses. I know that some of the information is used in national and regional databases, but mostly they want to make sure that they have covered all of the bases when it comes to learning about the patient. This exercise also gives you the chance to focus on something other than the impending doom that is quite obviously hanging over your head. (I would sugar-coat this for you, but it's like a band-aid. If you pull it off slowly, you're just going to cause more pain than is necessary.)

Once you have your diagnosis, you get to move onto phase II of the process which is the treatments. Congratulations, you've just completed your first day as a member of the Cancer Sucks Club. I would let you make a short acceptance speech, but you've got bigger fish to fry. Do NOT pass GO, do NOT collect $200.

Move directly to the Treatment chapter and begin the fun process of accepting the information that is being forced down your throat at the speed of light.

Chapter 3

Treatment

*"If you don't already have a degree in medicine, this would be a
REALLY good time to get one."*

One of the first issues that came up with our son was that of choosing a
treatment facility. We were not given a choice by the oncologists; however, my
father had some very good connections around the country and was prepared
to make recommendations to us regarding where we should go. After seeing the
local facility, he changed his mind and recommended staying put. This is an issue
that has the potential of being highly confusing to the average parent. Unless
you live in a bubble, you have heard of some of the larger more well-known
treatment facilities that have huge fundraising drives around the country. For
many people, the first instinct is to cut and run and get to one of those treatment
centers. In some cases, that is the correct instinct, however, in others, I believe
it to be a mistake. This is where it can get complicated. Navigating these waters
can definitely affect the outcome of your child's treatments, but not always in
the expected ways.

Having met many, many families while being treated in West Palm Beach,
I am of the opinion that most (I do not have an exact number for you) of the
children diagnosed, were placed on a specific protocol (or treatment plan) that
was dictated at the national level. This means that regardless of where they went
for treatment, they were going to get the same medicines. There are nationally
accepted treatment plans for most of the stages of most of the cancers that
exist. Now, having said that, there are other factors that come into play here. If
you are not familiar with hospital dynamics, then you probably are not aware

that larger university hospitals or teaching centers are usually much better staffed and more equipped to handle some of the issues that can arise during treatment. However, bigger is not always better. In our case, we could have traveled back and forth across this great land looking for the "perfect place", and all we would have accomplished is having wasted valuable time in getting started on our son's treatment. Time is almost always the enemy when it comes to this disease. Time without treatment can be deadly! The other factor that we were taking into consideration was that of support systems and quality of life. (Quality of Life could be a chapter on its own. I will definitely be explaining this further in future chapters.) By staying in West Palm Beach, we were able to keep Zachary close to home where we had a huge support network of friends. Also, our work was here.

Being able to keep some semblance of normalcy for Zachary was important to us. But, sometimes that just isn't possible. There are many cases where families are referred to specialists or facilities that have more experience with certain types of cancers. In those cases, you just have to make the best of things and tap into whatever family and friends are available as resources. The other comment that I would like to make regarding treatment facility choice is this: if the doctors are not able to pinpoint the diagnosis for you, it is time to find a facility or doctor that has more expertise. We saw this a few times, and usually the doctors are very good about knowing when they need to make the recommendation, but remember, you as the parent are the #1 advocate for your child. You need to speak up!

As I wrote earlier, we chose to stay local. We knew that by going elsewhere we would in essence be starting from scratch, and we didn't want to waste any time. The plan that we were given was a protocol that was being used everywhere for stage IV neuroblastoma patients. It included a variety of nasty chemotherapies, followed by the surgery, then transplant, and finally radiation. The first surgery for Zachary was the implantation of the port. If you are not familiar with ports, they are basically a device that is usually implanted into the chest wall that allows easy access to the patient's blood stream, without the risk of harming the veins. The port has a receptacle that sits just under the skin, and then a line that feeds directly into the blood stream. Nurses are able to numb the skin with a topical cream, and then access or insert their needle directly into the rubber-like receptacle end of the device. The patient will at most feel the needle go through the skin, but no discomfort once it penetrates. In most cases, the numbing cream prevents any pain. Psychologically, it can be very intimidating to have a nurse come at you with a ¾" needle that she is going to stick into your chest, but most of the children seem to adjust to the process well.

Once the needle is inserted, special dressings or bandages are placed over the needle to prevent germs from infiltrating the area. The needle is attached to an I.V. line that runs to an I.V. bag, hanging on a pole. The children are then "free" to roam about with the rolling pole. Their arms are not encumbered by an I.V. needle, so they can participate in games, activities, arts & crafts and the like. Having a foreign device implanted in the body increases the risk for infection so there are concerns that have to be addressed. For us, one was the "fever rule." Any fever over 100.5 was an automatic admission to the hospital for I.V. antibiotics. The risk of infection in the central line (or port) is a major concern. An infection can necessitate the removal of the port which is not a circumstance that you want to have happen. For more information about ports I would recommend either searching online, or asking someone who actually has some medical knowledge. (You are reading this stuff like I REALLY have expert knowledge about these things, and quite frankly it is freaking me out!)

Once you get the port implanted the fun REALLY begins. NOT! All chemotherapies are not created equally, and all patients don't react the same to any one chemotherapy agent, so you probably need to take most of what I write about here with a grain of salt. (I never understood the whole 'salt' thing. Isn't too much salt bad for you? Whatever.) In our case, the chemo was pretty nasty. And you KNOW that it's nasty when they come into the room wearing gowns and gloves to protect their skin as they hang the bag of medicine that is being pumped directly into your child's blood stream. We always thought that it was curious how no one wanted to risk getting that stuff on their clothes or hands, but they had no problem pumping Zachary full of it. I remember during our introduction to the world of chemotherapy, the doctors were explaining to us all of the possible side effects, and most of it was truly going in one ear and out the other. (It wasn't like we REALLY had any choice as to what course of action we were going to take.) I specifically recall the one side effect, the doctor said, "I should warn you, there is a really good chance that Zachary will never be able to have children." My response was, "Well, since he is only 6 years old right now anyway, let's find a way to keep him alive until he is old enough to worry about that, and then we'll just tell him to adopt!" Anyway, the chemo sucks. I figured I should warn you in case you hadn't heard it from someone else. The nausea sucks too. They try to combat it with a variety of medicines, but unless your child is some sort of freak of nature, there is going to be vomit, and lots of it! I don't remember how long it took before we got over rushing into the bathroom to help him throw up, but eventually the experience loses its appeal and mystery and you find yourself waiting for the retching to stop before you dare to enter and help with the clean up.

As for the cycle of chemo, once again it will vary depending upon your child and the types of chemo that they are getting. For us, we were pretty much on a cycle that had Zachary getting chemo for a week, and then he would have three weeks off. After the first week his blood counts would drop so low that he would get a fever just because. (Literally, his body would not be able to fight off the germs that exist in all of us.) The fever would get him admitted to the hospital where he would stay for anywhere from 3 to 7 days while they gave him antibiotics and waited for his counts to start to rebound. And then we would get almost a week at home, after which we would be back for another round. I know it doesn't sound like much fun, but I always thought of it as sort of a party. (Only without the music, dancing, food, or any enjoyment of course.) For Zachary, the many rounds of chemotherapy were interrupted occasionally by the bone marrow tests that had to be done. As I have written before, each cancer is different. Some require frequent spinal taps; we needed to keep an eye on his bone marrow.

At diagnosis, I believe his marrow was over 90% occluded with cancer cells. (That is NOT a good thing.) So, every so often the doctors would have Zachary put under anesthesia and they would bore large holes in his hips to suck out some marrow and a sliver of bone for review. We pretty much lived and died by those test results. Those tests and the scans that were being done were our lifeline. Not having the foresight to complete my degree in medicine, we were at the mercy of the doctors and the information that they were feeding us. Coming from a family that was medically savvy, I put a lot of weight on each and every blood test, scan, marrow test, etc. Rebecca was more of a "touchy feely" person, basing her evaluation on how Zachary was feeling and looking on any given day.

When we started to see a family therapist, I was given a rude awakening when I tried to rake her over the coals regarding test results. I was back at work pretty quickly, so my only lifeline to Zachary was through Rebecca and those reports. I would hang on each and every number, silently doing the math in my head, trying to ascertain what needed to happen for things to get better. There were many occasions where Rebecca did not have the numbers for me. I brought up this topic during therapy and fully expected the psychologist to take my side of the issue. Instead, I received a quick education regarding stress and how different people handle situations differently. The therapist made it very clear that while my comfort zone was fully entrenched in the numbers and results from tests, Rebecca's wasn't. What was good for me did her no good whatsoever. If I was "hung-up" on the numbers, then I needed to step up and make sure that the doctors were getting me those results. Rebecca was dealing with the stress in a way that worked for her. Neither way was wrong, we both had found our coping mechanism.

If you are reading this, looking for answers because you have been thrust into this situation, or perhaps a relative or loved one has, I implore you to take notice of that revelation. The attrition rate for couples in this situation is very high. I have heard that couples who lose a child to cancer divorce over 90% of the time. I am not sure what the rate is for couples that have not yet lost their child, but we have seen many casualties of war. Learning to find your coping system and to respect the system of your spouse can save your marriage and help you to create a bond that will enforce your team-like approach to fighting this disease.

The chemotherapy aspect of our treatment was full of ups and downs. Zachary had many fevers, and several setbacks. There were times when the doctors told us that the disease was progressing and that things were not looking good. This is par for the course. While some families are blessed with a smooth road, most are not. Fighting cancer is hard. It sucks. It sucks a lot! While riding the rollercoaster, you need to find a way to celebrate the minor victories that you will get, so that the defeats and low points won't suck you into an abyss that might otherwise prevent you from escaping. The ups and downs can happen daily, weekly, monthly . . . . there is no rhyme or reason to them. While at home in between treatments you will learn to clean your home in ways that you never dreamed possible. You will learn about masks that must be worn to prevent exposure to diseases. You will learn to screen visitors and visitor's relatives to make sure no chance of disease or illness crosses your threshold. (Why am I writing this like you are about to have a child diagnosed? That is QUITE morbid and depressing.) WE learned all of that, (is what I meant to write.) Zachary also lost his hair, another very common side-effect of most chemos.

In addition to the more commonly know side-effects of chemo, the low blood counts that result from those treatments necessitate special mention here. When the blood counts get too low (like zero for the white blood count), the doctors prescribe a drug called Neupogen (or GCSF). This drug is administered via injection which is usually given in the leg. After several days of injections, the GCSF will usually do its thing and help the patient to rebound with their WBC levels. This is a medicine that we as parents were allowed to administer at home. The only problem with that scenario is that Zachary never wanted to accept that we were "qualified" to give him the shots. We got REAL lucky with that episode when one of our neighbors, who was a nurse, offered to come over daily and give Zachary the injections. Zachary trusted her without question, and her visits usually went rather well, considering that we had a 6 year old who was getting stuck with needles each and every day for weeks at a time after chemo.

By June of 2000 we were finishing up the initial part of our protocol which was the chemo. There are cancers that have very short intense chemotherapy regimens, followed up by years of "maintenance" chemos. For information regarding those, I would recommend searching 'leukemia'. After our chemo, we were told that we needed to harvest stem cells for the upcoming transplant. We were sent to northern Florida where they do many of the transplants in our state at a university hospital up there. The harvest process consisted of a brief surgery where tubes were inserted in to Zachary's neck to give access to large blood vessels for transferring blood. Basically, the stem cells are a part of the blood . . . . a small part. You can't just take all of the blood to get enough stem cells, you would remove too much and the patient would die. So, what they do is remove the blood and run it through a machine that extracts the stem cells, and then returns the rest of the blood to the patient. This process can take many hours, or even days. We were told that most kids take two sessions spread over two days to harvest enough stem cells. Zachary was fortunate to complete his harvest on the first day.

The one "weak" point in this harvest in my opinion is whether or not the stem cells being recovered are truly "clean." The chemo was supposed to clean out his marrow enough to harvest clean cells, but you just never know what is going to sneak through in the process. After the harvest, we were sent home for the surgery to remove the original tumor. Neuroblastoma very often originates in one of the two adrenal glands. The adrenal glands are attached to the kidneys. Zachary's left adrenal gland had the tumor, and apparently it had grown so big, that it had atrophied (or shrunk) the left kidney to the point where it was not being used. Thankfully, his right kidney was functioning at 97% for the body, which meant that it was picking up the work load.

The surgery to remove the tumor was a major one. They had to slice open his belly to get access to the area. They removed a "green apple" sized tumor, the left adrenal gland, and a couple of the surrounding lymph nodes. The recovery from the surgery was no picnic either. The most common problem post operatively is pneumonia, from not working the lungs enough. Lying in bed for too long can be dangerous while getting up and walking can be outright painful. After about a week in ICU, Zachary was released.

The uncertainty here was that we needed him to be fully recovered from the surgery before the northern hospital would even allow us to begin the transplant process. The transplant floor there had adults and children sharing the same wing. The room allows one parent to stay with the child and it is kept immaculate. Every time that you leave or enter the room, you have to wash your hands, even if you just opened the door to call for a nurse. We rented a room at an Extended Stay America for the entire 9 weeks. I stayed for the first two weeks, and then I was flying back and forth on weekends so that I could work.

Meanwhile, we had family members coming in each week to help Rebecca out so that during the week she could get an occasional break to shower at the hotel or take a nap. The process wasn't perfect, but we made do. There were a couple of very scary days during transplant. One came when Zachary's platelets had dropped to 5,000, (normal is over 175,000) and he fell out of bed and landed on his head. He could easily have bled inside his brain from that one. The other came after Zachary was losing the nausea battle for several days. The doctors had tried several medicines without success to stop the nausea, but nothing was working. Apparently there is a little used medicine named Reglan that was used many years ago. The doctors decided to try it for Zachary. What they didn't tell us was that the reason Reglan was not being used as much anymore was that it had a very nasty side-effect that occurred a bit too often.

As we were watching Zachary, he slowly lost the ability to speak, and then his eyes rolled up and couldn't stay focused. His hands curled in an unnatural way, and he lost control of his body. At one point he started to cry, and we couldn't tell why. Finally, we were able to see that he had gone to the bathroom in his pants. Once we got him cleaned up, he started to cry again, and we were going out of our minds trying to figure out what was wrong. He had once again lost control of his bowels and had another accident. Once the nurses realized that he was having this reaction, they began to give him Benadryl in an attempt to "flush" his system of the Reglan. Unfortunately that process took about 7 or 8 hours. It was torture for us. I truly thought we were going to lose him. Watching him struggle with the inability to communicate to us was beyond anything that we had experienced before. Once again, I would not recommend letting your child get cancer. If you are unable to prevent that eventuality, MY ADVICE IS TO BE CAUTIOUS IF THEY RECOMMEND GIVING YOUR CHILD REGLAN!

There were some other minor glitches that took place. On at least two occasions, Rebecca prevented a mistake from occurring by noticing that a nurse was going to give Zachary either the wrong medicine, or the wrong dosage. Now, if your child has just been diagnosed with cancer, and you have no medical knowledge or understanding of medicines, I would imagine that it could be more than intimidating to think that as a parent, you are the "last stop" or "checkpoint" before disaster. Here is my advice on this. Pay attention and ask questions when nurses or doctors are administering medicines.

Rebecca had no prior education in medicine, she just got used to asking the right questions. So, when a nurse came in one day to hang a bag of medicine, Rebecca asked her what she was getting ready to give Zachary. The nurse looked at the bag and informed her that it was his daily antibiotic. Rebecca knew from the previous weeks of watching that the antibiotic had been coming in a syringe, NOT a whole bag. She mentioned this to the nurse, who was coincidentally new and still in training. The nurse went to get her supervisor, who then checked with the pharmacy and found out that they had indeed filled the prescription incorrectly. You really couldn't fault the nurse in training. She was given the medicine in the bag, for Zachary. A more seasoned nurse would probably have caught the error, but the fault was clearly with the pharmacy. Either way, Rebecca prevented a major problem from occurring. The lesson here is that by paying attention to your child's treatments, you can pick up on enough information to be an effective advocate for their well-being.

Slowly over the weeks the stem cells started to do their thing and Zachary's immune system started to rebuild itself. As Zachary began to regain strength, he was allowed out of his room more for walks and exercise. All of his progress was encouraging to us and gave us hope. And when you have watched your child lose about a third of their body weight, and go through an ordeal like a transplant, hope is something that you wrap up tightly around you and don't let go of. The last "scare" that we had during transplant happened at the very end. We were within a week of being released and the doctors had cleared Zachary to start taking his "home" medicines again. During transplant, the doctors will sometimes have the patient stop taking home medicines that can interfere or otherwise adversely affect the recovery process. Zachary was on a medicine for his mild asthma called Ah-Chew. It is a decongestant/antihistamine that is used for allergies, colds, flu and other breathing issues. Well, Zachary hadn't been given that medicine since starting his transplant. When we were cleared to start him back on it, the nurses just said, "Go ahead and give him his pill today." I was in the room with him, Rebecca was out in the hallway visiting with some other families, and Zachary took his pill. I was picking up some papers and not really paying attention to anything in particular when Zachary informed me that his head hurt and he didn't feel good. I responded (without looking at him) that I would get the nurse to bring him some Tylenol or something. He persisted and said, "I just don't feel right." I turned to look at him and nearly freaked out. His entire upper body, chest, arms, neck, face and head were bright red. I immediately pushed the call button, (and thankfully on the transplant floors when you push a call button, someone immediately asks what you need,) and when the nurse asked what I needed I said, "I need a nurse right away, Zachary is having some sort of reaction."

They came FLYING into the room. I mean, like within seconds there were several nurses surrounding him. They asked what had happened, and I told them about giving Zachary his Ah-Chew. They immediately injected his line with Benadryl and within seconds he was losing his red glow and feeling better. Apparently, (and don't take my word on this, ask around), transplants can sometimes sort of "reprogram" the patient's body to where they react differently to medicines after transplant than they did before transplant. The other interesting change that occurred much later, (or at least we didn't realize it until later), was that he no longer had mild asthma. That is another possible occurrence with the body's change.

Eventually, we got discharged and were sent back home to Jensen Beach. The last treatment phase of Zachary's protocol was the radiation. There had actually been a mild debate on the timing of the radiation. Some patients are radiated before transplant with heavy doses that are used in an attempt to eradicate any hidden or straggler cancer cells. The problem that we had was that Zachary's neuroblastoma had already shown itself to be very aggressive in nature, and the doctors were concerned that by doing the radiation first, we might actually have given some of the cells an opportunity to duplicate and grow. Overall, the protocol attempts to throw a wide variety of chemos, radiation and transplant at the disease, in an attempt to hit it from many different angles.

The downside to waiting on radiation for after transplant was that they couldn't give Zachary higher doses. If the doses were too high, his immune system (which was not fully recovered) would get damaged to the point where he would not recover. The coin was tossed, and the decision was made to do focal (or small area) radiation after transplant. The radiation was given over 15 days and thankfully there were no major side-effects or problems with that process. After radiation we were instructed to start Zachary on a 14 week cycle of an oral medicine called Accutane. Some of you may be aware of this drug; it has been in the news over the past several years for being controversial because of its side-effects. Accutane is an acne medicine that supposedly can cause depression. There have been a few highly publicized cases of teen suicide attributed to its use. Some researcher buried deep in a lab somewhere discovered that this drug can help neuroblastoma patients by the aging or killing of some cancer cells.

Zachary was only 6 years old at the time, so we really weren't too concerned about the teen depression issues. Besides, we were somewhat caught up with the whole, "Child fighting cancer" depression issues. I don't remember the exact dosage, but he was taking about 10 pills, three times each day for seven days, and then he would get two weeks off. Our main challenge with that drug was the size of the pills. Being only 6 years old, Zachary couldn't swallow them. The pills were rather large, and with a standard outer shell surrounding a yellow yolk-like medicine. The only method that we could use to get Zachary his dosage was to take a large gauge sterile needle to puncture the outer shell, and then we would squeeze the medicine into a small bowl. Once in the bowl, we would mix the drug with pudding or something similar that Zachary was likely to tolerate.

The main side-effect was the drying of the skin, which makes sense, since it is an acne medicine. We were about three or four rounds into the plan when Zachary was due for his post transplant bone marrow check. That was near the end of November, 2000. On or about November 25, 2000, the doctor called to inform us that the results were in and the news was NOT good. Zachary still had cancer cells in his marrow, and we should plan for the worst. Actually, they told us this. "Stop giving him the Accutane. Call the "wish" foundation and have his wish expedited, because within a month or maybe six weeks, he will be too sick to do anything, and within two months, he will be gone." HURRAY . . . . . what great news! And just in time for the holidays. (That was sarcasm in case you haven't caught on to my style of writing.)

I remember going out on the patio with Rebecca and the two of us sitting there trying to plan what kind of funeral arrangements would need to be made. That sucked. I mean cancer sucks of course, we've established that, but planning a funeral for your child REALLY sucks. So, we somehow got through that December without raiding our local pharmacy for Prozac or some other mind numbing medicine. Then in January something strange happened. We were at the doctor's office for a "normal" visit and the doctor was looking over Zachary, checking him out upside down and sideways, and he turned to us and made an interesting comment. He said, "I want to do another bone marrow test." My response was, "OK, why exactly are we going to put him through another test when you've already skipped to the last chapter and told us how this story is going to end?" He replied, (and I'll never forget this), "Zachary looks too good. He should be much sicker by now. I want to recheck his marrow." Rebecca and I looked at each other and then told him, "OK, have at it." Less than one week later we received a phone call telling us that they now believed Zachary was in remission . . . . and oh by the way . . . . start taking the Accutane again!

While being told that Zachary was in remission was incredible news to process, you must keep in mind that we were somewhat skeptical and leery of grasping onto false hopes. The doctor explained that he believed Zachary's bone marrow test in November had revealed "dying" neuroblastoma cells that appeared as viable and made it look like the disease was still running rampant. The newer bone marrow showed almost no disease, and thus brought them to the conclusion that he was truly in remission. Whatever the case was, as parents of a child with a life-threatening illness, you learn to take the victories and run with them . . . . even if they don't entirely make sense. So, we finished up the regimen of Accutane and Zachary slowly regained his weight, complexion, and overall well being.

And we lived happily ever after. (Yeah right, and if you believe THAT one, then I've got some swamp land here in Florida that I would just LOVE to sell to you.)

Chapter 4

Family & Friends

*"Not all family & friends are created equally. This is your complete
(or somewhat complete) guide to circling the wagons
and rounding up the troops."*

Every family dynamic is different. So, while you are reading this chapter, you need to keep in mind that while I have spoken to many families and based this information on multiple occurrences, these stories in no way constitute absolutes or definitive scenarios that you will face if your child has been diagnosed. (Did that sound too legalese? Like I REALLY care whether or not you read into this the wrong way.)

I have taken part in many, many parent support group discussions over the past eight years, and invariably, the conversations always include discussions about how family and friends react and deal with this disease. Too many times I have heard parents lament about how family members let them down, or didn't "step up to the plate", or just flat out disappeared when the going got rough. And with friends, the same things have happened, only exponentially.

We were very fortunate in that we had an amazing family support system that went above and beyond to help us. We also had incredible friends and acquaintances who assisted us in ways that we never dreamed possible. Zachary's school and our local community held multiple fund raisers, supplied us with ready-to-eat dinners, paid mortgage bills for us, and were there for us to vent our frustrations or to lend a shoulder to cry on. There was however a small select group of friends who very abruptly vanished into thin air. It was if they were there one day, and gone the next. I would never try to make excuses for anyone who would abandon a family member or friend who was going through this ordeal, but I do believe that I can help to explain it. I believe that some people are just unable to "deal" with the enormity of the issue, and they find themselves emotionally and intellectually unable to process right from wrong. It is almost as if the gravity of the situation overpowers any other emotion and renders them unable to offer help, or even kind words. Some people are just not equipped to communicate on issues this big. It truly does separate the men from the boys . . . . so to speak. Cancer is a serious illness. It is a tragic illness that is devastating. Cancer in a child is all of that and more. Not that a child's life is any more valuable or cherished than that of an adult, but the innocence of a child and the helplessness that is associated with this diagnosis is extremely powerful.

Some parents see your sick child and immediately see THEIR children in that situation so they shut down emotionally, to avoid having to face those demons. I have also heard many stories of families having to deal with friends and family members who became jealous of the attention that the sick child and family were getting. This may seem incredulous to you, but it happens! Children with life-threatening diseases ARE given special attention and they DO have gifts and special opportunities presented to them. All of this lends itself to me giving out unsolicited advice to family and friends of someone who has a child diagnosed with cancer.

In our situation, the treating hospital was about 45 minutes away. This presented some challenging obstacles to maintaining a somewhat "normal" existence while balancing Zachary's treatment schedule. We were fortunate that Zachary is and was an only child. Families with more than one child present a whole different set of challenges that I will discuss a little bit later. When Zachary was diagnosed, Rebecca was working 40 hours/week for a large company, and I was running my business with my partner. I was the primary source of income for our family, and Rebecca was the primary care-giver. Her employer was at first very understanding and allowed her adequate time off to deal with the nightmare that was thrust upon us. That honeymoon however, didn't last too long. At some point, companies need to move on and go about the business of being in business. So don't expect too much latitude from your employers. (There were parents who we met who had co-workers donating time off and vacation time to allow the parent time with their child . . . . there are good people out there . . . . you've just got to find them and align yourself with them if possible.) (Back to friends and family.)

If you are a family member, you're first job is to circle the wagons. There needs to be someone in the family who steps up and says, "We are here to support you, we need to know what we can do to help." Now, the only problem with that statement is this; when you first hear the diagnosis, you feel like a deer caught in the headlights. Because of this, you can actually find yourself at a loss of ideas as to how your friends and family can help you. I remember thinking, "I'm trying to keep my sanity together, I don't know whether to cry or wind my watch, and now I've got to come up with some way for these people to help me so that they feel appreciated." Part of the problem here is that families who are new to the diagnosis don't always KNOW what they need or will need in the future. Depending on your budget and the age of the child, here are some items that can be useful to folks who are newly diagnosed:

Gas cards—Fuel ain't cheap, and trips back and forth to treatment centers and doctors can be VERY expensive.

Grocery store gift cards—Food ain't cheap either! Long stays in the hospital can translate into food going bad and needing to be replaced.

Phone cards—Hospitals don't provide long distance service free of charge, and not everyone has a cell phone plan that will cover the huge amount of minutes that a parent will need.

Restaurant gift cards—Most pediatric oncology hospitals are in or near metropolitan centers that have a variety of restaurants. If for some reason the parents can't use them while inpatient, then they will get used at home.

Movie rental gift cards—Children who spend days and weeks at a time in the hospital tend to get bored. Movies can help to alleviate that issue.

Target/Wal-Mart gift cards—There are all sorts of items that you don't think about that can be purchased there . . . . hand sanitizer, masks, gloves, over-the-counter medicines, toys, books, clothing, etc.

Cash—Nothing says "I care about you" better than cold hard cash! (Seriously though, expenses will go up, cash can help.)

Now, if you are more of the "hands on" kind of person who doesn't like "impersonal" gift cards or cash, don't panic . . . . there are plenty of other ways that you can help. Shortly after Zachary was diagnosed, we were contacted by a friend who wanted to bring us dinner when we got out of the hospital. Not only did they want to provide dinner for us, they further informed us that they had coordinated a group of like 15 or 20 families (many of whom we didn't even know) who wanted to provide a dinner too. This is how it worked. We were to call the primary contact person (our friend) to keep them posted as to when we were coming home. They were in charge of organizing the dinners and making sure that any donating family was kept apprised of changes in our schedule that might pop up, like fevers or delayed exits from the hospital. What ended up transpiring when we returned home was nothing short of a miracle for our family.

Every night for the two weeks that we were home between treatments, at precisely 6:00pm, a different family would knock on the door and present us with a ready-to-eat dinner. This is a wonderful thing. Even though we only have one child, it was so helpful to Rebecca that she could walk in the door and not have to first be thinking about what to make for dinner, or whether or not we even had food in the refrigerator that was edible. I will warn you that pasta was a recurring theme on these nights, but the good news is that pasta freezes well, and reheats well, so you will have many dinners that you can get out of one visit. Most of the families also provided dessert, which was a nice treat for us. This is an easy, inexpensive way to help a family in need. It is an activity that you can involve your children in, teaching them the importance of giving and helping a neighbor. A dinner of bread, salad, pasta and dessert can be prepared for under $10 or $15 and can easily feed 3 to 5 people. The system that our friend set up worked so well, that we were able to tap into that resource during several of our home stays. So, if you are a friend of someone newly diagnosed, you can offer up this service and be the hero.

Other helpful ideas are:

Offering to cut the grass.—Unless they live in a palatial estate, it should take about an hour or so and is much appreciated.

Taking the siblings to or from school, or offering to watch them after school or on weekends.—Having more than one child can exponentially complicate the diagnosis.

Offering to get the mail or newspapers.—Remembering to suspend service is probably one of the last things that a parent in this situation will do. We have great neighbors who watch out for us.

Grocery shopping.—If you can't afford to buy them some groceries, you can offer to do the shopping for them while you are doing yours. It saves them a trip to the store. If their child is in the middle of treatment, it can be quite an ordeal with masks and such, getting them out of the house. Car rides frequently can cause nausea, so saving a child from unnecessary road trips is a good thing.

Babysitting.—This can be a bit dicey and it is NOT for the faint of heart. Babysitting a child with cancer when you don't have any formal medical training will definitely be intimidating for almost anyone out there. And truthfully, most parents in this situation are too freaked out to be away from their child to enjoy a night out. But, there will come a time when that tide turns, and you as a friend can be there ahead of everyone else with the offer on the table.

The other big issue that we faced after Zachary's diagnosis was the conveying of information and daily reports. We had so many caring friends and family who wanted to be kept in the loop that we had to come up with a system to keep them posted. At first, it was brutal. I used to sit at the end of the hallway so that Zachary wouldn't be able to hear my conversations, and I would be sobbing on the phone, while relaying the day's events to one person after another. Eventually, one of our close friends agreed to be the gatekeeper for our other friends. We would call them once daily, and then they would take care of getting the information out to everyone else. That still left me to deal with family, but it did ease the burden somewhat.

Years later we were introduced to CaringBridge.org. CaringBridge is a not-for-profit organization that provides free web pages to families going through difficult times. From life-threatening illnesses to premature births to military deployment, they allow families to keep loved ones and friends up to date with what is going on in their lives. The page allows photos to be uploaded, and it provides an area for visitors to sign messages of hope and greetings. They maintain a database of old journal entries, so if you are checking in on someone and have missed an update, you can go back and read the old ones first so that you have a better understanding of the chain of events. I created Zachary's CaringBridge page in May of 2002. In the six years following that first entry, he has had over 600,000 visitors and countless guest book entries.

The beauty of the page is that it allows us to write an update at our convenience, and then friends and family can check in on us without feeling like they are imposing or interrupting our lives. Some people are so fearful of interrupting or disturbing the family, that they never make the first call to see how they can help. If you are the parent of a child diagnosed with cancer then you should know that you can use your CaringBridge site to let people know what your needs are. Most parents are either too proud or too beaten down by this disease to ask for help. The web page makes it easy. You're already in there writing about what is going on, so all you do is add a comment about a particular need that your family has. Here is an example:

"Johnny had a rough day, he threw up seven times, and thankfully only two of them were on me. Oh, and we are out of money, so if anyone has an extra $2,984,166 lying around, please bring it by the hospital."

There, now wasn't that easy? It wasn't? OK . . . . here is a better example for you politically correct folks:

"Johnny had a rough day today, we're hoping tomorrow is better. We were told today that he needs to see a specialist in Hopetown, which is about 3 hours away. We are in need of gas cards to help us with the expense of traveling back and forth. Thanks in advance to anyone who can help."

OK . . . so maybe that way was more appropriate. I never claimed to be Mr. Appropriate. The point is that you can use the web page to accomplish a LOT of things. People LIKE to be kept in the loop, but medical jargon can be overwhelming. I used to take the time to explain everything in great detail, so that folks would have a clear understanding of what was going on. Because of that, I used to get several guest book entries and emails from people asking me to further clarify certain aspects of Zachary's treatment or illness. It was very therapeutic for me to become the "expert" on a variety of issues. The web page gave me a place to vent my frustrations and to celebrate our victories. There is nothing like crying on the shoulders of hundreds of people, all at one time!

In the previous chapter, I mentioned that we had family members who helped us during the transplant phase of Zachary's treatment. We also had a friend who made a huge sacrifice and helped us out. Jessica was 18 or 19 years old at the time, and she was in college. Her mom was working for me and had told Jessica about our situation. I was trying to find family members to fill four consecutive weeks where I wanted coverage for Rebecca while I was working. The plan was to have someone new each week stay in the hotel and relieve Rebecca during the day so that she could shower or rest. That way, Zachary would not be alone. I was coming up on weekends, so I was there to relieve her Friday thru Sunday. Jessica made herself available and she and her boyfriend made the trip up and helped us out. It wasn't until many months later that I found out that she had been dropped from her course at college for missing too many classes that week. I wrote a letter to the professor explaining what Jessica had done and what kind of character I believed her to possess to be so selfless in her actions. Even with my letter, the college refused to budge and Jessica had to retake the course.

Not all of your friends are going to be able to make such noble gestures. But some will! If you are in a position to take time off from work and to be away from family, you can be the difference for a family like ours. It is a HUGE sacrifice, but it is well worth it! Any donation of time, money or assistance can make the difference for a family in need. You should never hesitate to make the offer; the worst that can happen is that the family declines. There are numerous other examples of how you can reach out to a family that has a child with cancer. We had neighbors who offered to take Zachary for motorcycle rides, or rides in exotic cars that their friends owned. He had offers to take airplane rides, to go fishing, to take backstage tours at NASA, and many more. Sometimes you as a friend will have connections that you never really thought too much about. Maybe you know someone who is connected with a local sports team and you can get tickets for a game, or an introduction to one or more of the players. There are many ways that you can brighten the day for a child like this, not all of them are spectacular on the surface, but when you are facing seemingly endless treatments, and possible death, ANY diversion is welcome!

Families with more than one child can face unique challenges when dealing with this diagnosis. Not only do the parents have to deal with doctors, hospitals, etc, but they also have to factor in their other children. Siblings risk getting lost in the mix, and the last thing that you want is for them to become collateral damage. There are probably many books out there that address this specific subject, and with us only having one child, I would imagine that for once, I am NOT the expert to be writing about it. BUT, when has that EVER stopped me before?

Actually, we have several friends who we met on the cancer floor who were in this situation. Depending on the age of the siblings, friends and family can be invaluable in assisting with the day to day regimens that need to be followed to keep a family on track. I already mentioned transporting back and forth to school, and the after school and weekend issue, but just making sure that the siblings are getting attention and are made to feel needed and important are huge issues. Our experience with these families was one where the siblings were very involved with their sick brother or sister, and in some cases, Zachary actually became very close friends with the non-patient children. There are unique school issues that can arise with siblings of children who have cancer. Anger issues sometimes rear their ugly heads away from the home environment, and parents should have a contact at the school who looks out for any potential problems. Jealousy from siblings is another issue that we have seen. The amount of attention, presents and special treatment can become overwhelming to a sibling who has to sit back and watch. Some of the charities that we've dealt with are very good about including siblings in the mix, but I will go more into depth about that in the next chapter.

In the end, there is no magic wand that will help you with family and friends. You just need to remember that many of them will be "lost" as to what they can do to help. You can hand them a copy of this book for instance. (Not your copy, BUY a new one and give it to them. Or better yet, WRITE about it on your CaringBridge page so that thousands of new people will want to buy it!!!) (That was a pretty shameless attempt to sell books, wasn't it?) Even if you are not battling this disease, I recommend making the most out of the relationships that you have. First of all, life is WAY too short to be harboring grudges and fueling feuds. Second of all, you NEVER know when life is going to jump up and bite you in the ass with a diagnosis like this.

Chapter 5

Charities

"Don't try to tackle the monster on your own, enlist the help of those who have fought it before!"

Every town is different, and I have heard many stories about the various charities that support families who are going through this process. In this chapter, I am going to focus mainly on our personal experiences, and also try to offer ideas on finding local resources.

On day #1 of diagnosis, we were introduced to two different charities that were on site at the hospital, supporting the families. Connor Moran Children's Cancer Foundation and the P.O.S.T (Pediatric Oncology Support Team.) Both of these charities were very good at assisting the families in a variety of ways. P.O.S.T. was the first one that we came into contact with. They had a child-life specialist who was there to help us with telling Zachary about this cancer. We knew that this was going to be a dicey conversation. Zachary was only six at the time, but he knew about Rebecca's step father who had died from cancer of the brain three months before Zachary was born. (She had told Zachary about him many times.) So, armed with the child-life expert, we had "the conversation."

Upon hearing the word "cancer", Zachary immediately whipped his head around and looked at Rebecca and asked, "Isn't that what Grandpa Dan died from?" (WHACK . . . . it was a swing and a hit for the little guy.) (We persisted.) Our expert did her thing and immediately informed Zachary that Dan had an entirely different type of cancer, and that we were going to battle this one together. She also knew of Zachary's fascination with action figures and ninjas, so she likened the cancer cells to "bad" ninjas and then she described the chemotherapy as the "good" ninjas. Zachary was able to comprehend the concept that a war was going to take place inside of his body, and that he would feel the effects of that war, but we were going to give him medicines to help with those effects. All of this was very daunting to Rebecca and me. We were walking on eggshells, where the only thing keeping us going was Zachary's strength and courage.

That same expert was with us on day #2 when Zachary was in surgery to have his port implanted. I'll never forget sitting with her in the surgery waiting area trying to make small talk, when out of nowhere she says, "You know, Zachary will get a "wish" from one of the major wish foundations." (WHACK . . . . a swing and a hit, right between my eyes.) I remember immediately thinking that Zachary shouldn't need a wish, wishes like that are for sick kids. Zachary just has cancer, he isn't REALLY sick. (WRONG) Denial never cured anyone, remember that! OK, so eventually I accepted that he was sick, but that was a scary moment.

The Connor Moran Children's Cancer Foundation was introduced to us on the oncology floor. They were always there, doing art projects with the children, or bringing toys up to the floor, or just sitting with the parents and being a shoulder to cry on. Both charities offered assistance with bill management and insurance navigation. (That's a fancy way of saying, "Dealing with the bullshit.") We had the P.O.S.T. help us with that aspect of the experience, only because they were first to offer their services and we didn't want to have confusion arise from spreading the bills and notices between two agencies. Both charities had access to regional and national larger charities that offer financial assistance to families in this situation, and we were helped on more than one occasion with a bill. If you find yourself smack dab in the middle of this diagnosis, I highly recommend asking other parents while you are at the hospital or clinic about which charities are helpful.

I would also ask the doctors and nurses, they are usually dialed into which organizations will help out. You should also take some time to go online and research your child's specific disease. There will undoubtedly be national or regional organizations that may have services or advice to offer. One such organization is the National Children's Cancer Foundation. They have helped us on numerous occasions with travel expenses to and from out of state treatment facilities. They will usually pay for one parent and the patient to fly, along with a hotel allowance, food allowance, and in some cases, transportation expenses too. They do require a case manager or local charity to refer your needs to them, so that they can verify the legitimacy of the request. Having said that, N.C.C.S has ALWAYS been very helpful and timely in their efforts to assist us.

Depending on your child's illness, you will find that the more common the type of cancer, the higher probability that there is a large national charity/ organization out there waiting to help. The less common diseases usually have organizations also, but they can be harder to find. We were not made aware of the ones for Zachary's illness until several years into diagnosis. We actually found one totally by accident from another family and the other by attending a local fundraiser for childhood cancer. When we showed up for that one, it turned out that entire focus of the charity was neuroblastoma research. Apparently the father of the child works in pharmaceutical research and was actively trying to find a cure for this disease. Once we had that connection, we were able to contact them and learn of some ground-breaking research that was being done in some select facilities around the country.

At the time of my writing this chapter, we just returned from Boggy Creek. Boggy Creek Gang Camp is one of the Paul Newman 'Hole in the Wall Gang Camps.' They were founded years ago and funded in part from the proceeds of his line of foods. (Salad dressings, popcorn, etc.) The camps were set up as getaways for children fighting life-threatening illnesses. During the fall, winter and spring, the camp has weekend getaways for the entire family to attend that usually last from Friday evening to Sunday afternoon. Then, during the summer the camp hosts week-long camps for the children only. Each family weekend and summer week-long camp is illness specific, so that there is a common bond between the campers. There are several of these camps around the world, and we are fortunate enough to have one in Florida, about three hours from home. We first started attending as a family that first year that Zachary was diagnosed. The summer after that, he started going to the week-long camps by himself. Ever since then, we have been attending the cancer sessions whenever there have been openings.

I believe their policy is that the camper must be at least six years old, and they can be no longer than five years out of treatment. Fortunately (actually, unfortunately) for us, we have never been more than one year out of treatment, so we have always been eligible to attend. The camp is an amazing place. They have incredible facilities that were donated/built by a variety of major donors. From the Olympic-sized pool, to the fully functioning theater, to the gymnasium, Boggy Creek is just perfect. The "Patch" or hospital that they have is always staffed with medical personal who have training in the illness of the campers attending. They can do chemo and dialysis there, among other necessary treatments so that children with these illnesses can attend the camp.

The cabins are beautiful, the lake is stocked with bass, and the arts & crafts/wood working area is always full of supplies. They have putt-putt, archery, computers, and many more activities for the campers. I would highly recommend looking up this organization on the web and donating time, money, or resources to help them out. It is truly one of the bright spots in our adventure. Anyway, the reason that I brought up Boggy Creek at this point in the "Charities" chapter is that one of the parent activities we participate in is the parent break-out session. During this time, the men and women split into separate groups and we spend about 2 or 3 hours talking about issues that affect us and our children while fighting this disease. Being a "seasoned" professional, I end up leading a lot of the discussions. One of the points that I made over this past weekend was that parents need to be their child's advocate when it comes to medical treatments. (I wrote about this earlier.) Well, the same applies to charities. If you are fortunate enough, the charities will fall into your lap and provide you with everything that you need. But, the harsh reality is that there are a lot of families to be taken care of, and sometimes local charities get overwhelmed.

You can do a minimal amount of research and/or networking with other families and you will invariably be rewarded with information that may lead you to other organizations that can help. During this past weekend there were 28 families attending Boggy Creek's Cancer Weekend, and of those, 20 had never been there before. That was a HUGE number for them. Usually they have many more returning families. Now, obviously some of the new families have just recently been diagnosed, so they wouldn't have had a need for Boggy Creek, however, many of them just hadn't pursued the chance to attend, or they weren't aware of what an amazing resource and escape the camp can be.

Another interesting topic that came up during the breakout session came from the facilitator who was running the group. He is a doctoral candidate who has been going there for many years. He asked what hospitals could do to help families in our situation. My response was that there needs to be more of an environment where families can interact and help each other. When we were diagnosed in 2000, we had that environment. The families used to look out for each other, watch each other's children, share meals, and help each other get through the days. In more recent years, we have seen a very different atmosphere on the floor. Part of this is due to the newer HIPAA laws that protect the privacy of patients and the information regarding their treatments. Also, there is sometimes a risk of spreading infection or illness when a child is contagious. Apart from that obvious concern, families should be able to interact and support each other while on the floor. It was a MAJOR part of our success and retention of our sanity that we had other families to "buddy up" with when Zachary was an inpatient for so many weeks. (More on that later though.)

The two major "wish" foundations that we know of are the Make-A-Wish Foundation, and the Children's Wish Foundation. I am pretty sure that there are more organizations like these two; however I believe they are the larger ones out there. We ended up using the Children's Wish Foundation. I don't recall the difference between the two, but they are both wonderful organizations, and we have had many friends who have used both of them. (Not in the double dipping sense, but many different friends who have used one or the other.) With Children's Wish Foundation, Zachary was told to come up with three wishes, in order of choice, and then submit them. The idea being, if they can't grant the first one, then they have two backup wishes to look at. At the time of our writing the wish list, we were watching a lot of TV sports, and Zachary was fascinated with Tiger Woods. So, wish #1 was to meet Tiger Woods. Now, the thing about meeting celebrities, whether they are from the world of sports, or entertainment, is that you usually only get a very short amount of time with them.

It may seem unfair on the surface, but when you factor in the high profile status of some of these celebrities; it is easy to see where they would have no time for anything else if they were to grant long visits or interactions with every child who asked. Zachary's second wish was a Disney Cruise and vacation in Orlando. The third wish may as well have been a trip to the moon, because I just don't remember after all of these years, so you're out of luck on that one. Anyway, Zachary's first wish was granted. He was going to get to meet Tiger Woods. That was the good news. The bad news was that because Tiger is such a sought after celebrity, the encounter would not take place for about a year from when we submitted it. We submitted it about a month before we got the wonderful news that Zachary only had about a month or two to live.

(Hmmm . . . . . while I didn't major in math in college, I'm thinking that there is a part to that equation that doesn't work.) You may recall from an earlier chapter that the SECOND thing the doctor told us back in late November of 2000, after he informed us that Zachary wasn't going to make it was, "You need to expedite his wish." (So much for meeting Tiger.)

Tiger's people were notified and we were sent a very nice autographed 8 X 10 photo. Meanwhile, we started to plan for the Disney trip. They gave us 4 nights on the cruise, 1 "travel" day to Orlando, (it actually took us like 59 minutes to get there from Canaveral where the ship docks), and then 4 nights in Orlando with Disney park passes. We took the trip in late January, AFTER they told us that he was in remission, but slightly before he was recovered enough to fully enjoy the trip. We used a wheelchair when necessary, and we were given instant access to rides, so that was pretty cool. All-in-all it was a great wish/trip. The meet & greet with Tiger would have been cool, but it would have probably lasted about 30 minutes or so. The Disney trip was full of memories that no one can ever take from us.

Some of the families wait on their wishes until their child is old enough to take a more adventurous vacation. The problem we had was that we had already been given the scare of a lifetime, so we were not particularly in the gambling mood. (There's the old saying about a "bird in hand", and I think we were in that mode of making the most of the here and now.) Some of the wishes that we have heard other children get are computers, special parties with limousine rides, Hawaiian vacations, cars, room make-over's, etc.

Another great charity that we got involved with is the Children's Miracle Network. They were very active at our north Florida hospital, and when Zachary was first diagnosed, our local hospital used to interact with them a lot. Sadly, the

hospital went from being not-for-profit to for-profit, at which point the Children's
Miracle folks had to part ways. We had a local university that started a dance
marathon to benefit the charity before that happened, and we participated in
that every year for about 6 years. Even after our local hospital was no longer
receiving funds, we still joined them every year and had a blast with the college
students as they raised money for the charity.

Some parents shy away from the spotlight that can be cast upon you when
you take part in these events, we didn't. Zachary adjusted very well to the
attention, and we as a family felt like we were giving something back by lending
our story and experiences to the many charities that we feel helped us either
directly or indirectly. Before the hospital became "for profit", the parents used
to joke about how they had NO problem parading our little bald-headed kids in
front of the media when they needed to raise money, however, when we tried to
improve conditions on the floor, they would scream poverty. In that sense, you
need to be careful of where and when you allow your child's story to be used. As
I wrote earlier, we KNOW that we benefited from many organizations, so I had
no problem speaking in front of groups, or lending our story to help raise money.
No amount of money could ever fully alleviate the feelings of helplessness and
despair that you feel while living this nightmare, however, having organizations
reach out to assist during the ordeal was invaluable to us.

There were times where we lent our story to an organization that we knew
would never directly benefit us, but knowing that other families would get help
when they needed it was enough for us to give back. One such instance occurred
at Boggy Creek one summer while Zachary was there. There were representatives
from another state who were in the process of building a similar camp, and they
had been granted access to Boggy for taking photos to be used in promotional
materials and commercials. We got notified by them that they had a photo of
Zachary that they wanted to use in a commercial. We gladly agreed, knowing
that the camp would be helping children like Zachary, but in another state. They
ended up sending us a copy of the commercial and an autographed photo from
the race car driver who was sponsoring the camp. Zachary took a lot of pride
in showing that to his friends over the next several years.

In addition to charities, there were several local fundraisers that were
organized for our family. Zachary's elementary school did an amazing job,
setting up a charitable bank account for us, and then organizing and hosting
several fundraisers that produced enough funds to get us through transplant.
There are many moments from the past eight years that I will never forget, and
one in particular came when I first heard that there was going to be a benefit
for Zachary. I was driving home from the hospital so that I could work the next
day, and I got a call from Rebecca. We were talking about the normal everyday
things that parents talk about, you know, blood counts, chemotherapy, Pokémon,

vomiting, Nintendo, dehydration . . . . you know . . . the usual stuff. Anyway, in the middle of the conversation she says, "Hey, I got a call from Zachary's school; they are going to have a benefit for us." I started to cry. The gravity of it all just hit me, "My son is so sick that the community is coming together to have a benefit for us." I'll never forget that.

Shortly after word got around about Zachary, Jessica (our friend who helped us during transplant), her mom Phyllis (who worked for me for 11 years) and some of their friends, worked with a local motorcycle bar to organize a huge benefit for us. They had a limousine come and pick us up and take us to the plaza where the party was. They brought in a Santa Claus to give Zachary a bunch of toys, and they raised several thousand dollars to help with bills. We were truly blessed to have so many different people from our community helping us in our time of need. During that same time, Jessica was also putting out a table during local festivals and fairs, selling buttons and t-shirts to help raise extra money for us.

Nowadays, with the economy hurting, charities are battling each other for funds in an environment where people aren't giving as much, because they can't afford to. There is an old Star Trek quote from the character Spock, in a scene where he is about to sacrifice his life to save others, where he says, "The needs of the many, outweigh the needs of the few, or the one." In the world of charities, this holds true.

The more prevalent illnesses have much larger fundraising machines and they are able to use the public awareness of their plight to procure the funds that they need for research and such. Some of the larger national cancer charities are able to raise millions and millions of dollars each year and those funds can get spread out over many regions, illnesses, etc.

That is why I feel it is SO important to find the organizations that are doing research into the specific disease that your child (or the child you are trying to help) is fighting, or the charity that is assisting the families on a local level. The "wish" foundations and N.C.C.S. are helping on a local level. And when all else fails, you can just help a family yourself!

The last charitable entity that I want to mention here is the Quantum House. We actually didn't have access to them until after relapse, which is the next chapter, but they belong in this one too, so here is the skinny on them. When Zachary was diagnosed, our local hospital did not have a hospitality house for the families. When Zachary was an inpatient, Rebecca would sleep on the tiny imitation of a couch, and I would sleep on an air mattress on the floor. The good news was that we would all be together. The bad news was that you never would get a real good night's sleep. We would switch off, "being on call" with Zachary each night, however, if it was "your" night being off, that didn't mean that you wouldn't wake up every time he needed to pee, or when his IV started to beep. You just couldn't escape the reality of what was going on around you. Upon relapse, the Quantum House had been built and was up and running.

They had 10 luxurious rooms, a fully stocked kitchen, a play area, a business center, and a wonderful garden and outside play area. They would give us a room when he was an inpatient, and that allowed one of us each night to "escape" for a real shower, meal, and a good night's sleep. It made all of the difference in the world to us. Local organizations would come in several times each week and prepare a big dinner for all of the family members who were staying there. There were always holiday celebrations going on that included family members of all ages, and you just felt like you were "home" when you stayed there.

At the end of the book I provide a comprehensive list of the charities that have helped us, including their contact information.

Chapter 6

Relapse (Treatments—Take #2)

"Just when you thought it was safe to go about living life to its fullest, the monster returns. Ding, ding, we now enter the 'bonus' rounds of the treatment phase where the values and stakes are MUCH higher."

Before I get started into this uplifting and happy time from our saga, (yeah right) I feel obligated to attempt to clarify the whole "relapse" issue with us. The word 'relapse' is generally used to describe an illness that was in remission and then returned. Usually, with cancer to be in 'remission' there needs to be what they refer to as "NED" (or No Evidence of Disease.) With Zachary, this just never happened. There are specific tests that are done with neuroblastoma to monitor levels of disease. I already wrote about the bone marrow test, there are also some urine markers that can be indicative of activity with this cancer too. However, we have found that by far, the most powerful tool for evaluating this disease is a test called an MIBG scan. (Meta-iodobenzylguanidine . . . . THERE, aren't you glad that I cleared THAT one up for you?)

Basically what happens is, the doctors inject a radioactive isotope into the patient, then they wait for about 24 hours, then they do a very specific scan, like a bone scan, that will show "hot" spots where the isotope has attached itself to the more active neuroblastoma clusters. (Confused yet? I am.) OK, most of you have heard of C.A.T. scans or M.R.I.'s. Those tests are useful in measuring disease also, but they can't always differentiate "active" neuroblastoma cells versus "dying" or "inactive" clusters.

The MIBG is a proven method of showing those spots. The downside to MIBG scans is that they are not very detailed or specific in their results. In other words, you can't look at the results from one and say, "The tumor is 5cm long and 3cm deep. Also, there can be active cells that are not clustered that will NOT show up on the MIBG scan. In the end, it is mostly medicine, with a little bit of art interpretation mixed in just to keep it interesting. (What fun would cancer be without HUGE amounts of uncertainty?) So, where am I going with all of this medical mumbo jumbo?

Well, back in January of 2001 when the doctors redid the bone marrow test and told us that Zachary was "in remission," we weren't doing MIBG scans. I'm sure that in other parts of the country, the test was being used, but that is the luck of the draw . . . . our area wasn't using them. So, all we had to rely on was the bone marrow test. THAT test has its uses, but once again, they were drawing the marrow from the hips, (an area known to be highly active with neuroblastoma patients) but if the disease is lurking elsewhere, they may not have detected it. ("Ooops . . . sorry . . . . how were we to know that your child still had cancer?")

The point to that long-winded explanation is that we were operating under the assumption that Zachary was indeed in remission during 2001. His health was improving, he was getting stronger, and there was no sign of back pain or fevers, both of which the doctors told us to expect if/when there was a relapse or reoccurrence of the disease. For you Monday morning quarterbacks out there reading this, and wondering whether we could have been doing more treatments, I don't have a good answer for you. I suppose that if we were being treated in one of the major neuroblastoma centers (NYC, LA, Atlanta, Philadelphia, etc), then maybe there would have been additional testing and treatments offered. As luck (good or bad . . . you decide) would have it, we were on a national protocol that only included the treatments that I wrote about in the 'Treatment' chapter. One of our doctors has actually suggested that Zachary may have never reached remission.

Medically speaking, he is considered to have recurrent or relapsed neuroblastoma; however, his current condition (walking, breathing, living, etc) seems to defy the textbook description of life after relapse. But, I am getting ahead of myself, first things first, Zachary's relapse.

It was the best of times, it was the worst of times . . . . (wait, I think that has been used before . . . . let me start over.) Long, long ago in a galaxy far away . . . . (oh great . . . . I think that one was used as well.) OK, for real this time . . . .

In November of 2001 Rebecca and I made the decision to have Zachary's port removed. We weren't using it for administering medicines, and every time that his temperature hit the magic number of 100.5, he was admitted to the hospital. We were also operating under the assumption that if he ever did relapse, he would have a new port implanted, and he would have that one until he died. (Did I mention earlier about the 100% fatality rate in relapsed neuroblastoma?)

So, we decided to give Zachary a break from the monthly port accessing that was required to keep it from getting clogged. The surgery went fine, and Zachary started to enjoy his newfound freedom. In late January of 2002, barely 3 months later, Zachary started to have back pain again. The doctors had warned us two years prior to that about how this disease will usually present itself the same way at relapse as it did during original diagnosis. So, we were immediately freaked out by the back pain. Our doctors were also freaked out, so they ordered an immediate bone marrow test and MRI scan. Within a couple of days we were notified of the wonderful (NOT) news that the disease was back.

It had returned with a vengeance. The marrow was infiltrated, and there was bony disease in multiple locations. Our local doctor informed us that he was going to call a few of the neuroblastoma doctors around the country to get some opinions/ideas as to how we should proceed. One of those calls went to Zachary's transplant doctor, and the message from him was anything but good. According to our local doctor, this is what advice was given. "Zachary's already had a transplant, why would you give him anymore chemo? Tell the parents to take him home, keep him comfortable, and let him die."

Now, some of you are probably sitting there reading this with your mouths wide open in shock. What you have to keep in mind is that relapsed neuroblastoma is generally looked upon as a death certificate for the child. We were told years ago that virtually all children who relapse with this disease will be dead within one year, and the ones that survive longer will endure a horrific existence of constant hospital stays, pain, and misery. (HEY, where do we sign up?) Well, obviously we did NOT listen to Dr. Doom. We ended up opting for a phase II protocol that included some heavy hitting chemotherapies. (Hmmm, I just mentioned "phase II." I suppose I should launch into some sort of explanation about that.) OK, here goes the layman's version of drug phasing. If you Google "Drug Phasing" you will find many helpful links as to how the process works. Here is a brief description to help you understand. (Also, the last thing that I want is for you to put MY book down so that you can go read someone else's material.)

Phase I—During phase I trials, researchers have usually had some success in the laboratory setting with a drug. (Picture lots of dead rats.) Usually these trials are small, not more than 30 patients, and they are designed to determine the safe dosage of a drug. Most patients on phase I trials have exhausted all "standard" or "traditional" treatments. They are usually left without viable options. Obviously there are no promises or guarantees with phase I trials. This is like throwing stuff against the wall, and praying that something sticks. Side effects are being researched, and safe dosage levels are being determined.

Phase II—During phase II trials, more patients may be added to the study, sometimes upwards of 50. At this level, doctors and researchers are trying to determine which cancers might react favorably to the drug, and how effective the drug is with those cancers. More research into side effects can also be done at this level. Not all drugs make it from phase I to phase II.

Phase III—These trials compare new treatments with currently existing treatments. Remember, most of the initial treatment protocols are standardized based on disease type, level, and other factors. So, if a newer treatment comes down the pike that is MORE effective than the standard one, it could mean that it is time to trade the older model in for a newer one.

Phase IV—This is done on already licensed drugs when they are trying to gather more information about long term risks, side effects, etc.

Now that you are fully versed on drug phasing, please pull out your #2 pencil and write a 500 word essay describing the differences between the different phases. (CLOSE YOUR BOOKS FIRST.) Just kidding, do NOT close your book. Oh, and you don't have to write an essay either. So, where were we? Oh yeah, phase II, nasty chemo. We actually started our first round of chemo after relapse on my birthday. I know this because I was sitting with the nurses at the end of the hallway, filling out the necessary documents that needed to be signed, and one of them didn't know what day it was. I commented that I knew it was February 11, because it was my birthday. One of the other nurses looked at me and said, "How horrible, that he has to start chemo on your birthday." I pondered over that comment for a moment or two and then replied, "Is there any GOOD day to start chemo?"

Actually, that topic came up many times with families while we were on the oncology floor. I would hear families lamenting about how it was someone's birthday, or anniversary (Our wedding anniversary was the day before Zachary was diagnosed . . . . BOO HOO), or some important day in their family's history, and I would have to be the one who popped the misery balloon by saying, "You know what, this situation is bad enough without us trying to INCREASE the severity of it by focusing on the fact that our Great Aunt Edna once had a friend who's cat was born on this same day in 1902. We get it. It sucks! Let's not make it any worse than it is."

So, we started on our new horrible chemotherapy regimen and we were off and running. The new chemos were not unlike the ones that we had done two years prior. They would knock his counts down to nothing, cause fevers, make him miserable, and wreak havoc on our lives. His appetite got so bad from the nausea that we ended up giving him Marinol. For those of you who don't know that wonder drug, Marinol is the synthetic form of Marijuana. Usually they don't give it to the younger kids (Zachary was eight at the time), but when all else fails, you will try anything.

Well, Zachary went from being a shy, introverted sickly boy who was losing weight as you looked at him, to a partying, eating machine who actually gained weight in the first week after taking the medicine. He was dancing in the hallway with the girl patients, wearing their wigs, and eating up a storm. He definitely got the "munchies" side effect from that drug. I'm guessing that it may have saved his life. He had lost so much weight and was continually nauseated and vomiting, so we were lucky to have had a doctor who would think outside of the box.

One of the newer (at least to us) tests that we were using was a urine test to look for two specific markers that can indicate an increased amount of cancer activity with neuroblastoma patients. These two levels are known as the VMA and HVA. I have written numerous journal entries about these magical urine markers, many of which are included at the end of this chapter. When we were first told about the VMA & HVA levels, the doctors neglected to tell us that the levels are not what you would refer to as . . . . . hmmmm . . . . how do I say this delicately . . . . well, RELIABLE!!! They are to be used, sparingly, in conjunction with MUCH more reliable tests. They should never be used as a standalone measure of disease. We were not told this.

So, when Zachary's levels started to escalate rapidly after just a few months of treatments, we met with his local doctor and said that we wanted to look for another therapy. What you have to keep in mind here is that with relapsed neuroblastoma, some parents refuse treatment and take their kids home. Back in 2002, in our area, there was no playbook that we could read to figure out which direction to take. The treatment plan went from being "on the doctors," to being "on us!"

So, when we told the doctor that we were done with that chemo, he agreed and suggested that we try to get seen in NYC by one of the leading neuroblastoma doctors in the world. We quickly made those arrangements and traveled to NYC. We were able to stay in the Ronald McDonald house that was only a few blocks from the hospital where we stayed for a week of testing and consultation with the doctors. They determined the level of Zachary's disease, and promptly sent us home to try two rounds of a duel-chemo recipe (Cytoxan & Irinotecan) that they had been using with some success in reducing the level of disease in several children. We have been told on a few occasions that researchers sometimes find that two chemotherapy agents, when put together, have a synergistic effect that can outweigh the benefits of using them separately. It would be like saying chemo (A) has a value of 1, and chemo (B) has a value of 1, but when you use them together, you get a value of 3. (Instead of the expected 2.) Those numbers are for example only, you don't actually get a 50% increase in benefit, but you get the general idea.

In the case of the two chemos that we were using, one of them is a known commonly used "harsh" chemo, while the other was relatively new (in the neuroblastoma world) and was much less harsh. We were instructed to do two rounds with those drugs. Each round consisted of one week of chemo, and then three weeks off. Because of the harsher one, we knew that we were in store for fevers and slow recovery time on his blood counts. We completed the two rounds in just over two months and then returned to NYC for reevaluation. After another week in NYC, we were told that Zachary's level of disease had indeed improved, but unfortunately not enough to be eligible for the treatment plan that we were shooting for.

The doctor also informed us that they were working on a new protocol that included the elements of the plan that unfortunately we were not accepted for. There was no clear timetable as to when the new plan would be available. He suggested that we return to Florida and continue giving Zachary the second or less harsh chemo, (Irinotecan) on a cycle of 1 week on and then two weeks off without the harsher Cytoxan.

With no other plan in sight, we followed his advice and returned home to continue with the Irinotecan. That was August of 2002. We started on that drug and very quickly we realized that Zachary was not getting anywhere near as sick from the chemo as he had in the past. Apparently the Irinotecan is tolerated much better than some of the harsher drugs. Between August of 2002 and January of 2003, we kept him on that chemo. During that time, we only had some minor bumps in the road. His nausea level improved drastically. He would still get nauseated from car rides but over time that eased up as well.

In January of 2003 we were again invited to NYC to be reevaluated for the newer protocol that was getting ready to open. We again stayed for a week and AGAIN we were denied access to the new plan. While they were happy with his apparently stable condition, they still felt that his level of disease was slightly too high for their protocol. (There is a common belief among many of the parents out there in cancer land that while most doctors are pure of heart and soul, some may discourage or prevent access to treatment plans in an effort to protect their statistics. In other words, when kids die, they can REALLY screw up your success rates! In a perfect world, we wouldn't even entertain the possibility of that being a reality . . . . but then again, in a perfect world; kids wouldn't be dying from cancer either.) Having been rejected for a third time, we asked about our options.

The doctor there suggested that we consider another protocol that they were running that utilized Arsenic. (Hmmmm . . . . . isn't that a poison? Well, chemo is sort of a poison too . . . remember the whole gloves and gown thing? How bad can it be? Well . . . . just to be safe . . . . let's ask.) "So, Doc, how many kids have you tried this Arsenic protocol on?" "Well, we've had nine children like Zachary try it." "Nine WHOLE children, wow, that's inspiring. Um, just out of curiosity, how did those nine WHOLE children do on the Arsenic protocol?" "Well, seven of them died pretty quickly, two more lasted a couple of months, and the last one made it a little longer than that." "They died? When you gave them poison? Go figure? Um, we REALLY appreciate your offer of poisoning our son, believe me, we've considered doing it ourselves on more than one occasion, but I think we're going to pass on this offer . . . . if it's all the same to you."

(While that may NOT be the verbatim conversation that took place, it was pretty darn close.) We returned home, without a new plan. So, Rebecca and I decided to employ the tried and true theory that "If it isn't broken, don't fix it!" We kept him on the Irinotecan and went about the business of living our lives. One of the interesting things that we DID learn during our three all-expenses NOT paid trips to NYC was that you never, NEVER hang your hat on VMA/HVA urine numbers. The doctors there made it painfully clear that they would have NEVER stopped the original treatment that we began on my birthday (Boo Hoo), based solely on the urine numbers.

After doing more research into urine testing and those two particular markers, I learned that there are some obscure foods that can actually affect the levels of VMA/HVA in the urine. Some of these foods are so obscure and rare, that I hesitate to even mention them, because you would NEVER expect to see a child eating things like; orange juice, chocolate, bananas, chewing gum, etc. (If you think that I making this stuff up, you've got to Google it and see it for yourself . . . . it's just too surreal to believe.) So, at some point in early 2003, I informed the doctors that IF they wanted some of Zachary's urine, I would gladly provide it for them, HOWEVER, I could NOT guarantee that the sample they would be receiving didn't contain dog or cat piss . . . because I was OVER the whole urine thing. Strangely, after making that comment, they didn't bother us so much for his urine anymore . . . . hmmmm. Go figure.

Zachary's disease slowly improved on the Irinotecan over time. This was not what we were told to expect. The doctors in NYC were adamant that any improvement that we might have would be found during the early rounds of using the drug. Certainly, by 2003, they would not expect to see further improvement, maybe stability of disease, but not improvement. The other factor that came into play in early 2003 was the addition of a non-traditional health supplement to Zachary's diet. The subject of supplements is too involved NOT to dedicate an entire chapter to it, so I have done just that! In fact, the NEXT chapter is titled "Supplements & Alternative Treatments," so you will get to read all about that aspect of our world when you get there.

I only mentioned it here, because we DO feel that some of Zachary's success and improvement can be attributed to the supplements that we have used. Now, back to 2003. As I mentioned a moment ago, Zachary was slowly improving, and we were going about the business of defying the odds and enjoying his good health. Slowly over time, the bone marrow tests started to come back clean, with no signs of cancer cells. The scans still showed disease in his spine, hips, and on occasion skull, collar bone, ankle and femur, but the marrow was clean.

He remained asymptomatic, (no sign of symptoms for you non-medical folks out there), and we kept hoping and praying that maybe the disease would just forget about us and go away. (Yeah right.) After about 22 months of IV Irinotecan treatments, we started to wonder about the long term effects of the chemo. We knew from previous studies that chemotherapy can cause secondary cancers to appear, (isn't THAT wonderful, when the "cure" becomes the culprit?) so we were starting to get nervous about how long Zachary had been on the Irinotecan. You need to remember that we were not part of any study; we were just doing our own thing, minding our own business.

After doing some initial research, we learned that the standard protocol for Irinotecan was 12 months. (Like . . . . 1 year, or 52 weeks.) (Hmmmm . . . . isn't 22 months a LOT more than 12?) After consulting with my calculator I did indeed confirm that 22 is a much higher number than 12. So, being the thorough chap that I can sometimes be, I did some more digging and found out that none of the doctors who I spoke with had any patients who had gone for more than 12 months on this chemo. BUT, more importantly, no one had any idea as to what the long term effects of this chemo were.

One of the MANY dilemmas facing us at that time was the knowledge that once a chemo agent stops working at fighting the disease, you can't go back to it. The neuroblastoma cells are known, over time, to develop a resistance to chemotherapy agents. The analogy that we were given way back in the beginning was that the cells evolve over time and learn to "filter" out the chemo so as not to be destroyed. (Scary shit . . . . isn't it?)

So, going almost a year past the "accepted" time for taking the Irinotecan did NOT do anything to calm down our nerves. The flipside to wanting to stop the chemo because of the long term effect issue was that you fear stopping something that is still working. What to do, what to do?

Choice A). Keep giving the chemo until it possibly causes some irreversible damage.

Choice B). Stop giving the chemo when it quite possibly is the only thing keeping the cancer from killing your child.

(Oohhh . . . . I love games . . . . let me play, let me play!)

Being the responsible, logical, and carefully thought out type person that I am, we did the only thing that any other sane parent would do . . . . we flipped a coin. "Heads its choice (A), and Tails its choice (B). Actually we didn't do that.

What we DID do is spend the next two months researching possible alternatives to the Irinotecan. We knew that there were other chemotherapy agents out there that we could try, but all of them were much harsher than the Irinotecan. Because of the HUGE amounts of uncertainty in Zachary's prognosis, we were very hesitant to try anything that drastically reduced his quality of life.

Quality of life is a term that gets thrown around a lot in the cancer community. It sounds all warm and fuzzy, but until you walk the walk, it is hard to appreciate just how much those three words factor into the decisions that you make each and every day. Quality of life might mean that you choose three "good" or healthy months with your child instead of six "bad" months where your child has lived longer, but they have spent the majority of the time in a hospital, or in pain. These are the choices that parents are forced to make each and every day around the country while battling this disease. So, when you hear the words, "quality of life", take a moment and try to put yourself in the shoes of someone who is walking down this treacherous road. (Actually, don't do that . . . . this road sucks . . . . take a different road and avoid this one at all costs.)

After researching the options, we decided to stop the chemo and try an experimental drug that was available in pill form. The drug, Fenretinide is in the same class of drugs as the Accutane. You may recall that the Accutane was used post-transplant to age or kill off any remaining neuroblastoma cells. Well, the Fenretinide, taken in large doses, was shown to have a similar effect on the cancer cells. That was the good news. The bad news was that in order to get adequate quantities of the medicine into the blood stream, the patient (Zachary) needed to take 10 pills, 3 times each day, for 7 days. Then he would get 2 weeks off, before having to repeat the process.

If the disease stayed away, I believe that he could stay on the medicine for up to three years. Fortunately for us, Zachary was then at an age where he could swallow pills. In fact, he was able to swallow like 5 of these monster pills at a time. To give you an idea as to how big they were, they looked just like a Mike & Ike's candy, only white . . . not red. Being off of chemo was a good thing for Zachary. His strength slowly started to come back, and he was able to be more active. Sadly, we were only able to stay on the Fenretinide for about 5 months.

During one of his regularly scheduled scans, the doctors informed us that they believed that his disease was progressing again and that we needed to find another approach. As luck (good or bad . . . . you decide) would have it, at the same time we were looking for alternative treatment plans, our doctors had heard that someone at Duke had figured out that you could give the Irinotecan IV formula to kids, and have them drink it instead of injecting it into their veins. They felt that when consumed, it metabolized differently, and the children were experiencing a separate secondary medical benefit from its use. (Makes sense to me . . . . just because you're not supposed to touch this stuff, doesn't mean we shouldn't have our children drinking it . . . . right?) The REALLY good news was that unlike most medicines that taste horrible, this one tasted like gasoline! (That is probably not fair to gasoline; I'm told that in moderation it can be tolerated.) So the new challenge became trying to find something to mix the chemo in so that he could keep it down.

Now, I'm not one to keep score, but I'm guessing that if the Guinness Book of World Records kept track of the most amount of puking sessions by one child in a 22 month period, Zachary would have won hands down. Every time that we thought we had found the magic formula to make it tolerable, he would get tired of it and start having problems again. But being the trooper that he was, we somehow managed to keep on keeping on, and he did indeed have a benefit from it.

The new progression of the disease that had emerged fell back to the old levels, and he became stable again. (Not in remission. Stable! Lots of folks get confused by that. They see him walking around, going to school, and they say, "How long has he been in remission?" You need NED to be in remission.) (And NO, NED is NOT some guy named Ned . . . . it's that whole No Evidence of Disease thing that I explained earlier.)

In December of 2006 we started to have problems with Zachary's port. It was not flushing easily during the regular monthly visits, and the doctor made the observation that we really weren't using it for anything anyway, so we made the decision to remove it! My only regret is that we hadn't thought of taking that action sooner. It really freed Zachary up and improved his quality of life. Not only did he get to avoid those monthly port accessing sessions, but fevers were no longer an automatic ticket to the hospital for him.

Zachary enjoyed several months of "normal" life, taking his oral chemo and not worrying about his port. Zachary made it until May of 2007 before his disease started to show signs of progression again. He was at one of his normal MIBG 6 month checkups and they informed us that there were new "hot spots" and the disease was spreading. Once again we were caught with our pants down. We had no backup plan in place. We were always passively looking into alternative therapies, but we didn't have a real choice selected yet. So, I went into research mode and within 3 days I had called 5 of the top neuroblastoma doctors who I knew of from around the country. The consensus was that there were really only 3 good choices to choose from for Zachary. While checking into treatment centers (none of the "good" stuff is ever available locally), I learned that option #1 did not have any openings at that time. We could get on a wait list if we wanted to. Now, there were two problems with that option.

First of all, being on a waiting list meant that we would be giving the cancer more time to grow. (I'm no expert, but I'm guessing that that would NOT be a wise move.) The other problem with option # 1 was that being on a waiting list meant that we were waiting for another child to die, so a slot would open up. (Now, I'm not an overly superstitious person, but I've GOT to believe that waiting for another parent to lose their child is NOT good Karma.) Option #2 was looking really good, until they told us that he was not eligible for that drug because of certain medical factors in his background. (Translation = they didn't want to hurt their statistics with a kid that might die on them.) And who can blame them? I mean really, which is more important, the life of ONE MEASLY child, or their statistics?

SO . . . . how are you liking option #3 huh? . . . . Looking pretty good, isn't it? Oh yeah!!!

By default, we chose (or it chose us) option #3. This drug trial had just opened up as a phase II, which meant that they had already gone through phase I and they knew what dosage was appropriate for children. The other good news about this was that it came in pill form, like the Fenretinide did. The name of this drug is ABT-751. Somewhat of a letdown after all of those REALLY cool long medical names that I have been throwing around for the last couple of chapters. But, it is what it is . . . . a drug that hasn't received an official name yet.

The only facility that we could get the drug from was C.H.O.P. (Children's Hospital of Philadelphia). That meant flying back and forth to Philly for treatment. The good news was that the doctor in charge of the study for the entire country was based in Philly. The initial trip required us to stay for an entire week of studies to determine his level of disease prior to starting the medicine. After that, they said we would need to return every three weeks for reevaluation scans and blood work.

We stayed at the Ronald McDonald House which ended up being pretty cool; it was the first one built in the country. The house was only about 4 or 5 blocks from the hospital, so we had no problem getting around. Both the house and the hospital are smack dab in the middle of the campus of the University of Pennsylvania which meant that there were plenty of college students walking around, and that made us feel somewhat safe in the big city. While we were there for that weeklong visit, we saw the Franklin Museum, we ate cheese steaks, we took the tour around the historical district, and we got to visit with an old college friend of mine and his wife. All in all, it was a pleasant enough visit. Before leaving, they gave us our pills and set up our return visit dates for three week later. The pills were to be given on a 7 day cycle with two weeks off, so there wasn't any real hardship there with nasty drugs or anything.

We were forewarned that the major side effect of this particular drug was peripheral neuropathy. (I can see you guys running to your computers to go on WebMD to look that one up . . . . I'll save you the effort.) Peripheral neuropathy is pain in the periphery or outer limbs, like hands or feet. The other main side effect to watch for was constipation. Apparently, the nerves that help to control digestion and movement of waste through the bowels are similar to the nerves found in the hands and feet, and this drug is known to cause problems with that particular nerve type. The first round went rather smoothly. Zachary didn't exhibit any side effects or issues. In fact, when we returned to C.H.O.P. for our three week checkup, they were surprised and impressed to discover that he was already showing signs of improvement. The doctor was pleased, but she made it clear that they usually don't see improvement that quickly. Zachary was unique. (Hey, you take what good news you can get . . . . when you can get it.)

During the second round of the ABT-751 Zachary was at Boggy Creek for the week-long cancer camp. While there, he became preoccupied with having fun and chasing girls, and was NOT paying attention to the fact that he didn't poop for seven days. He returned from camp on a Wednesday, and started to feel poorly. We got him in to see his local doctor on Thursday, but he could find no major problems that would have prevented him from going on our annual family reunion trip that was scheduled for the next day. So, we headed off on Friday for Tennessee. The drive up for Zachary was tortuous. He was constantly nauseated and not happy about being in the truck for so long.

We gave him medicines to try and make him comfortable, but it was a rough trip. We arrived at the vacation house on Saturday morning, and Zachary was still not himself. By that evening, we were concerned enough to take him to the local E.R. that was about 30 minutes away. Even though it was a typical small town hospital, they were very receptive to treating him. We have had experiences where smaller local hospitals get intimidated with his diagnosis and seem at a loss as to how to treat him. They did an x-ray and quickly determined that he had enough poop inside of him to start a small war with. Apparently, not pooping for 9 days is a BAD thing . . . . who'd have known? They gave him an enema and evacuated copious amounts of debris from his colon, small intestine, large intestine, bowel, legs, arms, and everywhere else that the crap had backed up into. Immediately after that experience, he started to feel somewhat better. We were able to return to the vacation house for the night.

Sunday was a weird day for him. He seemed at times to be getting better, but then he would spike a fever for no apparent reason. His appetite was spotty at best, but we attributed that to the fact that they had flushed out like 857lbs of crap from his body the night before. By Monday morning we started to worry. His fever was not going away, and he was not eating. (Pretty much a recipe for dehydration.) We loaded up the truck and headed back to the local hospital.

Unfortunately, they were busier than two days previously when we had first visited them. The good news was that they all remembered him and got him right in to be seen. The first thing that they found was that his oxygen level was too low. (There is a slick little device known as a pulse oximeter that attaches to the outside of your finger and quickly will give the doctors an oxygen level reading.) Because of the low oxygen, they brought in a tank and hooked him up with nasal oxygen. He was seen by the doctor, and after about an hour or so, they told us that they wanted to transfer him to Knoxville Children's Hospital where they had a pediatric oncology unit. That hospital was about an hour away. They loaded him up in an ambulance with Rebecca, and I followed them down to enjoy a three night stay in beautiful Knoxville, Tennessee. We actually had an interesting "scare" there before we were admitted. We had spent about 7 hours in an E.R. room receiving wonderful care, when I happened to ask the nurse if she knew what time we would be getting up to the oncology floor. She informed us that they were still trying to decide whether or not Zachary would get admitted. (Sirens started to go off in my head . . . . what was the alternative for us?)

He was too sick to be anywhere but in the hospital. I actually asked that question, but in a calm adult manner. She went on to say that they were considering transferring him to his "treating" hospital. (Ahhh, for those of you in the cheap seats who haven't been paying attention, she was referring to C.H.O.P. in Philadelphia.) OK . . . . and HOW exactly would we get there? Apparently air ambulance for Zachary and Rebecca, and for me, a wonderful 15 hour or so drive. (Yikes!).

Luckily that never happened. They admitted us to the floor and while we would have much preferred to be enjoying our vacation, we were treated to an amazing stay in a wonderful hospital. The "Southern" hospitality was incredible. Every person from the doctor down to the cleaning staff knocks on your door and actually waits for a response before entering. They gave us a two patient-bed room with a couch, so that we could all stay together and not have to get a hotel room. The entire staff went out of their way to make us as comfortable as possible, given the circumstances.

By Wednesday afternoon Zachary's condition had improved greatly, and we were informed that we could leave on Thursday to get back to our vacation. Apparently he had indeed been dehydrated, and the diarrhea after the constipation hadn't helped matters. We got back to the vacation home early Thursday, and Zachary was able to enjoy two full days of water-skiing and fun before we had to head home on Saturday.

During the drive home, Zachary started to complain of discomfort in his feet. We (being this idiots that we are), wrote it off as something related to his skiing or sun exposure. By early the following week, we found out the hard way that he was having severe peripheral neuropathy. Within a week, he was in a wheelchair, unable to walk. The doctors put him on a medicine called Neurontin, which is used for this condition. The downside to using that drug is that it can cause drowsiness and lethargy because of how it "dulls the nerves." Zachary ended up using the wheel chair for a little bit over a month. During all of this we were constantly in touch with the doctors in Philly. They have very strict guidelines as to how much they will allow a patient to tolerate before yanking the ABT-751 away because of toxicity issues. They reduced the chemo and watched us closely. Meanwhile, he showed some more slight improvement and then leveled off to where they felt the disease was "stable." Not getting any worse, and not getting any better.

We were still on the three week plan, but by that time, Rebecca had gotten comfortable enough that she could travel without me. I had gone up once without her, and then she was able to take over that chore so that I could focus on selling my business and doing work. We came close a few times to having Philly pull the drug from us, but luckily we were able to find a balance with the nerve drug and controlling his pain. After a few more rounds without incident, Philly allowed us to bump the three week schedule to a six week schedule. This was a huge help to us. Rebecca had been taking a lot of time off from work, and it was becoming logistically difficult to be traveling every three weeks. The other interesting development that we had with his treatments was that for the first time since relapse, we had a backup plan for if/when the ABT-751 was no longer available to us.

The doctors in Philly are working on many different new and innovative treatment programs. Years ago they pioneered a treatment that uses the MIBG technology to attack the cancer cells. I don't know all of the details, but basically it sounds like they tapped into the fact that the MIBG isotope attaches itself to the cancer cells. Playing off of that, I guess they found a way to attack the cell, while they were attaching to it. (I REALLY dumbed that down for you guys, but keep in mind who my readers are . . . . no offense.) The bottom line is that they have been using that therapy for many years and have a few variations on it that work on children with varying levels of disease. The other interesting outcome from the ABT-751 would be if Zachary makes it through the entire 3 year cycle, because then there would be a chance that the doctors would allow us to keep giving him the drug on a compassionate basis. You just never know. Also, there are new treatments becoming available all of the time, so there is a chance that something new and promising will pop up between now and then. We are just happy (it's a relative thing in our world) that Zachary is tolerating the current treatment and that we have this backup plan.

This chapter on relapse sort of brings you up to date on where we are in the treatment phase of life. There were some other pain issues that we never fully understood, but were resolved, that came up late last year. He spent some time in the hospital on two occasions, and various medicines were added and removed from his current regimen, but in the end we were able to return to "normalcy."

I guess as an author (I use that term loosely when referring to myself, trust me), you get to take certain liberties when writing your book. One of those liberties would be to go back, after you have already finished your work, and add something new. At the time of writing these next several paragraphs, my edited book was being read by a literary agent in California. So, why would I mess with perfection you ask? Well, things in our world can change quickly. What better way to give you a glimpse into how drastically things can get turned upside down, than by continuing a previously completed chapter on Zachary's treatments. Two weeks prior to writing this next section, Zachary and Rebecca were in Philadelphia for our three-month checkup. Sadly, Zachary's cancer was shown to have spread and grown considerably. He had increased disease in his spine, legs, hips, and a lymph node in his groin. As bad luck would have it, the night they arrived in Philadelphia, Zachary started to have leg pain. He even commented to Rebecca that he had a bad feeling about the scans and that he thought we were going to get bad news. The doctors were able to confirm that the areas of pain that Zachary was experiencing were lighting up on the MIBG scan.

With the news of his disease spreading, the doctors immediately instructed us to stop the ABT-751 chemo that he had been taking for almost a year. While that was obviously a huge disappointment for us, we recognize that we were fortunate to have gotten a year of "stability" on that relatively "easy" chemo. Even with all of the side-effects that Zachary encountered, we were still able to maintain a high quality of life for him.

When Zachary heard the news, he called me from his cell phone and was very upset. His exact words were, "Dad, the scans were bad, the disease is spreading. I think we need to say we're just an unlucky family and that we won't beat this disease. I can't fight it anymore." (Feel free to cry at this time, I did.) Somehow, through the tears and the torture of hearing those words, I found myself telling him that we needed to listen to what options were being given to us, and then we would make a decision as a family. Thankfully, the doctor had set up a conference call so that I could be included with her, Rebecca, Zachary and one of the nurses. By the time we started the call, Zachary had calmed down somewhat, and didn't sound as depressed as he had earlier. The doctor laid out a couple of options for us, but the MIBG treatment was the focus of the discussion. They had pretty much pioneered that therapy in Philly, and were experiencing some great success stories with it. The doctor informed us that normally it would take 6-8 weeks to get on the schedule, and that because of the delay, the patient would need to do some high dose chemo in an attempt to keep the cancer from spreading even further. However, they were able to find an opening 2 weeks from that visit, so Zachary would not have to endure more chemo at that time.

The MIBG therapy would require admission to the hospital on a Monday afternoon. They would insert an I.V. line into his hand or arm and begin flushing him with fluids. Zachary would also have to begin drinking large quantities of the drops that are used to protect the thyroid from damage. On Tuesday, they would give him the I.V. infusion of the radioactive isotope, which would take about an hour. After that it would become a waiting game.

The room is specially designed to prevent the radiation from escaping. The patient has lead barriers on either side of the bed to help in that effort. One parent can be in the room with the child, but special precautions are required. Any toys, books, clothes, etc. that the child touches must be destroyed before leaving the room. Because of that, the parent changes the DVD's and game disks for the child. Once the radiation level drops below a federally mandated level, the patient is released and sent home. (Usually by Friday of that same week.) If you are craving a more in-depth explanation of the treatment, you can go online and search "MIBG therapy," and several links should pop up. We were able to find some that included photos of the room and the gowns that parents must wear while staying in there.

So, now you are REALLY up to date with our treatment saga. (At least as of 4/26/08.) As of the writing of this section, we are two days away from beginning that process. (Do you smell what I smell? A sequel for my book!)

[FLASHBACK TO CLASSIC JOURNAL ENTRIES]

Sunday, November 24, 2002 at 08:42 PM (CST)

Well, we made it to the Quantum House! The weekend with my folks was great, they were celebrating their 45th wedding anniversary and we got to be there with them. We will be at the doctor's office at 8am sharp tomorrow, and hopefully onto the hospital after that. Tuesday we're scheduled for the bone marrow. Now on to bigger topics . . . .

WELCOME TO THE FIRST EVER CSC NEWS LETTER!
(Cancer Sucks Club) (Inspired by Audra's response to my journal entry)

MINUTES FROM LAST MEETING: There have never been any meetings, so of course there are NO minutes. Plenty of long hours and days, but NO minutes!

MEMBERSHIP DRIVE: Some of you may be asking yourselves, "How do I join the CSC?" WELL SNAP OUT OF IT! This isn't something you elect to join . . . . IT JOINS YOU. It's kinda like winning the lottery, only without the money, and instead of being wonderful, it sucks!

DUES: Well, after much consideration, the board of directors, (that's just me right now, don't be too impressed) had taken the issue of dues under serious consideration, and then it was immediately dismissed. It was decided that the families who are unlucky enough to have joined this club, pay enough through pain, suffering, anguish, anxiety, fear, empathy, exhaustion, sweat, tears, and heartache, that they don't need to be coughing up money for some club.

CLUB MOTTO: Well yes, every club needs a motto. Something prophetic, well written, easy to remember, eloquent and appropriate. So, after much thought and many seconds of pondering, the quite prestigious board of directors came up with the following:

CANCER SUCKED YESTERDAY, CANCER SUCKED TODAY, AND CANCER WILL UNDOUBTEDLY SUCK TOMORROW!

Now, I know some of you out there in la la land are going to take umbrage (fancy word) with the director's choice of mottos. Being as this is going to be a democratic club, (meaning that anyone can offer their input, and I'll type what I darn well please,) I have decided to set up a board of appeals that will review any complaints regarding this motto. This board will have the final word in all matters regarding the motto, what they say will go! I have decided to appoint our dear friends Jeff and Kathy, (who lost their son to cancer one week ago today) to head this board. I'm going to go out on a limb here and say, "I'll be happy to go along with any decision they make." Anyone dumb enough to want to submit a complaint or "less severe" motto for review, just email it to me, I'll see that it gets the attention it deserves.

CLUB LOCATION: Well, unfortunately, club members are located throughout the world. Even if we limited membership to those who are U.S. citizens, they are still spread throughout the country, some at home, some in the hospital, some traveling constantly between the two. So, let's just say that if you are unlucky enough to have joined our club, feel free to add your two cents in the guestbook, anytime you like. As for those of you who are members because of a friend who is a member, we welcome you with open arms. Your dues are $2,549.00 per month. You may make the checks payable to any of the families who pulled the short straw like us. Just pick a new family each month, and send away your money!

Scott
CSC Member since 3/16/00 (son has neuroblastoma)

Wednesday, November 27, 2002 at 08:25 PM (CST)

Ok . . . first things first. The update!

Our doctor called us today with preliminary results from the bone marrow taken yesterday. There were samples taken from both hips. The left side is completely clean. The doctor was going to check what that side showed last time. The right side last time was between 5 and 10%, and this time it was less than 5%! AND, most of those cells were 'mature' cells, or 'not bad cells." So, it appears as though Zman is responding to the current therapy. We are still waiting for the urine results. The iron levels, which are used as a marker for neuroblastoma activity, have improved also. This level is supposed to be 0-450. In Sept., his level was 934. In Oct. it dropped to 911. Three weeks ago it was down to 867, and Monday it was 680. So, the trend is good, it's dropping. However, be warned. These markers are not definitive. Using any one marker to gauge activity is like reading tea leaves while looking through the wrong end of a pair of binoculars to determine who's going to win the super bowl.

Now, onto bigger news! The Cancer Sucks Club has drawn a wide variety of interest from across the globe! People from all over West Palm Beach and Hobe Sound have been bombarding our page with 4 whole comments! WOW, what a response! I may need to hire a full time secretary to monitor and respond to all of the inquiries. (That was sarcasm for those of you who don't know me.) Actually, several people have commented and said they did get something out of those journal entries . . . . so, here continues the saga.

We on the prestigious board of directors, (that's still just me, but it sounds more important this way,) have been doing some serious thinking about this cancer disease. It is amazing to us (me), that this diseases whole purpose is take over its host (our child), only to then end its own life when the child loses the battle. So, it is defying logic. Obviously, our children are not properly suited to host this disease. So, maybe we need to just find another life form that can do the honors. Now, I don't want members from PETA jumping down my throat when I make some suggestions. I'm just trying to think of a way to spare our children the agony of this horrendous disease! The first thing that comes to mind, are the fire ants! Would any of us really miss them? There are plenty of them around, so the different cancers can have at it! Pick and choose and end as many of THEIR lives as they want. Sure, it will take the fun out of walking barefooted in South Florida, but we can't have everything.

The next obvious choice would have to be the wasps and hornets! I know honey bees provide honey and help with the whole flower thing, but really folks, does anyone know what purpose wasps and hornets provide, other than freaking me out when they fly too close? Fine, it's settled . . . they've made the list.

Moving onto the animal world, I'm going to go out on a limb and offer up rats! Sure, they make great pets, if you're a witch, but for the rest of us, do we really need these disease carrying rodents that badly? I think not. And, if we're going to give rats cancer, why not let sharks join the party. I know they're an important part of the food chain, but ever since I saw Jaws as a kid, I've feared that I might become a link in that chain, so, bye bye sharks.

Well, now that all of that is settled, we just have to figure out a way to convince this nightmare to leave our children alone!

Happy Thanksgiving to everyone. May it be a healthy and happy day for all of you!

Saturday, November 30, 2002 at 12:44 PM (CST)

HOME AGAIN!

We made it home today after our whirlwind tour of West Palm Beach. The chemotherapy part of our stay was thankfully uneventful. Zachary is still tolerating this drug well enough for us to keep him on this regimen. Evaluating the benefits of continuing is where this all gets interesting.

The bone marrow results that I mentioned in my last entry remain encouraging. We are still waiting for NYC to take a look at the samples that were sent to them. Hopefully they will be pleased as well. The urine level this time did not come down, in fact, it went back up a little bit. This could be a diet related swing. The amount it went up was minor, so we're not pushing any panic buttons just yet. I guess we'll have to schedule a trip to NYC in January to let them do a full workup on Zachary so we have an accurate assessment as to where we stand. We'll probably decide on that trip near the 1st of the year.

I would like to make a "public" thank you to the Mathis family for including us in their Thanksgiving Day feast. We had a great day with our friends, we are truly lucky to have people in our lives who think of us during difficult times. I would also like to say thank you to the Charlton family. They were very kind to have included us in Matthew's party and to have kept us busy during our down times after chemo.

Zachary can be difficult to read sometimes. He has tolerated this chemo so well, that I think we sometimes take it for granted that he is "ok" with everything that we're doing. These past few weeks have been different. He started to lose his hair again. Of all the things that I would never have believed that would bother him, this was #1. He has been without hair for so long, that I'm used to it I guess. But, it was growing back nicely, and then all of a sudden, it started to fall out again. We were told that the current chemo we're doing doesn't always cause this, but it certainly can. I know this is a minor issue in the big scheme of things, but as a parent, you try to protect your child from anything that causes pain or grief. As a parent, you see your friends grieving over the loss of their child, and you KNOW there are bigger issues out there than hair loss. As an eight year old, who knows what makes them tick at any given time? Not me.

The Cancer Sucks Club has lost another child. Seth lost his battle with this disease last night at our local hospital. We did not get to know this family well, but make no mistake . . . . this was a loss for all of us! No child deserves this fate! No family deserves this agony! Our thoughts and prayers are with Ruthie and Scott and their family.

There are many good causes out there, save the whales, the trees, the aardvarks (I made that one up,) the owls, and the list goes on and on. But, what resource for our future is more important than our children? I can think of none. I don't know which organization is doing the "best" research into curing this disease; there are so many types of cancer, where do you begin? I do know that with a little bit of effort, you can make a difference. Do a little bit of web searching, find a university or facility that is working in a direction that YOU feel is helping, and make a difference, either through donations, or by helping to make others aware of who the "good guys" are. If you live near a hospitality house, (Quantum, MacDonald, Target,) call them up and ask what supplies they need. Or, cook a meal for some of the families. It's a great way to get involved, and you'll get to see your efforts make a difference. Sometimes sending a check doesn't have the same feeling! But, I'm sure any of these organizations would love your donations.

Ok, I'll climb down off my soapbox and get back to doing what I do best . . . . being sarcastic! The Cancer Sucks Club has its motto, and its bylaws, but, there have been some requests for a song. Well, I've given this some thought, (18 seconds exactly.) And, I've decided that no ONE song will fill the need. So, we will have songs that change with the seasons. Our first one needs to have words that go with a popular Christmas song. So, get to work. And for those of you smart a$$ess out there, I don't know any Hanukkah songs, and I HIGHLY doubt any of you know any! (I'm referring to my non-Jewish friends who read this page.) So, *we'll stick with the Xmas songs. I'll get over it. I've done one using Jingle Bells, so that one is off limits! Find your own darn song! My song is at the bottom of this journal entry.*

Scott

(sung to the tune of jingle bells)

CANCER SUCKS
CANCER SUCKS
CANCER SUCKS ALL DAY!

FOR ALL THE KIDS, IT TAKES FROM US,
WE WILL SURELY PRAY.

CANCER SUCKS
CANCER SUCKS
CANCER SUCKS ALL DAY!

FOR ALL THE KIDS, IT TAKES FROM US,
WE WILL SURELY PRAY.

LOSING ALL YOUR HAIR,
PUKING ALL DAY LONG,
FRIENDS THAT PASS AWAY,
BEING FAR FROM HOME,

NEEDLES IN YOUR ARM,
NEEDLES IN YOUR CHEST,
WHY DO WE COMPLAIN SO MUCH?
ISN'T CANCER JUST THE BEST? (sarcasm)

(REPEAT CHORUS UNTIL IT DEPRESSES YOU BEYOND REASON.)

Wednesday, December 04, 2002 at 03:13 PM (CST)

WOW!

I am truly impressed. The creative juices have obviously been flowing freely across this great land of ours. Keep the songs coming. (My newest entry is at the end of the journal entry.) As far as the touring with our songs idea goes . . . . it sounds good on paper, and I don't know about you guys, but I couldn't carry a tune if it was wrapped up nicely and stuck into a bag!

I haven't been sleeping well lately. I wake up and lie there, so last night, after my whopping 4 hours of sleep, I wrote today's journal entry in my head. (Lotta empty space in there folks.)

Zachary did not have ankle pain yesterday, so that was good. He did have some diarrhea, but that is easily controlled with meds, so we're not too concerned. I had the honor of meeting Scott and Ruthie (Seth's parents) last night. Unfortunately, it took place at the funeral home. I had been looking forward to meeting them on the floor at St. Mary's, so that Zman and Seth could meet and play together. One of the more frustrating aspects of this disease for us men is the total and complete lack of control that we have over our family's lives! (Men are control freaks . . . . like THAT is news.) Speaking for the Finestone family, our thoughts and prayers go out to Seth's family.

Cancer Sucks Club News!

The board of directors has been reviewing past journal entries, and it has decided to make two additions to the panel in charge of reviewing complaints about our club motto. For those of you that have forgotten, our motto is:

CANCER SUCKED YESTERDAY, CANCER SUCKED TODAY, AND CANCER WILL UNDOUBTABLY SUCK TOMORROW!

In addition to Jeff and Kathy, the board is placing Scott and Ruthie on this panel. The job of this panel is to review any complaints about the harshness of our motto. Furthermore, the board realized its mistake, in not having laid out guidelines for submitting complaints. So, here are the club guidelines for making those submission:

ALL COMPLAINTS REGARDING THE CLUB MOTTO MUST:

1). Be typed or computer printed on an 8.5" x 11" sheet of paper.
2). Top margin and bottom margin MUST be 5" each.
3). Left and Right margins MUST be 4" each. (We realize that this only leaves you 1" by 1.5", but if you can't get your point across in that amount of space, then you are just not trying hard enough.
4). Five copies must be sent. One for each panel member and one for the board of directors.

5). *After all five copies are done, soak them in gasoline and place them into a fire-safe can.*

6). *Wait for 15 seconds so the gasoline can soak in.*

7). *Toss a lit match into the can.*

8). *Wait for the flames to die down, then pour in one cup of cold water.*

9). *Stir well so that the ashes are mixed nicely with the water.*

10). *Pour the ash/water mix into water tight container and send to the address listed below.*

If you have followed these steps properly, the panel will be able to easily flush your complaint down the toilet, without causing any clogs.

(Address for complaints)

Cancer Sucks Club
Attn: Review Panel
123 Areunuts Lane
Battlecreek, MI 12345

(We're just down the street from the Kellogg's factory.)

Scott

P.S. Here is my latest.
Sung to the song, White Christmas. (Is no song safe?)

I'm dreaming of a cure for cancer,
No more sick kids in this fight.
Where the chemo and radiation, are figments of our imagination,
Boy, the future would be bright!

I'm dreaming of a cure for cancer, where our kids can run and play.
Wouldn't our days be merry and light?
No more Christmases in this fight!

Sunday, February 2, 2003 12:31 AM CST

Yes, we are home! We finished up with chemo today with no excitement. This is a good thing. Now, we've got a lot of things to cover today boys and girls, so sharpen your pencils and pay attention . . . . I don't want to have to repeat myself.

First, let's begin with the medical lesson for the day. I don't want to bore everyone with lots of details regarding the various treatment protocols that we are considering; however, I did want to share excerpts from one of the studies to give you a better understanding of what we are facing. The one that I will be quoting from is being done in a hospital up north. It is a promising study that is showing a benefit (whatever that means,) in just over 50% of the 90 children who have tried it. On page #1, there is a paragraph titled:

WHY IS THIS STUDY BEING DONE? (The answer they give . . . .)

"This study is being done to determine if high dose 131 I-MIBG at a dose of 18 mCi/kg is a safe and effective treatment for relapsed or resistant neuroblastoma."

"Currently there is no known effective treatment for your child's type of cancer. We want to see if we can more effectively treat your child's type of cancer with a new experimental treatment plan. This experimental plan uses 131I-MIBG given at high doses. The dose may be high enough to permanently injure your child's bone marrow and therefore many research participants will need a stem cell transplant."

Ahhhhhhhhhhhhhh, what great news they delivered . . . . I especially like the first sentence in paragraph #2 . . . . "Currently there is no known effective treatment for your child's type of cancer." That pretty much sums it all up, wouldn't you say? Ok . . . . lets not get bogged down now folks, we've got lots to cover . . . . moving right along to the end of the study. They have a helpful paragraph that reads as follows:

ARE THERE OTHER TREATMENT OPTIONS?

"Yes, there are other options for treatment. Instead of being in this study, other options include:"

1). *Treatment with an intensive chemotherapy regimen and stem cell support without 131I-MIBG. (Been there . . . . done that . . . . no thank you.)*
2). *Treatment with chemotherapy or other agents that do not require stem cell support. (Ahhhhhhh duh. That is what we are doing now.)*
3). *Other experimental therapies. (Ok . . . . fair enough . . . we're looking into those now.)*

4). No therapy at this time with palliative care to help your child feel more comfortable. (This is death, for those of you that weren't sure.)

"Your child's doctor will talk to you about these other treatment options."
(Not likely . . . we've pretty much had to figure it all out on our own.)

So, are you keeping up everyone? Making good notes? There may be a surprise exam on all of this at a later date.

To summarize, we are looking at several options that include NYC, Philadelphia, and two treatment plans that allow us to stay home. I'm trying to get more information before deciding. It's like having a party . . . only there's no music or dancing . . . . and yes you guessed it . . . . it sucks!

Now, onto bigger and better issues. Speaking of things sucking, we've recently had some dissention in our ranks. I've seen at least three or four entries from faithful club members asking about a "less harsh" word than "suck" that could be used on shirts and buttons so kids and squeamish folks could wear them. Well, hmmmmmmmmmmm . . . . this sounds like a job for our executive board. You remember them don't you? Jeff, Kathy, Scott and Ruthie. Well, I spent several days with Jeff last week while we were down for chemo, and I'm here to tell those of you who haven't met him, he's a large man! I really don't see ME being the one to try and convince him that cancer doesn't suck, it only stinks. He's liable to hurt me . . . . permanently! You know the kind of hurt that takes years of physical therapy and drinking through straws . . . . NO THANK YOU! Then, there is Scott. Well, I really don't know Scott too well, but he could easily be the type who looks quiet and easy going, only to turn into Sean Connery from the movie The Presidio. He'll be smiling coyly at you right before he says, "I'm only going to use my thumbs." Then you find your Adam's apple sticking out the back of your neck . . . . HECK NO . . . . not for me thank you. Of course there is always Ruthie and Kathy . . . . HEY, I'm no wimp or anything . . . . but I'll be 40 years old in 9 days . . . . and us older folks tend to bruise easily. I envision one of them holding me down while the other is beating the daylights out of me.

The bottom line here folks is that I didn't put the "suck" into this club . . . . the disease did. Anyone who wants my blessing to print more politically correct buttons or shirts, you've got it. I'll stick with what I've got. No offense to those of you who asked for a change, but my anger towards this illness is not likely to abate anytime soon.

Thursday, February 6, 2003 2:33 PM CST

(Ding, ding) Round 2.

For those of you feeling slighted by my lack of a journal entry yesterday. Guess what? I DID type a wonderful entry that could easily have won awards for the best journal entry ever. However, CaringBridge had some internal problems that caused many users to lose all new information that was entered after 11:50pm on Tuesday. So, my entry is gone forever! I know that I should be writing these in a program like Word, so that I don't encounter this problem again, so as of today, I am playing it safe!

Now, I'll make an attempt to dig into my near 40-year-old brain for all of the wit and sarcasm that accompanied my lost journal entry. I wonder if 50 years from now, someone will find that entry and sell it like a "lost Beetle's album." Anyways, here goes nothing . . . .

Medical News:

Well, I am STILL waiting to hear back from the CA doctor regarding details of her study. I'm convinced that if the numbers look as good as the other options, we'll go with the medicine from CA. We can do it at home, and it has very few side effects. If Zachary gets a good response from it, he can continue it for up to 30 rounds. That's 90 weeks!!!!

How great would that be? No chemo and a healthy child for almost 2 years, AND the possibility that the disease would leave us forever . . . . you never know.

Cancer Sucks Club:

Yesterday I was on the road for my business. While I drive the highways of South Florida, I tend to do a lot of thinking. This can be a bad thing for all of you, because once I start getting ideas, they usually end up here in the journal entries. I've come up with a bunch of ideas for the t-shirts. First of all, I need to announce that I've made a decision regarding the logo. I know I promised to put it to a vote, BUT, I've exercised executive privilege and made a choice to expedite the next order. I want to first thank Juliet and Marjie for taking the time to come up with some great ideas. However, I chose Joe's design. I ended up making some changes, but Joe was great at working with me to get the changes put into place. He has his hands full right now. Ryan is back at Duke to get treatment for his infection, so Joe is holding down the fort. Thank you Joe for your help!

So, the new logo is on a disk at the t-shirt shop getting ready to have a screen print made from it so it can be on the pocket of all shirts from now on. I still have 11 shirts left that have the original wording on the pocket, as shown in the photo album. Now, onto where all of you come in. I've decided that I need your input, (promises, promises) on which of my crazy ideas you like. Of course, I'll probably do whatever the heck tickles my fancy anyway, but I figure it's good for morale in the club to try and include everyone in these decisions. I've got 7 different "sayings" for the back of the shirts, including the one that is currently being used. What I propose is this. I will list and letter each of the ideas A thru G. I will provide a custom designed rating system (this ought to be good,) and you can post in the guest book by designating a letter, with a rating. An example appears below. The rating system will work as follows:

The scale will run from 1 to 5. This is how you choose a number.

1 = Scott is whacked on this idea. Not only would I NEVER wear that shirt, any friend or family member caught wearing it will be asked to leave my house!

2 = Scott must have been breathing exhaust fumes while writing this one, BUT, I won't kick anyone out that is seen wearing it. You just won't see me in it too often.

3 = Ok, I've seen worse. I might be tempted to wear this one, but probably only in winter months while traveling up north so I could cover it with a sweater or jacket.

4 = Now we're getting somewhere. This is a good example of Scott's insanity. I would wear this shirt without being too self-conscious.

5 = WOW! What an idea. Every person in America should have to wear this shirt at least once each week! (Maybe a little over the top, but you get the idea.)

The ideas are as follows: (Remember, the new logo will be on the pocket, these sayings will be on the back only.)

A). Cancer Sucks! Spread the word.
B). Cancer only sucks on days that end in "y"!
C). Someone I care about got cancer . . . . and all I got was this lousy t-shirt!
D). I hate cancer . . . . one day at a time!
E). Club Motto: Cancer sucked yesterday. Cancer sucks today. Cancer will undoubtedly suck tomorrow.

F). *Having cancer is like having a party. Only there's no music or fun, and it sucks!*
G). *Doctor's office visit co pay* .... *$ 20.00*
    Full body MRI scan .... *$ 5,400.00*
    5 days of chemotherapy .... *$ 16,800.00*
    Bone marrow transplant *$350,000.00*
    Finding a cure .... *A Godsend!*

Example of rating: A-5, B-5, C-5, D-5 . . . . you get the idea.

Do what the democrats say, "Vote early and vote often."

Disclaimer—The owners and management in no way endorse one political party over another. We are not trying to incite a political debate in any way, shape or form. Further, we do not endorse the rantings or ravings of Scott. He is solely responsible for all of the content on this page.

Friday, February 7, 2003 10:21 PM CST

Here we are at bedtime on a Friday night. Zman, Rebecca and I just got home from seeing Shanghai Knights. It was funny. I've thought about this journal entry all day, trying to figure out how to give an update without sounding upset. Unfortunately, it ain't gonna happen.

Medical News:

Last night I spoke with the doctor from CA about the study/medicine that we are interested in. The numbers she gave me were not too exciting. I did appreciate her taking the time to discuss some of the many protocols that are out there. This doctor is very knowledgeable and she has many contacts around the country doing research with a variety of new treatments. The common theme that was sadly repeated to me is, "There is currently no cure for your child." That pretty much sums it up folks. All of these studies that we're looking at have experienced some level of success with some patients. Putting that success into numbers is nearly impossible. Every child with this disease reacts differently, and progresses differently, so it is very difficult to compare results from one patient to another. The drug they are using has been tried on 39 children who have the same disease as Zachary. 16 of those got what they call a "positive response." Meaning, they were able to complete at least 8 rounds (or 24 weeks) before seeing progression of disease. So, about 40% of the kids "may" have gotten something out of the drug.

It is now on the verge of becoming a phase II study, meaning that they will look more closely at how well children respond. During phase I, the primary goal is dose escalation . . . . or, how much of the drug can we give the patient without hurting them. Most phase I patients are on their last resort.

After discussing this drug, the doctor informed me of another study that is being done at 8 hospitals. There are some very specific rules regarding eligibility. We are currently researching some of Zachary's past treatments to determine whether he is able to participate in this study or not. If he is, it would take us to Philadelphia, and we would probably go for it. If not, we're leaning towards continuing our current therapy until it has run its course, and then getting the drug from CA on a compassionate basis. (If the study hasn't opened as a phase II, they will send the drug anyway for children who are progressing without hope.)

The CA doctor has been using the chemotherapy that we are using for quite some time. Her experience with it shows that the children who do respond, usually get between 7 months and a year. Depending on many, many factors that can't be used to pinpoint a prediction for us. We have been using this drug for 5 months by itself and for 7 months if you count the two rounds that we did with Cytoxan.

All of this of course sucks . . . . in case anyone was wondering. I just tucked Zachary into bed, and when I do this, I can't help but wonder what is going on inside his fragile little body. Is there a war going on between the disease and the residual chemotherapy? Who is winning? Is the disease gaining ground? I hate this. I hate that there are no clear choices. I hate that he has to endure treatments like this probably for the rest of his life. I hate that my mind allows me to wonder whether he'll reach his 10th birthday. (He turns 9 on March 1.) I hate that I can't find a way to help my son beat this monster. I hate not knowing how long we have on this current chemotherapy. I hate that every time we think we've found an option that we can live with, the axe falls and we learn of horrible side effects or less than desirable success rates. I hate having to go to bed at night with a little less hope than I woke up with.

We hope to spend some time with friends tomorrow, and then on Sunday, we will go to church. We've missed church for 5 weeks because of chemo and traveling.

Scott

P.S. I apologize for the lack of humor today. I usually get my laughs, by thinking of ways to make all of you laugh. I just didn't have my A-game today folks. See you Monday.

Tuesday, April 8, 2003 5:33 PM CDT

How many times have I written about urine numbers?
How many times have I lamented about tough decisions?
How many times have I explained the nuances of reading into test results?
How many times have I allowed all of you to crawl inside our heads to see what we live with every day?

(Those were all rhetorical questions for those of you who have been keeping score. Do NOT feel obligated to research and answer them.)

In case you haven't guessed yet, the urine numbers are in from last week. I've been thinking about this all day, trying to come up with a good journal entry that would explain it all again so no one would have to go back and relearn the basics. I guess there is no way around it. So here we go.

Cancer Sucks 101.

Welcome to class everyone. I hope your three-week break was nice. For those of you who were sleeping last time, here is a quick review;

1). *The marker (or test) that we use for gauging the level of activity in Zachary's cancer is found in his urine. It is broken down in two levels that are called the HVA and VMA. (These both have very long medical names that would mean nothing to anyone except the guys who named them.)*
2). *Normally, when the cancer is more active, these levels will elevate. When the cancer is more stable, the levels will come down. (This is NOT an exact science. These levels can fluctuate from diet changes and medicine changes as well.)*
3). *The chemotherapy that Zachary has been using since August of last year has been used to "stabilize" the disease. It has kept the cancer at a fairly constant level, not allowing it to increase, yet not knocking it down any more either. Since approx. October, Zachary's urine levels have stayed fairly consistent, fluctuating only by a small percentage every three weeks.*
4). *The same chemotherapy mentioned in #3 has a history of being effective for 9-12 months on average. There are some children who get a benefit from it for much longer periods of time, (18 months or so,) and some children who only get a few months of benefit from it. All children on this chemotherapy will eventually find themselves battling a cancer that has worked its way around the medicine and has rebounded with a vengeance.*
5). *Zachary has been taking the Potion X for about 44 days now. One of the known effects of Potion X is an increase in the marker levels being used. This has been explained to us as a result of the cancer breaking apart and*

appearing to spread, when in actuality it is leaving the body. This is why it is recommended that you do not do scans or biopsies for at least three months after starting the Potion X. It needs time to do its thing.

6). The only other way to determine if the cancer is "taking over," is by observing Zachary's clinical condition. In other words, how does he look and feel? Well, right now he looks and feels great! You have all seen my updates as to how active he has been lately. So this is a good thing. The only caveat to that would be the fact that urine markers can increase to very high levels BEFORE clinical signs of disease start to rear their ugly heads again. (Pain, fevers from tumors, etc.) (All the good stuff.)

7). So, in summary, when looking at urine numbers you have to be conscious of the clinical condition as well as the possibility that the Potion X is delivering the goods as desired! At the same time, you get to be tortured along with us in NOT knowing whether we have bet everything on a "new" medicine that might not be working while allowing an aggressive, obnoxious, ugly, horrific, mean old nasty cancer a chance to take over our child.

Here is the breakdown of urine marker numbers over the past three samples.

TYPE—DATE—LEVEL—+/-%

HVA......2/17......23.2
HVA......3/10......27.6....... + 19
HVA......3/31 ......39.3 .... + 43

VMA.....2/17......9.8
VMA.....3/10......12.4....... + 27
VMA.....3/31 ......16.1 .... + 30

Ok, I'll admit that these numbers scare the $hit out of me. But having said that, I feel that I have reached somewhat of a turning point in my religious view of all of this. I think there is somewhat of a "leap of faith" that needs to take place here. It cannot be a coincidence that there is currently no medical way to definitively determine what the cancer is doing. Maybe this is somehow part of God's plan. Not in a cruel or malicious way, but simple a test of faith in the course of action that we chose. I don't know. I certainly have never been an overly religious individual. I didn't become one when Zachary got diagnosed. I could never envision a God who would appreciate a person who only has a use for him in times of trouble or extreme need. I have come to rely more on the comfort and solace that religion and church can provide in one's life. Until very recently I held a view that religion was useful only in laying the groundwork for ethical and moral values that might not otherwise be delivered to our youth. Now, I'm not so sure.

Tuesday, May 20, 2003 9:24 PM CDT

WAITING FOR RESULTS SUCKS!

GETTING BAD RESULTS SUCKS!

FINDING OUT THE SAMPLE WAS SENT TO THE WRONG LAB SUCKS!

FINDING OUT THE HOSPITAL IS TO BLAME FOR SENDING THE SAMPLE TO THE WRONG LAB SUCKS!

REALIZING THAT YOUR RESULTS ARE USELESS BECAUSE THEY WERE SENT TO A DIFFERENT LAB SUCKS!

KNOWING THAT YOU ARE HELPLESS TO PLOT A COURSE OF ACTION FOR YOUR CHILD BECAUSE YOU HAVE NO USEFUL RESULTS SUCKS!

RELYING ON HOSPITALS TO GET "IT" RIGHT, AND THEN BEING LET DOWN SUCKS!

HAVING TO WAIT AT LEAST ANOTHER WEEK BEFORE GETTING NEW RESULTS SUCKS!

NOT KNOWING WHAT IS HAPPENING TO YOUR CHILD BECAUSE OF USELESS REUSLTS SUCKS!

IT ALL SUCKS!

I'M SICK OF IT ALL!

CANCER SUCKS!

SCOTT

P.S. There is a photo of the new t-shirt in Zachary's album . . . . buy one . . . don't buy one . . . I just don't care anymore.

Wednesday, May 21, 2003 5:15 PM CDT

EVERYTHING I WROTE IN YESTERDAY'S JOURNAL ENTRY STILL HOLDS TRUE FOR TODAY . . . . ONLY NOW THAT I'VE HAD SOME MORE TIME TO STEW OVER IT . . . . IT SUCKS EVEN MORE.

AND.... IF THAT GARBAGE ISN'T ENOUGH TO REALLY DRIVE ME APE$HIT.... ZACHARY HAS HAD GROIN PAIN FOR TWO DAYS NOW, AND TODAY HE WOKE UP VERY CONGESTED. I'VE GOT AN APPOINTMENT SCHEDULED WITH THE LOCAL PEDIATRICIAN FOR TOMORROW.... MAYBE HE'LL IMPROVE OVER NIGHT.

FUN AND GAMES EACH AND EVERY DAY!

Monday, June 2, 2003 7:07 PM CDT

Well, I'm either the most paranoid person in the world, or there is a true conspiracy out there to drive me crazy. Every time I feel like one of our battles is coming to an end, a new one pops up in front of us and forces us to take notice.

I've written about the urine test and how I'm pretty much through with using it because of all of the aggravation that it has caused us. Well, I made the decision that we would schedule a bone marrow biopsy and aspiration along with an MIBG scan to try and get a handle on where we stand. Today, Zachary started chemo, so I took the opportunity to let the office staff know that we are shooting for the last week in June. That gives them three weeks to set things up. The only downside to that schedule is that we will be bumping Zachary's regularly scheduled chemo back by one week, but we won't be returning from Memphis until late Monday night that week, so chemo would have been messed up anyway. So far, so good, right? WRONG! One of the office secretaries came back to the treatment room and informed us that they need an entire week for the MIBG scan. Ok, at this point in the story, I'm tempted to go into a long dissertation regarding the specifics of MIBG testing and what we know from experience. However, in the interests of time and my blood pressure, I will simple say that Zachary has had this test done on three separate occasions, and it basically consists of a 2 minute injection on day #1, and a one-hour scan on day #2. That's all folks! After arguing about the timing issue for a few minutes, the secretary walked away. The nurse who was caring for Zachary had heard everything, and she said she would call nuclear medicine to confirm the details. Well, one phone call later we learn that our wonderful hospital is basing their scheduling on the wrong isotope. For those of you who don't remember, I had to enlighten our hospital and doctor's many, many months ago that they were using an outdated isotope when scanning for this disease. After arguing with me, they finally made some calls and got the situation fixed. But, they never bothered to find out that the newer isotope has a much faster absorption rate, so there is no need to scan after the second day. The bottom line here is that once again, I have to take a stance on an issue to enlighten people, so that my son can get the care he needs. I could roll over and play nice, but it would royally screw up Zachary's schedule more than I care to imagine.

Do I somehow ASK for this craziness? Am I somehow defective mentally? What prompts a secretary to completely ignore a parent who not only has had to endure the procedure with their son, but has taken the action that allowed their hospital to have the correct isotope for other families? I'm not saying people should listen "blindly" to my ramblings . . . . but why am I so quickly dismissed as a trouble maker? Do I exude an arrogance that just pisses people off? (Most of these questions are rhetorical . . . . answer them at your own risk . . . . I'm in NO mood for any help in making me look any nuttier than I do on my own.)

Ok. I'm sure most of you came here today to get an update, not to read my ramblings . . . . so; Zachary had a good first day of chemo. (Note to self—using the words "good" and "chemo" in the same sentence should be considered an oxymoron.) It is amazing what we get used to. "Oh yeah, we had a great day of chemo . . . . he only puked 6 times, and the diarrhea was limited to 4 times . . . ." (That last sentence was just me making light of how we live by new standards with this disease . . . . Zachary didn't have any problems today.)

One of our good friends mentioned to me the other day that they've noticed my journal entries have taken on a more "harsh" quality as of late. If I had time to visit my psychologist, I'm sure she would say that it is a defense mechanism that I am using to express my frustration and fear of what will happen when this current chemo stops working. We are in our eleventh month of Irinotecan. Of the children who get a response to this chemo like Zachary, the average amount of benefit is 9-12 months. Some children get longer. I've tried to use the urine as a tool to monitor progress, they've screwed that one up pretty well . . . I'll never trust it again. My backup was the MIBG . . . . and now that is in question.

I wouldn't be so paranoid if everyone wasn't out to get me.

Monday, August 18, 2003 8:53 AM CDT

You would think that after repeatedly having a bucket of crap thrown in my face when I walk out of the front door in the morning that I would learn to use a different exit. Surely I have not aged so much that I have surpassed my capacity to learn from trial and error. Why then have I yet again allowed myself to be sucked into the urine game, (or as I like to refer to it—THE BLACK VORTEX ABYSS OF DEATH) again? Who knows? I guess maybe the unrelenting badgering of the doctor's office to repeat the test had something to do with it. Someone famous

*once said, "Constantly being bothered by someone is like being nibbled to death
by a duck!" Well, regardless of my mental shortcomings, or the ethical status of
the lab and doctor's office, we once again have urine numbers to report.*

UNIVERSAL URINE REPORT DISCLAIMER

*The above referenced report should in no way be used for any purpose other than
that which is stated in the 'urine report purpose manual' which can be found in
any sewer or garbage dumpster of most major cities. Please make sure you cross
check your results with an equally incompetent lab or reporting agency so that your
level of aggravation remains at its peak. Per section B-12.9983 of the Universal
Urine Report Disclaimer all patients wishing to have accurate information on
their lab results should routinely play their state lottery, thus allowing them a
much greater chance of winning millions of dollars so they can buy or build their
own lab and get the results done correctly. (Purchasing of an existing lab does
not guarantee results, results may vary with stupidity.)*

*This is ONCE again our first report from this particular lab; so ONCE again keep
in mind that these are reference numbers to be compared against in the future.
They are not to be taken too seriously!!!!!!!!!!!!!!!!!!!!!!!!!*

VMA = 11.1
HVA = 26.8

VMA normal range = 0-9
HVA normal range = 0-15

*Ok, there it is. It's all out on the table now. These results are most effectively
understood if you first soak them thoroughly in gasoline or kerosene and then
toss them into a raging fire.*

Tuesday, August 19, 2003 7:02 AM CDT

*Ok, so you've read my entry from Monday 8/18/03 and you are able to sense
my anger and frustration with this never-ending urine saga. Maybe some of you
are even beginning to think that I'm a little bit crazy . . . . heck . . . . I always
write about fighting the system or trying to change some process that has been
used "successfully" for scores of other families . . . . "Why can't that Scott guy
just conform like everyone else?" "Wasn't it last year that he made the hospital
change the isotope that they were using for their MIBG scan because he found a
more effective one was being used in other parts of the country?" Yep . . . . that*

was me! And it looks like I have (in the immortal words of Brittany Spears) "Done it again."

Here is what has caused the latest hubbub in the ever-logical brain of Scott.

On the report from the lab there is a disclaimer paragraph that reads as follows:

"The VMA to creatinine ratio and HVA to creatinine ratio will be reported whenever the patient is under 18 years, the urine collection is random or other than 24 hours, and the urine volume is less than 400ml/24 hours."

At first glance it seems to be an innocuous enough statement, right? WRONG. Ok. Let's take this slowly. (I'll use small words so you don't all get lost.) The VMA and HVA ratios are exactly what we are looking for here. They are the ONLY part of the urine report that matters to us or our situation. So, having them be accurate is everything. The sentence above is written with three criteria as an INCLUSIVE group. You may have noticed the word 'and' after the second criteria, between the words, 'hours' and 'the' near the end. That single word 'and' had me interpreting the sentence to mean that our precious ratios will only be reported when all three of the criteria have been met. 1). Under 18 years. 2). Random non-24 hour collection. 3). Volume less than 400ml/24 hr.

Well, let's see how we did.

1). YES! Zachary is under 18 years. Hallelujah!
2). Ooops. This wasn't a random collection. In fact the doctor specifically ASKED for a 24 hour collection and pre-called the lab to make sure it would get reported correctly.
3). Double oops. Page one of the report is kind enough to show that we gave them a 740ml sample. Hmmmmmm. They can count to 740, but they can't determine whether or not that number is higher or lower than 400 . . . . **RED FLAD**, **RED FLAG** The lab can't count!!!!!!!

So, my first impression was this. Either the whole report is meaningless and useless because the component we are looking for can't be done by this lab if the sample is random and the volume is over 400ml, OR the verbiage is wrong, and that little word 'and' needs to be changed to a smaller word, 'or'. As luck would have it, I kept the apology letter from the director of lab services at our hospital. That letter included the phone number for the director. So, not being one to be shy, I called the man. After speaking with him for about 2 minutes, I quickly ascertained that he possessed more administrative knowledge than medical knowledge. He may have even said at one point, "Dammit Jim, I'm a pencil pusher . . . . not a doctor." (You Star Trek fans will love that one.) Anyway, he promised to call the lab and speak with the pathologist who oversees all of this nonsense. Before I let him off of the phone, I did get to say, "You need to ask the lab whether they were too stupid or lazy to change that word from 'and' to 'or', or whether this entire test is a farce and waste of time." Later that afternoon he got back to me. Guess what? That word 'and' was supposed to be the word 'or'. They didn't realize it was incorrect. They are going to change it! So, basically, all HVA and VMA reports have been misleading and confusing for years and none of their geniuses caught it.

I'm quite sure that I've aged about 15 years in the past 12 months. I must have been sucked into some sort of time/space continuum.

The urine is supposedly accurate. We will use this one as our baseline and go from there. They are promising that our next report will have the corrected text. These levels are higher than we would like them to be. It is possible that the Potion X is ridding Zachary's body of the remaining bone lesions and that this is causing the urine levels to appear higher than normal. Time will tell.

Tuesday, December 2, 2003 6:58 PM CST

What is it about scans that will absolutely drive you to the brink of insanity? Is it the uncertainty? Or maybe the way our minds wonder down roads that they should never have to travel. I don't know, but I DO know that we have gone over 15 months without Zachary having a fever . . . . actually, he came close once about 8 months ago, but that was it! No fevers in over a year. Then, all of a sudden, in perfect timing with the scans set up for next week, he starts having some neck pain and gets all the way up to just shy of 100.5. On two separate readings he was 100.3 and 100.5. He had just taken Tylenol, so the doctor allowed us to wait the 4 hours to retake his temperature. I woke him at midnight last night (that was fun) (NOT) and luckily he had not spiked anymore. He made it through the night without incident and was fine all of today. So, for no apparent reason, his body decided to give us a scare. Now, for many of you who have been through this nightmare before, or are currently going through this nightmare now, you know what it is like to wait for news of scans. I usually try not to put too much thought into this process, because I have seen firsthand the torture that it can inflict on a family. But, in the spirit of spreading the misery, I allowed myself to get sucked into the pre-scan blues.

There have been too many children who have had turns for the worse lately. We lost one child locally, and we have a few CaringBridge friends whose children have relapsed. All of this of course sucks. A lot! I suppose there is a more dignified way to convey my feelings toward this disease and the toll that it seems determined to take on our friends and family, but frankly Scarlet . . . . I don't give a _____!

Too many children diagnosed.
Too many children tortured by the treatments.
Too many families devastated by this illness.
Too many lives upended.
Too many children relapsing.
Too many young angels flying to heaven.

Other than yesterday, Zachary still feels great. I AM very grateful for this. We know from almost four years of this that we are truly lucky that he is still enjoying a high quality of life. The alternative is unthinkable. I've spoken with other families whose children are in extreme amounts of pain on a daily basis. They alternate between sobbing over their child, praying for an end to the pain, and praising God for giving them more quality time without the effects of the cancer impeding their child's life. What kind of existence is this?

Someone out there NEEDS to find a crystal ball or magical wand or pixie dust, and use it to make all of this go away. Far away!

Friday, February 13, 2004 2:26 PM CST

I used to like roller coasters when I was younger . . . . what happened? I mean, the ups and downs were exciting back then . . . . but lately they seem to have lost their luster. Anyway, Zachary's back pain has magically disappeared! He was in need of pain meds Monday, Tuesday, and Wednesday, and then all of a sudden he no longer was complaining. This is a good thing for those of you who weren't sure. Cancer pain does not usually just "go away" without help, so the pain he was experiencing was probably from overdoing it this past weekend at the dance. Before the pain decided to leave our lives, we had already set up testing for next week, so we are going to keep those dates and get his testing done about 3 weeks earlier than we had originally planned. I should have some results by the end of next week.

I have written many times and many ways about the pain and frustration that this illness inflicts upon families like ours. And every time that I think I've written enough about it, another thought pops into my tiny brain and compels me to *drop it into all of your laps. This past week sucked! (I didn't mean to sugar-coat that last assessment, but this IS a family page.) Not only have I been torturing myself with thoughts of funerals and misery because of Zachary's back pain, but a few of our friends are having a really tough time with their child's cancer . . . . and on top of that, one of our friends had their child's cancer relapse this week. I know that I should be better equipped mentally to handle a little back pain, but there is just no escaping the words that have been engraved into our heads by the doctors . . . . "When his cancer comes back you'll know, because it will present itself the same way as it did at original diagnosis . . . back pain." Or there is always this gem . . . "You've pretty much exhausted the conventional therapies out there . . . . we just don't have any effective treatments to offer when the cancer comes back." (My personal favorite . . . NOT.) So, we had our moments of weakness and allowed our minds to travel down those roads of doom and despair. The good news is that I've come up with a new axiom that describes my current train of thought . . . . for lack of a better name, I'm calling it:*

SCOTT'S AXIOM (Tada . . . . flashy . . . isn't it?)

Scott's Axiom reads as follows:

THE NUMBER OF QUALITY DAYS THAT A FAMILY IS ABLE TO BUY FOR THEIR CHILD WITH CONVENTIONAL AND/OR NON-CONVENTIONAL THERAPIES WILL ALWAYS BE AT LEAST ONE DAY SHORT OF THE NUMBER THAT THEY WANTED!

(Not exactly Einstein-like thinking here . . . . but it summarizes my thinking right about now.)

The other interesting quote that I have for you today comes from a novel that I just finished. (Don't get too excited . . . . I don't read non-fiction . . . this isn't going to be some biblical quote or fancy schmancy theological quote that is used to stir up religious debates.) The quote is from a spy novel and is from a character who is discussing with another character how things just aren't going their way . . . . they are commando's who have been trying to plan a raid . . . and they can't get things to work out the way they want to. So the wiser of the two says, "IF YOU WANT TO MAKE GOD LAUGH, TELL HIM YOUR PLANS." Now, before you all get up in arms with me and accuse me of being an atheist or something, let me explain what I got out of this quote. I take it as meaning that life does not always go as planned. You do your best and try to be prepared, but don't expect things to always go your way, because life has a funny way of "happening."

Tuesday, February 17, 2004 8:11 PM CST

WARNING***WARNING***WARNING***WARNING

THIS IS THE SECOND UPDATE TODAY. IF YOU MISSED THE EARLIER EDITION, PLEASE REFRAIN FROM READING BELOW THIS PARAGRAPH UNTIL YOU HAVE BEEN PROPERLY BRIEFED ON THE CONTENTS OF THE EARLIER ENTRY.

(If you are still reading these words and have NOT gone back to read the earlier entry then you either have no reading comprehension skills, or you are just plain stubborn.)

(Oh sure . . . . just throw your total lack of respect for my wishes in EVERYONE'S faces and keep on reading like none of the words I wrote up above even exist . . . . great!)

Well, where do I begin . . . . in the beginning I guess? We got to the doctor's office to have Zachary's blood counts checked and to get his port accessed for the isotope injection today. His counts were great! His exam went great! The doctor said he looks great! Great! Great! Great! Even his accessing went great! So, we're getting ready to walk out of the office and head over to the hospital to get the injection for tomorrow's MIBG scan and Rebecca asks the secretary to call over to Nuclear Medicine to make sure they are ready for us. Nuclear Medicine gets on the phone and informs us that there is NO APPOINTMENT FOR ZACHARY TODAY! Hmmmmm. This is odd. Here we are, standing there with a perfectly good needle sticking in our son's chest, expecting to actually use it for something other than a really cool clothing accessory, and we're fresh out of luck. The isotope that is needed for this particular scan ONLY can be delivered on Tuesdays, and ONLY if it is ordered the week before, so they have ample time to manufacture it. So, someone from the doctor's office dropped the ball and . . . . yada yada yada . . . . we're screwed. Nuclear Medicine said they cannot do the scan this week, because of the timing with the isotope. The doctor asked if we wanted to wait until next week, and reschedule. Well, as much as I like to torture Zachary by having ¾" needles jammed into his chest on a regular basis, I made an executive decision and opted for sticking with the bone marrow procedures for tomorrow and just bypassing the MIBG scan for now. The bone marrow is by far the most "telling" test that we do anyway. His MIBG scan was clean last time, so if the bone marrow is unchanged or improved, it is highly unlikely that the MIBG scan would show any new lesions anyway. And, since we are actually testing about 3 weeks ahead of schedule, we can always set up an MIBG scan for the middle of March if we really get a hankering for one. (Many of you are turning on your TV sets looking for news of some deranged dad going ballistic at a doctor's office right about now. That was the old me. This is the NEW calmer me. Just because we're facing a disease that the doctor's say we won't cure, and just because we have insurance companies that don't want to pay for the services that they are contractually bound to pay for, and just because I can't stay in touch with my family because the cell phone company is plotting to undermine what little sanity I have left, and just because the doctor's office can't properly order a simple test, and just because my hairline is receding . . . . there is no reason to freak out. Life is good. Besides, it could be worse . . . . it could be raining.)

Friday, March 26, 2004 10:57 PM CST

Another week under our belts and I am happy to report that we have gone two whole days without the crutches. (Zachary wants the wheels back for his rolling shoes . . . they have been in time-out for several days. I told him that he wouldn't get them back until he went at least 4 or 5 days without the crutches.) Miraculously he was healed. Wednesday was the ceremony for all of the children who made honor roll. Rebecca took video for me since I was on the road.

Tonight there was an impromptu gathering of some of the board members of the Cancer Sucks Club. Now, before anyone gets all up in arms, I was invited at the last minute and I was NOT the organizer . . . so don't give me grief about not announcing it earlier. The four families who were there represented four very different stages of this disease. One family represented the tragic loss of one of our children, Robert. One represented a veteran relapsed case, Zachary. Another family is newly relapsed, Cameron, and the last family represents our family in remission, Mitchell. Four families from very different walks of life, thrust together into a world that none of us knew existed until a few years ago.

I must report that of all of the CSC meetings that I've attended, this was by far the most productive and serious, in regards to discussions and accomplishments. I have listed a brief summary of the highlights from this meeting below so everyone can get up to speed on where we stand on some important issues.

1). If you take a bite-size pretzel and a bite-size potato chip and eat them together, you will enjoy a unique flavor that is lost when eating either of the two alone. (Scott was credited with bringing this gem to the table.)

2). When ordering pizza for a large group, make sure there is pepperoni, mushrooms, plain, and at least one veggie-style pizza.

3). Fresh baked chocolate chip oatmeal cookies are always a hit. Make sure you bake enough when entertaining a larger group.

4). *Chocolate covered key lime pie is STILL good. Eat them slowly though, splinters ARE a hazard.*

5). *Given half of a chance, any gathering of boys and girls that number over 6 and range in age from 5-10, will at some point deteriorate into a free for all with yelling, screaming, chasing, running, falling and crying . . . . basically a chaotic zoo.*

6). *Cancer STILL sucks.*

Now, if you feel that these notes aren't adequate to properly bring you up to speed, don't hesitate to organize your own impromptu CSC meeting. (Don't forget the chip trick though . . . . it can make or break your party.)

Thursday, April 15, 2004 4:41 PM CDT

Last night sucked! (The ceremony and video show about Jake were beautiful.) Having to see another family go through that sucked . . . . BIG TIME!

Mark and Susan Griffin have joined the growing list of board members for the CSC. They have lifetime exemptions from any dues that may ever arise, and they are officially on the team that gets to answer ANYONE who dares doubt the levels of sucktatude that cancer inflicts on a family. (Anyone questioning the validity of the word 'sucktatude' will ALSO have to answer to them . . . so BACK OFF!)

I wish there was some really brilliant or insightful thought about last night that I could write about, but I was overcome with emotion for most of the evening. Our hearts break every time we think about Jake being gone. By far, Zachary handled it better than anyone from our group.

I applaud all of the CSC families who were able to attend to be there for Mark and Susan. I know firsthand how difficult it is to attend these ceremonies and to allow yourself to envision your child's face on the pictures and remembrances in place of the child that is gone. I saw the pain in the faces of the parents who have buried their children during the past year or two and have already lived this nightmare. All of it sucks. Being there together to watch out for each other is the only thing that gets me through the night. Knowing that there are families out there who will drop everything to lend a shoulder to cry on is a huge saving grace to this life we live.

Medical Update:

We have had quite the chaotic week, and I would love nothing more than to rant and rave about the idiots at the hospital, the pharmacy, the doctor's office . . . . etc. Unfortunately, I am drained from the past couple of days. I will say this. We are at war with the company that manufacturers the isotope. They are an international conglomerate that supplies doctors, hospitals and pharmacies all over the world. They are the ONLY independent company that can make the isotope for Zachary's scan. (The larger teaching hospitals make their own.) We have had nothing but problems getting this isotope for his scans. We ended up starting another round of chemo, (this really pissed Zachary off and caused major battles on the home front,) and then stopping chemo after one day because the nuclear medicine dept. was able to convince the company to send the isotope one more time. So, Zachary did chemo on Monday. He had his SSKI drops Tuesday and Wednesday morning (protect thyroid), his injection yesterday, and his MIBG scan today. He resumes chemo tomorrow and will have it through Monday. (That totally messed up his weekend.) Then, he will get his bone marrow on Tuesday. (Those results will be over-nighted to California for review.) The most amazing thing through all of this is that Zachary is MOST upset about . . . . (drum roll please.) . . . . Missing school!

He hates missing school. I don't know if there is some really cute girl that he is watching all day, but he truly wants to be there with his friends. (I know he doesn't get that from me . . . . when I was his age . . . . I would have moved Heaven and Earth to miss school.)

So, we will be around this weekend, taking it easy . . . . trying to keep him occupied while he remains accessed with his needle and unable to do anything overly physical. (Blockbuster loves us.)

Wednesday, June 16, 2004 5:49 PM CDT

Wow! A whole week has passed since my last journal entry and no one has sent me a nasty message complaining about how lazy I have become. (Everyone is probably afraid that I might become ANGRY with them.)

Zachary finished his second round of Fenretinide Monday evening. He is once again super sensitive to the sunlight. (This coincides beautifully with his new day camp that he is attending. Camp Wet. Swimming in the ocean, fishing in the river, snorkeling, etc.) Other than the obvious sunburn under his eyes, he has done well to protect himself. He loves the camp and it keeps him out of trouble from 9am until 4pm. Yesterday he came home with a wicked rash on his thighs.

It looked as though he had been exposed to sea lice. (For those of you who don't have to deal with these wonderful creatures, they are actually miniature jelly fish that are nearly impossible to see with the naked eye. They get under your swim suit and start stinging as a defense to being "trapped." Well, it turns out that no other child had any problems, so it is more likely that Zachary is allergic to the material in his one new bathing suit.

An interesting side note here is that I looked up sea lice last night when we still believed that they were the culprit. The first line of defense that was given on every web page was, (drum roll please) . . . . SWIM NAKED! Evidently, these creatures will only sting if caught under clothing. I suppose if we had sent him to a Catholic day camp where priests acted as counselors, that would have gone over wonderfully. (9, 10 & 11 year old children running around the beach naked.) [PLEASE DIRECT ALL HATE MAIL REGARDING OFFENSIVE JOURNAL ENTRIES TO THE FOLLOWING ADDRESS:]

COMPLAINTS R US
2894405136990123 N. FLASTERBUMPHINGARTER AVE.
CHIPMUNK VALLEY, AZ 00001

(If for some reason your letter comes back undeliverable, then you probably missed a number in the street address and need to resend it with the correction made.)

SO, there we were on Sunday afternoon, sitting around enjoying a nice quiet day, when all of a sudden there is a knock on our door. Our friend Susan stopped by to say hello. (Of course there was another motive to the visit.) Susan is working on her mid-terms and needed to do some more testing on people to get the experience. Not being of sound mind, I once again volunteered to be the guinea pig. This time, ANGER was not the subject. Intelligence (or lack thereof) was. I was volunteering for a one hour I.Q. test. Susan ran home and got her paperwork and returned. We all decided to eat dinner before any testing was to be completed. Zachary has somewhat of a "sensitive" stomach from the new medicine he is on. So, during dinner, he excused himself and exited stage left into our bedroom and closed the door. About 3 seconds later the house shook on its foundation from a massive gaseous explosion that burst from his body. Rebecca, Susan and I all looked at each other in horror. Zachary returned to the table and was greeted with our laughter, which did little for his self-esteem. He immediately tried to defend himself by saying, "At least I left the room!" My response to that was, "Zachary, there are people in California looking nervously at each other RIGHT NOW, wondering if that vibration in the ground they just felt is the precursor to the "big one." Surprisingly, this too did little to ease his embarrassment. (All of those parenting 101 lessons down the drain.) Well, we got through dinner and

I started to take my test. After the one hour test ended . . . . 2.5 hours later . . . . Susan started to tabulate the results. I was of course curious as to what kind of score I would get. Susan quickly corrected me and said that she was taking a progressive NEW style of psychology that didn't use the "traditional" number scale that everyone was used to. That older style of scale was too humiliating for some folks, so a newer more "user friendly" scale had been developed. On this new scale, your score is translated into an animal class. Each class is then ranked so you know where in the animal kingdom you would fall. The order goes something like this:

Dolphin, Monkey, Ape, Dog, Pig, Horse, Cat, Goat, Cow, Kangaroo, Walrus, Seal, Moose, Squirrel, Duck, Chicken, Platypus, Parrot, Turkey, Toad, Fish, Butterfly, and Ant.

My score put me somewhere in between the Toad and the Turkey. I guess it could have been worse . . . . or better. Susan was supposed to further explain this new animal rating, but she somehow ran out of time and exited our house rather quickly. Oh well, I guess I did ok.

Wednesday, July 7, 2004 5:37 PM CDT

In the immortal words of Mars Almond Joy candy bars . . . . "Sometimes you feel like a nut, and sometimes you don't!"

ATTENTION***ATTENTION***ATTENTION***ATTENTION

ANYONE WHO READ YESTERDAY'S JOURNAL ENTRY AND WAS ENCOURAGED BY THE URINE RESULTS; PLEASE TAKE A DEEP BREATH AND READ ON!

Today we received a call from the fu#$^&!#@ doctor's office informing us that the &^%$&& #@&^$ @#^#^$& !^^#&$#* &$&$*#@# ?>*&%# urine results are wrong! (NO, that was NOT a typo. And NO, you have NOT flashed back to one of the 6 or 7 previous journal entries from the last two years where I reported urine test screw-ups.)*

This IS live. This IS real. THIS DOES SUCK!

The level of my anger has not been this high since . . . . well I don't know. But it's high! (When Susan said I was angry after taking that test . . . . I had NO idea what anger was.)

The last time we tested his urine, someone at the doctor's office sent the urine to the wrong lab . . . . again. (For the third or fourth time.) So, when I was comparing numbers in yesterday's entry, I was comparing apples to orangutans. You CANNOT compare from one lab to another. Sadly there is NO standard for testing procedures or ranges for results. So, when you compare the most recent results to the last results that actually came from this lab . . . . his levels are higher. (This is a bad thing. If you believe in urine numbers.)

HOW IN THE WORLD DID I ALLOW MYSELF TO GET SUCKED BACK INTO THE GREAT URINE SCAM OF THE TWENTY FIRST CENTURY?

I MUST BE THE DUMBEST, MOST GULLIBLE, GLUTTON FOR PUNISHMENT WHO HAS EVER LIVED!

(It's not like I have forgotten SWEARING off of relying on these tests for REAL information . . . . I REMEMBER doing that. So why then, have I allowed them to turn our world upside down . . . . AGAIN?)

Incompetent, lazy, foolish, error-prone, knuckle-headed, inconsiderate, uncaring, weak-minded idiots! (And that was just describing me! Imagine what I think of THEM?)

As I sit here and try to find the words to properly convey how upset this has made me, I am for once . . . . at a loss for more words. When I got the call today from Rebecca, I truly believed that my heart and head were going to explode from the stress and anger. I SHOULD HAVE KNOWN BETTER! I have failed myself, my family, and everyone who relies on this page for good information about Zachary's status. I may not have created this nightmare, but you would think that after being burned 6 or 7 times by the same flame, that I would learn a lesson. But NOOOOOOO . . . . I just look around on my hands for some new unscathed skin to torch and blister.

I guess the big lesson for all of you is this: Before you start to read an update, grab your condiments from off of the table . . . because you WILL need a large grain of salt to go with my journal entries.

Scott

P.S. Tomorrow Zachary will undergo an MIBG scan to evaluate his disease status. Had the urine debacle not taken place, we would have been able to get through this weekend with relative little stress as we wait for results. Now, we get to spend the next several days allowing our minds to wander down forbidden roads. Such is the life of a family on this path.

P.S.S. Before any of you geniuses advise me to stop giving urine samples like I did for most of 2003, I have already considered that option and dismissed it. The protocol that we are on REQUIRES regular urine testing. The lead doctor can remove us from the study and prevent us from receiving medicine if we don't follow the schedules of testing that help them to evaluate their drug. (Maybe I'll submit some cow or horse urine for them to study.)

Saturday, July 24, 2004 7:16 AM CDT

For all of you gullible, tarot card reading, UFO spotting, pet psychic believing, Bigfoot watching, Loch Ness monster seeing, flat-Earth following nut cases out there, the NEW urine numbers are in!

(wow) (I can hardly contain my excitement) (The drum roll must be deafening)

If there EVER was a more anti-climactic moment in the history of these journal entries, I don't know what it is!

The "correct" level that we have been looking for this whole time is the HVA/Creatinine Ratio, and the VMA/Creatinine Ratio.

HVA = 18. (Normal range = 4-15)

VMA = 8.3. (Normal range = 2-11)

So there you have it. Now you can all sleep soundly tonight with the warm and fuzzy knowledge that one of his levels is just barely over the normal range, and the other is safely tucked away inside of the normal range.

What does it all mean you ask? (Frankly at this point, I have a better chance of picking the winning lotto numbers in every lottery across the country on the same day, while at the same time becoming the first person to win the presidential election without being on any ballot . . . . anywhere, while also being selected to be the first "normal" citizen to join the next space shuttle crew, than figuring out urine numbers.) I'm not saying these things won't happen, I'm just saying that if YOU believe they are going to happen, then I will gladly send you a signed 8X10 glossy of myself once I receive your cashier's check or credit card payment in the amount of $1,000.00.

We are getting ready to head down to WPB for the meeting about forming a clinic for the oncology/hematology kids. This is a project that has been "in the works" since before Zachary was diagnosed. I can remember going to meetings with the board of directors and discussing sites, building plans, etc. 3 ½ years ago, it seemed like it was going to become a reality back then . . . . and then it sort of faded away. I hope the current group has made progress so our children can get this much needed facility. Clinics in other cities have been hugely successful and universally loved by the families that have access to them.

Tuesday, October 19, 2004 6:24 PM CDT

Rules.

Rules can be a good thing.

Rules can help us keep order in an otherwise disorderly world.

Let us take a moment to see what Webster says about rules.

Rule (n) Controlling power; an authoritative direction or statement which regulates the method of doing something; a standard procedure. (v) To have control over; to make a straight line using a ruler; to be in command.

Ok, for the sake of today's journal entry, let's disregard the 'straight line' part and stick with 'regulates the method of doing something' part. Zachary is on an experimental drug that is in phase II of its study life through the NIH. As with all drugs, this particular drug has rules. (Is that a collective groan I just heard from all of you visitors?) One of the many rules governing the use of the drug requires us to have Zachary scanned by nuclear medicine using I-123 (an isotope.) (There have been many "interesting" journal entries discussing isotopes and the various problems we've had over the past few years . . . . if you missed them, feel free to go back and amuse yourself.) The scan is called an MIBG scan. It involves Zachary being injected with the isotope on Tuesday, and then being scanned 24 hours later on Wednesday. Hmmmmmmm. Seems pretty simple right? (Nothing is simple in our world.)

The previously mentioned isotope is not easily acquired. You cannot simply go into your back yard and drain some I-123 from your radioactive isotope tree. Walgreen's and CVS don't stock it on the shelf in between the Tylenol and Aspirin. The isotope has to be carefully made in a special pharmacy. Once it is made, it only has a life span of several hours before it is no longer of any use to anyone.

So, now that we have finished with our lesson (Isotope 101), let us move on to today's events. Rebecca got Zachary out of school early so that he could drive the one hour ride to West Palm Beach to receive his injection. She called ahead to confirm the arrival time of the isotope from the lab in Miami. Everything was all set to go. Rebecca and Zachary sat in Nuclear Medicine for close to an hour waiting for the isotope to arrive, only to hear the phone ring and have a whole bunch of things go wrong . . . .

Miami was calling to inform our hospital that they had indeed made the isotope, but sadly the isotope had failed. Hmmmmm. What does that mean . . . failed? Does it mean the isotope was given an eye exam and couldn't read the gigantic E? Does it mean it gave a urine sample and the rabbit died? Or maybe the isotope took the SAT test and got a 38. I honestly don't know what constitutes a failure in the world of isotopes, but the bottom line was . . . . they weren't going to have a non-failing isotope for Zachary this week.

This revelation put into motion a couple of disturbing events.

1). The Nuclear Medicine doctor commented to Rebecca, "I wonder if that is what happened last week with that other neuroblastoma family." This is bad. This is very bad folks. Evidently, one of the two other neuroblastoma families who gets scanned at our hospital had received an MIBG scan last week, only to have it come back indicating that the disease had spread throughout the child's body . . . . stomach, bladder, thyroid, chest, etc. The child had been sent for further testing . . . . CAT scan, MRI, bone scan, only to have those tests come back negative. Imagine being the family and being told your child is now full of a rampant disease that is spreading out of control . . . . only to find out a couple of days later . . . . oops . . . . we may have been wrong! Like I said . . . . bad.

2). Rebecca called Zachary's doctor's office and informed them that the MIBG scan wasn't going to happen this week. (Zachary is scheduled to start his next round of medicine on Tuesday.) (The "rules" state that he cannot start the next round until they see a current MIBG scan that confirms the disease has not started spreading.) The nurse told Rebecca that we would have to postpone the next round until the following week, so that we could scan next week. (This is the part where I was made aware of the goings on.) (In other words . . . . this is where the $hit hit the fan.) Rebecca had to go into the doctor's office, so I gave her a calm, sedate, reasonable message to pass along to the nurse from me . . . . "UNLESS YOU WANT ME GOING TO WAR WITH YOU AND YOUR OFFICE, YOU WILL GIVE US HIS MEDICINE FOR NEXT WEEK AND FIGURE OUT THE SCAN SCHEDULE . . . WHEN YOU CAN FIGURE IT OUT."

My humble naïve opinion is this: Rules are great . . . . rules are wonderful . . . . they help to make the world go around. BUT, this particular rule is designed to keep a child from staying on an experimental drug past its point of usefulness. There is NO danger to Zachary if he takes an extra round and it turns out he didn't need it. (Keep in mind that his last scan showed improvement . . . . so it is unlikely that things turned bad this quickly.) However, I feel that there IS a danger when skipping a round or unnecessarily allowing a dangerous and aggressive disease to regain strength and start trouble again. In the big scheme of things, what difference does it make to them if the scan is a little bit late? Did I sleep through a logic class or something . . . . are we not trying to prolong a child's life . . . or possibly even save it? I mean . . . . I know their precious rules, are . . . . well . . . . precious . . . . but REALLY folks . . . . what the #$&@ are they thinking?

Needless to say, the doctor's office made a reasonable compromise . . . . they will give us the medicine for the next round . . . . and we will start it Wednesday evening . . . . (one day late), after the MIBG scan that has been rescheduled for next week. Interestingly enough, you may remember that I had several meetings with the hospital CEO trying to convince them to make the isotope at our hospital, to avoid the many problems associated with transporting it from Miami . . . . money of course was always a factor in our discussions. Today Rebecca learned that our hospital is going to start making the isotope and that quite possibly next week's dose will be made right there in West Palm Beach. Hmmmm. I wish I had thought of that.

Thursday, December 2, 2004 5:41 PM CST

ANGER

DISAPPOINTMENT

FRUSTRATION

DISMAY

HOPELESSNESS

FEAR

DESPERATION

DESPONDENCY

I would go on forever, but I fear that my journal would take a dangerous turn towards the R-rated expletives that are flying across my brain and attempting to make their way through my arms, into my fingers, and eventually onto the keyboard!

In case any of you EVER had any doubts . . . . CANCER SUCKS!

(New CSC t-shirt coming soon . . . . "CANCER SUCKS . . . ALWAYS HAS . . . ALWAYS WILL.")

This is the part of my journal entries where I usually start typing in the verbatim results of our testing . . . . maybe on some level I've believed in the past that by giving all of you the exact text, it will somehow make it more real or "official" when I give you news.

Well folks . . . . it doesn't get MUCH more real than the bad news we got today. The MIBG scan showed that the spine area was stable . . . (not surprising since we only scanned 4 weeks ago,) however, there appear to be two new sites of activity. The left hip and the top of the left femur (the bone that runs from the knee to the hip.) So, why do we have new growth in just four weeks? That my friends is the million dollar question. Our doctor is going to contact the doctor in California who is in charge of the protocol that we are on, but I see this as a mere formality. The protocol verbiage is pretty clear to me . . .

"Any disease progression will preclude the continuation of the Fenretinide." The plan right now is to do an MRI on Monday afternoon to get a "better" picture of the hip and femur, but, once again we have NOTHING to compare the images to, so I see them as more of a baseline scan for future use. I certainly DON'T want to continue on the Fenretinide for another month to wait for a repeat MRI if the consensus is that the drug is no longer effective on Zachary's cancer.

I would say that we are back to square one, but that might give you the false sense of hope/security that comes with "square one" being a starting point of a journey. We are somewhere between square 198 and square 3,206. We are in a maze that seems to change as we try to navigate our way around. Just when it looks like we have found an exit, a new wall pops up and forces us to travel far away in another direction in search of an alternate "safe" way out. It is almost like trying to get from point A to point B using a system where you are only allowed to cut the remaining distance in half, once each day. Sure, it seems like you are getting closer . . . . but you will never get there!

Zachary is still somehow pain-free. This is more than a saving grace for us right now. We are lamenting over this in ways that some of you have experienced, and hopefully many of you will never know.

I made it clear to the doctor today that we want to know the availability of the new protocol that we found BEFORE we get to the end of next week. I am fairly certain that the bone marrow report is not going to be kind to us. (This is not pessimism, it is reality.) Not being ready and wasting time are NOT an option that we want to entertain for even one second. I would love to be able to keep a positive outlook and "hope for the best", but ignorance is NO longer bliss.

I have been haunted recently by horrific nightmares that wake me out of a dead sleep and keep me up when I should be resting. This is a new added bonus to the whole "cancer lifestyle" that we are enjoying. I don't know if my friends who have been through this haven't had this problem, or if they were just secretly praying that it wouldn't happen to me, but needless to say, I had no warning that my brain (or lack thereof) would start to work against me. (It's probably all of those Sponge Bob episodes . . . . Barney and Sponge Bob are scary shows.)

Let's summarize:

1). *The scans were bad.*
2). *Cancer still SUCKS!*
3). *Zachary is pain-free.*
4). *Cancer sucks even more than when I wrote about it sucking back in #2.*
5). *We are looking into new therapies.*
6). *We have two days of testing next week. MRI on Monday, Bone marrow on Thurs.*
7). *I'll be investing in toothpicks for my eyes . . . . if they ain't closed . . . I won't sleep and have nightmares. (Scary smart . . . . eh?)*

Thursday, May 26, 2005 9:05 PM CDT

You know . . . . sometimes you go through life and you get to meet and interact with all sorts of people who come from a variety of different walks of life . . . . and I know that I have somewhat of a reputation for being cynical at times (maybe a little bit) . . . . but overall, I would like to believe that I am a fairly good judge of character.

(Where is all of this going?)

I'm thinking that the "doctor" (yes .... I REALLY did use quotes there) that read Zachary's most recent MIBG scan MUST have recently undergone a frontal lobotomy or some other major cranial surgery. I now have in my hands the typed report from that scan. It reads as follows:

Normal MIBG activity of the salivary glands is present. Multiple areas of accumulation of MIBG activity in the thoracolumbar spine region are less prominent than on the previous study. Abnormal area of activity in the left parietal bone also noted and slightly less prominent than on the previous study. Left acetabular activity has not re-appeared. Right acetabular activity persists. Activity in proximal femurs bilaterally persists and is less prominent than on the previous study.

IMPRESSION:

Multiple areas of MIBG activity involving the spine, pelvis, proximal femurs and skull as seen on the previous study with appearance of subtle decrease of nearly all areas of activity since the previous examination. The significance of this is uncertain and might possibly be related to technical factors as it is essentially a uniform decrease in all visualized regions. No other significant new finding is present.

Hmmmmmmmmmmmmmmmmmmmmmmmmmmmmmmmmmmmmmmmmmmmmmmmmmmm

Am I the only one who finds it somewhat odd that there is a "uniform" decrease in ALL areas? I mean .... I'm no statistician or expert in mathematical equations .... but what exactly are the odds of that occurring? Now remember ... we're not talking about one or two or three or even six isolated sites ... we're talking about close to ten different locations that have consistently lit up over the past several scans. So, is it more likely that A). All of Zachary's sites have improved by EXACTLY the same amount?, or B). The scan is somehow flawed? (uptake not complete .... or poor imaging).

Call me silly .... but I'm gonna vote for B! (Not because I don't have the capacity to accept good news when it is thrown at me ... but because I believe in math .... and science and because I'm a pretty good judge of a duck when it waddles by me quacking and crapping like a duck!)

So, the next logical question is .... "Why didn't the reporting doctor ask for another scan to verify the miraculous uniform improvement that he has found?"

I don't believe this guy would know an MIBG scan if it fell off of the shelf and hit him on the head. I believe he has taken the path of least resistance and signed off on the scan so he wouldn't (as chief of the dept.) have to deal with the fact that the hospital doesn't have a radiologist who has experience reading these scans.

Having said (or written) all of that . . . . it really doesn't matter. HAD the doctor requested a second scan . . . . I would have declined . . . . gracefully . . . . (or not gracefully) . . . . (probably not gracefully) . . . . we are not relying on these scans for any big decisions . . . . so why torture Zachary with any more tests than need be? Sadly . . . there are several other families who rely heavily on these scans . . . . I don't know how they fared with their last tests.

Sunday, June 19, 2005 7:49 PM CDT

Medical Update:

As I mentioned a few updates ago, Zachary is on a larger dose of chemotherapy. (The thinking there is that since he is tolerating it well, a larger dose may provide a larger benefit . . . . and should (theoretically) be tolerated well . . . . since the lower dose has been. Well, Zachary has had quite a bit of nausea this week. He has gotten sick a few times . . . . usually after car rides . . . . but overall he has been a trooper. We won't know about his blood counts and how they have been affected until tomorrow.

Yesterday we had a really good time. Connor Moran Children's Cancer Foundation has a connection with a very nice guy who takes kids fishing. Rebecca, Zachary and I drove to West Palm Beach and he met us at a marina that was very close to one of his fishing spots. After a very short ride, we were throwing live bait out and trying to entice some nice 16-25lb tarpon into biting. We ended up hooking into ten nice fish . . . . and we landed 2. (Tarpon have a very hard mouth and provide an amazing fight . . . . they are very acrobatic . . . . it is not uncommon to have a fish leap out of the water several times during a fight. Because of this, they can be very tricky to land.) We were using light tackle . . . . so the fish had a fighting chance. Several broke off the line by swimming around pilings. We ended up enduring a major storm that blew through, but it didn't dampen our enjoyment of the evening . . . it was a blast. When I get the pictures developed . . . I will post them in the gallery and let everyone know to look there.

Now, onto other news. I don't usually respond to guest book entries in my journals, but a recent one caught my eye and provoked me to write some thoughts about it. Here is the exact text from the entry in question:

"I consider myself a friend; however . . . . You never have a nice thing to say about a doctor or the medical field. Please stop for a minute and realize that without all these people that you so quickly ridicule you would not have your son this Father's Day. Maybe it's time to stop and deal with your pain another way."

A Friend
FL USA—Sunday, June 19, 2005 10:17 AM CDT

So, there you have it . . . . I am being chastised for being a curmudgeon who complains too much. Hmmmmm . . . . on the surface . . . . it's tough to argue with that reasoning . . . . I DO complain a lot. But, is it REALLY complaining . . . . or am I just relaying some of the frustrations that we've had to endure over the past 5 years, 3 months, 4 days, 8 hours, 3 minutes, and 25 seconds . . . . ?(Not that I'm counting or anything.) Gosh . . . . I can't imagine NOT responding to this entry . . . . so here goes.

Ok . . . . first of all . . . . we ARE very grateful to the doctors who have helped us during our battle. If you go back and read ALL of my entries, you will find where I have given credit to those who have contributed to our successes. Unfortunately, there are many others who have hindered us or otherwise contributed to this nightmare by their actions or words. For example. The doctor who ran the transplant program where Zachary had his stem cell transplant should be commended for managing a program and staff that got us through a VERY difficult time in his treatment . . . . BUT (and I do mean BUT), when Zachary relapsed, he was the first doctor who our local oncologist called to get advice for further treatment. His answer was, "Zachary has already had a transplant . . . . why would you give him more chemotherapy? Let him go." (That is pretty much an exact quote . . . I'll never forget our local doctor relaying that conversation to us.) Now, that was over three years ago . . . . had we listened to his "advice" . . . . yesterday we would have been visiting Zachary's gravesite . . . instead of fighting fish together in the river!

And how about the doctor in NYC? He is an amazing oncologist. His specialty is Neuroblastoma. When Zachary wasn't eligible for his treatment protocol, he offered to put us on a different one . . . . the Arsenic Protocol. When I questioned him about it . . . . he admitted that only nine kids had tried it . . . . 7 had died quickly . . . . one lasted a couple of months . . . . and one lasted four or five . . . . (not the most exciting results a parent could hear.) But his group stands to receive big bucks by having kids on THEIR protocols. He couldn't get us on the one that we wanted . . . . the one that was producing interesting results . . . . so he tried to KEEP us as a patient by offering up an alternative that even HE wasn't excited about once questioned about it.

Our most recent problem with our local hospital and the radiologist screw-up has turned into a MAJOR issue. Several families have been affected by this . . . . and it is completely unnecessary. If we hadn't been in this battle for as long as we have . . . . I could see "A Friend's" point . . . . but WE KNOW BETTER. I may be getting old . . . but I can clearly remember a time when things were drastically different.

Our local hospital got MAJOR press by teaming up with a major local foundation when they "built" the new children's hospital. But they didn't build a hospital . . . . they renovated the old wing . . . . some of it is amazing . . . . some of it sucks! I remember calling them and asking why the story in the newspaper stated that the oncology floor was going to be "Brand New" . . . . (we had heard rumors they were only going to redo the old floor.) . . . . well . . . . all they did was redo the old floor . . . . new paint . . . new windows . . . . new air systems . . . . new floors and beds . . . . but something got lost in the translation. One of our closest friends was on the floor this weekend . . . . and they told us how it is now. We were there a few months ago . . . . and we saw it for ourselves.

Because of the most recent screw-ups, we are now going to have to travel 3 hours across the state to get our next MIBG scans done . . . . it will require a hotel stay over there . . . . and time away from work . . . . but it is the only way that we can assure ourselves of getting the kind of professional opinion that we DESERVE! Maybe I'm being a little bit picky . . . . but isn't it our son's LIFE that we're talking about? What level of care should we expect? Keep in mind . . . . we have seen and experienced a level of care that does NOT seem to exist here locally anymore.

I don't want "A Friend" to take this personally . . . . or to feel like my tirade is directed at him . . . . I am merely defending my right to FREAK OUT each and every time the doctors, nurses, hospital staff . . . . or ANY OTHER medical personal drops the ball when caring for my son.

I've always promised myself that I would never second guess the decisions we've made medically for Zachary. Looking back and doing that can be very destructive mentally . . . . and it doesn't accomplish anything. However . . . . if I was to allow these injustices to take place without recourse or comment . . . . I KNOW it would haunt me in the future. This IS my therapy. If you are looking for a loving . . . . soft . . . . cuddly . . . . warm . . . . and fuzzy site . . . then I am truly sorry . . . . this is NOT one. I guess those folks who get queasy or uncomfortable when reading these entries could email us privately . . . . and we will gladly respond with a much more tame and calm report. (You don't seriously want me to put it up for a vote "A Friend" . . . . do you? . . . . I mean . . . . I will if you want me to . . . . but either way . . . . this site is therapy for me . . . . if everyone stops reading it . . . . I'd probably STILL write the entries . . . . just to keep sane.)

Scott (The Ungrateful.)

Wednesday, October 5, 2005 8:08 PM CDT

Life must be boring here in Jensen Beach.

Boring?

Well, I assume it must be boring . . . . I mean we have so little going on.

Just chemo two weeks out of every three.

Blood counts every week.

Exam every week.

School.

Sure . . . . I'd say life is pretty mundane around here . . . . and THAT must be why we are being blessed with some excitement.

Zachary is once again experiencing double vision, dizziness, headaches, and fatigue. Two weeks ago he had several days of this . . . . and he is once again being harassed by these symptoms. He has not been able to stay at school for very long. (And I KNOW he wanted to stay today, because it was the start of soccer practice . . . and staying all day at school was the tradeoff.) He only lasted about an hour. (Thank you Susan for helping us out by picking him up today.) (YES, I know there are several Susan's who read this journal entry . . . but I'm FAIRLY sure that THE Susan will know who she is.) So, Rebecca called the oncologist's office and they asked that Zachary be brought right in for an examination. While he was there, the doctor called the neuro-ophthamologist's office and consulted with that doctor. Since the N.O. is unable to see Zachary until next Wednesday, he asked that we get an MRI of the brain! (Singing gleefully) "Oh what fun it is to have cancer . . . . la la la . . . "

So, tomorrow afternoon we are shooting down to Jupiter to get an MRI. Hmmmmmm. Jupiter you say? NOT West Palm Beach? Very curious . . . . very curious indeed. But isn't Zachary's doctor's office AT the West Palm Beach campus? (Nodding) Hmmmmm. And you are going to Jupiter instead? YES I AM. Evidently the N.O. specialist doesn't want the MRI done at the WPB hospital. HAH! It isn't our paranoia. They suck! And evidently it is common knowledge.

Speaking of sucking . . . . I got a bill from the hospital on the west coast of Florida where we did scans in August. The bill showed $293.00 in charges . . . . and it very clearly stated that our insurance "REJECTED THE CLAIM." At the bottom of the sheet it stated that, "Your insurance has rejected this claim . . . . please remit payment within 15 days."

Hmmmmm. I'm pretty sure we met our maximum out of pocket about 28 seconds into the current year . . . . so we should NOT have any claims being rejected. So, I called our insurance company and they informed me that they have NEVER seen this claim. So they have NEVER rejected it. Hmmmm. How could this be? I jotted down the guy's phone numbers so when I called the hospital I could refer them to the actual person who had armed me with this tidbit of information.

I called the hospital.

The lady who answered the phone was NOT prepared to deal with the wrath of Scott.

I explained the situation and she pulled our file up on her screen. Evidently they HAD submitted a claim to our insurance company . . . . with inaccurate and incomplete information about Zachary. So the claim was returned (not rejected) as incomplete.

I very calmly expressed my mild frustration with the hospital's apparent lack of fair play for sending me a notice of supposed rejection when in fact, it was an incomplete claim. I STRONGLY recommended that they refrain from sending me any further such notices. She made a note in the file. (Probably something like—"Irate, irrational, lunatic father has threatened to cross the state and rearrange my internal organs if we don't stop harassing him.") Not really . . . . but you know me . . . . calm, cool and collected.

So . . . . back to the excitement in our lives. Apparently one of the chemos that Zachary is on has possible side-effects of dizziness, fatigue, vision problems . . . etc. It is also interesting that these symptoms started in the week following the last round of chemo . . . the round in which we last upped the dosage of this chemo. Hmmmmmm. I'm no Sherlock Holmes . . . . well . . . . I just thought that I should clear that up . . . . I'm no Sherlock Holmes . . . . you know . . . in case any of you were confused.

Scott

P.S. Here's hoping that it is merely a reaction to the chemo. (Wouldn't THAT be great, having to stop or reduce a much needed chemo . . . . MORE excitement?)

Thursday, April 12, 2007 10:25 PM CDT

I find myself in an awkward position . . . . sitting on a very short bed . . . . writing a journal entry . . . . while young Zachary is sleeping about three feet away getting IV fluids and antibiotics . . . . and Rebecca is about two thousand yards away sleeping at the Quantum House.

Yep . . . . you guessed it . . . . we're in the hospital!

How did this happen you ask?
Oh . . . . you didn't ask?

Well . . . . tough luck . . . . I'm more than likely going to tell you anyway.

Zachary . . . . as you all know . . . . had that bout with back pain several weeks ago. That went away . . . . but he started having pain while peeing. The doctors thought that maybe he had a urinary tract infection . . . . so they prescribed oral antibiotics . . . . that didn't seem to help.

Meanwhile . . . back at the ranch . . . . Zachary has been experiencing increased nausea and vomiting . . . . but . . . having been on oral chemo for the past two years . . . . how does one know WHAT is causing nausea. With good counts and no fevers . . . . we have been somewhat on cruise control.

Today . . . . Zachary vomited again this morning before school . . . . and then he was complaining of dizziness. Rebecca called the doctors . . . they suggested giving him fluids, (especially since he doesn't drink enough), ... and there you have it . . . . he's in the hospital.

But wait . . . . it gets better . . . . NOT.

The urine sample came back negative for the UTI (urinary tract infection.)
So, the doctor ordered an ultrasound of his bladder . . . . to see what was what.

That test requires no food for 6 hours, so they weren't able to administer it until about 8:30PM . . . . Rebecca was with him.

This is where the fun begins. I'm thinking that the best thing for me to do here . . . . would be to give you some examples of what NOT to say to a person while engaging in conversation . . . . especially if you are trying to avoid putting your foot into your mouth.

Example #1.

You are introduced to a woman with a rather large stomach, and you say . . .

"When is your baby due?"

. . . . and it turns out the woman is NOT pregnant . . . . just fat.

Example #2.

You are introduced to an older man with a younger woman, and you say . . .

"Your daughter is very lovely."

. . . . and it turns out that the younger woman is his younger girlfriend.

Example #3.

You are a technician doing an ultrasound on a young cancer patient with his mother present . . . . the patient has endured 7 years of battling a horrendous disease and has been given little hope by doctors too many times to count . . . . while doing said ultrasound . . . you notice an anomaly and you say . . . .

"When was your son's left kidney removed?"

. . . . and it turns out that it was NEVER removed!

So . . . . now you have a mother in panic . . . . a mother with lupus who needs stress like hospitals need more idiots . . . . and you have a 13 year old boy who hasn't been in a hospital in quite some time . . . . seeing a panicked look on the two adult faces in the room . . . . I'm guessing that all of you are painting a pretty ugly picture in your heads right about now.

So . . . . of course . . . . it's 8:30PM at night . . . . so NOTHING definitive is going to happen until tomorrow . . . . by chance . . . the oncologist calls into the floor and is told about this . . . . he obviously doesn't remember any kidneys or other organs being removed . . . . and says we'll look at the final report tomorrow.

So . . . . the good news is that we get to worry about this ALL NIGHT!

Scott

P.S. Darn teenagers . . . . if they're not chasing girls, or sneaking Ipods into school . . . . they're losing their vital organs.

Saturday, April 14, 2007 6:12 PM CDT

The missing kidney riddle has officially been solved . . . . sort of . . . . well . . . . not so much.

(If that first sentence means absolutely nothing to you . . . . then more than likely you missed my last journal entry . . . . for the sake of all of humanity . . . . or at least your ability to follow along . . . . I suggest that you STOP here . . . . GO BACK to my last journal entry . . . . and GET CAUGHT UP!)

For the rest of you . . . . read on.

As I wrote before . . . . the kidney mystery started at about 8:30PM with the genius tech who was performing the ultrasound. Rebecca and I both slept REALLY well Thursday night, NOT! So . . . . Friday morning . . . . before the doctor showed up for rounds . . . . the nurse was able to pull up the official report in her system that showed the doctor's notes and impression from the ultrasound. Here is the exact text from that report:

"Real time ultrasound examination of the abdomen shows no evidence of metastatic deposits in the liver. The liver, spleen and pancreas appear normal. The kidneys also appear normal. No evidence of retroperitoneal lymphadenopathy."

(Notice that the word 'kidneys' is pluralized . . . meaning more than one . . . . or both in this case.)

So there you have it . . . . the tech must have just read things incorrectly during the exam. Or not . . . . the plot thickens.

The oncologist showed up for rounds . . . . and having been informed the night before about our little kidney mystery, he had taken the proactive step of printing up Zachary's old MRI scan reports from back in 2001 and 2002 . . . . pretty much the follow up scans from the year after diagnosis.

The earliest one available had this to say about the kidneys:

"The right kidney appears normal in size and enhancement. There is severely atrophic or hypoplastic left kidney."

The next scan . . . . from about 7 months later reads as follows:

"The right kidney is within normal limits. The left kidney remains relatively atrophic with only a small amount of contrast excretion."

OK . . . . quick vocabulary lesson . . . .

Atrophy (or atrophic as used above)—The degeneration or wasting away of an organ or part of the body, as from disease or disuse.

Now . . . . at this point in the story I should mention that BEFORE getting copies of these reports . . . . I had already used my "phone-a-friend" to get the low down on how a kidney could disappear. My resident expert (dad) informed me that loss or lack of blood flow could cause a kidney to atrophy or die. That knowledge . . . . along with the knowledge that Zachary's original tumor was in his left adrenal gland . . . . which is of course attached to the left kidney, was just enough information to make me paranoid that the original surgery hadn't gotten all of the tumor . . . . and the disease had come back to claim the left kidney.

Fast forward to our oncologist reading these reports to us and like a light bulb going off . . . I remembered that back in 2001 and 2002 . . . . they HAD given us copies of those reports . . . . and we had briefly discussed the fact that Zachary's left kidney was probably not fully functioning. If I remember correctly . . . . at the time . . . . we had bigger fish to fry . . . and one healthy kidney was good for us . . . . the left was still showing some functionality . . . . so there was no reason to do anything.

SO . . . . my question to the oncologist was, "Could the disease have caused the atrophy in the kidney . . . since the tumor was right there in the neighborhood?" His response was, "That is not common . . . . but, do you remember how large the tumor was?" Of course I did, so I told him, "Yeah . . . it was about the size of a green apple . . . . or just under the size of a tennis ball." Having heard that, he said, "Well . . . . if it was that big . . . it could have cut off the blood flow to the kidney and caused it to atrophy."

It was all beginning to make sense . . . . we had just forgotten about the left kidney not being fully functioning . . . . so the tech's inappropriate comments had caught us off guard. BUT WAIT . . . . it gets better . . . . if you were paying attention, then you will have noticed something that does NOT add up at all. The first report that I quoted from in this entry was the one from the doctor at our hospital two days ago rendering his opinion about Zachary's ultrasound . . . . you don't have to scroll back . . . . I'll retype it for you:

"The kidneys also appear normal."

??

Well . . . . he may not be a REAL doctor . . . . but he DID stay at a Holiday Inn last night.

You know . . . . we are scheduled to go over to Ft. Myers next week for our 6 month MIBG test . . . . a test that we USED to have done in West Palm Beach at our local hospital. But having screwed up the test soooooo many times in the past . . . . we just stopped having them done here. While Zachary was in the hospital the other day, Rebecca and Zachary ran into the tech who used to perform that test for us . . . . Rebecca asked him if things had improved, and he told her, "NO . . . you are MUCH better off going elsewhere for your exam." AND HE IS THE GUY DOING THE TEST!!!!

I believe another important piece of information here is that unless Zachary is from another planet (and we're not ruling that out), then humans do NOT re-grow kidneys! So his atrophic left kidney from 2001, and 2002 . . . . is at BEST still atrophic and very low functioning . . . . and at worst . . . . not functioning at all and superfluous at this point. SO, I'd like to get my hands on the "Kidneys also appear normal" doctor so I could clean his glasses for him . . . . or maybe take away his glass of whiskey so he could concentrate on his job.

Now that we know the left kidney is either useless or close to it, we will need to see a nephrologist so we can get a kidney function test to make sure that the left kidney is not causing problems. If it is just dead . . . . and minding its own business . . . . then we'll leave it alone . . . . if it is acting up . . . . then it needs to be put into time out . . . . have its IPod taken away, and be grounded for eternity.

So there you have it . . . . the kidney mystery wrapped up in a nutshell . . . . the 'NUT' being the doctor who incorrectly read the ultrasound of course.

So I guess Zachary has been living with just one good working kidney since the tumor grew so large . . . . probably back near the end of 1999 or the beginning of 2000. I haven't had a chance to do any research into any changes in diet or hydration that we need to focus on as we move forward . . . . I'm guessing that the hydration thing is big . . . . but I'm sure the nephrologist will want to weigh in on that issue.

Scott

P.S. Zachary got home from the hospital about 30 minutes before our local American Cancer Society relay for life started . . . . we headed over . . . and he got to walk the survivor lap with his buddy Ty-Michael . . . . they played and hung out for about 3 hours . . . . it was a good night!

Tuesday, May 8, 2007 7:07 AM CDT

We read the guest book entries every day. We love to see the comments from all over the country (and the world.) Sometimes they make us laugh, sometimes they inspire us, but mostly they comfort us with a feeling of being connected to a large community of caring folks who follow our drama.

Occasionally, there is an entry that will prompt me to write a journal entry . . . . like today. This following entry was posted the other day, and after reading it, by pure coincidence, I read an article in the newspaper that got me thinking . . . .

Here is a small part of the entry:

"Gosh I have been reading Zachs journal forever and I feel like I missed something . . . I thought Zack was off treatment? I guess I need to re-read!"

We have MANY friends and customers who see Zachary and assume that because he has a full head of hair, is in school (until about 3 weeks ago), and is looking good . . . . that he is out of treatment. This has repeatedly produced an interesting dynamic in the conversations that we end up having about young Zachary.

All of that coupled with a recent story that I read about a woman who lied about her child having cancer to raise money has me wondering about what people who don't see what we face each day . . . . must be thinking.

Here is a brief recap of where we are:

Diagnosed: 3/16/00
Finished Treatment: 11/20/00
Relapsed (restarted treatment): 2/11/02

That is it! You will notice, (or you won't, and I will have to point it out), that since my birthday in 2002, Zachary has been on treatment. That is five years, two months, and 27 days. (Not that I'm keeping track.)

So . . . . why is it that Zachary has all of his hair?

Why is it that he has been able to stay in school for most of this year?

Why is it that he rarely has hospital stays for problems relating to treatment?

Why do most relapsed neuroblastoma kids die within the first year of relapse?

Why do most relapsed neuroblastoma kids endure horrible quality of life after relapse?

Why, why, why, why, why, why, why??????????????

The simple answer is this . . . . "I don't know."

I wish I had answers for everyone . . . . I wish I could transmit my thoughts into others, so that I wouldn't have to flip the mental coin every time that someone asks me, "How is Zachary doing?"

And what exactly is the mental coin . . . . you ask?

(You didn't ask? . . . . oh well . . . . here is the answer.)

The mental coin is flipped when I try to decide whether to say:

1). *"He's doing great!" (This is both true . . . and misleading . . . at the same time . . . . relative to most other kids with his illness, he is doing "beyond" great. But, in comparison to kids who do NOT have cancer and do NOT need to take chemotherapy 10 days out of every 21, and do NOT need to do testing every time he gets a small pain or anomaly, and do NOT need to be constantly looking out for new therapies and treatments . . . . well . . . . then I suppose he is NOT doing "beyond" great.)*

2). *"(Insert long complicated explanation of his current treatment, multitude of doctors visits, hospital stays, testing, testing results, etc.)" Usually, when I take this approach, the person listening gets this glassy eyed look that conveys to me a sense of regret for having asked in the first place. I can almost hear them saying, "I didn't want to go to medical school today . . . . I just wanted to hear you say 'He's fine.' . . . . I didn't REALLY want to know what was going on."*

So there you have it . . . . at the end of the day, there is no good answer . . . . or question for that matter. There is no wrong or right . . . . we are not offended by questions . . . . we welcome them . . . . but sometimes, if you ask a question . . . . be ready to get an answer. And if you don't want to risk getting an answer that you don't want to hear . . . . say something like; "I hope he is doing well . . . . we think of him often." Or "We'll add him to our prayer list." Or something along those lines.

As for the parent who lied about their child having cancer to make money . . . . I don't even know what to say about that. What does it say about a person who looks at a situation like this and thinks to themselves . . . . "WOW, they are SO lucky . . . . people are just falling over themselves to help them, and give them money . . . . if only MY kid could have been lucky enough to have gotten a life threatening illness . . . . boy, life is just NOT fair." That is one demented and twisted mindset . . . . to that person I guess I would say this:

"Good luck in hell . . . . dress for summer . . . . it's hot down there!"

Scott

P.S. We leave tomorrow for Ft. Myers for two days of testing. This week makes five without chemo or treatment . . . . we are still without a diagnosis for the belly pain. We are hoping that this testing will assist us in making a decision on future treatment plans.

Wednesday, July 4, 2007 10:48 AM CDT

*5 years
1 month
7 days
3 hours
32 minutes ago . . . . I started writing journal entries.*

. . . . . and after all of that time . . . . we have hit the 500,000 hit mark on Zachary's page. Now . . . . normally that would be some sort of milestone . . . . but you have to factor in the 493,887 times that Rebecca and I have clicked onto this page to check the guest book in the REMOTE chance that some lurker out there actually took 20 seconds of their precious time to leave us a message.

(Did that come across as bitter or scorned? Ooops.)

Thank you to everyone who has checked in on us over the past 5 years . . . . 1/2 million hits is amazing . . . . even IF Rebecca and I make up the majority of them!!! We appreciate the concern, the thoughts, and the prayers.

Now on to medical news . . . . such as it is.

When I wrote that last journal update, I didn't mention that Zachary started to experience some foot pain while we were driving home. I really didn't put a whole lot of thought into it, because he had been in bed sick for over a week, and then he got back to the vacation house and was skiing, tubing, swimming, etc. So, I figured that maybe he just over did it a little bit.

Well . . . . the pain in his feet has worsened . . . . and he has started to experience some pain in his hands as well. Those of you out there in Cancertown may recognize these symptoms as classic side effects of a drug called vincristine.

Here are some fun facts about vincristine:

"Vincristine may also affect the nerves in the intestines, causing gut movement to slow down. This effect can result in constipation, which in some cases may become serious."

"This medication commonly affects the nerves and muscles in your body. Most of these side effects go away after this medication is stopped, however some effects may persist for a long time. Tell your doctor immediately if any of these serious side effects occur: painful/difficult urination, change in the amount of urine, pain (e.g., in the joints, back, muscles, jaw), numbness/tingling/pain of the arms/legs, weakness, difficulty walking, loss of coordination/balance, inability to move your muscles (e.g., muscles of the face, other parts of your body), drooping eyelids, hoarseness, trouble speaking, mental/mood changes (e.g., depression, hallucinations, confusion)."

If you have been paying attention to my recent journal entries, you will notice that the constipation and the pain in the extremities are sounding familiar. Well . . . . this is no coincidence. Vincristine is in the same family of chemotherapies as the experimental drug that we are now giving Zachary. That is why the intestinal thing is so dangerous. This pain in the feet and hands is new to us. AND it is coming WAY late in the round of chemo . . . . we are technically supposed to be starting our next round today . . . but with the holiday, we had to postpone it for a week. The other "scare" that we had yesterday came from his most recent blood work. His platelets were about 600,000! Now . . . . I'm no platelet expert by any means . . . . but in seven years of playing parent/doctor/cancer treater . . . . I have never seen his platelets go over 400,000! Apparently, whatever infection we were fighting up in Knoxville could have caused this to happen. When the body is fighting an infection, the bone marrow can go into overdrive to compensate and after the infection is gone, and the other counts are returning to normal . . . the platelet count can have a "late" skyrocket" effect. The doctor said not to worry about this . . . . she saw no concern for clots . . . . and said even if it hit 1,000,000, she wouldn't want us to panic.

(My main disappointment came from the knowledge that he got his platelet count over 600,000 in a little under a week . . . . and you sorry lurkers could barely get his page hit count to 500,000 in just over 5 years . . . . pitiful!)

Did I say that out loud? . . . . Oh that's right . . . . I put it in parentheses, so it's like I was just "thinking" it to myself . . . . so no one will read that or get offended . . . . cool.

So . . . back to the pain . . . . the doctor suggested Tylenol around the clock . . . . which has not been working so far . . . . and after that, she said to have our local oncologist prescribe Oxycontin. (CRAP . . . I hate giving him hard drugs.) As luck . . . . (bad or good . . . . you choose) would have it . . . . we still have some Oxycontin from a previous bout with some pain issue that he had within the last few months or so . . . . so we gave him half of one of those . . . . and hopefully he will get some relief.

Other than that . . . . things are quiet around here. We are being lazy today . . . . hanging around the house . . . . I did yard work all morning, Rebecca has been doing laundry, (in a feigned attempt to get caught up from vacation), and Zachary has been lying around, playing some video games. We may go over to a friend's house here in the neighborhood to swim and barbecue . . . if Zachary feels up to it.

I hope everyone has a safe and enjoyable Fourth of July.

Chapter 7

Supplements & Alternative Treatments

"Three toad's feet, eyelids from a chicken, blood from a goat . . . .
mix it altogether and chant along with me . . . " (Oh yeah, and click
your heels together three times while you're doing that, just in case.)

This chapter will, by FAR, prove to be the most controversial. The use of supplements in cancer patients, and specifically children, was being debated long before we joined the party, and I imagine that it will rage on long after we are through playing with this disease. Our introduction into the world of alternative treatments came in the form of a visitor who we had at the hospital very early on in Zachary's treatment. I don't recall exactly how those folks made it into our lives, let alone into his room, but I DO remember what happened. Apparently the acquaintance of ours brought this non-English speaking friend in to say a blessing over Zachary. Before we knew what was happening, they had taken out a bottle of "blessed oil" and they were splashing it on Zachary's head and chanting in another language.

Zachary was six years old at the time, and I remember him looking at me like I was some sort of imbecile. He had this expression on his face as if to say, "Are you on drugs or something? Get this freak away from me." Thankfully, those words never came out of his mouth. He endured the "blessing" and we cleaned him up afterwards. Who knows, maybe that is why we are enjoying such great quality of life. You never know! (You'll read those three words repeatedly throughout this chapter . . . . it's what we authors call a "reoccurring theme.")

113

After that we became somewhat leery of offers for miracle cures and healers. We were fortunate that one of Zachary's doctors was very well informed when it came to alternative treatments. In addition to being a pediatric oncologist, he had microbiology experience. So, whenever someone offered us something to try, we would run it past him to see if there were any contraindications with any of Zachary's medicines.

There was a silver treatment being done in Canada that we were told about, and after asking the doctor about that one he replied, "DO NOT even think about it, it will KILL him." Then, there was a clinic in Mexico that some of the families had told us about. Once again, our doctor told us that it was a hoax. He had a patient who had gone there years before and died, after giving them thousands of dollars for nothing. So, for the first three years, we stayed away from anything that we couldn't wrap our scientific minds around.

After relapse, things started to change somewhat in our opinion of supplements. We had been hearing about some patients who were supposedly benefiting from a supplement that was very high in antioxidants. Most of the supplements that target the cancer community seem to have an amazing (beyond belief) story attached to them that is supposed to lend an air of authenticity. There almost always is a conspiracy involved where the government doesn't want to let the world know that there is some super cheap cure out there hidden from the public's view.

When your child has cancer, you WILL grasp at straws and take swings at windmills. It is the very nature of parenting to want to protect your child at all costs, against enemies foreign and domestic. (Wait, that might be the soldiers oath . . . . I always get the two confused.) Anyway, as a parent, you WANT to believe that you will be able to find that cure, even if it is somewhat . . . . well . . . . Unbelievable.

Back to the land of antioxidants. As I mentioned just a moment ago, late in 2002 we had been hearing stories about a supplement that I will refer to as Potion X. The down and dirty explanation was that some chemist in the 1930's or 40's had developed this formula that he believed had come to him from God, (hold on now . . . . I don't want to lose you on this . . . stick with it for the payoff at the end,) and that he felt it was his moral obligation to give it back to the people. Supposedly he had tried on several occasion to have it approved, but he had run into road block after road block because it was not hugely expensive to make, ergo, a drug company wasn't going to be able make big profits on it.

I'm told that for years, he would ship it at HIS expense to cancer patients around the country, not charging for it. This supposedly went on for years, with many people believing that it was a "hidden cure." At some point, he was shut down by the government because he was never able to garnish approval for it. Then, several years later, Congress passed an act that allowed companies to market and sell supplements as long as they didn't make specific medical claims and they passed standard FDA lab testing for safety. Well, this chemist already knew that it was safe; not only had he already done his own extensive testing, he had been using it for years and had many people who could attest to its safety. He also had in place a large number of folks who knew of its benefit and were waiting in the wings for it to become available again.

So, he changed the name and submitted it to one of the labs that was doing the FDA approval thing. By then, there were many companies submitting supplements for approval, so his, under a new name, was able to fly under the radar. It easily passed the approval process, as he knew it would, and it became available again. This time however, he had to charge a fee for it. I'm not sure if he immediately started selling it directly to the public, but I know that when we were introduced to it, the family of the chemist had licensed one company to market and sell the product. The only caveat was that they couldn't sell it for more than an agreed upon price. Supposedly, the family retained the proprietary ingredient list, and they supplied it to the distributor, at cost, for them to market and sell it. I actually met the surviving son and daughter of the chemist at an annual gathering of people who take this supplement, and they assured me that they do not profit in any way from the process. It was always their father's intention for his family NOT to profit from this "God given" gift.

The story of Potion X is an amazing one that always raises eyebrows when told to men (and women) of science. Doctors in particular are quick to laugh at you when you mention that you are thinking of giving your child a supplement. Coming from a medical family, I always felt that traditional medicine was the way to go. And then in January of 2003 we were at a holiday party in West Palm Beach for the cancer families. I'll never forget it, I was sitting next to a nice woman and we were discussing our children and their treatments. She told me the story of her son who had been diagnosed with a DPG, (Diffuse pontine glioma.) None of the childhood cancers are any fun, I believe that I have made that abundantly clear. However, DPG's are ESPECIALLY not fun. My understanding is that they are inoperable brain tumors that have a 100% fatality rate within the first 9 months. The doctors offer some radiation, which can buy a little bit of time, but the outcome is always bad.

Well, this woman's son was running around with the other children, and he was about a year or so out already, and feeling great! While talking with this woman, I never got the sense that she fell into that stereotypical image that I had in my head of someone who would use a supplement or witchcraft, or whatever to heal their child. She told me the story of Potion X and about how they had been using it for quite some time.

At some time during the conversation a light bulb went off in my head, and I distinctly remember thinking, "There is no way that I am going to bury my son without having tried this supplement." For about $120.00, I would have a month's supply, and I figured that by then I would know if it were helping us or not. We got home and I ordered a bottle. Within a few weeks of giving it Zachary, we noticed that his blood counts started to improve. We were sold. When we told our doctor that we had started to give it to Zachary, he actually got angry with us, and said that it was nonsense and that it wouldn't help.

Now here's the thing. Physiologically, maybe the supplements help and maybe they don't. We could argue this point until the end of time and probably never resolve the issue. But what you need to keep in mind is that as a parent of a child fighting cancer, your "control" over his/her well-being has pretty much been stripped from you. Actually, it has been stripped, doused in gasoline, burned to a crisp, run over by a steam roller, and then dissolved in acid. The feelings of helplessness that permeate your soul each and every day can be somewhat overwhelming. Because of that, you find yourself willing to grasp those straws, no matter how flimsy they appear to be. By giving Zachary a supplement, we as parents got to FEEL that we were being proactive. With no drug interactions to worry about, the only downside could be that we might be wasting money. But once again, I didn't want to stand over his grave and wonder what could have been.

The one big downside to the Potion X was the flavor. Apparently it is derived from clove, which has a taste that can only be described as horrible. I used to call it the "black oil of death." I don't know why, I guess because it is black like oil, stains like oil, and tastes slightly WORSE than oil. (We're talking about automotive oil here, NOT cooking oil.) Zachary got into a groove with it where he would go a month or so and be able to tolerate it with one drink, and then another, and then yet another. He always seemed to find a way to get through the 4 times a day that he needed to take it. We kept him on a rigid schedule and we went about the business of living.

There were times that he missed his dose, but mostly he did pretty well. Towards the middle of last year, he started to have stomach issues that made it difficult for him to tolerate the Potion X. That was also about the same time that the oral Irinotecan stopped working. So his stomach was under attack by the harsh tasting chemo, and the supplement. As luck would have it, I had a customer who was always asking about Zachary's condition, and he approached me about a friend of his who was getting ready to come to market with a new supplement that was supposedly very high in its antioxidant levels. By that time, Rebecca and I were believers of the benefits of antioxidants. We even had several of Zachary's doctors say to us, "We don't know what you are doing, but whatever it is . . . . do NOT stop!" (That included the naysayer. He even tried the Potion X one time while we were there getting tested. He told us that the bad taste from it took two days to get rid of.)

So, when this friend mentioned the new product, I asked for more information. He hooked me up with his friend, who told me about the product. Apparently it has been around in raw form for hundreds, if not thousands of years in Asia. It is derived from a mushroom that grows on a specific birch tree in Siberia. There have been books written about its use in cancer wards in Russia and China, and people have been known to chew the mushroom or make tea out of it. This company had done their homework and come up with a way to "brew" it using pi water so that the nutrients are not lost. This new friend sent us a bottle to use for Zachary just prior to the commercial release of the product.

The Potion X by that time had run its course. He was having such bad stomach issues that we couldn't justify making him take it any longer. The new supplement was much easier to take. It only required 10 drops, twice daily, and it could be mixed in any juice, tea, coffee, soda, etc. You could even put it on food. And the REAL bonus was that it didn't have a bad taste. I have mixed it in water and while it does change the flavor somewhat, it is not too bad.

Zachary started taking the new supplement about the same time that he began the new chemo. Within a few weeks, his blood counts were higher than they had been in over 4 years! We asked his treating doctors about that, and while they would not go on the record and say that his high counts could be attributed to our supplement, they did advise us NOT to stop taking whatever we were taking.

To this day, all three of us are taking this supplement. With all of the traveling between home and up north, we are always exposed to colds and flu on airplanes and around town. We believe in this product and we will continue to use it until someone can show definitive proof that it is harming us in some way. As for all of the other supplements out there, I will never again speak poorly of them. There are many different vitamin & dietary supplements that are available, and we have heard some amazing stories from folks who feel they are getting a benefit from taking them.

[FLASHBACK]

Wednesday, February 26, 2003 7:46 PM CST

5 NEW REASONS WHY CANCER SUCKS! (As if we needed anymore.)

1). "Mom, am I going to beat this cancer?"
2). "Mom, will I live long enough to learn how to drive?"
3). "Mom, will I live long enough to go to high school?"
4). "Mom, will I live long enough to get married?"
5). "Mom, will I live long enough to do my dream job?" (This week it is to be an undercover policeman.)

All five of these questions came last night before bedtime. (Anyone with dry eyes at this point is doing much better than I am.)

I suppose part of the blame for his renewed awareness of the gravity of the situation falls on us. We knew going into this new medicine that we would need his cooperation. It tastes like a dog turd that has been cooked in tar, soaked in gasoline, and then chopped up and thrown into a blender with cat piss. (Some of you are probably wondering how I would come to be able to reference such a flavor . . . . let's just say I've got an active imagination.)

Anyway, we needed him on the same page as us with taking a nasty medicine 4 times each day . . . . everyday! So, we explained that there was a chance that this would make the cancer go away. There were no guarantees, but we wanted to try. He is quite bright. I'm sure it was an easy job deducing that "trying to cure" meant, "we might not make it." So, he has been asking the hard questions.

I'm sure someone out there can explain to me why a 9 year old (Saturday is his birthday, he'll be 9,) should have to entertain these thoughts for one nanosecond. How is it possible that any of these children should be thinking about whether they are going to live or not? It's bad enough that they endure the treatments, but do they REALLY have to be tortured with the magnitude of this? Is it not bad enough that as parents we live the nightmare 24/7?

You don't have to answer that. I know the answers . . . . I just don't like any of them.

Thursday, February 27, 2003 6:47 PM CST

Oh boy am I ever in trouble! I always knew that my big sarcastic mouth would land me in trouble one day . . . . well folks . . . . welcome to THE DAY!

Before I go any further into my ramblings, I need to break the silence on something. I have had several inquiries into what "non-traditional" medicine we are trying with Zachary. I am now going to give you the name, and later on in this entry, I will give you the web page for the mom who has been using this for her son for 16 months. The supplement is called Potion X. (Changed for the book)

Now, back to me being in trouble. Being the sarcastic guy who I am, I sort of hinted the other night that Potion X might not taste too wonderful. Evidently, a few parents called our friend and were "put off" by my comments. They were worried about giving something that was so awful. Well, now I've got to eat crow.

(Hmmmm come to think of it . . . . mixing it with crow doesn't sound like a bad idea.) WHOA, WHOA . . . . there I go again . . . . right back into the sarcasm . . . . holy $%#& . . . . I've got to watch myself. Ok, this is what I said the other night. "It tastes like a dog turd that has been cooked in tar, soaked in gasoline, and then chopped up and thrown into a blender with cat piss." First let me say, that was a blatantly unfair analogy. You don't chop this stuff up! There, I cleared the air on that one.

WHAT? You want more? Ok, ok, ok. Look folks. There have been several thousand people from 3 year olds up to 80 year olds who have used this stuff with success. Somehow, they managed to take it 4 or 5 times a day (depending on the formula.) So, do your research. Read the testimonials, call some of the patients (many of them give their email and phone number and encourage calls,) and then, if you feel this is something you want for you or a loved one . . . . you WILL find a way to take it. Zachary has only been taking it for 2 ½ days, but he does not complain. (This is coming from a 9 year old who wouldn't lick a stamp if you gave him .50 cents.) So, don't dismiss this based on the ramblings of some 40-year-old sarcastic nutcase. I didn't even think people were reading this nonsense.

We don't know where this new adventure will lead us, but I will say this, Zachary has been asking some hard questions lately. Yesterday he got all excited and said, "The new medicine is working, it's working!" He has been a little constipated, and we had told him that sometimes Potion X can cause the cells to leave the body through the stool . . . . he somehow connected the two unrelated occurrences in his head, and decided that the medicine is already working. I explained that it was too early to tell, but that he had the right attitude. Now, how many of you feel it is important for him to have a positive outlook like that? What kind of value can YOU put on a child who somehow finds the mindset that he WILL be healed? (These are rhetorical questions for those of you who were getting ready to type.) The mind can do amazing things. I am grateful that he has a renewed hope for a future on this planet. Remember, quality time is just that, QUALITY TIME. No false hopes, just a positive attitude!

Saturday, October 11, 2003 8:17 PM CDT

1st an update . . . . 2nd . . . . ranting and raving.

Zachary still has a cold and cough. We've been treating it with over-the-counter medicines that have been allowing him to sleep well at night and get through the days without any complaints. (Knock on wood) Still no fever. Monday our chemo adventure will take a new and exciting turn. Zachary will get accessed in Palm

Beach and get his first round as usual, but after that the nurses will be coming to our house and finishing out the week. (If you call Vegas early enough you can probably get some interesting odds on the following: 1). Chemo showing up. 2). Other meds showing up. 3). Nurse showing up. 4). Nurse being competent. 5). My blood pressure not rising at least 45% over recommended levels.)

One of the web pages that we follow is for a young girl who is battling a brain tumor. She is a few years older than Zachary. We actually got to meet her and her family at the Potion X picnic several weeks ago. I was checking her update (she does her own) and was extremely pissed off by what I read. She was recounting her most recent visit to the doctor's office and wrote about what a nurse practitioner had said to her about using Potion X. Here is the quote from her web page:

"She gave me the "when this doesn't work" talk so that I wouldn't be too let down if it doesn't. In fact, she told me that a positive attitude combined with prayers doesn't work and not to depend on those two things too much to be cured. AHHH!"

Ok. Now, I can take a lot of crap. (I have already.) I can understand that modern medicine doesn't have all of the answers. I can understand that research doctors need terminal patients to use as lab rats to help future generations of cancer patients. I can understand doctors and nurses getting frustrated with the loss of children year after year. All of this I can understand on one level or another. But WHAT ON GOD'S GREEN EARTH POSESSES A HEALTH CARE WORKER TO USE THOSE WORDS WITH A CHILD BATTLING CANCER? If you can answer that, then I guess you win the big prize . . . because I'm at a loss. WHAT DO THESE PEOPLE HAVE TO GAIN BY TAKING AWAY HOPE FROM SOMEONE? I've written about this before. Maybe I'm starting to sound like a broken record.

I also heard from a little birdie that there are some doctors out there in la la land who are sooooooooo upset by the growing number of children using Potion X that they are considering "going after" the parents that write about it on their web pages or suggest it's use to other families. Hmmmmmm. Where were these "protectors" when doctors told us to stop giving Zachary chemo and let him die. That was 20 months ago. (He is going to school, running around . . . . LIVING . . . for those of you in the cheap seats.) Where were these "protectors" when the one doctor suggested that we put Zachary on the Arsenic regimen? (That was a winner . . . . NOT . . . . nine kids tried it . . . . I think one lived for a few extra months . . . .) Wow . . . . how encouraging. These advocate angels from heaven seem to be missing in action more often than not.

ONCE AGAIN I WILL STATE WHAT SHOULD BE OBVIOUS.

IF YOU DON'T AGREE WITH THE TREATMENT COURSE WE'RE GIVING OUR SON, THAT IS FINE . . . . BUT DO NOT JUDGE US. MODERN MEDICINE HAS ALREADY GIVEN UP ON US . . . . LET US CHOOSE OUR OWN PATH. THANK GOODNESS THAT GIRL HAS THE STRENGTH AND COURAGE TO DISMISS THOSE COMMENTS AND CONTINUE HER FIGHT.

Scott

P.S. Whenever I get down or depressed . . . . I just open up a package and bite into one of our chocolate covered key lime pie bars . . . . they're just like coming home!

Friday, December 12, 2003 8:10 PM CST

In case you all have been wondering . . . . I HATE TO WAIT FOR RESULTS!!!!!!!!!!

I will not torture you the way the doctor's office tortured me today.

The MIBG scan shows "No measurable disease."

The bone marrow (left side) shows "No evidence for involvement of neuroblastoma."

The bone marrow (right side) shows "Less than 2mm of maturing neuroblastoma with ganglionic . . . . "

What does this all mean?

The bottom line here is: NO ACTIVE CANCER IS FOUND!

The "maturing neuroblastoma" are aged cells that are hopefully dying. Basically, you hope that any treatment you are doing is aging the cells so they die off. Sometimes patients will show signs of mature cells for many months. They can sit there and do nothing for a long, long time.

Now, before we get toooooooooo far ahead of ourselves, it is important to keep in mind that "no measurable disease" does not guarantee that there are no viable cells hiding out somewhere. However, it DOES mean that he has had dramatic improvement over the past 9 months. 9 months? Hmmmmmmm. I'm sure there is some significance to that time frame . . . . give me a minute . . . . I'll figure it out . . . . maybe it's got something to do with the moon cycles . . . . no . . . . that isn't it . . . . wait now . . . don't rush me . . . . let's see . . . . well . . . . we started Potion X about 9 months ago . . . . but that COULDN'T be it . . . . that stuff is just nonsense according to the doctors . . . . so it's GOTTA be something else . . . . well . . . . I'm sure it will come to me sooner or later. (Reread previous sentence with heavy sarcasm for desired effect.)

So here we are . . . . in very, very, very uncharted waters. Rebecca and I have spent so much time planning for doom and gloom that we are finding ourselves confused as to how to feel. We want to jump for joy, (but joy's boyfriend said "hands off mister",) and we want to dance in the street, (but I've got 3 left feet,) we want to scream at the top of our lungs, (but Rebecca woke up today with no voice,) so, I guess we'll just go to bed and sleep a little easier for a change. None of us is promised any future for ourselves or for our loved ones. (If you've driven on our highways lately, you know as well as I do that life is precious and not to be taken for granted.) So, we are confident that if nothing else, we have bought some precious quality time. They can't take that away from us.

I've emailed two very respected doctors who have treated Zachary and are experts in this field . . . . it will be very interesting to see what they say.

Tuesday, December 16, 2003 8:42 PM CST

HOLY COW! I go for weeks where I only update once in awhile, and now you guys can't keep me away from the keyboard. "Step away from the computer. No one needs to get hurt."

Well, if you are just checking in for the first time in several weeks, you need to go back and read the past two entries. Now, for those of you who have faithfully followed my ramblings, here is some more interesting news.

I emailed one of the two doctors who I've been writing about and asked some VERY specific questions about Zachary and his current status. All of you know how much it has upset us that not only don't we get any acknowledgement of Potion X, but the credit is being given to a chemo that we were PROMISED could not deliver these kind of results. So, here are a few excerpts from the email I received. This doctor was kind enough to include my questions so I would know what he was answering. (But, since I've met many of you and know how confusing the English language can be, I will make it even easier to understand.)

Scott: "Have you had ANY children like Zachary who have experienced this kind of improvement after so many months without change?"

Doctor: "Not in my experience with neuroblastoma." [WOW]

Scott: [In reference to the current chemo having used up its usefulness.] "Do you mean he will probably not improve any more, or that this chemo will more than likely not contain the disease for much longer?"

Doctor: "I do not expect him to improve further. I suspect that he may stay in his current state for some time with continued Irinotecan, but not forever. You have achieved a "miraculous" event of a second partial remission after progression, after bone marrow transplant." [WOW AGAIN]

So, not only has he never seen this kind of response before, he is conceding that it is "miraculous."

Well folks the votes are in and they have been carefully tabulated. (We're in Florida; we take our vote counting very seriously.) All of the hanging chads have been accounted for, and here is how the voting broke down:

1). Should we keep using the Potion X?

Yes = 9,337,126 No = 2

(Both 'no' votes were from chemotherapy drug salesmen.)

2). Should we fly to NYC to retest?

Yes = 1 No = 9,337,125

(I threatened the one salesman, he switched sides.)

3). Should we totally annihilate Zachary's immune system during the worst flu season in 40 years, and then put him on an airplane (better known as a flying flu box) and travel to NYC the Mecca of international flu convergence, to spend three weeks living in a hospitality house that has 11 floors and 88 rooms chock full of disease carrying folks from every corner of the world, followed by immense pain and torture that at best, MIGHT help?

Yes = 1 No = 9,337,125

(The one doctor felt obligated to vote for his own facility.)

Even if the stars were lined up and there was no flu and money was no object, we just don't see it happening. We have gotten a miracle that other neuroblastoma children have missed. No one can take that away from us. For however long it lasts, this quality of life will always be special to us.

Monday, April 26, 2004 6:02 PM CDT

Once upon a time in a totally made up make believe land called Acirema (hold it up to a mirror . . . you'll get it.) there was a horrible disease called jockitchitis. This bad, bad disease was rampant throughout the nation and came in many forms, affecting young and old, men, women and children. There were people from all walks of life who were battling this disease. Doctors and researchers spent endless hours and billions of dollars looking for answers to the puzzle that was, jockitchitis. (If this is starting to sound like an analogy for cancer, it is COMPLETELY coincidental.) Many doctors and scientists came up with a system where they could "test" their new cures on patients by allowing them to take a special medicine when all other options had failed. Some patients were taking natural supplements (once again I feel obligated to deny that I am in ANY way referring to Potion X or any other supplement,) and yet other patients were taking nothing, and hoping for the healing hands of God to smile upon them. Some patients actually used a combination of these approaches to try and beat the monster that was jockitchitis. One family in particular, the Rhinestone family, (don't even go there . . . it was the most logical name I could come up with . . . . and it in NO way is supposed to be us,) was using a natural supplement while trying a somewhat experimental drug that was hard on their son. His name was Fred. (Aha . . . . I threw you off the scent by not using a name even remotely close to Zachary's . . . there's no way you'd ever know that I'm writing about us.) Anyway, Fred was tired of the hard medicine that he had been taking, and his family found out about a new experimental medicine that sounded like a good way to go for everyone. The Rhinestone family worked very hard with their doctors to get this new medicine for their son. They did special testing to make sure that Fred's jockitchitis was at a level where it had the best chance of responding favorably to the new medicine. Everything seemed to fall into place. Then the unthinkable happened. Evidently many of the doctors around Acirema had little or no faith in the natural supplements that Fred was using. In fact, most of them were SO adamantly against the supplement, they stated quite assertively and frequently that the supplement had NO positive effect on the jockitchitis, and that there was no way that it could possibly have helped make Fred any better. The Rhinestones were not sure what was giving them the blessing of excellent quality of life, so they were happy to keep Fred on the supplement while trying other more modern treatments. Well, the doctor who was in charge of the new medicine was very excited about getting Zachary on her treatment, but there was one BIG catch. The Rhinestone family had to STOP giving their son the supplement that they believed had been a HUGE part in their son's great progress. What confused the Rhinestone's the most was the Hippocratic line of reasoning that was being used against them. On one hand the doctors were saying that the supplement was useless, had no affect on anything, and that it was benign. On the other hand they were being told that to take the new medicine, they had to quit their supplement because the doctors wanted to see results that were unaffected by outside medicines. How could that be? How can a supplement be BOTH useless and an interference at the same time? It made no sense. Either it is working and should be accepted by the doctors as a viable treatment option, or it is a fantasy that families can throw their money towards at their own discretion. WELL, the Rhinestone family was very discouraged and distraught and disappointed and many other words that begin with 'dis', because they wanted to give Fred the best chance for a good life.

[STAY TUNED FOR MORE ADVENTURES OF THE (TOTALLY MADE UP AND NOT REAL) RHINESTONE FAMILY.]

Scott

P.S. Everything is great with us . . . (eyes rolling) . . . . couldn't be better . . . . (clearing throat loudly) . . . . love to all!

Chapter 8

School

"There's more to life than just fighting cancer . . . . a little bit of education never hurt anyone."

When Zachary was diagnosed way back in 2000, one of the first groups of people to step up and try to make our lives easier was his elementary school. The principal and vice-principal were among our first visitors. They brought notes and toys and conveyed to us a commitment towards helping our family in any way that they could. For that, we will always be grateful.

When your child is first diagnosed, the LAST thing that you worry about is "how am I going to get them to keep up with their schoolwork." (Walking, talking and breathing take precedence over schoolwork . . . . you can quote me on that.) So, while Rebecca and I were focused on trying to keep Zachary alive, we were instructed by the child-life specialist to try and maintain as much normalcy in Zachary's life as possible. The theory being, if the child's life is kept somewhat "normal", they will have a better chance of NOT allowing the diagnosis to define who they are. There is obviously no way to avoid the reality of how much it changes their life, but you can still try to keep some routines in place. I guess psychologically, if the child sees that they still have to do homework, they won't be thinking, "Hey, I must be dying. They stopped making me do my reading and math." (That may be somewhat of an oversimplification of the issue, but I think you get the concept.)

We were immediately made aware of the hospital homebound program that was and is still available through the county school board. Basically what it involves is having a teacher see the child about two times per week, for about an hour each visit. Now, on the surface, this doesn't seem like a whole lot of instruction compared to the 8am-2pm five days/week that most kids get. But what you have to keep in mind is that while the classroom setting does provide a lot of hours of instruction, it is NOT one-on-one. A teacher visiting the hospital or home can accomplish wonders with only a few hours each week.

The other factor that comes into play is the parents. The visiting teacher will almost always leave assignments and homework for the student to work on. If the parents put even a minimal effort in keeping their child involved, then they have a good chance of that child staying on grade with their classmates. Now, staying on grade is NOT going to be your #1 focus when your child is battling a life-threatening illness, I KNOW that. I've actually SAID that on many occasions. I remember distinctly saying, "I don't care if he gets several grades behind, I just want him to live!" The problem with THAT mindset (yes, I am guilty), is that quality of life includes aspects of a child's schooling that we as parents sometimes don't remember to factor in.

A child who has had friends for years and all of a sudden is no longer able to be "included" with those friends will be paying a price against the quality of life. We were very fortunate to avoid that scenario. The school got his classmates involved by having them write notes and make posters wishing him well and we posted those in his hospital room, so he would always know how many people out there were rooting for him. The notes from family and adult friends were wonderful too, but there is something special about seeing your classmates take the time to reach out and show that they are thinking about you.

Once Rebecca and I got onboard with the visiting teacher thing, we found our groove and let the process take its course. I never pushed the issue too hard, but Rebecca was able to find a healthy balance between keeping Zachary on course, and allowing him to deal with his treatments and diagnosis. Even though Zachary missed the last three months of kindergarten, he was able to move on to first grade with his peers. Unfortunately, first grade started while we were in northern Florida getting the bone marrow transplant. So we kept up with the homebound teaching program when we could. In 2001, Zachary was still recovering from the transplant, so he wasn't able to return to school until the last month or so of that year. One of the many talents that our local child-life specialist possesses is an expertise in being able to navigate and assist in the child's return to the classroom. Obviously, there are unique considerations that a child in that position will present. Some of those include:

- *Educating the staff regarding health issues.*—Most teachers and staff won't have experience in dealing with a pediatric cancer patient. Watching out for chicken pox, flu, and other communicable diseases so that the family can be forewarned is a very important issue. Making the staff aware of the child's physical and mental limitations is essential. Each and every child will present unique challenges. Zachary was still very weak, and he still had his port. Avoiding sports where a direct impact to the port area was possible was one of the issues that needed to be addressed.

- *Having an IEP in place.*—An Individual Education Plan is essential when a child like Zachary is returning to the normal classroom. This allows everyone, including the county nurse, administrators, teachers, and support staff to have a better understanding of the child's condition and expectations. Allowing for a calculator, or more time on tests are just two examples of issues that can be addressed in an IEP. There should also be a timeline for reevaluation. I believe we had one each year before school started, but if special situations arise, you can request more frequent ones as needed.

- *Reintroduction to the classmates.*—Our child-life specialist would go into the classroom and speak to the children about Zachary's condition and explain to them on a level that they could understand that he was fragile, and that he needed their help in making the process work. Our school required that a note be sent home to inform the parents that someone would be speaking to their children about cancer and specifically about Zachary, but we never had any issues there. Several of his classmates actually took it upon themselves to be his "helpers", making sure that he got work when he was out sick, or helping him in and around the classroom. Being bald, pale, and full of scars can be VERY intimidating to a child, especially in this day and age where image is such a focus of even our young children.

These are just a few of the many issues that will surely arise if you are reading this as a parent whose child is newly diagnosed. If you are reading this from any other perspective (and I hope that you are), then please keep in mind that as a parent, you can make sure that your child is understanding and compassionate when dealing with a classmate facing an illness such as cancer. That may seem like it should go without saying, but just wait until you read the section dealing with middle school.

OK, back to elementary school. Before returning to first grade, Rebecca and I started to notice that Zachary was not hearing us too well. For quite some time, we wrote it off as selective hearing, but before long, it became obvious that he needed to see a specialist. We had an audiology test preformed, and the results showed that he had lost about 50% of his hearing, mainly in the higher ranges. This is a common side effect from some of the more harsh chemotherapies. The damage is irreversible, but hearing aids do help. Unfortunately, they are bulky and make Zachary very self-conscious of kids staring at him. That coupled with his perpetual baldness made life very challenging.

So, those issues aside, Zachary was able to finish up first grade with his classmates, and then he was able to start second grade with them as well. You may recall, (or you may NOT recall, some of you are getting older and tend to forget more easily) that in November of 2001 Zachary had his port removed. That allowed him to participate in more school activities. Sadly, as I mentioned earlier, he relapsed in early 2002, so once again he was yanked out of school and placed back into the hospital homebound program.

He completed second grade and was advanced upward to third grade, but when that started, he was still too sick to attend school. We were able to keep him on track, constantly trying to find that balance of quality of life, and he eventually wanted to return to his classmates in early 2003. At that time, Zachary was receiving the IV Irinotecan on a 5 day cycle, with 16 days off. We were actually having a visiting nurse come to the house to administer the chemo. The doctor's office would access the port on day 1 and give the first treatment, and then we would be able to stay at home for the remainder of the treatments. The catch here was that the port would stay accessed for the entire 5 days. (Monday-Friday.)

Now, just to refresh your (aging) memories, the needle is about ¾" long and is placed inside the receptacle. On the outside of that, there is a plastic piece that has the tubing attached to it. The tubing is about 12" long and can be capped off to allow the patient mobility and "freedom." When the nurse or doctor needs to give medicine, they simply clean the end where the cap is with alcohol, (Not like Johnny Walker Red . . . . medicinal alcohol), and then they attach another tube or IV line that runs to the bag of medicine.

The actual infusion or drip of medicine would only take 30 or 40 minutes. Sometimes there would be the need to give him extra fluids, but overall the process usually didn't take more than an hour. When completed, the nurse would flush his line with saline and then heparin (to keep it from clotting) and then cap it off and tape the excess tubing to his chest so that it wasn't dangling around. (You've gotta believe that I'm telling all of this for a reason that SOMEHOW relates to this chapter right? Well, if you will just bear with me, the payoff is coming.) For those of you wanting to have more of a visual aid in picturing Zachary with his port accessed, just go to his CaringBridge web page, the front photo shows Zachary with his port capped off.

So, now that we have all completed Port-Accessing 101, we can move onto our next lesson which is titled, "Going to War with the County Nurse & Winning." (Hmmm, was that TOO revealing of a hint as to what happened in third grade?)

Before I tell that story, I want to make sure everyone understands that in this wonderful country of ours, federal law mandates that each and every child has a right to an education regardless of physical or mental limitations. (That isn't an exact quote, but I'm guessing that you get the gist of it.) During the IEP meeting that was setup to discuss Zachary's return to school, the focus of the meeting quickly turned to the fact that during the chemo infusion weeks, Zachary would be attending school with his port accessed, and the line capped off and taped to his chest, (under his shirt.) This was NOT some random idea that Rebecca and I had come up with in our spare time.

As parents, ALL decisions that involve the health and welfare of our child were run past Zachary's oncologists. If they didn't sign off on something, we didn't do it! So, going into the meeting, we already had Zachary's oncologist's approval for him to attend school with his port accessed. Our child-life specialist knew this, and was fully prepared to go to battle for us. When the topic came up, the county nurse immediately had issues with that scenario. Her concern was this, (and you REALLY should make sure that you are sitting down while reading this, because it packs quite the wallop), she was worried that while attending school with his port accessed, he might decide to DEACCESS himself, and then chase other kids around with the bloody needle.

Now, let me paint a picture for you. First of all, having a ¾" needle inserted into your chest region is not for the faint of heart. Almost all of the children who we met over the years had developed routines and processes that they made the nurses follow leading up to the needle insertion. This also applied to the REMOVAL of said needle.

While you wouldn't think that there would be pain associated with the pulling out of the needle, it was definitely somewhat traumatizing for many of the kids. So, the concept of Zachary de-accessing himself, and then using the needle to chase other kids with, was bizarre and beyond our comprehension. Putting that aside, I think that I was somewhat put off by the fact that her only concern was the possibility of him negatively affecting other kids, there was NO mention of the risks and issues facing Zachary.

The nurse could see that she was outnumbered, Rebecca, me, the child-life specialist, principal, vice-principal, and guidance counselor were all on the same page when it came to finding a way for Zachary to be with his classmates and back in school. In a weak effort to deflect the blame and stall for time, she "demanded" that the county doctor sign off on Zachary's being allowed to attend while accessed.

Our child-life specialist stepped up to the plate when the nurse brought this up, and she knocked one out of the park for us. Her comment went something like this, "Zachary's pediatric oncologist has ALREADY cleared Zachary to attend school with his port accessed. Now, if the county doctor possesses some higher level of expertise than the oncologist, I would like to hear about his qualifications." Before the nurse could reply, the principal chimed in with this beauty, "Look, the law is very clear on the fact that it is our responsibility to provide an education for Zachary.

His own doctor has cleared him to attend school with his port accessed, so UNTIL I hear from the county doctor where he will go on record saying that his expertise supersedes that of the oncologist, Zachary gets to come back to school!!!" (OH YEAH BABY . . . . . THAT'S WHAT I'M TALKING ABOUT!) I don't remember if the nurse immediately crawled into a hole and disappeared, or if she just wilted right there in her chair, but that settled the issue, it never came up again. And amazingly (not) Zachary never de-accessed himself or chased any kids around with a needle, (hmmm, go figure?)

Zachary "graduated" from third grade without any other major issues, and he was able to begin fourth grade with his classmates. Fourth grade also went on without too many hiccups. This turned out to be his first full year of school (with the exception of sick days of course.) He was still doing the IV Irinotecan, and we found a way to make it work for everyone, (except the county nurse . . . . she doesn't count.)

During Zachary's fifth grade year he had the change from IV chemo to the Fenretinide pill. That made it much easier for him to fit in and feel more like a "normal" child. When it came to graduate from elementary school we knew that it would be an emotional time for us. By then, Zachary was three years out from relapse, which meant that he had lived much longer than the one year maximum that they had given us. That coupled with the fact that we were able to keep him with his classmates made for a tear-jerker of a ceremony. During that graduation, they had announced that they would select one classroom at a time, and read each child's name. The child would then walk across the stage, receive their diploma, and then exit the stage to wait for their classmates. They asked the audience to hold their applause until all of the children from one classroom had gathered off stage.

Well, when it came time for Zachary, I was lucky to have been put on video camera duty. That gave me something to hide behind so that no one could see my tears. (Not that I, as a grown man ever cries, but apparently someone had added cayenne powder or pepper flakes to the ventilation system, and those particles amazingly only made their way into MY eyes, at PRECISELY the moment when Zachary was walking across stage. (Seems almost unbelievable . . . doesn't it?)

Well, when they announced, "Zachary Finestone", the parents, students, and staff gave him a standing ovation. He received his diploma and was trying to exit the stage when one of his favorite teachers grabbed him in a bear hug . . . . it was AT that point that several other members of the audience were affected by the rogue pepper. When you get to the chapter titled "Lifeline", you will know that Zachary's graduation day was VERY high above the survival line!

For us, (and most of the country I think), 6th, 7th & 8th grades are middle school grades. Before we signed Zachary up for middle school, we received a letter from the State of Florida informing us that because Zachary had an IEP in place, he was eligible for a special scholarship that allowed him to attend one of several private schools that were participating in the program.

The State would pick up the cost of attending, and Zachary would get to attend a school where the class sizes were much smaller, and theoretically he would have a better chance of assimilating into the middle school years. One of our concerns with public 6th grade was the large class size, and the fact that Zachary had been very "sheltered" when it came to socialization with his peers. Middle school can be brutal. Kids can be very hard on each other for a variety of reasons. Because of Zachary's baldness and hearing aids from chemo, we knew that he faced some serious challenges. We found a local church based program that was very close to home, and they made room for Zachary.

When we first met with the staff there, we once again brought our child-life expert, and the three of us made it PERFECTLY clear that Zachary needed to be treated like a normal kid. By that time, we had learned some very hard lessons about what happens when you spoil a sick kid. (Do the math in your head. You end up with a kid who is sick . . . . AND SPOILED. Not an ideal mixture.) I remember actually saying to them, "If he screws up, he needs to be punished the same way that you would punish any other child." (In retrospect, I should have picked up on the looks of astonishment that a few of his teachers were shooting at me. It was almost as if they were thinking, "What kind of monster would EVER punish a sick child?" (Great thinking . . . . while we're at it, let's give him an Uzi and couple of spare magazines full of ammo, that way whenever he doesn't like the way things are going, he can just mow down everyone that he's angry with.) We left that meeting somewhat comfortable with the situation. The director assured us that Zachary would be treated like the other kids and that no special accommodations would be made. (Yeah right.)

About one month into that school year, we were made aware of the fact that he was not being made to keep the same academic standards as the other children. I don't recall exactly what tipped us off; it may have been a lack of homework. Either way, I remember asking him what was going on during class, and he couldn't tell us. When we pushed further, he said that he would sit quietly and read his Harry Potter book while the other kids were working with the teacher. We FLEW to the school . . . . I mean, I don't think we could have gotten there any quicker if we had owned a teleportation machine. We expressed our concern to the Director, and she brought the teacher in for a consult with us.

The teacher, bless his heart, told us, "I know that Zachary is reading his book during class, I just didn't want to upset him, so I let him do his own thing." (Great . . . . . you're only mistake was forgetting to issue him the Uzi, so he could interfere with EVERYONE'S education.) That meeting produced one of the "deep breath" moments where you make sure that the next words out of your mouth don't land you in jail, or worse, eternal damnation. (It was a church school after all.) After re-educating the educators, we eventually got Zachary back on track. The problem was, they had opened the door for Zachary to see that he could easily manipulate them with very little effort. (At almost 12 years of age, manipulation is a tool that is NEVER too far from your arsenal.)

Zachary finished the 6th grade and was able to complete the necessary work to advance to the 7th grade. By that time, we had already made the decision that it was time for him to rejoin his classmates. And, the issue became moot when the church school had an uprising and it was announced that it would no longer exist after graduation. When we met with the middle school, we were very fortunate to have Zachary's case assigned to a very caring and understanding woman who watched over the children with special needs.

From the beginning, she made it clear that they wanted to help Zachary get back into public school with the least amount of friction or problems possible. Everything from his hearing aids, to his class schedule was addressed with her, and we always felt that she was looking out for Zachary's best interests. When it came time for the IEP meeting, Zachary's guardian angel made sure that not only did the administrators and teachers attend, but that the cafeteria and support staff was there as well. They even went as far to include a teacher from the 6th grade who was recovering from cancer himself; so that Zachary would have someone to speak with and relate to if he felt the need.

By early on in 7th grade, Zachary was feeling well enough to try out for the school soccer team. He had played when he was younger and wanted to be a part of the team. There were many children who showed up for the tryouts, some of whom Zachary had played soccer with in previous years during leagues. One of the steps to joining the team included writing an essay as to why the student felt that he/she should be accepted on the team.

Zachary wrote a very moving essay about his condition and how he would give 100% of his efforts to help the team. Apparently the coach was moved by this, because Zachary made the team. Because of his lack of stamina, he didn't get a whole lot of playing time, but he DID score a goal for the team during one of their matches, and curiously, a swarm of microscopic insects flew into my eyes and made them water when I saw him score and begin to celebrate.

Near the end of the season, he started to have some issues with bullies at the school. Apparently there is no shortage of moronic behavior at the middle school level, because a group of 3 or 4 boys started to torment Zachary about his illness. They were making comments like, "Ooh, don't touch Zachary, his cancer will rub off on you and then you'll get sick." and "My grandfather had cancer, it will kill you." Or my personal favorite, "Why don't you just get into your coffin now, you know you are going to die anyway?" After passing this information along to the administration, these boys were taken aside and reprimanded. It was made very clear to them that comments like those would

NOT be tolerated and that any future problems could result in suspensions. Thankfully, it didn't happen again.

7th grade ended and 8th grade began. But in the middle of that, we had switched chemos and had been dealing with all of the pain issues. Because of that, we decided to place Zachary on a half day schedule. We enrolled him in an online reading/writing class and left the rest of his courses to be taken at the middle school. But, within the first 70 days of school, Zachary had missed 35 due to illness or doctor appointments.

The teachers were being very helpful in their efforts to get us his schoolwork, but Zachary was missing out on that interaction with the instructor. We spoke with our contact at the school, and we agreed that the best course of action was to place Zachary back into the hospital homebound program. That way, he would STILL be getting the same schoolwork from the teachers, but he would ALSO be getting that one-on-one time with the instructor.

As luck would have it, the teacher who had helped us before during elementary school offered to return as his homebound instructor. She always was helpful in adjusting to our schedule. So, from late 2007 until present Zachary has been working at his own pace with the online class, and he has been trying to keep up with the other courses with the help of our homebound teacher. Zachary's goal is to graduate in May with his peers so that he can possibly attend high school with them in the fall.

[FLASHBACK]

Thursday, May 8, 2003 7:01 PM CDT

Once again I find myself impressed with the Zman!

We got back the results from the FCAT today. (For those of you who don't live in Florida, our esteemed politicians passed legislation that requires all third graders to achieve at least a level 2 out of 5 in both reading and math to graduate to the fourth grade.)

Zachary got a 3 in both areas! He scored above the national average in both areas as well! This all from a boy who has spent one week out of every three getting chemotherapy since school started. When we were home, he wasn't always able to meet with his homebound teacher. Sometimes our schedules didn't match up, and sometimes she was sick and didn't want to risk exposing Zachary to any bugs. The bottom line here is, Rebecca and Zachary worked hard for this, and they deserve the credit.

I will be praying extra hard (if that is possible) for the Potion X to rid my son of cancer. It would be surreal for me to be sending him off to the fourth grade in August.

No matter what happens, I am proud of the way he has worked to achieve this goal. Zachary's good friend Mitchell from Boynton Beach also passed his FCAT. He has been on homebound schooling while being treated for leukemia. These kids are amazing!

I keep thinking back to all of the wonderful experiences that we have been able to provide for Zachary while he has endured the constant medical testing and treatments. I know I've said it before, but we've been trying to provide the best quality of life while trying to keep him grounded in the fundamentals of being a nine-year old. We also have been trying to keep the trips, hockey games and special events in his life to balance out the hardships that he has endured.

Just when I thought I had Zachary all figured out, he surprises me again. What a great son!

Thursday, September 4, 2003 7:52 AM CDT

Week #2 of chemotherapy during the school year is proving to be more challenging than the previous one. Zachary is definitely feeling the effects more, and he is experiencing fatigue that is seriously affecting his demeanor. I guess we could take one of two roads at this point. Seeing as it is only the second week of this routine, we could push him a little harder and see if over time he adjusts to the schedule. Or, we could make the adjustment now and let him go onto dual enrollment. That would allow him to attend his regular class during the two weeks that he is off of chemo, and then he would be doing homebound schooling during the chemo weeks. The reason we had tried to avoid that setup is that our county only provides 2 hours of homebound education each week. We are very lucky that Zachary's teachers are extremely committed to helping him get through all of this. Rebecca is going to speak with them today to see if we can make the homebound system work without having Zachary fall behind the rest of his class to a point where he would not be able to catch up. (I don't know what I'd do with myself if everything just worked out smoothly for once . . . . I guess it would make for boring journal entries.)

I'm sure it will work out. Now onto bigger and better things . . . .

I was out shopping the other night when I ran into an old friend who was with someone I had never met. The friend asked how Zachary was doing, so I gave them a quick update that included the obvious comment, "He is still doing chemotherapy one week out of every three." Well, the friend of the friend asked a question at that point that caught me off guard. He said, "Why is he getting chemotherapy?" Well, hmmmmmm. I guess the obvious answer would have been, "He has cancer." But you guys know me. I used the 1.87352 seconds that followed their question to figure out all of the OTHER reasons you might give your child chemotherapy. So, in the spirit of our Cancer Christmas Songs that we all worked on last December, it is now time to come up with . . . . (drum roll please)

TOP REASONS YOU'D GIVE YOUR CHILD CHEMO . . . . OTHER THAN FOR TREATING CANCER.

Now, I know how shy some of you can be, so I've decided to get the ball rolling with some of the thoughts that popped into my mind during those precious 1.87352 seconds that I was given . . . . and here they are:

1). *Our son has a bizarre aversion to barber shops and scissors . . . . the chemo allows us to remove his hair without subjecting him to those tortures.*
2). *Our country is smack dab in the middle of an epidemic of overweight children. What better way to control their weight than to administer chemo once in awhile, thus insuring that diarrhea and vomiting will ensue to help shed those unwanted pounds?*
3). *Kids these days have WAY too much energy. Getting them to go to sleep on time can be a major battle. Chemo gives you the bonus effect of sucking the energy right out of your child, thus allowing you to get them to bed on time.*
4). *We live in a materialistic society. Way too many people are putting too much of an emphasis on income and possessions. Chemo treatments are an easy way to help keep your finances at rock bottom. Between co-pays and unexpected expenses from surprise hospital visits, you won't have ANY extra cash lying around to spend on frivolous items like food, clothing and home repairs.*

Ok, that should be enough. Now it's your turn. Let's see some creative new reasons why we give our children chemotherapy. I'm not promising a prize for the best ones, but you never know.

Monday, March 29, 2004 9:07 PM CST

The weekend is over and another week has begun. Yesterday we had a wonderful day. Our good friend Jeff got married in WPB and we were there to join in the festivities. It was absolutely a wonderful day for a wedding. Sunny, clear blue skies

*and nice light breeze. Afterwards we took Zachary over to his friend Matthew's
house so they could play together. We ended up having dinner with them and
getting home late.*

*Today has proven to be a bit more of an adventure compared with the relative
calm of the weekend. Let's see if we can bring you all up to date . . . .*

*FIRST, Zachary made it to school on time this morning . . . just slightly
over-tired from yesterdays hard playing . . . . SECOND, Zachary's teacher
approached Rebecca about 1 or 2 hours into the school day to inform her that one
of the other children in Zachary's class was at the nurses office with what looked
like FIFTH's disease. THIRD, Rebecca contacted the oncologist's office to get
their opinion, FOURTH, they said Zachary needed an infusion of immunogoblin
or is it immunoghost, or maybe ammogunpowder, or immunoglobulin . . . .
something like that . . . . anyway . . . . where was I? . . . . FOURTH, FIFTH,
SIXTH . . . . ????? I don't remember . . . . well . . . . he gets to the doctor's
office, gets his port accessed and heads over the hospital . . . . and who does
he find there? His friend Mitchell! Mitchell is there getting his port removed
(Thank you Lord) and Cam is there getting his put in . . . (Lord . . . . you try
our patience sometimes.) So naturally Zachary didn't want his friends stealing
all of the limelight today, so he gets exposed to some numbered illness. (Why
FIFTH's disease? Are FIRST through FOURTH already taken?) So, it takes
until 4pm for them to start the 6 hour infusion of this medicine. About 30 minutes
into the infusion, Rebecca finds a voice message on her phone from the school
nurse informing her that the boy with THREE HUNDRED EIGHTY SECOND'S
disease came BACK to school with a note from the doctor saying he doesn't
have that illness (Fifth's) at all. Hmmmmmm Very curious going's on . . . . Well,
before yanking the plug on Zachary's infusion and ruining his day by stopping
a wonderfully fun 6 hour treatment, I make my way home and find a different
message from the nurse informing us that she and another teacher are convinced
that the boy did indeed have the illness, and that not only does another child
in the school have it, but some other kids in our district have been diagnosed
with it as well. At this point, we're thinking we'll keep the IV running and hope
for the best. About 3 hours later, I finally get a chance to speak with Zachary's
teacher, and she informs me that at lunch today the staff was talking about the
MANY kids with strep throat, the kindergarten kids with chicken pox, and the
EIGHT THOUSAND SIX HUNDRED TWENTY THIRD disease that is going
around as well. Her recommendation is that we keep Zachary out of school the
rest of the week. (Next week is spring break and chemo anyway.) She promised
to have his school work ready for us tomorrow afternoon . . . . so he should be
fine with keeping up. Now all we have to do is prevent him from catching any
of these numbered and unnumbered illnesses. In other words . . . . "First and*

foremost our Second priority during the Third and Fourth weeks of the month will always be to avoid Fifth's disease at all costs."

[Finishing another journal entry is like being in SEVENTH heaven.]

Wednesday, May 5, 2004 9:37 PM CDT

No news yet on our medical drama with the new medicine. We are also still waiting for definitive news from California about our bone marrow results. (I don't want to get too far into it right now, but there IS a war brewing in my head with the doctors and support staff. I WILL devote some time in the near future to changing the way they communicate with families about the results for their children. The current system is unacceptable and I WILL be taking up this battle.)

About a month ago when Zachary missed three straight weeks of school, his class was given an assignment to write a story. They evidently worked on it over several days with guidance from the teacher. Zachary wasn't able to start his until about a week and a half ago. He had to finish it in time to be turned in with his classmate's stories. Zachary chose to write about cancer. The following text is his story in its entirety. His words. His thoughts. Please keep in mind that he has "remembered" events in his own way. The timeline may not be accurate, and some of the names and events have been "lost" in his recollection of the past four years. Here is his story.

WHY I HATE CANCER!

An original story by Zachary Finestone

Hey, my name is Zachary and I want to tell you my last four years fighting cancer. It all started when I was playing t-ball and my back hurt. The doctors said I must of pulled a muscle and just to take pain medicine for the pain. But obviously that didn't work. After that I decided that I hate the doctors. Then we went to get an MRI. Then I started getting low fevers. After about two months of that they said "That's it! We know what's bothering Zack he has a tumor called neuroblastoma." He also said that it is very rare and dangerous at this rate he may not make it. After that scare they said to take me to a hospital. That was so bad. It was a "D" .... which means dreadful!

About five months later I had my first friend, Robert. He likes fishing and playing cards. A week after that I had my first painful bone marrow, since then I hate them. *Especially when the nurses have to watch . . . . I'm surprised that they don't freak out. As always I hate bone marrows . . . . except the milk of amnesia, that stuff is so coooooooooooooool! After about a month we met a new kid named Mitchell. He is cool. He plays everything I play. Back then I was boring. When I first met Mitchell he had pneumonia and low counts. Plus fevers. And diarrhea. That mixed together makes him really sick.*

When I relapsed which means (the disease came back) I missed a lot of school. I also hated that. And they stuck me with so many needles in my port, my arm, my hand, and my legs. After weeks of nausea and vomiting I was just about to hurt somebody. And also my hair was falling out. That stunk. My hair was falling out because of all of the chemo the nurses and doctors were giving me while I was staying at the hospital. The ride to the hospital was a long one and I almost always got sick in the car. Another bad thing about the hospital is the pillows are flat and the nurses don't let you sleep all night. My room was always cold and I never liked the food there.

Since I was at the hospital so much, I had to leave me soccer team. They lost their best player . . . . ME! Not only did the chemo make my hair fall out but it gives me mouth sores. Mouth sores are VERY PAINFUL. They hurt when I eat and drink. When I get them the doctors give me magic mouthwash. It would numb the sores so that I could eat and drink. Sometimes it would not work and the doctors would give me morphine. The morphine would make me have bad dreams. It also made me grumpy. That would get me in trouble with my mom and dad every time. But when I was not being grumpy I was asleep. I would sleep during the day because of low blood counts. I sometimes sleep a lot during chemo.

But what makes me angry about cancer is . . . . when I lose a friend or a family member. I have lost many people I know to cancer. I will name a few for you. Robert, Jalen, Seth, Maya, Jake, and grandpa Dan. It is a mean disease. I wish cancer was not real. I don't think it is fair that kids get cancer and can die. I hope that I don't join them in heaven. I wrote this book to tell you why I hate cancer.

This is about why I hate cancer!

About the Author: Zachary Finestone is a 10 year old cancer survivor who lives in Jensen Beach with his parents. Zachary continues to fight his cancer to this day. To read more about Zachary's adventures go to his web page at www.caringbridge. org/fl/zacharyfinestone.

The end.

I know there are run-on sentences and mistakes . . . . but I can't imagine a story from him being any more "from the heart." There are many pictures in the book. The cover shows a needle with a big line through it . . . . (like a no smoking sign.) The first picture inside shows him holding his back saying, "My back hurts still." The second drawing shows two boys kicking a ball back and forth. Underneath it says, "That is me on the left." The third picture is of the bed and pillow. It says, "Nooooooo. Not the bed!" The fourth drawing shows Rebecca and me looking down at him and his arms are up in the air as if to say, "What did I do now?" The last drawing is of a tombstone that has "R.I.P." written on it.

Scott

P.S. Yes. I did buy shares of Kleenex before posting his story.

P.S.S. When he got his story back from his teacher, there was a post-it note attached that read: "You are the most amazing student I have ever met! 100"

Chapter 9

The Lifeline

"Your one-stop shop for learning what it is like to live in our world."

Being the parent of a child with cancer affords me certain philosophical freedoms when trying to relay to people what it is like to walk in our shoes. Over the years I have been interviewed many times for a variety of stories in the news. Everything from Zachary's diagnosis, to hospital dramas and charities that we have been involved with has been included as subject matter. Invariably, the question of what our life is like comes up.

It is very hard to describe in words to people what this existence is REALLY like. Many years ago I came up with a visual tool that I felt helped me explain to people what we are feeling. I used that tool in more than one interview, and I have been told that it does a pretty good job of conveying our mindset. I call it the "lifeline." (See Figure #1) The concept works like this. For "normal" families living "normal" lives, you exist on a daily/weekly/monthly/yearly basis above or below your lifeline. You will notice in the figure #1 that the lifeline splits the page pretty evenly.

In my opinion, everything good that happens to us occurs above that line, and conversely, everything bad that happens in our lives takes us below that line. All else being equal, our lives are lived somewhere in the middle. I have given several examples of life events that we all (most of us anyway) have experienced, and I have shown where they fall (relatively speaking) in relation to that core lifeline.

Figure #1

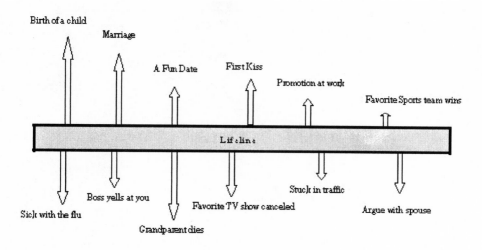

As you can see, it is a pretty easy concept. You may not rank the events the way that they are shown here, but the idea is that the degree to which an event affects your life, will determine how high above or far below that core lifeline they occur. Now, this is where the whole cancer thing comes into play. Obviously, the "event" of having your child diagnosed will occur WAY down below that life line. (I would hope that it would be fairly obvious that having a child diagnosed with cancer would be perceived as a "bad" event, but you never know who's reading your book, so you've got to keep things as simple as possible.) Now let's take a look at Figure #2 shown below.

Figure #2

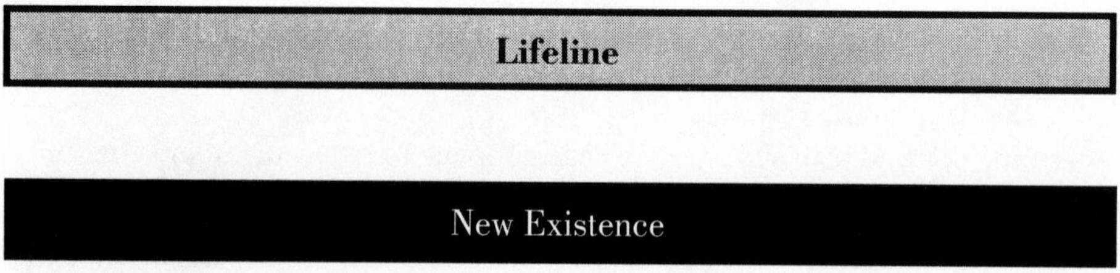

Lifeline

New Existence

You will notice a couple of things in this new diagram. For one, I have removed the life events. I did this so that we could focus only on the OTHER change that I made, which is adding a new lifeline which is shown with a black background.

My theory is this, when you have a child diagnosed with a life-threatening illness like cancer, your daily existence or lifeline changes. You no longer are able to function at that same middle ground that you've always been able to. Now, you are somewhere BELOW that line, trying to make it through life, one day at a time. The interesting (at least to me it was) part to this theory is that you can still have moments and events that will bring you up above your lifeline.

The problem is this, your base lifeline is now lower than that of someone NOT in this situation, those good events or life experiences that before were elevating you to "highs," are now quite often just bringing you to a level of "normalcy." Don't get me wrong, there are still genuine occasions where you make it above the original line, but there is NO escaping this diagnosis. There is no hiding from the hidden truth that lurks in the shadows of your mind and swirls through your consciousness always waiting for an opportune moment to yank you back into reality.

Some of you may interpret this as a sad commentary on me not being able to truly enjoy "the moment," (whatever the particular "moment" is.) That is not the case. There are many wonderful experiences and life events that we get to enjoy that lift our spirits and bring us happiness. The one intangible here is the underlying prognosis and uncertainty.

We have had many friends who we met through cancer whose children were able to complete their treatments, rid themselves of the cancer, obtain the label "NED" and move on with their lives. But if you were to call them today, (and some of them are several years into remission), they will all tell you that there is never a cough, ache, pain, or other anomaly with their child that doesn't have them losing sleep over the chance that this monster has returned.

With us, the monster never leaves. So every family reunion, birthday, holiday, celebration, etc., while enjoyed by all (including us of course), is also looked at as possibly being our last. Once again, many of you may view that as us being morbid or "glass half empty" kind of folks. I don't see it that way. For those of you who know us personally, you have seen us living life to its fullest and trying to make the most of an impossible situation.

So that is the lifeline and the theory that accompanies it. I hope that the visual aid has in some way brought you closer to appreciating what our life is like.

[FLASHBACK]

Thursday, August 22, 2002 at 05:06 PM (CDT)

Rumor has it that we've got an ANC of 60! For those of you that slept through my "Beginners Course to Blood Counts" several days ago . . . . shame on you! But, having an ANC above zero is a start. Anything over 500 means that Zman

has a fighting chance to fend off nasty bugs, and when it goes over 1500 . . . .
we generally party in the streets!

Zachary has not had a fever for 24 hours now, so if this trend continues, tomorrow
he will be allowed out of his room. [LOCK UP YOUR DAUGHTERS . . . . ZMAN
WILL BE PROWLING THE HALLS]

Today we had an adventure! Zachary was getting platelets (blood products for
you flunkies), and about halfway through the infusion, he threw up . . . I got
nervous, because he hasn't gotten sick since we arrived on Sunday, so I immediately
beeped the nurse. She arrived quickly after hearing the tension in my voice over
the speaker system, and together we noticed that he was breaking out in hives.
(Blood reaction). A lot of the kids get these, and after the first occurrence the nurses
have to pre-treat the kids with Benadryl before giving them blood products. Zman
has never had a reaction to a blood product before. The nurse immediately gave
him a whopping dose of Benadryl and a steroid. Within 5 minutes he was out
cold, and within 20 minutes the hives were gone. I'm glad his breathing wasn't
affected; the nurse had some epinephrine on hand though just in case. She never
felt that he was in danger, but it was very unnerving to see these bumps popping
up all over his neck, cheeks, chest, arm pits, sides, chin . . . etc. All in all, my
recommendation for everyone is; A). Don't get cancer. B). If you get cancer, get rid
of it quickly. C). If you can't get rid of it quickly, take your time, but don't have
complications while treating it. D). If you're going to have complications, you're
obviously a difficult person to deal with, so you'll be ignoring this sage advice
anyway! BUT, try not to have adverse reactions to drugs and blood products; it
just messes up everyone's day. (Like he had a choice.)

The good news is that he slept for 3 hours from the Benadryl, only waking up
once to relieve himself of the 3.5 gallons of pee that he had accumulated while
resting. (I think I'll take up juggling urinals as a hobby after we get out, I'm
getting quite adept at it.)

If the ANC trend continues, we might get out over the weekend or early next week,
I'll keep everyone informed.

Wednesday, August 28, 2002 at 07:07 PM (CDT)

Ok, close your eyes . . . . not literally you goof ball . . . you won't be able to read this. I
just want you to get a clear mental picture of what Zman treated me to this evening.

It all started with a long, long day on the road . . . . I know, I know, violins are playing everywhere for me. Ok, so I'll fast forward to after dinner. I'm lying on my bed, trying to relax. I KNOW Zman had a good day, because I've got a cell phone, so I get updates whenever I need my Zman fix! So, back to the relaxing on the bed. I'm zoning out . . . . sort of watching TV . . . there was some special on neuroblastoma on the Discovery channel, (we haven't lived the nightmare enough; we've got to torture ourselves with as much misery as possible . . . . just to keep our tear ducts flowing.) Anyway, where was I? Oh yeah, I'm lying on the bed, and I hear this little voice from the other room . . . .

. . . . It's Zman, he comes running into our room, all proud of something . . . . walks up to the bed and throws a wad of folded up toiled paper onto the comforter that I'm lying on and says, "Look inside, but don't REACH inside." So, I'm figuring he's killed a bug or spider or something. He knows I hate spiders. (I realize that this chink in my armor is a great disappointment to all of my fans out there, but yes, spiders and bees are my kryptonite.)

Anyway, I open this toilet paper expecting to find a bug, and what do I find, staring back at me??????????? A big blood stain!!!!!!!!!!!!!!!!!!!!!!!!! The problem with this stain was, there was NO BUG INSIDE!

Zman, being the careful cancer patient that he is, had checked the paper after wiping his behind . . . . he saw the blood, and being the platelet-conscience lad that he is, figured he would parade the results onto my bed. Now, I know my immediate parental response SHOULD have been to show concern for the possibility that his platelets might be a tad low, but I've got to be honest with all of you. All I could think was . . . GET THAT USED BLOODY BUTT WIPED TOILET PAPER OFF OF MY BED!

I realize that my image of being a sensitive caring father has just been thrown out of a window, landed in a mud puddle, run over by a car, and then lit on fire and burned beyond recognition . . . . but COME ON . . . . USED TOILET PAPER . . . PLEEEEEEEEEEEEEEAAAAAAAAAAAAAAAAAAAAAAAASSSSSSSS SSEEEEEE!.

Of course, once I regained my senses, I donned gloves and examined his behind . . . . resisting the urge to smack him for his efforts. I believe it was an anomaly . . . . he has no petechiae, and we recheck counts tomorrow morning, so I'm sure he's alright . . . . I however, may be scarred for life.

Thursday, November 21, 2002 at 06:23 PM (CST)

Robert's funeral was today.

Mitchell had a scare this week with his counts.

Cameron has been at Duke for transplant over 4 months now.

Ty-Michael has had numerous scares with relapse this year.

Ryan is still battling GVHD.

Jessica just started the long road of maintenance.

Genna finished chemo and is now doing therapy.

Zachary starts chemo again on Monday.

The list is endless.

CANCER SUCKS!!!!!!!

Sunday, March 23, 2003 8:22 PM CST

As if there were ever any doubt, Zachary won the hula hoop contest with a runaway performance. For those of you who have never seen him do the hula hoop, I can only say that clearly, he is a freak of nature. There is no logical explanation why any human being should be able to do the hula hoop with such ease. I consider myself a fairly athletic individual who possesses better than average coordination, but somehow, I cannot get a stupid plastic ring with a 3' diameter to go around my hips any more than 3 or 4 times. And, to add insult to injury, the ONLY reason that I successfully get the 3 or 4 rotations, is because of the force I use to start the ring moving! Zachary can make that hoop go around his waist for an eternity without expelling any more energy than I use to blink, yet when I try to hula hoop, I come dangerously close to dislocating my back. Not to mention the sweat and the abnormally high heart rate that I immediately incur.

The ONLY explanation for all of this that makes any sense is that Zachary was placed here on this planet by aliens to torment us with his freakish skills. I can live with this assessment, mainly because the alternative is accepting that a 9 year old somehow possesses a skill that has eluded me for 40 years.

The dance-a-thon at FAU was a blast. We met some new families, some new dancers, and had a great time. There was line dancing, games, food, and a great group of people who came together to raise money for the Children's Miracle Network. They raised over $8,000.00 this year! Five families showed up this year, a record! All of us shared our stories with the dancers so they could better appreciate how their efforts affect the lives of children and families in need. I actually made it through our story without coming close to tears. I may have found a new tactic for my speeches. I focus in my mind on how much we have to be thankful for, instead of focusing on the horrible details of what Zachary has been through. I even worked it into my speech. I told the dancers that it may sound odd for a parent of a child with a non-curable cancer to say they are "thankful." But, I explained that we have been blessed with an entire extra year that many doctors had told us we would never get. We are also blessed to be able to do this current chemotherapy on an outpatient basis. Zachary gets to sleep at the Quantum House with us, and we get to visit friends, see movies, and have lots of quality time away from the doctors and hospital while we are down in WPB. All in all, I believe that it went well. I don't know if it is a good thing, or a sad thing, that I can now tell this story without breaking down into a blubbering mess.

Sunday, June 15, 2003 1:12 PM CDT

Thank you for all of the Father's Day wishes and Happy Father's Day to all of the dads out there in the land of computers.

Sometimes I get the idea that my wonderful son spends at least 2 or 3 hours each day thinking of things he can do that will feed my creative process and prompt me to write about his exploits. Yesterday was once again one of those days. The phone rang at around 2pm. I looked at the caller ID and had a panic attack, it was Boggy Creek! During those first 2 seconds as I reached for the phone, a wide range of horrible scenarios raced through my mind. As I was lifting the receiver up to my ear I was going through the various things that could have gone wrong with Zman at camp. The girl on the other end of the line was Zachary's team leader. (They divide the camp into 4 or 5 cabin groups that do many team activities during the week.) The first thing she did was to calm my nerves by saying that Zachary is having a wonderful time at camp. Then she said that she had two questions for me.

What could those questions be? Obviously something of extreme importance for them to call us . . . . right? It must be one of the following:

1). What is Zachary's blood type? He needs a transfusion.

2). *Is Zachary allergic to antibiotics? He got bitten by a snake, a dog, a horse, a chicken, a cat, a squirrel, and a scorpion.*
3). *When Zachary wonders off into the woods alone, how long before he finds his way home?*
4). *Zachary was smoking cigarettes behind the cabins with the counselors and set the building on fire, do you have insurance to cover that kind of expense?*

Surely one of these scary situations or something similar to them should have prompted the call! NOT.

What did they need to know?

#1. The camp director wanted to confirm that we were picking Zachary up on Tuesday morning and that he was NOT riding the bus back. (This was indicated on the pre-camp forms so they should have known this, but I confirmed it for her anyway.) #2. Apparently Zachary has been bothered by some faint memory from his childhood. He remembers being in a store parking lot and "someone" hitting him with a shopping cart and then not apologizing to him. (At this point I got very quiet. What do you say to a statement like that? Rebecca and I had no recollection of anything CLOSE to that happening EVER! And why would he all of a sudden in the middle of camp think or be bothered by a thought like that?) I told her NO. We never hit him with a shopping cart. And if we had, we would have apologized. I also told her to inform the Zman that when we left camp Tuesday morning, we were driving straight to the nearest store so I could RUN HIM OVER WITH A SHOPPING CART! She giggled and informed me that she could NEVER say that to him. I tried to convince her that he understands my sense of humor, but she wasn't buying any of that. Oh well. It will have to be a surprise!

Sunday, June 29, 2003 10:11 PM CDT

NEW PHOTOS IN THE ALBUM

[IF YOU ARE LOOKING FOR TEST RESULTS, PLEASE SEE THE JOURNAL ENTRY FROM 6/27; IT HAS ALL OF THE INFORMATION THAT YOU SEEK]

Zachary started chemotherapy again today. We were up on the temporary floor at our local hospital. Our room left several things to be desired. The window was cracked severely, the A/C was NOT working, and there were ants all over the floor. The nurses quickly moved us to another room. All in all, the floor is not a total disaster. If it is truly a temporary home while we wait for new digs, then we will deal with it. We are home tonight, and Rebecca and Zachary will commute for the next four days to the doctor's office to get his chemo. Hopefully this will work out ok. He has already ripped the protective cover that surrounds his port and needle. I had to add another one to prevent germs from getting to the needle or his accessed port. (This is exactly the kind of thing that I was worried about when we first discussed coming home. If we were at Quantum House, we could have been up on the floor in a matter of minutes. The nurses would probably do the same thing I did.)

After chemotherapy today we went out to dinner with many of our Cancer Sucks Club friends. The dinner sort of evolved quickly over the past day and a half, so if anyone from the Palm Beach area is reading this and feeling left out . . . . it was NOT intentional. We had spoken with Kathy Charlton about "doing" dinner after chemo, and then Diane and Bo Mathis had asked if we could get together . . . . so we talked about all of us eating somewhere . . . . then I started to try and think of a place where we could eat and talk as a group, and I remembered that Matthew Charlton's birthday party was at this nice little Italian place that had a semi-private room . . . . one thing led to another and 24 hours later we were having dinner with Kathy and her three, Jessica, Christina, Matthew and Jordan (Christina's friend), Ed & Kathy with their two, Kyle and Colette, Bo & Diane with their two, Mitchell and Kaleigh, Ed and Laurie with their two, Amanda and Sydney, Tricia with Jessica, and then Genna came with the Mathis's and Kathy C's mom Barbara joined us as well. Oh, my gang was there too of course. (I seriously hope I didn't forget to mention anyone.) Anyway, it was a very nice evening. The restaurant was very good to us, and we had the room for as long as we wanted it. The kids all sat together and had fun and the parents were able to talk and relax for a few hours. I had run out earlier in the afternoon and gone to Publix to get a sheet cake. I had them write "Cancer Sucks Club" on it. We never got around to reading any minutes or voting on anything, but it was comforting to be with these people for an evening. I wish we could do that more often and I wish we could get more families involved. I believe it was good for everyone!

LESSON OF THE DAY:

Before I give my wisdom of the day, it is necessary to give some background information. Zachary loves to bowl. This is nothing new to anyone who knows him. He has gone bowling many times with his friends. Whenever one of the kids gets left with a 7-10 split, (or an equally impossible split,) I usually make a loud promise to pay them $500.00 if they somehow manage to make it. This has worked out to be a very safe bet for me in the past. That is, up until yesterday. Zachary bowls in a league on Saturdays. He has missed three weeks in a row because of *camp and traveling. The bowling alley is nice enough to allow the children to make up their "lost" weeks at their leisure, so we took Zachary yesterday morning to bowl six games so he could make up for three weeks of league play. (They bowl two games each week in league.) Well, in his last game he had a frame where his first ball knocked down seven pins, leaving a nasty 5-7-10 split. This is basically the 7-10 split (the hardest to make) with an extra pin off on the 7-pin side but just far enough away that a really good ball would need to be thrown to pick up those two pins. As far as the 10-pin, well, it would take an utterly amazing shot to make that as well. He needed to just barely nick the left side of the 5-pin so it could slide over all the way across and catch the 10-pin, while at the same time hoping that the impact from the 5 pin would send the ball far enough left to catch the 7 pin. Me and my arrogant big mouth blurted out, "$100.00 bucks if you make them all." Zachary is used to hearing these kinds of comments, so it didn't really rattle him. I followed that comment up with, "Seriously though, you should aim for the two pins that are on the left side, you might be able to at least get both of them." (Thinking that it would require a perfect shot, and that the 10-pin was completely out of the question.) Zachary stepped up to the line and everything slowed down like in the Matrix. As soon as the ball left his hand, I saw my wallet flash before my eyes . . . . the ball had barely touched the ground and I knew I was in trouble. Sure enough, the ball went straight to where it needed to go . . . . it kissed the 5-pin on the left side, sending it sliding off to tackle the 10-pin, and got just enough of a bump to pick up the 7-pin. So, now you know what that scream was on Saturday at around 10:12am . . . . Zachary jumping for joy.*

The moral of the story is, don't write checks your bank can't cash! I've opted for the monthly installment plan.

Sunday, September 28, 2003 8:15 PM CDT

The weekend has come to an end. Zachary is feeling good now that another round of chemo is over. Today was the Connor Moran Children's Cancer Foundation's annual Rapids Water Park outing. It was supposed to rain all day, but it turned out to be a perfect day for going to the water park. Zachary had a blast. We went on just about every ride they have there. Looking back over the day, I would have to say that the one ride that I could have lived without was the new ride that we took a chance on. It is basically a very short steep tight tube that gets you up to about 387 mph before shooting you into a toilet bowl shaped bowl that you zoom around and around in until you lose speed and "drain" out of the bottom like a turd in a toilet. You then drop into a 6.6' deep pool where you try to regain your senses before swimming to the edge. The tube part was so fast, I think that I actually traveled through time and briefly saw my future. (Oddly enough there was no repeat of that ride in MY future.) Once you shoot out of the tube, the dizzying effect is so overwhelming that you can't see straight. By the time you regain some of your senses, you are dropped (usually upside down) through the drain. This is the kind of ride that should have a tattoo kiosk at the exit, so you could give yourself permanent bragging rights by tattooing on your arm or chest that you survived it.

Yesterday Zachary and I had another one of those fun conversations that start off with him informing me that he is interested in stopping chemotherapy for a couple of months. I usually don't like to play along when he starts that game, but I decided to give him some extra rope to see just how far he would hang himself. Once he made the statement, I was forced to respond with the obvious question . . . . "What happens if we stop the chemo and the Potion X is unable to stop the cancer?" His immediate response was, "I die of course." (The beauty of these conversations is you can usually lead a nine-year old down the road that YOU want to travel. It's like an attorney; you never ask a question that you don't already know the answer to.) My next question (which I knew he would answer incorrectly) was, "Well, if that happened, who do you think would be affected by your death?" He responded with, "No one. I can't think of anyone." (Buzzzzzzzzzzzz wrong answer.) This is what I said. "Zachary, the decision that you are talking about making is an adult decision. Mommy and I have always tried to include you in these types of decisions. From now on, you will NOT be included." (This got me an immediate response.) "Why dad? Why not?" "Well", I said, "I asked you an easy question. You should be able to name hundreds of people who you KNOW care about you and would miss you if you died. But you chose to give me an answer that is NOT an adult answer, so you are showing me that you really DON'T want to have adult conversations." (He didn't like that. He said he was only kidding when he couldn't name anyone. But the bottom line was I got him to rethink his position.)

This is a dangerous game. You really don't want to instill a sense of guilt surrounding the whole death thing. Especially when that is the road that the doctors are promising you will eventually travel. On the other hand, you don't want to allow a child to disassociate themselves from loved ones and friends. That would only make it easier to give up. (I love walking the balance beam on these issues. It really makes life interesting when you get to have these discussions with your child.) NOT NOT NOT

Anyway, I think we've temporarily past that hurdle. In the meantime, we've made some inquiries into the possibility of doing Zachary's chemo up here near home. He would still have to travel to WPB for Day #1 to get counts done, get accessed, and get his first round. But after that we would be doing the remaining four days up here. It isn't finalized yet, but we're working on it. We're thinking it will give him more quality time up here, with less travel time to the doctor's office. I'll keep you posted.

Monday, November 24, 2003 8:55 PM CST

As founder and President of the Florida chapter of the Cancer Sucks Club, I am here to tell all of you that cancer does indeed still suck. A lot. A whole lot. Tons and tons of sucking by the cancer monster.

Through all of my joking and storytelling, I've never lost sight of what all of our families are going through or how far we've all come as a group in this battle. Tonight was a very sobering reminder of just how great a toll this battle is having on our lives. I attended the viewing and visitation of Maya. At 4 ½ years of age, she was definitely one of God's little angels. I'm sure there are those out there who have prophetic words of advice to pass along at times like these, but I am at a loss. The logical part of my brain is trying to convince me that this is part of the battle, that little soldiers will be lost, and that we just have to accept that for what it is. But the emotional part of my brain is furious. Why does this have to happen? Why? I just don't get it.

Zachary has two more days of chemo this week and then he will have a break for two weeks. We will be testing in two weeks, right before the next round. He is still hoping to somehow get clean scans so he can quit chemo.

Scott

P.S. Please keep Maya Pettit's family in your prayers. Please keep Zachary in your prayers. Please keep all of the little angels and soldiers who have fought this battle or are still fighting this battle in your prayers. (I know I am asking a lot of all of you, but it would mean a lot to me if you would follow up on this one.)

Saturday, November 29, 2003 11:36 AM CST

Thanksgiving has come and gone. The tryptophan knocked me out for 2.5 days, so that is why I haven't updated in awhile. (Are you buying any of this? Because if you are, I've got some chocolate covered key lime pie to sell you too.) Anyway, we had a wonderful day with the Mathis family in Boynton Beach. Plenty of food, fun, football, and games. Zachary had one little bump in the road on the way down, he got sick about one mile from our friend's house. (Car trips wreak havoc on his system.) He woke me up at 3:30am this morning for some Zofran. (Sometimes the chemo stays with him for a few days and keeps him off his normal game.)

We had an interesting conversation last night while driving to Blockbuster for some movies. Here are excerpts from that conversation:

Zachary: *"I'm going to travel around the world in an RV when I get older."*
Me: *"Around the world? How are you going to cross oceans in an RV?"*
Zachary: *"I'll have a boat too."*
Me: *"A boat? It's going to have to be a huge boat to hold your RV, isn't it?"*
Zachary: *"Yeah, a big boat and an RV."*
Me: *"Ok, sounds great. How exactly are you going to get enough money for a boat that large and an RV?"*
Zachary: *"I'm going to be running my organization, S.A.F.E. (Saving Animals For Everyone.) That's how!"*
Me: *"Oh, and that's going to make a lot of money? Isn't it going to be a charitable company?"*
Zachary: *"Yeah, but Mitchell is going to be a professional baseball player, and he's already said that after he makes a lot of money for a few years, he'll quit and come join me so we can do S.A.F.E. together."*
Me: *"Well, as long as you've got it all figured out . . . . I guess you're set."*

Amazing how the mind of a nine-year old works. Things are so clear and simple. No messy logic to muddy up or cloud your thoughts.

Tomorrow we're frying up a turkey for my folks and Rebecca's grandparents. I'm sure I'll be sleeping for another three days after that meal.

I hope everyone had a safe and delicious Thanksgiving.

Monday, January 19, 2004 6:38 PM CST

Sorry for the lack of journal entries . . . . I've been working double duty . . . . helping to keep things rolling with the fishing business and covering down at the fair with the key lime pie bars. So far we haven't "lit any fires" at the fair. Everyone loves the product, but there is SO much food there, you can get lost in the shuffle. We're on the opposite side of the fair from all of the rides, and that seems to be where the bulk of the crowds have been so far. Also, most of those folks are younger kids, and they're not typically our largest customer base. Tomorrow through Friday are Senior Citizen days, so maybe we'll get our demographic after all. We've had some great press. One of the local weather guys interviewed my one partner and ate a pie bar during the broadcast . . . talking about how great it tasted. And today one of the radio stations that is doing live feeds from the fair tried the bars and spoke highly of them too. We still have 13 days left, so we'll see what happens.

Zachary joined me and one of my partners today to help out and run the booth. (He also was looking for another chance to go on rides and try to win stuffed animals.) He talked my partner Randy into riding the big drop with him. It is basically a tower that has four sets of seats that are slowly pulled up to the top and then dropped, only to slow and brake at the very bottom. By the look on Randy's face afterwards, I'd say that Zachary fared better with that one than he did. Zachary and I threw some money away and won Rebecca a stuffed animal . . . . just what she needed. (We only need 2 or 3 more stuffed animals to break the indoor record for a house of this size.)

Zachary started on another weird thing today. Out of the blue, he asks me, "Dad, is it expensive to change your name?" I told him you have to go to court and it does cost something. So he said, "Ok . . . I want to change my name to Seth." I asked him why, but never really got a straight answer. Evidently Rebecca told him that when she was picking names before he was born, 'Seth' made the final two but lost out to 'Zachary.' I told him it sounded more like he was subconsciously trying to rid himself of the person who has cancer to become someone new who is not affected by the disease. He didn't know what 'subconscious' meant, so I had to explain it. He denied that that was the reason and offered this one up instead. "The name 'Seth' reminds me of the word 'snake,' and that reminds me of 'Charlie' (the snake we used to own,) and I miss Charlie.

Ok . . . . how we got from A to B to Q . . . . I don't know . . . . but this twisted logic was obviously coming from an overtired little man. When we were still at the fair, I told him that I would change his name to "Booger" if he wanted, but not to 'Seth.' He didn't like that too much. Just to aggravate him further, I told him that I was going to change my name to "MYNAMEISBOOGER', so when he wanted to get my attention, he would have to say, "MYNAMEISBOOGER", and that would of course be very embarrassing. He didn't like that idea much better. (I was only trying to help.)

Tomorrow it's back to school and back to the fishing business for me. I've got two days off from the fair . . . and then it's back to barking like the Yak woman. It's better than being the guy who has to sprinkle pixie dust at the 'tilt-a-whirl.' (A National Lampoon Vacation reference for you movie lovers.)

Sunday, March 14, 2004 8:22 PM CST

You know, these web sites are great. They really serve an important service for families like ours. Being able to reach out and communicate with everyone and give them updates from the comfort of our home is a beautiful thing. Of course, I don't imagine the wonderful folks at CaringBridge ever imagined that sick demented guys like me would be using these pages to convey more than just the usual medical occurrences. I have to say that in addition to being blessed with a wonderful child, I am TRULY blessed to have a son who provides me with daily material for my entries. Now before I continue, I feel obligated to provide you with one of my patented disclaimers. Most of you know that Zachary is not my biological son. Having said that, most of you who have met him know that he and I are very much alike. Whether he takes after me or whether I take after him can be debated for centuries without resolution, but the point is, most folks feel he is more like me than Rebecca. This next story reflects a part of our lives where I want to make it clear that Zachary does NOT take after me. Do you need to reread that last sentence? I am taking NO ownership for any of the comments that he made today.

It may come as a surprise to the women reading this page, but some men, (NOT ME,) feel it is cute, or manly, or clever, or something, to give their private parts a name. [IT IS IMPORTANT THAT YOU KNOW AND UNDERSTAND THAT I AM NOT ONE OF THESE KIND OF GUYS.] (With the possible exception of a lapse in judgment during college, I have never partaken in that particular ritual.)

So, here we are getting ready for our day of urine collection. Now, Zachary has peed in a variety of bottles, jars, and urinals during his various stays in hospitals. He has always required the help of either Rebecca or me because he was never able to hold the container and do his business. Well, he is older now. I guess I figured that a ten-year old could handle it. Especially considering the fact that the 24-hour collection bottle is a massive container that he could rest on the toilet seat and easily manage. So, you can imagine our surprise and shock today when Zachary asked for help, and I said "You can do it alone." . . . and then those magic words that every parent dreams of hearing came blurting out from the perfectly straight face of our boy. "I can't hold my Twinkie and the bottle at the same time."

I want to make it clear that I have NEVER referred to my unit as a Twinkie, Ho-ho, Ding Dong, Suzie Q, or ANY other cream filled pastry for that matter! This one falls totally in his lap . . . . (as it were.)

Well, the moral of the story is he did need help. It was either that or we would need to invest in some more mops and wipes to clean up the floor.

Saturday, April 17, 2004 6:02 PM CDT

Medical News:

Zachary is still doing his chemo. He finishes this round on Monday. We have NOT gotten any MIBG results . . . . the ONE doctor who reads those has been on vacation and didn't get back until yesterday or today. So, we will probably have the results early next week. Tuesday is the bone marrow test, and those results should be available by the end of the week. Blah, blah, blah, blah, blah . . . . and the beat goes on.

Now on to a much more important subject. I've been meaning to address this issue for quite some time; however, I couldn't find a way to approach the issue without upsetting people and causing mass panic. It's one thing to write every day or so about cancer and other such mundane subjects, but this is much more serious!

I really don't know where to begin. I don't know how long this epidemic has been growing in our country, but it is time that we searched out its roots and put an end to it NOW! Left unchecked, I fear we will be slaves to this latest phenomenon that is . . . .

. . . . . The "Punch Buggy—No Punch Back" game!

Zachary got hooked on this highly controversial game about a year ago. We very quickly put a stop to the actual "punching" that was taking place, but that hasn't slowed the intensity or competitive nature that this game provokes. For those of you who aren't familiar with this game, this is how it is played.

While you are driving around, anyone who spots a Volkswagen Bug, yells out the color, along with this phrase: (i.e. if it were yellow) "YELLOW PUNCH BUGGY—NO PUNCH BACKS." Then, theoretically, the "spotter" then has the right to punch someone. Well, even without the dreaded "punch," the game is equally damaging to the mind. For example, I now find myself looking wildly for these stupid cars even when I'm driving ALONE! (What the heck is that all about?) And when it comes to Zman, well let me just say this . . . . he can be in the middle of a sentence about anything, ANYTHING, and he will spot a bug, yell out the sentence . . . and get right back to his train of thought. (Of course with Zachary, there are all sorts of extra rules that are randomly put into play that make the game that much more difficult to follow.) If you or your family have not yet been afflicted with this game, my advice to you is DON'T DO IT! Save yourselves and forget the rest of us . . . . we're beyond help.

As with all diseases, it is of paramount importance to go back to the roots of the evil monster before finding a way to terminate it. I don't remember playing this game as a young child. Rebecca does. (She is of course 13 years younger than me . . . . but maybe I was sheltered.) How far back does this illness go? Where on Earth was it started? (Or was it started in Hell as a way for the devil to get back at us for inhabiting the planet that he was banished from?) Who came up with this madness? If you can answer any or all of these questions, you may be able to save us from ourselves.

I'll leave you with this thought. If we can't rid ourselves of this dreaded game, we may have to take a much more drastic action. I'm drafting legislation that will outlaw the ownership of Volkswagen Bugs. It will include heavy sanctions for those who violate the law and drive these freaks of nature on our roads and highways. Maybe a 10-20-Life law like the gun law. Get caught owning one . . . . 10 years in prison . . . . get caught sitting in one . . . . 20 years in prison . . . . get caught actually driving one . . . . you get Life in prison.

I'm not resting until we resolve this issue as a group. The whole "cancer" thing can wait. This is important stuff people!

Monday, December 5, 2005 7:39 PM CST

I wish the news from this weekend's soccer match was good . . . . unfortunately our team did not do so well. We lost 6 or 7 to 1 . . . . I lost track after the first few. We did so many things wrong . . . . it pains me to think about it. I imagine that Wednesday night's practice will be interesting.

Zachary still feels pretty good . . . . he has had some stomach pain that I think he got from pulling a muscle. It seems to be getting better, so I'm not too worried about it.

For those of you who remember the old "Who's on first?" comedy routine, this next story might amuse you. I will warn you in advance that if you suffer from anxiety, high blood pressure, or any other hypertension-like illness, that you do NOT try to repeat any of the things that I have done. On the other hand, if you have low blood pressure or are just lacking in excitement, you might want to contact your cell phone carrier to kick start your metabolism.

Cell phone carrier Company #1 recently purchased carrier Company #2.

This was in all of the papers.

It even was mentioned on TV.

A giant bought a monster.

Great things will come to all.

The world will be a better place.

(I wouldn't put too much credence in those previous comments.)

(But this is just me talking . . . . what do I know?)

I used to have 6 phone lines with Company #2 for my business. I believe I have written in previous journal entries about how frustrating they were to deal with. In my travels, I would constantly be without coverage . . . . which would put me out of touch with Rebecca and Zachary . . . . which would drive me up a $#%^&@ wall!

So, about 2 years ago we switched to another company. But. (There is always a 'but.') I kept the Company #2 account open because we had one person who was on our account who wanted to keep her line active with them. Since I didn't really have to deal with them anymore . . . it seemed like an easy enough arrangement . . . . they bill me . . . . we bill her . . . . I don't have to talk to them anymore. Then Company #1 went and bought them out.

Now, our bills all say "Company #1" on them. The contact phone number says, "Call Company #1—1-800-whatever. So, our friend decided that the plans with Company #1 are much more affordable than Company #2, and that she wanted to switch. Company #1 informed her that only a company owner was allowed to make those decisions . . . . in other words . . . . I was being thrown back into the game. (Without a helmet or cup for protection . . . . I might add.)

[This is where the "Who's on first?" thing comes into play.]

I called the phone number on my bill that says, "Contact Company #1."

They answered, "Company #2 . . . . how may I help you?"

Hmmmm . . . . I could see bad things were ahead of me.

I calmly explained the situation . . . . I had one phone number left on the account, and I wanted to switch it to a Company #1 line . . . . BUY a new phone . . . . and ADD time to the contract.

After wasting large amounts of oxygen . . . . she informed me that I needed to call Company #1. She was with Company #2. (Why did my bill say "Call Company #1."?) Who knows . . . . "Call Company #1, here is the number," she said.

So I called the number . . . waited on hold . . . . again . . . . and explained my needs to the Company #1 person . . . . again . . . . and after wasting more oxygen I was informed that I needed to speak with the business side of Company #1. "Here is the phone number in case you get disconnected . . . I'll transfer you."

I got disconnected.

Ahhhhhhh . . . . but she gave me the phone number.

I called the number.

I waited on hold again.

I explained our request . . . . again.

. . . . and the answer was . . . .

"You need to call Company #2 . . . . they can do that for you."

AHHHHHHHHHHHHHHHHHHHHHHHHHHHHHHHHHHHHHHHHHHHHHH

(I think I actually said that.)

So . . . . I started at point A . . . . was sent to point B . . . . and then to C . . . . only to be sent back to A.

I wasn't biting on that one . . . . I objected on the grounds of utter stupidity. She agreed that something was amiss and said she would transfer me to the business side of Company #1.

AHHHHHHHHHHHHHHHHHHHHHHHHHHHHHHHHHHHHHHH

"You ARE the business side of Company #1 . . . . I have your phone number right in front of me."

"Oh . . . . ok . . . . well . . . let me transfer you to someone who can fix this."

More waiting.

More waiting.

A little bit more waiting.

A lot more waiting.

Insane amounts of waiting.

A new "helper."

"How may I help you?"

I explained the problem . . . . again . . . but this time they took a new approach . . . . they tried to confuse me with a reverse Vulcan logic quagmire. I was at the point where I was trying to order the new cell phone that our friend wanted to get . . . . and this is EXACTLY what the phone bimbo said to me:

"You can't get a phone until you have a phone."

AHHHHHHHHHHHHHHHHHHHHHHHHHHHHHHHHHHHHHHHHHHHH HHHHHHHHHHHHHHHHHHHHHHHHHHHHHHHHHHHHHHHHHHHHH HHHHHHHHHHHHHHHHHHHHHHHHHHHHHHHHHHHHHHHHHHHHH HHHHHHHHH

So I said, "HOW IS THAT ENGLISH? SPEAK ENGLISH TO ME."

And her reply was . . . . "Sir . . . you cannot get a new phone until you have a phone."

AHHHHHHHHHHHHHHHHHHHHHHHHHHHHHHHHHHHHHHHHHHHH HHHHHHHHHHHHHHHHHHHHHHHHHHHHHHHHHHHHHHHHHHHHH HHHHHHHHHHHHHHHHHHHHHHHHHHHHHHHHHHHHHHHHHHHHH HHHHHHHHH

So I said.... "PLEASE USE SMALL WORDS AND SPEAK VERY SLOWLY. AND EXPLAIN TO ME HOW THAT MAKES SENSE."

"Sir.... until you have a Company #1 account, you cannot order a phone."

"Oh.... I can see where you could confuse the words, "phone" with "account"... I mean they are identical ... except for the fact that all of the letters are different and they sound nothing alike!"

Once we got past THAT debacle.... I told her that I would be happy to set up a new account.... and that is when we got disconnected... again.

About an hour later my friend called me on my cell phone and she had the Company #1 rep on the phone conferencing with us ... so we could work things out. The rep explained that we needed to open a Company #1 account for the business to make things work. "Fine.... lets rock and roll."

"Ok sir.... we'll need a credit card from you to cover the $5.00 fee for this transaction."

Silence.

More silence.

Finally my friend spoke up and said that she would be happy to pay the $5.00 fee on her credit card.

"I'm sorry sir.... we can only accept a credit card that has the same billing address as the cell phone account."

(I can see where this makes sense.... I mean.... $5.00 charged on some credit cards are different than $5.00 charged on other credit cards.... oh wait.... no they're not!)

IDIOT

"You have GOT to be kidding me. You want our money... but only if you can get it a certain way?"

"I'm sorry sir... that is the policy."

"Why can't you just add it to my bill . . . . I've paid thousands of dollars over the years to you guys . . . and NOW all of a sudden you want a credit card . . . . for FIVE DOLLARS?"

"You paid Company #2 that money . . . . we're Company #1."

"YOU BOUGHT THEM . . . . YOU'RE THE SAME IDIOTS NOW . . . . RIGHT?"

(I think maybe in retrospect that using words like idiot and moron can be counterproductive . . . . I've got to work on my people skills.)

I don't like to give credit card info over the cell phone . . . so I promised to call back when I was at a land line.

Over the weekend I remembered that I was due for some more aggravation, so I called Company #1 to complete the deal. I was told again that I needed to speak with the business division . . . . and was duly transferred . . . . where I remained on hold for several minutes . . . . before a recording picked up to inform me that the business division was closed on weekends.

AHHHHHHHHHHHHHHHHHHHHHHHHHHHHHHHHHHHHHHHHHHHHHH HHHHHHHHHHHHHHHHHHHHHHHHHHHHHHHHHHHHHHHHHHHHHHHH HHHHHHHHHHHHHHHHHHHHHHHHHHHHHHHHHHHHHHHHHHHHHHHHH HHHHHHHHH

I called back today.

I explained the situation . . . . again.

Somehow I must have called the Company #2 number again by accident.

The phone person told me this . . . .

"Sir . . . . we can't sell new phones this week. We are in training with Company #1. We can sell new phones next week.

"You mean to tell me that the entire country is shut off from giving Company #1 their money for a whole week?"

"Yes sir . . . . you can call Company #2 . . . . but here at Company #1 we can't help you . . . . because we were Company #2 . . . . and we're just learning how

to BECOME Company #1 . . . . so we can't sell you Company #1 phones until our Company #2 brains have been deprogrammed and then reprogrammed with Company #1 information."

(Ok . . . maybe that wasn't exactly what was said . . . . but that is what I heard.)

I called the other, other, other, other Company #1 phone number.

I waited again . . . . like an idiot.

I got another "person" on the phone.

Like a beaten mule I said, "I am ready to pay the $5.00 to open a new Company #1 account."

"Sir . . . . there is no $5.00 fee . . . . "

AHHHHHHHHHHHHHHHHHHHHHHHHHHHHHHHHHHHHHHHHHHHHHH HHHHHHHHHHHHHHHHHHHHHHHHHHHHHHHHHHHHHHHHHHHHHHH HHHHHHHHHHHHHHHHHHHHHHHHHHHHHHHHHHHHHHHHHHHHHHH HHHHHHHHH

"It will just be a minute sir . . . . hang on for me . . . . "

And then I got disconnected.

Saturday, September 15, 2007 8:18 AM CDT

You know, I'm a fairly well adjusted, middle aged kind of a guy. At 44 years of age, I still feel like I have most of my physical agility and sports-like skills from my youth. Sure, I recognize that I don't run quite as fast as I did years ago. And I am aware that if I don't stretch and get limber before exerting myself that I will pay the price the next day with sore muscles. But, I have always been able to either excel, or "hold my own" when it came to sports.

Water skiing, snow skiing, soccer, basketball, softball, baseball, football, street hockey, roller blade hockey, tennis, volleyball, racquetball, kayaking & swimming. These are just a few of the sports that I have either participated in on a recreational basis, or played competitively in a league or organized manner.

If you were to include some of the less physical "sports", I can add, pool, ping pong, bowling, darts, horseshoes & bocce, just to name a few.

So, suffice it to say, I have a pretty well rounded background when it comes to activities requiring coordination and skill.

Of all the activities that I listed above, I would have to say that the one that I have never gotten above average in is bowling. I took bowling in college for one of my electives, but I never took it seriously and never really had enough of an interest to pursue it further than the occasional outing. For years my best game was about 150, and then a few years back I was with friends and family and bowled an uncharacteristic 175. Other than that, I'm usually good for a score that will fall somewhere between 100 and 135. Not a stellar score, but it is what it is.

Now, Zachary started bowling when he was younger. (Maybe 6 or 7). He got some pointers from some friends and did OK. When he took his time, he could get over 100, sometimes 115 or 120. He hasn't bowled consistently for quite some time. About two weeks ago, he got interested in bowling again. Let me rephrase that. About two weeks ago, he got interested in some girls who were interested in bowling. (It's that whole math thing. A to B to C.) So, it didn't take much for these girls to talk Zachary into joining their bowling league which was getting ready to start. He signed up, and the first week he bowled like a 75, 95, 106. (Approx.) His ball from years ago was one of those ridiculously light plastic things. So of course, I was talked into getting him a new $85.00 ball that you could use spin with. All of this in my mind was a waste. Here I am thinking that he'll get bored with it, and we'll have something else to collect dust in the garage.

Well, that all started about two weeks ago. Since then, he has become obsessed with bowling. The other day, while bowling some practice games, he had a three game series that was: 141, 200 & 149.

Yes, I wrote that correctly. He bowled a 200.

This sucks.

Kids are NOT supposed to be better at stuff than their parents.

Certainly not better than me.

We went to Blazer Bowling over the weekend and bowled two games with friends. Zachary got a 149 and a 135. I never broke 120 on either game. Life is NOT fair.

He has somehow found a curve that snakes into the pocket on almost every ball. He is hitting at or near that front pin very consistently.

I'm toying with the idea of grounding him and taking away the ball. He hasn't done anything wrong; I just don't like being outdone by a 13 year old.

Wednesday, April 23, 2008 2:16 PM CDT

LOSING YOUR IDENTITY

No, this is not going to be a sermon on how to protect your credit cards and social security number from those who would steal your identity to rob you of your money. This is instead, a brief glimpse into the dark reaches of my mind.

Who are we? That simple question is probably easy enough to answer for most people. Think about it, if a reporter walked up to you on the street and stuck a microphone in your face and said, "Who are you?" Most of you would be able to answer that without too much difficulty. One of the following statements might even escape your lips in an effort to summarize your identity:

"I am a housewife."
"I am a student."
"I am a family man."
"I am a police officer."
"I am a doctor."
"I am a volunteer."

(I could go on and on . . . . but I'm guessing that you get the idea.)

I have recently come to the realization that Rebecca, Zachary and I may be facing a "hidden" challenge to our identities that we had never envisioned. On March 16, 2000, our identities were permanently affected by the diagnosis that we received that day. There is no escaping that fact, it's not even worth dwelling on, it is a part of the very fiber of our lives that will forever be ingrained in our psyche. The trick in moving forward and carrying on with life is to not let moments like that DEFINE who you are or how others view you. Don't get me wrong here, there is no shame or negative connotation that we, or others like us, are trying to avoid. I'm just making an observation that it is nearly impossible to escape or otherwise avoid what has happened to us. It affects so many aspects of our lives; we couldn't avoid it if we tried.

So, why the philosophical discussion all of a sudden? Well, I am beginning to notice something inside of me that is quite foreign and somewhat intimidating. I am starting to feel like I am no longer the person who I thought I was. (Could that last sentence have been any more cryptic or confusing?) And it's not just me; I believe that Rebecca and Zachary have been living in this "altered state" for quite some time, maybe even years. Why has it all of a sudden hit me? I don't know. Maybe I have been in denial for a long time and have avoided taking a hard long look in the mirror . . . . I don't know. (You know the old saying; "Denial is not just a river in Egypt."—[de-Nile . . . . get it?])

Why is it that I am feeling less and less like the person who I thought I was? Is it because this disease has been so much a part of our lives for SO many years? Is it because we go for a year, sometimes two, without any major drama, only to have the rug pulled out from underneath us time and time again? Zachary has been battling cancer for 8 years. 8 years, and he is only 14 years old! That is close to 60% his life. And when you factor in that it's the most RECENT 60% and that he doesn't have many memories from the first 40%, you start to see where on most days he is DEFINED by his illness. In a perfect world, Zachary would answer the "Who are you?" question like this:

"I am a bowler."
"I am a soccer player."
"I am a son."
"I am a student."
"I am a giving person."
"I am hopeful."
"I am looking forward to the future."

Instead, he is more likely to respond:

"I have cancer."
"I am tired."
"I am in pain."
"I am angry."
"I am frustrated."
"I am worried about my future."
"I am worried about my parents."
"I don't want to die."
"I miss the friends who have lost their battle with this disease."

As for Rebecca, I have never asked her what her perfect-world answers would look or sound like, but I can guess:

"I am a mother."
"I am a wife."
"I have a healthy family."
"I have a wonderful life."
"I want for nothing."

Instead, I think that she is faced daily with thoughts like:

"I have a son with cancer."
"I have health issues that prevent me from fully enjoying life."
"I am a mother who is worried that her son will predecease her."
"I am depressed most days."

As for me, I guess my perfect-world answers would sound like:

"I am a husband."
"I am a father."
"I have a healthy family."
"The future looks bright."

Instead, I feel mired in thoughts like:

"I am a husband who cannot alleviate the pain of his wife."
"I am a father who cannot find a cure for his son's cancer."
"I am a person who can't remember what it is like to be without worries."

None of us are above life challenges or personal anguish. I am not suggesting that my problems are any worse than the problems that all of you face. I am merely turning the magnifying glass around and peering into the deepest parts of my head in an attempt to see what it is that makes me tick. Like Zachary, my memories of life before cancer are fading more and more every day. I have told friends on many occasions that because of how long we have been doing this, cancer has become a way of life for us. Those words always seemed more like a tool for educating people as to what we are experiencing, but now they seem much more like a harsh reality that is becoming increasingly inescapable as the months and years pass. I'm guessing that Rebecca also has a difficult time remembering life before cancer, although she is 13 years younger than me, and her memory isn't as affected by old age as much as mine is. But all kidding aside, my sense is that she too is living in a state of consciousness that is firmly planted in this diagnosis.

How did we let this happen to us? I don't know the answer to that one either. Maybe it is like the cancer itself, in as much as it slowly seeps into your life with such subtle changes that you don't catch on, until it is too late. Am I saying that it is too late . . . . that we are beyond hope? No, I would never say that. I would like to believe that I am still an optimistic person by nature. I believe that the glass is half full. (Of 5-day old chocolate milk that my teenage son forgot to wash out, leaving me with the fun job of having to scrub it out for 45 minutes to try and get it clean.) I believe that sunny days are coming. (Global warming . . . . temperatures are rising, water is going to be in short supply . . . . we're all going to die.)

See? I can be a positive thinker!

I guess the burning question in my gut is, WHO AM I? I thought that I knew who I was. I thought that I knew EXACTLY who I was. Now, I am not so sure. Maybe I DID know who I was, but somehow, I let that person become someone else. Maybe we all change over time and become a different person as we age and travel through the various stages of life.

Baby
Infant
Toddler
Child
Adolescent
Teenager
Young Adult
Husband/Wife
Parent
Grandparent

So why does it seem like I should be adding the word "cancer" after many of those?

Zachary

Child "with cancer."
Adolescent "with cancer."
Teenager "with cancer."

Rebecca & Scott

Parent of a child "with cancer."
Parent of a teenager "with cancer."

Is there a difference between other people defining you a certain way and you defining yourself that same way? "There goes Scott & Rebecca, their son has cancer." Vs "Hey, nice to meet you, my name is Scott, this is my wife Rebecca, and that's our son Zachary over there, the one with cancer." (We don't do that of course, but you get the idea.) What is our identity? Can we live in this cancer world that we find ourselves in and somehow define ourselves without it? Will Zachary EVER get the chance again to be just 'Zachary'? When does Rebecca get to define a life for herself without this hanging over her head?

And then there is me . . . . if you have been reading my journal entries for any amount of time, then you surely know already that I am beyond hope or help of any kind. If the planet blew up tomorrow, and we were all lined up at the pearly gates, waiting for our turn with you-know-who, I'm guessing that he/she would get to me and start shaking his head, while saying, "Son, I'd love to let you in, but have you READ some of the things that you have written about other people in your journal entries?" And I would reply, "Well, yeah, but were you LISTENING to some of the idiotic things that those same people were saying to me?" And then he would probably say something like, "Have you not HEARD of forgiveness?" To which I would have to reply, "I forgive them for being imbeciles. I forgive them for being too stupid to know better. That kind of forgiveness?" And then he would most likely say something like, "The best that I can do is to place you on the waiting list. Take one of these vibrating drink coasters, when its red lights start flashing and it begins to vibrate, come back and we'll talk again."

I once heard that an economist can be compared to a person who stands on the back of a train, trying to determine where it is going, by watching where it has been. I'm guessing that what they were trying to say is that every once-in-a-while you should look out the FRONT of the train to see what is coming. I think that we are having trouble looking ahead, because we are so deeply entrenched in where we have been.

Scott

P.S. Please do NOT sign the guest book to tell me how wonderful things are or how great things are going to be. This journal entry was NOT meant as a pity party. I am just trying to do what I have always done, and that is to give you a glimpse into what we are experiencing.

Chapter 10

Insurance

"The evil doers are among us, beware!"

This is the one chapter that I have been dreading. There is SO much information swimming around in my head that I wish I could just vomit it all out and have it appear magically on these pages. I guess I should start by issuing some sort of disclaimer that protects me from being sued for slander. (Not that I would EVER speak in a derogatory fashion about the scum-sucking, bottom feeding, bastards that work for insurance companies. I would NEVER do that.) Where was I?

Oh yeah, the disclaimer. The views, stories and thoughts expressed in this chapter are mine and mine alone. They should in no way be interpreted as a blanket characterization of the insurance industry as a whole, or of every employee of any particular company that I plan to eviscerate over the next several pages. Furthermore, any name-calling or descriptive phrases that I use to convey to the readers an understanding of just how much like a pile of dog shit I liken the insurance folks, should NOT be taken in the wrong light. (Remember . . . . you can't polish a turd!)

Before I go any further, I want to say that I had already finished this chapter when I was advised against using any actual company names. Even though the views are strictly mine, as I have stated previously, I will err on the side of caution and NOT name any companies in my book.

Our insurance saga started incredibly the day after diagnosis. Zachary was diagnosed on a Thursday. On Friday, I had to return home to get more clothing and supplies for the long stay in the hospital that we were just informed of.

Upon returning home, I of course got the mail out of the mailbox. Amazingly, one of the letters in there was from our first insurance company (I'll change the names to protect the guilty . . . . let's see . . . hmmm, something not TOO derogatory . . . . OK . . . I've got it.) I'll call them Lifesuckingbottomfeeders. (Was that too inflammatory? Oh well, they'll get over it.) So anyway, back to the letter.

The letter was a standard type notice informing us of a change to our policy. As of some date PRIOR to my opening the letter and DEFINITELY prior to Zachary's diagnosis, the Lifesuckingbottomfeeders had decided to NO longer cover a variety of expenses relating to bone marrow transplants. Now, while I may have still been somewhat in shock from the previous day's diagnosis, I was able to reach down deep into the depths of my mind and recall that less than 24 hours prior to reading that letter, a doctor somewhere in Palm Beach had told me that Zachary was going to need a bone marrow transplant. It was as if they had a crystal ball and KNEW that we were going to get that diagnosis. THAT was our introduction into the wonderful world of insurance.

At the time of diagnosis, all three of us were covered on a policy that Rebecca had through her employer. You may recall (or you may NOT recall) that I was self-employed, being the co-owner of a small company. We didn't have health insurance. My partner's wife is a school teacher, so his family was covered by the school board policy.

One of the unique aspects of our story regarding insurance is the fact that Rebecca was BOTH the insured parent, AND the primary care giver. What that means is that she had the insurance through her job, but MY income was our primary source of money, so the bulk of the care giving for Zachary was going to fall on her shoulders. You may see where this is leading to. While Rebecca is talented, smart, determined and resourceful, she has YET to solve the dilemma of being in two places at the same time.

At first, her employer was very understanding and gave her a leave of absence. Then, eventually, they decided to move on and fired her. At some point while all of that was going on, we learned that the company was changing insurance carriers, supposedly because of us!!! Keep in mind, this was no small company. They had several hundred employees, and yet they were claiming that Zachary's situation had prompted their carrier to drop them. I don't believe that we'll ever get the whole story on what transpired there, but I seriously doubt that a company of that size would get dropped over one claim, no matter how large it was.

After the Lifesuckingbottomfeeders came (oh great, here we go again . . . I've got to get creative and come up with some replacement name for those idiots, so as NOT to name them directly . . . . OOOH, I've got it) the SFB Company. (Shit For Brains.) At first, the SFB Company was caring and supportive. They even assigned us a nurse specialist to help us navigate through all of the paper work. The problem was, the specialist never really had any expertise, and she was constantly lagging behind and trying to catch up. Over the years, we had many numerous bad experiences with the SFB Company. Some of my most memorable journal entries came from those experiences. So, rather than try to rewrite history, I think that it's best for you to read the journal entries from back then, so that you can get a proper "feel" as to what our emotions were when dealing with them. (No skipping ahead to the end of the chapter, they're not going anywhere. It's like the icing on the cupcake. You've GOT to eat the cake first before you get to the sweet part.)

In 1986 Congress passed the Consolidated Omnibus Budget Reconciliation Act (COBRA) health benefit provisions. COBRA contains provision giving certain former employees, retirees, spouses and dependent children the right to temporary continuation of health coverage at group rates. (www.cobrainsurance.com/COBRA_Law.htm)

I included that tidbit of information because we stayed with the SFB Company while Rebecca was still unemployed, and then when she was fired, we were introduced to the wonderful world of COBRA. We were immediately made aware of the fact that COBRA insurance was much more expensive than what we had before. What's interesting (and sad) is that during the course of our initial treatment year, we had been given advice from more than one social worker as to how we should proceed with Zachary's insurance. At two different hospitals this is what we were told: "Rebecca, you should divorce Scott and tell the State of Florida that you are caring for Zachary alone. That will allow you to go onto full public assistance. He doesn't even need to move out, it's not like they're ever going to come by and check."

How sad is that? Our medical system isn't screwed up enough, we've got to encourage people to find ways to circumvent and beat the system. Medicaid can be a useful and necessary tool for families in need. Our problem was that I was making slightly too much money to be eligible for public assistance. Also, we had heard from other families who were on Medicaid that if you needed to travel for treatment, especially out of State, things could get REAL dicey.

We also had to factor in the specialists who we were taking Zachary to. Some of them didn't participate in the Medicaid program, and that would have required a change that we didn't want to make. So, we resolved ourselves to finding a way of staying with COBRA. Because we had been with the SFB Company, the COBRA stayed with them. The other issue facing us at the time was the fact that you only get 18 months on COBRA before you need an alternative. There are circumstances where you can get a 9 month extension (and I've got journal entries that talk about that coming up here shortly), but eventually you NEED to find an alternative.

We DID end up getting an extension, and eventually we were placed on what is referred to as a Conversion Policy. I'm going to let you look that one up on the internet, because I just don't feel like dissecting it in this book. I will tell you this though, Zachary is self-insured with his conversion policy. Meaning that the policy is in his name, it is not a "sub-policy" of Rebecca's or mine. We are insured through different companies.

Those last sentences have probably sparked some questions in your mind. Like, "Why haven't you added Zachary to Rebecca's policy?" Well, the SFB Company may be a monster, but they are a KNOWN monster. Zachary has a lifetime maximum benefit of $1,000,000.00, of which he has used about $450,000.00. So, we are trying to keep things running as smoothly as possible without too much chaos. Also, the conversion policy is now only about $170.00/month, whereas the COBRA policy was about $500.00/month. (That's a BIG difference!)

When you get to the journal entries here in a second, you will find that I have addressed most of this in "real time," meaning that as it was happening to us, I was writing about it. I have also included my now "famous" (or not so famous) concept for helping to fix part of the insurance problems that we face here in Florida. Unfortunately, the insurance lobby is WAY bigger and stronger than any of the politicians who I sent my ideas to, so nothing is likely to change in the near future.

As for the new families who have just gotten diagnosed and have somehow been told to read this book, I will tell you that navigating the insurance quagmire is a daunting task. We were VERY fortunate that one of our local charities was there to help us with that problem. Aside from the obvious medical issues that are facing you, I would HIGHLY recommend finding a local organization that has experience in dealing with insurance companies.

There ARE stories out there of families who have had a smooth ride when it comes to dealing with their insurance company. (There are also stories out there about Santa Claus, The Easter Bunny, and honest politicians.) You may be lucky enough to have found a case manager who is working with you to solve your problems now, but people quit, get promoted, go on vacation, etc. This isn't a disease that takes kindly to delays. Weeks and days can make a huge difference. Remember the story I told earlier about our initial protocol? We were having Zachary's bone marrow tested after every other round of chemo and we would do 1 week of chemo, then Zachary would get sick and it would take 3 weeks before we could start the next round. THEN, after he recovered from that, we would have to test his marrow to make sure that the medicines were still working. Well, after about 2 months of that, Zachary had his marrow checked and was due to start the next round of chemo, but his counts didn't rebound and we got delayed for another 2 weeks. (14 days.) The doctor informed us that we needed to redo the marrow test before Zachary would be allowed to restart his chemo. The reason you ask? The protocol required that the doctors have an accurate evaluation of the level of disease in his marrow prior to starting the round of chemo. AND, in that doctor's experience, a 2 week delay gave the cancer enough time to progress exponentially.

We have many stories from our friends who have had children fighting this and other cancers, where a couple of days one way or the other, made a HUGE difference in the treatment. So, the last thing that you want to be doing is experiencing delays because of something that you could have helped prevent. Remember, you will ALWAYS be your child's #1 advocate.

[FLASHBACK]

Tuesday, December 24, 2002 at 10:45 AM (CST)

WARNINGWARNING***WARNING***WARNING***WARNING***

THIS JOURNAL ENTRY IS RATED 'R' FOR LANGUAGE AND CONTENT. NO ONE UNDER 17 IS PERMITTED WITHOUT AN ADULT.

First things first. We are NOT having a baby! All of your feeble attempts to goad me into revealing the secret ahead of time will not work . . . . it is a Zachary related surprise that has NOTHING to do with his health. It is an unexpected addition to his celebrity status . . . . and THAT is all I am going to say about that. (That last part I wrote in my Forrest Gump voice.) Now, time to slay the dragon.

[Brief history] Rebecca and Zachary are covered by THE SFB COMPANY insurance. Rebecca's old company switched a few years ago, so we've had to deal with these people for quite some time. I would like to officially go on record as saying:

THE PEOPLE AT THE SFB COMPANY ARE, SCUMBAG, LOWLIFE, HEARTLESS, CONNIVING, BOTTOM FEEDERS WHO, I WOULD NOT URINATE ON IF THEY WERE ON FIRE!!!!!!!!!!!!!!!!!!!!!!!!!!!!!

(For the record, I held back there in case younger eyes found their way to this page.)

These bacterial scum have been trying for over two years to get us to drop coverage on Zachary so they could be relieved of the financial responsibility regarding his health. They have repeatedly mailed cancel notices late, to not give us time to respond, and they have fought us on treatments too many times to mention. When we sought treatment in NYC, they fought for over a month, making us believe it WOULD NOT HAPPEN. Then, we found out that Zachary is protected by a Florida law that requires insurance companies to pay for cancer treatments out of state for children, if the treatment is not available in Florida. This was surely something they knew, but they were hoping we would go quietly into the night. Now, we are at the end of COBRA. (For those of you that don't know, COBRA is the insurance plan that is federally regulated, it guarantees that when you lose or quit a job, you will have an additional 18 months of insurance coverage so you can find another policy and not have a lapse in coverage.) Well, Rebecca is not back to work, so we are exercising our right to buy a conversion policy. (This is a more permanent policy that will cover us until we are able to get one elsewhere.) Well, we've had to beg over and over again to get the information. We filled out all of the paper work, dotting all of the "I's" and crossing all of the "T's." The paperwork came yesterday. They conveniently left Zachary's name off of all of the sheets!!!!!!!!!!!!!!!!!!

I called them this morning, and after being on hold for ten minutes, their excuse was, "Oops, we must have forgotten his name, we'll send you new paperwork." In the meantime, the clock is ticking . . . . tick, tick, tick. We only have sooooo many days to get this done . . . .

AS PRESIDENT OF THE CANCER SUCKS CLUB, I AM INVOKING MY EXECUTIVE PRIVILEGE AND DECLARING WAR ON THE SFB COMPANY! DO NOT BE FOOLED BY THEIR LOVEY DOVEY ADS IN MAGAZINES STATING HOW NICE THEY ARE TO CHILDREN AND FAMILIES. DO NOT LET THEIR LAME ATTEMPTS AT WINNING OVER THE PUBLIC FOOL YOU. FROM NOW ON, THE WORD 'THE SFB COMPANY' IN A CONVERSATION NEEDS TO BE FOLLOWED BY "A$$HOLE$" OR "$HITHEAD$." TAKE NO PRISONERS IN THIS BATTLE.

I realize that many of you have fought and won or lost numerous battles with insurance companies over the years. And, I'm sure that if I asked, you could fill our guestbook with page after page of stories about many different insurance companies. This is my little payback for the past few years of torture behind enemy lines. I may still be a POW in this battle, but I'm not going to lie down without a fight!

Scott

P.S. Yes, we do have a case manager with THE SFB COMPANY, and if all of their other employees are scumbag, lowlife, heartless, conniving, bottom feeders, then our case manager is the excrement that they release every so often. She is the queen of double talk. Have a nice day!

P.S.S. You've heard of the "Wrath of Khan." Welcome to the Wrath of Scott.

Saturday, December 28, 2002 at 09:42 AM (CST)

Ahhhhhhhh the weekend. No stress right? THINK AGAIN!!!!!

BATTLE STATIONS . . . . BATTLE STATIONS . . . . EVERYONE TO YOUR BATTLE STATIONS!!!!!!!!!!!!!!!!!!!!!!!!!!!!!!!!!!!!

Yesterday was yet ANOTHER stressful day in the battle with THE SFB COMPANY. I was consulting with my generals in the war room, formulating an attack plan, and we were hit with another sneak attack by the enemy. After complaining that they had conveniently left Zachary's name off of the enrollment form, THE SFB COMPANY very graciously sent a NEW form for us to use. And this time, they listed him as Rebecca's spouse! Now, FAR be it for me to judge couples with a large age difference, (I am 13 years older than Rebecca), but COME ON FOLKS, not only is Rebecca 18 years older than Zachary, she is his MOTHER. I believe Freud would have something to say about that kind of relationship. Well, I of course called the conversion policy office and asked for the inept young lady whom I had spoken with 3 days ago. She was of course NOT going to be in until Monday. So, I gambled with the yutz (that's a cool Yiddish word that I think means idiot/moron) and explained (using small words so as not to confuse him) that I did not appreciate the way THE SFB COMPANY was handling all of this. He of course pleaded the fifth, and said that they "have no knowledge of Zachary's illness or case, so they would never purposely cause us problems." (After I stopped laughing, I said) "You folks need to stop making this difficult. Zachary has received letters wishing him well from our Governor, two former Presidents, our Vice-President, and our current President, to name a few. I don't want to have to make some calls . . . these people will have the insurance police investigating more orifices than you knew you had!!!!!!!!!!!!" Well, needless to say, he didn't want any full body cavity searches done in the near future, so he faxed new forms.

But, this shows us all that these insurance companies will go to ANY lengths to avoid keeping patients like Zachary on the books. They care about nothing but the bottom line. If you are reading this journal entry, and you are currently in a similar battle, DO NOT LET YOUR GUARD DOWN. These folks will puck with you every chance they get. (Substitute the letter 'f' for the letter 'p' in that last sentence please. There is only one, you can figure it out.)

MEDICAL UPDATE:

Zachary slept well last night, and woke up energized and hungry. This is all good. We plan on relaxing today, maybe we'll watch some football, and tonight, we'll probably go to the rollerblade hockey rink. I play there when I get a chance, and Zachary likes to skate around and shoot the puck a little. When he's feeling good, it's a fun evening for him. Me, I try to avoid skating into the walls at more than 5 or 10 mph. It can leave marks. (On me, not the wall.) And, every once in awhile, I actually score a goal. Now, don't be impressed, my friend Eric always says, "Even a blind squirrel finds an acorn once in awhile."

CANCER SUCKS CLUB:

Well, for those of you who were wondering whether cancer still sucks, DO WE REALLY NEED TO ASK THAT QUESTION? If so, let's email Jeff or Kathy or Scott or Ruthie or any of the other parents or kids battling this crap.

Tuesday, January 14, 2003 at 09:44 PM (CST)

Ok folks, it's late, I'm tired, and I have to get up early for work tomorrow . . . so bear with me.

You know those movies, where everything seems to be going ok, then WHAM . . . something jumps out, or bombs start going off. . . . you get the idea. WELL, let me tell you about the phone call I got today. First let me say, that I really believed that I had the whole insurance thing under control. I sorted out the policy differences, sent them a whopping check for the conversion policy, and have just been waiting for the confirmation that we will be on the new policy soon. Well, there is a company that "sells" the policies to the company that Rebecca used to work for. They negotiate with the insurance companies and work with the employers. These folks have helped us many times over the past 3 years (has it really been that long . . . we should get a button or something for time served . . . . oh yeah . . . we did,) anyway, these people know their stuff. Well, I had called them when this whole conversion thing had blown up in my face. They were looking into things when I got my answers the hard way, so I hadn't talked with them since it was resolved. Well, the owner of that company called today and asked if Zachary was disabled, in the eyes of SSI. I said yes, based on his hearing, he is labeled as disabled. Well, she said, HEY, you're eligible for an extension of 11 months of

COBRA! I said, HEY, I asked that very question to Rebecca's old employer when I was trying to get information about the conversion policy, and they had said, NO, NO, NO . . . . you are NOT eligible for an extension.

So, my next question was, "The conversion policy is cheaper, shouldn't I be happy to get onto it, and off of COBRA?" She replied, "NO! The new policy doesn't come close to the coverage of COBRA!!!!!!!!!!!!!!!! You need to stay on COBRA as long as possible to use the benefits."

Ok, now I'm pissed. This is just bull$hit. How much of this crap are they going to throw at us? They absolutely don't want us around, and they will do anything to move us along. I think I just broke a personal record with my blood pressure while typing this story. This can't be good for my health.

I'm going to deliver my next insurance payment to them in pennies. I'll get a wheel barrow from Home Depot and roll it in and dump the load in their lap!

Scott

P.S. There is no P.S. today, I'm too pissed about the insurance thing . . . quit reading this sentence and move along.

Sunday, May 25, 2003 8:25 PM CDT

Thought of the day: IF IT ISN'T BROKEN . . . . DON'T FIX IT!

Zachary has been enduring his cold with the assistance of a 12-hour cough suppressant. The only downside to this medicine is that it has no decongestant, so he is blowing his nose all day long. In my infinite wisdom, I decided to try and give him a break from the runny nose by having him take a chewable Benadryl today for our friend's Indy 500 party. Well, it wiped him out. He was lethargic and cranky, not wanting to stay all day like we normally would do. Adding to his misery was my ban on swimming. All of the other children were playing in the pool having a great time, and Zachary's mean old nasty father would only let him dangle his feet in the water. He did brighten up when his driver came in third . . . . that coupled with the $30.00 prize livened him up a bit. Once we got into the car, he was asleep in less than two minutes as we pulled away. It took me a few nudges to wake him up when we got home ten minutes later. The three of us then took a power nap for a couple of hours.

Scott

Special bonus story

Once upon a time there was a state called Florida. In this fictitious state, there were many families who had children who were stricken with cancer. Some of these families were fortunate enough to be able to continue to afford insurance through their jobs and businesses. Sadly though, many of the families were unable to afford the high cost of co-pays or premiums that can come with insurance. Sometimes a couple would have to split their duties, with one parent becoming the primary care giver, and the other maintaining the income for the family. In other families, sometimes there only would be one parent to carry both duties. If one of these parents had to give up their job to care for their child, they would lose their insurance and be offered COBRA insurance at a very expensive rate. In most cases, the families in all of these scenarios would forgo the expensive insurance and settle for state assistance.

The magical state of Florida was prepared for these families. They knew that tragedy could strike, so they had a plan. They would have programs to offer that were based on a family's income that would provide insurance to cover the high cost of cancer treatments. Sadly though, the state didn't put a whole lot of thought into their plan. When a child gets diagnosed with cancer, several things will almost always happen.

1). The family will be hit with an amazing amount of financial burdens.
2). The child will require medical experts from many fields, including quite possibly some from out of state.
3). Decisions about treatments will have to be made sooner, rather than later.
4). Family members will have more than enough stress in their lives.

Keeping all of this in mind, this is what the bright state of Florida decided to do. They would allow families to go through the stress of losing their primary (better) insurance, and going onto state assistance through one of their programs. This was a bad plan on only two fronts . . . . 1). It cost the state millions of dollars each year to pay for treatments for these children, and 2). It forced the families to accept inferior medical coverage that could prove to be fatal in the event the family needed to quickly get to another state for a treatment that wasn't available in Florida. (Florida can be very, very slow in approving out of state treatments.) Other than that, it was a great plan! In addition to the aforementioned downside, there would be the added stress of making the families jump through hoops with paperwork, evaluations, phone calls, and threatening letters on a regular basis.
*   All of this went on for many, many years until one day, a mild mannered father of a boy named Zachary was backed into a corner. It seems that this*

father had somehow found a way to keep his son on the better, more expensive insurance throughout his battle with cancer. This proved to be quite difficult, with many expenses being thrust upon the family that insurance would not cover. Zachary made it into remission, but the COBRA payments became too high for this family, so they buckled and tried to get their son on state assistance. At that time, the state made the one bright decision in an otherwise dark and dismal history. They offered to pay Zachary's portion of the COBRA, thus allowing the family to maintain the better insurance, while at the same time capping out the states expenditure at the cost of the monthly premium. Shortly after making that decision, Zachary relapsed. His medical bills throughout the rest of that year would reach $500,000.00, while the state had spent a mere $3,500.00 to keep that coverage active. Almost a year to the day after relapse, the COBRA folks decided to raise their rates by 50%. The father immediately contacted the state folks to get the additional amount paid so he could maintain coverage for his son. Sadly, the state refused. It seems that when making the original decision to help, the state was unaware that Zachary had secondary insurance through public assistance. That policy was only being tapped for minor expenses, co-pays, a few prescriptions, etc. The bulk of the expense was going to the folks at COBRA. The father was confused. He asked the state employees, "Are you saying that you want to turn back the clock and recant your decision to pay those $3,500.00 in premiums? Because if so, then I want to recant my decision to be able to afford COBRA. That would have put Zachary on FULL state assistance, costing you $500,000.00!" The local office was not going to be fooled by this obviously slick hustler. They quite cleverly replied with, "Hey there smarty. That $500,000.00 wouldn't have come out of our local office's budget . . . that's state and federal money. The $3,500.00 DOES come out of our local budget. And not only that, if Zachary HAD gone on full state assistance, our local office would be compensated by the state to maintain and monitor his case." The father was stunned. He had connived and planned for years. First, he had to be lucky enough to have a child diagnosed with a life-threatening illness. Then he needed to have his wife lose her job, forcing the family to get creative in the way they pay bills. After that, he had to trick everyone, so he could find a way to give his son coverage that would be inferior, while at the same time cost the state hundreds of thousands of dollars. NOT!!!

In the end, this is what really happened. The father looked at the situation and said this. "When a child gets diagnosed with cancer, (or any other life-threatening illness) why doesn't the state jump right in and make sure the family is able to maintain their insurance. Even if the insured parent loses their job and they go on COBRA (like us), the state is still way ahead of the game financially if they simply pay the monthly premium, instead of paying the actual medical bills. Even if the state had to pony up and pay for non-covered items, co-pays, etc, they would still be hundreds of thousands of dollars ahead with each and every child. You *do the math. COBRA is only good for 18 months, unless you are able to get the 9-month extension. But, the majority of the expense for these children occurs in the first 18 months to 2 years anyway. They either make it into remission or die. In the meantime, the family is able to use the "better" insurance, allowing them the flexibility to travel out of state if needed. Even if the family hits their lifetime cap for the child on the private insurance, that buys them time without having to do battle with the state nightmare, and it saves the state a lot of money. (Most caps are in the range of $1,000,000.00.)*

How much does the average state worker make? Paying the premiums and incidentals for one child like Zachary for one year could save the state enough to pay about ten employees $40,000.00/year. These ten specialists could be positioned around the state, doing nothing else except helping families like ours maintain their insurance. If each employee only helped one family per year, they would generate between $400,000.00 and $900,000.00 in savings for the state, depending on the diagnosis and treatment of the child. Most of you reading this have walked in our shoes. You know what the expenses are like. Do the math. In Zachary's first 12 months of diagnosis, he underwent 12 full weeks of in-patient chemotherapy, another 6 weeks of in-patient care for fevers, innumerable blood transfusions, countless scans and x-rays, major abdominal surgery, harvesting of stem cells, a stem cell bone marrow transplant, two weeks of radiation, and countless doctor's office visits. I don't even know how much that first year added up to, but a rough guess would be close to $1,000,000.00!

We always paid our insurance premiums on time and in full! The insurance companies make their money! They have actuarial tables that factor in a certain number of children like Zachary. Why should they reap the benefits of our premiums, and then be able to dump us when the child becomes a burden to them? Maybe I am just a dreamer, but the solution seems obvious to me. The state could be the hero!

PAY OUT A FRACTION OF THE MONEY YOU ARE SPENDING NOW, AND HELP FAMILIES MAINTAIN BETTER COVERAGE FOR THEIR CHILD.

Sunday, July 27, 2003 3:40 PM CDT

Weekends, weekends, weekends. We're always working towards those wonderful weekends. Mondays we're thinking about how long a week we have ahead of us. Tuesdays we're glad to have Monday behind us but we still see three long days ahead of us. Wednesdays we are starting to see the light at the end of the tunnel. Thursdays the end is near and we start to get that "good" feeling that the weekend will be great. And then Friday we can taste it. Even the British have a saying about the approaching weekend. If someone is daydreaming on Friday or working to get out early, they say they've got "P.O.E.T.S" disease. Piss Off Early Tomorrows Saturday.

Yesterday Zachary had his bowling league. He is doing really well. I think there are only three weeks left, but he has learned so much that I believe it will continue to be one of his favorite hobbies/sports. Yesterday afternoon we drove down to Palm Beach and met up with the Charlton kids and the Mathis's. We took the kids for more bowling. Because of the little ones, we had the bumpers up. Amazingly, Zachary is able to keep the ball in the middle and NOT use the bumpers. He scored a personal best 129 without relying on the bumpers. Zachary's friend Mitchell bowled a great game as well. Even though he relies on the bumpers a little bit, his 155 was a fantastic score. He had 40 after 5 frames, and then he proceeded to get a "four bagger", four strikes in a row, followed by a spare in the tenth frame. They all had a blast. It is really great to see these kids who have endured so much out there enjoying normal activities and not having to think about the cancer. Weekends are great.

I had an interesting phone call on Friday that I forgot to write about the other day. [Flashback] When we first were preparing to travel to NYC over a year ago for testing, we had a major battle with our insurance company over whether or not they would cover the expenses. After a prolonged battle, we found out that the State of Florida has a law that requires insurance companies to pay for cancer treatments that are not available within the State of Florida. So, after enlightening them, they agreed to pay the NYC hospital at the in-network scale, so the hospital wouldn't be chasing after us for payment. This system worked until our most recent trip in January. We started receiving bills from that trip about 3 months ago. I have called and called and called and talked until I am blue in the face, and I just can't seem to get answers as to why they are chasing after us for payment. Finally our friends at the oncology support team solved the puzzle. Apparently our genius insurance company had some sort of internal error, (the person who was using the one brain that they have misplaced it) and they had changed our file so that they were paying NYC at the out of network scale, which is of course much less. So, NYC was asking us for a few thousand dollars to make up the difference. This is where it gets great. Our friends on the support team convinced the insurance company of their mistake and got them to agree to fix it . . . . almost. Evidently they refused to fix the mistake by resubmitting the bills for complete payment unless . . . . (drum roll please) . . . . they heard directly from me and got my permission to reprocess the bills. Hmmmmmmmmmm

Lets see . . . . WOW this so difficult . . . . what do I do? I'm not used to facing these sort of life changing decisions . . . . do I: A) Give them permission to reprocess the bills, thus correcting the situation and relieving us of thousands of dollars in bills, or B). Refuse to allow them to reprocess the bills and find some way to come up with the money ourselves. Decisions, decisions . . . . the pressure is too intense . . . . how do I decide?

Well, I guess I've got to weigh the choices carefully and come up with some sort of plan. First I'll have to figure out if I even COULD come up with that kind of money . . . . I guess I could sell something . . . . let's see . . . . BODY PARTS! That's it! Why didn't I think of that a long time ago . . . . I mean seriously . . . . there are lots of body parts that we have two of . . . . isn't that overkill? Two eyes . . . . do I really need two? How about kidneys . . . . how often do I use both? Surely there is a market out there for 40 year old body parts . . . . Jiminy Cricket . . . I must have like 10 or 15 teeth . . . . is there a market for them? Hair won't help me . . . . unless back hair is in demand . . . . but fingers . . . . well, I've been using the middle ones quite a bit lately . . . but the little ones seem superfluous. I'll have to give this all some serious thought . . . . maybe the smart thing to do would be to push the 11 numbers on the phone and say the few words they are waiting to hear . . . . "GO AHEAD AND PAY THE BILLS YOU MORONS!"

Monday, October 13, 2003 8:34 PM CDT

Ok. I've eaten 18 pie bars today and you know what? It hasn't removed any of the stress. I just got a tummy ache for all of my troubles.

I'm starting to believe that maybe it is some sort divine plan to keep me writing journal entries. Why else would we have so much bull$%@ thrown upon us so frequently?

If I recall correctly, (and I usually do) I just wrote recently about the odds of the home health agency getting our "chemo at home" plan correct the first time. (I should have called Vegas and bet BIG money . . . . I'd have made a fortune.)

I walked in the door tonight and Rebecca was on the phone, visibly upset. The call was from the home health nursing agency making arrangements for the nurse to come over to our house tomorrow to administer the Zofran to Zachary. (Some of you read that last sentence and probably didn't notice a problem . . . . others read it and are beginning to put two and two together to get five . . . just like the idiots at home health care did.) Zofran (for those of you that are unlucky enough to know) is one of the anti-nausea drugs that are used for chemo patients. So, the obvious question of the day is; "Why are they all set to administer Zofran, but they made no mention of chemo?" Hmmmmmmmm . . . . very curious indeed! After calming Rebecca down enough to get some information, I called the gentleman (I'm using that term loosely) from the home health company and asked why we were NOT getting a nurse for chemo? His reply was interesting.

"We don't have nurses who are chemo-certified."

Oh no . . . . hell no . . . . no, no, no, no, no, no. There is NO way that you idiots have had this doctor's order for a whole week, and you're just NOW realizing that the funny long word at the bottom is a chemotherapy agent. No f'ing way! How is that humanly possible?

"Well sir, we're just a sub-contractor that the OTHER company uses when they can't fill an order for nursing."

"Ok, give me their number." (Nothing like working up the ladder of bull$#@& to find the moron responsible for making your life miserable.) Company #2 . . . . batter up!

"Why is this happening to us?"

"Well, we are a division of the company that your insurance company uses for home health nursing. Unfortunately, your county is one of the ONLY counties in Florida where we do not have licensed nurses. So, when that happens, we always sub-contract out to the aforementioned company to provide home health care. Whoever gave that contract out, failed to realize that they were referring a chemotherapy order to a company that has NO CHEMO-CERTIFIED NURSES."

Ahhh . . . . the buck has been passed again. (Not quite.) Somehow I got a very sympathetic representative on the phone. She seemed genuinely upset by the predicament that we had been placed in. She promised to make it her life's mission to fix this problem tomorrow . . . EARLY. I told her that I wanted two things from her.

1). I want this fixed early tomorrow.
2). I want an apology letter from whoever did this to us. (I'm not looking for money . . . . just a letter from someone admitting they screwed up.) She assured me that she was taking notes and would make it happen. (Riiiiiiiiiiiiiiiiiig gggghhhhht.)

So, at 8:30pm our doorbell rang and a nice gentleman was standing there with a box full of medical supplies. IV pole, saline bags, syringes, Zofran, Benadryl, IV tubing, Heparin, all sorts of goodies . . . . BUT NO CHEMO!!!!!!!

Here we are, all dressed up for the chemo ball, and no chemo date to dance with. How sad.

Scott

P.S. If you turn back the memory clock, you might remember that twenty months ago when Zachary relapsed, the insurance company lied, cheated, and used every dirty trick in their bag in a lame effort to have us doing chemo at home. At that time, the chemo in question had a much stronger agent that required much more nurse and doctor supervision. Obviously, we declined vehemently and stuck with the hospital. Now, here we are, twenty months later, trying to make life better for Zachary, (and giving the insurance company a chance to save tens of thousands of dollars) and they can't get it right.

Saturday, October 18, 2003 9:01 AM CDT

Has everyone been waiting with bated breath for the outcome of our saga?

Sorry about not updating earlier in the week. Between battling with the insurance companies, home healthcare providers, state agencies, working at my regular company, trying to get a new company off of the ground, staying updated on our battle with the nuclear plant, and saving the world (not really . . . but that made me sound MUCH more important) I've been busy.

GOOD NEWS:

The sympathetic representative from one of the bazillion companies that I've talked with this week came through on her promise to move mountains and make things happen. Tuesday at 11:50am (about 15 minutes before Rebecca was going to leave to head to Palm Beach for chemo) she called and said that the chemo was being driven down from Orlando (about 1.5hrs. away) and that the chemo-certified nurse was driving up from North Palm Beach (about 40 minutes away.) So, mountains got moved, planets were shifted, stars were realigned, and Zachary got his chemo at home on Tuesday. The rest of the week fell into place rather nicely. The nurse was very good with Zachary. She worked with Rebecca well and actually showed her how to do some of the procedures in case of an emergency. She is supposed to be our nurse from now on. (I would offer to hold my breath, but blue has never been a good shade for me.)

Zachary hasn't gotten sick once this week. It could be that not driving has saved his delicate equilibrium, or it could be that the reduced stress of not having to deal with the doctor's office all week has helped. Either way, he has done very well this week. I'm not complaining (for once.)

Rebecca is at work this morning. Her last day is tomorrow. She had originally given notice because of another job opportunity at Zachary's school, but we have since learned that the additional income she is making will preclude us from being eligible for our secondary insurance. This is another wonderful catch-22 that many families face.

Zachary is now stable enough for Rebecca to work part-time. We obviously need the money. She finds not one, but two different jobs that offer her enough hours to make some nice extra money, but not enough hours to be eligible for insurance. The extra income puts us over the edge for eligibility, so we will lose our secondary insurance. That will end up costing us more in medical bills than Rebecca can earn working those hours.

Lady's and Gentlemen, let's do the CANCER FAMILY DANCE!

"TAKE ONE STEP FORWARDS . . . . NOW TWO STEPS BACK . . . . NOW TWO STEPS FORWARD . . . . AND FIVE STEPS BACK . . . . NOW THREE STEPS FORWARD . . . . AND TWO THOUSAND FIVE HUNDRED AND TWENTY EIGHT STEPS BACK."

If you weren't paying attention, you just back pedaled off of a cliff. Sorry for the inconvenience, I hope the impact didn't break EVERY bone in your body.

Someone once said that, "Every cloud has a silver lining."

I'm sure that is true, but what they failed to inform us all is that while every cloud MAY have a silver lining, silver can be melted down and made into bullets. Those bullets have only one real use, killing werewolves. Once you shoot a werewolf, you almost always attract vampires who are looking for an easy meal. They of course suck all of the blood and then realize that dying werewolf blood doesn't sit well on an empty stomach. THEY get cranky and go on a killing spree that leaves innocent villagers and farmers dead across the country side. That of course puts a damper on the harvesting of crops, because all of those families are busy making funeral arrangements. A bad crop season always knocks the DOW down and sends investors into a frenzy. One or two of those guys ends up jumping out of a building, and you never know if they're going to land on your head.

So, every cloud MAY indeed have a silver lining, but if you live in the big city, and a stock broker lands on your head, you'll know to blame it on the clouds.

Wednesday, June 9, 2004 7:08 PM CDT

I looked up the phrase "Glutton for punishment" in my Webster's Complete Desk Reference Book yesterday and was somewhat shocked to find a picture of myself staring back at me . . . . that should have been a clue.

Last night I agreed to take Zachary with me on my sales run for today. I have done this one other time, and on that occasion, Zachary and I forgot to bring his bag of goodies, (games, books, snacks) to keep him busy. On that day, everything went relatively smoothly. Today, Zachary was somewhat more restless than I anticipated. In retrospect, I'm thinking that I should have scheduled myself for some root canal, or perhaps a total body wax hair removal . . . . or better yet, a tonsillectomy done anusscopically (spelling?) through the rectum. I don't know exactly how many times I heard, "Are we there yet?" today, but suffice it to say, it was too many. (Actually we had a great day. I just needed something to write about. He was somewhat bored at times, but he read his book and played his Nintendo SP.)

So after my long hard day at work, I make it home in anticipation of a relaxing stress-free evening. And what do you suppose I find waiting for me on the counter? Today's mail. Well, there really only was ONE letter for me, and it was a certified letter from our homeowner's insurance company.

Let me take just one moment to comment on certified letters. It is my humble opinion that ANY certified letter from your bank, insurance company, doctor, neighbor, employer, employee, court, law enforcement agency, ex-spouse, or ANY taxing authority . . . . is a BAD thing!!!! So, here I am with a dilemma. Do I open it and ruin a perfectly good evening, or do I keep it closed and ruin a perfectly good evening with worry? Hmmmmmm . . . . ruin . . . . or ruin . . . . choices, choices. These are the types of decisions that real grown-ups and leaders make every day. Sadly, I rarely fall into either of those categories . . . . so I flipped the mental coin that resides quite comfortably in my head and opened the letter. Much to my surprise, it was GOOD news! The insurance company had decided that, in light of the fact that I live within 3,000 miles of the beach and am almost certainly directly in the path of any and all hurricanes that may come this way, that they are canceling ALL home owners' policies for this region. Whew! And I was worried. I mean . . . . these insurance companies are owned by shareholders. I would never want my need for insurance to stand in the way of these poor shareholders from profiting from their investments. I mean really . . . . if I actually NEEDED to make a claim, it could drastically reduce the value of the company. I tip my hat to them. I guess they will be insuring homes that aren't susceptible to hurricanes, tornados, earthquakes, flooding, fires, drought, locusts, wind, sun, rain, snow, freezing, terrorist attack, or any other manmade or natural occurrence. Who can blame them? I'm sure there are like . . . .

. . . . . five or ten homes in Idaho or Arkansas that fall into their criteria.

Although, now that I think about this a little more . . . . I'm starting to sense a trend. Ever since Zachary was diagnosed, our insurance company has done everything in its power to try and drop us. (Read back from the early journal entries if you dare.) Why should THEY have to insure sick people? It is much more profitable to insure folks who never need any medical coverage. (I need to get into this racket.)

All kidding aside, I've devised a somewhat foolproof plan for getting revenge on BOTH the medical and home owner's insurance companies. Tomorrow I am going to become a 15 pack a day cigarette smoker. Now, I've never been a smoker, so this may take some getting used to. The plan is, by mid September when my home owner's policy expires, I develop lung cancer. Then, one day before it expires, I "accidentally" leave a lit cigarette on the bed after we leave the house. BAM! Huge medical bills AND a new house! That'll teach em!

Scott

P.S. One of the perks of having Zachary all day was to hear him talk about various subjects. One that you may find amusing was his "list" of girls he likes. Now, to save him HUGE amounts of embarrassment, the list that I am posting is the celebrity list. The list of local classmates is very confidential and will never be posted here . . . . unless I run out of material one day. And . . . . the winners are:

In fourth place . . . . Britney Spears
In third place . . . . Lindsay Lohan
In second place . . . . The Olsen Twins
In first place . . . . Hilary Duff.

(I'm thinking the Olsen twins should probably count as two, but I can't tell them apart. But, if you are a stickler for detail . . . . he DOES favor blondes, so whoever is more blonde, is really in second . . . then the others all follow her.)

Sunday, January 9, 2005 9:04 AM CST

Let's talk for a minute about the 1996 HIPAA law and how it serves to protect us from ourselves.

As most of you in the CSC already know, the HIPAA laws are there to protect US. If you were to do a search online and type in 'HIPAA law', you would see (as I did) that there is more information about this heralded legislation than any one person could possibly hope to read in a lifetime. And yet, we are all safer (right), and better off with it firmly in place. (That's not your monitor leaking; it's the sarcasm literally pouring out of your computer.)

I'm sure that if I were so inclined, I could probably spend many months analyzing and picking apart the HIPAA law and how it fails to "serve" us on many fronts. For now, I feel inspired to focus on just one of the flaws that I have found.

The one part of the HIPAA law that I want to discuss is the section that deals with privacy and your local pharmacy. Hmmmm. This must be an important issue. Our local chain is the largest in the country, and they are taking it QUITE seriously. Every January I submit a request to our pharmacy for a printout showing what we've spent in the previous year on drugs for each of us. This information is useful when filing tax returns. (When your medical expenses regularly exceed $12,000/yr. you DON'T want to take the standard deductions.) So, back to the pharmacy. Every year they cooperate and print out the handy dandy year-end totals for me to submit to the accountant. THIS year, I ran into a small roadblock when I went in to retrieve the data. They handed over mine and Zachary's without question, (I am his father after all,) however, when it came to Rebecca's, the red flags went up, the alarms went off, and the HIPAA law book came crashing down on the counter. "YOU ARE NOT REBECCA!" (Thanks for clearing that one up . . . . I was confused about my identity until you sorted that out for me.) "ONLY REBECCA CAN RETRIEVE HER PERSONAL, PRIVATE, CONCEALED, SECRET, INDIVIDUAL, INFORMATION." "YOU ARE NOT ALLOWED TO SEE WHAT DRUGS SHE HAS BEEN TAKING OR HOW MUCH SHE IS SPENDING ON MEDICATIONS . . . . THAT IS HER PRIVATE BUSINESS."

WOW . . . . what a relief! I'm SO glad the HIPAA laws were there, firmly in place to protect Rebecca from my sinister plan of saving her an extra trip to the pharmacy!

Wait a minute! (Light bulb going off in my head.) I just realized that we need to call the HIPAA police. There has been a major infraction of all that is holy and safe in the world of HIPAA. How could this have happened?

Just two days prior to my attempt to violate the sanctity of the HIPAA realm by picking up some sheets of paper, I was in that VERY same pharmacy, dealing with the VERY same pharmacy techs . . . . and what was I doing there you ask? I was paying for, and picking up Rebecca's prescriptions. WHAT? Blasphemy! WHAT

KIND OF AN OUTRAGE HAVE I INFLICTED UPON THE MEMORY OF THE HIPAA LAW FOUNDERS? I was allowed to pay for and RECEIVE her drugs? Where were the laws protecting Rebecca from her evil husband? I'm sure I spirited the drugs away to a private location where I could sit and read all about what medicines she was taking . . . . medicines for her lupus . . . . SECRET medicines for her health . . . . "OHHHHH THE HUMANITY OF IT ALL!!!!!!!!!!!!!!

I could have tampered with them . . . . I have could sold her secrets to the tabloids for millions of dollars. I could have RULED THE WORLD WITH THAT INFORMATION! "Well, good luck with that!" (For you Sponge Bob fans.)

So there you have it. I confess. I, Scott the deceiver, of sound state of mind, (it's all relative), knowingly and willfully, purchased my wife's prescriptions for her to save her a trip to the pharmacy, KNOWING full well, that two days later I could hide like a coward behind the ingenious HIPAA laws to force her to make an extra trip later on to the pharmacy to retrieve private information about medicines that I already knew about. (That was one LONG sentence . . . . let's not ask our English teachers if it is punctuated properly please.)

I can only hope that the courts will go easy on me and take into consideration that while I may have MEANT well with my actions, I clearly caused irreparable harm to be inflicted upon the integrity of the HIPAA laws.

Saturday, January 15, 2005 8:48 AM CST

****TEST RESULTS ARE IN****

But first . . . . a follow up to my previous HIPAA Law journal entry. I had to go back to the pharmacy for some things, and I didn't know if Rebecca had gotten over there to pick up her top secret 2004 year-end information. So, being the inquisitive type, I meandered over to the pharmacy counter and asked the clerk (the same one who refused to hand over the info the last time) if Rebecca had picked it up yet. The clerk found the papers and said, "No, they are still here." Then he proceeded to place them BACK into the bin for safe keeping. The pharmacist on duty must have sensed trouble brewing, because she inched her way closer to the counter to intervene between me and the soon to be berated clerk. I looked at her and asked what the logic was behind their handing me Rebecca's drugs without Rebecca present, but NOT handing me a piece of paper that lists those same drugs. She shrugged and hid nicely behind the HIPAA Law that protects her right to be an imbecile. One of these days I'll track down a government worker who is well-informed on HIPAA regulations and query them as to the logic behind this policy.

So, test results are in huh? I suppose all of you are anxiously waiting for Master Scott to decipher, analyze, interpret, decode, and explain the latest and greatest news from our beloved hospital. Well, never being one who likes to disappoint, I WILL give you the results, but sadly, I don't know if I possess enough brain cells to adequately figure out the mess that IS, our test results. Here is the text from those results . . .

"There are two, three, nine, fifteen, one areas of increased, decreased, somewhat more or less greater or less than the average of the whole, or half of the part that is centrally located to the left of the right side of the top bottom part of the middle portion of the bone that is connected to that other bone that is beneath and on top of the section that is completely covered but NOT surrounded by the area that is worse than the part that is better."

Well, I hope that cleared it all up! NO? Why not? It seems fairly obvious to me that the text clearly indicates what is going on with Zachary's disease. You don't see it? Hmmmmmm. Very curious indeed!

Ok . . . . I'm not going to enter the entire text from the report . . . . suffice it to say that one area looks slightly improved, however, there are several NEW areas that are lighting up and several old areas that look worse. The spine remains unchanged. Virtually all of the new and worsening activity is in the hips. (Pelvis, sacrum, iliac, acetabulum.) Three weeks from now we will be two months out from our baseline MRI scans, so we will repeat those and see more definitive imaging of what if anything has changed. The bone marrow testing is only one month old, and since that was clean, there doesn't appear to be any reason to repeat those tests right now. The primary indicator for us remains to be Zachary's lack of symptoms or pain. The doctor is a little nervous about Zachary playing soccer twice weekly, (apparently the hips are used quite frequently when kicking and running . . . . who knew?), but, since Zachary thoroughly enjoys soccer, I don't see taking that away from him. If he truly IS getting worse, then he may never be able to play again . . . . I'm not going to rob him of this chance to enjoy his favorite activity. Zachary has two more regular season games left, and then there is a tournament of a few games . . . depending on how his team does.

Saturday, March 25, 2006 2:44 PM CST

Once again I am inspired to write another journal entry because of all of the great guest book entries! (Not really . . . . but I figure a little positive reinforcement never hurt anyone.) (Oh crap . . . . I guess then by writing "not really" you will figure out that I write when I write . . . . and regardless of how entertained I get from your posts . . . . sometimes I just don't have a journal entry in me.) (I've got to learn to stop typing everything that goes through my mind . . . . that is definitely going to get me into trouble one day.) (And why do I always put those thoughts into parentheses? I mean . . . . does that REALLY tell you that it is coming from the depths of my tiny brain?) (OK . . . . where was I?)

The SFB Company drama got interesting (or sad) yesterday. You may recall that I wrote about the incredibly funny phone satisfaction survey that I took the other night after writing about how much we hate The SFB Company and how useless they are. Well . . . . at the end of that phone call the surveyor asked if I wanted to hear from The SFB Company regarding my dissatisfaction with their company . . . . I of course am a glutton for punishment, so I agreed to another phone call. Well . . . . this lady Anne tried reaching me on Thursday. Unfortunately, I was on another phone call . . . . didn't recognize the number calling . . . . so I let it go to voice mail. The phone number on my caller ID was not a phone number that could be called back. (?) (How is that possible?) I dialed the number and got a recording from the phone company informing me that the number I was dialing was not in service. (OK . . . how is THAT possible?) The lady can call me from that number . . . but I can't call back. (Whatever.) So on Friday . . . . I told Rebecca that if she called back . . . . tell her to call my cell phone . . . . but tell her to wait like 5 minutes . . . . so Rebecca could call and warn me that she was calling . . . . that way I could get off of any other call that I was on. For once . . . . one of my plans worked out . . . . she called Rebecca and said that she would try my cell phone . . . but that if I didn't answer . . . she was NOT calling back again. (Nothing like customer service.)

Anne and I hit it off like nuns in a whore house. She was NOT the warmest individual in the world . . . . BUT . . . . she seemed pretty knowledgeable about The SFB Company and its inner workings. I went round and round with her over the semantics of how her company and the pharmacy that they own communicate . . . . (or don't communicate.) . . . . and she told me this.

"Zachary's plan is NOT a good plan. On his plan YOU are responsible for paying UP FRONT all medical and drug bills . . . . and then YOU are responsible for submitting claims to get reimbursed."

OK

Hmmmmmmm.

OK

My response: "Well . . . then how do we get treated at hospitals and doctor's offices without them demanding payment upfront?"

Attila The Hun: "Those types of providers file the claims as a courtesy to you. They very rarely will demand upfront payments."

Me: "OK. . . . then how did we get from February of last year until December of last year without the pharmacy demanding any payment . . . . once we reached our max out of pocket . . . they just took care of billing you?"

Attila: "They must have made an internal decision to take care of that for you . . . because of the large number of claims that you file in a year."

Me: "I remember very clearly the conversation I had with The SFB Company rep when we first started on this chemo plan over a year ago. I was complaining about how our local pharmacy wanted us to front the payment on thousands and thousands of dollars of medicines each and every week for us to receive the chemo. Then, we were supposed to submit the claims to The SFB Company, the way you are describing, and wait patiently for the refund. When I explained to THAT rep that I don't have tens of thousands of dollars to play that game, she recommended that I call their in-house pharmacy and set up an account for Zachary. As she explained it, the in-house pharmacy is owned by The SFB Company and they will process the claims in a manner that will take into consideration our out of pocket situation . . . . thus getting our medicine to us WITHOUT having to be the banker for The SFB Company or their pharmacy. Using their pharmacy was THE SFB COMPANY REP'S IDEA!!"

Attila: "That rep was wrong."

Me: "" (I was speechless at this point.)

Attila: "As I said before . . . . you chose a bad plan."

Me: "I didn't CHOOSE any plan. Zachary was on Cobra and we were forced to move to a conversion policy to avoid losing insurance altogether."

Attila: "Well . . . . those conversion policies aren't any good."

Me: "YA THINK?"

Attila: "Is there anything else that I can help you with?"

Me: (At this point I was tempted to ask her if she would humor me by trying to shove The SFB Company's insurance policy and their regulations up her A$$. But discretion is the better part of valor, so I just told her to %$#@ OFF!) Actually . . . . I asked for assistance in sorting out the mess revolving around the $715.40 that their in-house pharmacy hoodwinked out of me about a month ago.

Attila: "I can see where they may have processed some claims incorrectly . . . . it happens. I will review this and get The SFB Company to reimburse the pharmacy so that they can reimburse you."

Me: "Will I get back any interest for loaning them the money?" (I didn't actually ask that question . . . . but I can guarantee you that the thought crossed my mind.) (What I actually said was this.) "Thank you for your help . . . . may I ask what your title is?"

Attila: "Yes . . . . I am an elevated supervisor."

Me: "Elevated . . . . meaning your chair sits higher than the other supervisors?" (Once again . . . I didn't say that . . . but it's the thought that counts . . . . right?) (I asked if I could keep her phone number for future problems . . . . and she had no problem with that. She explained that she normally handles pharmacy issues . . . but she is very knowledgeable about EOB's and would be happy to help in any way possible.)

So . . . . that was my most recent The SFB Company drama. I'm not saying that The SFB Company is out to screw over any of its policy holders . . . . but I'm pretty sure the phone reps keep a copy of "How To Thoroughly Aggravate and Totally Piss Off Any and All Callers Who Might Be Trying To Do The Unthinkable . . . . Get Their Money's Worth . . . . in Three Easy Lessons."

Wednesday, March 29, 2006 5:52 PM CST

I am sorry.

I have to apologize to any of you lurkers who actually look forward to this time of year. I usually put a lot of planning and thought into an entertaining April fool's Day story . . . .

. . . but this year I have been so preoccupied by the insurance debacle that I have not had time to work on that tradition. It has truly gotten to the point where I

can't possibly come up with ANYTHING that rivals the nonsense that the insurance company keeps throwing at us. There is no prank, joke, story, or scenario that comes CLOSE to the reality of The SFB Company and their in-house pharmacy.

Today provided yet another amazing chapter in the ongoing saga. (Where to begin . . . where to begin?)

Let us start with the first phone call. (I suppose that the best way to write about this is to provide the actual dialog (as I remember it) so you can all just follow along.

Me: "Hello . . . . this is Scott."

Attila: "Hi Mr. Finestone, this is Anne from The SFB Company . . . . I promised to get back to you once I learned more about the $715.40 charge that you claimed the pharmacy wrongly billed you for."

(Let me pause here. If you haven't been reading my updates . . . then this isn't going to make a whole lot of sense to you. I hate to be repetitive, but you REALLY need to go back and read like the last 5 or 6 updates . . . . I know it gives you flashbacks to when you were given homework . . . . and for that I am sorry . . . . I hated homework . . . . but nothing sucks more than reading a story and realizing at the end that you needed to have read the prequel to fully understand the content.)

Me: "Yes Anne . . . . what were you able to find out?"

Attila: "After reviewing your account from 2005 I was able to determine that the pharmacy DID overcharge you and that you are due a refund of $715.40."

Me: "OK . . . . how do we make that happen?"

Attila: "Well, I have already issued a check to the pharmacy . . . . they received it on 3/25/06. That check includes several other claims that were processed incorrectly. Unfortunately, when I spoke with their representative, she informed me that the refund to them will NOT be posted in their system for at least two weeks."

Me: "OK . . . . so they will issue me a refund check in two weeks then . . . right?"

Attila: "Well . . . . no! . . . . It's not that simple. The pharmacy informed me that they will NOT issue you a refund based on my conversation with them. They will wait for you to call them and specifically request a refund."

Me: "OK . . . . I'm trying to look into the future . . . . and envision that phone call. When I do this . . . . I can clearly picture the phone rep informing me that they have NO record of any SFB Company check getting to them . . . . and that they don't know what I am talking about."

Attila: "OK . . . . I have thought of that already. I am going to give you the check number and amount, so you can let them know exactly what you are referencing. I am also going to give you the date of service . . . . so they should be able to find it easily."

Me: "OK . . . . good . . . . so I wait two weeks . . . . I call them up . . . . I give them all of this data . . . . and THEN they will issue me a refund check . . . . right?"

Attila: "Hmmmmm . . . actually it is not that simple. See . . . . that company does not usually write checks to anyone . . . . if you had paid for the bill on your credit card, they would simply refund your card . . . . but since you wrote an actual check . . . . they may try to issue the refund BACK to us (The SFB Company) and then have us write the check to you."

(I'm not sure . . . . but I think at this point in the conversation my head may have exploded. I didn't pass out or anything . . . . and I don't remember seeing any blood or brain fluid anywhere . . . . but I'm pretty sure something in my head erupted.)

Me: "OK . . . . I'm a little bit slow . . . . so let's go over this again . . . . for me to get a refund for the money that the pharmacy incorrectly billed me for . . . . you The SFB Company have to issue them a check . . . . which they then hold in their account for at least two weeks . . . . after which, they will write a check to you . . . . so you can then refund me?"

Attila: "I know it sounds bizarre . . . . and I'm trying to find a way around this . . . . there is a second level at that company where I believe I can get them to bypass the step where they issue a check to us . . . . but I won't know for sure for another day or two."

Me: "A LITTLE BIZARRE? A LITTLE BIZARRE? . . . . Lady . . . . it couldn't get any more bizarre unless your two companies required me to dance naked in the street with clothes pins on my nipples before processing this refund."

(OK . . . . maybe I didn't say that . . . . but you've got to admit, it would have been a great impact statement.)

Attila: "*Let me work some more on this . . . . the important thing is . . . . you will get your refund . . . . it just is going to take some time. Wait the two weeks . . . . then call them and let's see what happens after that.*"

Me: "*Well . . . . now that you mention it . . . . I really didn't want to rain on your parade of good news . . . . but there is another issue that has NOT been addressed here . . . and I believe it has a direct relevance to your plan.*"

Attila: "*What is that?*"

Me: "*Whenever my wife or I call the pharmacy company lately, they refuse to speak with us . . . because we are NOT Zachary Finestone . . . . and he is self-insured. We have explained that he is only 12 years old and that we are both his custodial guardians . . . . but that has not deterred them from requiring all sorts of bizarre authorizations before they will communicate with us. I can see what is going to happen . . . . I will call them and they won't want to speak with me.*"

Attila: "*That is just stupid. Here at The SFB Company we have a house policy that allows us to deal with custodial guardians of minor children.*"

Me: "*And when I call them . . . . they answer the phone . . . . 'The SFB Company—Pharmacy division.*'"

Attila: "*They are a different company from us . . . . I have explained this before.*"

Me: "*I'm not saying . . . . I'm just saying.*"

Attila: "*Well . . . . I can run interference for you. When you are ready to call them, call me first . . . . you may recall that our phone system will require that you leave me a voice mail . . . . I will then call you back . . . . and then we can conference call them and get through this.*"

Me: "*So . . . . let me get this straight. To get my money back . . . . the money that should never have left my bank account . . . . the money that I can't afford to be writing checks for . . . . the money that they illegally and immorally billed me for . . . . this is what I need to do: 1). I call your voice mail and leave you a message. 2). You call me back. 3). You then get them on the phone. 4). They and you and me . . . attempt to get on the same page regarding the date of service, billed amount, policy procedures, company rules . . . . and the square root of the azimuth of the sun when it is in its mid-summer position in the sky. 5). They THEN will likely inform us that they are issuing a refund to NOT ME . . . .*"

but you. 6). You will then have to wait for the money to get BACK to The SFB Company. 7). At some point you will call me again . . . . or simply issue a refund check BACK to me. 8). I then take the check for $715.40 and attempt to get a bank to process it, since by this time . . . . banks will no longer be dealing with checks . . . . the world will have gone to one currency . . . . and checks will have become a thing of the past."

(OK . . . . maybe some of that sarcasm that I have become know for was left out of that diatribe . . . . but let me assure you . . . that just because I wasn't saying those words . . . . it doesn't mean they weren't flowing through my brain.)

Attila: "If you ever need to call them . . . . and feel that there is going to be problem . . . .
. . . . call me first and I will mediate that call for you."

Me: "OK . . . . sounds like a plan."

Now . . . . that call took place this afternoon around 12pm or so. As I have written before . . . I just can't make this stuff up . . . . and it gets better.

At around 3pm, my cell phone rings . . . . and guess what . . . . it's The SFB Company . . . . a different rep calling to inform me that SHE has been working on my problems. (This is like the Twilight Zone . . . . I SWEAR I looked around to see if I was on Candid Camera.) So, here is the transcript from THAT phone call. (For comedy purposes . . . I am going to call this second rep . . . . Attila II.)

Attila II: "Hi Mr. Finestone, I am with The SFB Company . . . . and we spoke before . . . . I have been working on your problem with the overpayment and I have reviewed all of the claims from 2005. I believe that I have isolated the problem and that I have determined what has happened."

(The instinct here to let her go on and on and on and on and on and on about this was overwhelming . . . . but I felt a minute pang of guilt . . . . so I let her off of the hook . . . . or so I thought.)

Me: "Actually, I just spoke with Anne from your company . . . . and she informed me that your company has issued a refund check to the pharmacy and that I am just weeks away from getting a refund."

Attila II: "I see some notes in your file . . . . let me see if I can make heads or tails of this . . . . give me a few moments."

(At this juncture . . . . I must have been hit in the head with a stupid bat a few times, because I had a sudden urge to fill the awkward silence while she was reviewing our file . . . . I had NO idea what awkward was until I started opening my mouth.)

Me: "So . . . . I guess this Anne woman is some sort of elevated supervisor . . . or escalated supervisor for you guys . . . . I can't even remember how I got hooked up with her."

Attila II: "Actually . . . . she IS an elevated supervisor . . . . and she was brought into this because of the answers you gave during the phone survey that you took."

Me: *(Laughing)* "OH . . . . I did sort of have some bad things to say . . . . that guy asked me some ridiculous questions . . . ."

Attila II: "I have not yet seen your survey."

(Once again . . . . I should have quit while I was ahead . . . . or not behind . . . . or whatever . . . but somehow I just couldn't help myself.)

Me: "Well . . . . the survey guys was asking me to rate a previous call with one of your reps, and I gave the lowest marks possible . . . . actually I asked if I could give lower marks and he wouldn't let me."

Attila II: "I WILL get to see the survey . . . . it hasn't come down through the system yet . . . . you see . . . . I AM THE PHONE REP THAT THE SURVEY WAS BASED ON."

(That sound you are hearing now is the same pin dropping that I heard at approximately 3:13pm today.)

(How is this possible? How in the world do they allow the SAME person to call me back? AND HOW IS IT NOW THAT I AM FEELING LIKE THE BAD GUY?

I AM THE BAD GUY?

WHY DO I SUDDENLY FEEL GUILTY?

THIS SUCKS!

How did this get all turned around?

I must be the dumbest person on the planet.

I mean . . . . she opened the trap door . . . . she shined a light into the trap door.

She commented on how DEEP and dangerous the trap door looked.

And I leapt right through the opening and fell hard!

Me: "Well . . . . if it makes you feel any better . . . . we had spoken with like 5 or 6 reps that week, and my answers were based on all of those conversations."

Attila II: "We will be using your survey information as a learning and teaching tool for future phone calls."

(Oh crap.)

(Oh crap crap.)

(Crap crap crap crap crap crap.)

If this state wasn't so damn flat . . . . I'd climb the nearest mountain and jump off.

(I . . . . JUST . . . . CAN'T . . . . MAKE . . . . THIS . . . . STUFF . . . . UP!)

I am like a magnet for this garbage.

And I better NOT catch ANY of you laughing or giggling about any of this. You should be reading all of this nodding understandingly with a sympathetic expression FIRMLY planted on your face.

Tuesday, August 1, 2006 7:03 PM CDT

I hadn't planned to write another journal entry so soon, but I wanted to get this across while it was fresh in my mind. (Small minds are like that . . . . you have to empty them more often or you just lose the thoughts.)

Zachary has gained back his weight! I know this because his pink eye and sinus infection returned . . . . and I know THAT because he woke up Friday morning with eyes swollen shut and a stuffy nose . . . . so I got him an appointment with his local pediatrician. AND that . . . . is what prompted this story.

You see . . . . as loony as I am . . . . I am occasionally blessed with a logical thought or two. Here is what I came up with. I knew that Zachary's oncologist had called in eye drops for the pink eye that Zachary had finished with a week earlier. (There were still plenty of drops in the bottle . . . . the seven day course had ended.) I also knew that he did NOT have a fever, but was probably highly contagious with the pink eye. I didn't want to A). expose any other oncology kids to his pink eye, and B). make him sit in a car for a 45 minute drive down and then back again. So . . . . I called his local pediatrician (whom he had not seen in over a year) and made an appointment. I then called the oncologist's office and explained my plan. They agreed that going to the pediatrician was better for everyone and that they just wanted to be kept in the loop as to what the local doctor said.

So far . . . . everything was going as planned.

Now . . . . Zachary's local pediatrician had long ago packed his bags and left the state of Florida. He had been replaced with a couple of other doctors who we had heard good things about. A few minutes after making the appointment, that office called to inform us that they were getting a "Policy not active" message from The SFB Company when they tried to access their automated system to make sure that his insurance was still active. Hmmmmm. Rebecca reread the policy number to them and let them know that I would be bringing a copy of it with me. I arrived at the office about ten minutes early (always planning ahead) and again they said that his insurance was not active. Hmmmmm.

Not active.

Cancelled.

Not usable.

OK . . . . so . . . . if his insurance is "not active", then how in the hell is our local oncology office getting paid. I mean . . . we've been using the same policy for almost two years now . . . . so . . . . we've gone over to Ft. Myers for testing ($16,000 per trip), and we've had 25 rounds or so of chemo . . . . ($$$$$?????) . . . . so what gives?

They had me keep Zachary out in the lobby waiting area away from the other kids . . . . and they asked that I call The SFB Company and have them fax over confirmation that he is indeed insured. I called the phone number on the card . . . . and I went through the obligatory automated system. It asked for his ID number . . . . which I provided . . . . and it promptly informed me that his ID was, "Not a valid ID in their system."

(Oooooh . . . . that could prove to be a bit awkward.)

Because I am blessed with eternal patience . . . . I pressed the '0' key to get to a LIVE person. The automated system didn't like this . . . . it tried repeatedly to get me to make a selection OTHER than '0' so that it could "better route my call."

I DIDN'T WANT TO BE "BETTER ROUTED." I didn't want to be 'routed' at all! "Routing" didn't sound like a lot of fun to me. I wanted a human . . . . not another robot.

I finally got through to an operator . . . . and after explaining my dilemma; she informed me that "Your son's ID is not on file as being active." Hmmmmmm. (OK . . . . I will admit that at this point in the saga . . . . my eternal patience MAY have been stretched to its limits . . . . and my blood pressure MAY have escalated somewhat . . . .)

"Not on file as being active you say?"
"That is correct."
"That is NOT correct . . . . he is an oncology patient . . . . he gets seen by his oncologist every single week . . . . he gets chemo two out of every three weeks . . . . for the past two years we have been doing this . . . . with an ACTIVE account."
"Hmmmmmm . . . . please hold . . . . let me transfer you to a different dept."
"OK . . . . you do that."
(Insert Jeopardy music here.)
(Pause)
(Pause)
(Pause some more)
"Hi . . . . how may I help you?"
(Re-explain story.)
"Yes . . . . I see your son's ID right here . . . . his account is active and fine."
(Pause)
(Pause some more).

"OK.... could you please fax over something to his pediatrician so that I can get him treated for an illness?"
"Sure ... what is the phone number?"
(Providing phone number.)
"Good bye."
"Good bye."

So .... he had a sinus infection and needed an antibiotic .... and they had us continue with the eye drops. Both seemed to work ... because his eyes improved quickly.

I of course was NOT through with The SFB Company. When I had some free time, I called them back and once again the automated system couldn't find his ID.... and once again I tried to get an operator .... and once again the system fought me .... and once again I persisted .... and once again I got an operator .... and once again she couldn't find his account on file .... and once again I got transferred to another operator .... and once again that operator was able to find his ID. (Whew .... that took a lot of oxygen to say all of that.) So I casually explained that while I thoroughly enjoy playing games with The SFB Company all day long ... the sad truth is that occasionally Zachary needs to see a doctor OTHER than his oncologist .... and God forbid we needed an emergency room .... I would be VERY put out if I was told again that he did NOT have insurance coverage ... when we all know that he does. She agreed and asked that I hold so she could call the automated system herself to see what it did. She came back on after a minute or so and agreed that there was a glitch somewhere in the system. She, along with a supervisor informed me that they had never seen this before and that they had no idea as to how to fix the problem. They asked me for contact information and said that they were going to start making calls to higher ups, in an attempt to resolve the issue. They also said that they would call me back with results.

That all happened on Friday .... today is Tuesday .... I have not heard back from them yet.

BUT .... I did get a call yesterday evening from a survey company that was calling on behalf of The SFB Company and my most recent phone call with them. Hmmmmmm .... (You've got to be kidding me .... are they that stupid?)

What I love most about those The SFB Company surveys is that they only have a scale from 1 to 5. 1 being "poor" and 5 being "great." The other great thing is that they ask questions that are so generic it is almost impossible to give an intelligent answer.

For example . . . . if they ask, "How would you rate your call overall?"

"Well . . . . the operator was certainly sincere enough . . . she seemed to care about my problem and she wanted to find a solution . . . . however . . . . she was unable to remedy the problem . . . . so am I rating the operator on how she spoke with me . . . or on her ability to fix the problem?"

"Sir . . . . you need to rate the call overall with the scale from 1 to 5."

(Unbelievable.)

So . . . . I proceeded to give a series of ratings . . . . that were mostly generic . . . . and then she asked me about how I felt towards The SFB Company as a company . . . . big mistake . . . . I asked if I could use a number lower than '1' . . . . she didn't like that.

Idiots.

Basically . . . . they are asking questions that they have absolutely NO interest in hearing the answers to.

Oh well . . . . I will try to remember to update you if this saga ever ends . . . . don't hold your breath.

Today Zachary had his wellness checkup with the same pediatrician's office . . . . and as part of that exam . . . he needed to have his private area checked . . . . and Zachary is used to having his oncologist . . . . who is a man . . . . do that exam . . . . he is NOT used to . . . . ANY female examining him . . . . or even talking about seeing that area on him. Unfortunately, there no longer is a man at that office . . . . so we really didn't have a choice. Zachary was uncooperative . . . . to say the least . . . . he ended up getting grounded and lost many of his electronic devices . . . . including but not limited to his cell phone, his computer, his TV, and his Xbox.

He ended up getting the exam . . . . and living through it.

Wednesday, July 18, 2007 8:58 PM CDT

You want an update . . . . YOU CAN'T HANDLE AN UPDATE!

(I couldn't resist the "A Few Good Men" reference.)

Well . . . . I can give you an update . . . . but I am warning you now that there is definitely going to be some pieces to the puzzle that you will NOT get tonight . . . . tomorrow is D-Day.

BUT . . . . you've cried like little babies for an update . . . . so you'll get one.

Zachary has been walking and standing more and more each day. He is still using the wheel chair for longer distances, like around the mall, but around the house, he is showing improvement. I spoke with his Philly doctor yesterday, and she wants to see at least 51% non-wheel chair mobility. I believe that we are there, but tomorrow we return to the local oncologist's office for a professional evaluation.

Our Philly doctor asked about Zachary's pain, and when I explained that he has conveyed how the pain is intense when he first stands up or puts pressure on his feet, and then slowly, as he walks, it becomes more tolerable. She said that this is exactly how this neuropathy presents. It can take a huge psychological toll on the patient, because they have to somehow get over that MASSIVE hurdle of forcing themselves to endure a "known" pain, to get to an "unknown" area, of reduced pain after some time. She is convinced that his pain will not be with him long term, and that he has not gotten any permanent nerve damage. But, the doctors up there are very conscience of Zachary's quality of life, and they want to make sure that we can avoid these side-effects in the future.

There was another interesting development from our conversation yesterday. I had asked about the possibility of getting a certain Phase I drug on a compassionate basis if the pain issues weren't resolved enough to allow us to continue on the current chemo. The reason for this request was simple . . . . we feel that Zachary has been "beaten" up pretty badly over the past few weeks, and we are concerned that if we had to switch treatments, and go to the MIBG therapy, we would be knocking his immune system WAY down, possibly far enough to require stem cell recovery. So, we were thinking that a hiatus from the heavier chemo-like agents might be a good idea. Our doctor said that her team has been talking about Zachary and discussing options . . . . they feel that because his disease has presented itself as more of an indolent disease than an aggressive disease lately, that he could benefit from the lower dosage MIBG therapy that they have been perfecting lately. That treatment would only require a one day treatment, every six weeks. AND, it is much less likely to have any severe side-effects, like the need for stem cell recovery. In fact, his counts would probably not be knocked down too much at all. Originally, they were discussing giving him the one week MIBG therapy, which would have been very harsh on his system.

So, having heard of this back up plan, we are much more at ease with the knowledge that we may be at or near the end of our run with this current chemo. Having a backup plan makes getting through the day much, much easier.

So, tomorrow we will know what the final decision is. Our local doctor will examine Zachary and then communicate with the Philly doctor, and then we will know what we are doing.

Other than that, the only other news from today of interest was the phone call that I got while trying to eat dinner. Rebecca wrote down on a sheet of paper that The SFB Company was on the phone.

Here is the actual transcript from that call:

"Hello, this is Scott Finestone."

"Hi Mr. Finestone, this is Ms. Dipshit from The SFB Company." (OK . . . her actual name was probably NOT Ms. Dipshit, but I have changed her name to protect her from anyone out there who might not like the nature of the phone call.)

"Yes . . . . Ms. Dipshit . . . . what can I do for you?"

"Well, I spoke with you on 7/2/07, you called about a claim that had not been paid in full, do you remember this?"

[Sidebar] OK . . . . just to explain . . . . after our initial trip to Philly, we got a bill from the hospital saying that The SFB Company had only paid about 65% of the bill, and that the other $1,200.00 or so was on us! The reason for the denial of full benefits was, "No prior approval." I called them on 7/2/07 and explained that we were given no other options other than Philly and that my son's disease required us to get there quickly . . . . at that time, she informed me that it was not a problem and that they would resubmit the claim for further payment.

[Back to Ms. Dipshit.]

"Yes, I remember speaking with you."

"Well, we've reviewed the bill and found that we paid the correct amount, and that any other portion that remains is your responsibility."

"My responsibility? What is the reason for this."

"Well, it says here in the notes that because the injury was from a work-related incident, we are only going to pay the portion that we already paid."

"A work related injury you say? Are you kidding me?"

(Actually at this point in the conversation, I don't remember a whole lot . . . . I may have been screaming . . . . I know that blood was shooting out of my ears, and that I may have actually growled at her over the phone . . . . I'm not too sure.) *"An injury? How exactly did my 13 year old cancer patient son get a work-related injury when he does NOT work, and has been a cancer patient for over 7 years?"*

"Well . . . . I'm just reading from the notes . . . . it LOOKS like they have indicated that it was a work-related injury . . . . I'm not sure what this abbreviation means."

"Well . . . . I need to know what is going on here, because in 7 years, we have always met our out of pocket responsibility by the second or third week of January . . . . and the rest of the year is on YOU."

"Sir, I am going by the notes here, and they read that this is a comprehensive policy, not a PPO policy . . . . do you know what your coverage is as the insured parent?"

"Ahhhh . . . . yeah . . . . I'm NOT the insured parent . . . . Zachary has a conversion policy . . . . the same policy that he has had for several years . . . . he is self-insured . . . . as he has ALWAYS been."

"Well . . . . this comprehensive notation seems to indicate that we have paid our portion correctly."

"OK . . . . well . . . . how about you look again, because we have been to NYC three times, our local hospital numerous times, and to Ft. Myers about four times for this same scan . . . . so how come, all of a sudden, you are changing your requirements for approval on this scan? We need this scan . . . . WHEN WE NEED IT . . . . to keep him on the correct protocol . . . . "

"Oh . . . . wait . . . . I should have read further in the notes . . . . it says here that on 7/5/07 we made an additional payment. The bill was paid in full at the entire contract price . . . . there is no amount due by the insured party . . . . sorry."

" . . . . " (Yeah . . . I was speechless . . . . go figure.)

"Mr. Finestone . . . . are you there?"

" . . . . " (Still speechless.)

"Mr. Finestone . . . . I can give you a confirmation number that you can pass along to the provider if they need proof that we paid the balance . . . . do you have a pen?"

" . . . . " (Stunned silence . . . . shock . . . . high blood pressure . . . . you name it.)

"Are you ready to take down that number?"

"Yes . . . . please give me that number Ms. Dipshit . . . . and THANK you for ruining yet ANOTHER one of what is SURE to be my last days on this Earth."

Scott

P.S. Oh . . . by the way . . . . that entire script . . . . was basically word for word . . . . I may have embellished a little bit there at the end, but that is EXACTLY what happened.

Wednesday, August 29, 2007 12:17 AM CDT

Bucking the trend of only updating this page once per week, I have decided to give you all a "bonus" update today.

Over the years I have written several updates that have dealt with our experiences with The SFB Company. (Better known as the "Evil Doers.") So, in fairness to the "Evil Doers", I have decided to write something nice about them, sort of. We were contacted recently by our new case manager! (TA DA).

(That didn't have quite the impact that I was aiming for, did it?)

We have, in the past, been assigned a case manager on at least 3 other occasions that I can recall. Each and every time, the case manager had NO ability to manage ANYTHING, let alone our case. So you can appreciate why I may have been somewhat skeptical when we received news of yet another person who was there to help us. But, being the fair, calm, thoughtful, and understanding kind of guy that I am, I decided to give this new person the benefit of the doubt. (In other words, I was willing to give her just enough rope to hang herself.)

Thankfully, she has proven to be helpful so far. I have called and emailed her about a couple of bills that providers are claiming have not been paid properly, and she was able to address the problems and make the necessary adjustments.

The other interesting fact is that she is not only our case manager, but she specializes in oncology. (Hmmmmm.) (That might have been a way to lead into my next comments.)

About two weeks after we were contacted by our new case manager, we received an interesting packet from The SFB Company. It contained a variety of brochures along with a letter that read as follows:

Dear Member,

It has been brought to our attention that you may have been tested for and/or received medical treatment for a cancer diagnosis. Since our information is based on health claims records and not information provided directly by your physician or other treating providers, it may not accurately reflect your medical condition. If that is the case, please disregard this letter.

Enclosed are brochures that provide information about living a healthy lifestyle and ways to help prevent cancer. These brochures are provided to you as part of THE SFB COMPANY Healthcare oncology program.

If you or a family member is currently in active treatment for cancer and need assistance, please call THE SFB COMPANY Healthcare oncology program at (phone number.)

This program is designed to support participants and their families who are coping with a cancer diagnosis. Our goal is to help educate you and your family on your diagnosis, provide you with additional information about your treatment options and help you to minimize or avoid some of the side effects and complications of treatment. In addition, we will answer questions about your health benefit plan, and tell you about available resources and services that may benefit you or your family. As needed, an Oncology Program Specialist will help coordinate your health care services, as well as facilitate communication among your treating providers.

We hope you find the information in these brochures helpful.

Sincerely,

Oncology Program Specialist

WOW, they seem to have thought of everything! (Or have they?)

Let us take a closer look.

Where should I begin? Oh, let's see, I think I'll start with the letter, specifically the part where they are saying, "We believe you have cancer, unless we were misinformed, in which case, sorry for scaring the shit out of you."

(OK, in their defense, it wasn't written EXACTLY like that, but that's what I saw when I read it, so whatever.)

How is it that they are just NOW figuring out that Zachary has cancer? One would think that all of the chemotherapy over the years would have been somewhat of a clue as to what his diagnosis was. Although, I'm sure there is an entire subculture of street chemo users out there. NOT

What should we look at next? How about the helpful brochures? They seem like a logical place to start.

There were four brochures enclosed, I will start with the one titled:

"Eating More Fiber"

This one is actually pretty harmless. Zachary could use some more fiber in his diet, and this one basically tells you how to accomplish that feat. It does NOT however, explain how to get a 13 year old child to replace beef jerky, candy bars, fruit roll-ups, and macaroni & cheese with broccoli, nuts, asparagus, and fruit.

The second one is titled:

"Choosing Fats—They're Not All the Same."

This one deals mainly with trying to cuts fats, so that you can lose weight. Hmmmm. (Did I miss the memo where we were trying to get Zachary to lose weight?) I thought we were trying to keep the weight on, because of the loss of appetite that he occasionally experiences. (But what do I know, I'm just a parent. I guess we will start to cut back on his diet and try to get him to shed some of those excess pounds that they are so concerned about. After all, he's up to almost 112lbs. We certainly don't want him going over that 115 mark!)

The third one is titled:

"Get Walking! For Better Health at Any Age."

This one is chock full of cartoon images of older folks walking with canes, and trying to get exercise. Well, I guess we can start ignoring the potential of more peripheral neuropathy in the feet and listen to this brochure. After all, they MUST know better than our docs in Philly. And besides, a little pain in the feet that was registering about a 7 or 8 out of 10 is no big deal. We'll get him walking ASAP!

The fourth and final one is my favorite:

"How to Prevent and Detect Cancer."

This one starts out harmlessly enough with a section on eating right. Once again, they talk about a balanced nutritional diet that includes all of the right foods and none of the wrong foods. (I've never seen so much mention of wheat, fiber, lentils, and cabbage on one page before.) The second section deals with staying in shape. Once again, on the surface this appears to be a somewhat harmless bit of advice, IF we weren't scared out of our minds about aggravating his neuropathy. The third section is titled, "Stay in the Shade." This one deals with the dangers of skin cancer and how to avoid the sunlight. (I guess it's a good thing that we don't live in Florida, where the sun is about 50 feet over our heads and burning down on us at about 50,000,000,000 degrees!) The fourth section is titled, "Quit Smoking." Wow! Thank goodness they included this one, because we weren't sure whether or not to keep Zachary away from cigarettes. He did try those 2 or 3 cigarettes a couple of months ago, and he liked them, so we were tempted to start allowing him to continue with that habit, BUT, now that we see in this brochure that it is recommended NOT to smoke, we will make the right choice! The next section addresses healthy habits. One of the focuses here is limiting your intake of alcohol. Hmmmmm. (It's as if they KNOW Zachary personally and have tailored this brochure to HIM!) I guess the bad news is that he drinks beer, but the good news is that it was LIGHT beer, so he IS watching those excess calories, WHICH according to the earlier brochure, is WAY important! The last part of this gem deals with self-examination for signs of cancer. First they show what skin anomalies look like, and then they get into self examinations for women. This part actually shows illustrations of women (naked) and how they should examine themselves. After that, they go into male self-examinations, where they show a man fondling (examining) himself. I'm thinking that if I give this brochure to Zachary, he'll see the section on women examining themselves, and then we won't be able to get him to STOP examining himself! So, while I'm sure their intentions were good, the last thing that I want to hear from him is how *this brochure doesn't stack up to the Hustler magazine that we confiscated from him earlier this year. At the end of the brochure they include some charts that discuss at which ages you should do which type of testing for cancer. Amazingly, the first age range shown is 20-29.*

I'm guessing that these brochures were NOT written with pediatric oncology in mind! (But that's just me talking, what do I know?)

Scott

P.S. Rebecca just called from Philly while I was finishing up this entry. Zachary's MIBG scan from this morning shows that the disease is stable. There may be some lightening of the sites (slight improvement); however there is nothing definitive, so they are writing up the report to say that he is stable. (Stable is good. Stable is better than progression.)

Monday, November 5, 2007 9:08 PM CST

Lauren
Wayne
Ed
Donna
Jessica
Brett

Do these names mean anything to you?

No, it is NOT my new coed bowling team.
No, it is not my new coed pool team.
No, I am not putting together a volleyball team.
No, no, no, no, no.

I'll give you a hint.

If these six people were in a room, with no one else there. And if you were somehow able to electronically scan an image of their collective brains, without harming them of course, (or, go ahead and harm them, either way is good with me), and if, during your scan you were able to somehow measure the number of brain cells that they had, as a group. I promise you. I PROMISE you. You would be hard pressed to find two brain cells to rub together among the six of them.

Having said all of that, I believe that it is now fairly obvious that these folks all work for The SFB Company.

What makes this group of highly polished brainiacs different from all the other ones that I've spoken to over the years is that this group was interacted with ALL IN ONE DAY!

It all started with our special oncology support executive. (BULLSHIT). Sorry, I sneezed. I realize that my sneeze may have sounded like I was saying "Bullshit", but that would be inappropriate. It is purely coincidental that my sneeze sounded like the word "Bullshit." (Must be chilly in here or something.) Anyway, my day started with an email that I received from her. Basically, I had emailed her with a claim to investigate. I had received a bill from their pharmacy, and once again I was confused as to WHY I was receiving a bill, when we met our out of pocket maximum in January. There is no reason for them to be billing us for anything, this late in the year. I had called them, (a division of The SFB Company), and they had given me the information about the claim. I forwarded that information to our special little helper, and she was emailing me back. Her response was that she had spoken with someone named Heidi at the pharmacy company who had informed her that Zachary Finestone no longer was covered with insurance. His policy had, "Termed." Sorry, have a nice day! (BULLSHIT). Sorry, must be allergy season or something. I'm allergic to dust, smoke, and imbeciles.

So, not wanting to argue through email, I called The SFB Company.

Helper #2, (I'm counting our specialist as helper #1) started off the call on a bad note. "I'm sorry Mr. Finestone, you are NOT the policy holder, Zachary is. We will need to speak with Zachary about this issue." (BULLSHIT). There it goes again. Sorry, again. My bad.

ME: "Umm, Zachary is thirteen years old. He is a cancer patient. He is sitting about 10 feet from me, trying to eat something while he fights an incredibly intense pain that has yet to be diagnosed. How about we SKIP the part where you need to talk to him, especially considering that we've been to that dance about 10 times over the past 3 years, and you guys have never learned the steps." (Silence).

Helper #2, "Umm, OK, I'll speak with you then."

ME: [Thinking] (You chose wisely young grasshopper.)

ME: "I am trying to figure out why one of your reps is being told that Zachary's policy has "Termed." I am being billed for something from your pharmacy division, and it should have been covered."

Helper #2, "This is a pharmacy issue with them. I will transfer you to them, and they will straighten this out in no time."

ME: "BULLSHIT" "Excuse me, I sneezed, I will hold while you transfer me."

Helper #3: "Hi this is clueless Ed, how can I help you Zachary?"

ME: (&%$#@) "Actually, this is Scott, Zachary's custodial father. He is only thirteen years old and I need some help on his account."*

Helper #3: "Hmm, I really need to speak with Zachary; his name is on the account."

ME: (&^#%%@$@) "Thank you for offering to speak to Zachary, but, seeing that he is having another pain attack and is, as I said earlier, only thirteen, you will be speaking with me."

Helper #3: "Hmm. OK. What is the problem?"

ME: [I outlined the problem.]

Helper #3: "Hmm. I am looking at his account, and I don't see where there are any charges or outstanding balances due. Everything is coming up zeros."

ME: "Hmm. That is strange. I got an email message saying that his policy was 'Termed' and that he no longer had coverage."

Helper #3: "Hmm. Let me look. Oh yes. I see now. He does indeed no longer have any coverage for the pharmacy."

ME: [Deep breath] [Pause] [Another deep breath] "How is that possible?"

Helper #3: "It says here that his policy Termed on 4/30/07."

ME: "Why? Why did this happen, and why was I not notified?"

Helper #3: "I don't know, you need to speak with member services, let me transfer you over."

ME: "Whoa, whoa, whoa. Let us not get ahead of ourselves. I was transferred over from THEM to YOU, to help me fix this."

Helper #3: "Umm. Well, I just do pharmacy stuff. You need member services. Please hold while I transfer you."

ME: [%$#@]*

Helper #4: "Hi, this is Donna, how can I help you?"

ME: "Hi Donna, (fill in the rest.)"

Helper #4: "Is Zachary there? I need to verify that I can speak with you on this account?"

ME: (I actually paused here, and started to look around the room for the hidden Candid Cameras.) "NO, Zachary is not available, blah, blah, blah, blah, blah."

Helper #4: "Oh, sorry about that, no problem. Let us look at your account." "I see where the policy did change in May. Your one policy was terminated on 4/30 and the new one was put into effect on 5/1."

ME: "Why was my policy changed at all? I never received any notification."

Helper #4: "Hmm. I don't know. This is a conversion policy that falls under the Florida law requiring us to provide insurance if you are unable to get other insurance. It is still under the conversion policy, but it has changed from a 'Legacy' account to a 'Proclaim' account."
"Also, the claim that you are asking about took place during the 'Legacy' time of your account, you'll need to speak to the division that handles those policies. I will transfer you."

ME: "Before you transfer me, who can explain to me why this change took place?"

Helper #4: "Well, it is run by the state. Let me look for a phone number." (Pause for station identification.) "Well, the only number that I have comes with a caveat. It says here that the phone number is only active during August, which is when the policies can be changed. Sorry." "I'll transfer you now."

ME: "AHHHHHHHHHHHHHHHHHHHHHHHHHHHHHHHHHHHH"

Helper #5: "Hi, this is Jessica, how may I help you?"

ME: (I explained it all over again, only this time without the demand for Zachary to get on the phone.)

Helper #5: "Oh, I am in that division; however, I don't handle the Legacy accounts. You need a Legacy account specialist."

ME: "Of course I do. Let me guess. You will transfer me?"

Helper #5: "Yes, I will transfer you."

Helper #6: "Hi, this is Brett, blah blah blah."

ME: (What I said before.)

Helper #6: "Hmm. Well, I see where the account did change in May. It looks like you are now on the new Proclaim system."

ME: "Why the change? Why wasn't I notified? How can you change my policy without telling me?"

Helper #6: "The other phone reps were confused. This is not a policy change. This is a newer system that is handling these policies now. It would be like upgrading from an older version of Excel to a newer version. You still get the same functions, only with some new features. All of your old information and benefits transferred over. Only, we are having some difficulty in getting the system to recognize all of your out of pocket expenses and co-pay information. We are working on getting that information caught up. It appears as though your troubles MAY be related to that issue."

ME: "Hmm. YOU THINK???" "While I have you on the phone, how much of Zachary's $1,000,000.00 lifetime benefit have we used up?"

Helper #6: "Let me see. As of 11/1/07, you have used $402,899.84. But, there is good news." (This next part is hardly within the realm of belief. Given that we had already spoken at length about Zachary's cancer, his expensive treatments, how he meets his out of pocket within the first few weeks of each year, you will NOT believe what this guy said the 'good news' was.) "Every year that you have renewed your policy for your son, you get an EXTRA $1,000.00 of lifetime benefit."

ME: "He spends $1,000.00 on medical bills when he doesn't poop for three days. What am I going to do with $1,000.00?"

Helper #6: "I see your point. I just thought you would like to know that it gets added on."

ME: "I'll be sure to celebrate that little tidbit of news as soon as I come down off of my natural high from hearing how we've spent almost half of his lifetime benefit money already."

Helper #6: "I will investigate the error we spoke about earlier, and I will call you back when I find something out."

ME: "Okey Dokey."

All of that happened today!!!

Although, I do owe The SFB Company and their pharmacy an apology. It hurts me to say it, but I have been unnecessarily harsh on them over the years. I have repeatedly bashed them over their lack of communication, in light of the fact that The SFB Company owns the pharmacy. But today, I learned an interesting fact. There ARE mitigating circumstances relating to WHY there has never been strong communications between the two companies.

Apparently, they DO have the two empty soup cans to speak to each other with; however, they have been UNABLE to locate a string that is long enough to stretch between the buildings. So, we can't really blame them if the technology does NOT exist yet for them to easily speak with each other, now can we?

Medical News:

I already told you that we left the hospital yesterday. Last night was fairly quiet. Today however, was anything BUT quiet.

Early today, Zachary seemed to be having more frequent sharp pains. Then, around 11am I was walking by the room where he was online, playing a game, and I noticed that he went through about a minute of sharp pains every 2 to 3 seconds. They kept coming, one right after another. I asked him how long that had been going on, (because that never happened in the hospital the entire time we were there), and he said that during the night it happened a few times. Then, later, I was working with my business partner and I heard a bang from his room.

Now, when he is vomiting, he will bang the bath tub so that we know to join him in the bathroom to share in his vomiting experience. So, we went to check on him. He wasn't in the bathroom, so I opened his bedroom door. He had a cartoon on, his toys on the floor, and he was balled up, in INTENSE pain, clutching his side. He could not even speak, to tell me what was going on. The pain was that intense. I had my friend get the pulse oximeter, to see if he was getting enough oxygen. It came up to around 84 or 85, which is very low. I called the oncologist, (actually, I almost called 911, but he started to move and signal me.) The entire episode lasted about 4 minutes. It scared the crap out of me. I was almost crying, it was killing me to see him in that much pain. The oncologist offered to readmit him, but we never did find a pain medicine to stop those spasms. She was going to have me take him to the local E.R. if he wasn't breathing properly, but as soon as the pain subsided, he was back to normal. She ordered the anti-viral med used for shingles. (We won't know from his blood work whether that is the cause, for a couple of days. But at this point, we need to try something.) He had one more attack like that, only not as long, about an hour ago while we were out looking at video games.

I have been scared, and upset many times over the past 7 ½ years, but today was bad. Really bad.

Chapter 11

Religion

"I must be the BIGGEST glutton for punishment to have attempted tackling this issue."

When I originally laid out this book, I had not included a chapter on religion. The omission was NOT intentional, I just hadn't realized how important that ongoing "chapter" of our lives was. I guess some background information about our religious upbringing would help you to understand the decisions that we have made.

I was raised in a Jewish family. (Like my last name wasn't a hint to that!) We attended a Reform temple in Pittsburgh, PA. What is a Reform temple? (Oh great, now I have to explain religion to everyone?) Well, I am definitely the LAST person on the planet who should be educating ANYONE in the realm of religion.

At the risk of getting an explanation incorrect and facing eternal damnation (I don't even know if my religion has that,) I will leave teaching religion to the experts. If you are really curious you can go online and do some digging, OR, do what I did growing up and learn the bulk of it from Charlton Heston in the Ten Commandments! All of the good "Thou shalt not's" are in that movie, and if you follow them, you should be just fine in life.

Unlike me, Rebecca was raised in a household that was exposed to many different Christian religions. From what Rebecca has told me, "My mother changed religions all of the time. We were always joining and then leaving a new church." So, neither of us was raised in what I would consider an overly religious setting. However, we were BOTH raised with a respect for the moral and ethical standards that most religions follow. You know, the "Thou Shalt Not's."

When Zachary was diagnosed, we weren't part of any church or synagogue so we didn't have a "spiritual" leader to call on for help. At the time, our hospital in Palm Beach was a not-for-profit hospital that had nuns and a priest on staff. As luck would have it, the priest was a REALLY cool guy. He was by far one of the most unassuming, caring, and inclusive religious people who I have ever met. Father John would come up onto the oncology floor and sit with us for long periods of time, without ever bringing religion or faith into the conversation. He would be there for the families to help them cope with the daily drama that takes place within this diagnosis. There were times when I wanted to discuss religion, so Father John and I would sit at the end of the hallway, and talk about God, Zachary's condition, and what it all meant. And during those conversations, I never once felt that he was trying to convert me, or change any of my beliefs. He was simply trying to comfort us, and help us in any way that he could.

When the hospital was purchased by a large corporation and became "for profit", the nuns and priest left. At that time, the hospital brought in a few different religious counselors who would stop by to offer their help. Because of my last name, (and obviously Zachary's) every week or so a Rabbi would pop into the room. Now, I have nothing against Rabbi's. I have known some wonderful Rabbi's. The problem with the hospital Rabbi was that he was about 118 years old, and could relate to Zachary about as well as an ant relates to an elephant. They may co-exist, or even share the same relative space, but are they EVER going to really connect?

When Zachary relapsed, Rebecca and I knew that we were in trouble, in more ways than one. We had lived for the prior two years knowing that a relapse with this disease meant certain death. (When they tell you 100%, they mean EVERYONE!). We had no idea how long we were going to have with Zachary, and I started to think more and more about the end, and how it would play out. I started to envision the actual ceremony, and how a religious person would be up at a pulpit, talking about my son and his life. (In retrospect, I'm guessing that my psychologist would say that having those kinds of mental exercises is NOT a healthy thing to do, but my mind has always had a way of doing its own thing.) Aside from the obvious pain of envisioning your child's funeral, I somehow started to obsess over the concept of having a religious person up there who actually knew Zachary and wouldn't just be reading off of a sheet of paper about his life.

I don't know why this became so important to me; maybe it was a measure of control that I was seeking to compensate for the total LACK of control that I was experiencing with his cancer. Regardless of the motivating factors, Rebecca and I had reached a place where we wanted to have a religious connection. Our dilemma was that we had never found a Jewish temple that "worked" for us.

We had looked into a few when we got married, but we were turned off by the message we were receiving about having a mixed religious marriage.

(Some Rabbi's are more open about that issue than others.) And as for attending a church, I had my preconceptions that included everything from a revival-like atmosphere where people would be carrying Zachary up onto the stage to lay their hands on him and scream to the heavens, to a church where they would cut the heads off snakes and want to pour the blood onto Zachary's head. (OK, I'll admit that I MAY have been somewhat naïve as to what happens in church, maybe I read too many weird books or saw too many movies as a child.)

One of my strengths is the fact that I know when to ask for help. I am NOT afraid to ask directions, (I hate driving around aimlessly looking for something,) and I am NOT afraid to tap into local resources when looking for answers. So, I called some friends of ours to ask if they knew of a "low key", family-friendly church where we could have a good chance of benefiting from the religious community.

They immediately told me about a local church where the pastor was a very nice man who they recommended we meet. I took their advice, and decided to treat the process like an interview. I would lay it on the line with this pastor, and see how he reacted to what I felt our needs were. During our meeting I was very impressed with every aspect of his message. I had explained our situation explicitly. I told him that we were NOT looking to become some "pet" project for a church where everyone would always be pointing to us and saying, "Oh, there goes that poor Finestone family . . . . how sad." We also didn't want to have Zachary thrown up on a stage for weekly "healings." He had been freaked out enough by the crazy foreign woman splashing oil on his head shortly after getting diagnosed, he didn't need more chaos.

Basically, I made it clear that what we were looking for was a safe, friendly church that we could come to when Zachary was well enough, and not feel pressured or singled out because of our situation.

I never had to look for another church. Pastor Dale was our man. We had several years of wonderful experiences with that church. Dale and his wife used to visit us in the hospital when we were stuck there for treatment or illness. Dale would also stop by our home on occasion to check up on us. I somehow managed to attend church on a regular basis without being struck by lightning or violating any of my core beliefs.

During the ceremonies, if the congregation was reading something aloud that didn't "jive" with my beliefs, I would simply say one of the Jewish prayers that I had grown up with to myself, so as not to interfere or disrupt anyone near me. I never felt like I was betraying my upbringing either. Zachary would attend Sunday school when he was feeling up to it, and Rebecca seemed to appreciate being able to associate with her religious background. Sadly, our pastor retired a few years ago, and the church had a major uprising that split the congregation during a nasty battle that sent most of the families scattering among the other local churches. Since then, we have not found a new religious home.

As for the families out there looking to these pages for answers or direction, I can only advise you so far, eventually you are going to have to find the path that works for you and your family. We have had friends from the cancer community who were WAY more religious than we were. We even attended their church a few times and experienced religious practices that we had only seen in the movies.

For them, that atmosphere worked! When one family lost their child to cancer, it caused a "break" in their faith that may never be mended. When comparing that family with ours, you can see where the religious background that you bring into this ordeal won't always dictate the long term religious practices or beliefs that you will leave with. I don't believe that any of that is a reflection on the character of the person or the family that may change after diagnosis. I just think that this disease has far-reaching consequences that many of us never envisioned.

My recommendation to a new family that finds themselves smack dab in the middle of this diagnosis is to tap into ALL available resources for encouragement, help, prayers, and comfort. That may mean doing what we had to do and reaching out for help to find a religious entity to call "home."

Through some of my conversations with Father John and later with Pastor Dale, I was made aware of the fact that it is not uncommon for people to "find" religion when things are at their worst. In other words, "Our child has been diagnosed with cancer; we better align ourselves with God now, before it's too late." As I mentioned earlier, we didn't do that at first.

We did have numerous churches from around the country add Zachary's name to their prayer list. And while we could argue all day and into the night as to whether that had any effect on his longevity, I can tell you unequivocally that we as a family benefited through the knowledge that we were being prayed for by so many people. Zachary's CaringBridge site was particularly useful when it came to spreading the word about our daily sagas. Any mention in my journal entries of us needing help or good thoughts would prompt many guest book entries from across the country regarding Zachary being added to a church's prayer list.

Chapter 12

Life & Death

"Funerals are not pleasant. Avoid at ALL costs letting family
members or friends die!"

Don't panic. Nothing has changed with Zachary's condition since the chapter on "Relapse" where I wrote about the new MIBG therapy that we are doing now. I didn't come up with the title to this chapter to freak everyone out. I just wanted to devote some time in my book to the overall "Life & Death" theme that this illness forces a family to live and breathe.

If you read my old "Flashback" journal entries carefully, then you will have undoubtedly noticed that on more than one occasion I mention the death of a child from cancer. We hadn't experienced that side of this disease until after relapse, in 2002. At that time, we obviously were in a "different" place mentally, having been told ourselves that Zachary would not survive for long. Because of that, we found ourselves bonding to the other cancer families in a way that we never originally envisioned. Our connection just seemed to exist on a much deeper level, almost to the point where we were like one big extended family.

You may recall the numerous journal entries that covered the Cancer Sucks Club. Well, when I first wrote about the CSC, my intention was to vent about my hatred for the disease, while trying to make people laugh in light of the seriousness of what we were all experiencing. After just a few of those CSC entries, it didn't take me long to realize that we had a core group of families who would literally walk across broken glass or through flames for each other. We still had our families and friends who supported us throughout this ordeal, but the CSC group was something special. Through life and death experiences, we were celebrating our victories and comforting each other during our tragic losses.

When I think back to 2002, I can't help but wonder how we would have EVER gotten through that year without the support and friendship of the families who were going through treatments alongside us. Not only did we have each other to rely on at the local hospital, but in early 2003 when we traveled to NYC in search of new treatments, we were joined by another neuroblastoma family who we had known for almost a year. Being able to tap into that kind of resource is an amazing aspect of this horrific experience that we will NEVER forget.

When it comes to funerals and services for children, I can't imagine that there is much that I can write about those times that wouldn't be inherently obvious to anyone with an ounce of compassion. I do want to relay one experience that I will never forget about one of the local families who lost their child to cancer. We had already been to too many services over the year or so since relapse, and this one happened to be for a family that we knew, but we certainly weren't "super" close with. We had seen them on the floor at the hospital, but we had never really connected with them outside of there. Rebecca and Zachary could not make it to their service, I don't remember if he was sick or what was going on, but I do remember that I went alone. Since we really didn't know them too well, I didn't know anyone else who was attending the service. It was all family and friends of theirs.

I arrived after the larger crowds had already paid their respects, and I was lingering at the back of the visitation area, trying to stay "out of the way." Well, the mother and father of the child who had died caught sight of me, and immediately came over to get hugs and visit. I could see family and friends watching us, almost with a look of curiosity as to how they didn't know this stranger (me) who was garnishing so much attention from the grieving parents.

At that moment it dawned on me that the connection we have as families who are going through this or have already gone through this is beyond anything else that we had experienced in our lives. I don't remember how long we stood there hugging, crying and talking about Zachary and their lost child, but I felt like my attendance there had served a purpose, and that I had done something right for once.

I remember back in 2002 when they had told us (for the second time) that Zachary did not have long to live, and that we should plan for the worst. I took it upon myself to visit the local chapter of Hospice. (For those of you lucky enough to have never had a need for Hospice, they provide services for families who have a loved one who is terminally ill.) Some chapters do home visits to assist with care at the end of a patient's life, and some have inpatient facilities that make a person's last days as comfortable as possible. So I had decided that I couldn't hide anymore from the reality that we were being told was imminent.

I remember walking in and waiting patiently for the receptionist to recognize my presence. After a few moments, she asked what she could do for me. I replied that I was seeking information about Hospice for children. She immediately pointed to a rack of pamphlets and told me that there were several available that helped a child in dealing with the loss of a grandparent or other relative. I knew that she was going to feel "bad" when I corrected her, but I was REALLY in need of some information, so I calmly told her that I was not looking for information about how to help a child who has lost a relative, but rather I had a child who was facing a poor diagnosis and was probably going to need their help.

She turned gray and paused, before letting me know that they had only one employee qualified to handle such situations. She escorted me back to some remote corner of the office where a nice lady who dealt with children was seated in a small cubicle. Sadly, they did not have an active program in place to deal with children in Zachary's position. (On the other hand, maybe it was God's way of saying, "We're not ready for him anyway . . . . don't sweat it.") I thanked the nice lady for her help, and never looked back after leaving their office. Sure, I could have done some research and found a chapter that had more experience with children, but somehow I knew deep down that we just weren't ready for that outcome.

Every family that we have ever met during this adventure (or misadventure) has stories about how they got diagnosed and how they experienced bumps in the road. And if asked, every one of those families will tell you that they feel their child's story is a special one. We certainly would say that Zachary's longevity in light of the prognosis we have been given makes our story unique and special. The point here is ALL of the families and their stories are unique AND special. ALL of these children who have been thrust into this illness are special and deserve to be treated as such. The degree to which a family's life is turned upside down cannot be expressed adequately with mere words. The pain, anguish, fears and uncertainty that is inflicted upon a family when they receive this diagnosis is massive and overwhelming. "Life & Death" are not issues that you expect to discuss and literally LIVE through with your young child.

I hope that our experiences and my twisted style of conveying them to you have in some way shed light on what has been 8 years of us facing life with our son's cancer. We have said for quite some time that fighting cancer has become a way of life for us. I am 45 years old now, so I have been dealing with this for over 17% of my life. Rebecca is now 31, so she has been living this nightmare for over 25% of her life. And Zachary, our little warrior, has been fighting the monster for over 57% of his life. (When you ask a guy, you get math! . . . . Not that you asked, but the numbers are quite powerful when you put them into that perspective.)

Numbers alone cannot do justice to what this battle has meant to us. The childhood that was robbed from Zachary can never be replaced and the degrees to which this illness has changed Rebecca's and my life are so far reaching and all encompassing that I cannot envision a time when we won't be affected by it.

Appendix

List of Charities

Camp Boggy Creek
30500 Brantley Branch Road
Eustis, FL 32736
866-Go-Boggy
www.boggycreek.org

CaringBridge
1995 Rahn Cliff Court—Suite 200
Eagan, MN 55122
651-452-7940
www.caringbridge.org

Children's Miracle Network
4525 South 2300 East
Salt Lake City, UT 84117
801-278-8900
www.childrensmiraclenetwork.org

Children's Wish Foundation
8615 Roswell Rd.
Atlanta, GA 30350
800-323-Wish
www.childrenswish.org

Connor Moran Children's Foundation
825 US Hwy. 1—Suite 200
Jupiter, FL 33477
561-741-1144
www.connormoran.org

The Leukemia & Lymphoma Society
1311 Mamaroneck Ave.
White Plains, NY 10605
800-955-4572
www.leukemia-lymphoma.org

Little Smiles
13860 Wellington Trace—Suite 38-124
Wellington, FL 33414
877-294-KIDS
www.littlesmiles.org

Make-A-Wish Foundation
3550 North Central Ave.—Suite 300
Phoenix, AZ 85012
800-722-Wish
www.wish.org

National Children's Cancer Foundation
1 South Memorial Lane—Suite 800
St. Louis, MO 63102
314-241-1600
www.children-cancer.com

Pediatric Oncology Support Team
5325 Greenwood Ave. Suite 301
West Palm Beach, FL 33407
561-882-6336

Quantum House
901 45th Street
West Palm Beach, FL 33407
561-494-0515
www.quantumhouse.org

Ronald McDonald House
1 Kroc Drive
Oak Brook, IL 60523
630-623-7048
www.rmhc.org

The Super Jake Foundation
PO Box 477
Gurnee, IL 60031
847-625-0436
www.superjakefoundation.org